PAST PARTICIPLES
FROM LATIN TO ROMANCE

Past Participles
from Latin to Romance

Richard Laurent

UNIVERSITY OF CALIFORNIA PRESS
Berkeley • Los Angeles • London

UNIVERSITY OF CALIFORNIA PUBLICATIONS IN LINGUISTICS

Volume 133

UNIVERSITY OF CALIFORNIA PRESS
BERKELEY AND LOS ANGELES, CALIFORNIA

UNIVERSITY OF CALIFORNIA PRESS, LTD.
LONDON, ENGLAND

Library of Congress Cataloging-in-Publication Data

Laurent, Richard, 1953–
    Past participles from Latin to Romance / Richard Laurent.
      p.   cm. — (University of California publications in
linguistics ; v. 133)
    Includes bibliographical references and index.
    ISBN 0-520-09832-3 (paper : alk. paper)
    1. Romance languages—Participle. 2. Latin language—Participle.
3. Latin language—Influence on Romance. I. Title. II. Series
PC164.L38   1999
440'.045—dc21   99-36467
                                        CIP

In memory of

Margaret Lucado Goodwillie Garlick
Richard Cecil Garlick
Meta Glass
Arthur Goodwillie
Margaret Sandford Banister

Contents

Introduction

Chapter 1. Latin Past Participles, Inherited and Innovated

vii

Chapter 2. Reshaping of Verb Paradigms in Late Latin and Proto-Romance

Chapter 3. Past Participles in Eastern Romance

Chapter 4. Past Participles in Western Romance

Chapter 5. Synopsis of Data

Chapter 6. Theoretical Implications

Tables

TABLES IN APPENDIX 3

Abbreviations

LANGUAGES AND DIALECTS

Abru.	Abruzzese [It.]	ECat.	Eastern Catalan
Alg.	Alguerese [Cat.]	Elb.	Elban [It.]
Alt.	Altamura [Apul.]	Em.	Emiliano [It.]
Amp.	Ampezzo [Fri.]	Enga.	Engadin [RR]
Apul.	Apulian (Pugliese) [It.]	Engl.	English
Arag.	Aragonese [Sp.]	Fass.	Fassano [Lad.]
Args.	Aragüés Valley [Sp.]	Ferr.	Ferrarese [It.]
Arom.	Aromanian	FP	Franco-Provençal
Auv.	Auvergnat [Oc.]	Fr.	French
Av.	Avesnois [Pic.]	Fr.-It.	Franco-Italian
Bad.	Badiotto [Lad.]	Fri.	Friulian
Ban.	Banat [Mold.]	Fri-R	Friulian in Romania
Barr.	Barranquenho [Ptg.]	Gal.	Galician [Ptg.]
Berg.	Bergamese [It.]	Gar.	Gardenese [Lad.]
Bls.	Bielsa [Arag.]	Gasc.	Gascon [Oc.]
Br.	Brayon [Pic.]	Gen.	Genoese [It.]
Burg.	Burgundian [Fr.]	Germ.	German
Cal.	Calabrian [It.]	Gév.	Gévaudanais [Oc.]
Can.	Candama [Leon.]	Ggn.	Guignemicourt [Pic.]
Car.	Cartagena [Sp.]	Gk.	Greek
Cast.	nonstd. Castilian [Sp.]	Gor.	Gorizia [Fri.]
Cat.	Catalan	Goth.	Gothic
CI	Channel Islands [Nor.]	Gra.	Grado [Fri.]
CL	Classical Latin	IE	Indo-European
Clau.	Clauzetto [Fri.]	Ist-I	Istriano [It.]
Cmpa.	Campagnese [It.]	Ist-R	Istro-Romanian
Cmpi.	Campidanese [Sard.]	It.	Italian
Cod.	Codròipo [Fri.]	K	Kruševo [Arom.]
Cors.	Corsican [It.]	Lad.	Ladin
D	Dignanese [Ist-I]	Lang.	Languedocian [Oc.]
DR	Daco-Romanian	Laz.	Laziale [It.]

Leon.	Leonese [Sp.]	Ross.	Rossellonese [Cat.]
Lig.	Ligurian [It.]	RR	Ræto-Romance
Liv.	Livinallonghese [Lad.]	Russ.	Russian
LL	Late Latin	Sal.	Salento [It.]
Log.	Logudorese [Sard.]	Salm.	Salmantrino [Sp.]
Lomb.	Lombard [It.]	Sard.	Sardinian
Luca.	Lucanian [It.]	SCors.	South Corsican
Luca-GI	Gallo-Italian in Lucania	SF	Sot de Ferrer [Sp.]
Lucc.	Luccan [It.]	Sic.	Sicilian [It.]
Lun.	Lunigiana [It.]	Sien.	Sienese [It.]
Mara.	Maramur [Mold.]	Sis.	Sisco [Lig.]
Marb.	Marebbano [Lad.]	SIst-R	South Istro-Romanian
Marc.	Marchese [It.]	Skt.	Sanskrit
Meg.	Meglenoromanian [Arom.]	SLuca.	South Lucanian
Mil.	Milanese [It.]	SM	San Mango [Cal.]
Mold.	Moldavian [Rom.]	Sp.	Spanish
N	Naisey [FP]	Sto.	Saintongeais [Oc.]
Neap.	Neapolitan [Cal.]	Surs.	Surselvan [RR]
Nor.	Norman [Fr.]	Ţ	Ţărneca [Meg.]
Nuor.	Nuorese [Sard.]	Tam.	Tamaritan [Cat.]
Oc.	Occitan	Toch.	Tocharian
OL	Old Latin	Tud.	Tudanca [Leon.]
Oltn.	Oltenian [Rom.]	Tusc.	nonstd. Tuscan [It.]
Opo.	Oporto [Ptg.]	U	Uma [Meg.]
Pad.	Paduan [It.]	Ud.	Udine [Lad.]
Pch.	Percheron [Nor.]	UEnga.	Upper Engadin
Pers.	Persian	VA	Val d'Aosta [FP]
Pic.	Picard [Fr.]	Val.	Valencian [Cat.]
Pied.	Piedmontese [It.]	Vd.	Vaud [FP]
Pin.	Mt. Pindus area [Arom.]	VE	Val d'Echo [Arag.]
Poit.	Poitevin [Oc.]	Vegl.	Vegliote
Pol.	Polish	Ven.	Veneto [It.]
PR	Proto-Romance	VG	Val Graveglia [Lig.]
Prov.	Provençal [Oc.]	VP	Val del Pas [Leon.]
Ptg.	Portuguese	VS	Val de Saire [Nor.]
Rml.	Romagnolo [It.]	Vx.	Vaux [FP]
Rom.	(Daco-)Romanian	Z	Zara [Vegl.]

OTHER ABBREVIATIONS

LANGUAGE STAGES

Mid	Middle
Mod	Modern
O	Old

SYMBOLS

±	by analogy with
≠	does not continue
÷	regularized from
x	crossed with
>	develops into
<	develops from
*	unattested
?	doubtful
•	semilearnèd
!	notable oddity
#	competing with regular by-form
§	(sub)section
1	first-person
2	second-person
3	third-person

MORPHOSYNTAX

acc.	accusative
act.	active voice
adj.	adjective
adv.	adverb
aor.	aorist
conj.	conjugation
decl.	declension

dep.	deponent
fem.	feminine
f., fut.	future
freq.	frequentative
gen.	genitive
ger.	gerund
impf.	imperfect
indic.	indicative
infin.	infinitive
masc.	masculine
neut.	neuter
nom.	nominative
obl.	oblique
p., part.	participle
pass.	passive voice
pf.	perfect
pl.	plural
plup.	pluperfect
p.p.	past participle, past-participial
prep.	preposition
pres.	present
pret.	preterit
sg.	singular
subj.	subjunctive

OTHER TERMS

C	consonant
D	dental stop
L	liquid
o.o.o.	of obscure origin
std.	standard

Tabula Gratulatoria

So in life's wintertime thy thoughts take wing
In ink, reliving our childhood in spring.

Carl de Thursarin,
A Roman in the Hesperides

Begun as a sketch for a course in Late Latin taught by József Herman, *Past Participles from Latin to Romance* has developed into a stereopticon slide covering a range wider and narrower than back at the University of California at Berkeley. To shift metaphors: besides sliding under a theoretical foundation, I have braced the frame with cross-references, added a wing of new dialects, and carted away plaster and beams from the old monument. I leave to future collators the task of landscaping the grounds.

After my pen had gleaned forms from across Romance-speaking Europe (ROMANIA), I drew upon the past-participial competence of several native speakers: for Romanian and all trans-Adriatic Romance, Emil Vrabie; for Polish, Matthew Motyka; for Italian, Ruggero Stefanini and Andrea Malaguti; for French, Edwige Gamache and Sophie Marnette; for Spanish, Antonio Cortijo; for Catalan, Joan Sempere-Martínez; for Portuguese, Milton Azevedo. I have also drawn upon observations made by Thomas Walsh of Georgetown University and by two anonymous peer reviewers.

I remain grateful to professors at UC Berkeley: above all to Suzanne Fleischman, for reviewing the manuscript and for making comments that widened its scope and heightened its accuracy almost beyond measure; to Gary Holland, for bringing to bear his knowledge of Indo-European tongues, not least among them Latin and Greek; to Charles Faulhaber, Jerry Craddock, and Joseph Duggan, for serving as guides across lesser-known fields of Romance philology.

At UC Press on Berkeley Way, I thank Rose Anne White for coordinating each stage of turning unbound pages into a book, and Janet Mowery for copyediting beyond the call.

For letting me to look through their stacks in search of past participles, or for bringing them to me, I thank those estimable institutions Doe Library at Berkeley, Lauinger Library at Georgetown, and the Library of Congress. For help with formatting data in formats that first appeared passing strange, I thank Arthur Laurent, R. Wood Miles, and Robert Orlov. For help in another field, however it may have narrowed, I thank Mansour Armaly, Todd Severin, John Zacharia, and Fadi Nasrallah.

I thank my parents for having given me a love of learning, apprenticed me in the trade of writing, and taught me to tell the truth often. I thank each in a long line of teachers, starting in fall 1959 with Miss Rose Noble at Robert E. Lee Elementary in Alexandria, Virginia. And I wish to recall friends who used to gather at that grammar school at the other end of Jefferson Street: Nancy Becker, Dru Blair, Randy Causley, Deanna Greenwood, Kelly Kelso, Chip Land, John McKitterick, John Moncure, Deirdra Mooney, Margaret Richards, and Jenny Tindell.

For instilling the awareness and resolve to move west and back again, I thank Robert Denommé, Oron Hale, M. Roy Harris, and Natasha Moyle from Virginia days; Michael Blackwell, Lorraine Collier, Glennys George, and John Kay from IMF days; Francis Dinneen, Joseph O'Connor, Victoria Pedrick, and Shaligram Shukla from Georgetown days. For the examples they set at Pitt and Duke Streets before those days began, I wish to express continuing appreciation to Pat Beckington, Al and Louise Forstall, and David Abshire.

Anyone leafing through the index verborum at the end will find that *Past Participles from Latin to Romance* covers some 600 words from Latin and, from Romanian to Portuguese, six or seven times more than that. Any taxonomy has to have gotten jumbled now and then. As Morris Bishop says in *The Middle Ages*, the copyists' guild used to have its own trade demon, Titivillus, "whose business was to induce scribes to make mistakes" (259) and who, I am told, used to sit above church choirs writing down every wobbly note or false syllable sung. Since troubadour days, the demon seems unlikely to have stayed out of work for very long. So, as if whistling my way across a graveyard of the great, from Diez to Malkiel, I whisper this:

PRECOR NE ME INDUXERIT

TITIVILLUS IN PERMULTOS ERRORES

When apotropaic charms have run out, I alone remain responsible for any mistakes or misjudgments, up to and including mumpsimus, that still bespatter these pages from first to last. In advance I ask forgiveness for the year of publication, fated soon to look as archaic as a date with three digits does now.

But I really regret only one thing: having been unable to finish the book in Escondido, California.

RICHARD LAURENT

22 June 1999

Major Types of Past Participle in Romance, as Written
(after Iliescu and Mourin)

■ absent ▢ archaic ▨ now graphic only

Reflexes of Latin	arrhizotonic			rhizotonic				
	-ĀTU	-ŪTU	-ĪTU	-SU	-STU	-CTU	-PTU	'-ĪTU
ROMANIAN	–at	–ut	–it	–s	–st	–pt		
Aromanian	–ată	–ută	–ită	–să	■	–ptă		
Istro-Romanian	–at	–ut	–it	–s	–st	–pt		
Vegliote	–úot	–oit	–ait	–s	■	–t		
ITALIAN	–ato	–uto	–ito	–so	–sto	–tto		
Milanese	–aa	–uu	–ii	–s	–st	–tt		
Neapolitan	–ato	–uto	■	–so	–sto	–tto		'–eto
Lucanian	–at	–ut	■	–s	–st	–tt		'–ete
Sicilian	–atu	–utu	■	–su	■	–ttu		–(t)tu
SARDINIAN	–adu	■	–idu	–su	–stu	–ttu		'–idu
Friulian	–ât	–ût	–ît	■		–t		
Ladin	–at	–ù	–it	–s	–st	–t		
Engadin	–at	–eu		–s	–st	–t		
Surselvan	–at	–iu		–s	■	–tg	–t	
FRENCH	–é	–u	–i	–s	–st	–tt	–t	
CATALAN	–at	–ut	–it	–s	–st	–t		
SPANISH	–ado	–udo	–ido	–so	–sto	–cho	–to	
PORTUGUESE	–ado	–udo	–ido	–so	–sto	–(i)to		

Introduction

The Italian is pleasant, but without sinews,
as a still reflecting water; the French
delicate, but even nice as a woman, scarce
daring to open her lips for fear of marring
her countenance; the Spanish majestical but
fulsome, running too much on the *o*, and
terrible like the Devil in a play....

Richard Carew, *Epistle on the Excellency
of the English Tongue* (1605)

0.0. OVERVIEW

Since the time of the *Technē Grammatikē* ascribed to Dionysius Thrax (ca. 100 BCE), participles have been acknowledged in the West as a part of speech that shares features of verbs and nouns. In Greek as well as Latin, they were marked for case like nouns, for tense like verbs, and for number like both, but were never marked for person or mood like finite verbs (Robins, 38–39; Dinneen, 100). Of the several participles of Latin verbs, I am concerned here with the perfect or past participle (p.p.) that came to resemble syntactically those found in the English catch-phrase *been there, done that.*[1]

Across half of Europe and beyond since Romulus Augustulus was dethroned in 476 CE, speakers of neo-Latin languages have given a steadily greater role in the syntax of sentences to past participles coming down from Latin, which have themselves tended to become gradually more predictable in the ways they are formed, if not always in the same ways everywhere. During the twenty-first century, those past participles or variants of them will live on in speech from Bucharest to Brussels to Buenos Aires. Yet the story of how each thrived or died remains untold.

0.1. FILLING A GAP

It is astonishing how little the standard survey of Latin or Romance takes account of the morphology of past participles. Among general works in the field, Buck's *Comparative Grammar of Greek and Latin* (1933) devotes a page

---

[1] A late-twentieth-century locution connoting a surfeit of boredom. For a discussion of active and middle present and perfect participles in Indo-European languages, see Sihler, 613–21.

1

and a half to Greek verbal adjectives and Latin past participles (307–9). More
recently, Sihler's *New Comparative Grammar of Greek and Latin* (1995) has
some three pages on the subject (564–66), along with data on alignments of
perfect/p.p. stems. Iordan and Orr's *Introduction to Romance Linguistics* as
revised by Posner (1970) contains only two references to past participles, both
of them listed in the index under "past-definite, disappearance of" (583).

Among works on Gallo-Romance, Price's *French Language: Present and
Past* (1971) devotes four pages to past participles and another two pages to
compound tenses formed with them (221–26). Pope's revised *From Latin to
Modern French* (1952) has some two and a half pages about past participles
(385–87), though a number of others appear in Pope's verb tables.

Among works on Hispano-Romance, Lapesa's *Historia de la lengua
española* (9th ed., 1981) has a brief mention of the development of present-
perfect constructions in Late Latin (75), along with a brief mention of strong
past participles surviving into Old Spanish but not beyond (210). Lloyd's *From
Latin to Spanish* (1987) contains less than two pages on all Latin participles
(103–4), about a page on new compound tenses and past participles in Late
Latin (169–70), and about three pages on those in Old Spanish (313–15; 367–
68). Williams's revised *From Latin to Portuguese* (1962) has just over two
pages on past participles (184–86).

It should be noted that those books deal with Romance west of Italy.

A more general work, Hock's *Principles of Historical Linguistics* (1986),
contains no reference to past participles in the index, though in the text they
occasionally figure in examples of e.g. morphological leveling.

Authors of those works appear to consider that patterns of retention or
replacement of types of Latin past participles were perfectly natural. To be
sure, historical grammars deal with a broad spectrum of topics and can,
accordingly, devote only so much space to each one. Yet even Mourin's two
thorough studies, *Lees participes passés irréguliers* and *Les rapports entre les
formes irrégulières du parfait et du participe passé* (both 1968), while they cite
disused mediæval forms, make no attempt to describe changes within the
past system since classical times or to compare the morphology of Roman past
participles with that of their counterparts in Romance.

It is clear, therefore, that the morphology of past participles in neo-Latin
has not yet been investigated in historical depth, or with the comparative
breadth across the Romance-speaking areas of Europe (ROMANIA) that the
topic deserves. In the present work, I sketch the Latin system of p.p. formation
and review how later speakers have kept or lost or transformed the inventory
of past participles left to them by the legionnaires.

Several themes are treated in detail: first, the origins of past participles in
Classical Latin (CL) in one type of verbal adjective from Indo-European (IE);
second, outcomes of such verbal adjectives in some ancient and modern IE
languages; third, the past-participial system as constituted in CL, together with
a sketch of the whole perfectum system; fourth, the reshaping and
continuation of that system in Late Latin (LL) or Proto-Romance (PR); fifth,
past-participial outcomes during mediæval Romance and after the rise of

standardized Portuguese, Spanish, Catalan, French, Italian, and Romanian. Along the way, past participles in dialects that never acquired an army or a navy are reviewed as well.

By contrast with the lack of attention paid to past-participial morphology in Romance languages and dialects, extensive treatment has been given to two themes related to past participles across ROMANIA: whether they display agreement in number and gender with a subject or a direct object, and which auxiliary verb—reflexes of HABĒRE 'have' or ESSE 'be,' TENĒRE 'hold' or FIERĪ 'become'—they take in perfect and passive constructions. Here the theme of agreement is dealt with only in passing, in a review of the decline of gender and number marking on past participles in spoken French (§4.4.12); the theme of auxiliaries is also dealt with in passing.[2]

0.2. METHODS AND SOURCES

Along with a review of regular p.p. morphology, long lists of irregular past participles are supplied in some sources drawn upon for this study, like Blasco Ferrer's *Lingua sarda contemporanea* (1986), Bichelli's *Grammatica del dialetto napoletano* (1974), and Nicoli's *Grammatica milanese* (1983). Others sources prove less reader-friendly and require skimming to obtain survivals or innovations. Many such works are dictionaries, among them Buffière's *Dictionnaire occitan-français: dialecte gévaudanais* (1992), Consolino's *Vocabulario del dialetto di Vittoria* (1986), Lombard and Gâdei's *Dictionnaire morphologique de la langue roumaine* (1981), Godefroy's revised *Lexique de l'ancien français* (1982), and Blasi's *Dizionario dialettale di San Mango sur Calore* (1991). Then again, Oliva and Buxton's *Diccionari català-anglès* (1986) proves helpful in identifying defective verbs and obsolete variants. For verifying forms in standard Italian, Battaglia's *Grande Dizionario* (1961–) proves invaluable, above all in its indications of register.

More comprehensive works like Elcock's *Romance Languages* revised by Green (1975) and Tekavčić's *Grammatica storica dell'italiano* (1972), whose treatment of past participles is fuller than that of most others, provide a great many examples of reshaped verb paradigms. With regret, I have forgone using Jaberg and Jud's *Sprach- und Sachtatlas Italiens und der Südschweiz*. Since that compilation contains only eleven past participles that I could find, it would add little to a study of p.p. inventories across ROMANIA.

In the absence of two contributions to the literature, this study could not have been written: Harris and Vincent's *Romance Languages* (1988), likely to remain the scholar's workstation for neo-Latin, and Iliescu and Mourin's

---

[2] For a survey of agreement or nonagreement of past participles in compound perfects across Romance, see Posner, 257–61. For a survey of auxiliary selection in compound perfects, see Posner, 15–24. For a survey of passive morphology, including that of pseudoreflexive or SE-passives, see Posner, 179–81. For a study of auxiliary selection in Romance perfects and passives from Italian westward, see Squartini, 18–34. For a study of more than sixty Romance systems of p.p. agreement through the centuries, see Loporcaro 1998 (unreviewed at press time).

Typologie de la morphologie verbale romane (1991), highly informative for lesser-known languages and dialects.[3] Furthermore, Robert de Dardel's *Parfait fort en roman commun* (1930, 1958), particularly a chart on the spread of present-tense stems into the perfect (later preterit), served as the inspiration for undertaking a similar effort for past participles across the old Empire. To my regret, this study contains no illustrations of p.p. types from literature of the Middle Ages that could compare to Dardel's copious illustrations of preterit types from such sources.

For checking the survival of lexical items in Romance languages, the standard remains Meyer-Lübke's *Romanisches Etymologisches Wörterbuch* (*REW*).[4]

Theoretical works that have proved helpful include Bybee's *Morphology* (1985) and Aronoff's *Morphology by Itself* (1994) for stems of verbs in Latin. Moreover, Bybee, Perkins, and Pagliuca's *Evolution of Grammar* (1994) offers a worldwide perspective on the development of anteriors as well as perfectives; Heine's *Auxiliaries* (1993) surveys grammaticalization and the conceptual shifts involved; Carstairs's *Allomorphy in Inflexion* (1987) examines attempts to explain deviations from the ideal one-to-one match between meaning and form; Hall's *Morphology and Mind* (1992) reviews historical evidence for affix creation; Beard's *Lexeme-Morpheme Based Morphology* (1995) gives a syntactic test for distinguishing adjectives from past participles that have identical morphology. Articles about theory used here include Maiden's "Irregularity as a Determinant of Morphological Change" and Vincent's "Towards an Explanation of Some Analogies in Perfect and Past Participle Stems in Latin and Italian."

Regardless of the terminology, if any, used in a Romance language or dialect, verbs are classified according to Latin nomenclature so that the reader may make cross-linguistic comparisons more easily. Thus, reflexes of -ĀRE verbs are described as 1st-conjugation ones, reflexes of -ĒRE verbs as 2nd-conjugation ones, to reflexes of ʹ-ERE verbs as 3rd-conjugation ones, and reflexes of -ĪRE verbs as 4th-conjugation ones. When a language or dialect has blended, say, the 2nd and 3rd conjugations of Latin, such blends are marked with a solids: 2nd-/3rd-conj. verbs.

To help the reader further, the term **preterit** covers the Romanian aorist, the Italian *passato remoto*, the French *passé simple*, and of course the Catalan *pretèrit* and Spanish *pretérito*. Throughout, the term **infinitive** refers to the present active infinitive, the only one to survive into Romance

---

[3] Iliescu and Mourin promise a second volume tracing the historical evolution of verb forms.

[4] An anonymous reviewer has called Meyer-Lübke (and Elcock as well) "somewhat dated" sources. Perhaps so. One has to guard against Meyer-Lübke's neogrammarian assumption that sound laws admit of no exception, which leads him to assert e.g. that Sp. *nunca* 'never' < NUMQUAM (rather than "regular" *nonca*) must have come into being as a learnèd term. One has to guard against Meyer-Lübke's insouciance about marking entries with macrons or asterisks. Yet that anonymous reviewer has neglected to mention which work, if any, could have supplanted the *REW*. For a review of etymological approaches taken by neogrammarians, see Malkiel 1993b, 22–24.

except for the perfect passive infinitive (type AMĀTUM ESSE 'to have been loved'), which took on a present-tense value 'to be loved.'[5]

Unless otherwise stated, all Romance past participles are given in the masc.sg., descended from both masculine and neuter forms in Classical Latin. Remnants of noun-phrase marking by case have been ignored: Old French and Old Occitan past participles are given in the oblique, and Romanian past participles in the nominative/accusative.

Recalling how annoyed I used to get at authors' ascribing to their public a thorough knowledge of Walloon or Welsh or Vlach, I have supplied glosses for every form cited in this book, right down to Ptg. *grande* 'big.'

Custom dictates that macrons be written above long vowels in words from Classical Latin, in which length was phonemic. Yet CL words were not the direct ancestors of Romance words. Rather, the inventories of vowels (and consonants) in Romance come down from several patterns traceable to Late Latin, none of which precisely matched the CL pattern. Written on historical principles, this book nonetheless cuts corners. So when I put something like "Fr. *dit* < DICTU 'said, told'" or "Fr. *mis* 'put' < MISSU 'sent,'" I mean that the first item has stayed in what I call type 9 (tautic athematic) and the second item has stayed in what I call type 8 (sigmatic), not that the vowel in either past participle comes straight from Latin. Again, in Catalan, p.p. *escrit* < SCRĪPTU 'written' may look like a 4th-conj. form and p.p. *dut* 'carried' < DUCTU 'led' like a 2nd-/3rd-conj. form, but I rank both as type 9s still.

A methodological qualification is perhaps in order. Unlike linguists studying most other languages, researchers into Romance have the privilege of drawing upon texts in the ancient mother tongue as well as in the mediæval daughter tongues and modern granddaughter tongues. Between the Latin of Cæsar's *Commentaries* (before 44 BCE) and the Romance of the *Strasbourg Oaths* (842 CE), there nonetheless remains a wide gap both chronological and morphological. Bearing in mind Price's observation apropos of the spread of -ŪTUM p.p.s that "[i]t is in most cases impossible to determine whether this [reshaping] took place in V[ulgar] L[atin] or later and independently in the various Romance languages" (223), and noting difficulties in dating even approximately the emergence of other unclassical past participles eventually attested in Romance, I still assume that past-participial forms found (with suitable phonological adjustments) in more than one Romance language represent reflexes of creations by speakers of Late Latin or Proto-Romance, even if such creations have gone unattested so far.[6]

In any unattested variant, it would be the height of presumption to put a macron over a vowel; I have almost always refrained from doing so. Readers should regard starred forms as indicative rather than definitive.

After all, speakers might have remodeled parts of a given verb because of rhyming analogies or semantic similarities with another verb. They might have done so because of an unconscious wish to level outstanding though

---

[5] For a discussion of the origin and development of infinitives in Latin, see Sihler, 610–13.

[6] For details about the phonology of Latin, see Vincent 1988a, 28–33.

infrequent irregularities to the profit of irregular forms that remained, which thereby came to sound more distinctive. Especially when applied to a past participle appearing in only one language or dialect, a starred form should not be regarded as excluding any possibility of analogical remodeling in Proto-Romance, or indeed later.

When a work about a little-known dialect has listed no past participle for a verb and no survival of a Classical Latin form either, the most that one can say here is what the regular outcome would most likely be. In the absence of hypothetical reconstructions in such cases, readers may find that *Past Participles from Latin to Romance* slightly understates the trend toward sharper marking through time for past participles of most verbs that survived.

0.3. BACKGROUND

This section covers a few preliminary matters in the mother tongue of Romance: how words were stressed, and what kinds of endings the verbs had.

0.3.1. Word-Stress Rules in Latin

As long-term trends favored past participles clearly marked by class with a tonic vowel or [s], it will be well to review the rules governing stress. In Latin, stress could fall on the last syllable or **ultima**, on the second-to-last syllable or **penult**, or on the third-from-last syllable or **antepenult**. Two features determined where stress fell: the quantity (length) of the penult or antepenult vowel, and the number of consonants, if any, after that vowel. A syllable counted as long if it had a long vowel or a diphthong, or if it had a short vowel followed by two or more consonants.

All monosyllables were of course stressed on the single vowel or diphthong of their ultima; no CL past participle fell into that category. In disyllables like the p.p.s CURSUM 'run,' NĀTUM 'born,' and CLAUSUM 'closed,' stress fell on the first vowel, whether short or long.

In polysyllables, stress fell on the penult when that syllable counted as long, whether because of a long vowel as in the p.p.s VOLĀTUM 'flown,' DĒLĒTUM 'destroyed,' PETĪTUM 'asked,' and SOLŪTUM 'loosened,' or because of a short vowel followed by two or more consonants as in the p.p.s ASPERSUM 'sprinkled' and COOPERTUM 'covered.' Some polysyllables with penult stress, like the p.p.s SURRĒCTUM 'arisen' and PRŌTĒCTUM 'covered over,' had a long penult vowel before a consonant cluster, so that the tonic syllable also counted as long. However, when a polysyllabic word had a short penult vowel before only one consonant, stress fell on its antepenult, as in the p.p.s CÓGNĬTUM 'known,' NÓCĬTUM 'harmed,' and VÁLĬTUM 'been strong, been worth.'

By and large, words in Romance languages retain stress on the same syllable that was stressed in Latin. Owing to the disappearance of most final vowels in Romanian, Catalan, Occitan, and French, these languages have developed disyllables and polysyllables stressed on the last syllable. Thus, from penult-stressed AUDĪTUM 'heard' have come masc.sg. Rom. *auzit*, Cat. *oït*, OOc. *auzit*, and OFr. *ouï* with stress on the ultima. In contrast, their cognates It. *udito*, Sp. *oído*, and Ptg. *ouvido* have kept their final vowels and hence kept stress on the penult.

0.3.2. Verb Classes and Past-Participial Types in Latin

Morphologically, the most predictable types of CL past participle showed a stressed vowel from the stem of the **perfectum** (used to form perfect, pluperfect, and future-perfect tenses) or from the stem of the **infectum** (used to form present, imperfect, and future tenses). The two most predictable types had the same stressed vowel in most forms of both infectum and perfectum, stress falling on the penult of their past participles as well. In Latin, stressed [a:] and [i:] normally occurred in most forms of 1st-conj. verbs with infinitives ending in -ĀRE and in most forms of 4th-conj. verbs with infinitives ending in -ĪRE, respectively; for such verbs, those stressed vowels occurred throughout the perfectum, including the past participle.

For the 1st-conj. verb meaning 'like, love,' a few of the forms in stressed [a:] were infin. AMĀRE, 1pl. pres.indic.act. AMĀMUS, 2pl. imper. AMĀTE, 1sg. pf.indic.act. AMĀVĪ, p.p. AMĀTUM. For the 4th-conj. verb meaning 'end,' a few of the forms in stressed [i:] were infin. FĪNĪRE, 1pl. pres.indic.act. FĪNĪMUS, 2pl. imper. FĪNĪTE, 1sg. pf.indic.act. FĪNĪVĪ, p.p. FĪNĪTUM.

Rare in Latin, an apparently regular 2nd-conj. type with stressed [e:] throughout, as in infin. FLĒRE 'weep,' 1sg. pf.indic.act. FLĒVĪ, p.p. FLĒTUM, disappeared in Proto-Romance if not earlier. Also rare in Latin, verbs whose 1sg. pres.indic.act. ended in -UŌ or -VŌ regularly had p.p.s ending in -ŪTUM, though for a verb like SOLVERE 'loosen' vocalic [u:] occurred only in the fut.p. and in the p.p. SOLŪTUM. In Late Latin or Proto-Romance times, that -ŪTUM type spread to the past participles of many verbs belonging to the 2nd conjugation in -ĒRE or to the 3rd conjugation in ´-ĔRE, even though few if any finite verb forms in these classes acquired [u]. Verbs with past participles in stressed [a:], [i:], or [u:] (and also [e:]) after the root will be termed **arrhizotonic**.[7]

Three types of past participles in Latin were **rhizotonic**, bearing root stress. They could end in ´-ITUM, in ´-TUM, or in ´-(S)SUM. Verbs with perfects in -UĪ and roots ending in a liquid or nasal consonant normally had past participles in ´-ITUM, as witness pf. MONUĪ and p.p. MONITUM 'warned.' For some verbs, notably most 3rd-conj. ones, -TUM was suffixed directly to the

---

[7] The term a rrh i zot oni c may indicate that stress falls either before or after the stem. Thus, past participles in -ĀTU, -ĒTU, -ĪTU, and -ŪTU would more accurately be called post rh i zot oni c. For a review of the formation of long-vowel past participles in Latin, see Leumann, 617, and Sihler, 623–24.

root, with no theme vowel intervening, as in DOCTUM 'taught,' SECTUM 'cut,' CULTUM 'tilled' as against the perfect-tense forms DOCUĪ, SECUĪ, and COLUĪ. Other common examples were DICTUM 'said,' SCRĪPTUM 'written,' FACTUM 'done/made' as against the present-tense forms DĪCŌ, SCRĪBŌ, FACIŌ. I refer to the first type in ´-ITUM as **rhizotonic thematic** and to the second type in directly suffixed -TUM as **tautic athematic**.

When a dental stop (**D**) ended the stem, **D** + -TUM gave -(S)SUM; -SSUM was preserved if otherwise the root syllable would be light, as after a short vowel. Thus were formed the p.p.s MORSUM 'bitten' and FISSUM 'split,' contrasting with perfect-tense MOMORDĪ and FIDĪ, present-tense MORDEŌ, FINDŌ, which kept [d]. Such **sigmatic** past participles often occurred where a verb's perfect contained [s] as well, as in pf. CESSĪ and p.p. CESSUM as against pres. CEDŌ 'yield.'[8] By analogy with such past participles, other CL verbs acquired past participles of the same type like LĀPSUM 'slipped,' MULSUM 'milked,' FĪXUM 'fastened,' PULSUM 'throbbed,' and CĒNSUM 'deemed,' though the stems of these verbs' 1sg. pres.indic.act. forms LĀBOR, MULGEŌ, FĪGŌ, PELLŌ, and CĒNSEŌ ended in neither [t] nor [d] (Sihler, 625).

Another type of past participle, like GESTUM 'done, waged' (cf. pres. GERŌ), HAUSTUM 'drained, emptied' (pres. HAURIŌ), and USTUM 'charred' (pres. ŪRŌ) combined sigmatic with tautic athematic marking.[9] In such verbs, past participles and infectum forms had grown less alike because [s] had rhotacized when intervocalic but had stayed as such before e.g. [t]. I call this fairly rare type **sigmatic-tautic**.[10]

A final past-participial possibility for Latin verbs may startle readers who are better acquainted with Romance. As shown in Table 0–1 on page 9, more than a few Latin verbs were defective, in that they had no fourth principal part. In this book, Latin verbs lacking that part are marked **no CL p.p.**

Many defective verbs were inchoative, denoting the start of an action, like FLŌRĒSCERE 'burst into bloom.' Many others were stative, denoting ongoing conditions, like CALĒRE 'be hot' or MARCĒRE 'be faded.' Perhaps because of the temporal or aspectual ranges covered by inchoatives and statives, such verbs seldom had a past participle in Classical Latin, though they usually did have a finite perfectum. One hesitates to rank as necessarily inchoative or

---

[8] Strictly, the term sigmatic should refer only to forms whose markers are etymologically -s-, as in Gk. aorists like ἔλυσα 'I left' versus asigmatic present λύω 'I leave.' A more accurate term for forms like MORSUM 'bitten' and FISSUM 'split' would be secondary sigmatic.

[9] That [st] combination is therefore conservative. For a review of combinatory changes in consonant-final stems for past participles, and of the ´-ITU type of past participle, see Leumann, 615–17, and Sihler, 624–25.

[10] Earlier, a roughly comparable development had taken place in Greek. From verbal adjectives like πιστός 'to be trusted,' ζωστός 'girded,' the ending -στός spread to certain vowel-final stems unentitled to it on etymological grounds: thus, Homeric γνωτός 'understood' was replaced by sigmatic-tautic γνωστός (Sihler, 625). For Italian p.p.s in -sto, see §3.5.5.1.

Table 0–1

Latin Verbs Lacking Past Participles

High-Frequency	2nd Conjugation	3rd Conjugation
ESSE 'be'	CALĒRE 'be hot'	FERVERE 'boil'
POSSE 'be able'	FLŌRĒRE 'bloom'	NING(U)ERE 'snow'
SAPERE 'taste, know'	LŪCĒRE 'shine'	PLUERE 'rain'
VELLE 'want'	MARCĒRE 'be faded'	STRĪDERE 'creak'
	TIMĒRE 'fear'	TREMERE 'quake'

A few CL verbs had past participles that were suppletive, borrowed from other verbs. In this book, such verbs are also marked **no CL p.p.**, since their p.p.s were unrelated morphologically to their infectum or their finite perfectum. For verbs like BIBERE 'drink' (pf. BIBĪ, p.p. PŌTUM) and FERĪRE 'hit' (pf. ĪCĪ or PERCUSSĪ, p.p. ICTUM or PERCUSSUM), the term **no CL p.p.** should be understood to mean "no nonsuppletive past participle in Latin." That phrase never appears after suppletive FERRE TULĪ LĀTUM 'carry,' for with rare exceptions only the stem of its finite perfectum TULĪ (related to TOLLERE 'raise; remove') was to survive into Romance.

0.4. QUESTIONS TO BE ANSWERED

In *Past Participles from Latin to Romance*, I try to find answers to the following questions. Which types of CL past participle survived into Romance, and why did they do so? What older, "irregular" types disappeared? What older, "regular" types were generalized? What new types of participles emerged? How were past participles devised for verbs that had lacked them, and how were they devised? Where did reflexes of individual past participles survive, and why did they do so? Is it true that only ultra-high-frequency forms remained irregular? Which types of past participles proved popular in each part of ROMANIA?

Given that past participles started life as verbal adjectives (see §1.1), it may be understandable that some should have lost their membership in the verb phrase. Which past participles in Romance came to be restricted to adjectival use, like Engl. *molten, shaven, shrunken, drunken,* and *stricken* but unlike past-participial *melted, shaved, shrunk, drunk,* and *struck*? Which past participles lasted on adjectivally, perhaps in a set phrase or two, after their verbs went out of style, like Engl. *graven* 'carved,' *smitten* 'hit'? Which past participles went out of style along with their whole verbs, like Engl. *chidden* 'rebuked,' *trodden* 'walked on'? After all, forms resembling Germ. *alt* 'old' and *kalt* 'cold,' perhaps from old past participles meaning 'having grown up' and 'having cooled,' had already become adjectival by Common Germanic times (Lockwood, 163).

In Classical Latin also, old past participles had broken all semantic links with their verbs and turned into pure adjectives: CASTUM 'clean, pure' was the old past participle for pres. CAREŌ 'lack, abstain,' as CERTUM 'definite, reliable' was the old past participle for CERNŌ 'sift; decide,' and SALSUM 'salty, salted' was the old past participle for SAL(I)Ō 'salt.' Others wavered: CAUTUM '(been) watchful, careful' could be used either as a past participle or as an adjective (Flobert, 495). How did similar developments affect past participles through the centuries in Romance?[11] Could past participles shed their thematic marking and come to resemble adjectives, or, in some languages, 1st-person singular verbs from the present indicative?[12]

From east to west, the principal varieties of Romance dealt with here are Romanian, Italian, Sardinian, Friulian, Ladin, Ræto-Romance, French, Franco-Provençal, Occitan, Catalan, Spanish, and Portuguese. As far as evidence allows, I also treat Aromanian (and Meglenoromanian), Istro-Romanian, and extinct Vegliote in the Balkans. Within language groupings, certain dialects or separate languages are reviewed in detail. Romanian has two such dialects: Oltenian and Moldavian. West of Croatia and Slovenia, Gallo-Italian has six such dialects: Istriano, Lombard, Piedmontese, Ligurian, Romagnolo, and Lunigiana. Below the La Spezia–Rimini line, central-southern Italian has seven: Corsican, Calabrian, Abruzzese, Apulian, Lucanian, and Sicilian. Sardinian has three: Campidanese, Logudorese, and Nuorese. In Switzerland, Ræto-Romance has two: Engadin and Surselvan. To the northwest, French has three: Norman, Picard, and Burgundian. To the south, Franco-Provençal has four: Naisey, Vaux, Vaud, and Val d'Aosta. Farther south, Occitan has five: Gascon, Poitevin, Auvergnat, Gévaudanais, and Languedocian. Catalan has four: Rossellonese, Valencian, Tamaritan, and Alguerese. In the rest of Iberia, Spanish has two: Aragonese and Leonese.

---

[11] By CL times, CARĬTU 'lacked' and CRĒTU 'sifted; decided' (the latter also meaning 'grown,' from another verb) had developed as new fillers for two of those past-participial slots. A review of adjectivized and nominalized past participles appears in Leumann, 612–14. Some of these, like the p.p./adj. CONTENTU₁ 'contented,' are better linked to reflexive verbs, in this case SĒ CONTINERE, than to nonreflexive ones. Note also CONTENTU₂, purely past-participial for CONTENDERE 'strain, strive.' Other adjectives from past participles, like INULTU 'unavenged, unpunished' or IRRĬTU 'invalid, vain,' appear to have been used primarily in the negative (Joffre, 349, 350).

[12] In this book, I use the term **short-form** to describe past participles that look like adjectives or 1sg. pres.indic. verbs in Italian, Spanish, and Portuguese. The term is borrowed from Slavic morphology: in Russian, for instance, many adjectives and all passive participles have both long and short forms. For details, see Unbegaun, 97–100, 234–35, 246–47.

Portuguese has one: Galician. To increase granularity further, I scan subdialects, among them Val Graveglia within Ligurian, San Mango sul Calore within Calabrian, Sot de Ferrer within Spanish, and Barranquenho within (southern) Portuguese. I regret all gaps that persist in p.p. coverage.

The choice of dialects was determined in large part by the availability of published material at Berkeley, Georgetown, and the Library of Congress. Native speakers were consulted for major languages.[13]

0.5. SURVIVAL AND DISAPPEARANCE OF PAST-PARTICIPIAL TYPES

Can one detect any long-term trend in the success or failure of certain types of past participle in Romance? Contradicting Jespersen's view that the most efficient languages express the greatest amount of meaning with the simplest mechanisms, Aitchison notes that in certain tongues "true simplicity seems to be counterbalanced by ambiguity and cumbersomeness" (226). Moreover, a language that appears simple and regular in one respect is likely to be complex and confusing in others.[14] Little if any evidence exists that languages are making progress toward complete regularity. Instead, Aitchison observes "a continuous pull between the disruption and regularization of patterns" (227), so that an observer would be wrong to regard either leveling of irregularities as a step forward or disruption of patterns as a step backward.

Nevertheless, the view adopted in this study may be said to echo that of Jakobson: "The overlapping between territorially, socially, or functionally distinct linguistic patterns can be fully comprehended only from a teleological point of view, since every transition from one system to another necessarily bears a linguistic function" (2). As much as I can make sense out of that, I plan to highlight certain morphological changes through time and across space without aspiring to what Jakobson would call full comprehension. I avoid delving deeply, or at all, into any signification supposedly lurking beneath the changes, a task for which I have been rendered unfit by temperament and training alike.

Over the centuries, but especially in Late Latin and Proto-Romance times, there appears to have been interplay between two competing tendencies:

---

[13] At the risk of causing confusion with the Italian dialect Romagnolo (abbreviated Rml.), with Romansch (abbreviated RR for Ræto-Romance), or with Romance-speaking areas (ROMANIA in small capitals), I refer to the language spoken in what was once Dacia as Romanian (abbreviated Rom.). I then follow suit with Aromanian, Meglenoromanian, and Istro-Romanian. As an analyst born in what is now Moldova has put it, "No Romanian ever said that he or she is a *Ru-* and that he/she speaks *Ru-*. Not even the last countryman or shepherd in the Carpathians" (E. Vrabie, p.c.).

[14] Because this work deals with morphology far more than with phonetics or phonology, all cases of visible speech—known, reconstructed, or assumed—are expressed in broad transcriptions. In words from modern French, for instance, I never mention that [t], [d], and [n] are dental or that [r] is uvular. For words from Latin and Romance, I use [a] (instead of [ɑ]) to stand for the vowel heard in Engl. *father, wash*.

forces of tradition tended to preserve archaic types of past-participial formation, especially high-frequency ones, while analogical reshapings tended to move most past participles into more transparent classes, either with a stressed theme vowel or with sigmatic marking. Syntactically, past participles became for the first time a central part of the verb system, used to create a specifically perfect construction absent from Classical Latin as well as new passive constructions.

Table 0–2

Vowel Change in Irregular Romance Verbs

≠ does not continue CL form

language	1sg. Present Indicative	1sg. Preterit	Past Participle
French	tiens < TENEŌ	tins ≠ TENUĪ	tenu ≠ TENTU
Spanish	hago < *FACŌ	hize < FĒCĪ	hecho < FACTU
Catalan	veig < VIDEŌ	viu < VĪDĪ	vist ≠ VĪSU
Italian	ho < HABEŌ	ebbi < HABUĪ	avuto ≠ HABĬTU

In Romance, some of the most common verbs preserve or have evolved anomalous forms like ones that have been leveled through analogy in less common verbs. Already relics in CL times, for instance, few of the ablaut series in verbs have survived into Romance. Yet, even after stems for many preterits and past participles have been brought into line with each other, the alternations of tonic vowels have emerged in paradigms like the ones in Table 0–2 for French *tenir* 'hold,' Spanish *hacer* 'do/make,' Catalan *veure* 'see,' and Italian *avere* 'have.' Such alternations provide evidence that, irregularly, vowel change still distinguishes principal parts for verbs across ROMANIA.[15] In the chapters that follow, I investigate the emergence of new irregularities alongside the leveling of old anomalies.

---

[15] Several of the outcomes in Table 0–2 require explanation (not given here), for they cannot have developed straight from CL forms. If only for certain high-frequency verbs, vowel change clearly remains a marker of tense in Romance. It has even developed for verbs whose Latin originals displayed no such changes. Throughout this book, as noted in Chapter 6, I avoid considering Romance present-tense indicatives and subjunctives, which despite fairly recent leveling are often less regular than their Latin ancestors.

In Latin, a verb might form its past participle in one of nine ways. Every Romance language and dialect has fewer. Among standard languages, complexity generally remains greatest in the east, for Romanian and Italian both have seven types of past-participial formants, but then again so does Catalan; French has six types; Spanish and Portuguese have only four. Coincidentally, the two most successful Romance languages in number of speakers have the fewest p.p. irregularities.

If one excludes rhizotonic types, unproductive almost everywhere, speakers have reduced the number of past-participial classes to three in Romanian, Italian, Catalan, and French. Elsewhere, leveling has gone further still. In three areas—Lucanian, Calabrian, and Sicilian in southern Italy, Engadin and Surselvan in Switzerland, and Spanish and Portuguese in Iberia—speakers have reduced the number of classes for regular past participles to just two: one for reflexes of verbs in the 1st conjugation, the other for reflexes of verbs in the 2nd, 3rd, and 4th conjugations. No Romance speakers has yet gone so far as to have one regular type.

0.6. PREVIEW OF SUBSEQUENT
CHAPTER AND APPENDIXES

As adumbrated in Chapter 1 and discussed more fully in Chapter 2, speakers of Late Latin increasingly came to prefer arrhizotonic past participles, which had stress on their theme vowels like many other forms of regular verbs. Rhizotonic types of past participle were to become fewer still across most of ROMANIA, while the three arrhizotonic types in reflexes of [a:], [i:], and [u:] have flourished far more than they did in Latin. Lausberg's comment (251) that past participles marked in -S- or -SS- and past participles with -T- suffixed directly to the stem were leftovers from IE verbal adjectives and survive in Romance in no systematic way has thus been proved half right, given the spread of sigmatic marking in eastern Romance. Lausberg's comment could apply equally well to rhizotonic past participles ending in -ITUM, which have vanished outside Sardinia and parts of southern Italy.

Still retaining their adjectival function today—many old rhizotonics are extant only as adjectives—past participles have expanded their syntactic role to serve as markers of perfectivity par excellence from Portuguese to Romanian. How did this expansion come about? Chapter 2 examines in detail the reshaping of verb paradigms, particularly past-participial types, presumed to have taken place during Late Latin and Proto-Romance.

Chapters 3 and 4 review evidence across ROMANIA, from east to west, for both regular arrhizotonic formation and anomalous rhizotonic formation of past participles. As explained in detail, eastern Romance proves more conservative in keeping rhizotonic past participles, even evolving new sigmatic ones; western Romance retains fewer CL rhizotonics, with innovation tending toward generalization of arrhizotonic forms.[16]

In Chapter 5, the past-participial data gathered are examined to determine not merely which types survived where but also, perhaps, why certain types tended to flourish in one area while withering away in another. In Chapter 6, theoretical implications of the study are discussed, especially for the light that they may shed on speakers' changing past-participial preferences from one century to another, from one land to another.

Appendix 1 reviews popular and unpopular types of past participles in major languages across ROMANIA. Appendix 2 lists outcomes within a corpus of past participles for Latin verbs that survived. Appendix 3 quantifies the data gathered, even for probably unrepresentative corpora that highlight irregular forms more attractive to the connoisseur than to the statistician.

Next comes the list of references, not "sources," because I look at few if any primary sources here. Last comes a 100-page index verborum designed to pinpoint by section number each past participle from non-Latin languages, Latin, and Romance that appears between the start of the Introduction and the end of Chapter 6.

---

[16] Declining to open a particularly noisome can of worms, I make no attempt in this book to define the terms "Late Latin" and "Proto-Romance." In all likelihood I have allowed other terminological misconstructions, if not inexactitudes, to slip in here and there. For a review of sources of evidence about Latin, see Vincent 1988a, 26.

1

Latin Past Participles, Inherited and Innovated

We have no text which is a faithful record
of even one mode of contemporary speech.
The chisel of the stonemason, the pen of the
loquacious nun, and the chalk that scribbles
on the wall, disregard the tongue and move
self-willed in traditional patterns.

Palmer, *The Latin Language*

1.0. OVERVIEW

In this chapter, I trace the emergence of Latin perfect or past participles from
one type of verbal adjective in Indo-European (IE), and I sketch the syntactic
role played by past participles in Classical Latin (CL).[1] After considering
probable reshapings within the perfectum that took place before Latin was
written down, I review anomalies that endured and reshapings that occurred
after a literary standard was established. I then look at how speakers of Late
Latin developed specifically perfect verb forms and restricted old perfects to an
aorist or punctual sense.

Turning to other IE languages, I trace expansions in the syntactic roles
played by past participles, which at times—though never in Romance—have
crowded out earlier preterits to stand by themselves as past-tense verbs.
Likewise, I show that, in some of Romance, originally present-perfect
constructions like Fr. *j'ai été* 'I have been' have tended to displace reflexes of
Latin perfects like the Old French preterit *je fui* 'I was [once].'[2]

---

[1] For a survey of the Indo-European verb system, see Sihler, 442–53.

[2] Reduction to [i] of the ending from -ĪTUM could have sped the disappearance of OFr. 1sg.
prets. in [i̯] like *bui* 'drank,' *crui* 'believed,' which lost final yod but later acquired a graphic -s.

15

1.1. HISTORICAL SURVEY OF VERBAL ADJECTIVES: INDO-EUROPEAN TO LATIN

In Indo-European, certain nominal forms drawn from verbal stems could best be regarded as verbal adjectives used in apposition to any noun in a sentence (Meillet 1964, 374). Apparently corresponding in use to adjectives and nouns, they retained the functions of finite verbal forms (Lehmann, 208). Older IE languages like Greek and Sanskrit preserved that feature best. Thus, Greek present, aorist, or perfect participles could express an attribute of a noun they qualified; they could define the circumstances of an action; they could supplement the meaning of other verbs (Goodwin, 328).

Although verbal adjectives in IE might be built from a great variety of suffixes, some verbs had an adjectival type in *-tó- not belonging to any tense or to any voice (Buck, 307). IE forms in *-tó- became a type of Sanskrit participle with accented -tás and the Greek verbal adjective with accented -τός (masc.nom.sg.); they usually had passive force if derived from transitive roots, active force if derived from intransitive ones. In Sanskrit, then, active verbal adjectives like jātás 'born' and bhūtás 'having become, been' belonged to intransitive verbs, while a passive verbal adjective like dāntás 'tamed, subdued' belonged to a transitive verb.

In Greek, an active verbal adjective like ῥυτός 'flowing' belonged to the intransitive verb ῥέω 'flow.' A passive verbal adjective like γραπτός 'written' belonged to the transitive verb γράφω 'write.' A third type of verbal adjective, also belonging to transitive verbs, denoted possibility, with ὁρατός 'visible' belonging to ὁράω 'see,' ἀκουστός 'audible' belonging to ἀκούω 'hear,' νοητός 'thinkable' belonging to νοέω 'think.' That those last two categories could overlap is suggested by polysemy for the verbal adjective related to transitive αἱρέω 'take, catch': αἱρετός might mean either 'chosen, elected' or 'conquerable; intelligible.' Other Greek verbal adjectives displaying polysemy were μεμπτός 'blamed; blamable,' πιστός 'trusting in [rare]; trusted,' and ἀπρακτός 'doing nothing; not done' (Smyth, 157).

In Gothic, that suffix deriving from -tó- appeared as -þs in masc.nom.sg. past participles for one class of weak verbs. In preterit-present verbs, the suffix from athematic -tó- might appear as -þs in past participles like kunþs 'known' < IE *gnHtós, or as -ds in past participles like skulds 'owing, lawful' < *skḷtós, or else as -ts in þaúrfts 'useful,' adjectivized past participle of þarf 'need.' Thus, a cross-linguistic comparison of reflexes of the IE verbal adjective *statós, meaning 'standing, stood up,' would yield nom.sg. Skt. sthitás, Gk. στατός, CL STĂTUS, and Goth. staþs 'a place,' for which cf. Engl. stead (J. Wright, 163).

Verbs in IE had various ways of making presents, aorists, and perfects. Conjugational classes emerged in each daughter language according to different patterns. As will be shown, close morphological links between the perfect (later preterit) and the past participle have existed from CL times on, with differences between the stems for the two verb forms tending to narrow through the centuries in Romance. A similar development might have taken place in early Germanic: if the endings of Gothic weak preterits in (1sg.) *-ida* and *-ōda* and *-áida* did not represent remnants of an agglutinated periphrasis with reflexes of an old aorist *dhe:-* 'put, place' (cf. Gk. τίθημι, Engl. *d o*), as some analysts maintain, it is likely that the dental stop in past-tense verbs like *salbōda* 'anointed,' *þāhta* 'thought,' and *habáida* 'had' was closely related to the dental stop or interdental fricative of those verbs' past participles *salbōþs*, *þāhts*, and *habáiþs*, which themselves were certainly related to Latin verbal adjectives in -TUM.[3]

In addition to that dental suffix used for the past participles of weak verbs, Gothic had a suffix deriving from *-nó-* that gave endings on past participles for strong verbs, like *bitans* 'bitten,' *budans* 'bid, asked,' *numans* 'taken,' as also for some in Sanskrit like *t īrṇás* 'crossed,' and *h īnás* 'left, abandoned.' A reflex of that nasal suffix *-nó-* appeared in some Latin words like PLĒNUM 'full' and DŌNUM 'gift' (Safarewicz, 256; Braune, 103). A third type of verbal adjective in *-ró-*, with transitive or intransitive force, appeared in a few Latin words like CĀRUM 'dear' [earlier 'loving'?, 'being loved'?] and INTEGER 'whole, entire' [earlier 'untouched'?] (Sihler, 628). Nevertheless, reflexes of either *-nó-* or *-ró-* were never used to build past participles in Latin; only the *-tó-* type was so used (Leumann, 611). In certain Romance languages, from Istrian to Franco-Provençal, hardly a trace remains of that *-tó-* marker today.[4]

1.2. SYNTACTIC ROLE OF PAST PARTICIPLES IN LATIN

In Classical Latin, reflexes of the *-tó-* type of adjectival formant could be found not only on verbal bases but also on nominal ones, giving e.g. (neuter nom./acc. sg.) BARBĀTUM 'bearded' from BARBA 'beard,' ONUSTUM 'loaded, laden' from ONUS 'load, freight,' and SEXTUM 'sixth' from SEX 'six.' Only those drawn from verbal bases could become verbal adjectives, yet not every verb had its own adjective (Monteil, 347; Magnien, 405). By contrast with Greek, verbal adjectives were thoroughly integrated into the verb system of Latin (Meillet and Vendryes, 555). They came to serve as perfect or past participles, "originally denoting a completed action or state, i.e. corresponding to the perfective aspect of the Latin verbal system" (Harris 1978, 201), and were

---

[3] For a discussion of the origin of the Germanic dental preterit, with a detailed bibliography, see Braune, 109.

[4] Such an audible [t] survives only when deriving from a CL [kt] or [pt] cluster followed by CL final [a], which sequence became [tə] or [jtə] in Old French. Recall also that, like Germanic languages, Russian retains two types of past passive participle: one suffixed in [n] and one suffixed in [t] (Unbegaun, 176–78). That the [n] type should be productive and the [t] type unproductive in Russian today—the reverse of what applies in e.g. current English—shows how speakers in various areas have made different choices to expand or contract the scope of application for inherited morphemes.

identified by Roman grammarians as the fourth principal part of verbs. Syntactically, past participles were considered passive for transitive verbs but active for intransitive verbs and deponent verbs. An example of that last type is MENTĪTUM 'having lied' (cf. MENTĪRĪ 'tell lies'). However, some transitive verbs had past participles with active force: PŌTUM 'having drunk' or JŪRĀTUM 'having sworn.'[5]

Most commonly used in a predicative role to add new information about the subject, past participles usually suggested that the action they denoted happened before that of the main verb, as often in ablative-absolute constructions like CETHĒGUS, RECITĀTĪS LITTERĪS, REPENTE CONTICUIT 'when the letter had been **read out**, Cethegus suddenly fell silent.' Past participles might also suggest cause, concession, or condition, as in NŌN MIHI NISI ADMONITŌ VĒNISSET IN MENTEM 'it would not have entered my head unless I had been **reminded**.' In addition, past participles might mark events themselves, so that the passage VIOLĀTĪ HOSPITĒS, LĒGĀTĪ NECĀTĪ, FĀNA VEXĀTA HANC TANTAM EFFĒCĒRUNT VĀSTITĀTEM, literally '**violated** guests, **slaughtered** ambassadors, **ravaged** shrines brought about this massive devastation' would be better rendered by reshaping the past participles into nouns: 'the violation of guests, the slaughter of ambassadors, the destruction of shrines...' (Jones and Sidwell, 529–30). The latter rendering would sound more like Romance, famed for strings of noun phrases.

CL past participles also served to create passive verb forms in the perfectum (type MISSUM EST 'it was/has been sent,' MISSUM ERAT 'it had been sent,' MISSUM ERIT 'it will have been sent'). In contrast with Romance, the syntactic range of participles in CL remained rather narrow; generally speaking, they appear not to have been used to form active compound perfect verbs. Moreover, as Vincent remarks, past participles in Latin were related to the verb root by derivation instead of inflection. Vincent explains: "By this we mean that it was a related word built on the same root as the forms of the verb, but not a necessary part of the verbal paradigm required by the operation of general morphosyntactic rules" (1978, 54).

Resembling past participles morphologically were future active participles, almost always built on the same stem as the past participle plus a suffix -ŪR- before their adjectival endings. In certain instances, as Aronoff points out (33–35), verbs lacking a past participle did have a future active participle: ESSE 'be' had FUTŪRUM, CALĒRE 'be hot' had CALITŪRUM, and DOLĒRE 'be hurt' had DOLITŪRUM. Moreover, a few 1st-conj. verbs with irregular perfects had regular future participles, so that e.g. SONĀRE 'ring' with pf. SONUĪ and p.p.

---

[5] Sihler notes (622) that a very few CL adjectivized past participles seem to have once had present-tense meaning: CIRCUMSPECTUM 'cautious' (earlier 'looking around') and ĪNFĒNSUM 'hostile' (earlier 'attacking'). As Laughton points out (3), a few Latin p.p.s betrayed their adjectival origins in one of two ways: some like CĒNĀTUM 'dined,' PRĀNSUM 'brunched,' PŌTUM 'drunk,' and PRÆTERITUM 'gone by,' derived from verbs that were not passive; others like TACITUM 'been silent' and QUIĒTUM 'rested' did not imply past tense (or, as would be said today, anteriority).

SONITUM had fut.p. SONĀTŪRUM 'going to ring.' No future participles survived as such into Romance.[6]

Likewise resembling past participles morphologically, 4th-decl. verbal nouns called supines came down from a type suffixed in -*tu*- rather than -*tó*- and were ambiguous as to voice.[7] Supines in the accusative were used with verbs of motion to express purpose, as in MĪLITĒS MĪSIT PĀCEM PETĪTUM 's/he sent soldiers to ask for peace'; supines in the ablative of respect were used with a few adjectives, as in MĪRĀBILE DICTŪ 'wonderful to relate' (Jones and Sidwell, 459, 540). For the fourth principal part of most intransitive verbs like ĪTUM for ĪRE 'go' or VENTUM for VENĪRE 'come,' it is in fact the supine rather than the past participle that must be quoted (Sihler, 622). Rarely, as in p.p. STĂTUM as against supine STĀTUM 'stood,' the two forms differed in CL. Any such morphological distinction has long since vanished. From now on, therefore, I treat supines as past participles.[8]

1.3. PERSISTENT CONJUGATIONAL ANOMALIES IN THE PERFECTUM

It will be well to continue a review of the perfectum by examining the various types of perfect finite verb formation in Latin.

Four types were destined to remain popular. Two had clear marking with theme vowels: the 1st-conj. type with its -ĀVI pf. and its -ĀTUM p.p., and the 4th-conj. type with its -ĪVI pf. and its -ĪTUM p.p. A third type had its pf. in -UĪ (perhaps contracted from *-ŪVĪ) that, in CL, seldom matched another type of p.p. in -ŪTUM.[9] A fourth type had its perfect marked in -SĪ or -XĪ; its past participle most often bore either congruent sigmatic or contrastive tautic athematic marking.[10] All types except those four shrank through time. Notably, three types of perfect failed to thrive.

---

[6] Elcock (123) cites a few noun relics from future participles, like Fr. *aventure* < ADVENTŪRA 'things to come.' Note also Sp. *hechura* 'workmanship,' from FACTŪRA 'things to do/make.'

[7] That resemblance extended only to the accusative sg., where masc./neut. past participles and supines both had the ending -TUM. In the ablative sg., masc./neut. past participles ended in -TŌ and supines in -TŪ. Supines were used almost exclusively in the accusative and ablative sg., with a very rare "overtly dative supine" ending in -TUĪ probably being a secondary development (Sihler, 613). For other possible roles played by the supine in CL, see Sihler, 612.

[8] For a list of various types of nouns and verbs formed from the same stem as past participles —"the "third stem"—see Aronoff, 37–39. In this book, nouns from past participles are discussed in §3.1.5.3 (Romanian), §3.5.2 (Italian), §4.4.9 (French), §4.6.2.5 (Catalan), §4.7.7 (Spanish).

[9] For a discussion of long-vowel perfects in Latin, with bibliography, see Leumann, 589–91, 598–600. For a more theoretical approach, see Kurzová, 151.

[10] For a discussion of sigmatic perfects deriving from aorists in Latin, see Leumann, 591–93, and Sihler, 510–11, 582–84. Italic futures like OLat. FAXŌ 'will do/make' and CAPSŌ 'will take,' perhaps originally subjunctives of sigmatic aorists, are reviewed in Sihler, 558–59. For a more theoretical approach, see Kurzová, 150.

1.3.1. Reduplication

Some of these descended from assumed perfect forms in IE with reduplication of the initial consonant, like TETIGĪ 'I touched' and CUCURRĪ 'I ran' as against unreduplicated pres. TANGŌ and CURRŌ. The replacement of Old Latin TETINĪ 'I held' and SCICIDĪ 'I cut' by TENUĪ and SCIDĪ in Classical Latin (Kent, 114), and perhaps the replacement of *FIFIDĪ by FĪDĪ 'I split' as well (Ernout and Meillet, 235), indicates that reduplication became rarer toward Romance. It was to become rarer still.[11]

Appearing only sporadically in Latin perfects and never appearing in standard past participles, reduplication was a common feature of Gk. perfects like λέλοιπα 'have left' (CL cognate LICTUM) as against pres. λείπω, aor. ἔλιπον. Reduplication also appeared in the present tense of a few Gk. verbs like δίδωμι 'give' (CL cognate DŌ) and in that of a very few CL verbs like GIGNŌ 'beget.' In Tocharian, by contrast, reduplication was used to mark some past participles, like kākotu 'split,' kakätwu 'tricked,' pāpeku 'cooked,' sasruku 'killed,' tatärku 'given leave,' and wawu 'given' (Bader, 177–78). Reduplication thus appears to have been specialized in a different function in each language.[12]

1.3.2. Direct Suffixation

Another type of Latin perfect entailed suffixation of endings directly to the stem. Sometimes the stem vowel remained short in both present and perfect, as in VERTĪ 'turned' and FIDĪ 'split' as against pres. VERTŌ and FINDŌ. Sometimes the short stem vowel lengthened in perfects like SCĀBĪ 'scratched,' FŌDĪ 'dug,' SĒDĪ 'sat' as against pres. SCABŌ, FODIŌ, and SEDEŌ. Perhaps by analogy with the second type of perfect, there developed forms like long-vowel CĀVĪ 'avoided,' FĀVĪ 'favored,' JŪVĪ 'helped,' and MŌVĪ 'moved' as against the short-vowel presents CAVEŌ, FAVEŌ, JUVŌ, and MOVEŌ (Buck, 292–93).

Certain analysts claim that these perfects were only apparent or graphic ablauts, as Latin speakers disliked writing -VV- before another vowel. The four above would thus have been athematic -UĪ perfects pronounced [ka:wui:], [fa:wui:], [ju:wui:], [mo:wui:].[13] If so, perfects of that type would have provided morphological inspiration for the spread of -ŪTUM past participles

---

[11] In Late Latin, the absence of long theme vowels distinctive in the same environment, and the consonant clusters perhaps resulting from syncope of atonic vowels, would have sufficed to doom almost every reduplicated perfect to extinction.

[12] For a discussion of reduplicated perfects in Latin, with bibliography, see Leumann, 586–88. For a discussion of reduplication in IE languages generally and in Greek particularly, see Sihler, 487–90, 495–96. For a more theoretical approach, see Kurzová, 151.

[13] For a discussion of direct-suffixation perfects like MŌVĪ 'moved,' see Leumann, 595–96 and Sihler, 581–82. For a more theoretical approach, see Kurzová, 152.

in Late Latin; if not, such perfects would have come to be used less by each successive generation.

1.3.3. Vowel Change

A few common verbs had present stems in [a] and perfect stems in [e:], with the root vocalism of the past participle usually matching that of the infectum in quality and quantity. Such verbs included pf. CĒPĪ 'seized, took' with pres. CAPIŌ and p.p. CAPTUM, pf. JĒCĪ 'threw' with pres. JACIŌ and p.p. JACTUM, and pf. FĒCĪ 'did/made' with pres. FACIŌ and p.p. FACTUM. For verbs that appear not to fit that pattern, like pf. ĒGĪ 'drove; acted' with pres. AGŌ and p.p. ĀCTUM—where p.p. root vocalism matches that of the infectum in quality and that of the finite perfectum in quantity—see §1.3.4 below.

A third type of vowel-change perfect entailed simple lengthening of the present-stem vowel, like VĒNĪ 'came' with pres. VENIŌ (p.p. VENTUM) or LĒGĪ 'chose; read' with pres. LEGŌ (p.p. LĒCTUM). In verbs of that type, p.p. vocalism might match either that of the infectum or that of the finite perfectum.

Those variations in vowels had come down from IE ablauting verbs comparable to Engl. *sing sang sung*. Within the CL verb system, the instances of ablaut that survived had become unpredictable and unproductive.[14] By the time Romance vernaculars emerged, almost all vowel-change perfects had been everywhere remade: perhaps speakers came to feel that the morphology of those finite perfectum forms made them sound too little like infectum ones to be readily recognizable as part of the same paradigm.

1.3.4. Lachmann's Law, Amended

In CL, a long vowel in the past participle, as against a short vowel in the infectum, occurred in e.g. FŪSUM 'poured,' RĒCTUM 'ruled,' TĒCTUM 'covered,' STRŪCTUM 'put together,' FRĀCTUM 'shattered,' PĀCTUM 'agreed,' and TĀCTUM 'touched' as against pres. FUNDŌ, REGŌ, TEGŌ, STRUŌ, FRANGŌ, PACISCOR, and TANGŌ. Most of these long-vowel past participles had long-vowel perfects as well, but not all long-vowel perfects were accompanied by long-vowel past participles. Thus, pfs. like MĪSĪ 'sent,' FŌDĪ 'dug,' RŪPĪ 'broke,' and FĒCĪ 'did/made' differed in vocalism from p.p.s like short-voweled MISSUM, FOSSUM, RUPTUM, and FACTUM.

A long-ago attempt by Lachmann to explain such alternations phonologically—the stem vowel of a tautic athematic past participle being long if the stem ends in a voiced consonant, and short otherwise—does work for a great many p.p./pres. oppositions like FRICTUM : FRICŌ 'rub' versus FRĪCTUM : FRĪGŌ 'fry' (Vincent 1988, 30). However, as Watkins has observed,

---

[14] For a discussion of the decline of ablaut in Latin verbs, with bibliography, see Sommer, 605–7 and Leumann, 29–41. Ablaut in Latin past participles is reviewed in Leumann, 615.

several verbs whose stems end in [g] or [d], there being no examples in final [b], break Lachmann's Law. It cannot explain why tonic vowels in past participles like FICTUM 'shaped,' STRICTUM 'tightened,' SCISSUM 'split,' and also -SESSUM 'sat'[15] remain as short as those in pres. FINGŌ, STRINGŌ, SCINDŌ, and SEDEŌ.

Closer examination reveals analogies made within the perfectum before Latin was written down. (Here the symbol ± is to be read "by analogy with.") For instance, the p.p. CRĒTUM 'sifted; decided' ± pf. CRĒVĪ replaced older CERTUM, used only adjectivally in CL to mean 'settled, resolved.' An old p.p. EXFUTĪ 'poured out,' glossed as "modern" EFFŪSĪ by a Roman commentator, suggests that the old p.p. of FUNDŌ 'pour, spill' was *FUTUM (cf. the Gk. verbal adj. χυτόν 'poured, shed') and that the CL p.p. FŪSUM was made by analogy with pf. FŪDĪ, because verbs with dental-stop perfects usually had sigmatic past participles.

Moreover, the CL pf. FŌDĪ 'dug' (pres. FODIŌ) would have given a long-vowel p.p. *FŌSUM under Lachmann's Law, but the inherited short-vowel p.p. FOSSUM < IE *bhodh-to- suggests that pf. FŌDĪ was reshaped by rhyming analogy to present-perfect ŌDĪ 'hate.' Likewise, the CL pf. SĒDĪ 'sat' (pres. SEDEŌ) would have given a long-vowel p.p. *SĒSUM under Lachmann's Law, but the inherited p.p. -SESSUM 'sat' based on supine SESSUM < IE *sed-tu suggests that pf. SĒDĪ was reshaped by analogy to another vowel-lengthening perfect, though which one remains unclear. In view of those exceptions, says Watkins, Lachmann's Law ought to be revamped to state less sweepingly that "at a certain period in the prehistory of Latin, the morphological expression of the perfect passive [i.e., past participle] assumed an accessory mark of vocalic length, there where that same vocalic length served as the distinctive mark of the perfect active. When this relation could not hold true...no lengthening took place" (64).

Within the verb system as it stood in CL times, perfects and past participles displaying such vowel changes stood apart as morphological isolates. Ablaut had become unproductive.

1.3.5. Further Anomalies

Synchronically, speakers of Latin—unaware of the long history behind the words they used—might have noticed that the stressed vowel in p.p. SATUM 'sown, planted' matched neither that in pres. SERŌ nor that in pf. SĒVĪ, while the stressed vowel in p.p. STRĀTUM 'stretched out, spread out' matched that in pf. STRĀVĪ but not that in pres. STERNŌ.

At least two verbs had a perfect in [w] and a present in [n]: one may compare pf. LĪVĪ 'smeared' (no p.p.) and pres. LINŌ, and pf. SĪVĪ 'allowed' (p.p. SĬTUM) and pres. SINŌ. Somewhat resembling those two was another verb, with pf. SPRĒVĪ, p.p. SPRĒTUM 'spurned,' and pres. SPERNŌ. One with

---

[15] Watkins notes that the unprefixed past participle of SEDEŌ 'sit' is unattested.

unusual stem variation had pf. TRĪVĪ, p.p. TRĪTUM 'rubbed' and pres. TERŌ (cf. Gk. τρίβω 'rub').

Pleonastically, some CL verbs could display two types of perfective marking. Comparison of pfs. like MESSUĪ 'reaped' (p.p. MESSUM) with pres. METŌ, and of NEXUĪ 'bound' (p.p. NEXUM) with pres. NECTŌ, shows that these two perfects combined the sigmatic and the -UĪ type, even if the latter had an earlier straight sigmatic by-form in pf. NEXĪ. Moreover, pf. QUÆSĪVĪ and p.p. QUÆSĪTUM 'sought' combined the sigmatic and the 4th-conj.-style [i:] marking contrasted pres. QUÆRŌ, marked in neither [s] nor [i:][16]

Several CL verbs had short vowels in the past participle and perfect contrasting with long vowels in the present: the stressed vowels in past participles like CESSUM 'yielded' and USTUM 'charred' matched those in perfect CESSĪ and USSĪ but not those in pres. CĒDŌ and ŪRŌ. Other CL past participles showed vowel grades identical to those in finite perfectum forms, like ĒSUM 'eaten,' ĒMPTUM 'bought,' LĒCTUM 'chosen' with pf. ĒDĪ, ĒMĪ, LĒGĪ, but note the short stem vowels in the pres. EDŌ, EMŌ, LEGŌ. By contrast, short vowels in tautic athematic past participles like DICTUM 'said' and DUCTUM 'led' contrasted with long vowels both in pf. DĪXĪ, DŪXĪ and also in pres. DĪCŌ and DŪCŌ.[17] In Romance, especially in the west, the tautic athematic type of past participle was to be restricted to high-frequency verbs that thus turned into morphological isolates, subject to leveling.

Among suppletive verbs, all three of the principal parts of pres. FERŌ 'carry,' pf. TULĪ, and p.p. LĀTUM (earlier *tlātóm; cf. Doric τλᾶτόν 'durable') probably sounded unrelated to most native speakers. That verb had borrowed its perfectum forms from another, TOLLERE SUSTULĪ SUBLĀTUM 'lift, raise,' whose CL parts were prefixed in the perfectum but not in the infectum, another persistent anomaly. However, by CL times that verb's pf. TETULĪ, attested in Plautus, had lost its reduplicative prefix (Sihler, 580). Many forms of another high-frequency verb, EŌ 'go' with infin. ĪRE, pf. IĪ (later ĪVĪ) and p.p. ĬTUM, had been almost worn away by phonetic attrition. The most common and most irregular verb of all, SUM ESSE FUĪ 'be' (no p.p.), was put together from several different stems and was to retain substantial irregularity everywhere.[18]

---

[16] CL also had sigmatic QUÆSŌ 'seek; beg, entreat,' once meaning 'want to ask.' Next to VIDEŌ 'see' CL also had sigmatic VĪSŌ 'inspect,' once meaning 'want to see.' Both were relics of old desiderative formations marked with [s] (Leumann, 522–23). Sigmatic stems in Latin for both infectum and perfectum are reviewed in Kurzová, 181–86.

[17] Tautic athematic past participles in CL corresponded to Gk. verbal adjectives with -τό- directly suffixed to the stem. Two examples are λεκτός 'chooseable; chosen' from λέγω 'choose,' or like πεμπτός 'sendable, to be sent' from πέμπω 'send.'

[18] For a review of the origin and development of the irregular verbs POSSUM 'be able,' VOLŌ 'want' and compounds, FERŌ 'carry,' EŌ 'go,' EDŌ 'eat,' DŌ 'give,' FĪŌ 'become, be done/made,' AIŌ and INQUAM 'say,' and SUM 'be,' see Sihler, 538–54. By Romance times, all but DŌ would be remade or would disappear.

1.3.6. Unpredictabilities within Regularity

In CL verbs, morphological transparency was greatest for what had become regular members of the 1st conjugation and 4th conjugation. Verbs like JOCĀRE or JOCĀRĪ 'jest' usually had tonic [a:], and verbs like DORMĪRE 'sleep' usually had tonic [i:], in the infinitive, imperfect, perfect, and past participle, as well as other arrhizotonic verb forms like 1pl. and 2pl. present indicative and subjunctive.

Within those two classes, however, opacity at times prevailed over transparency. A small number of verbs in -ĀRE like CUBĀRE 'recline,' DOMĀRE 'tame,' NECĀRE 'slay,' VETĀRE 'forbid,' and SECĀRE 'slice, chop' had perfects in -UĪ, while such 1st-conj. infectum forms with typical 2nd-conj. perfectum forms could also have rhizotonic thematic past participles like CUBĬTUM, DOMĬTUM, and VETĬTUM or tautic athematic ones like NECTUM and SECTUM. Some verbs in -ĪRE like SALĪRE 'jump' and APERĪRE 'open' had anomalous -UĪ perfects as well but had the tautic athematic past participles SALTUM and APERTUM. Two other -ĪRE verbs, SANCĪRE 'bless' and VINCĪRE 'tie,' had the sigmatic pfs. SĀNXĪ and VĪNXĪ along with the tautic athematic past participles SĀNCTUM and VĪNCTUM.

Although 2nd-conj. verbs always had tonic [e:] in the infinitive and in many forms of the infectum, only some half-dozen—DĒLĒRE 'remove, destroy,' FLĒRE 'weep, lament,' NĒRE 'spin thread,' OLĒRE 'smell of,' -PLĒRE 'fill,' and VIĒRE 'weave together'—were predictable enough to retain that long vowel in pfs. like DĒLĒVĪ or p.p.s like DĒLĒTUM. Most often, 2nd-conj. verbs like HABĒRE 'have' and DĒBĒRE 'ought to' had perfects in -UĪ and rhizotonic past participles in -ĬTUM, marking each principal part with a different theme vowel. Pairs of verbs in the same infectum class, like MANĒRE 'stay' and AUGĒRE 'increase,' might both have sigmatic pfs. (MĀNSĪ, AUXĪ), but one might have a sigmatic p.p. (MĀNSUM) and the other a tautic athematic p.p. (AUCTUM). Yet another 2nd-conj. verb, TORRĒRE 'heat, parch,' did have the expected -UĪ pf. TORRUĪ but also had an irregular sigmatic-tautic p.p. TOSTUM, while 2nd-conj. CAVĒRE 'beware' had a direct-suffix pf. CĀVĪ with vowel lengthening and a tautic athematic p.p. CAUTUM.

Unpredictability was greatest within the 3rd conjugation, a ragbag of verbs fitted into one formal class by grammarians because of the infin. ending ´-ĔRE but actually representing several disparate paradigms (Buck, 270–72). Some, like GEMERE 'moan,' TEXERE 'weave,' and VOMERE 'throw up,' could also have -UĪ perfects as if they belonged to the 2nd conjugation, yet their past participles—rhizotonic thematic GEMĬTUM, VOMĬTUM but tautic athematic TEXTUM—could be inconsistent with one another. It was true that 3rd-conj. verbs always had a rhizotonic infinitive and normally a rhizotonic past participle, but the past participle might be rhizotonic thematic, tautic athematic, or sigmatic: PERDERE had PERDĬTUM 'lost,' TENDERE had TENTUM 'stretched,' FALLERE had FALSUM 'tricked,' and FINDERE had FISSUM 'split.'

Merely from a given 3rd-conj. infinitive, no speaker could tell whether its past participle was going to be thematic, sigmatic, or tautic athematic. No

speaker could tell from a given sigmatic perfect—say AUXĪ, DĪXĪ, or VĪNXĪ—
or from a given tautic athematic past participle—say AUCTUM, DICTUM, or
VĪNCTUM—that the first in each set matched 2nd-conj. AUGĒRE 'increase,'
that the second one matched 3rd-conj. DĪCERE 'say,' or that the third one
matched 4th-conj. VINCĪRE 'tie, bind' (examples from Tekavčić, 279). All in
all, CL perfects in -VĪ or -UĪ, reduplicated perfects, and lengthened-vowel
perfects were to be found in all four conjugations, perfects in -SĪ in all but the
1st. Again, CL past participles in -ĪTUM and direct-suffix -TUM were to be
found in all four conjugations, past participles in -SUM in all but the 1st.

Comparing the roots of infinitives with those of perfects and past
participles in CL, Tekavčić notes that any of the three forms might display
most of the following traits: reduplication, changes in vowel quality and in
vowel length of the root, appearance or disappearance of root-interior nasal
consonants, changes in voicing or quality of root-final consonants, different
theme vowels or none, and also the presence or absence of a sigmatic marker.
For verbs in Classical Latin, Tekavčić states that a full forty-one different
combinations of the above features could occur in the three stems for
infectum, finite perfectum, and past participle (287–89).

Yet anyone highlighting irregularities can risk losing sight of the big
picture. As Aronoff points out (43, 49), substantial regularity had already been
attained under the classical standard: given the infectum theme vowel, one
could usually predict other stems, although strictly the categories "2nd
conjugation" and "3rd conjugation" are valid only for infectum stems.
Drawing on data from Allen and Grenough's *New Latin Grammar* (1894), and
presumably counting as regular the 2nd-conj. verbs with -UĪ pfs. and -ĪTUM
p.p.s, and the 3rd-conj. verbs with -SUM p.p.s (3rd-conj. perfects are omitted),
Aronoff arrives at the distribution set forth in Table 1–1 on page 26. I have
added the approximate number of regular verbs in each class.

Aronoff concludes that more than three-quarters of the 710 simple verbs[19]
were regular within their conjugation, at least for past participles. I would add
that a clear majority of all simple verbs—385 out of 710, or 54 percent—were
regular members of the 1st or 4th conjugation. In that light, reduction of
allomorphy in Romance preterits and past participles would look like a
continuation of trends far advanced in Latin.

Aronoff goes on (52) to propose the CL default method of building the
perfectum: to make a default perfect, suffix *u* to the present stem; to make a
default past participle, suffix *t* to the present stem. A combination of Aronoff's
two default methods might explain why, in areas from Transalpine Gaul
through Italia to Dacia, most verbs outside the 1st and 4th conjugations came
to take past participles in reflexes of -ŪTUM, a development reviewed in §2.14.

Speakers' understanding of default verb morphology appears to have
shifted through time and space. For a depiction of paradigms generalized by
Late Latin speakers, see Table 2–4 on page 98.

---

[19] I.e., excluding intensive, iterative, or desiderative verbs and (I assume) prefixed verbs.

Table 1–1

Degree of Regularity in Latin Verbs, by Conjugation

(after Aronoff)

Conj.	Theme Vowel	Number of Simple Verbs	Proportion of Regular Verbs	Number of Regular Verbs
1st	Ā	360	96%	345
2nd	Ē	120	75%	90
3rd	Ĕ, Ĭ	170	35%	60
4th	Ī	60	67%	40
TOTAL	—	710	—	535

1.4. EARLY RESHAPING OF PERFECTUM PARADIGMS

Following a merger of aorist and perfect in Italic languages, the tense called perfect in Latin retained a great variety of stem types (Sihler, 579). Yet before Latin was recorded, some regularization of finite perfectum stems had taken place.[20] Verbs in CL show the same vowel extended throughout the singular and plural of perfect forms, unlike the different vowel grades existing in Proto-Indo-European verbs and in certain other older IE tongues. In Germanic, for instance, some old perfects retained vocalic variation: Gothic present-tense 1sg./3sg. *wait* contrasted with 1pl. *witum* 'know,' as Old Norse past-tense 1sg./3sg. *fann* < *fánþ* contrasted with 1pl. *fundum* < *fnðú m* 'found.'[21] However, CL 3sg. SĒDIT, 1pl. SĒDIMUS 'sat,' like CL 3sg. VĒNIT, 1pl. VĒNIMUS 'came' had tonic [e:] in both singular and plural (Kent, 391). Likewise, Sanskrit kept vocalic variation in 3sg. *véda* contrasted with 1pl. *vidmá*, as Greek did in 3sg. οἶδε contrasted with 1pl. ἴδμεν 'know,' but the CL

---

[20] For a survey of the IE perfect, there termed "stative and tenseless," see Sihler, 564–70.

[21] Germanic languages innovated some instances of vocalic variation in verbs, giving e.g. 1sg./3sg. *sat* but 1pl. *sētum* 'sat,' 1sg./3sg. *qam* but 1pl. *quēmum* 'came.' Latin leveled the ones it had inherited.

cognates VĪDIT and VĪDIMUS 'saw,' perhaps from old aorists, had tonic [i:] in both singular and plural (Buck, 286).

During the prehistory of Latin as in its posthistory, different parts of verb paradigms seem to have influenced other parts. As Sihler notes, "[t]he perf. and the pple. in effect belong to the same paradigm (to *ussit* act. the corresponding passive is *ustus est*), and there is [a] great deal of mutual influence between the two stems" (583).

In the following sections, each of the two principal parts of the perfectum will be shown to have influenced the other.

1.4.1. Influence of Perfects on Past Participles

Perhaps most often, certain CL past participles had been influenced by the stems of their finite perfectum. Thus, the p.p.s HÆSUM 'stuck,' MULSUM 'milked,' and PRESSUM 'squeezed' were aligned with the sigmatic pfs. HÆSĪ, MULSĪ, and PRESSĪ, there being no dental stop in pres. HÆREŌ, MULGEŌ, or PREMŌ. By CL times, the prefixed p.p. -PLĒTUM 'filled' had probably been remade from *PLATUM by analogy with its "regular" 2nd-conj. pf. -PLĒVĪ. In fact, most CL past participles with unexpected root vocalism had been patterned on the vowel found in their finite perfectum: FŪSUM 'poured' for *FUSSUM ± pf. FŪDĪ, and ĒSUM 'eaten' for *ESSUM ± pf. ĒDĪ. At times, the infectum could inspire such reshaping, as in p.p. ŪSUM 'used' for *ISSUM ± present ŪTOR.

1.4.2. Influence of Past Participles on Perfects

Certain CL perfects had been influenced by their past participles. Although the Old Latin diphthong OU usually reduced to Ū in the classical tongue, so that one would expect OL IOVSIT 's/he ordered' to give long-voweled *JŪSIT in CL, the attested pf. JUSSIT had a short root vowel by analogy with p.p. JUSSUM, and so did infin. JUBĒRE. Again, pf. VOLSĪ or VULSĪ 'plucked, pulled' had been remade sigmatically from OL VELLĪ (cf. pres. VELLŌ) by analogy with p.p. VOLSUM or VULSUM.

1.4.3. Influence of Infectum on Perfectum

Certain CL perfects had been influenced by their infectum stems. In pre-Latin, pf. GESSĪ 'displayed, waged' along with sigmatic-tautic p.p. GESTUM had acquired the short vowel extant in infectum forms like pres. GERŌ. Likewise, pf. JŪNXĪ 'joined' along with its tautic athematic p.p. JŪNCTUM had acquired the nasal infix extant in e.g. pres. JUNGŌ, as had the p.p. ĒMŪNCTUM and pf. ĒMŪNXĪ acquired the nasal extant in e.g. pres. ĒMUNGŌ 'blow one's nose.' Despite the existence of a non-nasal pf. PEPUGĪ, p.p. PŪNCTUM had also acquired the nasal in e.g. pres. PŪNGŌ 'sting, prick' (Meillet and Vendryes, 336). Still, if the nasal infix in pres. PINGŌ 'paint' and VINCIŌ 'bind, fetter' had

been extended into the pfs. PĪNXĪ and VĪNXĪ, it remained absent from the
p.p.s PĪCTUM and VICTUM. However, by-form VĪNCTUM seems attested, and
so is PINCTUM later on: cf. p.p.s like Fr. *peint*, It. (*di*)*pinto*, and now adjectival
Sp. *pinto*.[22]

1.4.4. Further Reshapings

By CL times, old reduplicated perfects like *LELIQUĪ 'forsook' and *FEFUGĪ
'fled' might have lost their prefixes to become LĪQUĪ and FŪGĪ (Palmer, 272).[23]
Leveling might also have taken place within 3rd-conj. CŪDERE CŪDĪ
CŪSUM/CUSSUM 'thresh grain; forge metal,' where CŪDĪ could have replaced
an old reduplicated perfect. Later on, speakers were to make a new sigmatic pf.
CŪSĪ ± p.p. CŪSUM. In another kind of leveling, the reduplicative pf.
FEFELLĪ 'tricked; failed' had been remade on the infectum stem, for had it
been old it would have been *FEBULĪ (Ernout and Meillet, 154, 213).

    Although the sigmatic type of perfect properly belonged to stems ending in
stop consonants, a few others like pf. VĪXĪ 'lived' (pres. VĪVŌ) and STRŪXĪ
'heaped up, built' (pres. STRUŌ) might well have been created by rhyming
analogy with OL pres. FĪVŌ (later FĪGŌ) or pf. FĪXĪ 'fasten' (Sihler, 583).

    Another sort of regularization had taken place in pre-Latin times: in CL,
pf. ĒMĪ 'bought' differed from pres. EMŌ merely by vowel lengthening in the
stem, but most compounds of that verb like DĒMŌ, CŌMŌ, PRŌMŌ, and
SŪMŌ had come to make their perfects with sigmatic suffixes, yielding more
sharply marked DĒMPSĪ 'subtracted,' CŌMPSĪ 'arranged,' PRŌMPSĪ
'produced,' and SŪMPSĪ 'took, obtained' (Kent, 117). Since the p.p.s DĒMPTUM,
CŌMPTUM, PRŌMPTUM, and SŪMPTUM still agreed with ĒMPTUM in being
tautic athematic rather than sigmatic, speakers appear to have brought those
compound verbs' perfectum into line with those of e.g. SCRĪPSĪ SCRĪPTUM
'wrote/written' or VEXĪ VECTUM 'conveyed,' which had a pf. suffix in [s] and a
p.p. suffix in [t] added directly to the stem, in contrast with the absence of
sigmatic or tautic marking across the infectum. Another such instance would
be p.p. CLEPTUM 'stolen' as against pf. CLEPSĪ and infin. CLEPERE (Monteil,
350–51).

    At times, remodeling took place because of fortuitous homonymy, as has
developed in Engl. *sewn* and *sown*: since intensive verbs were almost always
built on the p.p. stem of their simplex, SECTĀRĪ 'follow eagerly' proves the
prior existence of expected *SECTUM as the p.p. for SEQUĪ 'follow.' That
*SECTUM would have clashed with SECTUM 'cut' (infin. SECĀRE, pf. SECUĪ);

---

[22] Nasal marking originally appeared only in the infectum (imperfective aspect) and hence
never in past participles, which belonged to the perfective side. For a discussion of nasal
infixes in Latin verbs, see Leumann, 533–35 and Sihler, 498–501, 533–34.

[23] Sihler however suggests (580–81) that perfects like those two might well have been
reflexes of old root and thematic aorists.

the former was remade as CL SECŪTUM ± VOLŪTUM 'rolled' (Sihler, 127, 160–61, 623).[24]

In CL, PULSUM was the past participle for PELLERE 'throb; drive,' but the existence of an older p.p. *PULTUM may be inferred by the CL frequentative that had infin. PULTĀRE 'knock, beat.' As in the last example, similarity of meaning could provide a basis for analogical extension of p.p. formants. Thus, the morphology of the sigmatic p.p. LĀPSUM 'slipped' might have been influenced by (rare) CĀSUM 'fallen,' as someone who slipped often fell; the [n] of MĒNSUM 'measured' might have been influenced by that of PĒNSUM 'weighed,' commodities like grain being measured out by weight. In turn, the loss of [t] in CĒNSUM 'deemed' has been ascribed to the influence of MĒNSUM 'measured' (Kent, 134), for both required judgment. By CL times, then, analogies had somewhat increased predictability within the perfectum.[25]

1.4.5. The Latin Perfect in -V- or -U-

A great many CL perfects descended from specifically Latin creations with a suffix realized as [w] after a vowel, [u] after a consonant. Examples of the postvocalic type include CANTĀVĪ 'sang often,' FLĒVĪ 'wept,' DORMĪVĪ 'slept,' and COGNŌVĪ 'known,' all of them arrhizotonic. Examples of the postconsonantal type, mostly for stems ending in a liquid or nasal, included SALUĪ 'jumped,' MONUĪ 'warned,' SECUĪ 'cut,' and MOLUĪ 'ground,' all of them rhizotonic Yet in the pf. LUĪ 'loosened; atoned for,' -U- was part of the verb stem as in pres. LUŌ (cf. Gk. λύω) and hence should not be counted among the -UĪ perfects.[26] In Romance, perfects in stressed [a] and [i] were to prove the most popular of all; reflexes of the -UĪ pf. type thrived more in LL than they had in CL.

One view is that this [w] or [u] perfective marker might have developed from an IE root aorist *e-bhu-m that turned into Gk. ἔφυν 'I grew' (Kent, 118). This [w] type of perfect had apparently once been restricted to at most a few verb stems in Latin and had spread to other stems ending in a long vowel (Buck, 294), including most found in the extensive 1st and 4th conjugations; the [u] type occurred in most perfects belonging to the 2nd conjugation. Whatever its origins, [w] or [u] had thus become grammaticalized as the characteristic perfective marker of Latin; elided or absorbed, it was later to

---

[24] During Late Latin times, VOLŪTU 'rolled' was to be crowded out of its slot by another fortuitous homonymy, when *VOLUTU emerged in most areas as the new, regularly arrhizotonic past participle for 2nd-conj. *VOLERE 'want.' That starred form replaced CL VELLE, a verb that lacked a past participle but had many forms beginning with VOL-.

[25] For a survey of rapprochement between infectum and perfectum stems, see Leumann, 603–5.

[26] Buck states (295) that possible semantic analogies in the spread of -UĪ perfects included, first, MESSUĪ 'harvested' (pres. METŌ) ± early SERUĪ 'sowed' (pres. SERŌ), and, second, NEXUĪ 'tied, bound' (pres. NECTO) replacing early NEXĪ ± TEXUĪ 'wove' (pres. TEXŌ).

become degrammaticalized almost everywhere in ROMANIA for finite perfects that became preterits.[27]

Past participles ending in reflexes of -ŪTUM constitute the exception to the general degrammaticalization of [w] or [u]. Following their expansion in the Late Latin of most areas, though not on Sardinia, such forms became far more common than they had been in CL (see §2.14). From Romanian to Catalan, they constitute the default method of making past participles for 2nd-conj. and 3rd-conj. verbs today. Mediæval attestations of -*udo* past participles in Portuguese and Spanish suggest that reflexes of -ŪTUM were once popular nearly all the way across ROMANIA (see §4.7.4.1).

From my point of view, by far the most notable regularization of Latin verbs had taken place within the regular 1st and 4th conjugations. By CL times, the tonic theme vowel already shared by the infinitive and perfect in those conjugations had been extended to the verbal adjective marked with [t] that became the past participle (Monteil, 349).[28]

1.4.6. Prefixation of Archaic Verbs

A number of CL verbs existed only in prefixed versions or in inchoative ones. Of others, only the past participle remained. As shown in §2.2, prefixation of short verbs in LL was to allow some of them to survive.

One might regard some of those verbs as beginning with what Malkiel has called prefixoids, segments formally identical to prefixes but leaving no attested base when subtracted.[29] For instance, a verb *HENDŌ 'take hold of'? is unattested, but prefixed PRÆ- or PREHENDŌ PREHENDĪ PREHĒNSUM 'grab' was used widely and often came to mean merely 'take'; a verb *NĪDEŌ is likewise unattested, but RENĪDEŌ 'shine; smile' continued in CL. Unattested 3rd-conj. *VIDŌ 'split'? always appeared as part of the compound DĪVIDO DĪVĪSĪ DĪVĪSUM 'divided.' A 1st-conj. verb *TĀMINŌ, perhaps meaning 'touch,' was used only in prefixed CONTĀMINŌ 'contact, soil through contact' in CL. Two other 3rd-conj. verbs shared an infectum: of *CELLŌ$_1$ 'raise'? there survived only the adj. CELSUM 'high,' originally a past participle, but prefixed versions were extant, while *CELLŌ$_2$ 'hit, strike' could be used only in prefixed PERCELLŌ PERCULĪ PERCULSUM 'overturn, ruin.' Yet another verb meaning 'hit, strike,' 3rd-conj. *FENDŌ *FENDĪ *FĒNSUM, could be used only in compounds like DĒFĒNDŌ 'ward off, drive away.'

Other simple verbs from old Latium are attested only in CL glossaries. That held true for 3rd-conj. APŌ *ĒPĪ APTUM 'tie, attach,' though prefixed

---

[27] For a review of theories about the origin of perfects in [w] or [u], see the discussion and extensive bibliography in Leumann, 593–98. Sihler notes (585) that the [w] might first have been merely a glide separating stem from ending. For a more theoretical approach to the question, see also Kurzová, 150.

[28] For other reshapings of perfects, see Leumann, 603–4.

[29] Cf. English "lost positives" like *kempt,* an old p.p. for *to comb* now extant only in a negative adj. *unkempt.*

COĒPĪ 'began' and inchoative APĪSCOR 'reach for, attain' were widespread. It also held true for 2nd-conj. PLEŌ PLĒVĪ PLĒTUM 'fill,' replaced by prefixed variants like IMPLEŌ 'fill in' and COMPLEŌ 'fill up, fulfill' in CL. And it held true for deponent MINĪSCOR 'remember' (rare p.p. MENTUM), always prefixed in CL as in COMMINĪSCOR 'imagine, devise' or REMINĪSCOR 'recall.'

Still other simple verbs had almost passed out of use by themselves but still lived on in prefixed versions.[30] That held true for rare and archaic 3rd-conj. FLĪGŌ FLĪXĪ FLĪCTUM 'beat,' for SPECIŌ SPEXĪ SPECTUM 'look at, behold'—with a by-form infectum SPICIŌ backformed from compounds like CŌNSPICIŌ 'catch sight of'—and also for STINGUŌ STINXĪ STINCTUM 'extinguish, annihilate.' Deponent GRADIOR (pf./p.p. GRESSUM) 'walk' was rare in CL, being usually replaced by INGREDIOR (Ernout and Meillet, 39, 139, 111, 177, 224, 240, 279, 397, 515, 531, 570, 639, 649).

The existence of such verbs in Classical Latin foreshadowed a much greater use of prefixation in Late Latin, perhaps to give more phonetic body to short verbs like EDERE 'eat.' In fact, where any of the above verbs lived on in Romance, they did so only in prefixed variants.

1.5. NEW DISTINCTIONS IN THE PERFECTUM

The finite verb forms called perfect in CL, as one might expect from a category representing a blend of perfect and aorist stems and endings, made no distinction between stative and punctual meaning. At least one is tempted to reach that conclusion from reviewing samples drawn from the elaborated literary language. For instance, when the Roman historian Livy uses constructions like MULTŌ AURŌ ARGENTŌQUE ID [TEMPLUM] EXORNĀTUM HABĒBANT 'they held this [temple] decorated with gold and silver' (*Ab urbe condita libri* 26.11.9), only stative meaning is to be inferred from the last two words. Yet popular writers of the second century BCE, among them the playwrights Plautus and Terence, did use syntagms of HABEŌ plus past participle that might well have had perfect meaning. For instance, Plautus (*Pseudolus* 602) has ILLÆC OMNIA MISSA HABEŌ QUÆ ANTE AGERE OCCĒPĪ, best translated 'I have dispatched all the things that I undertook to do earlier'; Terence (*Eunuchus* 382) has QUÆ NŌS NOSTRAMQUE ADULESCENTIAM HABENT DĒSPICĀTAM 'who have looked down on us and our youth' (G. Holland, p.c.). In both, the past participle still agrees with the noun object. For whatever reason, perhaps owing to accidents of attestation, such constructions seldom appear in works dating from the Golden and Silver Ages. They reemerged under the later Empire, with the past participle now tending to be reoriented away from the nominal object and toward HABĒRE and thus tending to be invariable. Thus, Oribasius, physician to Roman emperor Julian the Apostate (died 363 CE), writes HÆC OMNIA PROBATUM HABEMUS 'we have shown all these things,' where neut.sg. PROBATUM does not agree with neut.pl. HÆC or OMNIA (Schwegler, 118–19).

---

[30] For fronting or raising of the expected stem vowel in prefixed verbs, see Buck, 100–2.

By limiting syntagms like PROBATUM HABEMUS to present-perfect meaning, speakers of LL restored or continued something like the aspectual distinction that had once been available to IE speakers and apparently to speakers of Italic also. They narrowed the temporal range of so-called perfects like CANTĀVĪ and DORMĪVĪ, by LL times better termed preterits, to approximately that of Greek aorists denoting one-time past actions without any present resonance. To express present-perfect or past-perfect aspects, they increasingly came to use syntagms built of grammaticalized HABEŌ etc. or HABĒBAM etc., both fated to undergo severe phonetic attrition in Romance, plus a semantically "full" past participle descended from adjectival formations in IE. Such new perfective constructions may be seen as part of a broader tendency in LL toward analytic verb constructions with modal or other auxiliaries (Fleischman 1982, 49). As Harris remarks, "a syntagm combining the present tense of an auxiliary verb (HABET 'has') with the perfective participle (FACTUM 'done/made')....[left] FĒCIT 'did/made' as the—now unambiguous—exponent of the past punctual category" (1978, 135). Over time, through a kind of situational metonymy, syntagms like HABEŌ LITTERĀS SCRĪPTĀS shifted from denoting states (= 'I have letters [that have been] written') to denoting results of actions (= 'I have written letters').[31]

Comrie notes that perfect constructions like those of LL have parallels in more than a few related and unrelated languages worldwide: "A common way of combining present and past meaning is to use the present tense of an auxiliary verb with a past participle: the present auxiliary conveys the present meaning, while the past participle conveys that of past action" (106–7). In such cross-linguistic periphrases, which may come to denote either retrospection/pastness or prospection/futurity, verbs like 'have,' 'be,' 'become,' or 'want,' while still capable of bearing a full semantic load, also commonly become grammaticalized as function words.[32] In addition, despite the survival of more than a few anomalously formed past participles into Late Latin and beyond, the new analytic constructions displayed far greater regularity than had the older synthetic ones. By contrast with the large number of ways to mark perfects in Classical Latin, and the still fairly large number of ways to mark preterits in Late Latin and Proto-Romance, the HABEŌ + p.p. syntagm was of "universal applicability" (Harris 1978, 135), i.e. usable for at least every transitive verb in the language, and far more predictable morphologically.

---

[31] According to Heine (30, 46–47), use of HABĒRE 'have' to make both new perfect constructions and new future constructions may be explained by grammaticalization not merely of HABĒRE but of whole periphrastic expressions: conjugated forms of HABĒRE plus past participle ("a static complement") were grammaticalized as perfects, while all infinitives ("dynamic concept[s]") plus conjugated forms of HABĒRE were eventually grammaticalized as futures in most areas.

[32] For a review of recent work on shifts from resultatives to perfectives in various languages, see Bybee, Perkins, and Pagliuca, 68–69.

Over the course of several centuries, then, speakers of LL moved toward creating specifically perfect syntagms by using a possessive verb together with old verbal adjectives. By Proto-Romance times, such syntagms were appearing even in legal documents. As Migliorini remarks (38), texts put together in a kind of Latin from eighth-century Italy already contain unclassical compound perfects built from conjugated forms of HABĒRE 'have' plus past participle, along with unclassical compound imperfective passives built from conjugated forms of ESSE 'be' plus past participle. Among other phrases, Migliorini cites SI NEGLECTUM NON HABUISSET 'if s/he had not failed to see to' from a law of 733; SI QUIS LANGOBARDUS HABET COMPARATAS TERRAS 'if any Lombard has bought lands' from a law of 780, and also IRAM DEI INCURRAT ET IN TARTARUM SIT CONSUMPTUS 'let him incur God's wrath and be burned in hell' from a document dated 767 where final <u>m</u> often indicates a mere orthographic reminiscence. In the last example, one may confidently identify the analytic phrase SIT CONSUMPTUS as a present-tense passive for CL synthetic CŌNSŪMITUR rather than a perfect-tense passive. Constructions like these, no doubt already current in Late Latin, have remained so in Romance ever since.

1.6. FURTHER MORPHOSYNTACTIC DEVELOPMENTS IN LATE LATIN

Besides new perfects made out of a conjugated form of HABĒRE 'have' plus a past participle, Late Latin speakers made major innovations in the verb system. Abandoning the old synthetic passives, they extended into the infectum the practice of building analytic passives from a conjugated form of ESSE(RE) 'be' plus a past participle. Also out of ESSE(RE) plus a past participle, they developed a new perfect for intransitive active verbs that appears in e.g. a tombstone inscription SORŌRĒS ŪNĀ DIĒ OBITÆ SUNT 'the sisters [have] passed away on one day.' Here the verb OBITÆ SUNT, presumably modeled on MORTUÆ SUNT 'died,' would have been OBIĒRUNT in CL. Again, in a passage rendered "they were now well stricken in age" by the King James Version (Luke 1:7), some manuscripts of the more demotic *Itala* version have the new plupf.indic. PROCESSI ERANT 'they had advanced' for what is rendered by a pluperfect subjunctive, PROCESSISSENT, in the more conservative *Vulgate* (Väänänen 1981, 145).

In most areas, speakers of Late Latin abandoned the CL future and future-perfect indicative forms—not the categories—along with the CL imperfect and perfect subjunctive.[33] In most areas, speakers also created a new future

---

[33] On Sardinia, the imperfect subjunctive continues in use to this day, one of the four tense/mood exponents rendered by a single word but used mainly as an inflected infinitive (Jones, 332–33). Likewise, the "personal infinitive" in Portuguese continues the imperfect subjunctive (Parkinson, 154). In Hispania, the future perfect indicative and the perfect subjunctive blended to form the Sp. and Ptg. future subjunctive, these days "almost extinct" in the former (Green, 102) but still flourishing in the latter (Parkinson, 164).

made of any infinitive plus a conjugated present-tense form of HABĒRE 'have.'[34] They also created what became a new conditional, made of any infinitive plus a conjugated imperfect-tense form of HABĒRE.[35] Most of these changes entailed the replacement of synthetic forms with analytic ones, though the futures and conditionals have been fused across most of ROMANIA since the earliest attestations.[36] By contrast, futures formed with prefixed *VOLERE 'want' or DĒBĒRE 'ought to' have not fused (Fleischman 1982, 50–52, 114). Neither have futures formed with prefixed VENĪRE AD 'come to.' Across millennia, it may be that synthetic forms tend to be replaced by analytic ones, some of which in turn become fused and end up being replaced by new analytic constructions.[37]

Speakers of Late Latin evidently made no attempt to establish aspectual distinctions between tenses other than for the perfect and aorist, where such distinctions are most commonly encountered worldwide. Thus, little if any nuance apparently existed between new pluperfects like *HABEBA CANTATU in Gallia and old ones like *CANTA(VE)RA in Iberia, or old ones in new uses like *CANTA(VI)SSE in Dacia. Derivatives of another new kind of pluperfect, type HABUIT FACTUM 'had done/made,' survive in e.g. It. *ebbe fatto*, Fr. *eut fait*, Sp. *hubo hecho* "only in a highly limited range of grammatical contexts, generally after certain temporal conjunctions" like the equivalents of "as soon as, just after," though the current state of affairs need not always have obtained (Harris 1978, 147; see also Squartini, 197–202).

Aside from such forms limited to what Harris terms past anterior, in almost every area of emergent Romance only one of the three pluperfect exponents that descended from e.g. 3sg. HABĒBAT CANTĀTUM, from plupf.indic. CANTĀ(VE)RAT, and from plupf.subj. CANTĀ(VI)SSET survived with pluperfect meaning by the time the local daughter language was first

---

[34] On Sardinia, new futures were built from a conjugated present-tense form of HABĒRE AD 'have to' or DĒBĒRE 'ought to' plus infinitive; in Rætia, from a conjugated present-tense form of VENĪRE AD 'come to' plus infinitive; in Dacia, from a conjugated present-tense form of *VOLERE 'want' plus infinitive. By the way, LL speakers often wrote future perfects (type CANTĀVERŌ 'I shall have sung') where CL would have had simple futures (type CANTĀBŌ 'I shall sing'). Could they have been transcribing, in a way acceptable to literati, post-CL futures that were also marked in [r]?

[35] On Sardinia, conditionals were built from a conjugated imperfect-tense form of HABĒRE AD 'have to' plus infinitive; in Rætia, from the CL pluperfect subjunctive; in Dacia, probably from a conjugated imperfect-tense form of *VOLERE 'want' plus infinitive. To express the future seen from the past, Italian is the only Romance language to use an analytic conditional: constructions like *disse che sarebbero venuti* 's/he said they would come' (literally, '...they would be come') go back at least to the *Decameron* . For a review of efforts to explain how the construction came about, see Maiden 1996.

[36] In Old Spanish and still in high-flown Portuguese, the two parts of futures remain(ed) detachable.

[37] Two modern examples of the trend toward analytic syntagms would be Fr. *je vais aller* 'I am going to go,' tending to replace fut. *j'irai* 'I will go' in many if not most idiomatic contexts, while Cat. *vaig anar* 'I am going to go' tends to replace pret. *aní* 'I went.' By Fleischman's Law, these syntagms are unlikely to fuse in the centuries to come.

attested. In old northern Gallia, the few survivals of old CL pluperfects in *St. Eulalia* (ca. 880), namely *auret* 'had' < HABUERAT 'had had,' *pouret* 'could' < POTUERAT 'had been able,' and *furet* 'was' < FUERAT 'had been,' had past value, and those survivals were hardly seen again after the tenth century. The Occitanizing *Passion du Christ* has preterit *agre* 'had' < HABUERAT and *fure(t)* 'was' < FUERAT, while the *Vie de St. Léger* has preterit *laisera* 'let, allowed' < LAXĀ(VE)RAT 'had widened, loosened' (Bartsch, 331–32).

Furthermore, the continuance in most of ROMANIA of only two of the four synthetic tenses of the CL subjunctive—as in pres. AMEM 'I may love' and plupf. AMĀ(VI)SSEM 'I might have loved'—could suggest that speakers of Late Latin blurred some earlier verb distinctions, like that between the old imperfect subjunctive, future perfect indicative, and perfect subjunctive that usually resulted in the disappearance of all three in Romance vernaculars. Yet those speakers developed a contrast between perfect and preterit unknown in the classical tongue. As already shown, they developed two other new verb forms combining tense and mood functions. Beginning as what Fleischman 1982 has called a future-of-the-past (type CANTĀRE HABUĪ in parts of Italia, CANTĀRE HABĒBAM elsewhere), the first of these went on to develop into a specifically conditional form unknown earlier, giving It. *canterei*, Sp. *cantaría*, Fr. *je chanterais* 'I would sing.'[38] The other, beginning as what Fleischman has called a future-perfect-of-the-past (type HABĒRE HABEŌ CANTĀTUM), evolved into a past conditional likewise unknown previously, giving It. *avrei cantato*, Sp. *habría cantado*, Fr. *j'aurais chanté* 'I would have sung.'

1.7. EVOLUTION OF PERFECTS IN OTHER INDO–EUROPEAN TONGUES

At about the same time as a periphrastic perfect was expanding in LL, periphrastic perfect conjugations started to develop in two languages in close contact with Latin, namely Germanic and Greek. Whether LL had any influence on those developments remains uncertain. According to Pisani (56), the emergence of periphrastic perfects in Germanic scarcely occurred in isolation, for he attributes it to the influence of LL and Romance. In an article republished in *Linguistique historique et linguistique générale* 2:120, Meillet also takes a cautious approach to the issue of perfective inspiration across languages: since Gothic had no compound perfects, one may suppose that Germanic dialects imitated the "tour romain" (cited by Maurer, 160). No scholar appears to have suggested any influence of Germanic upon Romance in developing specifically present-perfect verb forms, though more than a few

---

[38] In CL, contrary-to-fact assertions were normally expressed in the imperfect or perfect subjunctive, and "future-more-vivid" ones in the present (or perfect) subjunctive. In LL, a blurring of phonological distinctions between impf. and pf. subjunctive might have led speakers to refer unambiguous means of expressing such notions and hence to expand existing verb constructs while grammaticalizing new ones. For details of LL verb reshapings, see Vincent 1988a, 56–58.

Germanic speakers were granted land for settlements inside the Empire long before it fell. However, in reviewing the rise of periphrastic future, conditional, and perfect constructions like ModGk. ἔχο γράμμενο 'I have written,' Browning, incidentally performing metathesis of the auxiliary in reference to Romance, makes a comment about one such construction that might apply to the two others: "Whether there is any connection between this construction and the construction *habeo* plus infinitive, which gave rise to the future form in most Romance languages, is an open question" (33). In any event, remarkable similarities in tense formation among Germanic, Romance, and Greek might be attributable to the semantics of the verb 'to have' and could suggest the existence of common pathways of grammaticalization across languages. In fact, this appears to be a more compelling explanation than cross-linguistic influence.[39]

Other Indo-European tongues have undergone a similar evolution of syntax. Hittite, for instance, retained few traces of the old IE suffix in *-tó-*; it had only present- and past-tense finite verbs and only one participle, marked by -*ant*-. Yet Hittite speakers eked out their scanty tense system by forming periphrastic perfects/pluperfects in two ways. First, they could combine presents or pasts of the verb χαr(k)- 'hold, keep, have' (cf. Gk. ἀρκέω 'ward off,' CL ARCEŌ 'enclose; keep away') with the participle, yielding e.g. *nu m u ištamaštan kuit harkir* 'and because they had heard of me.' Second, they could combine presents or pasts of the verb *eš-* 'be' with the participle, yielding e.g. *natta kuiški pānza ēšta* 'no one had gone' (Sturtevant, 267–68). Parallels to both the 'have' type and the 'be' types of perfects from Hittite, as already noted, were to prove productive in Romance. Again, in a perfect construction in Breton like *gwelet am eus* 'I have seen,' *gwelet* is a past participle, and the auxiliary *am eus* represents an "inflected preposition" plus an old verb form used to express possession (Anderson, 337).

Developments in verbal morphosyntax in Persian may also shed light on the emergence of specifically perfect constructions in LL, even if Romance has not gone on to grammaticalize dative constructions originally denoting possession. In Old Persian, the expression of transitive perfects by passive constructions with the agent put into the genitive/dative case seems to have been based on possessive constructions. Thus, an OPers. possessive sentence like **manā pussa astiy*, literally 'to me [there] is a son' would be equivalent to CL MIHI FĪLIUS EST or HABEŌ FĪLIUM 'I have a son'; cf. Russ. *u menya syn* [u m(ɪ)nja sɨn] 'by/with me [is a] son' but, with a verb of possession, Russ. *imeyu pravo* 'I have the right.' Furthermore, an OPers. perfective sentence like *sa manā krtam astiy*, literally 'to/of me done it is' would be equivalent to CL MIHI FACTUM EST, itself equivalent to LL *HABEO FACTUM 'I have done.' Imitating the syntax of that possessive construction, the OPers. perfect

---

[39] For a review of common realizations of inherited grammatical tendencies, see McCray's *Advanced Principles of Historical Linguistics* on the Romance future (138–55), on aspect and the Romance past-tense system (155–71), and on the modal systems of Indo-European and Romance (171–88). For a review of past-tense aspect in varieties of Romance, see also Squartini, 152–89.

reproduces the literal meaning of the HABEŌ FACTUM type in Late Latin (Benveniste, 179–80).

In drawing a distinction between perfect and preterit but not e.g. between pluperfect imperfective and pluperfect perfective, speakers of LL behaved like speakers of many languages worldwide. As Comrie notes (71), when languages display aspectual distinctions, the tense most often evincing them is the past tense rather than the present, future, or pluperfect.

1.8. PAST PARTICIPLES BECOME PRETERITS IN OTHER INDO-EUROPEAN TONGUES

Certain IE languages may permit the observer to glimpse a possible end-stage for perfects built from HABEŌ 'have' or SUM 'be' plus past participle in Romance. One should recall that certain IE perfect verbs had already become present-perfects in certain daughter languages: *woida 'I have seen' came to mean 'I know' in e.g. Goth. *wait* and Gk. οἶδα. Moreover, as Meillet points out, the IE perfect as a distinct verbal form survived to be attested only in ancient Indo-Iranian and Greek; in their earliest attestations Italic, Celtic, and Germanic had obliterated the IE distinction between aorist and perfect and, except sometimes in the passive voice, had not yet evolved compound verb forms with specifically perfect meaning (1965, 154). After compound perfects developed, speakers of Slavic and Indo-Iranian reinterpreted perfective constructions by ceasing to use modal auxiliaries. Past participles became verbs in their own right.

Among speakers of Old Slavonic, two types of preterits seem to have been in use: a simple one called aorist like *n ešǔ* 'I carried' or *v ǔzbudixǔ* 'I awoke' and a less common compound one called perfect like *neslǔ jesmǐ* or *v ǔzbudilǔ jesmǐ,* formed from a conjugated present-tense form of 'to be' plus a past active participle marked in [l]. Endings on such participles remained adjectival (Meillet 1965, 153).[40] In Old Slavonic, that formant had been generalized to become the universal marker for past participles. In Russian as in some other Slavic languages, the simple preterit has failed to survive. Auxiliary verbs in periphrastic perfect-active constructions, at first tonic, wore away to clitics and then to zero. Thus, old Russian past participles like *vzyal* [vzjal] 'taken,' *shël* [ʃɔl] 'gone,' *videl* [vidjɪl] 'seen,' *sdelal* [zdjɛləl] 'done/made' have come to serve by themselves as (masc.sg.) past-tense verbs, both perfective and imperfective. Unlike present- and future-tense verbs marked by person and number, past-tense verbs in Russian still keep adjectival endings marked by gender and number (Vaillant, 3:83–85, 91).

---

[40] That [l] formant occurred in a few CL adjectives like CRĒDULUM 'believing' and PĒNDULUM 'hanging,' and in a few Umbrian future-perfect verb forms like 2sg. *apelus* and 3sg. *apelust* 'will have slaughtered' and 2sg. *entelus* and 2sg. *entelust* 'will have placed' (Poultney, 135).

A parallel development has occurred in Polish: an old pluperfect construction in use as late as the seventeenth century, type *on był powiedział*, literally 'he was said,' has lost its conjugated component *był* 'was' and become a simple perfective past in ModPol. *on powiedział* 'he said [once].' Compare nonstandard English *you seen it, they done this, I been there, my brother gi'n* [< given] *me this beer*; after the grammaticalized perfect auxiliary *have* or *has* reduced to [(ə)v] or [(ə)z] and then disappeared in speech, a few morphologically distinct past participles ending in [n] have come to bear the whole load of expressing perfectivity.[41]

In much the same way, during later Sanskrit and in its daughter languages like Prakrit, speakers came to denote past actions not by active preterits but by past passive participles, with the agent expressed in the instrumental case: Skt. *sa mayā dṛṣṭaaḥ*, literally 'he by me was seen,' was used for 'I saw him.' The old preterits disappeared in Middle Indic, and in modern Indic languages all preterit tenses are based on the old past passive participle (Burrow, 369).

In Old Persian, once again, both aorist and perfect tenses were commonly in use, but by Middle Persian both had vanished; the past tense in Middle Persian was expressed by a form based on the old verbal adjective in *-tá-*. Thus, the last two words of OPers. *ima tya manā kṛtam* 'what by me was done' became MidPers. *man kart* 'I did' (Meillet 1965, 153). As in Slavic, one past tense in Persian drove out the other. As in Slavic and Indic, past participles in Persian came to serve by themselves as past-tense verbs.

No Romance language has yet reached this stage. Still, in many modern languages and dialects, present-perfects coming from e.g. HABEŌ FACTUM 'I have done/made' have been encroaching on the domain of preterits descended from e.g. FĒCĪ 'I did/made [once].'[42]

Harris 1982 outlines four successive stages of this shift, using FĒCĪ to stand for all Latin perfects that became Romance preterits and using HABEŌ FACTUM for all present perfects. Each stage has been preserved in at least one modern tongue. At Stage I, typified by Sicilian and Calabrian and no doubt Late Latin itself, FĒCĪ still serves both preterit and perfect functions, with HABEŌ FACTUM restricted to present states resulting from past events. At

---

[41] In *Leveling of Irregular Past Participles in Military English* (1995), Brown notes that the great majority of Engl. verbs have the same form for preterit and past participle. Turning to verbs that have two different past-system slot-fillers in the standard language, Brown deals principally with use of finite past-tense forms to fill p.p. slots by U.S. soldiers in Germany. Most subject to leveling are verbs with three different vowels in the present, finite past, and past participle: *ring rang rung, drink drank drunk, sing sang sung,* or *swim swam swum.* Least subject to leveling are two other types. The first has three different vowels but a past participle ending in -(*e*)*n*: *write wrote written, fly flew flown.* The second type has two different vowels but a past participle in -(*e*)*n*, like *see saw seen, speak spoke spoken, freeze froze frozen,* or *steal stole stolen.* Suppletive *go went gone* showed a low tendency toward leveling; Brown did not test for *be was/were been.* Overall, then, the speakers surveyed strongly tend to level one type of outstanding allomorphy in English verb inflection.

[42] English maintenance of a distinction between *was* and *have been* would put the language at Harris's Stage III. As in other Germanic language, though, the past tense in English permits no morphological contrast between preterit and imperfect in most contexts.

Stage II, as in Galician-Portuguese, FĒCĪ keeps most of these functions listed under Stage I, but HABEŌ FACTUM starts developing perfect values in some contexts. At Stage III, as in Castilian, FĒCĪ is limited to preterit functions, with HABEŌ FACTUM acquiring its archetypal value of a past action with present relevance. At Stage IV, as in spoken French and Italian, standard Romanian, and Sardinian, FĒCĪ is limited to formal styles and may be lost; HABEŌ FACTUM serves as both preterit and present perfect. In this way, an aspectual distinction presumably extant in IE, definitely lost in Latin, and restored in most of Romance, has been lost once again in many daughter languages.[43]

Table 1–2

Merger and Remerger of Aspect/Tense Distinctions

Indo-European [aspect]	Classical Latin [tense >	Late Latin	Modern Spoken French, Italian, Romanian
aorist	perfect	preterit	*passé composé*, etc.
perfective		perfect	

Linked to the disappearance of preterit forms and the use of present-perfect verbs with preterit meaning has been the rise of "doubly compound" forms like Fr. passé surcomposé (type *j'ai eu fait* 'I have had made/done [before something else happened]').[44] Similarly, Moldavian dialects of Daco-Romanian have developed constructions like *m'am fost dus*, literally 'I have

---

[43] For distinctions in some Romance languages between the hodiernal past (expressed by old present perfects) and the pre-hodiernal past (expressed by preterits), see Bybee, Perkins, and Pagliuca, 101–2. In contrast to what has been going on in French, standard Italian, and Romanian, Vincent (1978, 56–57) states that, in the extreme south of Italy, preterits have shown signs of ousting the past-participial syntagm. Should that trend thrive and spread, this book may stir interest only in a preterist ("one who collects cold nests" —Nabokov, *Pale Fire*).

[44] Among examples of this type cited by Battye and Hintze (312) are *Je ne le sais pas mais je l'ai eu su* 'I don't know it now but I did once,' the last clause being literally '...but I have had known it' with a sequence of two past participles. Squartini (322) notes another surcomposé construction, more acceptable in Switzerland, for perfective counterfactual conditions like *Si j'avais payé ces cent francs tout de suite, ça m'aurait eu gêné*, literally 'If I had paid the 100 francs right away, it would have had bothered me.'

been gone,' current in the north in the sense 'I have gone' (Iordan and Orr, 336). Speakers thus reinforce old present-perfect verb forms no longer felt to convey perfectivity by themselves.

Though few would hold that speculation in philology has reached a degree of refinement that would enable a researcher to predict drift in any tongue, one might hypothesize a Stage V: past participles would stand alone as past-tense exponents in part of ROMANIA, just as they have come to do in Russia, Poland, northern India, and Iran, as well as in nonstandard English at times. One wonders how in that event the crucial grammatical information would be coded. Unlike Germanic languages, after all, every Romance language has so far maintained a sharp morphological contrast between past durative (imperfect) and past punctual (preterit or present perfect). Within the largest verb class in hypothetical Stage V French, though, passé composé forms would become homonymous with imperfect forms in four of the six slots: as a word-final contrast between [ɛ] and [e] has already been neutralized for many speakers, [ʃāte] would mean not only 'used to sing, was singing' in the sg. and 3pl. but also 'sang [once]' and 'has/have sung' across the six persons of the paradigm.[45] As the millennium turns, no such merger of tenses is occurring in any Romance tongue.

1.9. A PERSPECTIVE ON CHANGE

In this chapter, I have briefly looked briefly at the CL perfectum and the emergence of new compound tenses in Late Latin. Noting that past participles have come to replace preterits in some IE languages, I have reviewed the gradual replacement of preterits by present-perfect constructions in parts of ROMANIA and have sketched a scenario for the eventual disappearance of reflexes of HABEŌ 'have' in such constructions. To come back from the hypothetical future to the historical present, I am about to set sail on a voyage of discovery across 2,100 miles and 1,500 years. In the next chapter, I explore the remaking of verb paradigms, and within it the reshaping of past participles, that took place in Late Latin and Proto-Romance.[46]

---

[45] If reflexes of HABEŌ etc. were to vanish before past participles, past-system forms would remain quite distinct in Spanish, Italian, and Romanian. Thus, Spanish would have trios of (3sg.) preterits, (3sg.) imperfect indicatives, and (masc.sg.) past participles like 1st-conj. *cantó, cantaba, cantado* 'sang/sung' or trios like 4th-conj. *durmió, dormiba, dormido* 'slept.'

[46] In perusing this work, readers will note a lack of parallelism from one section to the next: a splitter rather than a lumper, I treat no two languages alike. By highlighting variance in p.p. inventories, I dab in a tinge of local color for accessible stages of each tongue, trying to show part of the wider spectrum brightened by each.

2

Reshaping Verb Paradigms
in Late Latin and Proto-Romance

To backward-straining, nostalgic eyes,
foreshortening confused the genres and the
styles. All the chests and cupboards of
Roman literature were ransacked to robe
these literary posturings, and the ageing
Muse found nothing incongruous in a
cosmetic which sanctioned the simultaneous
application of lipstick and woad.

Palmer, *The Latin Language*

2.0. OVERVIEW

Palmer's remark deals with the stylistics of Latin but may also be regarded in a
morphological light: the CL standard excluded a great many rustic or old-
fashioned forms that speakers still used, and it took little account of ongoing
changes in lexis and morphosyntax. In Late Latin, and indeed at Pompeii,
some of the suppressed rusticisms and new constructions came to be written
down. This chapter traces changes within the verb system of Late Latin and
Proto-Romance, notably the disappearance of many verbs that displayed
anomalous morphology and the recasting of more than a few anomalies that
survived in day-to-day speech.

During the first century BCE, Latin as written by Julius Cæsar appears to
have been thoroughly understandable to the unlettered when read aloud, as
political propaganda ought to be. How much did Cæsar's listeners (or readers)
observe CL standards themselves? Threshing wheat in Etruria, treading
grapes in Campania, peddling trinkets or snacks beneath the four-story
skyscrapers of Rome, speakers of Latin at that time could recognize and
respect such standards even if they were unable to abide by them.

Just as the Orontes was flowing into the Tiber, so the Tiber was flowing
into the Moselle and the Tagus, the Rhone and the Danube. When the
successors of Julius came to rule the circle of lands around the inland sea,
Rome won half those new lands to linguistic as well as military allegiance.

41

Across the Empire, more and more non-native speakers had to get by in Latin to pay taxes or evade them, bring lawsuits or fight them, buy goods or sell them. In time, Latin supplanted an untold number of tongues. Great-great-grandchildren of tribespeople in southern Europe became themselves native speakers of Late Latin, which kept shifting further and further away from the standard written by literati who commanded the classical tradition.

Now and again native speakers wrote or carved somewhat as they spoke. Now and again an antiquarian of the time disprized a novelty or two of theirs.

During the later Empire, the day-to-day speech of citizens and slaves and the lingua franca used with outsiders entailed among other innovations a wider use of past participles in perfective and passive constructions that were seldom written down. Unconscious linguistic preferences must have intensified the pressures already felt by native speakers toward regularizing morphology along innovative lines. Generations of native speakers of Late Latin together with generations learning the language for worldly or otherworldly success are unlikely to have limited themselves to the single CL past-participial exponent, often rhizotonic, chosen centuries earlier by literati at Rome. Often enough the literati had chosen none at all.

From now on, citation forms of past participles will appear with final -U rather than -UM unless in quotations. Citation forms of present participles, supines, and masculine or neuter nouns will also appear without -M, but SUM 'am' and prepositions or adverbs like CUM 'with,' CIRCUM 'around,' SURSUM 'up' will keep it.

2.1. POPULAR LATIN AS REFLECTED
IN FOUR WORKS

To illustrate the changes ongoing in Latin, analysts rely on several texts from the days of the Empire. Features of reported speech in the *Satyricon*, and features of informal writing in letters of Claudius Terentianus, the *Itinerarium Egeriæ*, and the *Mulomedicina Chironis*, are reviewed in detail for the light they shed on changing morphology, particularly that of past participles. After all, the presence of certain unclassical features both in Old Latin (OL) and in Romance suggests that they persisted among speakers without ever being allowed into the literary standard. In quotations below, the omission of macrons should not be taken as suggesting that oppositions of vowel quantity had already been neutralized when the works were written.

2.1.1. The *Satyricon*

Bearing in mind Palmer's warning about the mixture of archaism and innovation found in Late Latin, one may reach conclusions about Latin morphology during the first century CE by reviewing nonstandard forms used by characters in the *Cena Trimalchionis*, part of the *Satyricon* attributed to the satirist Petronius and datable to about 65 CE. In his edition of the *Cena* (18), Sedgwick notes that dinner guests speak in sermo plebeius or the uneducated, unpolished registers of Latin that could have lain behind Romance vernaculars. Used with caution, several features of their speech suggest ways in which Latin was evolving as early as Nero's reign.

As Sedgwick explains in his commentary (90–132), speakers at Trimalchio's dinner simplify some consonant clusters, reduce some diphthongs, syncopate some proparoxytones, interchange genders and declensions for various nouns, overuse diminutives, and Latinize Greek plurals like SCHEMAS 'figures of speech' (44.8) for SCHĒMATA.

Morphologically, Trimalchio and guests use verbs in the active voice where CL required deponents, for which see §2.9. They say LOQUIS 'you [sg.] speak' and ARGUTAT 'he chatters' (46.1) next to ARGUTAS (57.8), EXHORTAVIT 'he encouraged' (76.10), and NAUFRAGARUNT 'they were shipwrecked' (76.4); CL would have LOQUERIS, ARGUTĀTUR and ARGUTĀRIS, EXHORTĀTUS EST, and NAUFRAGĪ SUNT. In CONVIVARE 'to feast' for CONVĪVĀRĪ (57.2), an active infinitive replaces a deponent one, while in LAVARE 'to be washed' for LAVĀRĪ (42.2), an active infinitive replaces a passive one. Perhaps striving after imagined elegance through hypercorrection, speakers also turn some active verbs into deponents: DELECTARIS 'you delight' (64.2) and DELECTARETUR 'he might delight' (45.7), FASTIDIUM '[I] scorned' (48.4), RIDEATUR 'may laugh' (57.3), and SOMNIATUR 'whoever dreams' (74.13). In CL, the Trimalchian impf.subj. AMPLEXARET 'he welcomes' (63.8) would be deponent and pres.indic. AMPLEXĀTUR, though a rare active form is attested elsewhere (Sedgwick, 121). Confusion between active and deponent verbs foreshadows the complete disappearance of the latter in Romance.

A tendency among speakers to use more transparent verb forms is evident in MAVOLUIT 'he preferred' (77.5) for syncopated CL MĀLUIT < MAGE VOLUIT 'wanted more.'

While they dine, Trimalchio and guests mix up infectum and perfectum stems, or finite and participial stems within the perfectum. Some of their unclassical usages point to developments in Latin's daughter languages. The remarkable p.p. FEFELLITUS 'tricked' (61.8), for FALSUS, has reduplication carried over from finite perfectum forms like FEFELLĪ; but note nominalized FALSUM 'a mistaken idea' at 71.7.[1] Since reduplication was supposed to occur (if at all) only in finite verb forms, its hypercorrect extension to a past participle may be taken as a sign that this type of perfective marking was losing ground by ca. 65 CE.[2] No reflex of a reduplicated past participle exists in Romance.

---

[1] FALSU as an adjective meaning 'mistaken; untrue; lying' and a noun meaning 'mistake, lie,' was accepted under the CL standard. Cf. adj. ACŪTU 'sharp,' earlier p.p. 'sharpened.'

[2] Competing with CL GENITUS, the LL reduplicative p.p. GIGNITUS 'begotten' (Sommer, 601) was based on reduplicative infectum as in pres.indic. GIGNŌ. In LL, the reduplicative p.p.s PEPERCITUS and PEPERTUS 'spared' are attested ± pf. PEPERCĪ (Leumann, 617).

Across aspectual lines, in contrast, the Trimalchian pres.indic. VETUO 'I forbid' (53.8) for CL VETŌ suggests [ʊ] or [w] carried over from pf. VETUĪ; in Romance, the standard It. p.p. *vietato* ÷ VETITU and the OFr. 3sg. pret. *vead* < *VETAVIT ÷ VETUIT (*Chançun de Willame*, 3512) suggest regularization along infectum rather than perfectum lines, but regularization nonetheless. Likewise, the Trimalchian fut.p. VINCITURUM 'going to win' for VICTŪRUM (45.10) has a nasal infix retained from infectum forms like pres.indic. VINCŌ, pres.p. VINCENTE; these days, the nasal infix has spread into rhizotonic past participles like It. *vinto* and Lad. *vint*, as well as arrhizotonics like Fr. *vaincu* (see §2.14.5).[3] Nasal marking has also spread into the past participle of FINGERE 'shape, form,' which in CL had a nasal pf. FINXĪ but an non-nasal p.p. FICTU, yet attested FINCTUM (Väänänen 1981, 144) has given rise to It. *finto* and Fr. *feint* 'pretended' as against 4th-conj. Sp. *heñido*, 2nd-conj. Cat. *fenyut* 'kneaded.' Leveling of nasal and non-nasal variants could go the other way: inscriptionally attested LL p.p. DEFUCTUS 'defunct' lacks a nasal infix found in the standard, in this feature resembling standard RUPTU 'broken' (Carnoy, 178).[4]

Showing more morphological overlap between finite perfectum forms and past participles, the Trimalchian fut.pf. PARSERO 'I shall have spared' (58.5) for reduplicative PEPERCERŌ has [s] carried over from p.p. PARSU (by-form PARCĬTU). In Romance, words built on the same stem as PARCŌ have survived only rarely, e.g. in Oc. *parcer/parcir* and the It. adj. *parco* 'frugal, thrifty' < PARCU. In this verb, sigmatic marking has failed to thrive.

Of especial interest in the *Cena* is a regularized past participle seen in the phrase DOMATA SIT 'may she be tamed' (74.14) instead of CL rhizotonic DOMITA, which has been aligned with the 1st-conj. infectum DOMŌ DOMĀRE. It still is so aligned in (masc.sg.) past participles like It. *domato* and Cat. *domat* 'tamed.' Built on frequentative DOMITATU, past participles like Fr. *dompté* and Ptg. *dondado* 'idem' are as arrhizotonic as the other Romance forms.

At one point, Trimalchio speaks of buying up the rest of Campania and Calabria so that he can get all the way to Sicily by crossing his own estates. Now Petronius's mockery of arriviste ex-slaves makes it unwise to place full confidence in the forms listed above. Even if parodic exaggerations, they are still illuminating, for they show the kinds of analogical changes possibly encountered at the time in unmonitored or nonstandard usage. After all, several of those forms have left descendants in mediæval and modern Romance. They indicate that demotic Latin had already become fairly unclassical, if its spoken variants had ever become as standardized as purists might have wished, an unlikely development in any language.

---

[3] From this fut.p. VINCITURUM 'going to win,' one might hypothesize an unattested rhizotonic thematic p.p. *VINCITU, or, given the absence of macrons, even a regular 4th-conj. variant shaped like DORMĪTŪRU 'going to fall asleep.'

[4] Magnien notes (409) that nasal-infixed RUMPTUS appears in some manuscripts of Plautus; cf. the OFr. by-form *ront* 'broken.'

All in all, owing to borrowings from Greek (*credræ* < κέδρος 'cedar,' 38.1) and Semitic (*mapalia* 'shacks,' 58.13), the lexis of Latin was being enriched.[5] Owing to innovation, certain postclassical features of morphosyntax were already in evidence. Owing to conservatism, certain preclassical forms stigmatized in the literary language continued to flourish.

2.1.2. Letters of Claudius Terentianus

A Roman soldier stationed in Egypt who apparently retired there, Claudius Terentianus wrote, or dictated, letters home during the first quarter of the second century CE. His letters contain a few items of morphological interest.

For instance, one finds in the letters a pair of future active participles that seem to have been remodeled in a way likely to affect past participles as well. Though the absence of macrons makes certainty on this point impossible, the two future participles suggest that the atonic -ĬTU marker was growing in popularity. True, the letters contain several future participles entitled to that marker under classical norms, like EXITURUM 'about to go out' (467.8). They contain others. At least Claudius's MISSITURUM 'about to send' (468.22) is perfectum-based, though it has an extra syllable; CL would have MISSŪRUM, and Claudius does have MISSURUS elsewhere (467.23). By contrast, Claudius's (V)INCITURUM 'about to win' (468.37) has infectum-style nasality; here CL would have perfectum-based VICTŪRUM.

In reference to presumably rhizotonic thematic forms like the attested p.p. SEPELITUS for CL SEPULTUS 'buried'—but cf. infin. SEPELĪRE—Adams makes this comment (49): "The -ĬTUS type probably seen here tended to disappear [over the centuries], but in early Vulgar Latin at least it seems to have shown some productivity." Adams gives later examples of similar reshaping. Another infectum-based future participle SUBSCRIBITURIS, evidently for CL SUBSCRĪPTŪRUS 'about to sign' despite the oddity of its ending, is found in the *Tablettes Albertini* (iv.3). A regularized past participle TULITUS, for CL suppletive SUBLĀTUS 'taken away,' is found in a translation of parts of the fabulist Babrius (fourth century CE); cf. infin. TOLLERE.

In the letters of Claudius Terentianus, two finite verb forms offer clues to morphological trends underway in second-century Latin. First, pres.indic. POSSO 'I can' (469.15) for standard POSSUM has an Italianate look without a final -M and with a final -O. Second, pf.indic. COLLEXI 'I gathered' (471.12f.) for standard COLLĒGĪ suggests that at least some speakers were coming to prefer perfects marked by [s] rather than by vowel change and direct suffixation of endings. Were varieties of Latin still spoken in Egypt today, the rates of sigmatic retention or revival there might rival the rates observable in Romania (see §3.1.5).

---

[5] As stated below in §2.2, new lexical items came into Latin mainly from Greek, Celtic, and Germanic. Most of the contribution from Semitic came later, when Hebrew terms passed into the Christian vocabulary.

2.1.3. The *Itinerarium Egeriæ*

Formerly known as the *Peregrinatio Silviæ* or *Peregrinatio Ætheriæ*, the *Itinerarium* recounts part of a grand tour, made to sites mentioned in the Bible, by a woman from the western Roman Empire. She was probably a nun and could well have come from the future Galicia, in far northwestern Hispania. Written in a breezy style without pretension to literary worth, the work has been dated to between 381 and 384 CE (Väänänen 1987, 8).[6]

One unclassical past participle found in the *Itinerarium* is OSTENSUM 'shown' for CL OSTENTUM (11.4, and fourteen times more), a form suggesting hesitation between sigmatics and tautic athematics. Another is VENITUM 'come' for VENTUM (39.2); the CL standard form appears nine times (Bechtel, 91). The absence of macrons makes it impossible to ascertain whether that VENITUM ought to be assigned to the -ĬTU type or the -ĪTU type, but given its 4th-conj. infinitive VENĪRE as well as past participles like Sp. *venido*, Rom. *venit*, and above all OPtg. *vĩido*, the arrhizotonic option looks likely.

Confusion between active and deponent verb forms was continuing in the late fourth century CE. In OPTATI SUMUS (17.4) 'we chose' for CL OPTĀVIMUS, Egeria turns an active 1st-conj. perfect into a deponent; in EGREDERE (18.7) 'go out, go up' for ĒGREDĪ, she turns a deponent 3rd-conj. infinitive into an active one, though that verb does appear in deponent guise five other times. Instead of morphological passives, Egeria sometimes uses periphrases built of past participles plus infinitives in an infectum sense: for the verb in INTERPOSITÆ ORATIONES FIUNT (44.5) 'prayers are inserted,' CL would have required passive INTERPŌNUNTUR. Reflexive FACIT SE HORA QUINTA (38.5), literally 'it makes itself the fifth hour,' has a wholly Romance look to it. Here a writer more familiar with CL norms would have put FIT 'becomes, is done/made.'

Syntactically, Egeria often uses a conjugated form of HABĒRE 'have' plus a past participle, seemingly with anterior meaning. If CASTRA IBI FIXA HABUISSENT (19.7) could be read either as 'they might have [had] their camp set up there' or as 'they might have set up camp there,' another example—UBI IPSI CASTRA POSITA HABEBANT (25.30) should no doubt be read 'where they had set up their camp' and thus illustrates new perfect constructions. Then again, Egeria once uses a present participle for a past participle, so that in QUAM SEQUENTES FUERUNT (22.23) 'whom they followed,' CL would have had SECŪTĪ SUNT (Bechtel, 91–92, 125–26). Conceivably an imperfective sense is intended: 'whom they had been following.'

Under the CL standard, perfect, pluperfect, and future-perfect passives were built from a past participle plus infectum forms of ESSE 'be.' Signaling a change in speakers' interpretation of compound passives, Egeria's auxiliaries in such constructions almost always come from the perfectum of ESSE. Thus plupf.indic. FUERAT, pf.subj. FUERIT, fut.pf. FUERŌ, plupf.subj. FUISSET, and pf.infin. FUISSE appear rather than the impf.indic. ERAT, pres.subj. SIT, fut.

---

[6] References are to Edward Bechtel's 1902 edition, titled *Sanctæ Silviæ Peregrinatio*.

ERŌ, impf.indic. ESSET, and pres.infin. ESSE required by the classical tradition. Both the old and the new constructions are seen in FUERAT REVELATUM...FUERAT OSTENSUS...FACTUM EST (16.5) 'was revealed, was shown, was done.' As that last example indicates, however, Egeria seldom writes perfects like 3sg. FUIT 'was,' 3pl. FUĒRUNT 'were' in passives; the only two exceptions—evidently conforming to the literary standard—are MONACHI...QUI...NON FUERUNT IMPEDITI (3.4) 'monks who had not been hindered' and FUERUNT LAPIDE GIRATA (5.5) 'had been surrounded by a stone wall' (examples from Väänänen 1987, 62). By implication, speakers of Latin in the late fourth century were changing or had already changed their interpretation of passive syntagms like AMĀTUS SUM away from 'I was/have been loved' and toward 'I am loved,' which is how speakers of Romance interpret them today.

2.1.4. The *Mulomedicina Chironis*

Datable to the later Empire, the *Mulomedicina* (ca. 400 CE?) is a translation by Vegetius of a Greek handbook on how to treat illness in livestock, ascribed to one Apsyrtus.[7] The translation offers a picture of Late Latin, certain features of which foreshadow constructions in Romance.

Confusion between active and deponent verbs, to the advantage of the former, occurs in 1st-conj. REMEDIARE (189) for CL 2nd-conj. (RE)MEDĒRĪ 'heal, cure,' and also in UTERE (117, 128) for CL 3rd-conj. ŪTĪ 'use.'

Completing the shift hinted at in the *Intinerarium Egeriæ*, here passives with infectum forms of ESSE often have Romance-style imperfective values instead of CL-style perfective ones. Thus HAC RATIONE...QUOD INFRA SCRIPTUM EST should be read 'following the method that is described below' (117). In CL, SCRĪPTUM EST would have meant 'was described' or 'has been described'; here the method has not yet been set forth.

Also foreshadowing Romance, reflexive constructions are used with medio-passive value in the *Mulomedicina*. Thus Vegetius has UBI PRIMUM MORBUS SE ABSCONDIT 'where first the disease is concealed' (174) or STATIM SE MORBUS IN CONTRARIUM VERTIT 'the disease immediately turns for the worse' (119). Throughout, active and reflexive verbs often replace passives. In true passive constructions, past participles occur with a variety of auxiliaries (Ernout, 143–47). Which auxiliary to use was still being sorted out.

Divergences from the classical standard In the *Mulomedicina* may entail metaplasm, with 3rd-conj. verbs moving into more sharply marked classes. Instead of 3rd-conj. RABĒRE 'rage, be mad,' Vegetius has 1st-conj. RABIARE (84, et alibi), for which cf. prefixed Fr. *enrager* and It. *arrabbiare*. Instead of 3rd-conj. MĒIERE 'piss,' Vegetius has 1st-conj. MEIARE (69, et alibi), for which cf. Sp. *mear*. Again, 4th-conj. EXCUTIRE (72) and SINIRE (43) replace 3rd-conj. EXCUTERE 'shake out, drive out' and SINERE 'place, let, leave.' There appear suggestions of remaking of the irregular infins. VELLE and POSSE to 2nd-conj.

---

[7] References are to Eugen Oder's 1901 edition of the *Mulomedicina*.

*POTERE and *VOLERE in forms like fut. NOLĒBIS (157) for CL NOLĒS 'you [sg.] will not want' and apparently in impf.subj. POTERINT (174) for POSSENT 'they might be able' (the CL pf.subj. being POTUERINT).

Additional signs of the ebbing of unpopular morphology occur as well. Reduplication fails to occur in finite perfectum forms like the fut.pfs. PENDERIT 'will have hung' (198), TEGERIS 'will have touched' (276), and TENDERIT 'will have held' (77). Past participles for FRĪGERE 'fry' appear often as CL FRICTUS etc. but twice as FRIXUS (190, 261), its stem sigmatically aligned with that of pf. FRĪXĪ. The nasal consonant appearing in the infectum of RUMPERE 'break' appears in the 3sg. fut.pf. PRÆRUMPERIT (31) for PRÆRŪPERIT 'will have broken off in front.'

Among paradigm shifts, Vegetius writes a u-stem pf. SUBVENUIT (58) for direct-suffixation SUBVĒNIT 'succored, relieved.' That u-stem perfect, often matching u-stem past participles, suggests that it and its kind were expanding in Late Latin. Providing further evidence on u-stems, Brunot lists the following 3sg. pf.indic. forms gathered from the *Corpus Inscriptionum Latinarum*: REGUIT (V 923) for RĒXIT 'ruled,' CONVERTUIT (VIII 25) for CONVERTIT 'turned around,' and also BIBUIT and SAPUIT (XII 2040) for BIBIT 'drank' and SAPĪVIT or SAPIIT 'tasted, knew' (cf. OSp. *sope*, OFr. *sot*). Compare also the doubly marked 3sg. pf.indic. FECUIT for FĒCIT 'did/made' (III 6010, 137); shades of the ModRom. p.p. *făcut* 'done/made'!

Moreover, finite perfectum forms on the model of reduplicative DEDIT 's/he gave' found in the *Mulomedicina* include 3sg. EDIDERIT 'will have eaten' (86), along with 3pl. OSTENDIDERINT 'will have shown.' Forms resembling those three were to enjoy great success in some varieties of Romance, especially Occitan. Here they may represent hypercorrections.

Unclassical past participles are sigmatic ABSCONSA 'hidden' for CL ABSCONDITA (260), together with infectum-based DESINITUS 'ended' for DĒSĬTUS (222) and CERNITUM 'decided' for CRĒTUM (258). A new slot-filler is DEFRITUM 'broken [of fever]' (132, 138); FERVERE 'boil' had no CL p.p.[8] As with Egeria's VENITUM 'come,' the absence of macrons makes it impossible to ascertain whether by-form BATTITUM 'beaten' (233) for CL BATTŪTUM—and DESINITUS and CERNITUM for that matter—ought to be assigned to the -ĬTU type or the -ĪTU type. However, the second doubtful case was probably aligned with the new 4th-conj. infinitive SINĪRE, also appearing here.

Of especial interest in the *Mulomedicina* is a by-form past participle seen in the phrase FARINAM CONSPARTAM 'flour sprinkled around' (735) instead of the CL SPARSAM (Ernout and Meillet, 638). That form CŌNSPARTAM heralds variant past participles like It. *sparto* as against standard *sparso* 'spread, spilled,' or regional Rom. *spart* as against standard *spars* 'cracked, split.' More broadly, CŌNSPARTAM suggests a wavering between sigmatic and tautic athematic past participles for some verbs that has characterized Romance languages from French to Romanian. Indicative of the same

---

[8] The new p.p. also appears written DEFRICTUM (50), presumably with silent c̲.

hesitation in Vegetius is TERTAS 'wiped, cleaned' (258) for CL TERSĀS (Brunot, 85–89; Oder, 305–8).[9]

2.2. LEXICAL INNOVATIONS

Borrowings from other languages, notably Greek, Celtic, and Germanic, along with echoic words, enriched the inventory of verbs in Late Latin. For example, from Celtic as spoken in Gaul came a verb meaning 'change, exchange' that gave rise to Fri. *gam(y)á*, It. *cambiare*, Fr. *changer*, Cat. *canviar*, and OSp. *camear*.[10] That verb must have been borrowed early, for a prefixed reflex appears far to the east in Rom. *a schimba* 'exchange.' Later, from Germanic into Late Latin west of the Balkans, came loan-verbs like *warjan* 'defend' > It. *guarire*, OFr. *garir* (now *guérir*), Cat. *guarir* 'cure,' and Sp. *guarecer* 'shelter, keep safe'; yet reflexes of the old verb SĀNĀRE 'heal' survived in Ptg. *sarar*, OSp. *sanar*, and Sard./South It. *sanare*, if not in Rom. *a vindeca* < VINDICĀRE 'claim; avenge' (Rohlfs 1970, 19).

Perhaps of echoic origin was the interjection **toc* 'pow,' which acquired verb endings in the largest class to give a verb behind Rom. *a toca* 'knock,' probably the earliest verbal sense. In a softened sense 'touch,' the new verb replaced most reflexes of CL TANGERE, with its reduplicative pf. TETIGĪ and its rhizotonic long-vowel p.p. TĀCTU, to give It. *toccare*, Fri. *toká*, Fr. *toucher*, and Oc./Cat./Sp./Ptg. *tocar*; the old verb still survives in e.g. Oc. *tanher* 'become' with p.p. *tangut*, OSp. *tañer* 'touch' with p.p. *tañido* (*REW* nos. 8767, 8558).[11] In Late Latin or Proto-Romance, those verbs became predictable.

Certain verbs attested at the dawn of Latin poetry and prose but disallowed under the CL standard reappeared as the sun of empire set. That was the fate of onomatopoetic 4th-conj. MUTTĪRE 'mutter, mumble, murmur' or loosely 'speak,' with a regular finite perfectum but no past participle. Absent from texts since the days of Plautus and Terence (second century BCE), this verb MUTTĪRE turns up again ca. 400 CE in the Vulgate and has left descendants in Romance like OFr./Oc. *motir* 'speak' (Ernout and Meillet, 426–27).

In Late Latin, speakers tended to replace certain common verbs with more vigorous and active synonyms. Where CL had compounds of AGERE 'move, drive,' DŪCERE 'lead,' or FERRE 'carry,' speakers of Late Latin often had compounds of JACERE 'throw.' Instead of the old verb EXPELLERE 'drive out,' later speakers often used EXSPUERE 'spit out, get rid of'; instead of ĒMITTERE 'send away, let go,' they used ĒVOMERE 'spew out'; instead of COLLIGERE 'gather, gain,' they used CONRĀDERE 'scrape together' (Löfstedt, 27–29). Their drive toward more expressivity through lexical replacement was to leave traces across Romance.

---

[9] Cf. sigmatic TERSUS 'cleaned' in Plautus and tautic athematic TERTUS in Varro (Magnien, 410).

[10] Also postclassical and very rare 4th-conj. CAMBĪRE (Ernout and Meillet, 89).

[11] Sp. *tañer* now mainly means 'pluck, twang (a stringed instrument)' or 'peal, toll (a bell).' Spanish has a nominalized p.p. *tañido* 'plucking, twanging; pealing, tolling.'

2.2.1. Other Parts of Speech as Bases for New Verbs

A fair number of nouns borrowed from Greek were turned into verbs in Latin. From Gk. κόλαφος 'a blow, punch' came the early loanword COLAPHUS (already in Plautus), which in Late Latin or Proto-Romance produced the ancestor of 4th-conj. It. *colpire* 'strike, harm' and Cat. *colpir* 'impress, upset,' and of 1st-conj. OFr. *colper* 'cut, break,' now *couper*.[12]

During CL times, Gk. τόρνος 'drill, lathe' was borrowed as TORNUS and yielded TORNĀRE 'make on a lathe; turn,' with reflexes in Romance from Rom. *a turna* 'break open; pour' to Oc./Cat./Sp./Ptg. *tornar* 'turn, return; redo.' Again, Gk. στύππη 'tow, oakum'—a substance used to caulk and plug leaks in ships or barrels—was borrowed as STUPPA (cf. Fr. *étoupe*) and, the noun having come to mean 'cork,' was turned into a 1st-conj. verb meaning 'stop up' in Late Latin. Reflexes of that verb are found across Romance, from Rom. *a astupa* to Sp./Ptg. *estopar* (Ernout and Meillet, 131, 658–59, 695–96).

Native Latin nouns could likewise be turned into verbs, with almost all of them joining the largest and most productive conjugation. Attested under the Empire was 1st-conj. PECTINĀRE from PECTIN- 'a comb,' already replacing 3rd-conj. PECTERE PEXĪ PEXU 'comb, card' and flourishing in Romance from Rom. *a pieptena* to Ptg. *pentear*. Rustic in CL, denominal 1st-conj. SĒMINĀRE 'sow' from obl. SĒMIN- 'a seed' ended up eliminating in Romance almost every reflex of irregular 3rd-conj. SERERE SĒVĪ SATU 'sow,' with its three different tonic vowels (Ernout and Meillet, 491, 617–18).[13]

Verbs already extant might be reshaped on the basis of nouns related to them. In LL, regular 1st-conj. RŌRĀRE 'be wet with dew' was prefixed to give attested ARRŌRĀRE 'bedew, moisten,' but speakers seem to have felt that the prefixed variant had too many liquids.[14] In the northwestern part of the Empire, they remade the verb on the basis of nom.sg. RŌS 'dew': reflexes of the resulting dissimilation live on in Fr. *arroser*, Oc. *arozar*, and unprefixed Cat. *rosar* 'water' (Ernout and Meillet, 577; *REW* no. 677).[15]

---

[12] Sp. *golpear* 'knock, beat, pound' appears to have been built on the noun *golpe* 'hit, clash'; cf. also freq. *golpetear* 'strike or pound continually' < *golpeteo* 'knocking, pounding.'

[13] Reflexes of SERERE 'sow' apparently survive only in Logudorese, as in *siridu* 'sprouted, sprung up' (Meyer-Lübke, *REW* no. 7844). Confusion between cause and effect?

[14] A rough parallel might be found at an earlier stage of the language, when intervocalic [s] > [z] > [r]. If the next syllable already contained [r], rhotacism often failed to take place: CL CÆSARIĒS 'bushy-haired' and MISER 'wretched' kept intervocalic [s] (examples from Sihler, 172–73).

[15] Unprefixed RŌRĀRE has left offspring only in Rom. *a rura* 'drip' (*REW* no. 7373a). In *Word Formation in the Roman sermo plebeius*, Cooper reviews verbs attested pre- and postclassically: frequentatives (205–16), inchoatives (216–23), denominatives (225–30), and verbs lengthened with suffixes like -ICĀRE or -INĀRE (239–45). Only one verb extender grew less popular in Late Latin: desiderative marking in [s]. As Cooper points out (223–25), a number of desideratives are attested preclassically, but hardly any survive in Romance. For more on desiderative verbs, see notes 22 and 58 to this chapter. For sigmaticism in Romance, see §5.5.

As a part of speakers' inventiveness discussed in §2.11, past participles could serve as roots for new regular verbs in Late Latin or Proto-Romance. Now and then, a present participle might do the same: from a prefixed variant of PAVENTE, pres.p. of PAVĒRE 'quake with fear' (no CL p.p.), came It. *spaventare*, OFr. *espoenter* (now *épouvanter*), and Oc./Sp./Ptg. *espaventar*; a contracted variant gave Cat./Sp./Ptg. *espantar*. North of the Loire, prefixed OFr. *apaisenter* 'calm, appease' came from a variant of PĀCANTE, pres.p. of PĀCĀRE. South of the Pyrenees, Sp. *calentar* 'heat, warm' and *levantar* 'raise, lift' have also been built on old present participles. From something like CREPANTE, pres.p. of CREPĀRE in its LL sense 'burst,' have come OFr. *craventer* 'break open' and Sp./Ptg. *quebrantar* 'break, crush.' Finally, reflexes of RĒPERE 'crawl' and a 1st-conj. verb based on pres.p. RĒPENTE live on sporadically from Pistoia to Galicia (Ernout and Meillet, 489, 571; Harrington, 12; *REW* nos. 2312, 3035, 6133, 7221, 7222).

2.2.2. Longer Roots for Old Verbs

Containing another theme (semi-)vowel besides tonic [a], the 1st-conj. infinitive ending -IĀRE might also have been added to adjectives or nouns in Late Latin or Proto-Romance. Thus, an adjectivized p.p. ACŪTU 'sharp[ened],' once equipped with an -IĀRE ending, would have given the ancestor of It. *aguzzare*, Sp. *aguzar*, Cat. *agusar*, Fr. *aiguiser* 'sharpen.' Similarly, ALTU 'high, tall,' itself originally the past participle meaning 'grown-up' for ALERE 'nourish,' might have added -IĀRE to give the ancestor of Rom. *a înălţa*, It. *alzare*, Sp. *alzar*, Cat. *alçar*, and Fr. *hausser* 'lift, raise.' Verbs that survived across ROMANIA could have undergone the same treatment, creating by-forms that grew distinct semantically. Thus from the past participle of pan-Romance *COCERE 'cook' (CL COQUERE, p.p. COCTU) would have come an -IĀRE verb meaning 'cook, burn' that gave rise to OFr. *coissier* 'wound' and Ptg. *coçar* 'itch' (*REW* no. 2016).

According to Walsh's more recent view of such 1st-conj. verbs, mostly unattested, they derive from abstract nouns like CAPTIŌ 'a taking' and COCTIŌ 'a cooking' or from comparative adjectives like ALTIOR 'higher.' Already existing CL verbs on that second model were AMPLIĀRE 'widen,' (AB)BREVIĀRE 'shorten,' (AL)LEVIĀRE 'lighten,' LONGIĀRE 'lengthen,' and of course ALTIĀRE 'raise,' among others. LL speakers would have reinterpreted the yod in such forms as being part of the stem for new 1st-conj. verbs.[16] Moreover, many Romance verbs that analysts have retrojected to LL variants in *-IĀRE probably arose far later, from analogies made in individual languages. For example, OSp. speakers might have crossed still-current *cesar* 'stop; step back'—built from the stem of p.p. CESSU + -ĀRE—with its lexical opposite *puxar* 'push [ahead]' to give *cexar* > *cejar* 'give up, yield; slacken.'

---

[16] New verbs on that model included *CURTIARE 'shorten' > It. *raccorciare* to Cat. *acorsar* and Ptg. *encurtar* (but cf. Rom. *a scurta*); *BASSIARE 'lower' > Fr. *baisser* to Ptg. *baixar*; *ACUTIARE 'sharpen' > It. *aguzzare* to Ptg. *aguçar*, while Romanian has 4th-conj. *a ascuţi*.

Walsh's explanation would obviate any need to posit *CESSIARE as the prototype of *cejar*. It would also weaken my case for tracing shared Romance innovations all the way back to Late Latin.

Among LL speakers, what might be termed a long 1st-conj. infinitive ending -ICĀRE, already extant in a few CL verbs like CLAUDICĀRE 'limp, be lame' (cf. CLAUDĒRE 'idem') and FODICĀRE 'dig' (cf. FODERE or FODĪRE 'idem'), must have become increasingly common through time, for reflexes of -ICĀRE appear on verbs throughout Romance.[17] As in CL CLAUDICĀRE and FODICĀRE, that -ICĀRE ending might be added to a verb later on. Although a reflex of the verb FĪGERE FĪXĪ FĪCTU later FĪXU 'fasten' survives in conservative It. *figgere* (p.p. *fitto*), one must suppose a variant in -ICĀRE to derive Fr. *ficher* 'thrust, poke,' Oc./Ptg. *ficar* 'stay,' Cat. *ficar* 'put in.'[18]

From the bare verb FLECTERE 'bend' with its sigmatic pf. FLEXĪ and p.p. FLEXU, only a single reflex survives in Romance. However, a long-form variant in -ICĀRE lies behind OFr. *flechier* 'bend' (now *fléchir*) and Sic. *ñuttikari* 'fold.' If FŪRERE 'rave, be mad' has failed to thrive, a longer variant in -ICĀRE may lie behind OIt. *frucare*, OFr. *furgier*, Oc./Cat. *furgar*, Sp. *hurgar* 'rummage around,' perhaps earlier 'ransack' from the folkways of barbarian marauders. A diminutivized long-form variant gave It. *frucchiare* 'meddle.' Again, not deponent ORĪRĪ 'arise' or even an active form of it but instead a long-form variant in -ICĀRE may well have lain behind Rom. *a urca* 'go up,' with regular p.p. *urcat* (*REW* nos. 3289, 3365, 3366, 3597, 3598, 6098).

2.2.3. Lexicalization of By-Forms

Tending to replace 3rd-conj. PENDERE PEPENDĪ PĒNSU 'weigh; estimate' under the Empire was denominative 1st-conj. PĒNSĀRE from the same stem as PĒNSU 'weight.' Because most Romance reflexes retaining the [ns] cluster mean 'think,' while most reflexes simplifying the cluster to [s] or [z] mean 'weigh,' some analysts like R. Hall (1974) suppose that the erudite preserved the old form while the ignorant evolved the new one.

However, one should also take account of R. Wright's contention (13–16; 27–29) that so-called semilearnèd terms in Romance might occur in everyday contexts like feeding horses (Sp. *pensar*)[19] rather than weighing them (Sp. *pesar*).[20] If so, speakers across the future ROMANIA could sometimes have made a distinction in meaning between two variants of a verb still current at the time. Still, feeding and weighing both sound like activities of daily life.

---

[17] A 4th-conj. variant FODĪRE, attested in Cato and Plautus (Ernout and Meillet, 243), no doubt lies behind Fr. *fouir* 'burrow, dig [underground].' For other suffixes in -ĀRE verbs like LĒVIGĀRE 'smooth' and BUBULCITĀRĪ 'drive or keep oxen,' see Leumann, 550–52.

[18] Anomalous [n] in the OSp. cognate *fincar* might have arisen by analogy with the [n] in OSp. (*f*)*inojos* 'knees,' in the stock phrase *fincar los finojos* 'kneel down,' ModSp. *hincar la rodilla* or *hincarse de rodillas* (J. Craddock, p.c.).

[19] That sense resulted from a semantic narrowing of 'weigh' to 'weigh out fodder.'

[20] More plausibly, weighing the loads carried by horses to collect tolls or other fees.

As noted in §2.2.2, speakers might lengthen an old verb. From the same root as PENDERE came a variant *PENDICARE assumed for e.g. Fr. *pencher* 'hang, lean' and Oc./Cat. *penjar* > Sp. *pinjar* 'lean, bend.' A diminutivized variant resembling *PENDICULARE might have given It. *pencolare* 'totter, waver' (*REW* no. 6384).

2.3. REPLACEMENT OF VERBS

In a series of displacements, several verbs underwent shifts of meaning and were replaced by others in their earlier meanings. One such series involved the verbs EMERE, CAPERE, and PREHENDERE. When EMERE with its unusual pf. ĒMĪ and p.p. ĒMPTU lost the sense 'take,' still attested in Latin glossaries, and came to mean 'buy' as early as Plautus and Ennius (second century BCE), its place was taken by equally irregular CAPERE CĒPĪ CAPTU, earlier meaning 'seize, take in hand' and also 'contain.'[21] Through time, the semantic domain of CAPERE was encroached on by PRÆ- or PREHENDERE, which as CAPERE had already done widened from the sense 'seize, grasp' to the sense 'take.' Crowded out of that semantic slot, CAPERE remained in use in the narrower sense 'contain, fit into' (Ernout and Meillet, 95). Though EMERE, the earliest 'take' verb, vanished in Romance, the other two verbs lived on. Of the regularized reflexes of 3rd-conj. CAPERE, OIt. *capere* (also *crapire*), OFr. *chavoir*, Oc./Sp./Ptg. *caber*, and Cat. *cabre* (also *caber*) have kept the sense 'fit into'; ModIt. *capire* has shifted further to mean 'take in, understand,' while Log. *kabere* has been nominalized to mean 'property, possessions' (*REW* no. 1625). Today, at the old imperial frontiers, reflexes of PREHENDERE like Rom. *a prinde*, Cat. *prendre*, and Sp/Ptg. *prender* still mean 'catch, grasp.' At the imperial center, while still usable in the sense 'catch,' It. *prendere* and Fr. *prendre* have widened their semantic fields to become the standard verbs meaning 'take' in each tongue.

As discussed further in §2.10, frequentative or iterative or intensive verbs had a high likelihood of survival because they were completely regular and had greater phonetic body than verbs unsuffixed in -TĀRE or -SĀRE.[22] Derived from p.p. CAPTU 'taken,' the old 1st-conj. iterative CAPTĀRE 'hunt, covet, seize' has survived from Rom. *a cắta* 'seek' to It. *cattare* 'acquire' to Oc./Sp./Ptg. *catar* 'catch sight of.' Prefixed with AD-, CAPTĀRE has given It. *accattare* 'beg for,' Cat./Sp. *acatar* 'obey, respect,' and its Fr. reflex *acheter* has become the standard verb meaning 'buy.' An attested variant in yod,

---

[21] In compounds, EMERE still often kept the sense 'take': ADIMERE 'take away,' EXIMERE 'take out,' and INTERIMERE 'take away from the midst; destroy.'

[22] Frequentative verbs denote habitual actions (e.g. 'knock every day'); iterative verbs denote repeated actions (e.g. 'keep on knocking'); intensive verbs denote forceful actions (e.g. 'knock hard'). The three are not always easy to tell apart. At first built on the p.p. stem of a simple verb, many such verbs came to be formed by adding -ITĀRE to the bare infectum stem, resulting in e.g. AGITĀRE 'put in constant motion' from pres.indic. AGŌ 'move, drive' and ROGITĀRE 'ask often or eagerly' from pres.indic. ROGŌ 'ask' (Buck, 267–68).

CAPTIĀRE 'hunt' (cf. CAPTIŌ 'a taking'), has given Rom. *a acăţa* 'seize; begin' along with reflexes still meaning 'hunt' like It. *cacciare*, Fr. *chasser*, Sp. *cazar*, and Ptg. *caçar* (Ernout and Meillet, 95–96; *REW* nos. 1661, 1662).

Verbs conjugated according to patterns that came to seem increasingly anomalous, then, were to have one of three fates in Romance. The highest-frequency ones continued in use with their anomalies preserved; some, like EMERE, passed out of use; others, like CAPERE, were remade along more predictable lines entailing a stressed theme vowel.

2.3.1. Fatal Brevity

At times, a CL verb was doomed by the meagerness of its phonetic body, especially if it had forms already monosyllabic or that became so in Late Latin. Existing frequentative variants, more distinctive and more predictable, tended to prevail. Already under the Empire, speakers were replacing the short 3rd-conj. *u*-stem verb SPUERE SPUĪ SPŪTU 'spit' with longer 1st-conj. SPŪTĀRE (cf. It. *sputare*,[23] Fri. *spudá*, OFr. *espuer*, Oc. *espudar*), earlier a frequentative meaning 'spit out.' Speakers were also replacing SPECERE SPEXĪ SPECTU 'look at' with various prefixed versions or with the frequentative SPECTĀRE 'observe, stare,' itself often prefixed (cf. It. *aspettare* 'wait,' Rom. *a aştepta* and Ptg. *espeitar* 'look, glance').

Latin speakers might replace even a short 1st-conj. verb with a longer variant. When they still lived under the Empire, FLĀRE 'blow' was yielding to FLĀTĀRE (cf. It. *fiatare* 'breathe'), NĀRE 'swim' to NĀTĀRE > Oc./Cat./Sp./Ptg. *nadar*.[24] In an instance of brevity and unpredictability, 3rd-conj. VEHERE VĒXĪ VECTU 'convey, transport' failed to outlast the Empire, probably owing to its too-brief forms like infin. *VERE after syncope following loss of [h] as a phoneme. Another short verb never heard from again was QUĪRE QUĪVĪ QUĬTU 'be able, up to doing,' with its anomalous short-vowel past participle. Desiderative or frequentative forms of verbs had more body: thus, LACERE 'stimulate, seduce' is attested only in glossaries, but its desiderative LACESSĪRE 'provoke, exasperate' and its frequentative LACTĀRE 'wheedle, cajole' both flourished in Latin if not in Romance (Ernout and Meillet, 240–41, 346, 442–43, 555, 639–40, 644, 717).[25]

Unless prefixed or suffixed, some short verbs were lost; the old prefixes turned into Malkielian prefixoids. No Romance verb comes from the bare

---

[23] Also It. *sputacchiare* 'spit on, sputter,' from a diminutivized reflex of SPŪTĀRE 'spit.'

[24] From an obscure variant *NOTARE 'swim' come Rom. *a înota*, It. *nuotare*, and OFr. *noer* (*REW* no. 5846). Mod.Fr. *nager* 'swim' comes from NĀVIGĀRE 'sail,' already used by Ovid in the sense 'swim.' Conversely, NĀRE was used by Catullus in the sense 'sail.'

[25] Desiderative verbs denote intention and in IE languages are usually marked with [s], as in Skt. *pipāsāmi* 'I wish to drink' or CL 3rd-conj. CAPESSŌ 'lay hold of eagerly, strive for' from CAPIŌ 'take' (Buck, 279).

stem of EDERE or ĒSSE 'eat' with its p.p. ĒSU or ESTU.[26] Only in central-western Iberia have there survived reflexes of prefixed COMEDERE (meaning 'eat up' in CL) to give Sp./Ptg. *comer*, with regular non-*ar*-verb p.p. *comido*, though a semilearnèd by-form *comesto* endures, or used to, in Portuguese, and Old Spanish had a by-form *comudo*. Elsewhere, EDERE was replaced by a derivative of 3rd-conj. MANDERE MANDĪ MANSU 'chew,' used as early as Pliny (first century CE) to mean 'eat.' A suffixed 1st-conj. variant of MANDERE has yielded Rom. *a mânca*, Vegl. *manonka*, OIt. *manicare*, Log. *man(d)igare*, and Fr. *manger* (> It. *mangiare*, Cat. *menjar*, Ptg. *manjar*), all with regular p.p.s.

Likewise, unprefixed (G)NŌSCERE (G)NŌVĪ (G)NŌTU 'know' survives nowhere in ROMANIA, but reflexes of prefixed COGNŌSCERE—'get to know, recognize' in CL—survive in e.g. Rom. *a cunoaşte*, It. *conoscere*, Fr. *connaître*, Cat. *conèixer*, Sp. *conocer*, and Ptg. *conhecer* 'know, be acquainted with.' To be sure, the mere presence of a prefix could not guarantee long life for a verb: although COGNŌSCERE endured, its prefixed partner IGNŌSCERE 'overlook, forgive' was replaced in Romance by reflexes of easier-patterning 1st-conj. PERDŌNĀRE 'pardon'; a reflex of the old past participle survives in the It. semilearnèd adj. *ignoto* 'unknown' (Ernout and Meillet, 191, 308, 382, 445).

2.3.2. Fatal Homonymy

As for homonymy resulting from phonemic merger, speakers might have come to avoid the verb MÆRĒRE (rare pf. MÆRUĪ, p.p. MÆSTU) 'ail' because it sounded too much like MERĒRE (pf. MERUĪ, p.p. MERĬTU) 'earn, deserve' after [ai] had reduced to [ɛ]. In any event, MÆRĒRE did not survive and MERĒRE did. Even in CL times, MÆSTU apparently seemed less verbal than nominal and was spun off as an adjective meaning 'sad'; it failed to endure into Romance.

Another example of emerging homonymy affected the 3rd-conj. deponent QUERĪ QUESTU EST 'complain,' which once it had been remade as an active verb came to sound too much like the verb QUÆRERE QUÆSĪVĪ QUÆSĪTU 'seek,' at least in its infectum. As the first of these seems hardly to have been used after the first century CE, only reflexes of the second verb survive today (*REW* no. 2147; Ernout and Meillet, 377, 555).

2.3.3. Fatal Irregularity

Anomalies remaining in CL verbs often took the form of an infectum apparently belonging to one class and a perfectum apparently belonging to another. Often the morphology of a verb's past participle matched neither that of its finite perfectum nor that of its infectum. For speakers of Latin, each principal part of such verbs might have sounded as if it belonged to a

---

[26] P.p. ESTU 'eaten' is so listed, with no macron, by Ernout and Meillet. If old, this past participle would come from *a͞d-to-; if new, it would come from ĒSU with [t] added and thus be doubly marked like certain later -*sto* forms in Italian (see §3.5.5.1).

different conjugational class, though from my point of view the classes had come into being after the verbs themselves had. Again, many such verbs had meager phonetic body.

To return to verbs mentioned in §1.3.5, one thinks of 3rd-conj. LINŌ 'smear, daub' with its perfect either 2nd-conj.-style LĒVĪ or 4th-conj.-style LĪVĪ and its short-vowel p.p. LĬTU. One thinks of 3rd-conj. SINŌ 'let, leave' with either 4th-conj.-style SĪVĪ or reduplicative SISTĪ for its perfect and short-vowel SĬTU for its past participle. One thinks of 3rd-conj. SERŌ 'sow, plant' with its 2nd-conj.-style pf. SĒVĪ and its vowel-changing p.p. SĂTU. At times as well, infectum and perfectum belonged to different classes. To speakers of Latin, 3rd-conj. STERNŌ 'spread out' might have seemed to have in pf. STRĀVĪ and p.p. STRĀTU a 1st-conj. perfectum. Again, 3rd-conj. TERŌ 'rub, wear away' might have seemed to have in its pf. TRĪVĪ and its p.p. TRĪTU a 4th-conj. perfectum (but see §2.11.2). So might 3rd-conj. RUDŌ 'roar; bray' with its pf. RUDĪVĪ and p.p. RUDĪTU, and 3rd-conj. ARCESSŌ 'send for, summon' with its pf. ARCESSĪVĪ and p.p. ARCESSĪTU.[27]

2.3.4. Fatal Defectiveness

Verbs missing their fourth principal part might either acquire one in Late Latin or vanish altogether, none or almost none surviving into recorded Romance. Of the verbs that vanished, as noted above, many were short or irregular or both. Some belonged to the register of Roman religion and fell into disuse when the rituals themselves did; among that number were regular 1st-conj. LITĀRE 'obtain a favorable omen' and LĪBĀRE 'pour a libation' (Ernout and Meillet, 356, 363). Other verbs belonging to the registers of law, statecraft, and war fell into disuse when Roman soldiers no longer took the field against Franks, Burgundians, Vandals, and Goths.

Several verbs that vanished lacked a perfectum. If deponent FOR 'speak' did have a regular p.p. FĀTU (cf. infin. FĀRI, Gk. φημί) used to form all perfectum finite tenses, in the infectum it could be used only in the 3sg. and 3pl. pres.indic. and in the 1sg. and 3sg. fut.indic.; only reflexes of this verb's nominalized pres.p. INFANTE 'unable to speak' remain in Romance, in e.g. Fr. *enfant* 'child.' At least one verb had a functioning perfectum (ĪCĪ, ICTU 'struck') but a moribund infectum even in CL (ĪCŌ or ĪCIŌ, ĪCERE 'strike'); p.p. ICTU was the only form still in current use. One might hypothesize that, especially in compounds, ĪC(I)Ō sounded too much like JACIŌ 'throw' and was semantically similar as well, as someone ordered to strike often had to throw a weapon. Finite forms of the verb MEMINĪ 'remember' belonged morphologically to the perfectum yet had present, imperfect, or future

---

[27] A straight reflex of LINERE survives only in Surselvan *lená* 'smear,' one of SINERE only in Freiburg *sêdr* 'let, leave,' one from RUDERE only in Oc. *ruzer* 'grunt.' From ARCESSERE none survives. In contrast, STERNERE has reflexes in Rom. *a aşterne*, OFr. *esternir*, OPtg. *estrer*, and in many dialects, almost everywhere in the sense 'strewing litter' (*REW* nos. 5063, 7937a, 7418).

meaning, so that in effect the verb could not be used in a perfective sense, especially since it had only a quite rare form MENTU for its past participle.[28]

Likewise, in CL the verb ŌDĪ 'hate' had only perfectum forms with infectum meanings, except for its fut.p. ŌSŪRU; the OL p.p. ŌSU 'hated' found in Plautus had passed out of use.[29] Prefixed COĒPĪ 'began' could be used only in the perfectum, with perfective meaning, and despite the existence of a p.p. CŒPTU 'begun' was u nlikely to live on owing to its brevity.[30]

Being about to leave Classical Latin behind, I now abandon the Classicist's practice of using the 1sg. present active indicative as the citation form for verbs and follow the Romanist's practice of citing verbs in the infinitive.

2.4. FAVORED AND DISFAVORED TYPES WITHIN THE PERFECTUM

Throughout the history of Latin, speakers reshaped past participles i n accordance with various analogical patterns. I have gleaned fragments of reshaping in pre-Latin. In CL times, leveling took place within the perfectum of FĪGERE 'fasten' when the older p.p. FĪCTU was remade as FĪXU ± pf. FĪXĪ, with the remade form living on in It. *fisso* 'fixed, regular' and in semilearnèd Fr. *fixe* as in *prix fixe* 'fixed-price.' Also in CL times, the perfectum of NĪTĪ 'lean, rely on" changed when its old pf./p.p. NĪXU was remade as NĪSU ± ŪSU 'used,' a form similar semantically as well as morphologically. Although both new past participles were of the increasingly popular sigmatic type, neither NĪXU nor NĪSU was to live on in Romance (Ernout and Meillet, 234, 442).

In Late Latin, further regularizations took place. For instance, the CL infectum of 3rd-conj. PROSTERNERE 'debase, ruin' seemed not to match its 1st-conj.-style perfectum with pf. PROSTRĀVĪ and p.p. PROSTRĀTU. Forms like It. *prostrare*, Oc./Ptg. *prostrar*, Sp. *postrar* 'fall prostrate' suggests that the infinitive was remade along perfectum lines, PROSTRARE being attested as early as the seventh century in Isidore of Seville (Tekavčić, 329).

It is time to review observations made so far in this study. By Late Latin times, which types seemed likely to grow and spread within the past system? Which types seemed likely to shrink or die out?

---

[28] For a review of the morphology of unpredictable verbs in Latin, see Leumann, 521–32.

[29] Prefixed adjectives built from the old p.p. ŌSU 'hated,' like EXŌSU 'hating greatly' and PERŌSU 'hating; hated,' continued to be used in the literary language (Flobert, 502). Leumann cites an attested pf. ODIVI, as if regular for a 4th-conj. variant *ODIRE. In CL, that root was kept alive by the noun ODIU 'hatred' and the adj. ODIŌSU 'hateful.'

[30] OL infectum CŒPIŌ 'begin' was replaced by suppletive CL INCIPIŌ. Under the Empire, pres. CŒPIŌ 'begin' and ODIŌ 'hate' were (re)developed, but as neither left descendants in Romance one doubts they were popular. Also fated to vanish, MEMINĪ 'remember' had a fut. imperative MEMENTŌ 'be sure to remember'; a pres.p. MEMINĒNS 'remembering' was developed by writers but remained rare. Suppletive ICTU or PERCUSSU was used as the p.p. for FERĪRE 'hit, slay,' which itself lacked a perfectum (Ernout and Meillet, 305, 395, 458).

2.4.1. Types Disfavored Everywhere

Almost all perfects that entailed lengthening or raising of a vowel in the root syllable like FŪGĪ 'fled' (pres. FUGIŌ), and almost all perfects that entailed direct suffixation of person-number endings like INCENDĪ 'lit, kindled' (pres. INCENDŌ), were replaced by arrhizotonic or sigmatic types in Late Latin or Proto-Romance. Why did these two types grow rarer? For the direct-suffixation type, speakers might have felt that the finite perfectum forms sounded too much like infectum forms, making it difficult to distinguish tense in rapid speech; for the lengthened or raised-vowel type, speakers might have felt that the finite perfectum forms sounded too little like infectum forms, making it difficult to associate aspects of the same verb. True, some homonymy between infectum and perfectum was tolerated in the long run i n e.g. Sp. *cantamos* 'we sing/sang,' *salimos* 'we leave/left.' Yet among vowel-change direct-suffixation perfects, only reflexes of FĒCĪ 'did/made' have survived everywhere.

In view of the near disappearance in Romance of reduplicative perfects—though reflexes of high-frequency DEDĪ 'gave' and STETĪ 'stood, stayed' lived on—one doubts whether this type long remained popular among the plebs. Overall, like [w] infixation and vowel lengthening and/or raising, reduplication as a marker of the finite perfect or preterit may be said to have become degrammaticalized between Latin and Romance (Lloyd, 168). In LL, moreover, suppletive FERRE TULĪ LĀTU 'carry' acquired several variants of a more regular past participle attested as TOLLITU, TULITU, or apparently syncopated TULTU, for which last cf. It. *tolto* 'taken away' (Leumann, 617).

Everywhere, speakers grew less willing to use rhizotonic athematic past participles like CAPTU 'taken,' JACTU 'thrown,' TENTU 'held,' TEXTU 'woven,' or VENTU 'come,' again probably because such forms came to seem insufficiently marked as past participles. Only high-frequency forms of this type like FACTU 'done/made' and DICTU 'said, told' have resisted leveling, though the latter has often acquired a tonic [i] matching that of pf. DĪXĪ.

Other IE languages have undergone similar regularizations of verb morphology across aspectual lines. In Sanskrit, for instance, some participles were made by direct suffixation of an ending to the verb root, giving e.g. a p.p. *ma-ta-* 'thought,' while other verb forms were made by addition of a stem-forming suffix to this root, giving a 3sg. pres. *man-ya-te* 'thinks.' In Pali, speakers began to level such variation, so that Pali had *mañña-ti* for the 3sg. present and, for the past participle, both inherited *ma-ta-* and innovative *maññ-ita-*, which latter more closely resembled the pres. stem (Hock, 182–83). Romance stands to Latin as Pali does to Sanskrit.

2.4.2. Types Favored Everywhere

Owing to the rise of new perfect constructions, past participles became a central part of the verb system for the first time. Every verb needed a past participle. Not all verbs had had one in CL. To fill the gap, as noted, speakers living under the later Empire evolved new past participles for verbs they still used. As Vincent remarks (1988a, 56–57), they did so by building on means already available within the language: if a given verb had no past participle, one was created by analogy with other verbs that did.

What were the analogical patterns that speakers followed to form new past participles? Most notably, they preferred arrhizotonic types ending in -ĀTU, in -ĪTU, and in -ŪTU, corresponding to infinitives ending in -ĀRE, in -ĪRE, and in -ĒRE or ´-ERE respectively. For the first two of these paradigms, tonic [a] and [i] in both infinitive and past participle, and in other slots as well, made for easy conjugation. At a time when many verbs were wavering between the 2nd and 3rd conjugations, the usefulness of past participles in tonic [u] for either infinitive type enhanced morphological predictability, so that speakers reshaped many 2nd- and 3rd-conj. rhizotonic past participles along -ŪTU lines. From Romanian through Tuscan to French, Occitan, and Catalan, regular past participles end in reflexes of -ĀTU, -ĪTU, and -ŪTU. In Spanish and Portuguese, past-participial predictability has grown greater still since the Middle Ages, for aside from a handful of high-frequency rhizotonic past participles (and other learnèd ones) only reflexes of -ĀTU and -ĪTU remain in use today. Two arrhizotonic types have also prevailed elsewhere: in Surselvan and Engadin they are reflexes of -ĀTU and -ĪTU, while in Calabrian, Lucanian, and Sicilian they are reflexes of -ĀTU and -ŪTU.

Across ROMANIA, above all in Italia and Dacia, speakers of Late Latin or Proto-Romance tended to preserve sigmatic preterits and past participles like RĪSĪ and RĪSU 'laughed.' At times, speakers made the entire perfectum of a verb sigmatic, for some verbs acquired sigmatic preterits like attested ABSCŌNSĪ for CL ABSCONDĪ or ABSCONDIDĪ 'hid' and attested SORBSĪ for CL SORBUĪ 'swallowed' (Väänänen, 143). Even more than in Italy, speakers in Dacia remade sigmatically many preterits and past participles for 3rd-conj. verbs. Sigmatics survived into mediæval French and Spanish but are now unproductive in the first, extinct in the second.

2.4.3. Types Favored in Some Areas

A fourth type of arrhizotonic past participle, in -ĒTU, had no doubt been moribund in CL and soon died out, except in a few adjectivized past participles like QUIĒTU 'rested.' Often, surviving verbs from the 2nd conjugation that had that kind of past participle were moved into the 4th conjugation, producing e.g. Cat./Oc. *delir* 'melt [of snow]' from DĒLĒRE 'destroy, remove' (CL "regular" 2nd-conj. p.p. DĒLĒTU).

In a phonological sense, one might consider that tonic mid-front vowels did live on in verb morphology for part of ROMANIA. In Italian, old 2nd-conj. "regular" perfects in -ĒVIT etc. appear to lie behind preterits like 3sg. *credé* and 3pl. *crederono* 'believed,' unless *-e* has contracted from *-ai* < -ĀVIT etc. Again, if devoid of influence on past participles, the model of 3sg. DEDIT 's/he gave' was to prove powerful in preterit formation. It remains the basis for e.g. 3sg. preterits like Catalan ones in *-é* and Portuguese ones in *-eu*. In Occitan, the ending -*et* < -DEDIT (for CL -DIDIT) proved so popular that it was extended into 1st-conj. preterits like *amet* 's/he loved' ≠ AMĀVIT (Togeby, 14).

For a time, certain arrhizotonic past participles seem to have faced competition from rhizotonic thematic ones in -ĬTU. Unless they represent hypercorrections, or conceivably 4th-conj. variants as in Old Spanish, LL inscriptions containing forms like PROVITUS 'approved' for PROBĀTUS, VOCITUS 'called' for VOCĀTUS, and PROCITUM 'asked, demanded' for PROCĀTUM imply that for a while the old rhizotonic type of past participle in -ĬTU expanded, even for at least a few -ĀRE verbs already conjugable with complete predictability. Then again, if they are out-and-out 4th-conj. forms, they would resemble a few past participles that developed for 1st-conj. verbs in Old Spanish (§4.7.8). In Late Latin as well, past participles in -ĬTU arose for a few verbs that had lacked that principal part in CL. Forms like postclassical BIBĬTU 'drunk' suggest the vitality of the -ĬTU type (Planta, 440; Battisti, 260).

Indeed, though supplanted elsewhere, -ĬTU past participles live on today on Sardinia and in most of southern Italy. As that -ĬTU ending became increasingly common there, certain athematic rhizotonic past participles appear to have been replaced by thematic rhizotonic ones built from infectum stems. Their popularity may also be deduced from the survival into other Romance languages of more than a few nominalized past participles like Fr. *fente* 'slit' ≠ FISSA 'split' (infectum stem FIND-), the CL past participle surviving in Fr. *fesse* 'buttock.' Of the four rhyming OOc. past participles that syncopated from forms in -ĬTU, *mout* 'ground,' *sout* 'loosened,' *tout* 'taken away,' and *vout* 'rolled,' only the first comes down from a form accepted under the CL standard (Mann, 10).

Eventually, speakers across Dacia, Gaul, Hispania, and much of Italia grew less willing to use rhizotonic thematic past participles like HABĬTU 'had,' CRĒDĬTU 'believed,' DĒBĬTU 'had to,' or VENDĬTU 'sold,' which owing to syncope would have come to sound insufficiently distinctive as past participles, especially in what had been the western provinces. In French, for example, three of those four old past participles would have become homophonous with their verbs' 3sg. pres.indic. forms *croit, doit, vend*.

2.5. SURVIVAL OF REGULAR VERBS

In Late Latin if not earlier, certain 3rd-conj. verbs gave way to others belonging to more predictable conjugations. One such verb was FLUERE FLUXĪ FLUCTU/FLUXU 'flow,' replaced everywhere by 1st-conj. CŌLĀRE 'strain, filter.'[31] Across ROMANIA, the complex conjugation of suppletive FERRE TULĪ LĀTU 'carry' was no doubt one reason for its replacement by 1st-conj. PORTĀRE.[32]

---

[31] Readers may decide which of the two p.p. variants for infin. FLUERE 'flow' is older.

[32] In *REW* no. 3258, Meyer-Lübke notes that FERRE 'carry' survived in Old Campidanese on Sardinia and in an inscription on an Old Portuguese boundary marker: *ferit en terra de* 'brought onto the land of…' [?]. Meyer-Lübke gives glosses only at the headwords of entries.

Except for inkhorn terms resounding in epics written in Old French and Old Occitan—chansons de geste—the verb GERERE GESSĪ GESTU 'carry, hold; wage' with its sigmatic finite perfect and its sigmatic-tautic past participle was also replaced by PORTĀRE across the northwestern provinces of the old Empire. If LINQUERE LĪQUĪ LICTU 'leave, abandon' has one learnèd reflex in prefixed It. *delinquere* 'commit a crime,' the verb was replaced everywhere else by 1st-conj. LAXĀRE (CL 'loosen, widen'), or more accurately often by a metathesized variant with medial [sk][33] that also took over for irregular SINERE SĪVĪ SITU 'allow; place; leave.'

In Late Latin or Proto-Romance, CL NECTERE NEX(U)Ī NEXU 'bind' was replaced by reflexes of 1st-conj. LIGĀRE 'tie' or NŌDĀRE 'knot'; LIGĀRE also tended to replace 4th-conj. VINCĪRE VINXI VINCTU 'tie around, fetter,' with its sigmatic perfect and tautic athematic past participle. Likewise, 3rd-conj. OSTENDERE 'expose, show,' with a direct-suffix pf. OSTENDĪ and p.p. OSTENTU (nonstandard OSTĒNSU), yielded in Romance to reflexes of 1st-conj. MŌNSTRĀRE, which had no troublesome consonant changes for speakers to keep straight.

Moreover, owing to the triumph of two verbs borrowed from Greek, 1st-conj. TORNĀRE and GYRĀRE, unlearnèd reflexes of 3rd-conj. VERTERE VERTI VERSU 'turn' are poorly represented in Romance (but cf. Sp./Ptg. *verter* 'pour, flow'). Reflexes of the p.p. VERSU did come to be used nominally in various senses, and the p.p.-based frequentative VERSĀRE 'turn around often' lived on everywhere with nonfrequentative meaning, most often 'pour' or 'spill.' In Romance from Old French to Portuguese, past participles for semilearnèd *vertir* have been remade along regular 4th-conj. lines. In Italian, 3rd-conj. *vertere* still lacks a filler for the p.p. slot (Ernout and Meillet, 227, 241, 273, 361, 435, 470, 628, 725, 736).

Membership in the 1st conjugation could promote but never guarantee longevity for a verb. When almost completely regular POTĀRE POTĀVĪ POTĀTU/POTU 'drench; drink [heavily]' was replaced everywhere by reflexes of BIBERE 'drink,' for instance, speakers lost a semantic distinction that some would regard as essential.[34]

Generally, users of Late Latin shared three tendencies in revamping morphology: to mark nouns with diminutive endings, to turn nouns into verbs with predictable endings, and to give their verbs greater phonetic body in speech. All three tendencies come out in an instance of reshaping that lives on today. Most speakers of Late Latin chose to replace almost regular 4th-conj. SARĪRE 'hoe, weed' (rarely, p.p. SARTU next to regular SARĪTU) with pan-Romance SARCULĀRE derived from the diminutive-looking noun SARCULU 'light hoe,' or perhaps from a root SAR- plus -ICULĀRE. Their

---

[33] Cf. OEngl. *axian* and *ascian* 'ask.' Reflexes of both persist to this day, in std. *ask* and nonstd. *ax*. Had Louis XVI known English, he could have said "Don't ax me" to his jailers.

[34] Built on the stem PŌT- 'drink' (not PŎT- 'be able'), only derivatives of the noun PŌTIŌNE 'a drink' survive in Romance to give nouns like Fr. *poison* or OSp. *pozon* 'bane,' Ptg. *poção* 'medicine, physic'—the last archaic—and adjectives meaning 'potable' (*REW* no. 6699).

choice resulted in e.g. It. *sarchiare,* Fr. *sarcler,* North Cat. *sasclar,* and Sp./Ptg. *sachar,* all with regular past participles (Ernout and Meillet, 595; *REW* no. 7601).[35]

In the rest of this chapter, I look at how speakers of Latin and post-Latin languages dealt with unpredictability in other verbs. The focus shifts gradually from Latin toward Romance.

2.6. METAPLASM

In Late Latin or Proto-Romance, a number of verbs underwent metaplasm, shifting from one conjugation to another. How was metaplasm motivated within the history of Latin? It may be true that to point to the role of metaplasm merely gives a name to certain restructurings for infinitives (and preterits and past participles), nothing more. Nevertheless, avoiding abstract explication for now, I note that the verbs most susceptible to metaplasm belonged to the 3rd conjugation, and that many of them moved into more sharply marked classes. A smaller number turned rhizotonic.

Under the CL standard, several infinitives and hence their whole infectum system could belong to either the 2nd conjugation or the 3rd. Examples are TERGĒRE and TERGERE 'wipe, clean,' FERVĒRE and FERVERE 'boil,' FULGĒRE and FULGERE 'flash, gleam.'

In Late Latin or Proto-Romance, a few verbs went the other way: they shifted conjugation from 2nd to 3rd, especially the future Occitania and Catalonia. Thus RĪDĒRE 'laugh' changed to Fr./Oc. *rire* and Cat. *riure,* RESPONDĒRE 'answer' to Rom. *a răspunde,* It. *rispondere,* and OFr./Oc. *respondre,* VIDĒRE 'see' to Cat. *veure,* or again PLACĒRE 'please' to Cat. *plaure* and SEDĒRE 'sit' to Cat. *seure.* That the trend was far from universal is shown by Oc. 2nd-conj. *vezer* 'see,' *plazer* 'please,' *sezer* 'sit' and by Cat. 2nd-conj. *responder* 'answer,' resembling the Sp./Ptg. reflex.

Other verbs that underwent metaplasm shifted within arrhizotonic classes, especially from the 2nd conjugation to the 4th. Thus MERĒRE MERUĪ MERITU 'deserve' turned into OFr./Oc./OCat. *merir,* and SORBĒRE SORBUĪ SORBITU 'swallow, gulp down' turned into Rom. *a sorbi,* It. *sorbire,* and Oc./Cat. *sorbir,* even if Sp. *sorber* and Ptg. *sorver* apparently hold to the 2nd conjugation. In Romance, most of those verbs replaced their rhizotonic thematic past participles with regular ones belonging to the 4th conjugation.

As mentioned in §2.5, several verbs acquired sharper marking by class, to the detriment of the rhizotonic 3rd conjugation. Thus 3rd-conj. SAPERE 'taste, know' shifted stress to yield 2nd-conj. It. *sapere,* Fr. *savoir,* and Oc./Cat./Sp./Ptg. *saber.* So did CADERE 'fall' to yield Rom. *a cădea,* Vegl. *kadar,* It. *cadere,* OFr. *chëoir,* Oc. *cazer,* and Sp./OPtg. *caer,* but cf. still-3rd-conj. *caure* < *[kaðˈrə] in Catalan and 4th-conj. *cair* in Portuguese today.

---

[35] Reflexes of SARĪRE 'hoe, weed' survive in Friulian and Piedmontese *sari* (*REW* no. 7606). This verb should not be confused with SARCIRE SARSĪ SARTU 'mend, patch.'

Certain metaplasms assumed to date from LL or PR times may be explained by the emergence of yod in the powerful 1sg. present indicative, which inspired a move toward out-and-out 4th-conj. forms containing tonic [i]. Often, 3rd-conj. verbs with *i*-stems joined the 4th conjugation, with which they already had many forms in common.[36] Thus CAPERE 'take' (1sg. pres.indic. CAPIŌ) has given It. *capire* 'understand,' but compare 2nd(/3rd)-conj. Oc./Cat./Sp./Ptg. *caber* and still-3rd-conj. Cat. *cabre* 'contain, fit into.' Better examples are RAPERE 'snatch' (1sg. pres.indic. RAPIŌ) changing to Rom. *a răpi*, It. *rapire*, and Fr. *ravir*; CUPERE 'crave' (1sg. pres.indic. CUPIŌ) changing to attested CL CUPIRE, which gave OFr. *covir*, Oc. *cobir*, Log. *kubir*; and FUGERE 'flee' (1sg. pres.indic. FUGIŌ) changing to attested LL FUGIRE, which has left descendants all the way across Romance (Tekavčić, 329–30; Väänänen 1981, 135).

In addition, 3rd-conj. FREMERE 'howl, growl,' VOMERE 'throw up,' STERNERE 'spread out' became Fr. *frémir, vomir,* OFr. *esternir* with regular 4th-conj. past participles in *-i* rather than reflexes of rhizotonic FREMĬTU, VOMĬTU, and STRĀTU.[37] Here Italian has still-3rd-conj. *fremere* 'throb, shake, shudder' with p.p. *fremuto*, but cf. the proparoxytonic noun *frémito* 'throb, quiver.' Unless it arose from an old frequentative, It. 1st-conj. *vomitare* like Sp. *vomitar* has been formed from the noun *vomito* or *vómito* from 4th-decl. VOMITUS. It is altogether possible that a number of verbs now regularized derive from deverbal nouns. That derivational pathway is scarcely explored here. In §§3.1.5, 3.5.2, 4.4.9, 4.6.2.5, and 4.7.7, I discuss Romance adjectives and nouns, mostly sigmatic, whose morphology mirrors that of the corresponding past participles.

Back to regularization. Judging by It. *carpire* 'seize,' Log. *karpire* 'split,' OFr. *charpir* 'pull, twitch,' and Oc./Cat./Sp./Ptg. *carpir* 'tear up, pull off,' the evidence seems conclusive that 3rd-conj. CARPERE 'pluck, tear off,' with sigmatic pf. CARPSĪ and tautic athematic p.p. CARPTU was remade nearly everywhere as a regular 4th-conj. verb, though cf. Sic. 1st-conj. *karpari* 'seize, grasp.' Further proof of morphological realignment within the perfectum is provided by past-participial outcomes for this verb: straight reflexes of CARPTU appear to have survived nowhere, but a sigmatic variant prefixed with EX- gave rise to adjectives like It. *scarso*, Oc./Cat. *escas*, Sp./Ptg. *escaso* 'scanty, scarce,' and Fr. *échars* 'underweight [of coins]' (*REW* nos. 1711, 2961).

Verbs remade into the 4th conjugation included 2nd-conj. LŪCĒRE LŪXĪ (no CL p.p.) 'shine,' which gave a 4th-conj. OFr. by-form *luisir* (now only

---

[36] Early on, such *i*-stem verbs were tending to shift into the 4th conjugation. CL PARERE 'produce, give birth,' with 1sg. pres.indic. PARIŌ, had a 4th-conj. variant PARĪRE in Old Latin (Ernout and Meillet, 483).

[37] As is well known, nominalized reflexes of that past participle of STERNERE 'spread out,' deriving from the phrase STRĀTA VIA 'paved road,' have lived on in It. *strada* (from northern dialects), OFr. *estrée*, Cat./Sp./Ptg. *estrada* 'road,' as well as Engl. *street*, and Germ. *Straße*. Likewise, nominalized reflexes of the p.p. RUPTA 'broken,' deriving from the phrase RUPTA VIA 'broken-through, cleared road,' live on in It. *rotta* 'course' and Fr. *route* 'road, highway' (*REW* nos. 7442, 8291).

luire), Oc./Ptg. *luzir*, Cat. *lluir*, Sp. *lucir*, and perhaps Rom. *a luci*, a verb unknown to my consultant; cf. 3rd-conj. It. *rilucere*. Remade as well was MARCĒRE (no perfectum) 'be faded, withered,' which gave 4th-conj. It. *marcire*, OFr. *marcir*, and Cat. *marsir* (*REW* nos. 5136, 5345).

At times, the 4th-conj. perfectum of a verb that had a CL 3rd-conj. infectum might attract the latter into its orbit. On the fringes of Romance, PETERE PETĪVĪ PETĪTU 'ask' has given Rom. *a peţi*, Log. *pedire*, Sp./Ptg. *pedir*.[38] Then again, a verb that already had a 4th-conj. infectum and a 4th-conj. finite perfectum in CL might have a past participle of another type that came to sound anomalous and was replaced. Thus, SEPELĪRE SEPELĪVĪ SEPULTU 'bury, entomb' became It. *seppelire*, OFr. *sevelir* (now *ensevelir*), Oc. *sebellir*, Cat. *sebollir*, and OSp. *sebellir* or *sebollir*. All have regular past participles (*REW* nos. 6444, 7287). In Italian, regularized *sepellito* competes with conservative if not archaizing *sepolto*.

Between Latin and Romance, many verbs shifted from the 2nd conjugation to the 4th. Nevertheless, the importance of some of those that remained—HABĒRE 'have,' SEDĒRE 'sit,' and TENĒRE 'hold, have'—grew remarkably (Malkiel 1987, 167). When texts like the postclassical Vulgate (ca. 400 CE) are compared with versions in Romance languages, moreover, 2nd-conj. verbs are used more often than 4th-conj. ones. Therefore, "l'état de choses que Malkiel attribue à la période s'étendant du IVe au VIe siècle dure, en réalité, jusqu'à nos jours" (Mańczak, 199) [the state of affairs that Malkiel assigns to the fourth through sixth centuries has actually lasted up to our own times]. Indeed, in Spanish and Portuguese, the 2nd conjugation seems to have engulfed the 3rd. Everywhere else, most notably in Catalan and modern Occitan, the 2nd conjugation has shrunk. In Sardinian, often the odd language out, the 3rd conjugation has engulfed the 2nd.

In *A Prosodic Template in Historical Change*, Davis and Napoli try to explain the decline of 2nd-conj. verbs from Latin to nearly all of Romance. Noting that post-hoc explanations based on ambiguity, analogy, attraction, semantics, or differentiation are largely confined to one language, Davis and Napoli look for a reason that will apply across Romance. The one they find (12) is phonotactic: "Latin verbs in the second conjugation that had a monosyllabic root containing no sonorant consonant preceding the nucleus of the root syllable (what we call a "prevocalic sonorant") and ending in a single consonant...stayed together and went into a special conjugation class in each Romance language." Later, Davis and Napoli add that, for a verb to come down in the 2nd conjugation, it has to have had a light or monomoraic syllable containing the root vowel. Almost all verbs that failed to meet the two criteria went into other classes or were lost (143). As one might expect, this hypothesis is best supported for Italian, the living language closest to

---

[38] Yodless PETŌ (1sg. pres.indic. of PETERE) can hardly have played a part in the metaplasm. Malkiel 1954 contends that, in Ibero-Romance, PETERE 'seek, ask' coalesced with 4th-conj. EXPEDĪRE 'disentangle, set free; clear up, explain.' Presumably the prefix would have been optional; in 1sg. pres.indic. and other forms, yod would have been obligatory.

Latin. It is also supported by an increasing likelihood through time that anomalous verbs either will move into another class (like OIt. *pentere* 'repent,' now *pentire*) or will tend to disappear (like Fr. *manoir* or *remanoir* 'stay,' now obsolete, or *mouvoir* 'move,' restricted to literary use). Unfortunately for the past-participial purposes of this book, Davis and Napoli practically limit their discussion to infinitives in Latin and Romance.

In what might be called mutual metaplasm, each of a pair of verbs could influence the other in different ways in LL or PR. When 1sg. TENEŌ 'hold' came to rhyme with VENIŌ 'come' as *[tɛnjo] and *[βɛnjo], the 4th-conj. infin. VENĪRE > Rom. *a veni*, It. *venire*, Fr./Cat./Sp. *venir* inspired TENĒRE to shift to *tenir* in France and Catalonia, even if It. *tenere*, Sp. *tener* hold true to their 2nd-conj. origins and Rom. *a ţine* has joined the 3rd. By contrast, it was the pf. TENUĪ that gave rise to a perfect in -UĪ for direct-suffix VĒNĪ, as attested. In turn, both perfects in -UĪ inspired past participles ending in -ŪTU to replace rhizotonic athematic TENTU and VENTU. The first remodeling has given It. *tenuto*, Fr. *tenu*, Cat. *tingut*, and even OSp. *tenudo*; the second remodeling has given It. *venuto*, Fr. *venu*, Cat. *vingut*, and even OPtg. *vĩudo*. However, the new -ŪTU past participles clash conjugationally with infins. like Fr./Cat. *venir*, *tenir* and It. *venire*, so that morphological transparency for them remains only partial. In Spanish, infins. *tener* and *venir* may not rhyme, but p.p.s *tenido* and *venido* do. Romanian has followed the trend far enough to choose arrhizotonics: if *ţinut* and *venit* belong to two different classes, they are regular for infinitives *a ţine* and *a veni*.

Now Ptg. *vindo* [vĩdu] might appear to derive straight from VENTU, with nasal raising of the tonic vowel. However, the attested OPtg. graphies *vĩido* and *viindo* imply instead that Lusitanians inherited a 4th-conj. form resembling that in Sp. *venido*, nasalized its first vowel, and, once intervocalic [n] had fallen, assimilated that nasal vowel to the following [i] while maintaining nasality (Martins Sequeira, 195; Williams, 242).[39] Yet what used to be that past participle's partner, Ptg. *tido* 'had,' no longer rhymes with it owing to syncope of the pretonic syllable and the disappearance of nasality. Despite the emergence of such new anomalies between infinitive and past participle, speakers throughout ROMANIA originally chose an arrhizotonic past participle for VENĪRE.

Most LL metaplasms involved verbs from the 2nd and 3rd conjugations; some involved verbs from the 4th conjugation. Meanwhile, the largest verb class continued to attract new members, as it does today. On the way to French, for instance, already arrhizotonic PAVĪRE 'pound, flatten' became 1st-conj. *paver* 'pave.' In the sixteenth century, Fr. *puir* 'stink' began to yield to 1st-conj. *puer*, while *toussir* 'cough' < TUSSĪRE began to yield to 1st-conj. *tousser* (Darmesteter, 4:139–40). Across Iberia and to the north, 2nd-conj. TORRĒRE TORRUĪ TOSTU 'burn, parch' assumed a 1st-conj. guise, turning into Oc./Cat./Ptg. *torrar* and Sp. *turrar*, while the old past participle spun off as an adverb in literary It. *tosto*, OFr./OCat. *tost* 'soon' (*REW* no. 8801).

---

[39] An -ŪTU past participle also survived in OPtg. *vĩudo* < *VENUTU. See §4.7.4.1.

Replacing reflexes of MINUERE 'lessen' across ROMANIA was a 1st-conj. variant to which cf. attested MINUĀTIŌ 'a lessening' (Ernout and Meillet, 404–5). By and large, the 1st conjugation has become the only productive one in modern Romance, except perhaps for the originally inchoative -ĒSCERE type in Hispania and, to some degree, for the 4th conjugation everywhere.

2.7. PAST PARTICIPLES FOR THREE HIGH-FREQUENCY VERBS

Besides having anomalous infinitives in which rhotacism had not occurred, three high-frequency CL verbs had finite perfectum forms but lacked past participles. One was POSSE 'be able' with pf. stem POTU-. Another was VELLE 'want' with pf. stem VOLU-. The third was the most common verb of all, ESSE 'be' with pf. stem FU-. Speakers of Late Latin regularized all three of these infinitives to the -RE pattern that had become standard, while eliminating all other unrhotacized infinitives like NOLLE 'not want' and MALLE 'prefer.'

In reshaping POSSE 'be able' and VELLE 'want,' speakers used the existing pf. stems POTU- and VOLU-, minus the perfectivizing velar vowel but by analogy with the CL pres.p. POTENTE and VOLENTE, to create the regular 2nd-conj. infins. POTĒRE and VOLĒRE.[40] Such forms are perhaps first attested in the eighth-century *Codice paleografico lombardo*, where they appear as such, less the macrons, but are used for 3sg. impf.subj. forms without final t and have replaced CL POSSET and VELLET (Politzer, 101).[41] In any event, Romance reflexes of those infins. are Rom. *a putea, a vrea*, It. *potere, volere*, Oc./Cat. *voler, poder*, and OFr. *pooir, voloir* (now *pouvoir, vouloir* with [v]).

In the third instance, they hypercharacterized their most common infinitive by adding the -RE infinitivizer—itself deriving from -SE after a vowel—to the CL infin. ESSE. First attested in a Visigothic text perhaps as early as the seventh century (Väänänen 1981, 136), LL ESSERE has remained current in It. *essere*, Log. *èssere*, Fr. *être*, and Oc./Cat. *ésser*. In Dacia, speakers abandoned infin. ESSE(RE) altogether, expressing the notion 'be' with another infinitive, Rom. *a fi* < FIERĪ 'become, happen, be made' in CL. In northern Italy, Old Lombard *fi* was also used as a passive auxiliary.

Since every verb now had to have a past participle, how did speakers go about creating such forms for verbs that lacked them? As Table 2–1 shows,

---

[40] In CL, the stem POT- 'be able' also occurred in pres.indic. 2sg., 3sg., and 2pl. and in the impf.indic. and future; the stem VOL- 'want' also occurred in pres.indic. 1sg., 1pl., and 3pl. and in the impf.indic. and future. Probably all verb forms in POT- or VOL- contributed to the generalization of one stem throughout each paradigm in most areas. Italian still has 1sg. *posso*, 1pl. *possiamo*, 3pl. *possono*, but the special Fr. 1sg. *puis* comes from something like *[pɔtsjo].

[41] In CL, and perhaps in Proto-Romance in parts of Italy, impf.subj. verbs were built from the pres.infin. stem. Both are still marked with [r] Sardinian today, as witness the following pairs of infinitives and 3sg. imperfect subjunctives: 1st-conj. *kantare* 'sing' and *kantaret*, 2nd-/3rd-conj. *tímere* 'fear' and *timeret*, 4th-conj. *pulire* 'clean' and *puliret* (Jones, 331–32).

they based new past participles on the infectum, on the finite perfectum, or on both together where these were already isomorphous.

Table 2–1

Creation of Past Participles from Finite Stems

(after Dardel, 78)

Suppletive forms are italicized

CLASSICAL LATIN			LATE LATIN/PROTO-ROMANCE	
Infectum Stem	Perfectum Stem	Past Participle	Assimilation of Past Participle to Finite Stem	Anomaly
BIB-	BIB-	*PŌTU, PŌTĀTU*	BIBITU, *BIBUTU	—
FERĪ-	*ĪC-, PERCUSS-*	*ICTU, PERCUSSU*	*FERITU	*FERUTU
FLŌRĒ-	FLŌRU-	—	—	*FLORITU
POT-	POTU-	—	*POTUTU	—
PŪTĒ-	PŪTU-	—	*PUTITU	—
SAP-	SAPI-	—	*SAPUTU	—
VOL-	VOLU-	—	*VOLUTU	—

In forming a past participle for *POTERE, speakers of Late Latin used a newly popular type in -ŪTU, predecessor of Rom. *putut*, It. *potuto*, Surs. *pudiu*, Cat. *pogut*, Fr. *pu* 'been able.' One ending already familiar to Latin speakers was built of two verb suffixes, classifier -Ū- and p.p. marker -TU-. Perhaps unconsciously seeking a means of creating a new type of arrhizotonic past participle, speakers reinterpreted the compound as a single marker, -ŪTU. From eastern Iberia all the way to Dacia, and probably for centuries across the rest of Iberia, they added -ŪTU and its reflexes to a great number of past-participial roots, themselves more frequently based on the infectum stem than they had been in Classical Latin (see Table 2–1 above).

Notable among these creations was a past participle for *VOLERE 'want,'
even though an attested fut.p. VOLITŪRUS 'going to want' might suggest that
a rhizotonic thematic filler had potentially been found for the past-participial
slot. However that may be, the filler turned out to end in reflexes of -ŪTU in
most areas, as witness Rom. *vrut* (also *voit*), It. *voluto*, Surs. *vuliu*, Fr. *voulu*,
and Cat. *volgut*. In central-western Iberia, replacement of VELLE or *VOLERE
by reflexes of QUÆRERE 'seek' has left no evidence to support either
hypothesis. For two verbs, Table 2–1 simplifies perhaps too much: POSSE 'be
able' and VELLE 'want' each had more than one infectum stem. But I wish to
keep the focus fixed on the fourth principal part of verbs.

For the third verb lacking a past participle, ESSE 'be,' some speakers of
Proto-Italian evolved a 3rd-conj. form, which after aphæresis survived for
centuries as *suto* on the Italian peninsula but seems never to have flourished
beyond its confines. To express the notion 'been,' speakers of Late Latin or
Proto-Romance in most areas except Dacia chose to take over the regular 1st-
conj. past participle of another verb, STATU 'stood,' which has yielded
standard It. *stato*, Cat. *estat*, Fr. *été*, and Sp. *estado* beside *sido* < OSp. *seido*, no
doubt from a 4th-conj. variant of -SESSU 'sat' (infectum stem SED-).

In Dacia, while keeping *stat* in the sense 'stood, stayed,' speakers evolved
fost in the sense 'been.' The form appears scarcely derivable from the CL p.p.
FACTU of both FIERĪ 'become, be made' and FACERE 'do/make' or from
conjugated forms of *a fi*, all of which have [i] as their tonic vowel in
Romanian today. More probably, long-ago Dacians based their new past
participle on surviving perfectum forms of ESSE starting with FU-, like plupf.
subj. FUISSET (cf. also It. 2sg. pret. *fosti* < FU(I)STĪ), from which they might
have created a nonfinite form by adding a past-participial marker in [t]. This
is in fact roughly the explanation proposed by Marin and Rusnac (234),
though they maintain that *fost* was created by analogy with 2pl. pf. FU(I)STIS
'you were/have been.' A possible parallel for such a shift, though in a
different tense, would be Sp. 2sg. *eres* 'you [sg.] are,' apparently continuing fut.
ERIS 'you [sg.] will be' like OFr. *(i)ers*, which latter retained its future sense. It
would however have been quite anomalous for a finite verb form other than
the "unmarked" 3sg. to have inspired past-participial remodeling.

According to Lausberg (252), though, Proto-Romanians had the infin. **fire*
(now *a fi*) < FIERĪ 'become, be made' and formed its p.p. *fost* ± POSTU 'put,'
already a syncopated by-form in CL for POSITU. Unfortunately for Lausberg's
theory, the Romanian outcome for POSTU is *pus*, influenced anaphonically by
1sg. perfect (later preterit) POSUĪ and losing its [t] along the way. Why then
would assumed *FOSTU not have yielded imaginary **fus*, after undergoing
metaphony inspired by the final vowel in FUĪ >*fui*?

A more likely origin would be a form based on the finite perfectum stem
FU- but with the regular 2nd-/3rd-conj. past-participial ending to give *FUTU,
a form proposed by Bartoli (404) as the etymon for Vegl. *fóit* 'been.' How
*FUTU would subsequently have become sigmatic-tautic in Dacia remains
unclear.

Nevertheless, after all that remodeling, speakers of postclassical Latin had developed high-frequency past participles equivalent to 'been,' 'wanted,' and 'been able,' all usable in new constructions like the present perfect.

2.8. CREATION OF MORE PAST PARTICIPLES

Verbs past-participially defective amount to almost 10 percent of the Latin corpus in Appendixes 2 and 3, which was gathered in part to highlight every such verb fated to survive.[42] For many defective verbs, new nonsuppletive past participles in -ŪTU prevailed across most of the Empire (see §2.14).

How did speakers deal with one missing form and two anomalies? Well, first, SAPERE 'taste; know' had no past participle. Second, CADERE 'fall' with reduplicative pf. CECIDĪ had a rare p.p. CĀSU, with vowel lengthening and sigmaticism. Third, BIBERE 'drink' had a suppletive p.p. PŌTU and later, based on the infectum/perfectum stem BIB-, rhizotonic thematic BIBITU, barely attested before the third century CE (Ernout and Meillet, 70).

Romanian, almost alone in remaining faithful to a reflex *a şti* of regular 4th-conj. SCĪRE 'know' (p.p. SCĪTU), gave its p.p. *ştiut* a reflex of the old -ŪTU ending, thus acquiring a doubly marked filler for that slot with a 4th-conj. theme vowel before a 2nd-/3rd-conj. one. Elsewhere in ROMANIA, verbs that joined the 2nd conjugation usually developed past participles in -ŪTU, like the ancestor of It. *saputo*, Surs. *saviu*, Cat. *sabut*, Fr. *su*, and even OSp. *sabudo* (now *sabido*) 'known,' or the ancestor of Rom. *băut*, It. *bevuto*, Surs. *buiu*, Cat. *begut*, Fr. *bu*, and even OSp. *bevudo* (now *bebido*) 'drunk.'[43] For CADERE, most speakers of Late Latin or Proto-Romance chose an infectum-based past participle in -ŪTU, ancestor of Rom. *căzut*, Lad. *rekadù*, It. *caduto*, Cat. *caigut*, Oc. *cazut*, OFr. *chëu*, and even OSp. *caudo* (now *caído*) 'fallen.'

Two weather verbs in CL lacked past participles. Across much of ROMANIA but not in still-3rd-conj. It. *piovere*, reflexes of PLUERE 'rain' moved into the 2nd conjugation and seem to have made their past participles by drawing upon the stem of finite pf. forms like PLŪVIT (also PLUIT). Resulting past participles in -ŪTU include It. *piovuto*, Lad. *piovù*, Cat. *plogut*, and Fr. *plu*, but not Sp. *llovido* or Ptg. *chovido*. Here Rom. *plouat* shows that the Dacian reflex of PLUERE joined the 1st conjugation. The second weather verb, NING(U)ERE 'snow,' likewise with no CL past participle, was replaced throughout most of ROMANIA by derivatives of the noun meaning 'snow,' obl. NIVE: a 1st-conj. infinitive gave rise to past participles like Cat. *nevat* and Sp./Ptg. *nevado*, and a long-form variant infinitive gave rise to past participles like It. *nevicato* and Fr. *neigé*. In far-eastern Romania, though, the old infinitive survived as 3rd-conj. *a ninge*, and, in line with a development

---

[42] As always, knowledge of such forms depends in part upon accidents of attestation. One will seldom see in an official inscription the equivalent of Engl. verbs like *cram, gunk up, guzzle,* or *splurge*. How often would one see such verbs on a wall, assuming the wall survived?

[43] Also OPtg. *bebesto* 'drunk' ± innovative *comesto* 'eaten.' My consultant had never heard of either *-esto* variant.

seen in many other verbs, the stem of its sigmatic pf. NĪNXĪ was extended to form a p.p. *nins*.

In the sense 'boil' CL had two by-forms: either 2nd-conj. FERVĒRE with an anomalous pf. FERBUĪ in [b], or 3rd-conj. FERVERE with less anomalous direct-suffixing FERVĪ. Both lacked a past participle. Dacians kept their reflex a 3rd-conj. verb but, perhaps borrowing [b] from the 2nd-conj.-style finite perfectum, developed the infin. *a fierbe*. That Romanian verb's past participle, *fiert*, might have come from a rhizotonic thematic form; synchronically, that past participle may now be regarded as a tautic athematic one like COCTU 'cooked' > Rom. *copt*. By contrast, most speakers in Hispania of course moved the verb into an arrhizotonic class, giving Sp. *hervir* and Ptg. *ferver*, with regular non-*ar* past participles *hervido* and *fervido*. In the central areas of Gallia and Italia, speakers replaced FERVERE with reflexes of regular 4th-conj. BULLĪRE 'well up, bubble,' as also in Sard. *buḍḍire* and Cat. *bullir*, all of them again with regular past participles for that class.

Another verb lacking a past participle in CL was 2nd-conj. FLŌRĒRE 'bloom' with pf. FLŌRUĪ. One might expect reflexes of *FLORUTU in most of Romance by extension of the *u*-stem pf., but speakers of LL moved the whole verb into the 4th conjugation, no doubt because of the yod that emerged in 1sg. pres.indic. *[flọrjo] < FLŌREŌ. On the basis of an attested LL infin. variant FLORIRE (Väänänen 1981, 135), that remade 4th-conj. verb has developed regular past participles for its class from Rom. (*în*)*florit* through It. *fiorito* and Fr. *fleuri* to Cat. *florit*. Spanish has 2nd-/3rd-conj. *florecer* with p.p. *florecido* next to adj. *florido* 'flowery,' but cf. rhizotonic FLŌRĬDU 'idem.' Another remade verb was MŪCĒRE 'become moldy,' with a possible pf. MŪCUĪ[44] and no past participle, though there was a related adj. MŪCĬDU 'sniveling; moldy.' That verb joined the 4th conjugation in Fr. *moisir* with regular p.p. *moisi* but stayed true to the 2nd in Oc. *mozer*, whose past participle proved unfindable (*REW* no. 5710).

For two 2nd-conj. verbs now meaning 'stink' chosen in different provinces of the Empire, speakers evolved the missing parts along regular lines. In Italia and in central-western Iberia, FŒTĒRE 'stink,' with no attested perfectum, has lived on in Sic. *fetiri*, Sp. *heder* (p.p. *hedido*) and Ptg. *feder* (p.p. *fedido*); cf. also Cat. *feda* 'fertilized ewe.' To the north and east, PŪTĒRE 'be rotten' (no attested perfectum) has lived on in Rom. *a puţi*, archaic It. *putire*, Log. *pudire*, Oc./Cat./OSp. *pudir*, OFr. *puïr* (now *puer*), and finally It. *puzzare* with metaplasm as in French but perhaps based on the noun *puzzo* or *puzza* 'stench.' Inchoative PŪTRĒSCERE 'spoil, rot,' i.e. 'start stinking,' has given Sp. *podrecer* and prefixed Ptg. *apodrecer*, among others (*REW* nos. 3407, 6876, 6885). All have acquired regular preterits and past participles; instances of the latter are Rom. *puţit*, Cat. *pudit*, and OFr. *puï* (now *pué*).

One verb already belonging to the 4th conjugation, FERĪRE 'hit,' lacked a past participle of its own and used suppletive PERCUSSU or ICTU.[45] In Late

---

[44] Put into parentheses with a question mark by Ernout and Meillet, 417.

[45] But cf. regular 4th-conj. LL fut.p. FERĪTŪRUS 'going to strike' (Ernout and Meillet, 227).

Latin or Proto-Romance, FERĪRE was remade along nonsuppletive lines: It. *ferito*, Cat. *ferit*, Sp. *herido*, Ptg. *ferido* 'hit,' and Rom. *ferit* 'forbidden' have regular 4th-conj. past participles, yet OFr. preferred the -ŪTU p.p. *feru*, and OIt. had a by-form *feruto*. The verb thus resembles Rom. *a şti*, It. *venire*, and Fr. *venir, tenir, vêtir* in (optionally) having an anomalous past participle.

In Late Latin or Proto-Romance, speakers evolved some past participles for 2nd-conj. verbs by extending the perfect root, often one in -UĪ. For the verb CALĒRE 'be warm/hot' with pf. CALUĪ and no past participle in CL,[46] speakers seem to have extended the perfect stem to the past participle to create the ancestor of It. *caluto*, Cat. *calgut* (3rd-conj. infin. *caldre*), and OFr. *chalu*, but anomalously not of 4th-conj. Rom. *încălzit* or of arch. Rom. *încărit*. Sp. *calentado* has joined the 1st conjugation and evidently derives from the adj. *caliente* 'hot,' itself originally a present participle.[47] For TIMĒRE 'fear' (pf. TIMUĪ), speakers created another -ŪTU past participle, ancestor of Rom. *temut*, It. *temuto*, Cat. *temut*, and OSp. *temudo* (now *temido*).

Among the suppletive verbs of Latin, those acquiring greater predictability included FERRE TULĪ LĀTU 'carry,' with a remade past participle based more clearly on TOLLERE 'remove, take away.' For the first word in a Christian inscription TULITA EST DE SÆCLŌ 'she has been taken away from the world,' CL would have had ĒLĀTA (Grossi Gondi, 418). Often, TOLLERE itself was remade as a 4th-conj. arrhizotonic, in e.g. OFr./Cat. *tolir* and Sp. *tullir* but not in still-3rd-conj. It. *togliere* or 2nd-/3rd-conj. Ptg. *tolher* (Meyer-Lübke 1974, 161); the OSp. p.p. *tolludo* likewise suggests a 2nd-/3rd-conj. infinitive. Another suppletive verb was OFFERRE OBTULĪ OBLĀTU 'offer,' for which a present-based if still rhizotonic LL p.p. OFFERTU is attested in glossaries (Väänänen 1981, 144) and gave It. *offerto*, Fr. *offert*, Cat. *ofert*. Farther west, the verb was remade along inchoative lines to give Sp. *ofrecer*, Ptg. *oferecer*, with the regular non-*ar*-verb p.p. *of(e)recido*.

In that light, I wish to look at Aronoff's statement (52) that the default method of making CL perfects was to suffix -UĪ to the present stem and that the default method of making CL past participles was to suffix -TU to the present stem. Aronoff's view helps to explain the spread of -UĪ perfects in Late Latin, when the same rule would probably still have held true, but does little to explain the concurrent spread of perfects in -SĪ and past participles in -SU. Furthermore, the LL spread of past participles in -ŪTU suggests that, however valid for the classical tongue, Aronoff's default method for past participles would have been replaced by the twilight of empire. It is at any rate noteworthy that, even in Classical Latin, Aronoff's default methods entail suffixation of the infectum stem. In Late Latin, both suffixation in [s] and suffixation in [w] or [u] promoted sharper marking within the perfectum: perfects and preterits became more like one another if at times less like corresponding forms in the infectum.

---

[46] But cf. the fut.p. CALITŪRU 'going to be hot' (Ernout and Meillet, 89).

[47] Finite forms of OFr. *chaloir* 'care' have not survived. Neither has p.p. *chalu*. Now a "lost positive," a negative reflex of the old pres.p. still exists in the adj. *nonchalant* 'carefree.'

Generally speaking, in developing new past participles for verbs lacking them in CL, and in developing arrhizotonic past participles to replace ones that had been rhizotonic or suppletive, speakers west of Catalonia have come to select exponents whose endings derive from -ĪTU, while speakers from Catalonia eastward and northward have selected exponents whose endings derive from -ŪTU. For some common verbs that have developed arrhizotonic past participles, anomalies between infinitive class and p.p. class remain to this day. Preterit morphology has continued to exert strong influence on p.p. morphology.

2.9. REMAKING DEPONENTS AS ACTIVE VERBS

Classical Latin had a large number of deponent verbs, passive in form but active in meaning.[48] Originally, as Harris explains, such verbs had been "middle in meaning, *ie* denoting an action concerning or affecting the subject, [but they] gradually came to be reinterpreted as active and were, in popular speech, rapidly replaced by analogical active forms, as was appropriate to their new meaning" (1978, 187). That shift began earlier than CL times, for speakers had remade an earlier infin. DĒDĪ 'surrender' as active (SĒ) DĒDERE, with reduplicative pf. DĒDIDĪ and rhizotonic p.p. DĒDITU.[49]

In CL, some fluctuation occurred between active and deponent paradigms in e.g. RŪRĀRE and RŪRĀRĪ 'live in the countryside,' POPULĀRE and POPULĀRĪ 'ravage, devastate,' PARTĪRE and PARTĪRĪ 'share out, divide.' Confusion between active and deponent forms was not uncommon, as witness FLAGRATUS SUM 'I burned' in an inscription for standard FLAGRĀVĪ, and also the OL active by-form OPĪNĀRE 'suppose, conjecture' found in Plautus for what had to be OPĪNĀRĪ under the CL standard (Ernout and Meillet, 238, 462).

In addition, Latin had verbs termed semideponent, which had active forms in the infectum but passive-looking ones in the perfectum.[50] Here too there could be fluctuation between active and deponent in the perfectum of a verb like TÆDĒRE between TÆDUIT and TÆSU EST 'it was boring,' of a verb like LIBĒRE between LIBUIT and LIBITU EST 'it was pleasing, agreeable,' or of a verb like PUDĒRE between PUDUIT and PUDITU EST 'it was shameful.' Likewise, the verb PIGĒRE might have either PIGITU EST or PIGUIT 'it disgusted' for its very rare perfect. At times, moreover, early writers used

---

[48] In *Les verbes déponents latins,* Flobert puts the number of fully deponent verbs in CL at 884. If one adds deponent variants, semideponents, and (hypercorrect?) "neodeponents" like VERSOR for standard VERSŌ 'twist, shake,' the figure climbs to about 1,600.

[49] A 1st-conj. variant of SĒ DĒDERE lives on in Rom. *a se dada* 'surrender' (*REW* no. 2511). About that last gloss, coming from Fr. *se rendre,* I wonder: has English borrowed any other verbs that incorporate a reflexive pronoun from Romance? And, *render* being a good English verb on its own, would that *sur-* qualify as a Malkielian prefixoid?

[50] CL also had a few verbs that were deponent in the infectum but active in the perfectum (Aronoff, 54). What these verbs might have been I cannot say.

active pf. forms for semideponent verbs: in the second century BCE, Cato wrote SOLUĪ 'I got used to' and AUSĪ 'I dared' instead of the SOLITUS SUM, AUSUS SUM required by the CL standard, and the sixth-century grammarian Priscian notes that "antiquissimi" [early writers] used active perfects like GĀVĪSĪ 'I rejoiced' and FĪSĪ 'I trusted' instead of the GĀVĪSUS SUM, FĪSUS SUM required by the CL standard (Cremaschi, 74; Flobert, 498–99; Zumpt, 156).

In or before 79 CE, someone wrote on a wall at Pompeii ITIS FORAS RIXSATIS 'go brawl outside!' for what under the CL standard would have been ĪTE FORIS RIXĀMINĪ. Incidentally, ITIS and RIXSATIS show a takeover of the 2pl. pres. imperative by the 2pl. pres. indicative that was to endure in Romanian and French, though in passive or deponent verbs those two forms did have the same ending, -MINĪ, in CL (Haadsma and Nuchelmans, 56, 89).

Long-term drift disfavored deponents. With the disappearance of synthetic passives from the infectum—and since none survives anywhere in ROMANIA one may confidently assign an early date to their disappearance—most deponent verbs vanished from the language, taking their past participles (if any) with them.

Deponents that lived on into Late Latin and beyond were remade as active verbs. Most expired. For example, 1st-conj. deponent CŌNĀRĪ 'try' might well have been remade in the active voice, but of it only a derivative may survive in Log. *konos* 'sickly feeling.' Then again, 1st-conj. deponent CŪNCTĀRĪ 'delay' appears to have been remade in an active and suffixed form but, if so, survives only in Mac. *acumtina*, and ORom. *a cuntina* now 4th-conj. *a conteni* 'cease, stop' (*REW* nos. 2109a, 2391a).

Attested reshapings of deponents include AGGREDIRI for AGGREDĪ 'go to, approach,' which shifted to the 4th conjugation (Väänänen 1981, 135). One may compare the EGREDERE written by Egeria for ĒGREDĪ 'go out, go up,' which may belong either to the 2nd conjugation or to the 3rd but is definitely active.

Almost every remade deponent still thriving has an arrhizotonic past participle descending from -ĀTU or -ĪTU types in Latin. One would expect reflexes of deponents in the two classes to have matching past participles. For Romance descendants of MINĀRĪ 'jut out; threaten; drive,' for instance, a nondeponent variant in Late Latin must be assumed as the source of It. *menare*, Cat./Oc. *menar*, and Fr. *mener*, all having acquired the sense 'lead' (also 'hit' in Italian), though Rom. *a mâna* still means 'drive, guide'; Romance past participles for this verb descend directly from the old pf./p.p. MINĀTU. Similarly, not MORĀRĪ 'wait; reside' but a nondeponent variant must be assumed for Sp./Ptg. *demorar*, Cat. *morar*, Fr. *demeurer*, It. *dimorare*; a nondeponent variant of LUCTĀRĪ 'struggle' for Rom. *a lupta*, It. *lottare*, Fr. *lutter*, Oc./Sp. *luchar*, Cat. *lluitar*, and Ptg. *luitar*;[51] a nondeponent variant of MĪRĀRĪ 'look at' for Rom. *a mira* 'be surprised,' Oc./Cat./Sp./Ptg. *mirar* 'look at,' and It. *mirare* 'point, aim' in the standard and 'look at' only in dialects. Finally, ARGŪTĀRĪ 'chatter' had to have been remade actively to give e.g. OFr.

[51] Active LUCTĀRE 'struggle' is attested from Old Latin times (Ernout and Meillet, 368).

arguer 'find fault with,' OSp. *argudarse* 'hurry' (*REW* no. 643). Meanwhile, MINĀTU, MORĀTU, LUCTĀTU, MĪRĀTU, and ARGŪTĀTU were limited to past-participial use, and finite perfectum forms in -ĀVĪ etc. were created by analogy with ones already found in active 1st-conj. verbs.

Once transformed into active verbs, some old 3rd-conj. deponents shifted into the 4th conjugation, while some already 4th-conj. deponents underwent reshaping of their past participles along more regular lines. Thus Romance infins. like It. *ringhiare* or *rignare* 'growl, show teeth,' Cat. *renyir*, Sp. *reñir*, Ptg. *renhir* 'quarrel,' all of them with regular past participles, suggest not only that the 3rd-conj. infinitive RINGĪ 'show teeth, snarl' was remade actively and arrhizotonically but also that its old pf./p.p. RI(N)CTU was remade as a regular 1st- or 4th-conj. form: It. *ringhiato* or *rignato*, Cat. *renyit*, Sp. *reñido*, Ptg. *renhido*. In somewhat the same way, the 4th-conj. deponent infin. ŌRDĪRĪ 'warp cloth' could easily be transformed into a pan-Romance active verb (*REW* nos. 6093, 7325). Meanwhile, its sigmatic p.p. ŌRSU was replaced by regular 4th-conj. ORDĪTU, already attested in the Vulgate (Ernout and Meillet, 467). The regularized replacement gave rise to past participles like Rom. *urzit*, It. *ordito*, Fr. *ourdi*, Cat. *ordit*, and Sp./Ptg. *urdido*.

According to Elcock (116), CL MORĪ 'die' was twice remade: from 4th-conj. passive MORĪRI, as found in Plautus and Ovid, it became 4th-conj. active MORIRE, attested only after the Empire's fall. That second reshaping served as a base for Romance reflexes from Rom. *a muri* to Sp. *morir*, if not quite Ptg. 2nd-/3rd-conj. *morrer* or Sard. 3rd-conj. *mórrere*. Even after this infinitive had been brought into the 4th conjugation in most areas, owing no doubt to a powerful yod in the 1sg. pres.indic.act., rhizotonic past participles descended from tautic athematic MORTUU 'died' (minus one of its U's) have flourished almost everywhere in e.g. It. *morto*, Fr. *mort*, Sp. *muerto*. In Romanian, *mort* has been limited to the adjectival or nominal sense 'dead (person),' and regularized *murit* has taken over as the past participle meaning 'died'; Portuguese has developed a similar by-form p.p. *morrido* 'died; killed.'

Certain reshapings have continued only at the geographical extremes of Romance, or at the center. A nondeponent variant of 4th-conj. MĒTĪRĪ 'measure' survives in Sp./Cat. *medir* and Rom. *a meti*, having died out in standard Italian and French. There MĒTĪRĪ was replaced by reflexes of a denominal 1st-conj. verb with the stem of MĒNSŪRA 'a measuring,' reflexes perhaps influenced by MĒTĪRĪ's pf./p.p. MĒNSU, to give It. *misurare* and Fr. *mesurer* (cf. also by-forms like Rom. *a măsura*, Oc./Cat./Sp./Ptg. *mesurar*). A nondeponent variant of FĀBULĀRĪ 'tell fables, lie; talk' survives mainly in Ptg. *falar*, Sp. *hablar*, and Sard. *faeḍḍare* 'speak,' though It. *favellare* and OFr. *faveler* keep the older sense. Again, a nondeponent variant of VĒNĀRĪ 'hunt' survives in Rom. *a vâna*, Fri. *vinar*, Fr. *vener*.

Of course, when a verb had both active and deponent variants, speakers merely had to select the former. Thus PARTĪRE not PARTĪRĪ 'split' survives mainly in It. *partire* and Fr./Oc./Cat./Sp./Ptg. *partir* 'leave,' still also meaning 'split' in Iberia as in It. *spartire*, *ripartire* (*REW* nos. 3125, 5503, 5552, 6259,

9186). Past participles for such 1st- and 4th-conj. verbs have stayed as regular as their old perfects/p.p.s used to be.

Other verbs survive in the west, at the center, and in the east. CL 3rd-conj. PATĪ 'suffer, undergo'—note the yod in 1sg. pres.indic. PATIOR—with its sigmatic p.p. PASSU must have been remade as a nondeponent arrhizotonic. In fact, remade PATIRE is attested in the eighth-century *Codice paleografico lombardo* (Politzer, 101). Later outcomes are Rom. *a pắţi*, It. *patire*, OSp./OCat. *padir*, or else as an inchoative with an [sk] infix judging by Sp./Ptg. *padecer*; ModCat. *patir* with unlenited [t]. A less neat example is PRECĀRĪ 'beg, request, pray,' surviving actively in the center as OFr. *proier* (now *prier*), It. *pregare*, Sic. *priari*, and Vegl. *prekur*, as against Oc./Cat./Sp./Ptg. *rogar*, Rom. *a ruga* (Rohlfs 1970, 19). Still, compare OFr. *rover* 'demand' and the It. law term *rogare* 'draw up a contract' < ROGĀRE 'ask, pray'; OSp. still had "central" *pregar*.[52] Whether survivals or replacements, all these Romance verbs now have regular past participles descending from arrhizotonic -ĀTU or -ĪTU types.

Rarely, reflexes survive in Romance of both a CL semideponent infinitive and a CL perfect/past participle, though the latter no longer has any perfective value by itself. In the case of 2nd-conj. SOLĒRE 'be used to,' with rhizotonic pf./p.p. SOLITU, OFr. displays both a reflex of the old infinitive, *soloir*, though a by-form *soldre* appears to come from a 3rd-conj. variant, and perhaps a syncopated reflex of the old p.p., *solt*. Both forms have since vanished from French, though OFr. had a by-form p.p. *solu*. In Italian, proparoxytonic *solito*, listed as the past participle for *solere*, survives mainly as an adjective meaning 'customary' or a noun meaning 'habit, custom'; cf. also semilearnèd Sp. *insólito* 'unusual, unaccustomed.' Given that Sp. *soler* and It. *solere* are used mainly in the present and imperfect, the p.p.s *solido* and *solito* are seldom heard.

Having moved into a more common conjugational class, most old semideponent verbs that survived moved closer to the ideal state of a one-to-one match between meaning and form. At the same time, speakers tended to remake such verbs' past participles on the basis of the infectum stem. Thus, 2nd-conj. GAUDĒRE 'rejoice, enjoy' (pf./p.p. GĀVĪSU) sometimes joined the 4th conjugation and acquired regular past participles like Fr. *(en)joui* and Ptg. *gouvido*. In standard Italian, the verb stayed in the same conjugation as *godere*, but acquired an -ŪTU p.p. *goduto* (cf. Lad. *godù*). A long-form 1st-conj. variant like *GAUDICARE lies behind Cat. *gojar* and Sp. *gozar* with regular p.p.s *gojat* and *gozado*. In the same way, across the contiguous Romance area 3rd-conj. FĪDERE 'trust' (pf./p.p. FĪSU) was remade as a regular verb in -ĀRE, judging by past participles like It. *fidato*, Fr. *fié*, Cat. *fiat*, and Sp./Ptg. *fiado*. For such verbs, the old sigmatic past participles appear to have left vanished without a trace: no one but a Latinist remembers GĀVĪSU 'enjoyed' or FĪSU 'trusted' today.

---

[52] Ernout and Meillet say that, west of Dacia, ROGĀRE 'ask' lived on only in learnèd forms (576). Even if one grants semilearnèd status to Sp. *rogar* 'pray, ask, beg' with its intervocalic -g-, OFr. *rover* with its probably anti-hiatic [v] would cast doubt on that view.

2.10. FREQUENTATIVES, ITERATIVES, INTENSIVES AS SURVIVORS

Notable for their predictable conjugation, with masc.acc.sg. and neut. nom./acc.sg. past participles ending almost always in -TĀTU or in -SĀTU, frequentatives and iteratives furnished a rich source of 1st-conj. active verbs in Late Latin or Proto-Romance. Their frequentative or iterative meaning lost, most that avoided extinction flourished so luxuriantly that across ROMANIA they ended up supplanting their predecessors from CL.

On occasion, speakers remade a verb already belonging to the productive 1st conjugation, on the basis of its frequentative. For example, prefixed ADJUVĀRE 'help' (itself continued in It. *giovare*) had a p.p. ADJŪTU and a frequentative ADJŪTĀRE. That second form stands behind Rom. *a ajuta*, It. *aiutare*, Ptg./Cat./Oc. *ajudar*, Sp. *ayudar*, and Fr. *aider*, all of them with regular past participles for reflexes of the -ĀRE class. Similarly, though the simple verb *RUGERE 'burp' is attested only in the prefixed form ĒRŪGERE, its intensive variant (Ē)RŪCTĀRE 'belch out' lies behind It./Log. *ruttare*, Fr. *roter*, Oc./Cat. *rotar*, and Ptg. *arrotar*; cf. Sp. semilearnèd *eructar* with [kt] (*REW* no. 7416).

Bearing a morphological resemblance to the past participles CANTU 'sung,' PĒNSU 'weighed,' and PULSU 'beaten, throbbed' were frequentative CANTĀRE, PĒNSĀRE, and PULSĀRE.[53] Romance reflexes of all three of the latter group survive in nonfrequentative Rom. *a cânta*, It. *cantare*, Ptg./Sp./Cat./Oc. *cantar*, and Fr. *chanter*, in It. *pesare*, Ptg./Sp./Cat. *pesar*, Oc. *pezar*, Fr. *peser*, and in Ptg. *puxar*, Sp. (*e m*)*pujar*, Oc. *polsar*, and Fr. *pousser*, having dispensed with reduplication in the preterit. All have stayed members of the largest verb class. So have perhaps semilearnèd reflexes of PĒNSĀRE meaning 'think' like Sp. *pensar*, also meaning 'feed livestock.' Unlike CANERE 'sing,' the simplex DĪCERE 'say, tell' survives nearly everywhere; several reflexes of freq. DICTĀRE 'dictate, arrange' survive in It. *dettare* 'dictate; write' and in OFr. *ditier*, OOc. *dechar* 'endite, compose poetry' (*REW* no. 2630).

Also widely represented in Romance is a rare CL verb built on the p.p. QUIĒTU 'been quiet' of QUIĒSCERE. Frequentative QUIĒTĀRE 'stay quiet' has given It. *chetare* 'quiet, calm,' Oc. *quezar* 'be quiet,' Cat./Sp./Ptg. *quedar* 'stay.' A longer variant in -IĀRE gave OFr. *coisier* 'be quiet' (Ernout and Meillet, 557; *REW* nos. 6956, 6957). For more verbs built similarly, see §2.11.

Despite the general popularity of -ŪTU past participles for *u*-stem verbs in Late Latin (see §2.14), such verbs could die away and be replaced by their iteratives. That happened to STERNUERE STERNUĪ STERNŪTU 'sneeze,' for Romance has kept almost exclusively reflexes of STERNŪTĀRE 'sneeze over

---

[53] As Buck remarks (268), some originally frequentative verbs lost all frequentative force and were remade as double frequentatives: CANERE to CANTĀRE to CANTITĀRE 'sing or play repeatedly,' or DĪCERE to DICTĀRE to DICTITĀRE 'say again and again, insist.' Another set of verb triplets is CURRERE to CURSĀRE to CURSITĀRE 'run up and down.'

and over' in e.g. Rom. *a strănuta*, It. *starnutare*, Fr. *éternuer*, Oc./Cat./Sp. *estornudar* (*REW* no. 8250).[54] The Rom. p.p. *strănut* < STERNŪTU used to keep up the Latin tradition, but apparently came to sound anomalous for a 1st-conj. verb with infin. *a strănuta*, in fact identical to the 1sg. present indicative. Speakers have regularized that past participle to *strănutat* 'sneezed.'

Verbs with a sigmatic perfectum that were remade in part of ROMANIA include UNG(U)ERE 'oil' (pf. ŪNXĪ) and JUNGERE 'join' (pf. JŪNXĪ). These verbs' tautic athematic p.p.s ŪNCTU, JŪNCTU formed the basis for frequentative-looking 1st-conj. variants that lay behind Sp./Ptg. *untar, juntar* (p.p.s *untado, juntado*), if not It. *ungere, giungere*, Fr. *oindre, joindre*, or Rom. *a unge, a junge*. Conceivably, the attested frequentative ŪNCTITĀRE could have syncopated to give one of those Sp./Ptg. forms and inspire the other.[55] Reflexes of JUNGERE also survive in 4th-conj. variants: in Catalan as *junyir* (p.p. *junyit*), in Spanish as *uñir* or *uncir* (p.p.s *uñido, uncido*) and in Portuguese as *jungir* 'yoke' (p.p. *jungido*), all of them regular (*REW* no. 4620).

Among major Romance languages, unprefixed past-participial reflexes of 3rd-conj. VERTERE 'turn' survive only in Sp./Ptg. *vertido* 'spilt, poured' which cannot continue the p.p. VERSU and represents a regularization based on the present stem. Yet, as noted, freq. VERSĀRE 'turn round and round' has left behind Rom. *a vărsa*, It. *versare*, Fr. *verser*, Oc./Sp. *versar*, Cat./Ptg. *vessar*, most also meaning 'spill, overturn' and all endowed with past participles whose endings derive from -ĀTU.

In examining reflexes of 3rd-conj. PREMERE 'squeeze,' itself surviving as It./Log. *premere*, OFr. *priembre*, and Oc./Cat./OSp./Ptg. *premer*, one cannot know whether pf. PRESSĪ or p.p. PRESSU formed the basis for frequentative PRESSĀRE, itself the ancestor of 1st-conj. It. *pressare*, Fr. *presser*, and Sp./Ptg. hypercorrect *prensar*, which seems to reverse the [ns] > [s] shift that took place in most LL areas.[56] How could one decide whether the CL perfect or the CL past participle of 3rd-conj. QUATERE 'shake' provided the model for Romance forms? Either its pf. QUASSĪ or its p.p. QUASSU, or most likely both together, could have supplied the root for frequentative QUASSĀRE 'shatter.' One need not attribute the stems of such verbs to either the finite perfectum or the past participle by itself. Both appear to have influenced Romance developments. Then again, no frequentatives were formed from roots that unambiguously belonged to the perfect later preterit, so that the finite perfectum probably did no more than strengthen a morphological tendency already strong. However it was shaped, QUASSĀRE lay behind Fr. *casser*, Oc./Sp. *casar*, Cat. *cassar* 'break, shatter' and It. *cassare* 'erase, cancel,' behind a prefixed variant that gave It. *squassare* 'shake violently, wreck' (also *sconquassare*), and behind a

---

[54] With metaplasm, Italian also has variant *starnutire* 'sneeze' ± *tossire* 'cough.'

[55] Long-form UNCTITĀRE is found in Plautus and Cato (Ernout and Meillet, 747).

[56] Evidently, Sp. *prensar* was formed from the noun *prensa*, borrowed from Cat. *premsa* 'press' (*REW* no. 6741). In turn, unless the result of mere scribal rapprochement, the form *premsa* looks like a blend of the infectum stem of PREMERE with the p.p. stem of PRESSU.

long-form variant ending in -ICĀRE that gave Sp./Cat. *cascar* 'crack.' For quite
a while, reflexes of the old p.p. QUASSU survived as adjectival OIt. *casso*, OFr.
cas or *quas*, and OOc. *cas* 'broken.' One still survives, with another [ns] cluster,
in Sp. *canso* 'tired' (*REW* no. 6942).

Truly anomalous CL verbs had vowel change and direct suffixation of
endings in their finite perfects or past participles, or both. Two higher-
frequency ones were JACERE 'throw' (pf. JĒCĪ, p.p. JACTU) and prefixed
CŌGERE 'drive together' (pf. COĒGĪ, p.p. COĀCTU). If unprefixed AGŌ ĒGĪ
ĀCTU 'go, move, drive' left no descendants, neither did JACERE or CŌGERE,
directly. One might argue that neither could have been expected to do so, in
the light of a growing preference for regularity in word-formation among
speakers of Late Latin and Proto-Romance. Not at all from the attested
frequentative JACTĀRE, but rather from one that combined a past-participial
root JECT- with a 1st-conj. ending, must derive It. *gettare*, Log. *bettare*, Sp.
echar, Cat. *gitar*, Fr. *jeter*, and Ptg. *geitar* now *deitar* 'throw.' Not from the
attested frequentative CŌACTĀRE 'compel' but from a variant contracted like
CL CŌGERE < CUM + AGERE, derive 1st-conj. verbs like OFr. *coitier*, OOc.
coitar 'oppress,' Cat. *cuitar* and OSp. *cocharse* 'hurry,' and OPtg. *coitarse*
'worry' (*REW* nos. 2015, 4568).

In at least one instance, a basic verb and its frequentative have both
endured into Romance. Thus SALĪRE 'jump' (with p.p. SALTU) yields Rom. *a
sări* and It. *salire* 'climb,' Sp. *salir* and Ptg. *saír* 'go out,' Fr. *saillir* 'stand out,'
and, perhaps from a long-form variant, Cat. *salicar* 'spurt, gush' (with by-form
saliquejar). Frequentative SALTĀRE yields It. *saltare*, OSp. *sotar*, Sp./Cat.
saltar, and Fr. *sauter*, all of them having acquired the old sense 'jump.' All
have regular 1st-conj. or 4th-conj. past participles.

Examples of CL verbs where perfect endings were added directly to the
stem, a rhizotonic and hence decreasingly popular type in Late Latin and
Proto-Romance, include RUERE 'rush; fall down.'[57] In CL, this verb's pf. RUĪ
and p.p. RUTU both had tonic [ʊ], but cf. its fut.p. RUITŪRU with tonic [u:]. An
unattested frequentative resembling *RUTĀRE might lie behind Fr. *ruer* 'rush'
and diminutivized It. *ruzzolare* 'tumble.' A more likely instance of such
remaking would be that of VOVĒRE 'vow' (pf. VŌVĪ), which itself survives
nowhere but whose p.p. VŌTU, or the noun VŌTU 'a vow, prayer,' served as
the root for a frequentative-looking 1st-conj. verb. That verb still flourishes in
It. *votare*, Fr. *vouer*, Oc. *vodar*, and Sp. *votar*, even if the unlenited [t] in the
Spanish form gives it a tinge of cultismo and suggests revival rather than
survival on the Iberian peninsula.

As always, outcomes could vary across ROMANIA. Common in Latin, the
2nd-conj. verb MONĒRE 'remind, warn' with a -UĪ perfect and a rhizotonic
thematic p.p. MONITU has survived only in remade 4th-conj. Sp. *muñir*
'invite' (p.p. *muñido*): 1sg. pres.indic. MONEŌ > [mɔnjo] must have come to
sound like a 4th-conj. form in LL times. Reflexes of an attested LL
frequentative MONITĀRE have a marginally better survival rate, for prefixed

---

[57] RUERE 'tumble, rush' seems to survive as such only in Log. *ruere* 'fall' (*REW* no. 7423).

versions may be found in Sic. *ammunitari* 'admonish' and in Rom. *a dezmânta* 'dissuade.'

Frequentative morphology alone could not guarantee long life for a verb. Except in resuscitations by the learnèd—with that [ks] cluster intact—regular 1st-conj. VEXĀRE 'jostle, toss; disquiet' vanished everywhere in Romance. So did its irregular nonfrequentative VEHERE 'carry, convey' with a sigmatic pf. VĒXĪ and a direct-suffixation p.p. VECTU (Ernout and Meillet, 412, 717, 730; *REW* nos. 5658, 5661, 9294, 9456). Still, it seems clear that speakers often preferred frequentative variants because of their greater phonological body and more predictable conjugation.

2.11. PAST PARTICIPLES AS MODELS FOR VERB PARADIGMS

As early as CL times, some past participles had spun off as independent verbs: ASSU 'grilled, broiled,' from a demotic variant of ĀRSU 'burned' in which [rs] > [s:], gave attested 1st-conj. ASSARE starting with Apuleius in the second century CE. Reflexes of ASSĀRE are found in Sp. *asar* and Ptg. *assar* 'roast,' with regular p.p. *as[s]ado*. A diminutivized variant resembling *ASSULARE has given Fr. *hâler* 'dry hemp; sunburn.'

In CL as well, speakers tended to replace the fairly rare verb TRŪDERE TRŪSĪ TRŪSU 'push' with TRŪSĀRE, an old frequentative with sigmatic marking like the whole perfectum of the simplex that yielded Oc. *truzar* (*REW* nos. 737, 8957). It is altogether possible that many verbs in Romance that appear to derive from Latin past participles actually derive from unattested frequentatives. Because frequentatives were built on the same stems as past participles and almost always belonged to the 1st conjugation— an exception being 3rd-conj. VĪSERE 'look into, see after, visit' from VĪSU 'seen'—one cannot ascertain by morphology alone how such verbs arose.[58]

In Late Latin, VELLERE 'tear out, pluck' tended to fall to VULSĀRE, an unclassical form with the same stem as p.p. VULSU (Ernout and Meillet, 718).[59] Also presumably in LL, or in PR, a 1st-conj. verb with the same stem as the attested p.p. ABSCŌNSU 'hidden' for CL ABSCONDITU lay behind OFr. *esconser* 'hide' and OSp. *esconsar* 'warp, slant,' with a change of prefix to EX- (Ernout and Meillet, 4; *REW* no. 41). In Romance, speakers have gone on making new infinitives out of such stems.

---

[58] Unlike 2nd-conj. VIDĒRE 'see' (pf. VĪDĪ), freq. VĪSERE 'inspect' had a sigmatic finite perfectum VĪSĪ. Both verbs shared the p.p. VĪSU. A 1st-conj. variant of VĪSERE gave Fr. *viser* 'aim at, sight on,' also 'issue a visa, counterstamp,' the latter now the main meaning of Sp./Ptg. *visar* (*REW* no. 9372). With its sigmatic marking, the verb VĪSERE probably once had a desiderative meaning 'want to see,' much as QUÆSERE 'seek; beg, entreat' earlier meant 'want to ask'; cf. QUÆRŌ 'seek' (Leumann, 533).

[59] Whole verbs built from p.p. VULSU 'plucked' are found in Franche-Comté, Switzerland, and Lorraine (*REW* no. 9465). The CL pf. of VELLERE was usually VELLĪ but could also be sigmatic VULSĪ or VOLSĪ. (Cf. similar wavering in VULVA or VOLVA 'husk, wrapper.')

Just as one cannot tell whether a CL frequentative verb was based on its finite perfectum or on its past participle, when the two stems were the same, so one cannot tell whether the stem of an unattested 1st-conj. verb in LL or PR came from a past participle or from an identical adjective or noun. For that matter, one may hardly know whether speakers shaped such a verb after the Empire fell in the west but before anyone began to write in Italian, Spanish, or French. Where evidence is lacking, I presume that a Romance verb that looks as if it came from a CL past participle has followed that derivational pathway.

Why did certain past participles come to serve as models for whole verb paradigms? One may seek the answer in the coexistence in CL of nonfrequentative and frequentative verbs like CANERE 'sing' and CANTĀRE 'sing over and over'; such pairs of past participles as CANTU and CANTĀTU likewise coexisted. Given the still-adjectival nature of past participles in CL, a function they have kept to this day (cf. Fr. *des photos osées* 'racy pictures'), and given the total regularity of conjugation of frequentatives, speakers tended through time to restrict the CANTU type to adjectival use. Speakers also tended to prefer the CANTĀTU type, no longer felt to denote frequency, for use as past participles in perfective and passive syntagms. Further attempts to answer the question are made at the end of §2.11 and in §6.4.

2.11.1. (Semi)Deponent Perfects/Participles as Models

Among past participles for deponents or semideponents, three had great success as bases for new verbs. At least two others had some success.

First, in CL sigmatic AUSU was merely the pf./p.p. for 2nd-conj. AUDĒRE 'dare.' In LL, AUSU became the basis for *AUSARE. Itself perhaps reinforced by the noun AUSU 'a daring deed,' the new infinitive served as the progenitor of It. *osare*, Fr. *oser*, Cat. *gosar*, Sp. *osar*, Ptg. *ousar*.[60] Romance verbs with this pedigree still indicate their origin by keeping the old sigmatic marker throughout, including remade past participles like It. *osato*, Fr. *osé*, Cat. *gosat*, Sp. *osado*, and Ptg. *ousado* 'dared.' Meanwhile, the old p.p. AUSU survived adjectivally in e.g. OIt. *oso* and OFr. *os* 'daring'; as stated above, the latter has now yielded to *osé*, restoring identity of form between adjective and past participle.

Second, in CL sigmatic ŪSU—cf. the literary It. adj. *uso* 'accustomed'—was merely the past participle for deponent ŪTĪ 'use.' In LL, perhaps reinforced by 4th-decl. ŪSU 'use[fulness],' p.p. ŪSU became the basis for *USARE, ancestor of It. *usare*, Cat./Sp./Ptg. *usar*, and Fr. *user*. All forms of the verb, including past participles like It. *usato*, Fr. *usé*, Cat. *usat*, and Sp./Ptg. *usado*, also remain sigmatic, with similar Rom. *uzat* 'worn out, used up' being a neologism.

---

[60] As in Catalan, reflexes of *AUSARE 'dare' have acquired an initial consonant in Lombard *volsá* or *golsá*, and in Béarnais *gausá*. A long-form variant in -ICĀRE is presumed for forms attested in northern Italian dialects and in Alpine Romance (*REW* nos. 801, 804).

Third, in CL unclassifiable OBLĪTU (resembling a 4th-conj. type) was the past participle for deponent OBLĪVISCĪ 'forget.' In LL, OBLĪTU became the basis for *OBLITARE, ancestor of Rom. *a uita*, Olt. *ubbiare*, Sp. *olvidar* (borrowed into Portuguese), Cat./Oc. *oblidar*, Fr. *oublier* (borrowed as literary It. *obliare*), and Surs. *amblidá*.⁶¹ Remade past participles like Rom. *uitat*, Fr. *oublié*, Cat. *oblidat*, and Sp. *olvidado* are regular.

Other deponents undergoing the same transformation included TUĒRĪ 'protect,' whose CL p.p. TŪTU (rather than its by-form TUITU) became the basis for an attested frequentative variant TŪTĀRE, ancestor of Fr. *tuer* > Oc. *tuar* 'kill,' along with Fri. *tudá* 'exhaust,' Oc. *tudar* 'put out (fire),' Cat. *tudar* 'destroy,' and prefixed Vegl. *stotuor* 'extinguish,' all of them in overlapping semantic fields.⁶² Again, past participles like Fr. *tué* 'killed' are regular. In Italy around 1300, the religious poet Jacopone da Todi used prefixed *stutare* in the sense 'stifle, distress,' a form likewise built on the Latin past participle but prefixed with EX- (R. Stefanini, p.c.). Metaplasm has taken place in prefixed 4th-conj. It. *attutire* 'throw down' with p.p. *attutito* and Cat. *atuir* 'knock down' with p.p. *atuit*.

For all these verbs, most Romance languages have continued reflexes of remade -ĀTU past participles. They have turned into predictable members of the 1st conjugation (Elcock, 116; *REW* nos. 801, 6015, 9018, 9093).

If many verbs in the 2nd and 3rd conjugations tended to acquire past participles in -ŪTU as time went on, some old -ŪTU forms failed to outlast the Empire in most areas. Thus, as noted in §2.14.4, the old pf./p.p. SECŪTU of deponent SEQUĪ 'follow' tended to be remade along 4th-conj. lines, as was its infinitive in most areas. Yet p.p. SECŪTU served as the base for a 1st-conj. infinitive behind Log. *segudare*, and Oc. *segudar* 'follow' along with similar reflexes in Italian dialects from Sicilian to Corsican and perhaps also in Cat. *sotjar* 'spy on; watch for' (*REW* no. 7778).

2.11.2. Past Participles of Active Verbs as Models

Among principal parts of active verbs in Latin, certain past participles have come to serve as models for whole paradigms. In Spanish, two instances of the trend toward infinitivizing past participles involve FARTU 'stuffed' (infin. FARCĪRE)⁶³ and FĪXU 'fastened' (infin. FĪGERE). These past participles themselves evolved normally to still-current *harto* 'fed up,' and *fijo* 'fixed, settled,' now mostly adjectival; from these old forms have been devised the

---

⁶¹ Other verbs meaning 'forget' were built from prefixed variants like *EXOBLITARE, *DISMEMORARE, and *DEMENTICARE (Ernout and Meillet, 455). Cf. nonstd. Engl. *disremember* 'forget.'

⁶² Semantically, Fr. *tuer* 'kill' and related verbs developed either from a notion of banking a fire or from one of slaking thirst (Posner, 321). I prefer the image of a flame shielded too well.

⁶³ In LL, a regular 4th-conj. p.p. developed in attested FARCITU 'stuffed' (Ernout and Meillet, 216). In central ROMANIA, that regularization lies behind Fr. *farci*, It. *farcito*.

regular 1st-conj. verbs *hartar* 'stuff' and *fijar* 'fasten' with regular p.p.s *hartado, fijado*. Also from FĪXU came It. *fissare*, 'fasten; gaze.'

Defective in CL, the verb FRENDERE (no pf.) FRĒ(N)SU 'grind, gnash' must have adopted an infinitive based on its past participle to give Fr. *fraiser* 'frill, mill, drill,' Oc. *frezar* 'husk beans,' and It. (< Fr.) *fresare* 'drill, cut [metal].' Cf. also arch. It. 3rd-conj. *frendere* 'gnash,' a revival lacking a past participle.[64] Again, if INVENĪRE 'find' (p.p. INVENTU) left no unprefixed reflexes, p.p.-derived or frequentative 1st-conj. INVENTĀRE is represented in ROMANIA, and It. has 4th-conj. *rinvenire* 'find' with p.p. *rinvenuto* (Ernout and Meillet, 253, 321).

Among the rare nonlearnèd reflexes in Romance of LÆDERE LÆSĪ LÆSU 'wound, damage' are Sp. *lisiar* and Ptg. *lesar*, sigmatic like the old CL perfectum but now moved in the 1st conjugation. The Sp. form comes from a variant containing yod; cf. the noun LÆSIŌ 'oratorical attack.'

Outcomes have at times varied across ROMANIA. For example, CL PĒDERE 'fart' itself survived to give OIt. *pedere*, Oc. *peire*, Sp. *peer*, and OFr. *poire*.[65] That verb's CL p.p. PĒDITU had the same form as the noun PĒDITU 'a fart,' which seems to have syncopated to produce nouns like It. *peto*, Fr./Oc./Cat. *pet*, and Ptg. *peido*. From those nouns, or from past participles, were reshaped 1st-conj. infinitives like Fr. *peter* or *péter* (p.p. *peté, pété*) and Cat. *petar* (p.p. *petat*), none of which shows any sign of the intervocalic lenition of [d] to [ð] in Catalan and Old French and to zero in French today that one would expect from reflexes of infin. PĒDERE. In the far west, Ptg. *peidar* (p.p. *peidado*) also has the same stem as its noun, or the old past participle. On that point, prefixed and suffixed It. *spetezzare* (p.p. *spetezzato*) gives no help.[66] Another verb with similar meaning, regular 4th-conj. VISSĪRE 'fart,' stayed in that class to give Rom. *a băși* (p.p. *bășit*). Farther west, new infinitives apparently based on nouns gave 1st-conj. Fr. *vesser* 'fart silently,' It. *svesciare* 'chatter, yak' (*REW* nos. 4842, 6345, 9382).[67]

One verb based on a past participle seems to have evolved only in French. Elsewhere, SARCĪRE SARSĪ SARTU 'mend, patch, repair' survived as a regularized 4th-conj. verb, modeled entirely on the infectum stem, that has given past participles like It. (*ri*)*sarcito*, Cat. *sargit*, and anomalous Sp. *zurcido*,

---

[64] Meyer-Lübke also derives It. *fregiare* 'adorn, decorate' from Oc. *frezar* in the sense 'wreathe' (*REW* no. 3498). A long set of semantic leaps would be needed to get from 'gnashing' to 'adorning.' For another set of leaps, see note 69 to this chapter.

[65] In Old French, infin. *poire* < PĒDERE 'fart' sounded the same as noun *poire* < PIRA 'pear.' That homonymy might explain why, in the fabliau *De Jouglet*, a parvenu peasant about to marry the daughter of an indebted vavasor is induced to climb into a pear tree and eat plenty of pears, so that during his wedding night he disgraces himself fecally.

[66] In parts of Upper Aragon (see §4.7.12), lenition of intervocalic stops failed to take place, giving *petar* 'crack, pop' as the local reflex; the std. Italian form has been borrowed from Veneto *spetezar* (*REW* no. 6358).

[67] In all likelihood, speakers of Latin made a distinction between PĒDERE and VISSĪRE. On phonosymbolic grounds, one could conjecture that the first was more booming and the second more shrill, or perhaps silent.

all of which keep the general sense of the Latin avatar. North of the Loire, OFr. *sartir* (now *sertir*) 'inset [stones, panes, jewels]' derives from the p.p. root SART- plus regular 4th-conj. endings and has narrowed its semantic scope. It does have a regular remade p.p., *serti*.[68]

Romance has other verbs deriving from Latin past participles, most of them belonging to that ragbag called the 3rd conjugation. From Iberia come Sp. 1st-conj. *(a)tusar* and Ptg. *tosar* 'trim, comb, smooth hair,' paralleling It. *tosare* and OFr. *toser* 'clip, crop,' all three deriving from the past participle of 3rd-conj. TONDERE TOTONDĪ TŌNSU 'shave, shear,' as does *toso* or *tosa* 'kid; little shaver' in dialects of Gallo-Italian. From equally 3rd-conj. TUNDERE TUTUDĪ TŪ(N)SU 'hit, beat' came a variant based on the p.p. stem, prefixed with PER- 'through' and containing yod that gave 1st-conj. It. *pertugiare*, Fr. *percer*, and Oc. *pertusar* 'bore through, pierce.' Still-3rd-conj. Rom. *a pătrunde* 'pierce' comes from the old infin. PERTUNDERE, whose sigmatic p.p. PERTŪNSU has given the Rom. p.p. *pătruns*, a survival contrasting with regularized forms in use elsewhere (*REW* nos. 6436, 7599, 8781, 9012).

From the central area of ROMANIA comes It. 1st-conj. *tritare* 'chop, grind, mince' (p.p. *tritato*) along with Fr. *trier* 'sort, pick out' (p.p. *trié*), the latter borrowed as Oc./Cat. *triar* and OIt. *triare*. The stem of this verb appears to have come from the p.p. of TERERE TRĪVĪ TRĪTU 'rub, wear away' (*REW* no. 8922).[69]

Still more past participles came to serve as models for verb paradigms. Fr. 1st-conj. *raser* 'shave' (p.p. *rasé*) seems to have been built on p.p. RĀSU, perhaps helped along by the sigmatic pf. RĀSĪ, rather than the infin. RĀDERE, for which cf. Cat. *raure* < *[raðrə].[70] Verbs resembling *raser* survive from Italy to Portugal, while CL frequentative RĀSITĀRE gave Fr. *rader* (p.p. *radé*) 'level off [as a bushelful of grain],' though one has to suppose early syncope of the pretonic syllable. A long-form variant in -ICĀRE has left variants of its own in Sp./Ptg. *rascar* 'scratch, scrape' versus *rasgar* 'tear, rip,' with p.p.s *rascado*, *rasgado* (*REW* nos. 7070, 7074, 7075).

For some Romance verbs related to the CL infin. PASCERE 'feed, keep, tend' and its irregular pf. PĀVĪ, the irregular p.p. PĀSTU served as the basis for a 1st-conj. variant behind Sp. *pastar* (p.p. *pastado*), unless it was backformed from the noun *pastor* 'shepherd[ess]' or from a reflex of the 4th-decl. noun PASTU 'pasture, feeding.'[71] Elsewhere, 3rd-conj. PASCERE lived on in It.

---

[68] From a fem.sg. or neut.pl. form of p.p. SARTU 'mended' derives the Sp./Ptg. noun *sarta* 'string of pearls; rosary,' now used more generally to mean 'string, series, row' (*REW* no. 7615).

[69] Whether metal, wood, cloth, or flesh was involved, the semantic gap between 'rub away' and 'select' appears as wide as the one between 'gnash' and 'adorn'; see note 64.

[70] A verb form *RASARE is presumed as the base for CL RĀSĀMEN 'scraper' as well as the frequentative verb RĀSITĀRE found in Suetonius (Ernout and Meillet, 563). Cf. also adj. RĀSILE 'scraped, smoothed.'

[71] Normally one expects longer words to be shaped from shorter ones, so that upon Engl. *write, kill, love* are built agentive *writer, killer, lover*. In backformation, speakers clip longer words to shape shorter ones, as in Engl. *to burgle* from *to burglar*, or *to peddle* from *pedlar*.

pascere (p.p. *pasciuto*), OFr. *paistre* (p.p. *pëu*), and Cat. *péixer* (p.p. *pascut*).[72] All three preserve an older tradition, or used to, for their infinitives if not for their past participles. Cat. *pasturat* has been backformed from the noun *pastura* 'grazing-land.' An archaic Cat. infin. variant *pasquer* comes down with metaplasm from PASCERE; the Sp. doublet *pacer* (p.p. *pacido*), and Ptg. *pascer* (p.p. *pascido*) belong to the 2nd/3rd conjugation (*REW* no. 6263).

Again in Spanish and Catalan, the local reflex *pinto* or *pint* 'painted' of attested if macronless LL PINCTUM (Väänänen 1981, 144)—a variant of CL PICTU 'painted' including the nasal present in infin. PINGERE, pf. PĪNXĪ— gave rise to a 1st-conj. infin. *pintar* with its regular new p.p. *pintado* or *pintat*. Short-form *pint(o)* has been restricted to the adjectival sense 'spotted,' while fem. *pinta* has been restricted to the nominal sense 'spot, mark' (*REW* no. 6481). Several examples of creeping nasality appear in Table 2–2 below.

Table 2–2

Spread of Nasal Marking into Past Participles

(after Dardel, 78)

CLASSICAL LATIN			LATE LATIN/PROTO-ROMANCE	
Infectum Stem	Perfectum Stem	Past Participle	Assimilation of Past Participle to Finite Stem	Anomaly
FING-	FĪNX-	FICTU	*FINCTU	*FINGITU
PING-	PĪNX-	PICTU	PINCTU	*PINCTATU
VINC-	VĪC-	VICTU	*VINCTU	*VINCUTU

Another infinitivized past participle might seem to be CL (RE)GRESSU as the stem for the ancestor of Sp. *regresar* and Cat./Ptg. *regressar* 'go back, come back' with regular p.p.s *regresado, regressat, regressado*. In Italian, the CL infin. REGREDĪ has been remade as active 4th-conj. *regredire*, which usually has regularized *regredito* for its past participle, but the verb's elevated meaning 'regress' instead of the everyday one 'go back' suggests learnèd influence. In fact, the *REW* has no mention of any reflex of (RE)GREDĪ or its past participle. The work does confirm (no. 7725) that, in Iberia, sigmatic

---

[72] Cf. Cat. 1st-conj. *peixar* 'feed, nourish,' as in *un home ben peixat* 'a well-fed man' (Oliva and Buxton, 624). The verb *peixar* could well have formed from *peix* 'fish' by that maritime people, but might also have been influenced by the verb stem *peix-* < PASCERE.

SCISSU 'torn, split'—or rather an unattested variant in [s] not [s:], with compensatory lengthening of [I] to [i:]—has taken over the whole 1st-conj. paradigm in Sp./Ptg. *sisar* and Ptg. *sizar* 'pilfer, filch,' with regular p.p.s *sisado* and *sizado*. Nowhere has the 3rd-conj. infin. SCINDERE 'tear, split' left offspring of its own.

Across ROMANIA, still more past participles could become models for whole paradigms. An example would be the CL past participle for 3rd-conj. ŪRERE 'singe, char' (pf. USSĪ): sigmatic-tautic USTU spun off 1st-conj. diminutive-based USTULĀRE > Rom. *a ustura* 'burn, itch,' It. *ustolare* 'burn with desire; long for,' Oc. *usclar* and OFr. *usler* 'burn.'[73] It. *strinare* 'scorch, singe' appears to come from one more unattested variant of the same verb. A variant in -ICĀRE might have given Rom. *a usca* 'dry' with regular p.p. *uscat*. More probably, that verb derives from EXSŪC(C)ĀRE, itself from SŪCU 'sap,' like It. *asciugare*, Fr. *essuyer*, Cat. *aixugar*, Sp. *enjugar*, and Ptg. *enxugar*; a variant prefixed with PER- is assumed for It. *prosciugare* 'drain; dry up' and its derivative *prosciutto* 'ham' (*REW* nos. 3073, 6407, 9096).

Turning again to a sigmatic, from the p.p. SPŌNSU 'pledged, engaged' (infin. SPONDĒRE, pf. SPOPONDĪ) as well as from the nominalized pair SPŌNSA and SPŌNSU 'bride and groom' came a 1st-conj. infinitive yielding It. *sposare*, Fr. *épouser*, Oc. *espozar*, Cat./Ptg. *esposar* 'marry,' and semantically shifted Sp. *esposar* 'shackle'; cf. colloquial Engl. *get hitched* 'marry.'[74]

One CL 3rd-conj. verb had two by-forms for its finite perfectum and three by-forms for its past participle: PĪNSERE PĪNSĪ/PĪNSUĪ PĪNSU/PĪNSITU/PISTU 'crush, stamp' also had an attested 1st-conj. doublet PĪ(N)SĀRE, just as FODERE 'dig' had a doublet FODĀRE (Ernout and Meillet, 508–9).[75] According to the *REW*, nos. 6517 and 6518, there survived into Romance 1st-conj. PĪ(N)SĀRE and a variant with yod before tonic [a]. The former has given Rom. *a pisa* 'tread, flatten' (p.p. *pisat*), Oc./Ptg. *pizar* (p.p. *pizat, pizado*), and Cat./Sp. *pisar* (p.p. *pisat, pisado*), together with Fr. *piser* (p.p. *pisé*); the latter has given It. *pigiare* 'squeeze, press' (p.p. *pigiato*). Once again, modern reflexes suggest that long-ago speakers preferred regular verbs, where they had a choice.

When a CL verb had two stems, one throughout its perfectum and the other throughout its infectum, speakers of LL or PR sometimes built a new verb on the perfectum stem and eliminated the infectum one. Thus 3rd-conj. DĪVIDERE 'divide' had a sigmatic pf. DĪVĪSĪ and a sigmatic p.p. DĪVĪSU: from

---

[73] Both It. *uzzoli* 'lasciviousness' (*REW* no. 9081) and It. *uzzolo* 'whim, caprice' also seem to derive from p.p. USTU 'heated,' with metathesis of the medial cluster to [ts], lengthening of the stop to [t:], and the addition of a diminutive ending.

[74] The verb NŪBERE NŪPSĪ NUPTU 'veil; marry [of women]' has survived nowhere in Romance (Ernout and Meillet, 449). Across Iberia, it was replaced by *casar* 'move into a new house,' deriving from CASA 'hut, shack' in CL. Romanian also has *a însura* 'marry [of men]' from UXOR 'wife.' Meanwhile, MARĪTĀRE 'marry' survives from Rom. *a mărita* to Ptg. *maridar* (*REW* nos. 1728, 5361, 9107). Despite the existence of a noun SPŌNSIŌ 'solemn promise; wager,' no infinitive with yod like *[sposjare] seems to have arisen under the Empire.

[75] Latin derivatives of this word all lacked [n] (which, before [s], would have made the preceding vowel long): PISTILLU 'pestle,' PISTOR 'miller; baker,' PISTRĪNA 'bakery.'

that perfectum stem was created a new verb *DIVISARE > It. *divisare* 'plan, scheme,' OFr. *deviser* 'explain, arrange,' Oc. *devizar* 'idem,' and Ptg. *divizar* 'recognize.'[76] Surviving in Logudorese is *mesare* 'mow, reap' < attested 1st-conj. MESSĀRE 'reap, harvest,' also surviving in Sp. *mesar* 'pluck out hair.' Neither could come from the CL 3rd-conj. infin. METERE 'reap,' but consider its sigmatic perfectum made up of rare pf. MESSUĪ and p.p. MESSU, no doubt helped along by the (obl.) noun MESSIŌNE 'harvest' > Fr. *moisson*. Given that reflexes of the old verb METERE also survive, as in It. *mietere* and Oc. *meire*, the victory of sigmatics must here be accounted incomplete (*REW* nos. 2706, 5541, 5550).

I have already wondered why such past participles came to serve as the basis for whole paradigms. A plausible answer, for deponent verbs, would be that many already had CL frequentatives with the same stems as their past participles; for non-deponents, one might suppose that speakers used them largely in newly popular perfective constructions. A third reason would be that the new verbs or the by-forms that won out were both arrhizotonic, i.e. clearly marked by class, and less subject to phonetic attrition than verbs that faded out of speakers' minds during the twilight of empire.

2.12. PRETERITS AS MODELS
FOR PAST PARTICIPLES

In Late Latin or Proto-Romance, as I have remarked, some 2nd-conj. verbs evolved past participles that they had lacked in CL by extension of the finite perfect root. A precedent was set by verbs like 2nd-conj. ARDĒRE 'burn' with both a sigmatic pf. ĀRSĪ and a sigmatic p.p. ĀRSU, which when Latin speakers stopped distinguishing between Ā and Ă became a solidly sigmatic perfectum with [a] throughout. Brief as it was, that verb's past participle turned into It. *arso* and Rom./Surs./Enga./OCat./OFr. *ars*, since replaced by *cremat* and *brûlé* in the last two tongues.

Noting that, in Latin, the many sigmatic perfects derived from IE sigmatic aorists and that the relatively few sigmatic past participles were secondary, Vincent 1978 distinguishes three stages in morphological attraction exerted by perfects (later preterits) and past participles on each other. First, in Old and Classical Latin, some tautic athematic past participles were remade sigmatically by analogy with their sigmatic perfects. Thus CL MERSU replaced *MERTU 'sunk' (cf. OL MERTĀRE), and MĀNSU replaced *MANTU 'stayed' (cf. CL freq. MANTĀRE). Battisti (262) adds that CL PULSU replaced *PULTU 'throbbed' (cf. OL PULTĀRE).[77] At that stage, perfects were a central part of the

---

[76] If one accepts the neogrammarian belief that sound laws admit of no exception, verbs like Fr. *diviser* and Sp./Cat. *dividir* 'divide' would have to be semilearnèd. So would It. *dividere*: Following all the rules, DĪVIDERE would have given something like LL [divédere], which in French would eventually have become homophonous with *devoir* < DĒBĒRE 'ought to.'

[77] Both MERTĀRE and PULTĀRE might actually be old frequentatives, such verbs being almost always built from the same stem as the past participle of the simplex.

verb system, but past participles were still peripheral. Second, in Late Latin as shown by current Italian forms, some preterits were remade sigmatically by analogy with their sigmatic past participles: examples include *responsi* 'answered,' *presi* 'took,' and *corsi* 'run' ± RESPŌNSU, PREHĒNSU, CURSU.[78] At that stage, past participles had been integrated into the verb system.

When new preterit and present-perfect constructions coexisted, Vincent makes the following observation: "The preterite [was] therefore submitted to pressures in two directions: to extend its link with the participle and to differentiate itself from the present stem in those cases where it was not already distinct" (57).

During the third stage, in Italian and especially in Tuscan, sigmatic preterits tended to replace some that had come down from forms in -UĪ. An example is mediæval *volsi* 'wanted' for still-current *volli* < VOLUĪ. At that stage, the perfect had as it were regained morphological strength to influence some past participles like *vissuto* 'lived' and *valso* 'been worth.' After three stages of sigmatic remodeling, though, Italian still retains verbs like *dire* 'say,' *vincere* 'win,' *leggere* 'read,' and *togliere* 'take away,' whose sigmatic preterits contrast with their tautic athematic past participles, as well as a few like *chiedere* 'ask' and literary *porre* 'put' whose sigmatic preterits contrast with their sigmatic-tautic past participles *chiesto* and *posto*.

By all odds, the prize for influence of preterits on past participles must be given to Romanian, as discussed most fully in §3.1.5. Like Italian, though, Romanian still has verbs in which tautic athematic past participles contrast with sigmatic preterits.

In Proto-French as in other emerging varieties of Romance, vowels in a few preterit stems must have been extended into past-participial stems. From the tonic vowels in MĪSĪ and PRĒ(N)SĪ, the second of which underwent anaphony, derive the ModFr. *mis* 'put' and *pris* 'taken,' two of the remaining sigmatic past participles in the language today. Compare OSp. *mes[s]o, preso* < MISSU, PRĒ(N)SU, since superseded as past participles by infectum-based forms ending in -*ido*.[79] In Italian, both pret. *misi* and p.p. *messo* appear to have influenced the other in nonstandard forms: an OIt. p.p. *miso* was clearly based on the preterit stem—like the OSp. by-form *mis[s]o*—and an dialectal pret. *messi* has just as clearly been based on the p.p. stem. By contrast, although 2nd-conj. URG(U)ĒRE 'urge' lacked a past participle but did have a pf. URSĪ, no sigmatic forms seem to have been built on the pret. stem in Romance: standard It. 3rd-conj. *urgere* now lacks any preterit or past participle, though tautic athematic *urto* occurred in OIt. and survives as a

---

[78] As Vincent says (1978, 53 n.), CURSU had already been remade from expected *CURTU.

[79] By anticipation of the high front vowel [i] at the end of a LL pret. PRĒSĪ 'caught; took,' speakers of Proto-French raised the tonic vowel [e] to [i] as well, later extending that vowel into the past participle that turned into OFr. *pris* [pris]. Not content with that, speakers extended the already high first vowel of MĪSĪ > (*je*) *mis* into p.p. MISSU > *mis*. Their subsequent dropping of almost every final vowel but [a] > [ə] has veiled that anaphony in the decent obscurity of Romance philology, for more on which see the final note to this chapter.

noun meaning 'bump; clash.'[80] Learned-looking Cat./Sp./Ptg. 4th-conj.
urgir—with unlikely retention of a reflex of [g] before [i]—has a regular non-
ar-verb outcome for its past participle in Cat. *urgit* and Sp./Ptg. *urgido*.

In every Romance language, finite and participial forms within the
perfectum have influenced each other, for certain verbs; in every language,
the present stem has influenced both, for certain verbs. Which verbs where
came to have the same stem throughout? In Chapters 3 and 4, evidence for
further paradigm reshaping is reviewed in detail.

2.13. SHIFT TOWARD ARRHIZOTONIC PAST PARTICIPLES

Just as rhizotonic infinitives became less and less popular in most areas,
though they survived everywhere but central-western Iberia, so rhizotonic
past participles became less popular through time. Across ROMANIA, the
following stem-stressed past participles have probably left no direct
descendants among verb forms, though the verbs themselves live on: VENTU
'come,' TEXTU 'woven,' TENTU 'held,' SALTU 'jumped,' PĀSTU 'fed, kept,'
MŌTU 'moved,' CRĒTU 'grown' or 'sifted,' CĀSU 'fallen,' CAPTU 'taken.' One
could expand that list of everyday verbs to include strong past participles like
AUSU 'dared,' OBLĪTU 'forgotten,' and ŪSU 'used' that left progeny of whole
verbal paradigms but have themselves failed to thrive as past participles.

As Väänänen remarks (1981: 144), rhizotonic forms kept in Late Latin were
restricted to reflexes of ĀRSU 'burned,' CLAUSU 'shut,' DICTU 'said,' FACTU
'done/made,' LĒCTU 'read,' MORSU 'bitten,' PRĒNSU 'taken,' PŪNCTU 'stung,'
RĪSU 'laughed,' TĒNSU 'stretched,' TŌNSU 'shorn,' TORTU 'twisted,' and VĪSU
'seen.' Chapters 3 and 4 show that the list would have to be shortened for the
Romance west but lengthened for the Romance far east.

Speakers' diminishing inclination to use rhizotonic past participles,
whether athematic like those above or thematic like PERDITU 'lost' and
COGNITU 'known,' which likewise survive almost nowhere as past participles
in that form, was bound to play havoc with the conjugational system of CL
and lead to morphological innovation. In the discussion that follows, I try to
view irregularities traceable to IE as they would have appeared to speakers of
Latin unacquainted with diachronic linguistics.

2.13.1. Classical Hesitations

Not every verb form was fixed in the literary language of Rome. If a verb had
two past participles competing, one might be inherited, the other influenced
by its finite perfectum. By-forms might entail the presence or absence of

---

[80] More probably, LL *HURTARE 'push, thrust, kick' from Germanic gave rise to OFr.
hurter (now *heurter*) and Oc. *urtar* > It. *urtare*. It. *urto* would thus be a short-form 1st-conj. past
participle. In fact, only two Romance dialects seem to have kept straight reflexes of URGERE
'urge,' but semilearnèd forms have been revived in literary standards (*REW* nos. 4244, 9083).

certain features: a nasal consonant as in MICTU and MĪNCTU 'pissed' (cf. pf.
MIXĪ or MĪNXĪ),[81] a stop consonant as in deponent NĪSU and NĪXU 'leaned,
relied on,' or an atonic theme vowel as in ALTU and ALITU 'nourished.'
Alternation between the clusters [kt] and [ks] occurred in e.g. FLUCTU and
FLUXU 'flowed,' for which cf. pf. FLUXĪ (Holl, passim).

In addition, alternations in endings could occur depending on whether a
verb was prefixed by a preposition. Certain perfects formed by reduplication
and direct suffixation of endings acquired, in compounds, a *u*-stem
perfectivizer as in OCCINUĪ 'sang inauspiciously' as against unprefixed CECINĪ
'sang.' Other such perfects acquired, in compounds, a sigmatic marker as in
PRÆMORSĪ 'bit off' as against MOMORDĪ 'bit,' EXPŪNXĪ 'pricked out, canceled'
as against PEPUGĪ 'stung,' or EXPULSĪ 'drove out' as against PEPULĪ 'knocked,
beat' (Bader, 179). Although reduplication was almost to vanish in Romance,
the other two types of perfect marking were to expand at least for a time.

Already under the CL standard, paradigms were being regularized. For
instance, the perfectum of 1st-conj. PLICĀRE 'fold' could have either
rhizotonic pf. PLICUĪ and p.p. PLICITU or arrhizotonic pf. PLICĀVĪ and p.p.
PLICĀTU. During the first century BCE, Horace could write either arrhizotonic
IMPLICATA (*Epodes* 5.15) or presumably rhizotonic IMPLICITUM (*Ars Poetica*
424) in the sense 'enfolded, entwined, entangled,' and Horace could write
either arrhizotonic NECATUS (*Carmina* 1.29.6) or definitely rhizotonic
ENECTUS (*Epistulæ* 1.7.87) in the sense 'killed' for the first and 'worn out,
tired' for the second (Safarewicz, 259). Yet under the CL standard for FRICĀRE
'rub down,' the unusual pf. FRICUĪ competed against regular if less common
FRICĀVĪ; the verb's past participle could be standard tautic athematic FRICTU,
less common sigmatic FRIXU, or regularized FRICĀTU; moreover, PŌTĀRE
'drink [heavily]' had a regular pf. PŌTAVĪ and a regularized p.p. PŌTĀTU
alongside short-form PŌTU.

Such hesitations foreshadowed the disappearance of some anomalies fated
to take place when literary standards no longer delayed leveling. As things
stand now, all Romance reflexes of those verbs have joined the regular 1st-
conjugation paradigm.

2.13.2. Postclassical Remodeling

Toward the end of Empire, leveling included 1st-conj. SECATU 'cut, sawn' and
perhaps 4th-conj. METITU 'reaped, harvested' for CL SECTU and MESSU, both
from the Itala; cf. the CL infins. SECĀRE and METERE (Haadsma and
Nuchelmans, 62). Sigmatic perfects also expanded in Late Latin. From
inscriptions come FUNXIT for the CL deponent FŪNCTU EST 'has died, carried
it through to the end,' and also (E)LEXIT 'chose' for (Ē)LĒGIT. Two others are
3sg. MORSIT 'bit'—from a gloss MOMORDIT MELIUS DICIMUS QUAM MORSIT
'we better say MOMORDIT than MORSIT'—and 1sg. PRESI 'seized, took' for
PRENDIDĪ, from a Latin translation of the Salic Law. The third sigmatic

---

[81] Italian has a semilearnèd p.p. *minto* 'pissed' for its high-flown 3rd-conj. infin. *mingere*.

perfect, MORSIT, was clearly inspired by p.p. MORSU; the fourth one, PRESI, represents a sigmatic reshaping of the whole perfectum; the first and second show a spread of the already common pattern of perfects in [ks] contrasting with past participles in [kt]; the second also shows a reshaping of the unpopular vowel-change-plus-direct-suffixation type of perfect.

Two other arrhizotonic remakings come from the Itala. Pf. SALIVI 'jumped' has been aligned with its 4th-conj. infinitive SALĪRE, unlike the rhizotonic CL pf. SALUĪ and p.p. SALTU. Pf. SILEVI 'was silent' has been aligned with its 2nd-conj. infinitive SILĒRE rather than continuing pf. SILUĪ; the verb had no CL p.p., but an attested variant pf. SILEVI suggests that -ĒVĪ perfects might still have been marginally productive under the later Empire (Haadsma and Nuchelmans, 61).

2.13.3. Later Remodeling

Regularization of 1st-conj. past participles in Late Latin or Proto-Romance led to the standard It. p.p.s *covato* 'brooded, hatched' *crepato* 'burst,' *fregato* 'rubbed,' *segato* 'cut,' *s(u)onato* 'sounded,' *t(u)onato* 'thundered' (OIt. *tronato*), and *vietato* 'forbidden,' most of them paralleled from Romanian to Portuguese. Short-vowel 1st-conj. DĂTU 'given' and STĂTU 'stood' (but cf. supine STĀTU) might have been regularized as well, but the merger of [a] and [a:] across ROMANIA makes it impossible to tell.

Again, regularization of almost all 4th-conj. past-participial variants led to the standard It. p.p.s *salito*, *sentito*, and -*vertito* (Ewert, 225), reshapings also paralleled elsewhere. If 4th-conj. SENTĪRE 'feel' survives in the same infin. class in Fr./Sp./Cat. *sentir*, It. *sentire*, Rom. *a simţi*, its past participles—Fr. *senti*, Sp. *sentido*, Cat. *sentit*, It. *sentito*, and Rom. *simţit*—presuppose a regular infectum-based form replacing SĒNSU (Tekavčić, 287–89). Here even sigmatic-loving Italian and Romanian have refrained from continuing the old past participle.

In making the two largest verb classes more predictable, speakers promoted regularization across other classes (see §2.6). Allomorphy has never fallen to zero in any language, much less across language barriers. As shown by the spread of infectum marking into the perfectum (Tables 2–2 and 2–3), isomorphy between infinitives and past participles has risen since CL days.

That the trend toward arrhizotonicity was far from universal is shown by reflexes of PRŪRĪRE 'itch': Ptg./Cat. *pruir* and rare Oc. *pruzir* remain in the same class, but not 3rd-conj. It. *prudere* or more usual 2nd-conj. Oc. *pruzer*. On Sardinia and in southern Italy, 3rd-conj. variants were so greatly favored that they sometimes ousted 4th-conj. ones, resulting in Sard. *abérrere* 'open' and *kobérrere* 'cover' ≠ APERĪRE, COOPERĪRE and Sard./Cal. *véstere* 'clothe, dress' ≠ VESTĪRE, along with Abru. *sérvere* 'serve' ≠ SERVĪRE and Neap. *pártere* 'leave' ≠ PARTĪRE. In Occitania and Catalonia, too, verbs that had belonged to the 2nd conjugation in CL were often reshaped according to 3rd-conj. norms, giving e.g. Cat. *deure* 'ought to' ≠ DĒBĒRE, *moure* 'move' ≠ MOVĒRE, *doure* 'grieve, hurt' ≠ DOLĒRE.

Table 2–3

Spread of Non-Nasal Infectum Marking

(after Dardel, 78)

CLASSICAL LATIN		LATE LATIN/PROTO-ROMANCE		
Infectum Stem	Past Participle	CL Form Kept as P.p.?	Assimilation of Past Participle to Infectum Stem	Anomaly
CAD-	CĀSU	no	*CADUTU	—
CERN-	CRĒTU	no	*CERNUTU	—
CRĒSC-	CRĒTU	no	*CRESCUTU	—
MOV-	MŌTU	no	*MOVUTU	—
SED-	-SESSU	no	*SEDUTU	—
VID-	VĪSU	yes	*VIDUTU	*VISTU

Elsewhere, analogies made with other verbs might slow the trend toward clear thematic marking. For instance, in OFr. 4th-conj. *engloutir* 'gulp down' < IN + GLŪTĪRE had a 3rd-conj. by-form *engloutre*, possibly under the influence of *foutre* < FUT(U)ERE (Meyer-Lübke 1974, 168–73), for which cf. perhaps Engl. *snatch* 'pudendum'; only *engloutir* exists in French today.

Two rhizotonic thematic past participles in Latin were JACITU, VALITU for 2nd-conj. JACĒRE 'lie resting,' and VALĒRE 'be strong, be worth,' which had perfects in -UĪ; 2nd-conj. DOLĒRE 'grieve, hurt,' with no p.p. but fut.p. DOLITŪRU, also had a perfect in -UĪ. Most speakers of Late Latin or Proto-Romance seem to have extended perfect stems to serve as bases for these verbs' new past participles. In this way, the theme vowel in pf. DOLUĪ came to serve as well for Rom. *durut*, It. *doluto*, Cat. *dolgut* (3rd-conj. infin. *doldre*), and OFr. *dolu*, but not for Sp. *dolido* 'hurt' or of Ptg. *doido* 'crazy.' Along the same lines, while OOc. *jait* may derive from an anomalous syncopated variant of JACITU, most speakers elsewhere extended the stem in pf. JACUĪ, sometimes borrowing a palatal consonant from the infinitive, to create the ancestor of Rom. *zăcut*, It. *giaciuto*, and OFr. *geü*, but not of Sp. *yacido* or Ptg. *jazido* 'lain.' To replace VALITU 'been strong, been worth,' speakers in some areas extended the stem in pf. VALUĪ to serve as well for Fri. *valût*, Cat. *valgut*, and Fr. *valu*. A sigmatic stem was used in It. *valso*, even if neither of these lay behind Sp./Ptg. *valido*.

One may conclude that, in Proto-Romance, speakers preferred past participles with clear marking, whether arrhizotonic or sigmatic. Nearly everywhere, they remade several high-frequency past participles that had ended in -ĪTU or in -CTU (where C stands for any other consonant but [s]).

2.14. SPREAD OF PAST PARTICIPLES IN –ŪTU

Seen in a handful of CL past participles for 3rd-conj. verbs, like SŪTU 'sewn' (infin. SUERE), the -ŪTU ending applied only to *u*-stem verbs to which the [t] suffix was added directly (Buck, 308). Similar morphology existed in certain Gk. verbal adjs. like ἀδάκρυτος 'without tears' from the *u*-stem verb δακρύω 'weep, cry.' Save for their rarity, Latin *u*-stem past participles had arrhizotonicity in common with *a*-stem past participles like JOCĀTU 'joked' and *i*-stem past participles like DORMĪTU 'slept.'

Further examples from CL included unprefixed ARGŪTU 'shown, proven' (cf. infin. ARGUERE), STATŪTU 'set up' (STATUERE), and TRIBŪTU 'allotted' (TRIBUERE), as well as the popular pair SOLŪTU 'loosened' (SOLVERE) and VOLŪTU 'rolled' (VOLVERE, freq. VOLŪTĀRE 'roll around, tumble about'). Already adjectival in CL were the old *u*-stem p.p.s ACŪTU 'sharpened; sharp' (infin. ACUERE) and MINŪTU 'lessened; small' (MINUERE).

Prefixed past participles in this class included ABLŪTU 'washed, cleansed' (cf. infin. ABLUERE), IMBŪTU 'steeped, stained' (IMBUERE), along with the twins INDŪTU 'put on, clothed' and EXŪTU 'taken off, stripped' (INDUERE, EXUERE) and the triplets ADNŪTU 'nodded to, agreed' and ABNŪTU or RENŪTU 'denied, refused' (ADNUERE, ABNUERE, RENUERE).

As Tekavčić observes (326), to these *u*-stem verbs in CL may be added two others, which because of their semantic fields and affective contents must have been popular and most certainly have lived on: BATTUERE 'beat' and FUTUERE 'fuck' had the p.p.s BATTŪTU and FUTŪTU, reflexes of which still thrive from the Danube to the Ebro.

2.14.1. Attestations in Latin

Postclassical attestations of new past participles in -ŪTU are fairly sparse, perhaps because writers if not speakers regarded them as uncouth. Still, macronless ones may be found, notably REDDUTUS for CL REDDITUS 'given back,' INCENDUTA for INCĒNSA 'lit, set afire,' MOLUTUS for MOLITUS 'ground,' and PENDUTUS for PĒNSUS 'hung.' To these may be compared the Fr. p.p.s *rendu, moulu,* and *pendu.* Attested LL cognomina like feminine CREDUTA and masculine VENUTUS, from the same stems as CL CRĒTA 'believed' and VENTUS 'come,' suggest similar developments for other verbs (Väänänen 1981, 144–45), as still in the corresponding It. p.p.s *creduto* and *venuto.* Another infectum-based LL reshaping is DECERNUTUS for CL DĒCRĒTUS 'decided, determined' (Ronjat, 217, after citing further *u*-stem names). Minus the prefix, Rom/Cat. *cernut* 'sifted' continues that reshaping.

Postclassical inscriptions offer clues as well. In Hispania at least, once [t] and [k] had both come to be said [ts] before a front vowel, gens-names (nomina) that ended in -ATIUS, -ECIUS, -ICIUS, and -UCIUS in CL came to have by-forms spelled -ATIUS, -ETIUS, or -UTIUS. These variants were apparently inspired by adjectives or past participles in -ĀTU, -ĪTU or -ĬTU, and -ŪTU. Attested LL names like ALBUTIUS and MUTIUS suggest that the last type of ending was commonplace in Hispania at the time (Carnoy, 153).

2.14.2. Postimperial Developments

Across several centuries, the fairly common -UĪ suffix underwent a fate quite different from that of the rare -ŪTU suffix. The latter expanded in the future Catalonia, France, Italy, and Romania, but not at all on Sardinia and possibly only somewhat in the future Castile and Portugal, as Tekavčić maintains: "Infatti, l'assenza dei participi in -ŪTU del sardo e praticamente anche delle lingue iberoromanze da una parte, e la loro frequenza nella Romània centrale dall'altra, provano che essi rappresentano una evoluzione seriore rispetto ai participi in -ĬTU, che constituiscono lo strato anteriore, più antico" (452). [Indeed, the absence of -ŪTU participles from Sardinian and their near absence from Spanish and Portuguese, on the one hand, and their high frequency in central Romance, on the other, prove that they represent a later stage than -ĬTU participles do.]

As should be clear by now, I am willing to grant that -ŪTU past participles never took root on Sardinia or in southern Italy or in a few Swiss valleys. I decline to believe that they never flourished across mediæval Iberia.

With fair plausibility, Elcock outlines three stages for the trend toward past participles in -ŪTU. First affected would have been high-frequency verbs with a CL rhizotonic thematic past participle in -ĬTU, for—outside Sardinia, southern Italy, and possibly central-western Iberia—assumed forms ending in -ŪTU must have lain behind Romance past participles for those verbs. Second to obtain such past participles would have been verbs that developed a -UĪ perfect in Late Latin. Unattested new LL perfects of the -UĪ type included *CURRUI 'ran' for CL CUCURRĪ, and *VINCUI 'won,' with nasal infix, for CL VĪCĪ. From such unclassical perfects in -UĪ would have come the third stage: LL past participles in [u] like *BIBUTU 'drunk,' *CURRUTU 'run,' *CADUTU 'fallen,' *VINCUTU 'won,' and *LEGUTU 'chosen; read,' many of them abundantly attested in later Romance from Catalonia eastward, and more than a few in Old Spanish and Old Portuguese as well (see §4.7.4.1).

If neither provable nor disprovable, Elcock's three-stage scenario might well be revised as follows for most of ROMANIA. At the first stage, an expansion of -ŪTU past participles to verbs with -UĪ perfects would have promoted comparable marking for verbs mostly belonging to the 2nd conjugation. At the second stage, an expansion of both -ŪTU past participles and -UĪ perfects to verbs with -ITU past participles and various kinds of perfect would have further promoted such marking within the past system for 3rd-conj. verbs. At the third stage, centered in the future France and Catalonia and what were to become dialects of northern Italy, -ŪTU would have become the default ending for building past participles outside the 1st and 4th conjugations. At any rate, both Elcock's scenario and my rewriting of it lend support to the contention that speakers of Late Latin and Proto-Romance were unconsciously trying to heighten morphological predictability across the perfectum, notably for 2nd- and 3rd-conj. verbs.

After the trend toward past participles in -ŪTU for such verbs had gotten under way, it carried along most past participles in -ĬTU, whether primary or secondary, that did not correspond to perfects ending in -UĪ. That trend toward -ŪTU past participles seems to have been most noticeable in northern Gaul. Among those slightly remade since then, Old French developed *creü* 'believed; grew' ≠ CRĒDITU and CRĒTU, *eü* 'had' ≠ HABITU, and *veü* 'seen' ≠ VĪSU. Among those still keeping their OFr. garb were *fendu* 'split' ≠ FISSU, *fondu* 'melted' ≠ FŪSU 'poured,' *pendu* 'weighed, hung' ≠ PĒNSU, *tendu* 'stretched, held out' ≠ TĒNSU or TENTU, and *tondu* 'shorn' ≠ TŌNSU. Among those subsequently lost were OFr. *(e)issu* 'gone out' ≠ EXĬTU (Ewert, 225).

2.14.3. The Fate of Perfects in –UĪ

New participles in -ŪTU were supported morphologically within the past system by already extant perfects in -UĪ, which themselves grew more common for a time. Indeed, as Togeby notes (141), the expanded type of perfect (later preterit) formation in -UĪ was the only one to reach another very archaic language, Romanian, which has a great many past participles in -*ut*.

Apparently, the -UĪ type of perfect extended its range for generations but then, except in the future Catalonia and Occitania, became increasingly unacceptable as a marker of perfectivity in finite verb forms across most of ROMANIA.

In Dacia, to be sure, -UĪ perfects that lay behind "aorists" like 1sg. *băui* 'drank' ≠ BIBĪ, *căzui* 'fell' ≠ CECIDĪ, *crezui* 'believed' ≠ CRĒDIDĪ, *născui* 'was born' ≠ deponent NĀTU, and *stătui* 'stood; stayed' ≠ STETĪ appear to have kept their endings unchanged (Tagliavini 1923, 214), though those forms in tonic [u] appear rather to have been based on their past participles in -*ut*.

Devising an explanation for a postclassical reshaping of many non-1st-conj. perfects along -UĪ lines, Bourciez (83) relies on rhyming analogies and on semantic similarities between pairs of verbs.[82] He observes that there developed CAPUĪ 'took' (attested in St. Clement, third century CE) for CL CĒPĪ ± RAPTU RAPUĪ 'seized, grabbed'; there developed LEGUĪ 'chose; read' and REGUĪ 'ruled' (both attested in the *Corpus Inscriptionum Latinarum*) for LĒGĪ, RĒXĪ ± DOCTU DOCUĪ 'taught.' Perfects like VENUĪ (cf. VENUERIT in the Salic Law) for CL VĒNĪ 'came' ± TENUĪ 'held, had' no doubt appeared fairly early, Bourciez writes (83), but only later did there appear -UĪ perfects replacing CRĒDIDĪ 'believed,' CECIDĪ 'fell,' and VĪDĪ 'saw.'

---

[82] For a recent rhyming analogy in American English that has yielded a new preterit/past participle, cf. *plead:pled ± bleed:bled.*

In fairly conservative Italian, where the normal outcome of -CUĪ is reinforced [k:wi], inherited *giacqui* 'lay' < JACUĪ, *nocqui* 'harmed' < NOCUĪ, *piacqui* < PLACUĪ, and *tacqui* 'kept still' < TACUĪ gave rise to analogical *nacqui* 'was born' < *NACUI for CL NĀTU. Except after [k], normally LL posttonic [Cwi] gave It. [C:i], so that rhizotonic 1sg., 3sg., and 3pl. preterits like VOLUĪ > *volli* 'wanted,' TENUĪ > *tenni* 'held' represent regular outcomes.[83] Liquids tended not to geminate in such forms, where [w] > [v]: compare 3sg. *parve* 'it appeared' < *[parβe] < PARUIT and OIt. *dolve* 'it hurt' < *[dolβe] < DOLUIT, now sigmatic *dolse*. As Tekavčić observes (387), raising of the tonic vowel in *ebbi* 'had' < HABUĪ "non è ancora definitivamente chiarito" [has not yet been cleared up], any more than it has in *seppi* 'knew' < *SAPUI for CL SAPIĪ or SAPĪVĪ—unless one assumes anticipatory vowel assimilation—the consonants in both have evolved regularly from attested or assumed ones in Latin.

Other Italian preterits with geminated consonants like *stetti* 'stood,' *venni* 'came,' *crebbi* 'grew,' *conobbi* 'knew,' *ruppi* 'broke,' *bevvi* 'drank,' and *caddi* 'fell' presuppose LL perfects in -UĪ that replaced CL STETĪ, VĒNĪ, CRĒVĪ, COGNŌVĪ, RŪPĪ, BIBĪ, and CECIDĪ, all with reduplication, vowel change, or vowel lengthening. In the same vein, It. *piovve* 'it rained' presupposes an innovative pf. in -UIT for CL PLUIT or PLŪVIT (Tekavčić, 386). Moreover, the existence of another preterit of the same type, *TULUI 'taken away' ≠ SUSTULĪ, may be inferred by the It. form *tulle*, very rare in the Middle Ages and now remade as sigmatic *tolsi* (Dardel, 102).

According to Price (210–11), several OFr. preterits whose 1sg. still ended in [i̯] < [i:], not counting inherited *poi* 'could' < POTUĪ or *fui* 'was' < FUĪ, must have come from LL reshapings like *LEGUI > *lui* 'read,' *BIBUI > *bui* 'drank,' *COGNOVUI > *conui* 'knew,' *RECIPUI > *reçui* 'received,' *SAPUI > *[sau̯i] *soi* 'knew,' *CREDUI > *crui* 'believed'—for LĒGĪ, BIBĪ, COGNŌVĪ, RECĒPĪ, SAPĪVĪ or SAPIĪ, and CREDIDĪ—all but the last attached to the 3rd conjugation in CL. To this list of OFr. 1sg. preterits, Bourciez (341) adds CL-derived *ploi* 'pleased' < PLACUĪ, *toi* 'was quiet' < TACUĪ, where [o̯i] < [a] + [wi], and LL/PR-derived *crui* 'grew' < *CREVUI, *estui* 'stopped, stayed' < *STETUI, *jui* 'threw' < *JECUI, and *mui* 'moved' < *MOVUI for CL CRĒVĪ, STETĪ, JĒCĪ, and MŌVĪ. To these Ewert (217) adds OFr. *poi* 'fed, kept' < *PAVUI for rare PĀVĪ, besides *chui* 'fell' < *CADUI for CECIDĪ. As with many other retrojected reconstructions, the most that one may state with certainty is that such preterits were remade at some time during or after the fragmentation of Empire.

By the end of the Middle Ages in France and Spain, only a few descendants of -UĪ preterits had escaped extinction. Those few, like OSp. *sope* < *saupe* < *SAPUI 'I knew' and OFr. *oi* < *aui* < HABUĪ 'I had,' were transformed almost beyond recognition. So were Italian preterits with lengthened consonants like *crebbi* < *CREVUI 'I grew' and *bevvi* < *BIBUI 'I drank.' Both still in use, their earlier morphology has been disguised by orthographic gemination.

---

[83] Here and henceforth, C = consonant (except [s]).

2.14.4. Loss or Syncope of –ŪTU Past Participles

Once again, membership in an increasingly popular morphological class could not guarantee survival for a verb, even when it had a past participle in line with the trend toward arrhizotonicity. Deponent LOQUĪ 'speak' had pf./p.p. LOCŪTU, but all unlearnèd forms of the verb died out on the way to Romance. Again, failure to thrive by the *u*-stem verb METUERE 'fear' meant doom as well for its fairly rare p.p. METŪTU, appearing in Lucretius, *De rerum natura* v.1139 (Zumpt, 158). A related noun did survive in e.g. Sp. *miedo* < METU 'fear,' one 4th-decl. noun with a different stem from that of the corresponding past participle.

In Late Latin if not before, deponent SEQUĪ 'follow' with p.p. SECŪTU acquired active forms. Romance reflexes have generally joined the 4th conjugation. Agreeing with infins. like It. *seguire* and Sp. *seguir* are regular p.p.s *seguito* and *seguido*; irregularly evolving Fr. *suivre* has a 4th-conj.-style p.p. *suivi*, though OFr. *seü* seems to have come straight down from SECŪTU.

CL VOLVERE 'roll' had a p.p. VOLŪTU that one would have expected to thrive east of Castile, as one would have expected SOLŪTU 'loosened' to thrive. Perhaps what happened to the old p.p. VOLŪTU 'rolled' was this: in Late Latin, it was crowded out of its slot by higher-frequency *VOLUTU 'wanted' (> It. *voluto* etc.) but fell back on a rhizotonic thematic by-form *VOLVITU that appears to lie behind It. *volto* and Sp. *vuelto*. Also derived from a rhizotonic thematic p.p. variant are a pair of adjectives, It. *sciolto* and Sp. *suelto* 'loose[ned]' ≠ SOLŪTU. Other pairs with the same unclassical look are Surs. *viult* and Enga. *vout* along with Surs. *siult* and Enga. *scholt*.

Two of those syncopated past participles have a long history behind them. In the eighth-century *Codice paleografico lombardo*, document no. 21 has the form PERSOLTA ≠ PERSOLŪTA 'paid off,' and document no. 17 has the form TULTUS 'taken away' ≠ SUBLĀTUS (Politzer, 101).

One must not, then, overstate the attractiveness of arrhizotonicity. When speakers refashioned their verb system during and after the decline and fall, it might happen beyond the confines of Sardinia, Sicily, and southern Italy that a rhizotonic past participle emerged where no rhizotonic past participle had gone before.

2.14.5. Current Distribution of –ŪTU Past Participles

In western Romance, French keeps many past participles in -*u* that used to accompany 1sg. preterits in -*ui*. Of those given in §2.14.5, there survive *couru* 'run,' *vaincu* 'won,' and *lu* 'read' cited by Elcock; *plu* 'pleased,' *tu* 'been silent,' *crû* 'grown,' and *mû* 'moved' cited by Bourciez (though the last two are bookish); and *bu* 'drunk,' *connu* 'knew,' *reçu* 'received,' *su* 'known,' and *cru* 'believed' cited by Price. Most have cognates in Cat. *corregut* 'run,' *vençut* 'won,' *plagut* pleased,' *cregut* 'believed,' *crescut* 'grown,' and *mogut* 'moved.' In eastern Romance, aside from matching -UĪ perfects mentioned by Tekavčić, standard Italian and Romanian share a large number of -ŪTU past participles: *avuto* and *avut* 'had,' *bevuto* and *băut* 'drunk,' *conosciuto* and *cunoscut* 'known,' *creduto* and *crezut* 'believed,' *cresciuto* and *crescut* 'grown,' *giaciuto* and *zăcut* 'lain,' *piaciuto* and *plăcut* 'pleased,' *seduto* and *şezut* 'sat,' *taciuto* and *tăcut* 'been silent,' *tenuto* and *ţinut* 'held.' To that list one might add nonstd. It. *nasciuto* and std. Rom. *născut* 'born.'

Results across Romance seldom present so sharp a picture. Today, for instance, 3rd-conj. VINCERE 'win' has reflexes in It. *vincere* and Fr. *vaincre*, while reflexes farther west have undergone metaplasm to the 2nd conjugation in Oc. *vencer*, Cat. *vèncer*, and of course Sp. *vencer*. The verb's CL p.p. VICTU (short i̲) has survived as a rhizotonic form only in It. *vinto* and sigmatic Rom. *învins*. For this verb's past participle, -ŪTU forms have been preferred in Fr. *vaincu*, Cat. *vençut*, and OOc. *vencut*, while Spanish has ended up with an -ĪTU derivative in *vencido* (but cf. OSp. *vençudo*). All show a nasal infix from the old infectum stem VINC-.

For certain high-frequency 2nd- or 3rd-conj. verbs, then, past participles in -ŪTU have triumphed only in part of ROMANIA. As noted, SOLŪTU 'loosened' and VOLŪTU 'rolled' were remade rhizotonically in most areas. One would expect CŌNSŪTU 'sewn' to join the 4th conjugation in Sp. *cosido* but hardly in It. *cucito*, with an irregular affricate besides.

Although legitimate offspring of rhizotonic CAPTU 'taken' are found nowhere but in Dantean *catto*, both It. *capito* 'understood' and Sp. *cabido* 'fit into' come from a regular 4th-conj. innovation, as does Fri. *capît* 'taken.' By contrast, neighboring Lad. *čapat* 'taken' comes from a regular 1st-conj. innovation. Only Cat. *cabut* 'fit into' and OFr. *chavu* 'seized' come from a regular 2nd- or 3rd-conj. innovation.

For several verbs, past participles with endings from -ŪTU stop short of the Pyrenees. That does not mean they always did. For a few verbs, undeniably, the overwhelming Sp./Ptg. preference for past participles in -*ido* has reached Catalan on the east coast of Iberia. Rhizotonic athematic TEXTU 'woven' has been replaced by a regular 2nd- or 3rd-conj. innovation in Rom. *ţesut*, It. *tessuto*, Lad. *tesù*, OFr. *tissu* (now *tissé*), and Oc. *tescut*, but Cat. *teixit* agrees with Sp. *tejido*, Ptg. *tecido* in sharing a 4th-conj. innovation. A reflex of TĒNSU has been kept in It. *(s)teso* 'stretched,' but Fr. *tendu*. Rom. *ţinut* contrast with 4th-conj.-style Cat. *tendit*, Sp. *tendido*, though Catalan still has p.p. -*tès* in compounds. Perhaps on that sigmatic basis, a reflex of the postclassical equation REDDITU x TĒ(N)SU or PRĒ(N)SU = *RENSU has been kept in standard It. *reso* 'given back,' but a regular 2nd- or 3rd-conj. innovation has arisen in OIt. *renduto*, Lad. *rendù*, and Fr. *rendu*, in contrast with Cat. *rendit* and Sp./Ptg. *rendido*. Meanwhile, Rom. *redat* has joined the ever-productive 1st conjugation and failed to acquire infectum-style nasal marking as the rest did.

What were the results of all the reshaping outlined above? Below, Table 2–4 portrays the default morphology emerging for perfects and past participles in most areas where Late Latin was spoken.

Table 2–4

Heightened Isomorphy in Late Latin Verbs

Conj.	Infinitive	Preterit	Past Participle
1st	- ĀRE	-ĀVĪ	- ĀTU
2nd, 3rd	-ĒRE, ´-ĔRE	-UĪ. —— -SĪ	-ŪTU —— -SU
4th	-ĪRE	-ĪVĪ	-ĪTU

Despite observed differences between languages—to be reviewed in detail in §2.15—the regular conjugational classes created within Latin continued to expand across most of ROMANIA.

As the perfect ending -UĪ might have come from [u:wi:], perhaps still a current pronunciation in CL, one detects morphological symmetry across two conjugations already large, and one glimpses a combined conjugation coming into being. Perhaps potentially present in the minds of speakers back then, those patterns were later to become predominant.

To be sure, sigmatics proved far more popular toward the east; past participles in -so were to disappear from central-western Iberia, along with forms in -udo. As often happened, Sardinia and southern Italy were to go their own ways, keeping p.p. reflexes of rhizotonic thematics in -ĪTU. Most notably, of course, Table 2–4 ignores the survival of Latin past participles in reflexes of [pt] and [kt], both of them realized as [pt] in Romanian, as [t:] in Italian, as simple [t] in French, Catalan, and Portuguese; Spanish still distinguishes between [t] < [pt] and [tʃ] < [kt]. Undeniably, though, arrhizotonic or sigmatic types were fated to thrive as time went by.

2.15. A FEW DIFFERENCES AMONG ROMANCE LANGUAGES

Analysts continue to disagree about when and where divergences arose among varieties of the Latin koine and how fast the language(s) changed in each province. For a discussion of views on territorial differentiation within Latin, based on a review of epigraphic and literary evidence, three articles in

Herman 1990 (29–34, 55–61, and 62–92) provide the best guide. The same work contains evidence gathered from Sardinia (183–94), Gaul (147–63), and Dalmatia (121–46), together with evidence from Noricum, Pannonia, and North Africa where spoken Latin was to die out and be replaced by German, Hungarian, and Arabic respectively. For inscriptional evidence from Hispania, the standard work remains Carnoy 1903.

Certainly by the time Romance languages were first attested, they differed somewhat in the types of past participles that each favored or disfavored. Despite a shared tendency toward arrhizotonicity (or sigmaticism), they differ more than somewhat today. In Chapters 3 and 4, I review in detail the morphology of past participles coming down from Latin across the lands of southern Europe. For the moment, I want to review a few differences that have evolved for past participles in standard languages spoken in several parts of ROMANIA.

2.15.1. Are Analogies Predictable?

As results of verb remodeling have diverged somewhat across ROMANIA, I have proceeded on the assumption that the pathways along which analogy will flow, while ascertainable after the fact, can hardly be foretold. However, according to Kuryłowicz's "celebrated simile," a higher degree of precision ought to be attainable: "Il en est comme de l'eau de pluie qui doit prendre un chemin prévu (gouttières, égouts, conduits) *une fois qu'il pleut*. Mais la pluie n'est pas une nécessité. De même les actions prévues de l'«analogie» ne sont pas des nécessités" (cited in Vincent 1978, 60) [It is like rainwater, which has to follow a set path (gutters, sewers, pipes) *once it rains*. But rain does not have to fall. Likewise, the expected workings of "analogy" do not always take place]. Vincent (63–64) goes further still, maintaining that analysts should strive to predict directions of analogical change; meteorologists should know when it is going to rain. To pursue Kuryłowicz's simile, I wonder whether analysts ought to take it for granted that gutters, sewers, and pipes are laid out along the same plan in every language.

In pursuit of the goal of predicting analogies, Vincent suggests, Mańczak's idea that frequency of occurrence determines the direction in which analogy will operate ought to be modified: unmarked forms are more frequent because they have unmarked morphological structure, but many of the least regular verbs are among the highest-frequency ones. In Late Latin, full integration of the past participle into the verb system made such forms more and more frequent in patterns learned by each generation. Whether a given past participle was leveled along arrhizotonic or sigmatic lines, or whether it was "permitted to persist in [its] exceptionality" depended in part on frequency and in part on the rules of each stage of Late Latin and Romance languages. Changing through time and space, those rules largely determined the directions that analogies would follow.[84]

---

[84] Vincent's next book is provisionally titled *Morphological Change: from Latin to Romance.*

In offering these views, Vincent is presumably considering analogies made unconsciously by native speakers and only later pondered by analysts. Here I review past participles for verbs that have survived, some of which gained or lost sigmatic marking, and for one verb that has been revived. I try to chart the conduits along which analogy has flowed in each language. From Moldavia to Portugal, do they all run parallel in retrospect?

2.15.2. Outcomes for SANCĪRE 'bless'

Although speakers reshaped rhizotonic perfects and past participles for many verbs that had arrhizotonic infinitives, SANCĪRE SĀNXĪ SĀNCTU 'hallow, bless' survives not at all as a verb except in semilearnèd It. *sancire* 'ratify, sanction.' Judging by attested SANTUS, from the *Corpus Inscriptionum Latinarum* II 2395, that verb's past participle had lost its interconsonantal [k] early on (Carnoy, 172, 178). Owing to Christian usage, reflexes of SĀNCTU have long been used west of Dacia in the adjectival sense 'holy' or the nominal one 'saint,' in e.g. Sp. *san(to)*.[85] The OSp. adjective *sencido* 'uninjured, unharmed' (now *cencido*) suggests however that LL speakers in part of Hispania might have remade the verb's past participle along the arrhizotonic lines of its 4th-conj. infectum (*REW* no. 7566a). Such a remaking seems to have occurred in the form SANCITUS in Lucretius, *De rerum natura* 1.587, despite the absence of macrons.

In Romance, reflexes of SĀNCTU have become morphological isolates. Replacement verbs for SANCĪRE 'bless' have been built on compounds of BENE 'well' and a verb meaning 'say.' Typified by their past participles as usual, such replacements include Rom. *binecuvântat*, It. *benedetto*, Fr. *béni*, Cat. *beneit* (arch. *beneït*), and Sp. *bendito* or regularized *bendecido*.

2.15.3. Outcomes for FALLERE 'trick; fail'

Romance outcomes might vary across space as well as time. For instance, 3rd-conj. FALLERE 'trick; fail' had a p.p. FALSU of the sigmatic type (already adjectivized) that grew less popular in much of Romance. Reflexes of FALSU survive only as adjectives today, in e.g. It. *falso*, Oc./Cat. *fals*, and Fr. *faux*. Although OFr. still had a 3rd-conj. reflex of FALLERE in *faudre*, two other arrhizotonic variants live on in French today: 2nd-conj. *falloir* 'be required' and 4th-conj. *faillir* 'almost do.' Their regular, arrhizotonic past participles imply that—in northern Gaul at least—FALSU might have had a competitor in -ŪTU to yield Fr. *fallu* 'been required'; in most areas, FALSU had to have had a competitor in -ĪTU as well, which yielded *failli* 'almost done' as well as Rom. *fălit*, It. *fallito*, and Cat. *fallit* 'failed,' along with the Sp. adj. *fallido* 'disappointed, frustrated.' For that verb, central-western Iberia has preferred an old inchoative variant that has given Sp./Ptg. *fallecer* 'die' with regular non-*ar*-verb p.p. *fallecido*, though from the same verb there has also emerged

---

[85] Romanian has *sfint* 'blessed, holy' from Slavic (cf. Russ. *svyatoy*).

probably denominal *faltar* 'lack,' perhaps drawn from an unattested rhizotonic thematic past participle *FALLITA that also gave Fr. *faute* 'mistake.' Further past-participial relics are unearthed in §4.4.9 for French, §4.6.2.5 for Catalan, and §4.7.7 for Spanish.

2.15.4. Outcomes for LINGERE and LAMBERE 'lick'

If well-traveled pathways of conjugation appear to have become still more heavily traveled through time, morphology has not been destiny any more than geography has been. Two Latin verbs meaning 'lick' illustrate the point. Reflexes of at least a score of CL verbs with presents in [ŋg], perfects in [ŋks], and past participles in [ŋkt] remain popular, above all in Italy and France in local versions of e.g. UNG(U)ERE 'oil' and JUNGERE 'join.' However, reflexes of 3rd-conj. LINGERE LINXĪ LĪNCTU 'lick' survive only in Rom. *a linge*, Sic. *línčiri*, Log. *língere*, and Fri. *léndzi*, the first with the remade sigmatic p.p. *lins*. I have been unable to find past participles for the other two.

Reflexes of the other CL verb meaning 'lick,' 3rd-conj. LAMBERE LAMBĪ LAMBĬTU, survive only in Log. *lámbere*, Sp. *lamer*, and Ptg. *lamber*, the last two of which at least have regular preterits and the past participles *lamido* and *lambido* (*REW*, nos. 4865, 5066).[86] From the Appenines to the Pyrenees, meanwhile, both LINGERE and LAMBERE have succumbed to competition from a Germanic intruder related to Engl. *lick* and adapted into the 1st conjugation as verbs with the p.p.s *leccato*, *léché*, *lecat*.[87]

2.15.5. Outcomes for TORQUĒRE 'twist'

Morphologically rather than lexically, reflexes of 2nd-conj. TORQUĒRE 'twist' and its p.p. TORTU demonstrate even more variable remodeling of verbs across ROMANIA. Assuming simplification from [kw] to [k] in the infinitive, one may postulate a common Daco-Italo-Hispanic form. The Romanian reflex has undergone metaplasm to the 3rd conjugation in infin. *a toarce* 'spin thread' and for its past participle has developed sigmatic *tors* (and *întors* 'turned'), though archaic *tort* is attested; farther west, Fri. *stuars* has the same sigmatic marking. Like Romanian, Italian moved the verb into the 3rd conjugation as *torcere*, but kept the old p.p. *torto*. Along the Alps, Ladin *stort* and Enga. *stüert* also remain tautic athematic. Like the two great eastern

---

[86] LAMBERE 'lick' was first used in reference to dogs, later to people. LINGERE 'lick' also meant 'feed on, gloat over; lust after' and had an asigmatic desiderative LIGURRĪRE 'feel like licking' (Ernout and Meillet, 338, 360). Given the third sense of the simplex, one conjectures that LIGURRĪRE may not have been restricted to animal referents.

[87] Using Occam's razor, I must disagree with Meyer-Lübke's derivation of such verbs from unattested *LIGICARE (*REW* no. 5027)—presumably a non-nasal and suffixed variant of LINGERE—rather than from something like Germ. *lecken* 'lick.' From another Teutonic term, Frankish *lippa* 'lip,' comes Cat. *llepar* 'lick' (perhaps earlier 'slurp up') as well as the Fr. adj. *lippu* 'blubber-lipped' (*REW* no. 5075).

varieties of Romance, Catalan developed 3rd-conj. *tòrcer* with either a surviving rhizotonic p.p., *tort* (now also used adjectivally for 'bent, crooked'), or an arrhizotonic one, *torçut*, with the same root as that in present-tense forms. Spanish and Portuguese kept the infinitive in the 2nd(/3rd) conjugation as *torcer, trocer* but (predictably?) regularized the past participle to *torcido, trocido*, with the old past participle extant adjectivally in Sp. *tuerto* 'one-eyed' and Ptg. *torto*.

For infinitives, OFr. has early *tortre*, later *tordre* with voicing, apparently based on a 3rd-conj. variant with its root drawn from p.p. TORTU; a surviving noun *tordoir* 'rope-tightener; wringer' appears to come from the old 2nd-conj. infinitive. In OFr., this verb's innovative past participle could be either sigmatic *tors*, inspired no doubt by pret. *tors* < TORSĪ (still surviving adjectivally in a few phrases like *jambes torses* 'bandy legs'), or conservatively tautic athematic *tort* < TORTU, now used only as a noun meaning 'wrong.'[88] As past participles, both of these have since yielded to infinitive-based *tordu*, analogical with other regular 3rd-conj. forms, though Old French already had *tortu*. There have developed verbs from an assumed 1st-conj. variant in yod, which gave OIt. *torciare*, Cat. *trossar* 'draw in, tighten up' > Sp. *trozar*, and also Ptg. *trouser* 'wind threads around a spindle.' A diminutivized form of that verb yielded Fr. *tortiller* 'twist, twirl' (*REW* nos. 8798, 8803, 8804).

In a pattern seen across ROMANIA, eastern tongues have preserved or evolved rhizotonic past participles, and western tongues have evolved arrhizotonic ones. As for the consonant found after [r] in past-participial reflexes of TORTU, one may compare the [s] found in Rom. *tors*, Fri. *stuars*, and Cat. *torçut* with the [t] found in It. *torto* and Lad. *stort*, with the [d] found in ModFr. *tordu*, and with the [θ] found in standard Sp. *torcido*. Put another way, regularity of conjugation may have increased within a given language, but during a time of relative isolation each language went its separate way.

2.15.6. Outcomes for MULGERE 'milk'

Rivaling TORQUĒRE 'twist' in the diversity of its past-participial reflexes has been MULGERE 'milk,' which had a by-form MUNGERE in demotic Latin. The verb had two CL by-forms for its past participle: MULSU or MULCTU. Results differed across ROMANIA, with the verb dying out in parts of the west.

Helped no doubt by the sigmatic pf. MULSĪ, p.p. variant MULSU survived in Dacia to yield *muls*, also encountered in Surs. *muls*. Variant MULCTU survived on Sardinia to yield Log. *murtu* and also in the Tyrol to yield Lad. *mëut* or *mot*. A variant containing both a nasal marker and a sigmatic one lives on in Enga. *muns*. Std. It. *munto* appears to have the same demotic origin but has become tautic athematic, or might have syncopated from a rhizotonic thematic variant itself built on a nasal variant of the infectum stem.

---

[88] In what might be an instance of parallel evolution, Engl. *wrong* also used to mean 'twisted' Cf. *to wring* and Germ. *ringen* 'wrestle, strive.'

In western ROMANIA, where speakers tended to prefer arrhizotonic past participles, one has to suppose that an optionally prefixed 4th-conj. variant was the ancestor of Cat. *(es)munyit* and Ptg. *mungido* 'milked.' In French, the verb has been replaced by *traire* (p.p. *trait* < TRACTU 'drawn, pulled') and, these days, by 1st-conj. *tirer* 'pull' as well. In central-western Iberia, the verb has been replaced by Sp. *ordeñar*, Ptg. *ordenhar* with regular p.p.s *ordeñado*, *ordenhado* < ORDINĀTU 'set in order.' In the Romance far east, though, Rom. *a urdina* with p.p. *urdinat* still means 'prepare, arrange' (*REW* no. 6091).

2.15.7. Outcomes for VĪVERE 'live'

If infinitive reflexes of VĪVERE 'live' like It. *vivere*, Cat./OOc. *viure*, and Fr. *vivre* have held true to their 3rd-conj. origins in Latin, all three languages have nonetheless replaced the CL p.p. VĪCTU (long i) with variants of arrhizotonic innovations like It. *vissuto*, Cat. *viscut*, and Fr. *vécu* < *vescu*, with "extension of the -ŪTU suffix to the already sigmatic Latin perfect from VIXĪ" (Vincent 1988b, 297). For that verb, clearly, speakers in many areas preferred a doubly marked past participle.[89]

Not all did, however: present-tense stems serve for Fri. *vivût* and Olt. *vivuto*, while another Olt. form, *visso*, was built on the stem of pf. VĪXĪ (> It. *vissi*) with no theme vowel. In Spanish and Portuguese, the infin. *vivir* has gone over to the 4th conjugation and acquired a regular p.p. *vivido*. From the same stem, Romanian has evolved 1st-conj. *înviar* 'bring to life' (p.p. *înviat*), as it has evolved 1st-conj. *învolburar* 'overflow' as against CL 3rd-conj. VOLVERE 'roll.'

2.15.8. Old Sigmatic Participles

Reflexes of sigmatic VĪSU 'seen,' marked by both vowel lengthening and consonant change compared with 2nd-conj. VIDĒRE (pf. VĪDĪ), have thrived only in dialectal It. *viso*, Enga. *vis*, and the OFr. and OOc. by-forms *vis*. Another innovation in Late Latin or Proto-Romance, a sigmatic-tautic variant of merely sigmatic VĪSU, might well have been syncopated from CL VĪSĬTU 'inspected' (Tekavčić, 436). In any event, something like it has yielded It./Sp./Ptg. *visto*, Cat. *vist*, and another OOc. by-form *vist*. Only in Rom. *văzut*, Arom. *vidzută*, Lad. *vedù*, Fri. *viodût*, Surs. *viu*, Fr. *vu*, and in by-forms like It. *veduto* and OOc. *vezut* have reflexes of an infectum-based variant in -ŪTU imposed themselves.

Apparent reflexes of the old p.p. DĒFĒNSU 'fought off' remain in It. *difeso*, Enga. *defais*, and Cat. *defès* (less common than *defensat*), as also in OSp. and ModPtg. *defeso* 'forbidden,' so that regular 2nd- or 3rd-conj. innovations are

---

[89] In the unlikely event that this rhizotonic athematic p.p. had survived in far northern Gaul, it would have given OFr. [vit], homophonous with the noun *vit* 'penis,' and then ModFr. [vi], homophonous with the noun *vie* < VĪTA 'life.'

current only in Fri. *difindût*, Lad. *deféndù*, OOc. *defendut*, and Fr. *défendu*, and to be sure Sp./Ptg. *defendido* 'fought off.' Even where arrhizotonic past participles prevail, noun reflexes have survived to indicate an earlier sigmatic state of affairs: OFr. *defois* 'forbidden place,' OCat. *devesa* along with Sp. *dehesa* '[fenced-in] pasture,' and Ptg. *defesa* or *devesa* 'pasture; forest' (*REW* no. 2518).

For reflexes of TENDERE 'stretch' and FINDERE 'split,' certain survivals endure from p.p.s TĒNSU and FISSU. Thus Rom. *întins*, Arom. *teasă*, It. (s)*teso*, and Enga. *tais*, all from TĒNSU, remain rhizotonic and sigmatic; compare Sp. adj. *tieso* 'stiff.' Likewise sigmatic are Surs. *fess*, Cat. *fes*, and an old-fashioned It. by-form *fesso*. In Catalan, one should be no more surprised at the survival of sigmatic *fes* than at that of *entès* 'understood' < INTĒNSU, *encès* 'lit' < INCĒNSU, or *tos* 'shorn' < TŌNSU.

For reflexes of CURRERE 'run,' reflexes of the old sigmatic p.p. CURSU have lasted across eastern Romance in e.g. Rom. *curs*, It. *corso*, and a Lad. by-form *cors*; At the eastern end of Gallo-Italian, Istriano has sigmatic-tautic *koresto*. Going its own way as usual, Sardinian has kept or evolved tautic athematic *curtu*. Though Old Occitan still had sigmatic *cors*, speakers farther west have preferred arrhizotonic past participles for this verb, giving e.g. Fr. *couru*, Cat. *corregut*, and Sp. *corrido* (see §2.14.5).

2.15.9. New Sigmatic Participles

Though most often encountered in Dacia, sigmatic past participles could replace other types of rhizotonics at least as far as the Pyrenees. In fact, certain verbs in Latin had acquired sigmatic past participles through time. As noted in §2.12, it is likely that old *MANTU 'stayed' was remade as MĀNSU, old *MERTU 'sunk' as MERSU, and old *PULTU 'throbbed' as PULSU.

During LL times, CL rhizotonic ABSCONDITU 'hidden' was remade as attested ABSCŌNSU, which yielded Rom. *ascuns* and Olt. *ascoso*. Still current in bookish registers, *ascoso* has been prefixed and suffixed to give more common It. *nascosto*, somewhat resembling OOc. *escos(t)*. Other sigmatic reshapings in LL were based on finite perfectum stems. Thus LL FARSU 'stuffed' and SARSU 'repaired' look little like CL FARTU and SARTU but much like pfs. FARSĪ and SARSĪ. Moreover, the LL p.p. INDULSU 'been forbearing,' for a slot evidently left empty in CL, borrowed the sigmatic marking of pf. INDULSĪ (Ronjat, 217).

Two other new sigmatics might have arisen in Italy but, if so, spread beyond its confines. Replacing direct-suffixation MŌTU 'moved' was sigmatic It. *mosso*, with siblings in Enga. *moss* (Ræto-Romance) and in Vaud *mosu* (Franco-Provençal). Replacing rhizotonic thematic PERDITU 'lost' was an It. by-form *perso*, with siblings in Enga. *pers*, Surs. *piars*, and an OFr. by-form *pers*.

Not from p.p. SUBMONITU 'reminded, warned' but from a sigmatic variant came OOc. *somo(n)s* > OFr. *semons* 'urged,' infinitivized in its turn to give

ModFr. *semoncer* 'rebuke' (p.p. *semoncé*) and nominalized to give the Engl. law term *summons* 'demand for a witness to appear in court.'

In CL, 2nd-conj. PĀRĒRE 'appear' had a *u*-stem pf. PĀRUĪ and another rhizotonic thematic p.p. PĀRITU. Sardinian (Log.) *pássidu* remains rhizotonic but has acquired sigmatic marking. Italian kept the infinitive in the same class, giving *parere* (like OOc. *parer*) with pret. *parvi* < PĀRUĪ and new sigmatic p.p. *parso*, though in OIt. *paruto* also occurred. Istriano *paresto* has the *-sto* ending commonly seen on past participles in Gallo-Italian dialects across the Veneto and also farther south on the peninsula.

Speakers in parts of ROMANIA acquired new sigmatic past participles; speakers in other parts eliminated many or most of the ones they had. For an attempt to explain why both developments occurred where they did, see §5.5.

2.15.10. Outcomes for Learnèd Revivals of CĒDERE 'go, yield'

What has happened to the infinitival and past-participial morphology of a verb revived across Romance? A direct descendant of 3rd-conj. CĒDERE 'go, yield,' with sigmatic pf. CESSĪ and p.p. CESSU, survives only in the Log. adjectivized p.p. *akessidu* 'tired' (< *ADCESSITU?) and in a few dialects from southern Italy (*REW* no. 1798).

Elsewhere, the revived verb's past participles have almost all been remade asigmatically and arrhizotonically, but in different ways. French has 1st-conj. *céder* (p.p. *cédé*), Spanish has 2nd-/3rd-conj. *ceder* (p.p. *cedido*), and Catalan has 4th-conj. *cedir* (p.p. *cedit*).[90] Standard Italian has 3rd-conj. *cedere* (p.p. *ceduto*), with a conservative p.p. variant *-cesso* used only in certain prefixed compounds like *concedere* 'grant' (p.p. *concesso*); yet *recedere* 'recede' and *eccedere* 'go too far' have the *-uto* p.p.s *receduto, ecceduto*, while *retrocedere* 'demote' has the p.p. by-forms *retrocesso* and *retroceduto*.

All of the above verbs appear at least semilearnèd. However, Ladin has unclassical-looking *zedù* 'stopped.' Meanwhile, the old p.p. CESSU served as the stem of frequentative CESSĀRE 'give over, leave off,' surviving as It. *cessare*, Fr. *cesser*, Oc./Cat./Ptg. *cessar* and Sp. *cesar* 'stop, cease.'

Why did revivifiers of the verb CĒDERE assign the revivals to the classes they did? How was the choice motivated within the history of each language? I plead ignorance. And here I have been dealing with choices made in a mere handful of literary standards.

2.15.11. Flawless Hindsight

Upon reviewing all outcomes gathered in §2.15.1–§2.15.10, I am unable after the fact to discover what has swayed speakers to keep or shift the morphology of each form in the daughter languages of Latin. I am especially mindful of

---

[90] Here etymological wariness appears eminently justified. A straight reflex of CĒDERE 'yield, go' would have given early OFr. **ceidre* [tsei̯ðrə] then ModFr. **çoire* [swar]. Romanian has adapted the Fr. 1st-conj. version of the verb to produce *a ceda*, with p.p. *cedat*.

the fate of SANCĪRE 'bless,' which speakers could have reshaped along 4th-conj. lines, and did, but which they ended up forsaking for another, compound verb.[91]

How much success, I wonder, would a Roman grammarian have had at accounting before the fact for these outcomes? Of course, Rome fell long before the advent of scientific linguistics. All right, then: today, how much success would a Romance linguist have at telling p.p. fortunes for the next thousand years? I would settle for a hundred, or ten.

Alas, we cannot live our dreams. I am content to unearth old waterways along which analogy has already flowed. I can never find out how analogy will flow again, or why it should flow as it will.[92]

2.16. THE HERITAGE OF LATIN

From the time Latin came into being along the Tiber until it changed enough across southwestern Europe to be called Romance, fifty generations of speakers of the language had been shaping in successive stages, out of a verbal adjective that played a small part in their syntax, a past participle that played a large part and that plays a still larger one now.

Without knowing it, speakers also chose which Latin verbs would live and which would die. They fought the ravages of phonetic wear-and-tear by replacing some short verbs and by making others longer than before. They switched some verbs into more productive conjugations, namely the 1st and 4th. They used past-participial roots as models for whole paradigms of verbs that survived. They smoothed out roughnesses of conjugation in verbs they used less often but kept a few, and evolved more, in verbs they used all the time. Almost everywhere, they remodeled their old rhizotonic thematic past participles ending in -ĬTU; everywhere in what might still have borne traces of a Sprachbund, they remodeled most of their old tautic athematic forms in -CTU. Almost everywhere, they reduced allomorphy across whole verbs by using more past participles in -ĀTU, -ŪTU, -ĪTU to accompany perfect-preterits in -ĀVĪ, -UĪ, -ĪVĪ and infinitives in -ĀRĒ, -ĒRĒ or ´-ERE, and -ĪRE. Especially in the east, they reduced allomorphy within the past system by using more past participles in -SU to accompany perfect-preterits in -SĪ.

All in all, speakers of Late Latin and Proto-Romance widened the scope of certain past-participial types while narrowing the scope of others or allowing them to fade from the mind. In somewhat divergent ways since Romance began, speakers of each language have further reduced allomorphy in past participles for verbs they have kept alive until today.

---

[91] The semantics of It. *sancire* 'ratify, establish' (p.p. *sancito*) suggest semilearnèd revival.

[92] To many, the observations made in §2.15 must sound antiquated as a minuet. Readers will have found that historical linguistics arouses little interest these days among trend setters or trend followers, probably because work in the field requires ratiocination rather than assertion. For reasons behind a decline in the status accorded to etymology, see Malkiel 1993b, 135–42.

3

Past Participles in Eastern Romance

> He decided that they were speaking a late form of
> Vulgar Latin, rather more than halfway from the
> language of Cicero to that of Dante. He had never
> even tried to speak this hybrid. But by dredging his
> memory for his knowledge of sound changes, he
> could make a stab at it: *Omnia Gallia e devisa en
> parte trei, quaro una encolont Belge, alia...*
>
> L. Sprague de Camp, *Lest Darkness Fall*[1]

3.0. OVERVIEW

In this study, Eastern Romance is taken as including Daco-Romanian, Aromanian, and Meglenoromanian in the Balkans; Istro-Romanian and Vegliote in Dalmatia; Italian in its Tuscan, central-southern, and deep-southern varieties as well as its northern varieties termed Gallo-Italian; and finally Sardinian. Phonologically, this last language is often classed with western Romance on grounds like retention of final [s] and lenition of intervocalic stops (in most dialects), but, morphologically, Sardinian past participles have more in common with ones found in Sicily, Calabria, and Apulia than with ones found in Spain and France, or for that matter along the Po valley. For geographic convenience, this chapter also examines past participles from various Gallo-Italian dialects, including Istriano, spoken north of the La Spezia–Rimini line and south of the Alps.

In this chapter and the next, orthography generally follows the conventions observed in published materials. To promote readability without sacrificing clarity, though, many nonstandard forms appear stripped of their diacritical adornments and are spelled approximately as they would be in Romanian, Italian, or French.

---

[1] The novel being set in Rome in 535 CE, one may doubt particulars in that up-to-date rendition of Cæsar's Latin—preservation of intervocalic [mn] and final [nt] clusters, as well as relative pronoun *quaro* 'of which/whom,' pronoun *alia* '[an]other,' and old-style word order—without doubting its plausibility in general. While Latin was gradually turning into Romance, those who knew how went on trying to write if not speak by CL norms.

Here and there in Chapters 3 and 4, I mention adjectives and nouns that have the same morphology as past participles, old or new. Such double-barreled forms—mostly sigmatic innovations in Romanian, inheritances in Italian, relics in French and Spanish—are discussed only briefly, as part of the coverage of major languages.

3.0.1. Verbs in the East, Center, and West

If, as noted below, dozens of common verbs in Latin have vanished from Romania but been kept in Italy, Iberia, and France, perhaps a score have lived on only in far eastern and far western ROMANIA. Others survive in the far east alone. In calculating rates of retention, one should look back at the fourth century CE, when Lyon and Milan became the largest cities in the Latin-speaking half of the empire. Apparently, speakers in and around those cities started using old verbs in new senses or stopped using verbs maintained beyond the Pyrenees and the Carpathians.

Lexically though not phonologically, ROMANIA may thus be split into a central Gallo-Italian area, a western wing in Iberia, and an eastern wing in Dacia. I illustrate with a few past participles. Instead of innovative It. *trovato* and Fr. *trouvé* < *TROPATU 'troped,' Rom. *aflat* 'found' matches Ptg. *achado*, Sp. *hallado* < AFFLĀTU 'sniffed out.' Instead of It. *bollito* or Fr. *bouilli* 'boiled' < BULLĪTU 'bubbled,' Rom. *fiert* 'boiled' matches Ptg. *fervido* and Sp. *hervido* (no CL p.p. but cf. infin. by-forms FERVERE and FERVĒRE 'boil'). Instead of It. *domandato* or Fr. *demandé* 'asked' < DĒMANDĀTU 'entrusted, committed,' Rom. *pețit* 'asked to marry, proposed' matches Sp. *pedido* 'asked, demanded, proposed' < PETĪTU 'sought, asked for.' Reflexes of TRĀJECTU 'crossed' survive (as past participles) only in Rom. *trecut* and Ptg. *tragido* 'passed, gone,' each of them remade arrhizotonically in a different way, and apparently also in Rom. *petrecut* 'spent' < PER + TRĀJECTU, a form suggestive of throwing one's money away. Another past participle, Rom. *inceput* 'begun,' represents a rare survival of the root of INCEPTU 'taken in hand, begun,' though it too has been remade arrhizotonically.

Also vanishing at the center but remaining at the periphery was a regularized variant of SUBIGERE 'drive up from below; break up soil, work at.' Across ROMANIA, probable reflexes of the verb are attested only in rustic Rom. *a soage* 'knead, shape loaves' without any past participle, and in Sp. *sobar*, Ptg. *sovar* 'knead' with p.p.s *sobado, sovado* (*REW* no. 8362).[2]

Reflexes of PŌNERE 'put, set' (p.p. POSITU > POSTU) and MITTERE 'let go, send' (p.p. MISSU) provide a less neat example of innovation at the hub of Romance and conservatism at the rims. Rom. *a pune* matches Sp. *poner* and Ptg. *pôr* in keeping the old sense 'put,' but It. *porre* has been restricted to the

---

[2] No past participle is given under *a soage* in vol. 10 of the Romanian Academy's dictionary (1992 ed.). In view of Magyar *szoggatani*, it is unclear whether the verb comes from Latin. By analogy with, say, infin. *a suge* 'suck' and its p.p. *supt*, one could hypothesize a p.p. *sopt* 'kneaded' for *a soage*. That form would not be popularly recognized (E. Vrabie, p.c.).

literary register, Fr. *pondre* to the sense 'lay eggs.' Elsewhere, in central ROMANIA It. *mettere* and Fr. *mettre* have shifted to mean 'put,' while Sp. *meter* has narrowed to the sense 'put into,' and Rom. *-mite* 'send' has been restricted to compounds (Ernout and Meillet, 407, 490, 520).

At times, morphological innovations east and west have been similar as well. Like Cat. *mossegat*, Rom. *muşcat* 'bitten' comes from a long-form variant of the sigmatic p.p. MORSU remade into the 1st conjugation; cf. also It. *morsicato* 'nibbled' and Sic. *muzzikatu* 'bitten.' Moreover, Rom. *cernut* 'sifted' matches Cat. *cernut* 'idem,' neither of them from CRĒTU but cf. infin. CERNERE.

Other resemblances between past participles in Dacia and Iberia may have come into being by chance. Rom. *venit* and Sp. *venido* 'come,' Rom. *suferit* and Sp. *sofrido* 'suffered,' along with Rom. *murit* and Ptg. *morrido* 'died' show that languages at both peripheries of Romance have regularized their past participles for reflexes of the 4th-conj. infin. VENĪRE and for 4th-conj. variants of suppletive SUFFERRE and deponent MORĪ.

3.0.2. Romanian Verbs

Those at home on one branch of the Romance tree will remark that verbs known to them may be lacking from a second branch but may reappear on a third branch or a fourth. Yet certain verbs evolved in Romanian and nowhere else among major Romance languages.

Among originally prefixed verbs, Romanian has 1st-conj. *a împătra* 'be taken in by something' < IMPETRĀRE 'get by asking,' *a împuta* 'reproach' < IMPUTĀRE 'reckon as,' and, deriving from an adverb-plus-verb combination, *a îndemna* 'spur, incite' < INDE MINĀRE 'drive from there.' Note also 4th-conj. *a copleşi* 'overwhelm' from a reshaping of COMPLEXĀRĪ 'contain, constrain' (*REW* nos. 2102, 4306a, 4324, 4371a). Rather than a reflex of DĒFENDERE 'fight off,' Romanian has *a apăra* < ADPARĀRE 'arm, get ready'; rather than a reflex of MERĒRE 'earn, deserve,' Romanian has *a câstiga* < CASTIGĀRE 'set right; chasten' (Iliescu, 113). Merit appears to have been hard-won in Dacia.

Certain other verbs in the Romanian wordstock are lacking from standard Italian, Spanish, and French, yet shared with other languages or dialects like Friulian, Neapolitan, Abruzzese, and Engadin. One may compare Fri. *discanta* and Rom. *a discînta* 'cast a spell over' < DĒ + EX + CANTĀRE 'sing,' together with Fri. *sesela* and Rom. *a secera* 'cut, harvest' from a 1st-conj. denominal based on SĪCĪLE 'sickle.' One may compare Rom. *a (se) însura*, Neap. *nzurare*, Abru. *nzurar* 'get married' < IN + UXOR 'wife' + -ĀRE. Finally, Enga. *incler* and Rom. *a înţelege* 'understand' are practically the sole survivals across ROMANIA of the verb INTELLEGERE 'perceive, become aware, know thoroughly' (Du Nay, 40–41).

3.1. EVIDENCE FROM DACO-ROMANIAN

Aside from Moldavian and related dialects within Daco-Romanian, there exist or did exist several other varieties of Balkan Romance in enclaves of the peninsula between Trieste in northeastern Italy and Salonika in northeastern Greece. Past participles in those enclaves are reviewed in §§3.2–3.4.

3.1.0. Preliminaries

Despite replacement of vocabulary on a large scale, Romanian remains morphologically recognizable as a neo-Latin tongue. Regular masc.sg. past participles end in *-at* for descendants of the 1st conjugation, in *-ut* for descendants of the 2nd and some of the 3rd, and in *-it* for most descendants of the 4th, with a variant *-ît* [ɨt] usual when the root of a verb in this last class ends in [r]. Thus, from the 1st conjugation come *cântat* 'sung,' *mâncat* 'eaten,' and *rugat* 'prayed' (infins. *a cânta, a mânca, a ruga*). From the 2nd conjugation come *căzut* 'fallen' and *tăcut* 'been silent' (infins. *a cădea, a tăcea*). From the 3rd conjugation come *cerut* 'asked for' and *pascut* 'fed, kept' (infins. *a cere, a paşte*). From the 4th conjugation come *dormit* 'slept,' *metit* 'measured,' and *nutrit* 'fed' (infins. *a dormi, a meti, a nutri*).

From the earliest attestations, such have been the patterns followed by speakers of Romanian. As transcribed from the Cyrillic, a letter from the boyar Neacşu of Câmpulung in 1521 contains the following past participles: *auzit* 'heard,' *dat* 'given,' *dus* 'taken away,' *eşit* 'gone out,' *trecut* 'passed,' *văzut* 'seen,' and *venit* 'come.' A sigmatic was seen in *prins* 'taken, conveyed,' a labialized outcome of [kt] in *înţelept* 'understood,' now only adjectival (Sampson, 207). Except for *eşit*, now *ieşit*, all are identical to modern forms.

3.1.1. Borrowing, Retention, Revival

While keeping its own inventory of verbs derived from Latin, standard Daco-Romanian has borrowed numerous verbs from tongues spoken nearby and has adapted them to the conjugational system inherited from Latin: *a citi* 'read,' *a omorî* 'kill,' and *a plăti* 'pay' from Slavic, *a sosi* 'arrive' and *a lipsi* 'be missing' from Greek, *a hotărî* 'decide' and *a se întâlni* 'meet' from Hungarian all belong to the 4th conjugation. In the same way, *a bucura* 'enjoy' from Albanian has been fitted into the 1st conjugation (Cioranescu, passim).

Besides borrowing verbs from outside, speakers in Dacia abandoned verbs assumed to have existed in Late Latin because they survived almost everywhere else: past participles like APERTU 'opened,' freq. JECTĀTU 'thrown' have been replaced by *deschis, coborît*. It may dishearten any teacher to realize that the Romanian regular 1st-conj. p.p. *învăţat* 'taught' ultimately comes from VITIU 'blemish, flaw.' Among LL/PR past participles that became 1st-conj. verb roots (§2.11), Rom. *uitat* 'forgotten; looked at' < *OBLITATU thrives, but bookish *uzat* 'worn-out' represents a nineteenth-century borrowing from French rather than a survival of *USATU 'used,' and nothing like *AUSATU 'dared' or AUDĒRE for that matter seems ever to have passed current in the far east of Romance.

Efforts by nineteenth-century scholars to revive Latin verbs long defunct, often in a French or Italian guise, have enlarged the learnèd lexicon. Certain revivals, with regular past participles, have become standard among ordinary speakers today.[3]

Still, in Ernout and Meillet's *Dictionnaire étymologique de la langue latine*, one encounters the tag "panroman, sauf roumain" for entry after entry. Verbs thus marked include 1st-conj. APPELLĀRE 'call, name,' ERRĀRE 'wander,' NEGĀRE 'deny, refuse,' ORNĀRE 'equip, garnish,' LL PAUSĀRE 'stop, halt,' PLŌRĀRE 'lament, weep,' PRÆSTĀRE 'furnish, lend,' PŪRGĀRE 'cleanse, purify' and TEMPTĀRE 'grope; test, try'; 2nd-conj. MOVĒRE 'move,' NOCĒRE 'harm,' SOLĒRE 'do often,' and VALĒRE 'be strong, be worth'; 3rd-conj. FALLERE 'trick, fail,' FINDERE 'split,' MOLERE 'grind,' reshaped SEQUĪ 'follow,' and TREMERE 'tremble'; and 4th-conj. POLĪRE 'clean, buff.'

Many of the Latin verbs that do survive exist only in variants with prefixes, or prefixoids. Most popular is *în-* < IN-, appearing in e.g. *a încinge* 'gird' < IN + CINGERE and *a întinge* 'dip' < IN + TINGERE 'dye.' Also popular is *z-* or *s-* < EX-, appearing in e.g. *a zbura* 'fly, glide' < EX + VOLĀRE.[4]

At times, the disappearance of verbs may plausibly be attributed to homonymic clash. Thus, both regularly developing 1sg. pres.indic AMŌ 'like, love' and irregularly developing 1sg. pres.indic. HABEŌ 'have' would have come out *a m* in Romanian. Only the second survives, the less common verb passing out of use. (It was replaced by Slavic-derived *iubi*.) Given after the fact, explications such as these seem difficult to prove; see §2.15 for more such.

3.1.2. Verb Morphology: General Considerations

Like other Romance languages, Romanian bears witness to LL/PR regularization of verb paradigms. There have developed regular 1st-conj. p.p.s like *crǎpat* 'burst,' *frecat* 'rubbed,' *sunat* 'rang,' *tunat* 'thundered' ≠ CREPĬTU, FRICTU (also FRICĀTU), SONĬTU, TONĬTU. There have developed regular 4th-conj. p.p.s like *acoperit* 'covered,' *fugit* 'fled,' *învertit* 'turned,' *rǎpit* 'seized,' *sorbit* 'swallowed' ≠ COOPERTU, FUGĬTU, VERSU, RAPTU, SORBĬTU. A trace of the old inchoative infix -SC- appears in *putrezit* 'rotted' (no CL p.p.). As they do elsewhere, past participles grouped under the 3rd

---

[3] See Mallinson, "Romanian," 415–18, for a fuller discussion of scholars' re-Latinization of the Dacian wordstock before and after Romania gained independence from the Turks in 1878.

[4] Being interpreted, Ernout and Meillet's tag "panroman, sauf roumain" [pan-Romance except Romanian] means that a word has died out east of the Adriatic. Of 305 CL p.p. slots traced in Appendix 2 of this book, fewer than half (146) survive in Romanian. For a discussion of dialect geography within ROMANIA, especially Bartoli's unearthing of lexical similarities between Ibero-Romance and Daco-Romance missing from the Franco–Catalano–Italian center, see Malkiel 1993b, 84–94.

conjugation evince the least predictability: they may reflect either forms from Classical Latin, already assignable to several classes, or forms originating in Late Latin or Proto-Romance (Pop, 264).[5]

Contrary to a trend toward arrhizotonicity in infinitives throughout western ROMANIA, above all in Portugal and Spain, but consistent with a trend the other way observed in parts of southern Italy, some speakers of Daco-Romanian are tending to shift 2nd-conj. infinitives into the 3rd conjugation, so that e.g. *a putea* 'be able' is being replaced by *a poate* (Mallinson, 405). The effects, if any, of that shift on past participles remain uncertain, as both types of infinitive take the same type of regular past participle in -*ut*..

3.1.3. Past Participles in −*ut*

As happened from Italian through French and Occitan to Catalan, and probably in Spanish and Portuguese for a time, Romanian verbs in the 2nd and 3rd conjugations tended to acquire past participles in reflexes of -ŪTU, a fairly rare type in Classical Latin (see §2.14).

Such participles now include not only inherited *bătut* 'beaten' < BATTŪTU, *cusut* 'sewn' < CŌNSŪTU, and *futut* 'fucked' < FUTŪTU, but also later innovations like *băut* 'drunk' ≠ LL BIBITU and *părut* 'appeared' ≠ CL PĀRITU, which replaced rhizotonic thematics. Others in that class—*durut* 'hurt,' *putut* 'been able,' *vrut* 'wanted'—were past-participially defective in Latin, but *născut* 'born' has come to replace archaic *nat* < NĀTU, which had the ORom. sense 'person.' Today, infin. *a vrea* 'want' (p.p. *vrut*) has a 4th-conj. by-form *a voi* (p.p. *voit*) used mainly in Wallachia; it may derive either from the Romance noun *voie* 'will' or from a Slavic verb *voliti* 'want' (Pop, 273).

Certain lexical items look less than transparent. Rom. *mărunt*, the adjectival reflex of MINŪTU 'lessened,' derives from something like *MINUNT, perhaps influenced by MINIMU 'least,' and has passed out of the -ŪTU class; speakers feel nothing verbal in the word today (E. Vrabie, p.c.). Bookish *acut* 'acute' does not constitute a survival of ACŪTU 'sharp[ened].'

Other standard -ŪTU past participles today, such as *avut* 'had,' *vândut* 'sold,' *crezut* 'believed,' *pierdut* 'lost,' and *tăcut* 'been silent' can hardly have come straight from rhizotonic thematic HABITU, VENDITU, CRĒDITU, PERDITU, and TACITU, even if most such -ŪTU types are or were paralleled farther west. Likewise, *ţinut* 'held' and *ţesut* 'woven' cannot come from rhizotonic athematic TENTU or TEXTU. Nor can *crescut* 'grown' or *cunoscut* 'known,' forms with an [sk] infix, have derived from perfect stems seen in CRĒVĪ and COGNŌVĪ but rather from present-tense stems seen in CRĒSCŌ and COGNOSCŌ, plus the 2nd-/3rd-conj. ending -ŪTU. A "regular" 2nd-conj. p.p. has been remade in *umplut* 'filled' ≠ IMPLĒTU; for reflexes of the same

---

[5] According to spelling changes recently decreed by the Romanian Academy, the high central vowel [ɨ] is to be consistently written *â*, except in the prefix *în*- and in endings for certain 4th-conj. verbs.

verb farther west, compare the Italian by-forms *empiuto* and *empito* but Fr. *(r)empli*, Sp. *henchido*.

In Romanian, current past participles like *cerut* 'asked' and *văzut* 'seen' must come from present-based variants in -ŪTU rather than from QUÆSĪTU and VĪSU or even assumed variants that gave rise to forms current in It. *chiesto* or OSp. *quisto* 'sought' and Sp./It. *visto* 'seen.' The existence of dialectal allegro forms like *văst* 'seen,' *căst* 'fallen,' and *șest* 'sat' (Pop, 264)— suggestive of Cat. *vist* 'seen' or *post* 'set, laid' and It. *rimasto* 'stayed' and *nascosto* 'hidden'—may imply that such regularization as now prevails was achieved in the fairly recent past (see §3.1.6).

3.1.4. Other Kinds of Arrhizotonic Past Participles

Though often close to forms found farther west, Romanian past participles have their own distinctiveness. Their most striking quirk may have resulted from mere phonological conditioning. Floating in a Slavic sea, descendants of Dacians have evolved a kind of arrhizotonic past participle marked by a distinctive high-central tonic vowel [ɨ], conceivably borrowed from Slavic,[6] as in Slavic-derived *omorît* 'killed' and also *urît* 'hated < LL/PR *HORRITU 'bristled, been rough' for the verb HORRĒRE with no CL p.p. (Mallinson, 403, 406). The phoneme [ɨ] also figures in related words, such as *omorâtor* 'killer' and (I suppose) *urât* 'ugly' but, oddly, not in *ură* 'hatred.'

Two further morphological features illustrate the distinctiveness of Romanian. Other major Romance languages have kept reflexes of FACTU 'done/made.' For that high-frequency past participle, Romanian stands alone in preferring regularized *făcut*, with rhizotonic *fapt* < FACTU extant in the language only as a noun meaning 'deed.' The only widely spoken Romance language to retain in *a şti* a reflex of 4th-conj. SCĪRE 'know' (though cf. Log. Sard. *iskire*), Romanian has expanded its reflex of that verb's regular p.p. SCĪTU. Remade *ştiut* 'known' is the only past participle of a 4th-conj. verb to belong to the -ŪTU class (Pop, 286), but it keeps a morphological trace of its origins: absolutely regular *ştit* never evolved. Regularization has its limits.

If *a lua* 'take' < LEVĀRE 'lift' (with p.p. *luat*) has stayed in the same class but shifted semantically like Vegl. *levur* 'take' and Sp. *llevar* 'carry, bring, take'—cf. Engl. slang *lift* 'steal'—certain verbs in Dacia as elsewhere have undergone metaplasm through time. For instance, all surviving reflexes of Latin inchoatives in -ĒSCERE have moved from the 3rd to the 4th conjugation, so that e.g. *a numi* 'name' comes from a variant of 1st-conj. NŌMINĀRE.[7] New past-participial members of the 1st conjugation include *plouat* 'rained' (no CL p.p., infin. PLUERE), perhaps based on the noun *ploaie* 'rain,' as against 2nd-/3rd-conj. It. *piovuto*, Fr. *plu*, Cat. *plogut* and regular

---

[6] Although Russian has [ɨ] as a phoneme (written ы), no South Slavic language does.

[7] All other Romance reflexes of NŌMINĀRE 'name' have stayed in the 1st conjugation, from *numerari* in "Macedonian" [viz., Aromanian not Slavic Macedonian] through *lumenare* in Logudorese Sardinian to *nomear* in Portuguese (*REW* no. 5950).

non-*ar*-verb Sp. *llovido,* Ptg. *chovido.* Moreover, Rom. 1st-conj. *strâmtat* 'narrowed' has been based on *strâmt* 'narrow,' itself from a nasal variant of STRICTU (cf. infin. STRINGERE, pf. STRĪNXĪ) that lives on adjectivally. Rom. *strâmt* contrasts with non-nasal It. *stretto,* Fr. *étroit,* Cat. *estret,* Sp. *estrecho,* and Ptg. *estreito* 'narrow,' but cf. Olt. *strinto,* Lad. *strent,* Log. *istrintu* 'idem,' all with infectum [n] (*REW* no. 8305). Explanations for irregular Rom. *fost* 'been' are reviewed in §2.7.

Among neologisms, *cedat* 'yielded' has been inspired by Fr. *cedé,* as has *divizat* 'divided' by *divisé.* They indicate no survival of CESSU or DĪVĪSU, which owing to their sigmaticism could have been expected to survive in Dacia if anywhere (see §2.15.10). Rustic speakers do however have prefixed *purces* 'begun' < PRŌCESSU 'gone ahead; turned out.'

New past participles in the 4th conjugation include bookish *oferit* and popular *suferit* ≠ OBLĀTU, SUBLĀTU. As *suferit* 'suffered' presupposes a 4th-conj. reshaping of SUFFERRE, the p.p. *prânzit* 'lunched' ≠ PRĀNSU presupposes a 4th-conj. reshaping of PRANDERE. At least four other past participles in *-it,* namely *ferit* 'forbidden,' archaic *incarit* 'warmed oneself,' still current *încălzit* 'warmed up,' and *înflorit* 'bloomed' have evolved for local reflexes of FERĪRE 'hit,' CALĒRE 'be warm,' and FLORĒRE 'bloom,' verbs past-participially defective in Latin.

3.1.5. Rhizotonic Past Participles, Especially Sigmatics

Among rhizotonic past participles, Romanian has kept or evolved a number in [pt]. Those partly labialized from [kt] include *copt* 'baked' < COCTU 'cooked,' *fript* 'roasted, fried' < FRĪCTU, and, almost uniquely, *supt* 'sucked' < SUCTU (but cf. OSard. *suttu,* Elban *sutto* 'idem'). Those still with [pt] include *rupt* 'torn' < RUPTU 'broken' and arch. *scriptu* 'written' < SCRĪPTU. Most parallel Italian past participles in [t:] like *cotto* 'cooked,' *fritto* 'fried,' *rotto* 'broken,' and *scritto* 'written.'

Among the few other tautic athematic participles are *fiert* 'boiled,' perhaps from a late innovation in *-ĪTU* (no CL p.p.); *frânt* 'broken,' from a nasalized variant of FRĀCTU 'shattered' like OFr. *fraint;* and nominalized, outdated *nat* 'person' < NĀTU 'born,' with an arrhizotonic replacing the old past participle.

3.1.5.1. Sigmatic Drift

In its retention or evolution of sigmatic past participles, Romanian outstrips any other Romance tongue. More than a few sigmatics come down straight from Latin, like *mers* 'gone, walked' < MERSU 'sunk,' *ucis* 'killed' < OCCĪSU, *prins* 'seized' < PREHĒNSU, *râs* 'laughed' < RĪSU, *rămas* 'stayed' < REMĀNSU, *şters* "wiped (off)' < EXTERSU, and *trimis* 'sent' < TRĀMISSU 'sent across.' Also inherited are *ars* 'burned' < ĀRSU, *deştins* 'gone down' < DĒSCĒNSU, and *muls* 'milked' < by-form MULSU.

At times, as with *ras* 'shaved' or *râs* 'laughed' or *ros* 'gnawn,' the Latin verbs had sigmatic perfects and sigmatic past participles both: pf. RĀSĪ and p.p. RĀSU, pf. RĪSĪ and p.p. RĪSU, pf. RŌSĪ and p.p. RŌSU. Thus one can scarcely know which was responsible for the current sigmatic past participle. Likewise, either a sigmatic pf. resembling EXCUSSĪ or a sigmatic p.p. resembling EXCUSSU 'shaken out, knocked away' may have lain behind modern *scos* 'taken out' (cf. It. *scosso* 'shaken') and its 3sg. aorist *scoase*. Probably both forms reinforced each other, promoting greater uniformity across the past system for other verbs as well.

Romanian has developed on its own a few dozen past participles ending in |s| (Mendeloff, 60). No doubt this trend started with analogical extension of sigmatic stems from the perfect (later preterit), locally termed "aorist." At times, as noted above, both perfect and past participle were sigmatic in Latin: modern 3sg. preterits like *arse* 'burned' < ĀRSIT, *merse* 'went, walked' < MERSIT 'sank,' *rase* 'shaved' < RĀSIT, *ucise* 'killed' < OCCĪSIT, *roase* 'gnawed' < RŌSIT, and *râse* 'laughed' < RĪSIT merely preserve the sigmatic tradition, and their stems match sigmatic past participles without final -*e* that likewise preserve the tradition.

A few aorists have clearly borrowed |s| from their past participles, at least judging by the CL norm: *răspunse* 'answered' ≠ RESPONDIT but cf. p.p. *răspuns* < RESPŌNSU. More often, the roots of sigmatic past participles have been borrowed from sigmatic perfects in Latin (Rosetti, 156). Examples most likely include metaphonic *pus* 'put' and *spus* 'said' based on the stem of pf. (EX)POSUĪ rather than that of p.p. (EX)POSITU.

Additional sigmatic past participles inspired by sigmatic perfects are *adjuns* 'arrived' based on ADJŪNXĪ not ADJŪNCTU, *dus* 'taken away' based on DŪXĪ not DUCTU 'led,' *distrus* 'destroyed' based on DĒSTRUXĪ not DĒSTRUCTU, *plâns* 'wept' based on PLĀNXĪ not PLĀNCTU, *tras* 'pulled' based on pf. TRĀXĪ rather than p.p. TRACTU, and *zis* 'said' based on pf. DĪXĪ rather than p.p. DICTU. Similarly, p.p. *dres* 'guided' has been based on pf. DĪRĒXĪ not p.p. DĪRĒCTU, though *drept* survives nominally (see §3.1.5.2). P.p. *atins* 'reached' has been based on a nasal and sigmatic variant of pf. ATTIGĪ not p.p. ATTĀCTU, for which cf. pres. ATTINGŌ.

Lacking evidence to the contrary, I like to date p.p. innovations as far back as possible. However, these sigmatic reshapings cannot all go back to Late Latin days in Dacia, north or south of the Danube. In Old Romanian, when final -*u* was still written, greater allomorphy used to prevail across the past system for such verbs (see Table 3–1, next page). Thus, the p.p. *scris* 'written' would seem to be based on pf. SCRĪPSĪ rather than p.p. SCRĪPTU, but cf. ORom. *scriptu*. The form *ales* 'chosen' also represents a fairly recent innovation, and so may *cules* 'gathered' given the related p.p.s ADLĒCTU and COLLĒCTU.[8] With better etymological justification, aorists for these Romanian verbs are equally sigmatic: the ones heard most often include 3sg. *puse* 'put' and *spuse* 'said' < (EX)POSUIT, *scrise* 'wrote' < SCRĪPSIT, *trase* 'pulled' < TRĀXIT, and *zise* 'said' < DĪXIT.

---

[8] Cf. the It. 3sg. prets. *colse* ≠ COLLĒGIT 'gathered,' *corse* ≠ CUCURRIT 'run,' *dolse* ≠ DOLUIT 'hurt,' *lesse* ≠ LĒGIT 'read,' and *volse* ≠ VOLVIT 'rolled.' For more such, see §3.5.3.2.

Table 3–1

New Sigmatic Past Participles in Romanian

CL perfect	CL past participle	LL/PR reshaping of pf.-p.p. stem?	Rom. past participle	but cf. ORom.
ALLĒGĪ	ALLĒCTU		ales	aleptu
ATTIGĪ	ATTĀCTU	*ATTINX-?	atins	—
COLLĒGĪ	COLLĒCTU		cules	culeptu
DĒSTRŪXĪ	DĒSTRUCTU	*DESTRUX-?	distrus	—
DĪRĒXĪ	DĪRĒCTU		dres	dreptu
DĪXĪ	DICTU	*DIX-?	zis	—
DŪXĪ	DUCTU	*DUX-?	dus	—
SCRĪPSĪ	SCRĪPTU		scris	scriptu
TORSĪ	TORTU		tors	tortu
TRĀXĪ	TRACTU		tras	traptu
ŪNXĪ	ŪNCTU		uns	untu

Scanty ORom. texts contain more survivals of tautic athematic past participles that have since gone sigmatic. Thus, *tors* 'spun thread' and *întors* 'turned,' apparently based on pf. TORSĪ not p.p. TORTU 'twisted,' have been innovated fairly recently, given ORom. *tortu*. Similarly, *uns* 'oiled' may resemble pf. ŪNXI´ more than it does p.p. ŪNCTU, but ORom. *untu* shows that that form too has been innovated. Again, such verbs usually have aorists as sigmatic as their past participles, as witness (3sg.) *drese, duse, mulse, (în)toarse, alese,* and *culese.* Former asigmatics are still to be found.

Among morphological oddities, the sigmatic p.p. *deschis* 'opened' has apparently been based on a sigmatic perfect built from DĒ + EX + CLAUSU 'un-dis-opened' instead of on the simple CL p.p. CLAUSU 'shut,' which itself was prefixed to give Rom. *închis* 'shut.' A more likely etymon was -CLŪSU, usable only in compounds under the CL norm. Thereafter, the stem of both *deschis* and *închis* underwent metaphony, the vowel in the penult of pf. CLAUSĪ rising to meet the high front vowel of its ultima, which then disappeared. In any event, both perfect and past participle were already sigmatic in Latin.

Since Rom. *curs* 'run' clearly comes from the stem of p.p. CURSU not pf. CUCURRĪ, the asigmatic CL perfect could have borne no responsibility for that Rom form. Yet the existence of pairs in Italian like 3sg. pret. *corse* and p.p. *corso* could suggest that the whole perfectum of CURRERE 'run' tended to be remade sigmatically in Late Latin or Proto-Romance, at least toward the east. Over time, such realignments could triumph because of their greater predictability across the perfectum.

3.1.5.2. Differentiation

During the past few centuries, sigmatics have been gaining ground. As mentioned in §3.1.5.1, the presence in old texts of tautic athematic p.p.s like *untu* 'oiled,' *tortu* 'twisted,' and *scriptu* 'written,' all now sigmatic in the standard, suggests that many such past participles have been remade fairly recently. Nowadays, certain old tautic athematic variants survive only as nouns: *unt* 'butter,' *fapt* 'deed,' *tort* 'tow, oakum.' Moreover, the coexistence of standard *spars* < SPARSU with dialectal *spart* 'split, cracked'—but cf. std. *spart* 'cracked,' purely adjectival—suggests that speakers of the standard have assigned one function to each variant. For more on [s]- [t] variance, see §6.5.

Romanians have differentiated adj. *strâmt* 'narrow' from p.p. *strâns* 'tightened, squeezed' but may optionally use the second form as an adjective meaning 'stingy'; the first is clearly closer to STRICTU, though with infectum nasality already present in pf. STRĪNXĪ. On that past participle has been built a verb with p.p. *strâmtat* 'squeezed, shrunk' (Marin and Rusnac, 234–35). Romanians have done so for adj. *înţelept* 'wise' versus p.p. *înţeles* 'understood,' the last also in use as a noun ('sense, meaning') but the first closer to p.p. INTELLĒCTU 'perceived.' Romanians have done so with two nouns: inherited *drept* 'law, right' (also adj. 'straight; true, fair') contrasts with p.p.-based *dres* 'mending, repairing' but also 'adulteration of wine; seasoning of borshch, usu. with sour cream.' Romanians may appear to have done so with noun *incintă* 'interior, compass' versus p.p. *încins* 'girded,' but the first, closer to CĪNCTU, has been borrowed from Fr. *enceinte* or perhaps It. *incinta* and has the same meaning. In such pairs, a morphological distinction mirrors a semantic one.[9]

Yet Romanians still tolerate a great deal of morphological bivalence: *fript* 'fried; a roast' serves as both past participle and noun, and *copt* 'cooked, baked; ripe, mellow' serves as both past participle and adjective. So do *deschis* 'opened; bright' and *închis* 'shut; dark-colored.'

3.1.5.3. Nouns from Past Participles

Somewhat as CL masc.nom.sg. past participles were often identical to 4th-decl. nouns, Romanian has spun off past participles as nouns, almost all of them masculine. These may be arrhizotonic, like 1st-conj.-style *tăiat* 'a cutting,' or

---

[9] Cf. std. It. *sparso* and an OIt. by-form *sparto,* competing for the same p.p. slot.

2nd-/3rd-conj.-style *şezut* 'buttocks,' or 4th-conj.-style *venit* 'income, revenue.' They may be tautic athematic, like multivalent *copt* 'baking' and *fript* 'frying' above. As noted in §3.1.8, many verbs draw upon "long infinitives" for their verbal nouns. Nevertheless, when a verb has a sigmatic past participle, any noun derived from that verb tends to be sigmatic.

Three such bivalent forms can be plausibly traced back to Latin: *răspuns* 'answer' < RESPŌNSU, *râs* 'laughter' < RĪSU, and *ras* 'a shave' < RĀSU. The p.p. ancestor of Rom. *mers* 'pace, gait' used to be marked in [s] but, like most, seems to have had no direct ancestor among Latin nouns.[10] Most probably, at times now unrecoverable, speakers of Romanian innovated most sigmatic nouns that are isomorphic with past participles.

Today, sigmatic nouns identical to past-participial innovations include *cules* 'gathering,' *dus* 'going,' *înţeles* 'sense, meaning,' *plâns* 'weeping, tears,' and *tors* 'spinning.' Two agent nouns are *ajuns* 'arriviste, social climber' and a neologism *trimis* 'envoy, messenger,' the latter replacing Slavic-derived ORom. *sol* (cf. Russ. *slat'* 'send'). One noun still sigmatic but lacking the [t] of EXPOSITU 'put out' is feminine *spusă* 'hearsay, report,' generally said in the plural, *spuse*. Past participles occasionally pressed into service as nouns include *împuns* 'butted, rammed' and *străpuns* 'pierced, thrust through.'

I do not know whether masc. *curs* 'course, flow' represents a calque from French or Italian rather than a continuation in Dacia of CURSU 'run.' That sigmatic marking remains productive is shown by the new verb *a permite* 'allow,' whose sigmatic p.p. *permis* also serves as a noun meaning 'license'; cf. bivalent Fr. *permis*.

Several nominalized sigmatics may suffix -*oare*, giving *muls* or *mulsoare* 'milking,' *ninsoare* 'snow,' *prinsoare* 'bet, wager,' *scris* or *scrisoare* 'handwriting,' *tuns* or *tunsoare* 'shearing,' *unsoare* 'grease, ointment.' Speakers have built nouns of this type from both *strâmt* 'narrow' and *strâns* 'squeezed': from the first comes *strâmtoare* 'mountain pass' (also, more abstractly, 'difficult situation'), and from the second comes *strânsoare* 'embracing.' Whether speakers are aware of a link between the two nouns is best left to phonosymbolists.

Whether a verb has overlapping p.p./noun morphology turns out to be lexically determined. Certain new verbs have only long-infinitive nouns: *a admite* with p.p. *admis* and *a constrânge* with p.p. *constrâns* have *admitere* 'admission, admittance,' and *constrângere* 'constraint, compulsion.' Other new verbs have nouns with endings neither infinitival nor purely sigmatic: *a promite* with p.p. *promis* has semilearnèd *promisiune* 'promise,' and hemi-neologistic *a interzice* 'forbid' with p.p. *interzis* has semilearnèd *interdicţie*

---

[10] According to consultant Christopher Brunelle at Vanderbilt, the 4th-decl. noun RĀSU 'a shave, shaving' is attested only once, in Varro (first century BCE). Apparently, p.p. MERSU 'sunk' never developed any *u*-stem noun identical to itself. Neither did p.p. RŌSU 'gnawn.' Might those two nominal slots have been preempted? If so, by which lexical items? Compare the extant fem.nom.sg. MERS, a variant of MERX 'goods, wares' (citation form MERCE), and the extant masc.nom.sg. RŌS 'dew' (citation form RŌRE).

'prohibition'; cf. PRŌMISSIŌNE, INTERDICTIŌNE. Still other new verbs have nouns of both types, with semantic differentiation: *a restrânge* with p.p. *restrâns* has both *restrângere* 'limitation' and *restricţiune* 'restraint' (*Dicţionar invers*, 600 et seq.).

Speakers of Romanian have built nouns by stretching sigmaticism beyond the finite perfectum and past participle. Speakers of Italian have done the same, if less often (see §3.5.3.2); speakers of Catalan, less often still (§4.6.2.5). By contrast, sigmatic nouns in French (§4.4.9) and Spanish (§4.7.7) stand apart as true relics, for they preserve a type of p.p. marking that has become unproductive in the first tongue and obsolete in the second one.

Now I wish to foreshadow a feature that sets apart the far east from the far west. In Romanian, many p.p. relics are asigmatic, while a great many past participles are sigmatic; many p.p. relics are sigmatic in Spanish and Portuguese, while not a single past participle is sigmatic. Nevertheless, in Spanish and Portuguese all plural nouns and 2sg. verbs end in -s, but no plural nouns or 2sg. verbs end in -s in Romanian. In §5.5, I try to offer an explanation, no doubt partial in both senses, for that morphological chiasmus at the two geographical extremes of ROMANIA.

3.1.6. Morphological Leveling within the Past System

In Romanian as elsewhere in ROMANIA, preterits and past participles look more like each other than they did in Latin. Inexplicably regarding perfects in tonic [u] as "strong" i.e. rhizotonic, Dardel goes so far as to say, "Dans aucune langue romane...le parfait fort et le participe passé ne sont aussi étroitement liés que dans le couple *avui—avut* du roumain" (148) [In no other Romance language are strong perfects and past participles so tightly bound as in the Romanian pair *avui—avut* 'had']. Thus, speakers remade expected 1sg. **avi* as *avui* by borrowing the stem of arrhizotonic forms. Dardel goes on to hypothesize that inherited 2sg. pf. **[aβésti]* 'had' was remade as **[avústi]* then *avuşi* by analogy with p.p. *avut*, itself long since remade from HABITU. Likewise, says Dardel, inherited 2sg. **[kantásti]* 'sang' was remade as *cântaşi* by analogy with p.p. *cântat* 'sung.'

Indeed, Dardel (149) considers that the type of preterit in tonic [u] is still expanding in Romanian. Late arrivals include doubly marked (1sg.) *dădui* 'gave' and *stătui* 'stood, stayed,' a by-form *stătut* < STATŪTU 'stood up' having become archaic. Here a memory of reduplication from DEDĪ and STETĪ remains morphologically entombed, but new marking in a high back vowel has been built alongside. Indeed, reduplication has not only been kept in (3sg.) plupf.indic. *dăduse* 'had given' from plupf.subj. DEDISSET but has spread into another past tense, impf. *dădea* 'was giving, used to give' ≠ DABAT, part of the infectum in Latin but now with reduplicated perfectum marking (Ernout and Meillet, 178). Even half-remade according to a more productive pattern, though, the new finite past-system forms still clash morphologically with inherited p.p.s *dat* 'given' and *stat* 'stood, stayed.' By contrast, Dardel notes (149), already remade *făcui* ≠ FĒCĪ 'did/made' has inspired the creation of a new p.p. form *făcut* ≠ FACTU 'done/made,' both of them fully in line with infin. *a face* 'do/make.'

Nor has past-participial influence on preterits, or the other way around, been limited to arrhizotonics. A great many Romanian verbs now featuring a wholly sigmatic perfect system have had past-participial inspiration for that reshaping, though inspiration has come more often from the finite perfectum. Yet as Cioranescu explains (267), in reference to aorists for a new verb *a curge* 'flow' derived from *a cure* 'run' < CURRERE, older asigmatic aorists have been modified in accordance with a group of verbs that have identical stems for both past participle and preterit. Thus, the old aorist stem *curg-* has been rebuilt on the stem of p.p. *curs*, just as *merg-, şterg-, ung-, sting-, împung-, dreg-,* and others have been sigmatically reconstructed.[11]

In the former Dacia, sigmatic past participles often occur after a nasal-final root, retention of [ns] clusters being rare farther west in demotic words. Besides *prins* 'caught, taken' < PR(EH)ĒNSU 'grabbed' and *întins* 'dipped' or 'held' ≠ IN + TĪNCTU or TENTU (but cf. TĒNSU 'stretched'), past participles in that class are *ascuns* 'hidden'—based on an attested LL p.p. ABSCŌNSU rather than on pf. ABSCONDĪ or ABSCONDIDĪ or on p.p. ABSCONDITU—*încins* 'girded' or 'lit' based on CĪNXĪ not CĪNCTU but also on INCĒNSU not INCENDĪ, *plâns* 'wept, mourned' based on PLĀNXĪ not PLĀNCTU, *stins* 'put out (fire)' based on EXSTĪNXĪ not EXSTĪNCTU, *ajuns* 'arrived' based on ADJŪNXĪ not ADJŪNCTU, *lins* 'licked' based on LĪNXĪ not LĪNCTU, *împuns* 'butted, rammed' based on PŪNXĪ not PŪNCTU, *uns* 'oiled' based on ŪNXĪ not ŪNCTU, and *învins* 'won' based on a nasal variant of VĪCĪ but not VICTU (cf. infin. VINCERE). Another past participle with the same form, *învins* 'lived,' cannot have come straight from either pret. VĪXĪ or p.p. VĪCTU, or from infin. VĪVERE either. Was there a partial merger with the stem of VINCERE 'win'?

Most of those sigmatics contrast with tautic athematics farther west like It. *cinto, stinto, giunto, punto, unto,* and *vinto,* but cf. also sigmatic It. *acceso* 'lit' and OIt. *nascoso* 'hidden.' Again, these verbs' 3sg. aorists are also usually sigmatic in Romanian. A small sample is *stinse* < EXSTĪNXIT, *ajunse* < ADJŪNXIT, and *plânse* < PLĀNXIT. Where Latin offered past-participial by-forms like TĒNSU and TENTU, Romanian like Italian generally picked the sigmatic one, so that *întins* 'bent, stretched' has become standard, as has It. *(s)teso.* On the other hand, like *curs* 'run,' Rom. *tuns* 'shorn' has to come more from p.p. TŌNSU than from reduplicated pf. TUTUDĪ or 3rd-conj. infin. TONDERE; cf. *toso* or *tosa* 'kid, little shaver' from dialects of northern Italian.

In further examples of leveling within the perfectum, Rom. 3sg. aorists where [d] > [z] as in Occitan, like *căzu* 'fell,' *crezu* 'believed,' *şezu* 'sat,' *văzu* 'saw,' have come to match their p.p.s *căzut, crezut, şezut,* and *văzut,* all

---

[11] *REW* no. 2415 suggests that *a cure* 'run' may have been remade as *a curge* ± *a merge* 'go, walk.' The suggestion looks plausible semantically if unprovable historically. A Rom. homonym, fem. *cursă* 'snare,' comes from Modern Greek and, in that sense, has nothing do do with p.p. CURSU 'run'; in the sense 'fare,' though, it has probably been borrowed from It. *corsa* 'race, trip, fare.'

deriving from infectum-based -ŪTU variants. Those aorists cannot have continued CL perfects like reduplicated CECIDIT, CRĒDIDIT or direct-suffixation SĒDIT, and VĪDIT. Still less can they have continued CL past participles like sigmatic CĀSU, -SESSU, VĪSU or rhizotonic thematic CRĒDITU. Rather, the reshaping of Rom. 2nd-/3rd-conj. past participles along -ŪTU lines provided a model for reshaping aorists along -UĪ lines. Thus, the (3sg.) aorists *bău* 'drank' ≠ BIBIT and *vru* 'wanted' ≠ VOLUIT are now aligned with the p.p.s *băut* and *vrut*, themselves probably innovations dating from Late Latin.

Workings of analogy have sometimes favored an -ŪTU p.p., so that *învăncut* 'won' supposedly coexists with sigmatic *învins*, though the first variant is unknown to the consultant. Furthermore, the p.p. *înțelegut* 'understood' ≠ INTELLĒCTU—itself continued in adjectival *înțelept* 'wise,' an archaic p.p.—has been made ± *priceput* 'figured out' ≠ PRÆCEPTU 'known in advance; warned; taught' (Rosetti, 567). From a sigmatic stem of the same verb has come a noun *înțeles* 'sense, meaning.'

After all that leveling, aorists in -ps- still sometimes have past participles in -pt, matching Italian past-system sets in -ss- and -tt- like *cosse* and *cotto* 'cooked.' Most Romanian aorists containing an -ns- or -rs- cluster have acquired past participles ending in -ns or in -rs as well. Only a few such aorists have kept or evolved a tautic athematic past participle not containing [p]: *frânt* 'broken,' *fiert* 'boiled,' and dial. *spart* 'cracked' (Mourin, 178–79).

3.1.7. Leveling throughout Verb Stems

In the Romanian verb system, regular reflexes of the 1st, 2nd, and 4th conjugations like *a pleca* 'leave' < PLICĀRE 'fold' (cf. Sp. *llegar*, Ptg. *chegar* 'arrive'),[12] *a putea* 'be able' < *POTERE, and *a veni* 'come' < VENĪRE have a predictable stem for infinitive, aorist, and past participle. By contrast, a rhizotonic 3rd-conj. reflex like *a merge* 'go, walk' or *a rupe* 'tear' may have either a sigmatic past participle like *mers* or a tautic athematic one like *rupt*; the former type has sigmatic markers in both its past participle and its aorist, but the latter has tautic athematic markers only in its past participle. After roots ending in [p], such a split between a sigmatic aorist and a tautic athematic past participle has been inherited to become practically standard, as witness not only aor. *rupse* 'tore' and p.p. *rupt* 'torn' below but also *fripse* and *fript* 'roasted, fried,' *înfipse* and *înfipt* 'thrust, stuck,' *supse* and *supt* 'sucked,' and with vowel alternation aor. *coapse* and p.p. *copt* 'baked.' Another instance of such a divide would be *a fierbe* 'boil,' with 3sg. aorist *fierse* but p.p. *fiert*. Therefore, despite successive waves of regularization, usually along sigmatic lines, one cannot predict whether a given 3rd-conj. verb's past participle will be sigmatic or tautic athematic except, often, by etymology.

---

12 Evidently, two different narrowings of meaning were at work for reflexes of PLICĀRE 'fold': in Dacia, soldiers' folding up tents before decamping; in Iberia, sailors' folding up sails upon docking. In the central zone, Fr. *plier*, Cat. *plegar*, and It. *piegare* still mean 'bend, fold.'

Compared with the CL standard, zones of transparency have expanded. Patches of opacity persist.

Some Latin verbs like RUMPERE RŪPĪ RUPTU 'break' had a nasal infix only in the infectum and had thus preserved the IE trait of showing nasal marking only in the imperfective aspect, comparable to the infectum. In verbs like PINGERE PĪNXĪ PICTU 'paint,' the nasal infix had reached the perfect finite without touching the past participle, though it did in LL PINCTUM 'painted.' In verbs like PLANGERE PLĀNXĪ PLĀNCTU 'lament,' the nasal infix had spread to all three parts. Now in standard Romanian, the verb *a rupe* 'tear' has 1sg. aorist *rupsei* and p.p. *rupt*, all of them without a nasal consonant; a regional variant *a rumpe* has 1sg. aorist *rumpsei* and p.p. *rumpt*, all of them with the nasal consonant (Lombard and Gâdei, 2:103). Either way, consistency in nasal marking has become greater than it was in RUMPERE.

Anomalous verb paradigms are still being regularized. Perhaps surviving only in Romanian but if so in use no longer, the verb *a adaoge* 'add' < ADAUGĒRE with its p.p. *adaos* or *adaus* would have been inherited from a perfect-based sigmatic variant of ADAUCTU 'increased' and its 3sg. aorist *adaose* < ADAUXIT. Unknown to the consultant, that verb has in any event been supplanted by 1st-conj. *a adăuga* with regular p.p. *adăugat* 'added,' a recent creation not admitted into the first volume of the *Dicţionarul Academiei Române* (1913). There also survives an archaic by-form adapted to the 4th conjugation, *a adăugi*, with regular p.p. *adăugit* (Cioranescu, 6).

A second regularization has involved the old verb *a la* 'wash, shampoo' < LAVĀRE with its irregular p.p. *lăut* < *LAVUTU?, possibly a rare post-Latin instance of an -ĀRE verb's acquiring a past participle from another conjugation.[13] However, besides regular LAVĀTU, the CL standard allowed by-form p.p.s LAUTU or LŌTU, so conceivably a stress change could explain *lăut*. Since the sixteenth century, as Cioranescu explains (461), the derivative *a spăla* < EX + PER + LAVARE?, a predictable 1st-conj. verb, has been gaining ground in the flatlands against brief *a la* 'wash,' so that conjugated forms of the latter are now heard only in the mountains of Muntenia, in part of Transylvania, and in Moldavia.[14] In everyday speech elsewhere, the old p.p. *lăut* survives, especially in the negative compound *nelăut* or *nelat* 'unwashed.' That form having become an isolate, speakers use *a spăla* in all moods and tenses (Tagliavini 1923, 184).

3.1.8. Slots Still Unfilled; Metaplasm; Past Participles as Gerunds

Despite ongoing standardization, a few Romanian verbs remain defective, lacking an aorist and a past participle. Almost all of them—*divide* 'divide,' *concede* 'grant, yield,' *inflige* 'inflict,' and *protege* 'protect, promote'—belong to the still somewhat unpredictable 3rd conjugation (Lombard and Gâdei,

---

[13] Compare 4th-conj. Rom. *a şti* 'know' with its doubly marked p.p. *ştiut*.

[14] *EXPERLAVARE is in fact the etymon for *a spăla* proposed in *REW* no. 3044.

2:103). These have a learnèd look to them, like many defective verbs in Italian (§3.5.10). However, rustic *a soage* 'shape dough' also lacks a past participle.

Also as in Italian, a few Romanian verbs survive in two different conjugations: dialectal 1st-conj. *a discerna* 'discern' has been brought into the largest class, but the standard still prefers 3rd-conj. *a discerne*. Crossover may also happen between the 4th and 3rd conjugations, as in *a despărți* against *a desparte* 'separate,' both of them apparently standard. Other 1st-conj. verbs today have recognized 4th-conj. by-forms, like *a aciua* and *a aciui* 'shelter,' *a îmbuna* and *a îmbuni* 'appease,' and *a prefera* and *a preferi* 'prefer'; with a stylistic distinction, literary *a băuni* contrasts with dialectal *a băuna* 'shout' (Pop, 281–86). Regrettably, both *a băuni* and *a băuna* are unknown to the consultant.

Straight reflexes of Latin infinitives in -RE, known as "long infinitives," are now used as verbal nouns in Romanian. As has happened elsewhere (cf. Fr. *savoir* 'skill,' *pouvoir* 'power'), infinitives have been nominalized. In Romanian, some have gone on to lose almost all verbal force, giving e.g. *conducere* 'leadership,' *mâncare* 'food,' *fire* 'nature, character,' *știre* 'news.' In addition, certain old infinitives have been largely displaced as verbal nouns by out-and-out nouns, so that e.g. *credere* yields to *credință* in the sense 'belief,' *legare* to *legătură* in the sense 'connection' (Augerot and Popescu, 173). The syntactic gap thus created has partly been filled by past participles. Syntactically, the past participle in Romanian "has become the verbal substantive par excellence (the so-called supine), esp. as prepositional object....it functions rather like a Romance infinitive: *e greu de aflat* 'it is hard to find,' *se puse pe pictat* 'he began to paint' " (Georges, 3). Three more instances are *trebuie făcut* 'it must be done,' *am de legat* 'I have to tie,' and *e de mirat* 'it's something to be surprised at' (Du Nay, 56). It is doubtful whether such forms continue Latin supines, which would have had to die out everywhere but the Romance far east. (However, imperfect subjunctives survive on Sardinia; see §3.7).

Past participles have come to replace "long infinitives" ending in -re as verbal nouns. Thus, *lucrare* 'working,' remade from deponent LUCRĀRĪ 'gain, profit,' continues in use as a gerund to this day, unlike p.p. *lucrat*,[15] but *dormire* 'sleeping' has yielded fairly recently to p.p. *dormit* in that sense (E. Vrabie, p.c.). Could it have been a growing use of sigmatic past participles as deverbal nouns, as outlined in §3.1.5.2, that promoted an expansion of the syntactic role played by arrhizotonic past participles?

At all events, a somewhat different development has occurred in Istro-Romanian. As explained in §3.3.2, long-form past participles like *durmitu* 'sleeping' are used there as gerunds, but they remain morphologically and syntactically distinct from short-form past participles like *durmit* 'slept.'

Easternmost of major Romance languages, cut off for a thousand years from morphological currents flowing through the Sprachbund of

---

[15] *Lucrare* has also become nominalized in the sense 'work, paper, report' (*Dicționarul limbii române,* 510).

contiguous ROMANIA, Daco-Romanian like most of its cousins has undergone an expansion of p.p. types in -ĀTU, -ĪTU, and -ŪTU. More than any of its cousins, Daco-Romanian has undergone an expansion in the number of sigmatic past participles inspired by sigmatic preterits. Of major Romance languages, Italian comes in a close second sigmatically (see §3.5.3.2).

3.2. DIALECTS OF DACO-ROMANIAN

3.2.1. Oltenian

Dialects from the south and west of Daco-Romania are called Oltenian (Oltn.). One of them, spoken in the province of Gorj, is briefly described in Popescu's *Graiul Gorjenilor*.

Various metaplasms have taken place in Gorj compared with standard Daco-Romanian (DR). Verbs having shifted from 4th to 1st conjugation include *apipiiá* 'grope, paw,' *gătá* 'cook, finish,' *spovedá* 'confess sins,' and *ursá* 'foretell.' Verbs having shifted from 1st to 4th conjugation include *ardeii* 'spice with pepper' and *îmbuní* 'soften, appease.' Verbs having shifted from 3rd to 1st conjugation include *scriiá* 'write and *țăsá* 'weave' (Popescu, 78). What effect, if any, these metaplasms have had on past-participial formation remains uncertain, for Popescu gives no past participles for any of these verbs in their Oltenian embodiments.

A few verbs in Gorj have by-form past participles. In the pairs that follow, the first item looks like the standard exponent, while the second shows innovation: *rămîns* and *rămînit* 'stayed,' *şezut* and *şedut* 'sat,' *dat* and *dădut* 'given,' *stat* and *stătut* 'stood, stayed.' Among the Oltn. innovations, *rămînit* and *şedut* are based on the present stem, *dădut* and *stătut* on the still-reduplicative aorist stem. Moreover, *rămînit* is an arrhizotonic innovation.

At times, speakers in Gorj use a long infinitive where one would expect a past participle: *am venire* 'I have come' instead of standard-looking *am venit*. For the Romanian supine, speakers in Gorj may use either the long infinitive or the past participle. They thus have available alternatives like *Mai ai de-a cosi* or *...de cosit*, both variants meaning 'You have more to cut' (Popescu, 88–89). I cannot tell whether speakers make any distinction, stylistic or otherwise, between the two variants, but true synonyms are rare anywhere.

3.2.2. Moldavian and Related Dialects

Besides Moldavian itself, spoken northeast of the River Prut, varieties of these dialects include Maramureş, spoken in northern Transylvania centering on Sighet, as well as Banat, spoken in western Transylvania centering on Timişoara. Data for each come respectively from Lăzărescu's "Subdialectul moldovean," Vulpe's "Subdialectul maramureşean," and Neagoe's "Subdialectul banaţean," all found in *Tratat de dialectologie românească* edited by Valeriu Rusu.

At the risk of lending support from beyond the grave, as it were, to Soviet-era imperialists who granted Moldavian a separate, equal status and wrote it in Cyrillic, in this section I highlight ways in which Moldavian past participles differ from those in the Bucharest-based standard. No doubt Moldavian would better be termed "Mold-R" by analogy with Ist-R for Istro-Romanian in §3.3.2.

Like other dialects of Daco-Romanian, Moldavian evinces a degree of metaplasm vis-à-vis the standard. Reversing a trend observed in the standard, speakers of Moldavian have shifted some 3rd-conj. verbs into the 2nd conjugation, so that e.g. *a rămânié* 'stay' and *a ținié* 'hold' are used instead of std. *a rămâne* and *a ține* (Lăzărescu, 227). As in the standard, such metaplasms are unlikely to affect past-participial morphology. In the Banat, by contrast, the ever-expanding 1st conjugation has attracted new members, either throughout their paradigms or only in their past participles. Metaplasm has been complete in e.g. Latin-derived *a scria* 'write' with its regular p.p. *scriat* 'written' (cf. std. 3rd-conj. *a scrie* with p.p. *scris*), besides Slavic-derived *a trebuia* 'demand, require' with its p.p. *trebuiat* (cf. std. 4th-conj. *a trebui*, p.p. *trebuit*) and also Greek-derived *a mirosa* 'smell; feel' with its p.p. *mirosat* (cf. std. 4th-conj. *a mirosi*, p.p. *mirosit*). Sometimes, though, only the past participle has been swept into the largest class: compare the Banat by-form *rămânat* 'stayed' next to standard-looking *rămas* for the 3rd-conj. infin. *a rămâne* (Neagoe, 264). My native-speaker consultant, born in Moldavia, believes that only a young child could come up with any such metaplasmatic regularizations.

In an outcome like those found from the Seine to the Po along what Schürr has called the Romance backbone, Moldavian 1st-conj. past participles end in *-ét*, instead of DR *-at*. That shift has occurred because in Moldavian phonotactics [at] fronts after yod or a palatal consonant. Instances of fronting are *aprokiĭét* 'brought nearer,' *împărekét* 'paired off,' *spărijét* 'shocked, scared,' and *tăĭét* 'cut'; cf. the std. Rom. p.p.s *apropiat*, *împerechiat*, *speriat*, *tăiat*. However, throughout Moldova, the verb *a îngrăşa* 'fatten' has the p.p. *îngrăşăt*, a front vowel being disallowed after [ʃ] or [ʒ]. In Moldavian, there also survives an archaic variant, tautic athematic *zmult* 'pulled out, yanked out' prefixed with a reflex of EX-, as against std. sigmatic *zmuls* (Lăzărescu, 227). Both apparently derive from ĒMULSU 'drained, exhausted,' literally 'milked out,' or from a variant.

Across much of the Moldavian dialect area, one encounters allegro forms of past participles, especially in folkloric materials. Allegro forms gathered so far include *găst* 'found,' *şăst* 'sat,' and *văst* 'seen.' In the Banat, *vint* 'come,' a reflex unique in ROMANIA of CL VENTU though reminiscent at least in form of Ptg. *vindo* 'idem,' remains in common use (Neagoe, 264). Could this *vint* represent another syncopated variant that once ended in -ĬTU? In any event, recall that standard Daco-Romanian has arrhizotonics for these verbs' past participles: *găsit* 'found,' *şezut* 'sat,' *văzut* 'seen,' *vinit* 'come.' Finally, in Maramureş, the allegro form *fo* 'been' occurs commonly alongside standard-looking *fost* 'idem' (Vulpe, 338). A muting of final consonants, French style?

3.3. EVIDENCE FROM MINOR LANGUAGES
IN BALKAN ROMANCE

Outside Romania and Moldova, three varieties of Balkan Romance survive, or used to, in enclaves surrounded by Slavic, Albanian, and Greek. Each variety has a great deal in common with Daco-Romanian. As Vrabie writes in *Aromanian: Grammar, Lexicon, and an English-Aromanian Dictionary* (1999): "In spite of their territorial discontinuity at present, these four totally independent Romance entities...share a long series of important phonetic, morphological, syntactic and lexico-semantic features that lead back to Common Romanian." It is of course their morphological similarities, especially past-participial ones, that allure us here. For reasons explained in §3.3.3, so does a variety of Gallo-Italian found along the west coast of Istria.[16]

3.3.1. Aromanian (Macedo-Romanian)

Soon after the Common Era began, the ancestors of Romanians and Aromanians formed a Latin-speaking continuum that reached from the Adriatic to the Black Sea, but the fifth-century migration of Slavs into the Balkans split that continuum apart and eventually drove the Aromanians southward.[17] Data come from Papahagi's *Dicţionarul dialectului aromân general şi etimologic* (1974; abbrev. *DDA*), from Capidan's *Aromânii* (1932), and from Vrabie 1999. Orthography has been standardized, an apostrophe after a consonant denoting palatalization. Stress remains unmarked.

Like other languages of the Balkans, Aromanian has almost no use for an infinitive, generally replacing it with a subjunctive syntagm; the 1sg. pres.indic. serves as the citation form for verbs. As in Romanian, reflexes of old infinitives survive as nouns. Examples are *cîntare* 'singing, song,' *cădeare* 'fall[ing],' *dzîţeare* or *dzîţire* 'saying,' and *durn'ire* 'sleep[ing].' A few others are *amintare* 'gain < AUGMENTĀRE, *gărire* 'humming' < GARRĪRE 'chatter,' and *voamire* or *vumeare* 'throwing up' from the stem of VOMERE.[18]

---

[16] More about the essential unity of the several Romanians is to be found in Petrovici 1964 and in Gheţie 1986, 1987a, and 1987b.

[17] Two Arom. terms will serve to indicate the scope of language contact in the Balkans. The noun *aracĭŭ* 'plowman' combines Latin-derived *ar* 'plow' (< ARŌ or something like it) with South Slavic [oratʃ] or [uratʃ] 'plowman.' Again, the noun phrase *maţŭ kĭor* 'vermiform appendix'—literally 'blind gut'—combines a reflex of CL MATTEA 'meat delicacy' < Gk. ματτύη with a reflex of Turkish *kör* 'blind' (Vrabie 1993, 214–16).

[18] Lexically, Arom. *loc* 'place, land, earth' fills both of the slots occupied by Daco-Romanian *ţară* 'country, land' and *loc* 'place.' Owing to homonymic clash with the local reflex of QUÆRERE 'seek,' Arom. *ţer* 'sky' tends to yield to Gk.-derived *urano*, while for Daco-Romanians *cer* 'sky' remains current even if it sounds like the root *cer* 'ask, beg, demand.' From a suffixed variant of ANIMAL come both Arom. *nămal'ĭŭ* 'sheep, goat' and Rom. *nămaie* 'horned animal' (Vrabie 1999, passim). For more old Arom. infinitives in *-re* now restricted to

If the *DDA* is to be trusted, *lǎlǎtoare* 'weekday' comes not from LABŌRĀRE as one might think, but from something like *LABORATORIA.

In one semantic field for verbs, speakers of Aromanian still use reflexes of p.p. NASCERE 'be born' with "infinitive" *nascu* (p.p. *nǎscut* ≠ NĀTU). Speakers also use a verb based on 4th-decl. FĒTU 'offspring,' which has given "infinitive" *fet* and p.p. *fitat* 'born.' Other synonyms for 'be born' are *amintu* (p.p. *amintat* < AUGMENTĀTU 'increased'), *dizvoc* (p.p. *dizvucat* < DIS- plus a variant of VACĀTU 'been empty' or, being interpreted, 'emptied out'), and finally *nfaşu* (p.p. *nfaş[e]at* < IN- + FASCIA 'bundle' + -ĀTU), built from an image of swaddling a newborn rather than on one of wrapping sticks. In a different semantic field, Aromanian resembles its cousins far to the west. As a frequentative for *n'ergu* 'go, walk,' locals use *imnu* (p.p. *imnat* 'gone' < AMBULĀTU 'ambled'), the verb that reportedly contracted in contrastive ways to yield It. *andare* and Fr. *aller* 'go' among others.

Phonotactically, labials were velarized or palatalized before an old yod, which then generally vanished but at times left palatalized traces, written with an apostrophe.[19] These changes turn up in Aromanian past participles like *kirut* 'lost, destroyed' ≠ PERDITU 'lost,' and *n'ersu* 'gone' < MERSU 'sunk' for what have come out as *pierdut* and *mers* in Daco-Romanian. These changes also turn up in a pair of almost Gascon-looking Arom. past participles *h'ertu* 'boiled' (no CL p.p.) and *h'iptu* 'driven in' < FĪCTU 'fastened'; cf. Rom. *fiert* and *înfipt* with [f] preserved.[20]

Morphologically, Aromanian past participles have come out looking nearly the same as Romanian ones, but base forms keep a whisper of Latin -U. All words ending in a single consonant are followed by an off-glide lip rounding that customarily goes unwritten; after two consonants, the lip-rounding becomes syllabic and is usually written -u̱.[21] Local reflexes for arrhizotonic past participles are: 1st-conj. ones in -*at*, 2nd- and 3rd-conj. ones in -*ut*, 4th-conj. ones in -*it*.

---

nominal use, like *bişare* 'kiss[ing]' < BASIĀRE and *sǎrcl'are* 'weeding out' < SARCULĀRE, see Vrabie 1999, §49.

[19] Dabbing in a touch of local color, I wish to linger over the consonant changes typical of Aromanian and found nowhere else in Romance. Bilabial stops become velar stops: [p] > [k'] in e.g. Arom. *k'in* 'pine' from PĪNU, and also [b] > [g̠] in e.g. *g̠ini* 'good, fine' from adv. BENE 'well.' Labiodental fricatives become velar fricatives: [f] > [χ] in e.g. *hiu* 'to be' from FIŌ 'become, happen, be made,' and [w] > [v'] > [γ] (written y̠), in e.g. *yiu* 'alive' from VĪVU 'idem.' Bilabial nasals become palatal nasals: [m] > [ɲ] in e.g. *n'ergu* 'go' from MERGŌ 'I sink.'

[20] In Arom. *yinghiţ* or *yiyinţ* 'twenty,' the first variant apparently comes from a doubly nasal by-form for VĪGINTĪ but may well have resulted from metathesis, neither form displaying two [n]'s. Though surviving everywhere across contiguous ROMANIA, in e.g. It. *venti* and Sp. *veinte*, reflexes of the old Latin numeral have been preserved nowhere else in the Balkans. Rom. *douǎzeci*, literally 'two tens,' has been calqued from Slavic (*DDA*, passim). In some environments, if [f] > [χ] in Aromanian, it leaves no trace in Meglenoromanian (see §3.3.1.1).

[21] In the Farsherot type of Aromanian, words ending in two consonants commonly occur without the support vowel -*u* that is always present in other types (E. Vrabie, p.c.).

Looking through the past-participial inventory of Aromanian, any Romanist will recognize all endings at once and most stems soon after. From the 1st conjugation come *acăţat* 'hunted, caught,' *cîntat* 'sung,' *cripat* 'burst,' *dat* 'given,' and *lucrat* 'worked.' Resembling Rom. *spălat* (and Ist-R *spelat*) is Arom. *aspilat* 'washed,' no doubt built from doubly prefixed EX + PER + LAVĀTU 'idem.' In a (semantic) class by itself is trisyllabic *diucl'at* 'hit by the evil eye,' with what Malkiel would call a prefixoid. From the 2nd and 3rd conjugations come *avut* 'had,' disyllabic *biut* 'drunk,' *cădzut* 'fallen,' *criscut* 'grown,' *durut* 'hurt, grieved,' *putut* 'been able,' *tacŭt* 'been silent,' *vindut* 'sold,' *vidzut* 'seen,' and *vrut* 'wanted.' From the 4th conjugation come *acupirit* 'covered,' *apirit* 'opened,' *işit* 'gone out,' and *păţît* 'undergone, suffered,' all regularized from COOPERTU, APERTU, EXĬTU, and PASSU. If 4th-conj. *durn'it* 'slept' comes from the Romans, *mutrit* 'looked at' comes from the Slavs (cf. the OCS infin. *motriti* 'look'). Like Daco-Romanian, Aromanian has a type of 4th-conj. past participle in high central [ɨ], giving e.g. *avdzît* 'heard' and trisyllabic *aurît* 'hated.'

Less familiar illustrations would have to include the 4th-conj. Arom. p.p. *h'ivrit* 'been feverish' from FEBRĪTU. Though it is tempting to trace the word's initial consonant all the way back to Latin—cf. the attested dialectal doublet HEBRE for standard FEBRE 'fever' in Latin (Ernout and Meillet, 222)[22] —the temptation ought to be resisted, and in any event Arom. ẖ stands for [χ] not [h]. Still, the most common verb in the language, with "infinitive" *hiu* 'be' as against p.p. *fut* 'been,' shows a contrast between initial consonants. From the same source as Vegl. *foit*, the past participle seems to have been built from the stem of e.g. 3sg. pf. FUIT (no CL p.p.) plus the ending -ŪTU. Now resembling a 3sg. passé simple in French for the same verb, that Arom. form *fut* lacks the [s] that has arisen in Rom./Ist-R *fost*.

Among rhizotonics, Aromanian has kept certain forms tautic athematic. Straight survivals include *aleptu* 'chosen' < ĒLĒCTU (but cf. Rom. *ales*), *aruptu* 'torn' < RUPTU 'broken,' *astimtu* 'put out (fire)' < EXSTĪNCTU, *culeptu* 'gathered' < COLLĒCTU, *coptu* 'baked' < COCTU, *friptu* 'fried' < FRĪCTU, *plîmtu* 'wept' < PLĀNCTU, *suptu* 'sucked' < SUCTU, *traptu* 'pulled' < TRACTU, and *ţimtu* or *aţimtu* 'girded' < CĪNCTU. Built from EX + VICTU, *asvimtu* 'won' has borrowed nasality from its infectum. Other old tautic athematics survive only as adjectives or adverbs, like *d(i)reptu* 'straight' < DĪRĒCTU 'guided,' though the language does have a prefixed p.p. *ndreptu* 'arranged, prepared' ("infin." *ndreg*). Less innovatively, Aromanian keeps *faptu* 'done/made,' replaced by *făcut* north of the Danube, and keeps *mort* 'died; dead,' replaced in the former sense by p.p. *murit* farther north.

---

[22] Wavering between initial [f] and [h] occurred in other Latin words, as in std. HORDEU versus dialectal FORDEU 'barley' (Ernout and Meillet, 299). Only by-forms in [f] would start with a consonant in Romance. Later, labiodental [f] moved back to laryngeal [h] in Gascon (§4.6.1.5) and in Castilian, from which latter tongue [h] has since vanished as a phoneme.

By-forms have come into being as well. Alongside expected 4th-conj. *fudzit* 'fled,' remade from a tautic thematic, is innovative 1st-conj. *fugat*. Remade from a tautic athematic is trisyllabic 1st-conj. *scriirat* 'written,' which however appears to compete against sigmatic *scris* (an entry I have to mark as doubtful).

Aromanian keeps a number of sigmatics, and, like Daco-Romanian, has evolved more than a few unknown to the classical tongue. Inheritances include *arîs* 'laughed' < RĪSU, *ar(ă)mas* 'stayed' < REMĀNSU, *arsu* 'burned' < ĀRSU, and already cited *n'ersu* 'walked, gone' < MERSU 'sunk.' Even *mulsu* 'milked' comes from a Latin by-form MULSU, no doubt influenced by the sigmatic pf. MULSĪ. Others are p.p.s *scos* 'taken out' < EX + QUASSU 'shaken out,' *aştersu* 'wiped, scoured' < EX + TERSU, and unclassical *dişcl'is* 'opened; educated' < DĒ + EX + -CLŪSU 'shut,' which compound might at first have sounded about the way 'un-shut-out' sounds to us. As in standard Romanian, many past participles here have been remade on the basis of their sigmatic perfects: *dzîs* 'said, told' ≠ DICTU but cf. pf. DĪXĪ; *dus* or *adus* 'brought' ≠ (AD)DUCTU 'led [to]' but cf. pf. (AD)DŪXĪ; *torsu* 'twisted' ≠ TORTU but cf. pf. TORSĪ. Raising of the tonic vowel from [o] to [u] in *dipus* 'gone down, lowered' ≠ DĒPOSITU 'laid down, put down' and also in *aspus* 'shown, said' < EXPOS(I)TU 'set forth,' no doubt began with anaphony in pf. POSUĪ, just as it did in Rom. *pus* 'put,' but the former competes with 1st-conj.-style Arom. *dipunat*. Like its verb *a depune*, the corresponding Rom. p.p. *depus* 'set (of the sun)' is unknown to most speakers (E. Vrabie, p.c.). Certainly the two preterits *streş* 'squeezed' and *teş* 'stretched' have been influenced by the morphology of their (by-form) sigmatic p.p.s *stres* and *tes*.

Changes in p.p. marking have not always gone toward the sigmatic side. Newly tautic athematic are Arom. *aspartu* 'scattered' ≠ SPARSU, *primtu* 'understood' ≠ PRĒNSU 'grabbed,' and *pitrumtu* 'pierced' ≠ PERTŪNSU (cf. Rom. *spart* but *pătruns*). Nasal marking has spread all the way to several past participles in Aromanian. Compare *frîmtu* 'broken' and FRĀCTU, but note infin. FRANGERE. Compare *strimtu* 'narrowed' and STRICTU, but note infin. STRINGERE and pf. STRĪNXĪ.[23] Especially compare *(î)nvinsu* 'won' and non-nasal VICTU, but note the vowel in pf. VĪCĪ and the nasal in infin. VINCERE, not to mention the unclassical fut.p. VINCITURUM 'going to win' overheard at Trimalchio's feast (§2.1.1). A combining form of PANGERE 'fasten, drive in,' namely -PINGERE, has been spun off as a separate verb to produce Arom. *pingu* 'push' with p.p. *pimtu* ≠ PĀCTU, the Latin p.p. itself having been borrowed from the related verb PACISCOR 'make a deal, strike a bargain.'

Continued hesitation between sigmatic and tautic athematic past participles is revealed by several current by-forms going back to a similar hesitation in Latin. Compare prefixed variants found in sigmatic Rom. *împins* and in tautic athematic It. *spinto* 'pushed.' Thus, innovative Arom. *timsu* coexists with presumably conservative *timtu* < TENTU 'held [out]'; its close relative *tes*< TĒNSU survives adjectivally and past-participially as well.

---

[23] Daco-Romanian also has adj. *strict* 'idem,' a neologism from French or Latin.

Other past participles evincing the same hesitation between sigmatic and tautic variants are *agŭmtu* and *agŭmsu* 'reached,' *alimtu* and *alimsu* 'licked,' *aprimtu* and *aprimsu* 'lit,' *ascumtu* and *ascunsu* 'hidden,' trisyllabic *aumtu* and *aumsu* 'oiled, greased,' and *tumsu* and *tumtu* 'shorn,' the last pair also serving as adjectives meaning 'unfortunate; simpleminded.' Generally, tautic athematic by-forms appear to go back to p.p.s like ADJŬNCTU 'joined,' LĪNCTU 'licked,' ŪNCTU 'oiled' (though cf. also LL ABSCŌNSU 'hidden'), while sigmatic by-forms resemble pfs. ADJŬNXĪ, LĪNXĪ, ŪNXĪ. For reflexes of TONDĒRE, the sigmatic by-form goes back to p.p. TŌNSU 'shorn,' but the tautic athematic form can hardly go back to pf. TOTONDĪ; while p.p. *ascumtu* could conceivably go back to CL ABSCONDITU 'hidden,' it is probably analogical with other verbs displaying similar alternations (see Table 3–2).

Table 3–2

Consonant Marking in the Aromanian Past System

for selected 3rd-conjugation verbs

gloss	"infinitive"	preterit (1sg.)	past participle
preterit in [ʃ], past participle in [s]			
'bring'	aduc	aduş	adus
'burn'	ardu	arşu	arsu
'laugh'	arîd	arîş	arîs
'show, say'	aspun	aspuş	aspus
'wipe'	aştergu	aşterşu	aştersu
preterit in [ʃ], past participle in [t]			
'choose'	aleg	alepşu	aleptu
'tear'	arup	arupşu	aruptu
'break'	aspargu	asparşu	aspartu
'put out (fire)'	astingu	astimşu	astimtu

Most p.p. variation here entails different tonic vowels. They include *andrupît* or *andrupat* for "infin." *andrupắscu* 'lean, support' from Slavic, and *nţirnat* or *nţernut* for "infin." *nţernu* 'sift'; cf. the form *cernut* 'sifted' shared orthographically by Romanian and Catalan.[24] In at least one instance, though, competition entails a rhizotonic and an arrhizotonic, so that "infin." *dipun* 'set, go down' has both *dipus* and *dipunat* for past participles. In one verb, Aromanian has another kind of alternation involving a consonant in the stem rather than the ending: *yin* 'come' (where y = [ɣ]) may have for its p.p. either *vinit* or *vin'it*. Here there are two by-form preterits, but both have palatal nasals: *vin'* and *vin'ii*.[25]

Two other past-system irregularities go back to Latin. If Arom. *dau* 'give' has a regular p.p. *dat*, its preterit *ded* < DEDĪ preserves the ancient perfective reduplication. So, evidently, does the by-form pret. *fregi* 'broke' [fredʒ] < FRĒGĪ (also *frîmşu*) preserve an old vowel-change direct-suffixation perfect from Latin.

As shown in Table 3–2, Aromanian 3rd-conj. verbs usually have preterit [ʃ] as against past-participial [s] or [t]. Verbs listed have only a single filler for the p.p. slot; only a small sample is given here. That preterit [ʃ] might have resulted from palatalization of [s] before a final front vowel like 1sg. [i], which vowel has since disappeared. At all events, verbs with sigmatic past systems in Aromanian have developed a morphological contrast absent from Romanian, which for such verbs has a wholly sigmatic past system; compare the morphological review in §3.1.5.[26]

Turning to past participles as roots for whole paradigms, at least one verb in Aromanian could have been built on a Latin p.p., USTU 'singed, scorched,' rather than on its infin. ŪRERE. A long-form verb built on the Latin p.p. stem might have lain behind the regular Arom. verb that has p.p. *uscat* 'dried.' More plausibly, it comes from something like EX + *SUCCARE (cf. SŪCU or SŪCCU 'sap') crossed with OB + SICCĀRE 'dry out.' Arom. *uscat* somewhat resembles OFr. *uslé* 'burned,' a regular form deriving from an attested diminutive USTULĀTU 'scorched, singed.'

As has happened elsewhere, Aromanian past participles have come to be used in adjectival or nominal senses. Some of the adjectival ones will occasion little surprise: *aurît* 'hated' also means 'hateful,' *biut* 'drunk' also means 'drunken,' *putut* 'been able' also means 'powerful,' *tắcut* 'been quiet' also means 'close-mouthed,' and by-form *tes* 'stretched' also has an adjectival sense (cf. Sp. *tieso* 'stiff'). Some nominalized past participles look as

---

[24] However, the *DDA* (159) gives *andrupît* 'upheld' as the only past participle for the Arom. verb *andrupắscu,* from Bulg. *dopiram.*

[25] Aromanian and Daco-Romanian differ phonologically for inherited front vowels after labial consonants. Arom. e and i remain as such, but DR has undergone depalatalization from e to ắ and from i to î (â). Contrast Arom. *betrîn* and DR *bắtrân* 'old' < VETERĀNU 'old, veteran,' or Arom. *vimtu* and DR *vânt* 'wind' < VENTU (E. Vrabie, p.c.).

[26] For a complete list of irregular preterits and past participles in Aromanian—all for 3rd-conj. verbs—see Vrabie 1999, §32 and §41.

straightforward: *faptă* meaning 'deed, act,' *fudzită* meaning 'departure,' *işită* or *inşită* meaning 'outcome, result,' *loată* meaning 'a taking' (cf. Fr. *prise*), and certainly *mulsă* meaning 'milking [of sheep]'; *dzîcă* 'word, speech' looks more distantly connected to p.p. *dzîs*. Semantic shifts in other adjectivized past participles are fairly easy to grasp: *avdzît* 'heard' also meaning 'famous,' *avut* 'had' also meaning 'rich,' *cripat* 'burst' also meaning 'sad, anxious,' or *durut* 'hurt; desired' meaning 'sweet, dear.' Again, to understand the Arom. fem. noun *cripată* 'dawn,' one need merely recall Engl. *daybreak*. If p.p. *vrut* 'wanted' also has an adjectival sense 'beloved,' an adverbial one 'affectionately,' and a nominal one 'lover,' each appears readily comprehensible. Compare p.p.s like Sp. *querido* or Fr. *chéri* 'darling,' meaning respectively 'wanted' and 'cherished.' Yet other nominalized past participles in Aromanian practically require a semantic leap of faith: *faptu* from 'done/made' to 'charm, enchantment' (but cf. Sp. *hechizo* 'idem'); fem. *scriată* from 'written' to 'fate, destiny'; and *loat* from 'taken' to 'crazy' or 'paralyzed.' Related to a by-form masc. p.p. *apres*, fem. *apreasă* means not only 'lit, kindled' but also 'rising [of planets or stars]' (Capidan 1932, 478–79). Who but an Aromanian would liken the rising of a star to a twig's bursting into flame?

At Kruševo in the new Republic of Macedonia, noteworthy Arom. past participles include *h'ertu* 'cooked' (no CL p.p. for FERVERE 'boil') as well as unpalatal *nes* 'walked' < MERSU. In *kədzut* 'fallen' and *vidzut* 'seen,' intervocalic [d] has affricated to [dz] as in some DR dialects but not deaffricated to [z] as in standard Romanian. Initial [d] has affricated in Kruševo *dzës* 'said, told.' Finally, Latin [i] has sometimes become Aromanian [ə] initially, at least before [n], in the p.p.s *ənkl'is* 'shut' and *əndreptu* 'arranged, prepared' (Gołąb, 130; Vrabie, p.c.).

Into a cabinet of morphological curios one would have to put a pair of past participles from the area around Mt. Pindus in northern Greece. Much like speakers of Late Latin in northern Gaul (§4.4.0), those speakers of Aromanian have put so much stress on tonic vowels that, in rapid speech, they tend to syncopate atonic vowels. Thus, from the roots of "infinitives" *fug* 'run' and *adun* 'gather,' speakers have elided and assimilated the verbs' 1st-conj. past participles to end up with the allegro forms *vgat* 'run' and *annat* 'gathered.' To be sure, the elided vowels reappear in slower speech, giving *adunat* and *fugat* (DDA, 109, 1262). Curios *vgat* and *annat* will serve as a farewell to Aromanian.

3.3.1.1. Meglenoromanian

According to authorities west of the Adriatic, Meglenoromanian yet survives.[27] In that light, I follow convention so far as to give Meglenoromanian its own subsection and to refer to it in the present tense.[28]

---

[27] The sole textual mention accorded to Meglenoromanian in Harris and Vincent's *Romance Languages* (23) says that it is "spoken by a few thousand speakers." In the same work, a map of

True, Meglenoromanian differs a bit from Aromanian. In *Meglenromânii* (169), Capidan states that Meglenoromanian keeps verbal uses of infinitives like 1st-conj. *cîntari* 'sing,' 2nd-conj. *cădeari* 'fall,' rhizotonic 3rd-conj. *batiri* 'beat,' and 4th-conj. *durmiri* 'sleep.' And "standard" Meglenoromanian drops any final vowel on (masc.sg.) past participles. And several past participles in Meglenoromanian are built differently from their Aromanian counterparts.

In *Compendiu de dialectologie română*, though, Caragiu makes three remarks worth repeating. First, Caragiu says (280) that with few exceptions the verb morphology of Meglenoromanian is identical to that of the Aromanian. Second, discussing Meg. preterits, Caragiu notes (281) that differences between Aromanian and Meglenoromanian are limited to phonetics. Third, Caragiu says (284) that, again except for phonetics, the morphology of Meg. past participles does not pose any problems different from those already encountered under Aromanian. Certainly as regards the past system of verbs, Caragiu as good as says that while it was alive Meglenoromanian ranked as a dialect of Aromanian. Its similarities and dissimilarities vis-à-vis the "standard" should nonetheless prove enlightening.

Undifferentiated by dialect, or subdialect, two dozen past participles are supplied by Caragiu and about as many by Capidan. Regular 1st-conj. forms are *cântat* 'sung' and *lucrat* 'worked.' Regular 2nd-/3rd-conj. ones are *bătut* 'beaten,' *căzut* 'fallen,' *cunuscut* 'known,' *putut* 'been able,' *şăzut* 'sat,' and *vizut* 'seen.' Regular 4th-conj. ones are *durmit* 'slept,' *fuzit* 'fled,' and *ndulţit* 'sweetened' (cf. Rom. *îndulcit*). Fitted into the same class is Slavic-derived *lipit* 'glued,' as in Romanian.

In the corpus, only five Meglenoromanian past participles bear tautic athematic marking. Three look like Romanian: *copt* 'baked,' *rupt* 'torn,' and *supt* 'sucked.' Less close is [f]-less *iert* 'boiled.' Perhaps [p]-less *fat* 'done/made,' for expected **fapt*, was reshaped by analogy with *dat* 'given.'

As one would expect in eastern ROMANIA, sigmatics far outnumber other athematic types. Relics of a first wave of sigmaticism in Latin, most such p.p. inheritances have present roots ending in a dental stop: *ancl'is* 'shut in,' *ars* 'burned,' *scos* 'taken out,' *trimes* 'sent,' *tuns* 'shorn,' *uţis* 'killed.' Relics of a second wave of sigmaticism in Latin, other inherited past participles have present roots ending in a velar stop: *mers* 'gone,' *muls* 'milked,' *spars* 'shattered,' *tors* 'spun.' Three have present roots ending in [n]: *pus* 'put,' *rămas* 'stayed,' *spus* 'said.' By analogy with such forms, a third wave of sigmaticism has washed over Meglenoromanian past participles (I omit etyma for verb prefixes): *andires* 'guided' ≠ DĪRĒCTU, disyllabic *daus* 'added' ≠

Balkan Romance has an area marked off for Meglenoromanian (487). Closer to the reputed homeland, Coteanu's *Elemente de dialectologie a limbii române* of 1961 likewise has a map of the southern Balkans with an area marked off for Meglenoromanian (117).

[28] Owing to a diaspora of speakers beginning after World War I, Meglenoromanian survives on the pages of researchers if hardly any longer on the lips of speakers. For details, see Saramandu's chapter (476 et seq.) in the compilation edited by Rusu, *Tratat de dialectologie românească*.

AUCTU, *dus* 'carried,' ≠ DUCTU, *fris* 'fried' ≠ FRĪCTU but cf. LL FRIXU, *les* 'chosen' ≠ ĒLĒCTU, and *tras* 'pulled' ≠ TRACTU.

Nor does p.p. sigmaticism stop there. Inspired by inheritances like *pătruns* 'pierced' ≠ PERTŪNSU, *prins* 'caught, taken' < PREHĒNSU, *tuns* 'shorn' < TŌNSU, and *scuns* 'hidden' < LL ABSCONSU, all Meglenoromanian verbs with stems ending in [n] + [t] or [d] have remade their past participles in [ns]: *anţins* 'girded' ≠ CĪNCTU and *anvins* 'won' ≠ VICTU. With these compare Arom. *aleptu* 'chosen,' *asvimtu* 'won,' *friptu* 'fried,' *ţimtu* 'girded,' *traptu* 'pulled,' and 1st-conj. Rom. *adăugat* 'added,' but also Log. (Sard.) *frissu* 'fried.' Any adjective matching Rom. *înţelept* 'wise' having been lost from Meglenoromanian, the sigmatic p.p. *anţiles* 'understood' ≠ INTELLĒCTU has acquired an adjectival sense (Capidan 1925, 169–70).

Open back [ɔ] has somehow developed from close front [i] in some 3rd- and 4th-conj. Meg. forms whose stems end in [r], [ʃ], [j], [z], or [ts]: *işɔt* 'gone out,' *rɔs* 'laughed,' *sfărşɔt* 'ended,' *urɔt* 'hated,' and *uzɔt* 'heard.' Compare Rom. *ieşit, râs, sfîrşit, urît,* and *auzit.* Of the Meg. by-forms *frɔns* and *frɔnt* 'broken,' the second at least from a variant of FRĀCTU with nasality imported from its infectum, and Meg. *plɔns* 'wept' has come from already nasal if asigmatic PLĀNCTU; both of course had tonic [a:] in Latin. Relative to Daco-Romanian, initial a̱- has been lost in *cupirit* 'covered,' *flat* 'found,' and *scuns* 'hidden,' and for the second and third of these relative to Latin as well in view of the etyma AFFLĀTU 'sniffed out' and ABSCONDITU 'hidden.'

Two (sub)dialects of Meglenoromanian, spoken in Ţărnareca and Uma, differ mainly in phonetics. Though two or three arrhizotonic types are popular everywhere else in ROMANIA, hardly any of the few past participles gathered here are arrhizotonics. Such accidents of attestation lead one to suspect that the p.p. sample below—from Atanasov's "Meglenoromâna" in *Tratat de dialectologie românească*(1982)—may play up irregularity, downplay regularity. As always, the unusual draws stares.

At Ţărnareca, masc.sg. past participles resemble those of "standard" Aromanian in that they normally end in -u̱ [ə]. Rhizotonic tautic athematic examples are *faptu* 'done/made,' *ruptu* 'torn,' *frămtu* 'broken,' *plămtu* 'thrust, planted,' and *tumtu* 'shorn, cut.' A familiar sigmatic is *arsu* 'burned.' A 2nd-/3rd-conj. example is *dzăcutu* been silent,' like Rom. *tăcut.* This subdialect has been heavily influenced by Aromanian (Atanasov 1990, 211).

At Uma, a 2nd-/3rd-conj. past participle is *ţirut* 'asked, begged,' which resembles Rom. *cerut* ≠ QUÆSĪTU 'sought' in being based on the present stem as in infin. QUÆRERE. Here masc.sg. past participles normally have a zero ending while fem.sg. ones end in -ă̱ [ə], so that e.g. *fat* contrasts with *fată* 'done/made.' However, as in dialects of Franco-Provençal (§4.5), some Uma past participles differ in tonic vocalism according to gender. Here masc. [ɔ] contrasts with fem. [ə] or [i]: compare *frɔnt* and *frăntă* 'broken,' *plɔns* and *plănsă* 'grieved, lamented,' *işɔt* and *işită* 'gone out,' and *uzɔt* and *uzătă* 'heard,' with which last compare *avdzătu* in Ţărnareca. Part of the phonotactics of the Uma dialect—as of Aromanian—provides that in masc.sg. past participles final [u] rather than zero occurs in   environments incorporating consonant clusters. Examples are *spartu* 'shattered,' *unsu* 'oiled'—also *umtu*—and last, *arsu* 'burned' (Atanasov 1982, 523–24).

In his 1990 work, *Le mégleno-roumain de nos jours*, Atanasov furnishes more past participles. From the 1st conjugation come *culcat* 'lain,' *dunat* 'gathered,' *ligat* 'tied,' *măncat* 'eaten,' *scăpat* 'escaped,' and *vătămat* 'wounded.' From the 2nd/3rd conjugation come *ţirut* 'asked, sought,' *vut* 'had,' and *vrut* 'loved.' From the 4th conjugation come *murit* 'died' ≠ MORTUU, *sirbit* 'worked' = SERVĪTU, *tricut* 'passed,' and *venit* 'come' ≠ VENTU. A familiar-looking sigmatic for eastern Romance is remade *uns* 'oiled.' More past participles that sport an ending in -*ǫt*, assigned to the 4th conjugation though their infinitives end in -*ări*, are Meg. *ănmurţǫt* 'chilled, benumbed,' *ămpuţǫt* 'spoiled, rotted,' *ăncăldzǫt* 'heated,' and *ănvirdzǫt* 'turned green.'

In this later work, Atanasov specifies the conditions for final [ə]. With the auxiliary *veári* 'have,' past participles always have that ending in Uma and Ţărnareca, except in cases of the "inverse perfect" where participle precedes auxiliary. In other dialects, no such final [ə] ever occurs. With the auxiliary *iri* 'be,' past participles never have final [ə] in Uma or Ţărnareca either. In both locales, though, final [u] is pronounced after certain consonant clusters (Atanasov 1990, 210). A support vowel, final [u] plays a role analogous to that played by -*e* [ə] after Old French clusters that speakers would otherwise have found unpronounceable.

3.3.2. Istro-Romanian

Since the extinction of Vegliote, mourned in §3.4, Istro-Romanian (Ist-R) has become the sole shred remaining from a tapestry of Latin spoken long ago between Italia and Dacia, across lands now renamed Slovenia, Croatia, and Serbia. This Istro-Romanian branch of Latinity should not be confused with Istriano, a dialect of Gallo-Italian dealt with in §3.3.3. Data discussed here come from Puşcariu's *Studii istroromâne* of the 1920s, from Kovačec's *Descrierea istroromânei actuale*(1971) and "Istroromâna" (1984), and from Sârbu's *Texte istroromâne* (1992).[29]

Phonologically, Istro-Romanian and Daco-Romanian sound much alike. Before a front vowel in both, Latin [d] turns into [z], and Latin [s] turns into [ʃ]. One difference is that, again before a front vowel, both Latin [k] and Latin [t] give Ist-R [ts], but the former gives [tʃ] in Romanian. Morphologically, the past-participial inventory of Istro-Romanian looks almost indistinguishable from that of Daco-Romanian. In masc.sg., regular 1st-conj. forms end in -*at*, 2nd-/3rd-conj. forms end in -*ut*, and 4th-conj. forms end in -*it*. Just as in Romanian, survivors and new members of the sigmatic class end in -*s*; tautic athematic types preserve -*t* after another consonant; survivors of the Latin type in [kt] have come to end in -*pt*.

---

[29] I simplify Ist-R spelling, which only outsiders use, by declining to write the invariably labialized reflexes of tonic [a] as <u>å</u>, standing for [ɔ] or the like, and by declining to mark stress.

Among Ist-R past participles graphically identical to those in Daco-Romanian are 1st-conj. *arat* 'plowed,' *dat* 'given,' *gustat* 'eaten,' *legat* 'tied,' and *lucrat* 'worked.' A few not encountered in §3.1 but likewise identical are *m ăritat* 'married,' *săturat* 'eaten enough,' and *stricat* 'spoiled, wrecked'; the verb represented here by p.p. *visat* 'dreamed' has been built on the stem of p.p. VĪSU 'seen.' Still, the form *udat* 'wetted' must be ranked as doubtful, given the preference expressed by some speakers for using adj. *u d* 'wet' alone in constructions where others preferred that past participle.

Regular 2nd-/3rd-conj. forms shared by Daco-Romanian and Istro-Romanian are *crezut* 'believed,' *putut* 'been able,' *şezut* 'sat,' *temut* 'feared,' and *trecut* 'passed.' One could add *avut* 'had,' *cunoscut* 'known,' *cusut* 'sewn,' *ţesut* 'woven,' and *vrut* 'wanted,' but, as discussed below, the first three have by-forms and the third an allegro form. A shared 4th-conj. past participle is *murit* 'died.'

Sigmatic Ist-R *dus* 'brought' contrasts semantically if not morphologically with Rom. *dus* 'taken away,' the Rom. past participle used for 'brought' being prefixed *adus*. Nonetheless, Ist-R *ars* 'burned,' *ales* 'chosen,' *încins* 'girded,' *prins* 'caught,' *pus* 'put,' *rămas* 'stayed,' *tras* 'pulled, dragged,' *ucis* 'killed,' and *zis* 'said' look exactly like their opposite numbers in Romanian. So do *lins* 'licked,' *ros* 'gnawn,' *spus* 'said,' and by-form *tors* 'spun.' As in Daco-Romanian, many Ist-R sigmatics used to be asigmatic. Tautic athematics labialized from [kt] are by-form *copt* 'cooked' and *supt* 'sucked,' the latter possibly with a by-form as well. A highly unpredictable form shared by both is *fost* 'been,' but in Istro-Romanian it has the triplet allegro forms *fos, fs, os*.

At times, different exponents have been chosen for one past-participial slot. Dialectal in Romania, *spart* 'scattered, shattered' is widely used in Istria, with by-form *spars*—standard in Romania—being extremely rare in Istria. In contrast, Istro-Romanian uses the verb represented by p.p. *ţersit* to mean both 'asked' and 'begged [for alms].' Here Romanian distinguishes between the two semantic fields in e.g. p.p. *cerut* 'asked' as against p.p. *cerşit* 'begged,' the latter keeping something of the sigmaticism of its avatar QUÆSĪTU 'sought' though introducing [r] from the infectum stem.

Among past participles nearly identical to those in Daco-Romanian, several have different unstressed vowels. Judging by orthography, atonic <u>a</u> and <u>e</u> have not centralized to [ə]. An Ist-R form with <u>e</u> is *vezut* 'seen.' Ist-R̄ forms with <u>a</u> are *batut* or *abatut* 'beaten, hurt,' *cazut* 'fallen,' *facut* 'done/made,' *lasat* 'left,' *nascut* 'born,' *pascut* 'fed, kept,' *tacut* 'been silent,' and by-form *zacut* 'lain.' (Similar old-fashioned forms are found in parts of Moldova.) In all of these, the first vowel is written <u>ă</u> [ə] in Daco-Romanian. That phoneme is however present in the Ist-R p.p. *căntat* 'sung,' differing from Rom. *cântat* with its high central vowel. Istro-Romanian has that vowel in p.p. *plâns*, identical to Rom. *plâns* 'wept,' but lacks it in p.p. *vindut*, differing from Rom. *vândut* 'sold.' Again in pretonic vowels, Ist-R *cuvintat* 'said' contrasts with Rom. *cuvântat* 'uttered,' both of them built from reflexes of CONVENTU 'agreement.' Further differences in atonic vowels occur in Ist-R *spelat* 'washed' differing from Rom. *spălat*, in Ist-R *tremes* 'sent' differing from Rom. *trimis*, and in Ist-R *bęįut* 'drunk' differing from Rom. *băut*. There also exist Ist-R by-forms *conoscut* 'known' and *cosut* 'sewn,' along with 4th-conj. Ist-R *durmit* 'slept,' this last differing from Rom. *dormit*.

At times more conservative with its vowels than Daco-Romanian, Istro-Romanian proves more innovative with its consonants. As happened in Late Latin, liquids may vanish before another consonant: [r] has fallen in Ist-R *mes* 'gone' but not in Rom. *mers*, and [l] has fallen in *ăncaţat* 'shod,' *cucat* 'lain,' and by-form *ascutat* 'listened' but not in Rom. *încălţat, culcat, ascultat*. Vocalization of [l] here is due to Serbo-Croatian influence; cf. Russ. *kal* versus Serbo-Croatian *kao* 'mud.' What looks like a contrary development, insertion of palatal [λ] into the Ist-R by-form *pl'erdut* 'lost'—compared with Rom. *pierdut*—has also been plausibly ascribed to Slavic influence; more Ist-R by-forms for the same past participle are *predut* and *preidut* with metathesis, and southern *pl'erzut* with [z] before a high back vowel (Puşcariu, 3:128). Probably related to those developments are acquired liquids. In Ist-R *măcirat* 'ground,' *ţirut* 'held,' and *verit* 'come,' intervocalic [n] has rhotacized; compare Rom. *măcinat* (and It. *macinato*), *ţinut*, and *venit*. In this vein, note Ist-R *cirat* 'dined,' as against Rom. *cinat* < CĒNĀTU. Rhotacism of [l] in Ist-R *durut* 'hurt, grieved' occurs also in Daco-Romanian and Aromanian; cf. It. *doluto* 'idem.'

For sibilants, the picture looks less clear. Sometimes Ist-R [s] contrasts with Rom. [ʃ]; sometimes Rom. [s] contrasts with Ist-R [ʃ]. Each possibility is illustrated by Ist-R *şculat* as against Rom. *sculat* 'gotten up, arisen,' then by Ist-R *muscat* as against Rom. *muşcat* 'bitten.' Ist-R by-forms *scutat* and *şcutat* 'listened' would suggest continued hesitation between the two fricatives, at least before [k].[30] Under the same heading go two past participles meaning 'fled,' both regularized from FUGĪTU: Ist-R *fuzĭt* with [ʒ] and Rom. *fugit* with [dʒ].

In one environment, Istro-Romanian resembles Modern Greek, for speakers have turned a high back vowel into a labiodental fricative. Thus, in the Ist-R p.p.s *cavtat* 'looked for' and *avzit* 'heard,' the off-glide kept in trisyllabic Rom. *căutat* and *auzit* has turned into the more or less homorganic fricative. Compare also Ist-R *stivut* 'known' with Rom. *ştiut* 'idem,' where [v] may be an antihiatic excrescence like the one in OFr. *rové* 'asked' < ROGĀTU.

In the realm of morphology, the presence or absence of a prefix may set apart these two forms of eastern Romance. In a series of verbs, typified by their past participles as usual, the Rom. prefix *în*- has undergone aphæresis to become Ist-R *n*-, as also in Aromanian. Thus, Ist-R *nsurat* 'married,' *nţeles* 'understood,' and *nveţat* or *nmeţat* 'taught, prepared' look like shadows of Rom. *însurat, înţeles,* and *învăţat*. In Ist-R *tors* 'spun' as against Rom. *întors*, the prefix appears to have worn away to nothing, or never developed; another prefix may have done likewise in Ist-R *scuns* 'hidden' as against Rom. *ascuns*.

---

[30] Also before a voiceless stop, [s] often palatalizes in Venetian, Friulian, and even Croatian (E. Vrabie, p.c.). Another splinter of the "Romance backbone" near Germany (§3.2.2)?

Among past participles unlike those in Daco-Romanian are the Ist-R by-forms *cocut* 'cooked,' rare *scotut* 'taken out,' and rare *torcut* 'spun,' all three of them regularized along arrhizotonic lines. On the other hand, the Ist-R by-form *aveit* 'had' looks like something lifted out of early Old French, where the ending came from -ĒCTU (§4.4.4). Regularized along 1st-conj. lines have been two rare Ist-R by-forms exemplified by their regular p.p.s, but *zaţat* 'lain' and *tacắt* 'been silent,' are usually found only in the speech of children (Kovačec 1971, 133). As shown in §3.3.1, Aromanian has a few allegro forms of its own. The Ist-R allegro-form oddity *ţắst* 'woven' is apparently unknown elsewhere, except for OCat. *test* 'idem.' I intuitively doubt that either represents a direct survival of TEXTU 'woven.' As with Rom. *fiert* 'boiled,' I could accept a rhizotonic thematic variant in -ĪTU as the hypothetical etymon for at least the Catalan oddity. See §§3.2.2, 3.3.3, 3.5.2, 4.4.9.2, 4.6.2, and 4.7.7.2 for probable and possible -ĪTU survivors across Romance.

Unfortunately, the Ist-R by-form *suptat* 'sucked' might be unknown to native speakers and must be marked doubtful (Puşcariu, 3:135). If in use, it would closely resemble 1st-conj. Sicilian *sukatu* 'sucked' and, less closely, Fr. *sucé* 'idem.'

Minor differences add up to distinctiveness. Related to the Rom. negative adjective *nelắut* 'unwashed' is the Ist-R p.p. *lat* 'washed' < LAVĀTU 'idem.' Moreover, Ist-R *facut* 'done/made' has been so thoroughly regularized arrhizotonically that no rhizotonic variant like Rom. *fapt* 'deed' < FACTU seems to survive. It would be idle to add past participles for verbs borrowed from Slavic.

One morphological oddity deserves recognition. Ist-R past participles retain a distinct neut.sg. form, so that the infin. *ara* 'plow' has masc.sg. *arat* and pl. *araţ*, fem.sg. *arata* and pl. *arate*, and also neut.sg. *arato*. Readers will recall that, in Daco-Romanian, gerunds used to end in -*re*, though past participles are coming into use in that function. In an adapted Romanian transcription, most verbal nouns in Istro-Romanian end in -*atu*, -*utu*, or -*itu*, somewhat like old-fashioned past participles. Examples include *aratu* 'plowing,' *bejutu* 'drinking,' *durmitu* 'sleeping,' and *cositu* 'sewing'; modern past participles for infins. *ara, be, durmi, cosi* are *arắt, bejut, durmit,* and *cosit*. According to Kovačec, the verb *cocĕ* 'cook, bake' has a regularized p.p. *cocut*, while the inherited p.p. *copt* < COCTU serves only as a verbal adjective; however, Puşcariu lists the two as by-form past participles.

Equally revelatory of the current state of Istro-Romanian are two hybrid verbs represented here by their past participles. The second syllables of both *rascl'is* 'opened' and *zacl'is* 'shut' come from combining form -CLŪSU 'shut,' while the first syllables of both have been borrowed from Slavic.

From surrounding Croatian, Istro-Romanian has taken more than words. Sârbu (41–43) gives renewed evidence that at least some Ist-R verbs have developed aspectual contrasts long typical of verbs in Slavic languages (see Table 3–3). In Russian, for instance, the imperfective infinitive *videt'* 'be seeing' contrasts with the perfective infinitive *uvidet'* 'catch sight of,' which has *u-* prefixed; each verb has its own finite forms and its own participles besides. Now Istro-Romanian has evolved two ways of making such contrasts on its own. For some verbs, speakers express imperfectivity with a Romance etymon and perfectivity with the same verb prefixed Slavic-style. For other verbs, speakers express imperfectivity with a Romance etymon but perfectivity by a loan-verb from nearby [Serbo-]Croatian fitted into the local conjugational system. In the last form in the Table 3–3, morphology has been somewhat camouflaged by syncope: *zori* comes from *za + ori* 'plow.'

Table 3–3

Aspectual Pairs in Istro-Romanian

Slavic prefixes are underlined

gloss	Imperfective	Perfective
Type 1: Perfective with Slavic prefix		
'tie'	lega	<u>raz</u>lega
'weep'	plânge	<u>za</u>plânge
'sleep'	durmi	<u>za</u>durmi
'kill'	ucide	<u>zau</u>cide
'steal'	fura	<u>po</u>fura
'bark'	latra	<u>raz</u>latra
'spin'	torce	<u>po</u>torce
'eat'	mânca	<u>na</u>mânca
Type 2: Perfective with Slavic verb		
'drink'	be	<u>po</u>pi
'plow'	ara	<u>z</u>ori

Posner (93) offers another suppletive pair: Latin-derived *mânca* 'eat' < *MANDUCARE and Slavic-derived *poidii* with a *po-* prefix (cf. unprefixed Russ. *yest'* 'eat'). Such borrowing of an aspectual category could well represent, as

Posner says, "a sign of imminent 'language death,' when speakers are shifting their loyalty from one language to another." Yet another sign that Istro-Romanian has become moribund comes from a startling note by Kovačec: "Verbele cu formanţii infinitivali *-á, -é, ´-e* şi o parte din cele in *-i*...sunt de origine latină şi nu sunt productive" (1971, 131) [Verbs with infinitives ending in *-á, -é, ´-e*, and some of those in *-i*...are of Latin origin and are unproductive]. Put otherwise, a feature of Latin verb morphology that has remained constant in every other neo-Latin language—the productivity of the -ĀRE class under various guises—has passed out of existence in Istro-Romanian.

Long before the twenty-first century ends, Istro-Romanian seems destined to be swallowed by Croatian.[31] Soon enough, the past participles gathered here will come to resemble autumn leaves pressed in wax paper.

3.3.3. Istriano (part of Gallo-Italian)

As a glance at the morphology of its past participles makes clear, Istriano belongs to the Gallo-Italian continuum dealt with in §3.6.1. Still, Istriano is spoken along the west coast of the Istrian peninsula, part of Italia irredenta whether ruled by speakers of German or Slavic. For geographical convenience rather than morphological exactitude, then, I group Istriano with Balkan Romance. To avoid confusion with Istro-Romanian (Ist-R) in §3.3.2, I abbreviate the term Istriano as though it stood for "Istro-Italian" (Ist-I).

Data appearing here come from Ive's *I Dialetti ladino-veneti dell'Istria*, which does not refer to Ladin (§4.2), and from Iliescu and Mourin's *Typologie*.

In masc.sg., no reflex of intervocalic dental marking survives: regular past participles end in *-a* for 1st-conj. verbs, in *-u* for 2nd- and 3rd-conj. ones, and in *-i* for 4th-conj. ones. More conservatively, the corresponding fem.sg. forms end in *-ada, -uda*, and *-ida*. As in Sardinian, the preterit has vanished in Istriano and so gives no help in deducing any influence on p.p. formation (Iliescu and Mourin, 395).

Among local semantic oddities, *dezmerto* 'wasted' (infin. *dezmerzi*) appears related to std. It. *smerciato* 'sold out'; *nverto* 'opened' (infin. *nvérzi*) may have come from a past participle meaning 'turned in'; *spento* 'pushed' (infin. *spenzi*) resembles It. *spento* 'quenched, slaked.'

For Ist-I *cŏlto* 'taken' (infin. *cŏ*), compare not only the std. It. p.p. *tolto* 'removed' but also Ven. *ciapar* 'take,' It. *acchiappare* 'grab, seize' from Germ. *klappen* (cf. ModGerm. *Klappe* 'flap; valve'). Exemplars from Germanic and Romance might have blended in that p.p. *cŏlto*. Among local morphological oddities, past participles retain a distinct neuter singular form, so that the infin. *ară* 'plow' has masc.sg. *arăt* and pl. *arăţ*, fem.sg. *arăta* and pl. *arăte*, and also neut.sg. *arăto* (Kovačec, 574).

---

[31] For details of how Croatian has been encroaching on Istro-Romanian, see Coteanu's *Cum dispare o limbă* (*istroromâna*) ['How a Language Vanishes'], dating from 1957.

As in Latin, sigmatic past participles in Istriano usually occur for verbs whose present-tense roots end in a dental stop: *messo* 'put' < MISSU (infin. *méti*), and *perso* 'lost' ≠ PERDITU (infin. *perdi*), for both of which cf. standard Italian. Between vowels, [s] voices to [z], giving e.g. *divizo* 'divided' < DĪVĪSU (infin. *dividi*).

Never with long [t:], tautic athematic past participles include some that once had [kt] like *destruto* 'destroyed' < DĒSTRŪCTU (infin. *destruzi*), *dito* 'said' < DICTU with anaphony (infin. *di*), *fato* 'done/made' < FACTU (infin. *fa*), *frito* 'fried' < FRĪCTU (infin. *frizi*), *leto* 'read' < LĒCTU (infin. *lezi*), and *koleto* 'gathered' < COLLĒCTU (infin. *kolzi*). Other tautic athematic past participles come from Latin forms containing [pt] like *roto* 'broken' < RUPTU (infin. *rómpi*) and *skrit* 'written' < SCRĪPTU (infin. *skrivi*). Several in -nt- survive more or less intact from Latin days: *ponto* 'stung' < PŪNCTU (infin. *ponzi*), *onto* 'oiled' < ŪNCTU (infin. *onzi*), and *strento* 'clasped' < STRICTU plus present-based [n] (infin. *strenzi*). So do some past participles in -rt- like *koverto* 'covered' (infin. *koverzi*) and *morto* 'died' (infin. *murî*). At least one sigmatic-tautic survives from Late Latin or Proto-Romance: *visto* 'seen' (infin. *vedi*).

The Ist-I verb *dezmerzi* 'waste' with p.p. *dezmerto* might come from DĒMERGERE 'plunged into, dipped under,' with EX interposed, and if so would have acquired a tautic athematic past participle ≠ DĒMERSU along the way. The Ist-I oddity *zerto* 'sifted' looks almost like CRĒTU 'idem.' As with Ist-R *tăst* 'woven' in §3.3.2, I decline to accept the notion that *zerto* has come straight from Latin and would prefer some (unattested) rhizotonic thematic variant as its etymon. Compare Ist-I *skonto* 'hidden,' one of the data from Ive brought forward later in this section.

Two other common forms, belonging to 2nd-conj. infinitives, are sigmatic: *pusú* 'been able' (infin. *podé*) competes with an -esto p.p., and so does *(v)usu* 'wanted' (infin. *voré*). Raising of the first vowel in both past participles might have been caused by partial assimilation to now lost preterits like 1sg. *potsi* and *volsi*.

Other 3rd-conj. past participles now ending in atonic [u], namely *vindu* 'sold' < VENDITU (infin. *vendi*), *bi(v)u* 'drunk' < LL BIBITU (infin. *bevi*), and *kuñusu* 'known' ≠ COGNITU (infin. *koñosi*), seem to derive from old forms in atonic -ĬTU, though not invariably the ones attested in Latin. All likewise show raising of the first vowel, and in the last instance raising of the second vowel as well, unlike e.g. 1pl. pres.indic. *vendemo, bevemo*, and *koñosemo*.

In Istriano as elsewhere in ROMANIA, many high-frequency verbs show suppletion. For example, the p.p. *sta* 'been' < STATU 'stood, stayed' sounds nothing like infin. *ési* < LL ESSERE. Then again, neither do It. *stato* 'been' and *essere* 'be.' More strikingly, the apocopated Ist-I p.p. *bu* 'had' (cf. OFr. *eü* [əÿ]) sounds little like infin. *vé* < HABĒRE. On the other hand, p.p. *zi* 'gone' ≠ ĬTU now has the same form as infin. *zi* < ĪRE, but cf. 3sg. pres.indic. *va*.

Istriano resembles Venetian in having many past participles in -esto. As shown in §3.6.1, more past participles marked in [st] are found in Gallo-Italian than anywhere else in Romance. Most often occurring for 3rd-conj. verbs, such Ist-I forms as *koresto* 'run' (infin. *kori*), *pyovesto* 'rained' (infin. *pyovi*), *rendesto* 'given back' (infin. *rendi*), *respondesto* 'answered' (infin. *respondi*), *tazesto* 'been silent' (infin. *tazi*), and *vivesto* 'lived' (infin. *vivi*) are as standard as any forms can be in a dialect. Among 3rd-conj. by-forms in *-esto* are *lezesto* 'read' (infin. *lezi*), *ponzesto* 'stung' (infin. *ponzi*). That type also occurs for some 2nd-conj. verbs: the forms *paresto* 'appeared' (infin. *paré*), *savesto* 'known' (infin. *savé*), and *valesto* 'been worth' (infin. *valé*) are again the only ones listed. Among 2nd-conj. by-forms in *-esto* are *podesto* 'been able' (infin. *podé*), and *voresto* 'wanted' (infin. *voré*). There also exists *-isto*, a 4th-conj. variant seen in e.g. *dulisto* 'hurt' (infin. *duli*). So far, that [st] marker has not spread into the 1st conjugation: Istriano has no past participles ending in **-asto*.

Of irregular past participles, the two most common types are rhizotonic ones in [t] or [z] and arrhizotonic ones ending in *-esto*. Sometimes the two types compete for the same verb (*leto/lezesto* 'read,' *ponto/ponzesto* 'stung'). Among sigmatics, there are rhizotonic past participles like *perso* 'lost' and arrhizotonic ones like *vusú* 'wanted.' Finally, two weak types may compete as past participles for the same verb, like *podést* and *pusú* 'been able' (Iliescu and Mourin, 426–28).

Ive (53–54) supplies past participles for the two most common verbs in Istriano: *sta* 'been' and *bou* 'had.' Another, *skonto* 'hidden,' seems to have syncopated from something like de-prefixed ABSCONDITU. If so, it would stand as a rare survival outside Sardinia and southern Italy of the rhizotonic thematic type ending in -ITU. Compare It. *spanto* 'spread' and Rom. *fiert* 'boiled,' neither from CL etyma.

According to Ive, Istriano further displays its individuality by having developed past participles that end in *-us*, equivalent to std. It. *-oso*. Uniquely in Romance, an ending purely adjectival elsewhere has been here applied to past participles. Such forms include *raspus* 'answered' and *naskus* 'born.' One might seek the origin of that ending in Late Latin, when the muting of [n] before [s] made the rare p.p. ending -ŌNSU homophonous with the common adj. ending -ŌSU. While *raspus* 'answered' could thus go back more or less to RESPŌNSU, innovative *naskus* 'born' could not possibly go back to NĀTU. Clearly, speakers made unconscious analogies when extending the *-us* ending to a number of past participles unentitled to it on etymological grounds, but it remains unclear what those analogies were.

As if one needed further proof that Istriano belongs to Gallo-Italian, Ive furnishes still more Ist-I past participles ending in *-sto*, with -e̯- rather than -i̯- as their tonic vowel. Most of them go with verbs that belong to the 2nd or 3rd conjugation everywhere else: *ardisto* 'burned,' *duvisto* 'had to,' *gudisto* 'enjoyed,' *kuristo* 'run,' *piazisto* 'pleased,' *sadisto* 'yielded' (= std. It. *ceduto*), *savisto* 'known,' *skunfundisto* 'confused,' and *vulisto* 'wanted.' However, *durmisto* 'slept' belongs to a verb that belongs to the 4th conjugation everywhere, and so does *uldisto* 'heard' (= std. It. *udito*) with intrusive [l]; *muristo* 'died' would as usual be a special case. Two of these have syncopated by-forms: *uldó* 'heard' and *vusió* 'wanted.'

Finally, Ive supplies three other such forms—*kardisto, spurzisto* and *tukisto*—whose meanings I do not know, Ive omitting glosses for them. (The first may mean 'believed,' the second 'fetched.') In fact, readers ought to beware of the glosses I have blithely supplied above.

3.4. EVIDENCE FROM VEGLIOTE (DALMATIAN)

When the Republic of Venice won much of the eastern Adriatic coast and the islands offshore, northeastern Gallo-Italian came to serve as a superstrate for Vegliote. As a result, Bartoli when researching *Das dalmastische* was at times unable to determine whether a given lexical item had developed indigenously or been borrowed and adapted to local phonology. Less trustworthy items are here followed by a question mark. (Strictly, Vegliote refers only to Romance spoken on the island of Veglia, but I apply it also to the speech of Zara, now Zadar)

Among verbs in Bartoli's corpus that had undergone semantic shifts were *destruar* 'awake, rouse' < DĒ + EXCITĀRE 'arouse,'[32] *dramuor* 'butcher, slaughter' < DĒ + denominal *RAMARE based on RĀMU 'branch,'[33] *skutro* 'remove' < EXCUTERE 'knock out, shake out,'[34] *stentuar* 'work' < EX + TEMPTĀRE 'try out,' and *truar* 'throw' < TRAHERE 'pull, drag.'[35] Related to infin. *puoskro* 'graze' < PASCERE, the verb *pasnur* 'transplant' had been based on the stem of p.p. PĀSTU 'fed, tended, kept.'[36] That Vegliote belonged on the fringes of ROMANIA rather than at its Franco-Italian center is suggested by the semantic shift in Vegl. *levur* 'take' (cf. Rom. *a lua*, Cat./Sp. *llevar*, and Ptg. *levar* 'take [away]'); It. *levare* and Fr. *lever* 'raise, lift' keep the sense of LEVĀRE. However, in western-looking *faul(ar)* 'speak,' Vegliote also had a reflex of FĀBULĀRĪ 'tell fables, lie, chatter' like Sp. *hablar* and Ptg. *falar* instead of something like Rom. *spune* < EXPŌNERE 'put out; display; explain.' In Vegl. *spangro* 'push' < EXPINGERE 'push out,' though, Vegliote had something like It. *spingere* and OFr. *espeindre* 'drive out' or the useful Cat. verb *espenyar* 'throw off a cliff' (p.p. *espenyat*).

To see how Vegliote differed from other Romance languages, one could consider reflexes of infinitives from the four conjugations of Latin. All the originally free tonic long vowels had shifted, though according to partly unpredictable patterns. From the 1st conjugation, -ĀRE usually became -*uar* after a nasal but became -*uor* in other environments, giving e.g. *klamuar* 'call' < CLĀMĀRE, *sonuar* 'ring' < SONĀRE, and *fermuar* 'secure' < FIRMĀRE but also *kakuor* 'shit' < CACĀRE and *stotuor* 'extinguish' < EX + TŪTĀRE

---

[32] Reflexes of this verb also appear in Rom. *a deştepta* and It. *destare* (*REW* no. 2515).

[33] Reflexes of this verb also appear in OFr. *deramer* and Oc. *demaurar* 'strip off branches' as well as in Engadin and Surselvan (*REW* no. 2578).

[34] Reflexes of this verb have the same meaning in Rom. *a scoate*, but not in OFr. *escourre* or Oc. *escoire* 'thresh' or in OSp. *escudir* 'shiver, shake' (*REW* no. 2998).

[35] Rom. *a trage* < *TRAGERE (for TRAHERE) 'pull, drag') also means 'throw, shoot.'

[36] Cf. It. *pastinare* 'transplant' and Fri. *pastana* 'put shoots in the ground' (*REW* no. 6276).

'protect.' In some 1st-conj. infinitives, *-ur* alone sufficed: *kenur* 'sup, dine' < CĒNĀRE 'have a meal,' *menur* 'lead' < MINĀRE 'threaten; drive,' *maknur* 'grind' < MACHINĀRE, and *pakur* 'pay' < PACĀRE, along with *moitur(o)* 'move' < MŪTĀRE. From the 2nd conjugation, -ĒRE turned into *-ar*, giving e.g. *avar* 'have' < HABĒRE, *emplar* 'fill' < IMPLĒRE, and *ardar* 'burn' < ARDĒRE, and was joined by *bar* 'drink' < BIBERE (cf. It. *bere*, Rom. *a bea*), but then again that *-ar* ending might have *-o* optionally suffixed as in *valar(o)* 'be worth' < VALĒRE. From the 3rd conjugation, ´-ĔRE often turned into *-ro*, giving e.g. *dekro* 'say, tell' < DĪCERE, *spangro* 'push' < EXPINGERE 'push out,' and *skutro* 'remove' < EXCUTERE 'knock out, shake out.' Here again, *-ur* might appear: *fregur* 'fry' < FRĪGERE and *fur* 'make' < FACERE. From the 4th conjugation, -ĪRE often turned into *-er*, giving e.g. *senter* 'feel, perceive' < SENTĪRE, *dormer* 'sleep' < DORMĪRE, and *morer* 'die' from an active variant of CL MORĪ; however, note *apiar* 'open' < APERĪRE, which had perhaps joined the 2nd conjugation. To make Vegliote morphology more bewildering still, that *-er* ending was evidently optional on certain verbs like *piand(er)* 'hang,' *piard(er)* 'lose' (Fisher, passim). Infinitives in Vegliote might therefore take one of nine endings: *-uar*, *-uor*, *-ur*, *-uro*, *-ar*, *-aro*, *-ro*, *-er*, or zero. Bartoli views the following outcomes as regular for infinitive endings: -ĀRE > *-úr* (*-úor*), -ĒRE > *-ár*, ´-ERE > ´*-ro*, and -ĪRE > *-ér*.[37]

Arrhizotonic past participles appear to have had only three kinds of ending. Among those gathered were 1st-conj. *sekúot* 'dried' < SICCĀTU, 4th-conj. *fenáit* 'ended' < FĪNĪTU, and 2nd-/3rd-conj. *naskóit* 'born' ≠ NĀTU, demonstrating extreme diphthongization of free tonic vowels in all three types. Another 1st-conj. p.p. was *krepuát* 'burst,' regularized from CREPĬTU. Other 2nd-/3rd-conj. p.p.s were *avóit* 'had' ≠ HABĬTU, *blóit* 'wanted' and *sapoit* 'known' (no CL p.p.s). Other 4th-conj. past participles were *dormáit* 'slept' < DORMĪTU, *báit* 'drunk' ≠ LL BIBITU, *sentáit* 'felt' ≠ SĒNSU, and *záit* 'gone,' regularized (sort of) from ĬTU. Three verbs had p.p. by-forms among non-1st-conj. types: *potait* and *potóit* been able,' *vedóit* and *vedáit* 'seen,' *venóit* and *venáit* 'come.' Bartoli considers *desendoit* 'gone down' and *metoit* 'put' to have been innovations inspired by northern Italian forms. Certainly indigenous was *fóit* 'been' < *FUTU (cf. Arom. *fută*), but Bartoli regards homonymous *?fóit* 'fled' ≠ FUGITU as less certain, perhaps because of the Olt. noun *futa* 'flight' ≠ FUGA.

Among rhizotonic past participles in Bartoli's corpus are tautic athematic *apiárt* 'opened' < APERTU, *kopiárt* 'covered' < COOPERTU, and *dut* of *det* 'said' < DICTU. Possibly influenced by Italian—but with un-Italian vocalism—are interrogatively marked *?cŭolt* 'removed' ≠ SUBLĀTU, *?fuát* 'done/made' < FACTU, *?friát* 'fried' < FRĪCTU, *?kuát* 'cooked' < COCTU, *?plant* 'complained' < PLĀNCTU, *?ruát* 'broken' < RUPTU, and *?skrit* 'written' < SCRĪPTU. Sigmatics

---

[37]Bartoli might have had difficulty in transcribing dental consonants as enunciated by his toothless consultant. No such difficulties ought to have arisen when he transcribed vowels or [r], which no one needs teeth to pronounce. Bartoli (402) judges the infinitive endings *-ure*, *-are*, and *-ere* to be "toskanisierend" [Tuscanizing], though std. Italian has no infinitive in *-ure*.

are *mais* 'put' < MISSU, *piárs* 'lost' ≠ PERDITU, and *práis* 'taken, caught' < PRĒNSU. Another sigmatic, *stras* 'narrowed, tightened,' may be contrasted with std. It. *stretto* < STRICTU (Bartoli, 403–4).[38]

Yet more Vegliote past participles deriving from -ĀTU included *mudúot* 'moved' from something like *MOVITĀTU, providing further proof that plain MOVĒRE 'move' vanished east of the Adriatic.[39] In the same class were the adjectivized pair *dúot* 'wet' from a variant 1st-conj. past participle based on adj. ŪDU < UVIDU[40] and *blasmuát* 'bad' from a variant *BLASTIMATU for BLASPHEMĀTU 'blasphemed.' For this last lexical item, the original sense has been kept in It. *bestimmiato*, if not in Fr. *blâmé* and Cat. *blasmat* 'blamed' or in Sp./Ptg. *lastimado* 'hurt, injured.' Deriving from an adjective in -ŪTU, Vegliote had nominalized *karnoit* 'viper' < CORNŪTU 'horned'; cf. also *kroit* 'raw' < CRŪDU. Old sigmatic past participles were represented by adj. *fuals* 'untrue' < FALSU, old tautic athematics by *muárt* 'dead' < MORT(U)U— homonymous with *muárt* 'death' < obl. MORTE—and by adjectivized *sot* 'dry' < EXSUCTU 'sucked out,' for which cf. It. *asciutto* 'narrow-chested,' Sp. *enjuto* and Ptg. *enxuto* 'lean, drawn.' What would have happened to the -ĒTU type, had it survived, is suggested by *akait* 'vinegar' < ACĒTU or by *drat* 'straight' < DĪRĒCTU, where [e:] had become [a] or [ai̯] (Fisher, 33, 37, 43, 44, 48–49, 56, 62, 72–73, 94).

Older records from farther south along the Adriatic shore reveal the survival of more rhizotonic past participles. In a letter from a nobleman on Zara in 1325, the following forms appear: *ditu* 'told' < DICTU, *respwast* 'answered' < RESPŌNSU, and sigmatic *pjers* 'lost' ≠ PERDITU. In the letter, 1st-conj. p.p.s also end in -*uot* given *portuot* 'took,' and 4th-conj. past participles also end in -*ait* given *fenait* 'ended.' In one respect, Zara Dalmatian appears to have resembled other Romance tongues more than Vegliote did: 2nd-/3rd-conj. past participles used to end in -*ut* farther down the Adriatic, given *avut* 'had' and *inparut* 'learned,' *favlut* 'spoken' and *spozut* 'married,' though the last two of these show metaplasm away from the 1st conjugation (Sampson, 203–6).

All in all, fragments of Vegliote gathered at the end of the nineteenth century allow one to catch sight of a realm that remains forever out of reach: how would Romance languages between the Danube and the Adriatic have evolved if they had lasted till today? One might as well ask which morphosyntactic features of Latin might have lasted in a hypothetical Romance spoken across Morocco, Algeria, Tunisia, and half of Libya if

---

[38] Bartoli (403) contrasts the Vegl. by-form *det* 'said, told,' a straight reflex of DICTU, with Ven. *dito* and Fr. *dit*, with [i:] carried over from the finite perfectum DĪXĪ etc. Cf. the Vegl. p.p.s *mais* 'put' ± pf. MĪSĪ and *prais* 'taken' ± pf. *PRESI for PRENDIDĪ.

[39] Long-form *MOVITARE had reflexes in Old Venetian and western Occitan (*REW* no. 5705). Replaced by reflexes of MŪTĀRE 'change,' reflexes of MOVĒRE 'move' failed to survive in Dacia.

[40] Reflexes of that contracted adjective ŪDU 'wet' live on in Romance, if only in Rom. *ud* and Vegl. *yoit* 'wet' (*REW* no. 9030).

colonists along that thin green strip had gone on speaking the language in their own way. One might as well ask which features of Latin might have lasted in a hypothetical Romance spoken in Britannia long after the legionnaires withdrew in 410 CE.

3.5. EVIDENCE FROM STANDARD ITALIAN

Morphologically speaking, if the conservatism of Italian has resulted in part from transplants out of the classical garden, a botanist paying a visit of inspection will remark that the landscape looks nearly the same as it did fifteen hundred years ago. Italian has been laid out according to the most latinate plan available today. Examples in standard Italian come mainly from Battaglia's *Grande Dizionario della Lingua italiana* (1961–) and Tekavčić's *Grammatica storica dell'italiano*.

3.5.0. Preliminaries

Lexically, Italian has failed to continue certain verbs from Latin. If past participles may stand for whole verbs, Italian has replaced OBLĪTU 'forgotten' with *dimenticato* and *scordato* (but cf. OIt. *ubbiato*) and replaced PETĪTU 'asked' with *chiesto* and *domandato* (though a reflex of its old present participle survives as *pezzente* 'beggar'). In the sense 'learned,' Italian has *imparato* < IN + PARĀTU 'prepared.' Morphologically, regular past participles end in *-ato* < -ĀTU for 1st-conj. verbs, in *-uto* < -ŪTU for 2nd- and 3rd-conj. verbs, and in *-ito* < -ĪTU for 4th-conj. verbs.

Italian often seems little changed from Late Latin. Examples are 1st-conj. *giocato* 'played' and *parato* 'readied,' 2nd- and 3rd-conj. *battuto* 'beaten' and *fottuto* 'fucked,' 4th-conj. *nutrito* 'fed,' *tossito* 'coughed,' and *udito* 'heard.'[41]

Despite this deep morphological conservatism, speakers of Italian have remade a number of past participles along arrhizotonic lines. Most such remakings resemble those found elsewhere. They include 2nd-/3rd-conj.-style *tessuto* 'woven' ≠ TEXTU and *venduto* 'sold' ≠ VENDĬTU. They also include 4th-conj.-style *aderito* 'stuck' ≠ ADHÆSU, *carpito* 'plucked' ≠ CARPTU, *patito* 'undergone' ≠ PASSU, *perito* 'perished' ≠ PERĬTU, *rapito* 'seized' ≠ RAPTU, *sarcito* 'mended' ≠ SARTU, and *sorbito* 'swallowed' ≠ SORBĬTU. Note the 4th-conj.-style pair *concepito* 'imagined' and *percepito* 'perceived' ≠ CONCEPTU, PERCEPTU. A few of these, like *marcito* 'faded, withered' and *putito* 'stunk' (also *puzzato*), had no filler for the slot in Latin.

In p.p. lexis, std. *andato* 'walked, gone' contrasts with literary *gito* 'gone' (cf. dial. *ito*); std. *macinato* 'ground' contrasts with dialectal 4th-conj. *molito*

---

[41] Generalizing from ever-popular FACTU 'done/made' and perhaps also DICTU 'said, told,' speakers of certain Italian dialects have developed 1st-conj. p.p.s with endings as if from -ACTU, and sometimes also 4th-conj. p.p.s with endings as if from -ICTU. For details, see Rohlfs 1968, 368–69. Relics of a similar type in French, from -ECTU, appear in §4.4.9.3.

remade from MOLĬTU. From a single stem come usual std. *meschiato* and rare std. *mesciuto* 'mixed, mingled'; cf. also OIt. *meschitato*. Other literary p.p.s are *mirato* 'looked at' and French-inspired *obliato* 'forgotten,' rare *funto* 'performed' < FŪNCTU, poetic *fratto* 'broken' < FRĀCTU, and finally *misto* 'mingled' < MIXTU.

Italian marks stress only on oxytones like *città* 'city' or *tribù* 'tribe.' In §§3.5.1–3.5.10, I have added acute accents to mark proparoxytones like *spéndita* 'spending' or *pérdita* 'loss.' Paroxytones remain unmarked.

3.5.1. Features of the Italian Past System

Drawing a comparison between the infinitives, perfects, and past participles of Latin and Italian verbs, Tekavčić notes in *Grammatica storica dell'italiano* (376) that, in Latin, tonic vowels ran parallel for common 1st-conj. -ĀRE -ĀVĪ -ĀTU, for rare 2nd-conj. -ĒRE -ĒVĪ -ĒTU, and for common 4th-conj. -ĪRE -ĪVĪ -ĪTU. Owing to the disappearance of the -ĒRE type of perfect and past participle and the rise of preterits in -*ei* or -*etti* based on DEDĪ or a -UĪ variant for STETĪ, Italian has in effect reestablished the arrhizotonic symmetry that once existed in most Latin verbs, although by different means. For infinitives and (1sg.) preterits, Tekavčić remarks, Italian still has such parallels in 1st-conj. -*are* and -*ai*, 4th-conj. -*ire* and -*ii* and has evolved such parallels in 2nd-conj. and 3rd-conj. -*ére*/ ´-*ere* and -*ei*/-*etti*. For past participles, regular 1st-conj. -*ato* and regular 4th-conj. -*ito* match the tonic vowels in their infinitives and preterits.

Yet the impression of regularity conveyed by Tekavčić's schemata remains in part illusory. Despite his admission (376) that preterits like *vendei* 'I sold' and *potei* 'I could' have merely a "somiglianza apparente" [apparent similarity] with the old -ĒVĪ class of perfects, which have either vanished or joined other classes, one feels constrained to point out that scarcely half a dozen -ĒRE verbs in Latin kept tonic [e] in the perfectum, that not a single verb form coming down from -ĒTU survives as a past participle, and that fifteen hundred years of analogical remodeling have failed to make 2nd- or 3rd-conj. past participles morphologically transparent in Italian. That is, such past participles commonly end in -*uto*, but only a few syncopated infinitives, chiefly compounds built from reflexes of DŪCERE like *condurre* 'drive,' contain tonic [u]. Other contracted infinitives—*bere* 'drink,' *dire* 'say, tell,' *fare* 'do/make,' literary *porre* 'put'—may go along with uncontracted past participles or with inherited irregular ones (see §3.5.4).[42]

As in other Romance languages, regularization of Italian past participles has tended to take place along arrhizotonic lines. Among 1st-conj. forms, *vietato* 'forbidden' does not directly continue rhizotonic thematic VETĬTU, just as now-standard *suonato* 'sounded' and *tuonato* 'thundered' do not directly continue SONĬTU and TONĬTU. Besides acquiring regular -*ato*

---

[42] With full etymological justification, Italian infinitives ending in -*durre* have p.p.s ending in -*dotto* < DUCTU 'led.'

endings, all three have been part of a horizontal diffusion of diphthongs regularly evolving in rhizotonic forms like pres.subj.sg. *suoni* and *tuoni*. There also exist regular by-form p.p.s *sonato* and *tonato*.

Italian has extended -ĀTU to other -ĀRE verbs that had -ĬTU past participles in Latin (Meyer-Lübke 1931, 202). Most also had -UĪ perfects, but all have -*ai* preterits now. Instances are modern *crepato* 'burst,' *covato* 'brooded, hatched,' *domato* 'tamed,' and *spiegato* 'explained,' as against CREPITU, CUBITU, DOMITU, EXPLICITU, though EXPLICĀRE 'unfold' could optionally take an arrhizotonic -ĀVĪ pf. and an -ĀTU p.p. Note also 1st-conj. *rovesciato* 'overturned,' no doubt built on the same stem, RUP-, as p.p. *rotto* 'broken.'

In another regularization, stem-final consonants in past participles have been aligned with those in infinitives. As part of the drive toward greater transparency of form, at least eight -ŪTU p.p.s in Italian descending from inchoative etyma in [sk] or from other etyma in [k] now have palatal [ʃ] or [tʃ] even before a back vowel. They have been brought into line with their infinitive stems, where [ʃ] or [tʃ] comes from [sk] or [k] before a front vowel. Examples include 3rd-conj. *cresciuto* 'grown' (not **crescuto*) agreeing with infin. *crescere*, *conosciuto* 'known' (not **conoscuto*) with *conoscere*, *giaciuto* 'lain' (not **giacuto*) with *giacere*, nonstandard *nasciuto* 'born' (not **nascuto*) with *nascere*, *nociuto* 'harmed' (not **nocuto*) with *nuocere*, and *pasciuto* 'fed, kept' (not **pascuto*) with *pascere*. Two examples from the 2nd conjugation are *piaciuto* 'pleased' (not **piacuto*) agreeing with infin. *piacere*, and *taciuto* 'been silent' (not **tacuto*) agreeing with *tacere*. Though palatal consonants may alternate with nonpalatal ones in verb forms like the pres.indic. for 'end' or 'say'—1sg. *finisco* with [sk] as against 2sg. *finisci* with [ʃ], 1sg. *dico* with [k] as against 2sg. *dici* with [tʃ]—speakers have achieved consonantal parallelism between the above infinitives and their past participles.[43]

After centuries of leveling within the past system, a fair amount of morphological predictability has come about. As Vincent observes (1988b, 296), "very few verbs have an irregular preterit and a regular past participle, and even fewer have an irregular past participle and a regular preterit."

3.5.2. Old Past Participles in –ĬTU

Unlike Sardinian or dialects south of Rome, standard Italian resembles French, Portuguese, Spanish, Catalan, and Romanian in having almost no direct descendants of rhizotonic -ĬTU past participles kept in that function. Italian does retain several syncopated lexical items that once belonged to that type (§3.5.2.1). More conservatively, Italian has several unsyncopated nouns in atonic ´-*ito* or ´-*ita*, none of them serving any longer as a past participle (§3.5.2.2).

---

[43] Old Italian had a great many more present-tense stem alternations between palatal and nonpalatal consonants. For examples involving *venire* 'come,' *salire* 'go up,' *vedere* 'see,' *leggere* 'read,' *vincere* 'win,' *pugnere* 'sting,' and *cogliere* 'gather,' among others, see Maiden 1992, 292–93. Most of these have been leveled on nonpalatal lines.

3.5.2.1. Syncopated

Once belonging to a single class in Latin, Italian past participles like *erto* 'raised' ≠ ĒRĒCTU (next to the evidently learnèd adj. *eretto* 'erect'), *porto* 'handed over' ≠ PORRĒCTU 'fetched,' and *sorto* 'arisen' ≠ SURRĒCTU (see Table 3–4). All now contain an [rt] cluster. Resembling those three in form are

Table 3–4

Syncope in Italian Past Participles

( )   archaic as past participles

Latin	Proto-Italian	Italian	cf. Spanish (archaic)
Old forms in -ECTU			
COLLĒCTU	*COLLITU	colto	(cogecho)
ĒRĒCTU	*ERITU	erto	(erecho)
EX+ĒLĒCTU	*EXELITU	scelto	—
PORRĒCTU	*PORRITU	porto	—
SURRĒCTU	*SORRITU	sorto	—
Old forms in - UTU			
SOLŪTU	SOLVITU	solto	(suelto)
VOLŪTU	VOLVITU	volto	vuelto
New sigmatic-tautic			
VĪSU	VISITU	visto	visto
Old suppletive			
SUBLĀTU₁	TOLLITU	tolto	(tuelto)

syncopated *colto* 'gathered' ≠ COLLĒCTU (cf. infin. *cogliere*), alongside *tolto* 'removed' ≠ SUBLĀTU 'raised' (cf. *togliere*), and perhaps also tautic athematic *svelto* or *divelto* 'uprooted' ≠ ĒVULSU (cf. 3rd-conj. EX + ĒVELLERE > It. *svellere*). All now contain an [lt] cluster; the last is oddly unsigmatic. The first of these should not be confused with adjectival *colto* 'learnèd' < CULTU, and the last should not be confused with adjectival *svelto* 'quick,' which a lexicographer has to mark o.o.o.

Meyer-Lübke states (1931, 205) that such past participles syncopated from mostly attested variants, rhizotonic and proparoxytonic, although it is of course his interpretation that the variants should be put into that class. (I say "mostly attested" because, when it comes to macrons and asterisks, even Meyer-Lübke nods.) Such p.p. variants include TOLLĬTU 'taken away,' VOLVĬTU 'rolled,' SOLVĬTU 'loosened,' and QUÆSĬTU 'sought'; note also std. VĪSĬTU 'inspected.' Some of those lay behind Spanish past participles or adjectives like *vuelto* 'rolled,' *suelto* 'loose,' and *visto* 'seen.' They suggest that LL speakers in Italia, and elsewhere, tended to prefer past participles marked by a theme vowel, even if that vowel was unstressed.

Their descendants grew less fond of -ĬTU as a p.p. marker, again because it must have come to sound insufficiently distinctive to play that morphological role. Only syncope has saved several such forms from regularization. One is old-fashioned *arroto* 'added, made whole' from a variant of 1st-conj. ADROGĀTU 'claimed; adjudged,' and speakers have largely limited *arroto* to adjectival use.

3.5.2.2. Unsyncopated

In Italian, the presence of more than a few nouns built from -ĬTU p.p.s implies that current preferences in morphology did not always prevail along the Arno, any more than it did along the Seine, the Danube, or the Ebro. As Georges remarks: "Consequently, the category of p.-ptc. nouns comprises a multi-layered detritus of fossilized derivational patterns, often invaluable for reconstructing morphological mechanisms no longer directly observable" (15). In §4.4.9 for French and §4.7.7 for Spanish, I undertake two further digs into the layers of p.p. detritus.

Sometimes, from a whole verb only a past participle seems to have lived on: It. *lécito* 'permissible' < LICĬTU (not regularly evolving *leceto*) endures adjectivally, and also nominally in the sense 'right,' but no other form of LICĒRE 'be allowed' is to be found here.

Several other rhizotonic nouns in Italian, on which stress is marked below, have by-forms identical with past-participial exponents currently in vogue. Alongside fem. *cresciúta* 'growth [of plants]' and *spesa* 'cost; shopping,' the former an arrhizotonic innovation (if rare now) and the latter a continuation of CL EXPÉNSA,[44] descendants of past participles in -ĬTA like *créscita* 'growth, outgrowth' and *spéndita* 'spending' point to related forms in Late Latin or Proto-Romance. Compare the Cal. noun *críscita* 'yeast' (Rohlfs 1968, 375). Again, though, perfectly regular evolution would have given *-eta*.

---

[44] Also surviving in OFr. *espoise* 'cost' (*REW* no. 3042). Cf. the semilearnèd ModFr. p.p. *dépensé* 'spent,' with half its [ns] cluster engulfed by nasalization of the preceding vowel.

Perhaps *spéndita* was formed by analogy with *véndita* 'sale' < p.p. VENDITA on semantic grounds,[45] but the latter still sharply contrasts with the regularized arrhizotonic p.p. *vendúto* 'sold.' Note also the std. Italian noun *débito* 'debt' as against p.p. *dovúto* 'owed,' much like the noun *pérdita* 'loss' < p.p. PERDITA as against p.p. *perduto* (also *perso*). Much the same, though with infectum nasality absent from REDDITU 'given back,' is *réndita* 'rent, income' as against the sigmatic p.p. *reso*. A similar if syncopated contrast used to be evident in the OIt. noun *futa* 'fleeing, flight,' syncopated from the CL p.p. FUGĬTA but underivable from the CL 1st-decl. noun FUGA 'flight.' Compare the It. p.p. *fuggito*, remade arrhizotonically as it was everywhere in Romance (*REW* no. 3552).[46]

Nowadays, the by-form infins. *acquistare* and *acquisire* 'acquire' have regular past participles, in *-ato* and *-ito* respectively, yet the masc. noun *acquísto* 'purchase, acquisition' looks close to the French p.p. *acquis* 'acquired' and implies a syncopated LL/PR variant for CL ACQUĪSĪTU. The fem. noun *cérnita* 'sorting, selection' is based on the present stem of archaic 3rd-conj. *cernere* —with relatives in Portugal, Spain, Catalonia, Occitania, and Romania—and *cérnita* suggests a LL/PR present-based rhizotonic variant of CRĒTU 'sifted' based on the infectum stem; cf. the OIt. p.p. *cernuto* 'sifted.'[47] Again, the masc. noun *préstito* 'loan' as against regular 1st-conj. *prestare* 'lend' with an *-ato* p.p. suggests that, for a while in Italia, there survived a reflex of rhizotonic thematic PRÆSTITU 'provided, lent' (examples from Georges, 15).[48]

3.5.3. Other Rhizotonic Past Participles

As Elcock comments (131), of all parts of ROMANIA, Italy proved most amenable to retaining rhizotonic past participles. Italy even evolved new rhizotonics by means other than syncope. I go through dozens of them below.

3.5.3.1. Tautics and Double-Tautics

Italian keeps more than a few past participles in long [t:]. At times this characteristically Italian phoneme comes from CL [pt] as in *scritto* 'written' <

---

[45] Also surviving in Ptg. *venda* and Fr. *vente* 'sale' (*REW* no. 9190).

[46] Syncope involving a past participle occurred in the name of a mediæval Florentine institution *Lo spedale a' Pinti* 'Repenters' Hospital,' where *pinti* comes from 4th-conj. *pentiti/pintiti*. Nowadays, regular infin. *pentire* 'repent; change one's mind' and regular p.p. *pentito* have won out in the standard, but variance endures in two nonstandard by-forms: 2nd-conj. *pentere* and 3rd-conj. *pentre* (R. Stefanini, p.c.).

[47] A reflex of CERNERE 'sift' also survived in OFr. *serdre* (*REW* no. 1832). Givern Rom./Cat. *cernut* 'sifted,' one would expect that Fr. verb's p.p. to be regular *serdu*, but I have been unable to find any attestation of such a form in chansons de geste or fabliaux.

[48] On the phrase *dare in prestito* 'lend' was build the It. proparoxytonic noun *imprestito* 'loan,' borrowed as Sp. *empréstito* with its giveaway intervocalic -t- (*REW* no. 6725).

SCRĪPTU or *rotto* 'broken' < RUPTU. Most often, long [t:] comes from CL [kt] as in *fritto* 'fried' < FRĪCTU, *detto* 'said' < DICTU, *fatto* 'done/made' < FACTU, *stretto* 'tightened' < STRICTU, or *tratto* 'pulled' < TRACTU.

Several Italian past participles descended from LL etyma are formed with a simple [t] suffix, like *gionto* or *giunto* 'arrived' < JŪNCTU 'joined,' *morto* 'died' < MORT(U)U, and *pianto* 'complained' < PLĀNCTU, with the first and third of these deriving from reduction and assimilation of a CL [ŋkt] cluster to [nt] (Mendeloff, 53). Given that these verbs' semantic fields lie outside the spheres of law, war, religion, and administration, one might expect any tautic athematic past participle to represent a survival rather than a revival. That type also occurs after [r], as in the pair *aperto* 'opened' < APERTU and *coperto* 'covered' < COOPERTU (with syncopated infins. *aprire, coprire*) and the pair *offerto* 'offered' and *sofferto* 'suffered.' Other tautic athematics after [n] are *cinto* < CĪNCTU 'girded' (infin. *cingere*), and *tinto* 'dyed' with its privative partner *stinto* 'faded' < (EX)TĪNCTU 'dyed' (infin. *tingere*), alongside *estinto* 'passed away' < EXSTĪNCTU 'annihilated' (infin. *estinguere*), as in the phrase *caro estinto* 'dear departed.'[49]

In this class, [n] from the old infectum stem has found its way into some Italian past participles. Nasal victories extend to It. *(in)franto* 'crushed' instead of arch. *fratto* < FRĀCTU; compare OFr. nasal *fraint* vying with non-nasal *frait*. Two other Italian past participles with infectious nasality are It. *finto* 'feigned' resembling Fr. *feint* (cf. CL FICTU but LL FINCTU), also used adjectivally in the sense 'fake' or 'hypocritical,' and *dipinto* 'painted' resembling Fr. *peint* (cf. CL PICTU but LL PINCTU), itself also used nominally in the sense 'painting' in Italian. Archaic *minto* 'pissed' comes from by-form MINCTU, already with present-stem [n] (cf. infin. *mingere* < MINGERE), but that verb probably represents a revival by savants rather than a survival among the plebs.

Among tautic athematic past participles, some regularization has occurred through time. Old-fashioned *ricetto* 'received' < RECEPTU, still surviving in the family name *Benericetti*, has been replaced as a past participle by *ricevuto* built on the present stem. Meanwhile, masc. *ricetto* 'repair' < RECEPTU 'received' and fem. *ricetta* 'recipe; prescription' < RECEPTA both serve as nouns.[50]

As noted in Chapter 2, FERĪRE 'hit; kill' had two suppletive past participles. In Italian, a semantic distinction has arisen along with a morphological one between the two past participles for 4th-conj. infin. *inferire* 'infer; inflict.' Regular *inferito* means 'inferred,' and syncopated *inferto* means 'inflicted.' Readers may decide which variant sounds older.

---

[49] Since the *REW* has no entry for EXSTĪNCTU 'put out (fire)' anywhere in Romance, It. *estinto* may appear learnèd. Yet p.p.s like OFr. *esteint*, ModFr. *éteint* 'put out (fire)'—now extended to 'turned off (electrical gadget)'—strongly suggest that, in northern Gaul, ordinary speakers kept alive a verb for an activity of daily familiarity. Here Meyer-Lübke nods.

[50] Reflexes of RECEPTU also survive in poetic It. *ricetto* and in OFr./Oc. *recet* 'place of refuge' (*REW* no. 7112).

3.5.3.2. Sigmatics

Descending straight from Latin, Italian retains a great many sigmatic past participles like *arso* 'burned' < ĀRSU, *chiuso* 'shut' < -CLŪSU, *corso* 'run' < CURSU, *messo* 'put' < MISSU 'sent,' *morso* 'bitten' < MORSU, *raso* 'shaved' < RĀSU, *riso* 'laughed' < RĪSU, *roso* 'gnawn' < RŌSU, and *(s)teso* 'stretched out' < (EX)TĒNSU. Another sigmatic, *sparso* 'scattered' < SPARSU, has something of a by-form in archaic, tautic athematic *sparto*; to which compare the coexistence in Romanian of *spars* and *spart* 'cracked' (§3.1.5.2). Conservative It. *terso* 'clear, clean' < TERSU 'wiped, scrubbed' has been limited to adjectival use, but prefixed *deterso* still serves as the past participle for *detergere* 'cleanse, wipe.' Also surviving, marginally, is an old-fashioned adjective *pasto* 'fed,' reflecting sigmatic-tautic PĀSTU 'fed, kept.'

For other verbs in Italian, assimilation of [ks] to [s:] in the preterit stem has been extended to the past participle. Hence current *vissuto* 'lived' resembles the CL pf. VIXĪ + -ŪTU far more than it does the CL p.p. VĬCTU. In Italian, this last root VĬCT- appears both with semilearnèd [i] and with regular [e] < [ĭ], so that *vitto* 'victuals' for **vetto*, never usable as a past participle today, contrasts with pl. *vettovaglie* 'food supplies.'[51] Like *vissuto*, the stem of semilearnèd *flesso* 'bent' resembles the CL pf. FLEXĪ, but cf. p.p. FLEXU. Given the 3rd-conj. infin. *riflettere*, the etymological p.p. *riflesso* 'reflected' may appear to compete with regularized *riflettuto*, but the two have been made semantically distinct: the first has the literal meaning 'bent back [of light],' the second the more abstract meaning 'thought over.' Both, however, look semilearnèd because they keep an [fl] cluster normally remade as [fj], in e.g. *fiore* < FLŌRE 'bloom.' Indeed, the *REW* lists no direct descendants of REFLECTERE 'turn back, bend back' anywhere in ROMANIA; any such descendants would at all events be phonologically anomalous in Italian.

Like *steso* "stretched' mentioned above, certain sigmatic past participles in Italian appear to come from prefixed variants of Latin exponents. Another is *scosso* 'shaken' < EXCUSSU (cf. QUASSU 'shaken'). Conversely, a few appear to have dropped a CL prefix, like *sceso* and *disceso* 'gone down' < DĒSCĒNSU.[52]

As in Latin, sigmatic past participles often accompany 3rd-conj. infinitive roots ending in a dental stop. Thus, literary *assiso* 'sat' (cf. infin. *assidersi*), *alluso* 'alluded' (*alludere*), *annesso* 'attached' (*annettere*), *concesso* 'granted' (*concedere*), poetic *conquiso* and OIt. *conqueso* 'conquered' (*conquidere*), *deciso* 'decided' (*decidere*), *difeso* 'defended' (*difendere*), *discusso* 'discussed' (*discutere*), *eliso* 'annulled' (*elidere*), *evaso* 'escaped' (*evadere*), *intriso* 'kneaded; soaked' (*intridere*), and *ucciso* 'killed' (*uccidere*) all belong to this class. So do the related forms *appeso* 'hung,' *dipeso* 'relied,' and *sospeso* 'overhung' (cf. infins. *appendere, dipendere, sospendere*). So do learnèd-

---

[51] Cf. semilearnèd It. *cibo* 'food, meal' for what would have regularly evolved to **cevo* < CĬBU.

[52] Without prefixed *di-* but with reversal of meaning, It. *scendere* 'go/come down' has practically resumed the shape of rare CL SCANDERE 'go/come up' (Ernout and Meillet, 599).

looking *espanso* 'swelled,' *esploso* 'blew up,' and *espulso* 'driven out' (cf. infins. *espandere, esplodere, espellere*), the last of which continues a sigmatic reshaping from Latin times. Attached to the 2nd-conj. infin. *persuadere* is p.p. *persuaso* 'persuaded.' Equally sigmatic are *leso* 'harmed, injured' < LÆSU (cf. *ledere* < LÆDERE) and the p.p.-derived adjective *illeso* 'unharmed.' Archaic and still dialectal *creso* 'believed' (cf. *credere*) and *nascoso* 'hidden' (cf. *nascondere*) used to belong; the former cannot have continued CRĒDITU; the second did continue LL ABSCONSU (cf. OIt. *ascoso*) with partial aphæresis of prefixed IN-.

In the forms above, certain phonological features hint at learnèd retention or revival: the consonant clusters [ns] or [pl], a vowel before "impure s̲," or vowels suspiciously identical to those in the CL originals. After all, unprefixed infinitives like 3rd-conj. *cedere*, archaic *fendere, pendere*, and 2nd-conj. *sedere* tend to have past participles in reflexes of -ŪTU like *ceduto* 'yielded,' *fenduto* 'split' (also *fesso*), *penduto* 'hung' (but *-peso* in compounds), and *seduto* 'sat.' Meanwhile, arrhizotonic *creduto* 'believed' rather than sigmatic *creso* has become standard.

Actually, no straight reflexes have survived anywhere of ALLŪDERE 'caress, fondle,' CONCĒDERE 'withdraw, yield,' DĒCIDERE 'cut off; arrange,' ĒLĪDERE 'knock out,' EXPLAUDERE 'hiss off [the stage],' ĒVĀDERE 'go forth, escape,' or PERSUĀDĒRE 'prevail upon, convince,' according to the *REW*. Those verbs appear inessential to the business of daily life. Speakers of a post- or preliterary language could get along without them well enough. Nevertheless, a morphological pattern from Latin has remained in Italian: many rhizotonic infinitives with stems ending in a dental stop have past participles marked with [s(:)], as witness high-flown *assiso* 'seated,' p.p. for 3rd-conj. *assidersi*.[53] Absent recourse to Latin, the morphology of such Italian past participles would remain inexplicable.

In a development reminiscent of Romanian (§3.1.5), some sigmatic past participles now in Italian belonged to other classes or were lacking from the CL inventory. After sigmatic markers spread into the rhizotonic perfectum of a large number of verbs (Vincent 1988b, 296), notable instances of creeping sigmaticism have been *mosso* 'moved' ≠ MŌTU (though Old Italian still had *moto*), *parso* 'seemed' ≠ PĀRITU (but pf. PĀRUĪ > It. *parvi*), by-form *perso* 'lost' ≠ PERDITU, *valso* 'been worth' ≠ VALITU, and *reso* 'given back' from REDDITU 'idem' crossed with TĒNSU 'held out' or PRĒNSU 'taken' (see Table 3–5). Prefixed *arreso* 'surrendered' belongs here, too.

In the preterit, locally termed "passato remoto," all but one of these sigmatic past participles have sigmatic fillers for 1sg., 3sg., and 3pl., from which inspiration for sigmatic marking might have sprung: *mosso* 'moved,' *perso* 'lost,' *reso* 'given back,' and *valso* 'been worth' match the corresponding (1sg.) preterits *mossi, persi* (also *perdei, perdetti*), *resi* (also *rendei, rendetti*),

---

[53] Another sigmatic survival in the literary register is 1sg. pret. *alsi* 'felt cold' < ALSĪ (infin. ALGĒRE), used in the punning phrase *alsi e(d) arsi* 'I froze and burned [from love]' in madrigals and melodramas (R. Stefanini, p.c.). Normally in Italian, [ns] > [s] and [pl] > [pj].

and *valsi*. Since pfs. MŌVĪ, PERDIDĪ, REDIDĪ, VALUĪ were all asigmatic in Latin, it is hard to know whether perfect influenced past participle or vice versa or, again, whether both slipped into sigmaticism together.

Table 3–5

New Sigmatic Past Participles in Italian

* competes with present-based arrhizotonic

Latin	Italian	French	Spanish	Romanian
MŌTU	mosso	mû	movido	—
PĀRITU	parso	paru	parecido	părut
PERDITU	perso*	perdu	perdido	pierdut
REDDITU	reso	rendu	rendido	redat
VALITU	valso	valu	valido	—

Among the past participles chosen, sigmatic forms in Italian contrast with one arrhizotonic type in French and another in Spanish. For once, the Romanian forms cited are unmarked in [s].

Now and then, speakers have built nouns out of their sigmatic innovations. One is It. *mossa* 'movement, move' ≠ MŌTU 'moved'; see §3.1.5.3 for similar sigmatics in Romanian. More often, such nouns remain rhizotonic thematic, a type no longer acceptable for past participles: *réndita* 'income' and *pérdita* 'loss' (see §3.5.2.2). Note also the nonstandard p.p. *valuto* and a fem. noun of the same type, *valuta* 'currency; value.'

Most Italian sigmatic nouns identical to past participles represent continuations from Latin. Two are 4th-decl. CURSU 'a running' > *corso* 'course' and MORSU 'bite, biting' > *morso* 'bite, bit [for horses].' Like Romanian, Italian has innovated a number of sigmatic nouns; unlike Romanian, Italian has made many such nouns feminine (see §3.1.5.3). Examples are It. *possesso* 'ownership,' *presa* 'hold, grip,' and *tesa* 'snare, net.' However, the Italian noun *sorso* 'sip' seems to come from a postclassical innovation found also in the OFr./Oc. p.p. *sors* 'arisen.' At the same time, a syncopated variety of CL SURRĒCTU 'sprung up, arisen' has given the Italian p.p. *sorto* 'idem' (see §3.5.3.1).

Today, the semilearnèd noun *responso* 'decision, report,' retaining an [ns] cluster, clashes morphologically with remade *risposto* 'answered,' now sigmatic-tautic. Moreover, the Italian nouns *cessa* 'letup, pause' and *spesa* 'shopping' clash morphologically with the corresponding past participles, arrhizotonic *ceduto* 'yielded,' *penduto* 'hung.' Held down for a time, sigmatic p.p. by-forms may bob up again in prefixed versions of the verb, one of them typified by p.p. *speso* 'spent.'

By contrast, for 3rd-conj. infin. (EX)TENDERE 'hold (out),' where LL usage seems to have hesitated between (EX)TĒNSU and (EX)TENTU as past participles, Italian has naturally chosen the sigmatic one: standard (*s*)*teso* matches 1sg. preterit (*s*)*tesi*, quite unlike direct-suffix EXTENDĪ or reduplicative TETENDĪ. Prefixed *atteso* 'awaited,' *disteso* 'stretched out,' and *disatteso* 'ignored, disregarded' are equally sigmatic. Perhaps a rhyming analogy has been at work, for both p.p. *teso* and pret. *tesi* now rhyme with *preso* 'taken' < PRĒNSU and *presi* 'I took' ≠ PRE(HE)NDĪ, though they were once far apart. In turn, other past participles like ACCĒNSU 'lit' and EXPĒNSU 'spent' could have served as a sigmatic model for the variant behind *reso*. Here past-participial marking has influenced preterit morphology.

3.5.4. Regularities and Irregularities in the Past System

Synchronically viewed, Italian 3rd-conj. infinitives whose roots end in [dʒ] or [d:ʒ] show far less past-participial regularity than one might expect after fifteen hundred years of remodeling. Most verbs in the former group have tautic athematic past participles, but whether those have short [t] or long [t:] is to a degree lexically determined. Following a root-final consonant cluster [rdʒ] or [ndʒ] in the infinitive, the past participle normally has [rt] or [nt], never phonotactically disallowed *[rt:] or *[nt:]. Thus, *attingere, ergere, frangere, giungere, mingere, piangere, porgere, scorgere,* and *sorgere* have the p.p.s *attinto* 'drawn [water],' *erto* 'erected,' (*in*)*franto* 'crushed,' *giunto* 'arrived,' *minto* 'pissed,' *pianto* 'mourned,' *porto* 'handed over,' *scorto* 'discerned,' and *sorto* 'arisen.' Yet *stringere* has p.p. *stretto* 'tightened' instead of *strinto*, which survives adjectivally and participially in Florentine dialect.

Several 3rd-conjugation infinitives with the same consonant clusters as those listed above, like *convergere* 'incline together,' *emergere* 'surface; loom,' *rifulgere* 'flash,' and *spargere* 'sprinkle' have the sigmatic p.p.s *converso, emerso, rifulso,* and *sparso*. Most of the latter group with infinitives in [d:ʒ] have past participles in [t:], as witness *afflitto* 'distressed' (cf. infin. *affliggere*), *letto* 'read' (*leggere*), *retto* 'withstood' (*reggere*), and *strutto* 'melted' (*struggere*). However, *affiggere* has sigmatic *affisso* 'posted.' Three infinitives in [dʒ], *diligere, prediligere,* and *dirigere*, have the double-tautic p.p.s *diletto* 'beloved' (only adjectival now), *prediletto* 'preferred' (both adj. and p.p.) and *diretto* 'led' (also used adjectivally to mean 'straight, right'). Moreover, *esigere* 'demand, require' has borrowed previously and still adjectival *esatto* 'precise' < EXĀCTU 'driven through; completed' for its p.p., no doubt ± *redigere* with its suspiciously conservative p.p. *redatto* 'compiled' < REDĀCTU 'driven back; collected.' For verbs such as these, etymology provides a surer guide than current infinitive morphology, especially since many verbs in this group look semilearnèd. Indeed, the *REW* lists no straight verbal survivals anywhere in Romance of CONVERGERE, ĒMERGERE, REFULGERE, AFFLIGERE, STRUERE, DĒLIGERE, or REDIGERE; the verb EXIGERE has failed to survive in Italy.[54] Again, none of those verbs appears essential to peasants, fishers, or traders in carrying out the affairs of daily life.

Putting aside eloquent verbs for prosaic ones, I turn to variation within preterit stems. If a great many Italian preterits for rhizotonic 1sg., 3sg., and 3pl. continue LL etyma with adaptations (cf. *tenni* 'held' < TENUĪ, *volli* 'wanted' < VOLUĪ), preterits for arrhizotonic 2sg., 1pl., and 2pl. have postradical stress and have been remodeled on their present-tense stems. For some of these verbs, 2sg. forms like *volesti* 'wanted,' *tenesti* 'held,' *venisti* 'came,' *bevesti* 'drank,' and *cadesti* 'fell' display single consonants where the 1sg. forms display geminates; compare infins. *volere, tenere, venire, bere* < *bevere*, and *cadere*. Other variations, mostly consonantal but some vocalic, are more striking to the ear or eye. Thus, 2sg. *sapesti* 'knew' has [p] rather than 1sg. [p:], 2sg. *avesti* 'had' has [v] rather than 1sg. [b:], and 2sg. *rompesti* has [mp] rather than 1sg. [p:]. All three display different initial vowels from those in 1sg. *seppi, ebbi,* and *ruppi*; compare infins. *sapere, avere, rompere*.

Several further types of consonantal variation exist. In one of them, 2sg. *giacesti* 'lay,' *nocesti* 'harmed,' *piacesti* 'pleased,' and *nascesti* 'were born' have [tʃ] as against the [k:w] in 1sg. *giacqui, nocqui, piacqui, nacqui*. In another kind of variation, 2sg. *crescesti* 'grew' and *conoscesti* 'knew' have [ʃ] as against the [b:] in 1sg. *crebbi, conobbi*. In a third kind, zero contrasts with something, for 2sg. *stesti* 'stayed, stood' has no consonant as against the [t:] in 1sg. *stetti,* and 2sg. *paresti* 'seemed' has no consonant as against the [v] in 1sg. *parvi*. Again, 2sg. *dolesti* 'hurt, grieved' has no consonant after [l] as against the [s] in 1sg. *dolsi* or the [v] in OIt. *dolvi*. Almost all of the corresponding infinitives— *giacere, piacere, nascere, crescere, conoscere, parere, dolere*—match the stem for those verbs' 2sg., 1pl., and 2pl. preterits; the rare exceptions are 3rd-conj. *nuocere* with tonic [wɔ] and 1st-conj. *stare,* each with an inherited preterit irregularity. Yet given that all CL verbs had a single stem across their finite perfectum, morphological transparency has clouded over in such Italian preterits.

Across the past system, certain irregularities endure. Today, some forty verbs from Mourin's sample have both preterits and past participles in [s], and perhaps ten have both in long [s:]. One verb, *mettere* 'put,' contrasts a preterit in [s] with a past participle in [s:]. Seventeen verbs contrast preterits in [s] with past participles in [t], and sixteen contrast preterits in [s:] with past participles in [t:]. Five verbs contrast sigmatic preterits with sigmatic-tautic past participles. All remaining consonantal contrasts, like those between 3sg. pret. *parve* and p.p. *parso* 'seemed,' between pret. *ruppe* 'broke' and p.p. *rotto* 'broken,' between pret. *vide* 'saw' and p.p. *visto* 'seen,' and between pret. *nacque* and p.p. *nato* 'born,' must be ranked as unpredictable synchronically.

---

[54] An unlearnèd reflex of EXIGERE 'drive away; drive through' survives only in Upper Engadin *echar* (*REW* no. 3014), now apparently a member of the 1st conjugation.

So must a few contrasts entailing both vocalic and consonantal alternations like those between pret. *fece* 'did/made' and p.p. *fatto* 'done/made' or between *diede* or *dette* 'gave' and p.p. *dato* 'given.' Finally, fifteen verbs have irregular preterits like *dolse* 'hurt,' *piacque* 'pleased,' *bevve* 'drank,' *conobbe* 'knew,' *venne* 'came,' and *volle* 'wanted' but regular past participles. Four verbs have irregular past participles like *morto* 'died' but regular preterits (Mourin, 174–75). As shown in §3.6, most so-called dialects of Italian have achieved far greater regularity within the past system.

3.5.5. Analogies in Reshaping Past Participles

Many remodelings of standard Italian past participles seem to have taken place by analogy with past participles for other verbs. Undaunted by the difficulties inherent in trying to read the minds of the dead, Meyer-Lübke (1931, 204) suggests that on the model *ridere risi riso* 'laugh' were formed *intridere intrisi intriso* 'soak; knead' ≠ INTERERE INTRĪVĪ INTRĪTU 'rub, crumble,' and *perdere persi perso* 'lose' ≠ PERDIDĪ PERDITU. Similarly, *corso* 'run' < CURSU inspired *parso* 'seemed' and *apparso* 'appeared' ≠ [AP]PĀRITU, and the preterit-p.p. pair *pressi presso* 'squeezed' < PRESSĪ PRESSU inspired *mossi mosso* 'moved' ≠ MŌVĪ MŌTU. At times, phonetically isolated past participles joined a larger class: regularly evolving *fisso* < FĪXU 'fastened' became *fiso* (now literary) because Italian had no other past participles in *-isso* but a great many in *-iso*.

Signs of other remakings within the perfect system, Meyer-Lübke goes on (1931, 204), are that the sigmatic-tautic perfective pairs *svelsi svelto* 'uprooted' and *spansi spanto* 'spread' do not continue CL ĒVELLĪ ĒVULSU or EXPANDĪ EXPĀNSU: the sigmatic past participle has been remade tautically, and, presumably later, the asigmatic preterit has been remade sigmatically.[55] If the learnèd p.p. *espanso* remains sigmatic, it might simply be a Latinism; *spanto* would therefore be older. Among partial regularizations, on the infin.-p.p. model *aprire aperto* 'open[ed]' < APERĪRE APERTU were formed *offrire offerto* 'offer[ed]' and its partner *soffrire sofferto* 'suffer[ed]' ≠ suppletive OBLĀTU, SUBLĀTU. Total regularization would have given 4th-conj. **aprito*, **offrito*, **soffrito*. The reasoning is plausible if unprovable.

Tekavčić (435) states that for the literary verb *figgere* 'fasten, thrust' < FĪGERE with sigmatic pret. *fissi* < FIXĪ, the tautic athematic p.p. *fitto* cannot continue CL FĪXU (cf. *fiso*) and contrasts with prefixed *affisso* < AFFĪXU.[56]

---

[55] An example of the variant for *spanso* occurs in G. B. Casti, from the late eighteenth century: *E robe spante, rovesciate e rotte* 'property squandered, turned inside out, and broken' (R. Stefanini, p.c.).

[56] Actually, in CL FĪCTU 'driven in, fastened' was the older form, remade as FĪXU ± pf. FĪXĪ (Ernout and Meillet, 234). Compare It. *crocifiggere* 'crucify,' with expected p.p. *crocifisso*; however, Jacopone da Todi (1236–1306) wrote *alla croce fitto* 'nailed to the cross' (R. Stefanini, p.c.). The pair *fisso* and *fitto* indicates wavering between sigmatic and tautic athematic forms, wavering evident as well in pairs like Rom. *spars* and *spart*, It. *sparso* and *sparto* 'scattered, shattered,' and a number of twin or triplet by-forms in Old Sardinian (see Table 3–8, page 196).

Italian *fitto* was remade, says Tekavčić, by analogy with such past participles as *retto* 'guided,' -*dotto* 'led,' and *letto* 'read,' which have the long-sigmatic preterits *ressi*, -*dussi* < RĒXĪ, DŪXĪ, and *lessi* ≠ LĒGĪ. By implication, the CL pf. LĒGĪ 'read' was remade as sigmatic *lessi*, perhaps ± *ressi* < RĒXĪ 'ruled, guided.' Further inspiration for the sigmatic shift may have come from prefixed CL pfs. like INTELLĒXĪ 'realized, understood.'

Similarly, Meyer-Lübke tries to explain (1931, 205) how further analogical remodelings of past participles might have taken place. On the model *piansi piantô* 'lamented' < PLĀNXĪ PLĀNCTU, with Italian preterits marked with [s] and past participles marked with [t], and taking into account already sigmatic preterits like *accorsi*, *sorsi*, *porsi*, *colsi*, and *scelsi*, were formed the tautic athematic p.p.s *accorto* 'realized,' *sorto* 'arisen,' *porto* 'handed over,' *colto* 'gathered,' and *scelto* 'chosen' ≠ EX + ĒLĒCTU. These forms probably go back to partly attested variants ending in atonic -ĬTU, others being the uncontracted ancestors of modern std. *tolto* 'removed,' *volto* 'turned,' *visto* 'seen.' Compare these verbs' 1sg. prets.: *tolsi* ≠ TULĪ, *volsi* ≠ VOLVĪ have become sigmatic, but—like OFr. *v i(t)*, Sp. *v i*, and Cat. *viu*—std. It. *vidi* < VĪDĪ 'saw' continues the Latin tradition.

Being unable to quarrel with Tekavčić's or Meyer-Lübke's reasoning, I must repeat that at this late date no one's pen can glean the teeming brains of LL speakers.

Ocasionally, specialists acknowledge that the haze of years has obscured the working of analogical forces. Thus, the replacement of VALUĪ 'was worth' and VOLVĪ 'rolled' by sigmatics like *valsi* and *volsi* was quite "imprevedibili" (Tekavčić, 342) [unforeseeable]. Yet the first of these preterits inspired the standard sigmatic p.p. *valso* ≠ VALITU, contrasting with the standard tautic athematic p.p. *volto* ≠ VOLŪTU. Nonstandard Florentine has also developed the sigmatic prets. *volsi* and *vorsi* 'wanted' against std. *volli*; the still current Florentine preterit *m i trattiensi* 'I stayed over' suggests that sigmatic *tiensi* 'held' once existed for current Florentine and also std. *tenni*, unless it has resulted from a recent analogy (R. Stefanini, p.c.).

In another reshaping, CL STRĪDĒRE 'creak, hiss,' had a direct-suffixation pf. STRĪDĪ that was bound to be replaced, and no filler for its past-participial slot. Today, 3rd-conj. *stridere* 'shriek, squeak' has preterits like 1sg. *stridei* or *stridetti*, no doubt resulting from generalization of the endings in reduplicative DEDĪ 'gave' or STETĪ 'stood, stayed.' Even if such preterit forms could have inspired the rare std. p.p. *striduto* 'shrieked, squeaked,' they could hardly have provided a model for the more common standard sigmatic p.p. *striso*, or for the sigmatic pret. *strisi* still used in modern Florentine dialect. Inspiration for *striso* could have come from any similar-sounding 3rd-conj. verb with a sigmatic past participle, such as *assidere* 'seat,' *conquidere* 'conquer,' *decidere* 'decide,' *dividere* 'divide,' *elidere* 'annul,' *intridere* 'soak; knead,' or *uccidere* 'kill.' Regrettably, many of them belong to formal registers. On semantic grounds, the best candidate by far would be 3rd-conj. *ridere* (p.p. *riso*) 'laugh,' which also rhymes with *stridere*.

3.5.5.1. Spread of Past Participles in −sto

At first glance, a few past participles in Italian seem to have developed an unetymological [st] suffix. By analogy with CL POSTU, syncopated from POSITU and giving literary It. *posto* 'put,' the p.p. *visto* 'seen' could have been formed by insertion of [t] into CL VĪSU; cf. Cat. *post* and *vist*, Sp. *puesto* and *visto*, Ptg. *pôsto* and *visto*. More probably, frequentative VĪSITĀRE 'see often, visit' was crucial for the creation of a rhizotonic thematic p.p. *VISITU or might itself presuppose the existence of the latter, which would later have syncopated to yield attested Romance forms. Other past participles in [st] may have arisen by analogy with syncopations like It. *chiesto* 'asked' (also evident in p.p.s like OFr. *quest*, OSp. *quisto* ≠ QUÆSĪTU). If the older form appears to live on in It. *quesito* 'question, problem,' the *REW* contains no reflex of QUÆSĪTU though a great many reflexes of QUÆRERE.

Since Late Latin times, this [st] suffix has spread to a few other past participles. Reprefixed *nascosto* 'hidden' cannot come straight from LL ABSCONSU, any more than *risposto* 'answered' and *rimasto* 'remained' can have come straight from RESPŌNSU or REMĀNSU. In the doubly marked form *risposto*, as Vincent comments, "the -S- is the reflex of the Indo-European -tom formation and the -T- is due to the Late Latin analogical extension of the same formative" (1988b, 296). Vincent's explanation would extend to *nascosto* and to *rimasto*, no doubt with a lag of a few centuries. In these last two instances, [t] was suffixed fairly recently, the past participles of *rimanere*, *nascondere* having often been *rimaso*, *nascoso* during the Middle Ages; cf. Rom. *rămas*, *răspuns*, *ascuns* without [t] but OFr. *respos(t)* with optional [t]. Today, the t̲-less Italian noun *rimasuglio* 'leftover' supplies a morphological clue to the earlier state of affairs.

In nonstandard varieties of Italian today, the *mosto* 'moved' and *chiusto* 'closed' heard in Tuscany, the *muostə* 'moved' heard in Abruzzi, and the *misto* 'put' heard in the Marches suggest that insertion of [t] into already sigmatic past participles may still be a productive means of word formation (Tekavčić, 436–37).

3.5.6. Arrhizotonic Remodelings

Like Romanian, Catalan, and French, Italian has a great many past participles whose enidngs derive from -ŪTU. As happened almost everywhere else, the rhizotonic thematic type was particularly disfavored in Tuscany, as witness *avuto* 'had' ≠ HABITU, *dovuto* 'owed' ≠ DĒBITU, and rare *gemuto* 'groaned' ≠ GEMITU.

Yet, at least in the elaborated literary language, one is struck above all by the multiplicity of morphological means still available to shape Italian past participles, and by the ongoing popularity of the tautic athematic type highlighted in Table 3–6. (Each infinitive belongs to the 3rd conjugation.)

Table 3–6

Conservatism in Standard Italian Past Participles

Latin	Standard Italian	Nonstd. Tuscan	Cf. Std. Infinitive
COCTU	cotto	cociuto	cuocere
LĒCTU	letto	leggiuto	leggere
NĀTU	nato	nasciuto	nascere
PLĀNCTU	pianto	piangiuto	piangere
VICTU	vinto	vinciuto	vincere

Among the unliterary, the popularity of that type has proved lower. Thus, in Table 3–6, all the standard forms in the second column come straight from Latin, except that the last one has incorporated the nasal consonant already present across the CL infectum. From Giannelli's *Toscana*, all the nonstandard forms in the second column are purely infectum-based.

Overwhelmingly, arrhizotonic remodelings have come to end in -*uto*.

Despite an Italian predilection for sigmatic past participles rivaling that in Romanian and far exceeding any in western Romance, some sigmatic forms attested in Latin have joined an arrhizotonic class.[57] Sigmatic -SESSU 'seated' has yielded to unprefixed *seduto*; compare *posseduto* 'owned' ≠ POSSESSU. Likewise, rare CĀSU 'fallen' has yielded to *caduto*; and tautic athematic VENTU 'come' has yielded to *venuto*. Besides creating a past participle for ESSE(RE) 'be' out of STATU 'stood' to yield current *stato*, speakers of Proto-Italian devised a regular 3rd-conj. form *essuto*, which after aphæresis became Olt. *suto* 'been' and remained in use as late as Machiavelli's time (Tekavčić, 327).

As Elcock observes, suffixation of -*uto* to a few inchoative infinitive stems instead of perfect ones in e.g. *cresciuto* 'grown' and *conosciuto* 'known' "may be taken to indicate that during the Middle Ages it was still gaining ground"

---

[57] Why does Vincent (1988b, 296) speak of the "relative paucity" of sigmatic past participles in Italian? What is his standard of comparison? Among major Romance tongues, only Romanian has more sigmatics. Perhaps, having noted that p.p. -*s*- is original with verbs whose stems end in a dental stop (original from Latin times, that is), Vincent has miswritten "past participles" for "preterits." Yet he has already stated that pret. -*s*- goes back to Indo-European and has spread into certain Italian preterits whose CL avatars were asigmatic. As usual, an attempt to practice telepathy proves unavailing.

(130). More precisely, both CRĒSCERE and COGNOSCERE had formed their past participles in ways that lost popularity among speakers of Late Latin: CRĒTU 'grown' had belonged to the [e:] class, COGNITU 'known' to the rhizotonic thematic class. They were almost bound to be replaced by more regular forms.

That -*uto* past participles remained productive during the Middle Ages is suggested by the nonce-form *malastrudha* 'star-crossed' in the work of Bonvesin. In fact, dialects north and south contain innumerable remodeled forms whose opposite numbers have been kept rhizotonic in the standard (see §§3.6.1–3.6.2).

3.5.7. Wavering between −*uto* and −*ito*

Through time, speakers or at least writers of Italian have hesitated for some past participles between -*uto* and -*ito*, though never apparently between either of these and the class in -*ato*. For *vestire* < VESTĪRE, the modern standard has p.p. *vestito* 'clothed, dressed' straight from VESTĪTU, but older writers often had *vestuto*. Compare the anomalous Fr. cognate p.p. *vêtu* with its mediæval competitor in [i] then written *vesti*, a regular past participle for 4th-conj. *vestir* >*vêtir*.

According to Meyer-Lübke (1931, 203), several -*uto* past participles for standard ones in -*ito*, like *vestuto* 'clothed, dressed,' *sentuto* 'felt; heard,' and *storduto* 'bewildered, dazed,' used to and may still thrive in Lucanian, in the Basilicata. Another pair of by-forms exists in the std. p.p. *sparito* 'disappeared' (infin. *sparire*) alongside old past-participial and now adjectival *sparuto* 'lean, wan, meager'; CL PĀRĒRE 'appear' had no past participle (Tekavčić, 452).

During the Middle Ages and Renaissance, variants occurred more often. Old Tuscan had a great many past participles in -*uto* where the modern standard allows only -*ito*: besides *vestuto* 'clothed,' examples include *falluto* 'failed,' *finuto* 'ended,' *feruto* 'struck,' *patuto* 'suffered,' *pentuto* 'repented,' *peruto* 'perished,' *saluto* 'climbed,' *sentuto* 'felt,' *servuto* 'needed,' *smarruto* 'gotten lost,' *sparuto* 'vanished,' and *traduto* 'betrayed.' Note also OTusc. *giuto* 'gone,' now *andato*. Fluctuations could also occur between variants of p.p.-derived nouns, as when Jacopone da Todi wrote *feruta* 'wound' for what today would be only *ferita*.

To this day, the p.p. *moruto* 'died'—for what one would expect to be 4th-conj. *morito*, given infin. *morire*—remains dialectal in Tuscany. Nearby, Luccan and Pisan used to have *riusciuto* 'succeeded' and again *storduto* 'bewildered' (Rohlfs 1949, 422). In Tuscany, rustics still say *sentuto* 'felt; heard' instead of std. *sentito* (Giannelli, 34). Of course, in standard Italian, the 4th-conj. verb meaning 'come' still displays a similar vocalic alternation in infin. *venire* as against p.p. *venuto*.

Arrhizotonic remodelings now suppressed in the standard include OIt. *fonduto* 'melted' and OIt. *renduto* 'given back.' Each has been replaced by a sigmatic (*fuso, reso*); compare Fr. *fondu* and *rendu*. Even It. *essere* 'be' used to have a past participle regularized along 2nd-/3rd-conj. lines in Olt. *essuto*, but the standard now allows only *stato* in the sense 'been.'

3.5.8. Further Variation among Old Italian Past Participles

Like Tuscan rustics with their *vorsuto* 'wanted,' writers of the older literary language used variant past participles in *-uto*, in *-so*, or in diploid *-suto* that have passed out of the standard. In the sixteenth century, Cellini wrote *volsuto* 'wanted.' In the fourteenth century, Boccaccio wrote present-based *vagliuto* 'been worth'; another variant was *valsuto*. On occasion, writers during the Middle Ages and Renaissance used sigmatic rhizotonic past participles built on preterit roots. In the fourteenth century, Dante wrote *miso* 'put,' and Petrarch wrote *visso* 'lived'; cf. the 3sg. preterits *mise* and *visse*. Some interchange of stems occurred when Buonarroti (fifteenth–sixteenth century) wrote *volso* 'wanted,' for which cf. the std. 3sg. preterit *volse* 'turned' but std. *volle*. Another such set was *dolso* and *dolsuto* 'hurt, grieved'; cf. 3sg. preterit *dolse*. Moderns using standard Italian must have asigmatic *voluto* 'wanted' and *doluto* 'hurt,' sigmatic *valso* 'been worth,' and doubly marked *vissuto* 'lived,' the last still built on a preterit root.

Again, the fifteenth–sixteenth century writer Ariosto put *possuto* 'been able,' seemingly based on a present stem as in 1sg. pres.indic. *posso*, subj. *possa*, but more likely by analogy with other past participles like *vissuto* 'lived.' Yet another past participle used by the Renaissance writers Boiardo and Frezzi, *cresco* 'grown,' might have been based either on the present stem, in e.g. its 3rd-conj. infin. *crescere* or the now-standard p.p. *cresciuto*, or on the arrhizotonic preterit stem, in e.g. 2sg. *crescesti*. It could hardly have been based on the rhizotonic preterit stem in e.g. 1sg. *crebbi*. Likewise, the old p.p. *vivuto* 'lived' was based either on the present stem, in e.g. its 3rd-conj. infin. *vivere* or on the arrhizotonic preterit stem in e.g. 2sg. *vivesti*. It could hardly have been based on the rhizotonic pret. stem in e.g. 1sg. *vissi* (D'Ovidio and Meyer-Lübke, 152–53). Two other remodelinigs had sigmatic marking: Olt. *cosso* 'cooked' and *resso* 'given back' were definitely based on the stems of prets. *ressi* and *cossi* (Rohlfs 1968, 374).

One basic verb has been driven out by a foreign variant. Olt. *manicare* 'eat' (p.p. *manicato*) has yielded to *mangiare* (p.p. *mangiato*), adapted from Fr. *manger* and hence an emblem of Gallic preeminence in cuisine.

3.5.9. Short-Form 1st-Conjugation Past Participles

At times, syncope has occurred in the absence of similar syllables. In an outcome like one in Portuguese and Spanish (§4.7.8), some 1st-conjugation past participles in Old Italian had short forms lacking [at]. They included *tocco* 'touched' and the Germanic-derived duo *guasto* 'laid waste' and nominalized *urto* 'shoved; crashed,' with which cf. Fr. *heurté*, earlier *hurté*. Such short forms as these contrast with the standard p.p.s *toccato*, *guastato*, and *urtato*, with *guasto* now only adjectival in the sense 'out of order.' That three verbs taken over from Germanic acquired short-form past participles suggests that there might have been more of them in Proto-Italian than appear in extant attestations.

As Meyer-Lübke says (1931, 203), such participles turn up more in the spoken than in the written language. Indeed, peasants dwelling near Florence still commonly use short-form past participles like *compro* 'bought,' *busco* 'gotten, gained,' *mangio* 'eaten,' and *lavo* 'washed.' To these one may add *porto* 'carried' and *sento* 'marked, branded,' for std. *portato* and *segnato* (Giannelli, 42, 82). Belonging to oral registers of Italian—like most -ŪTU p.p.s in CL—short-form past participles have rarely appeared in print.[58]

As for explanations for the rise of such shortened forms, Tekavčić (438) regards *tocco* etc. as true past participles, not verbal adjectives like their relatives in Greek. While admitting that *urto* might have been made by analogy with *letto* 'read,' and *guasto* with *fatto* 'done/made,' Tekavčić attributes the true origin of such short forms to the coexistence in Latin of simple verbs having rhizotonic athematic past participles and their frequentative or iterative derivatives in -ĀRE having regular past participles in -ĀTUM. Just as, in Latin days, CANTUM 'sung' and AUSUM 'dared' had coexisted with CANTĀTUM 'sung often' and nonstandard *AUSATU (fated to enjoy a great future), so in Old Italian certain short variants coexisted with their long counterparts *toccato* 'touched' and *guastato* 'wasted,' which latter have become standard.

Somewhat as Williams does in *From Latin to Portuguese*, Meyer-Lübke (1931, 203) ascribes the origin of short-form past participles to the coexistence of (masc.nom.sg.) adjectives or nouns in -US and past participles in -ĀTUS, both built from the same stem. Two further examples of such coexistence are ALBUS 'dull white' next to ALBĀTUS 'clothed in white' and DICTUS 'said, told' next to DICTĀTUS 'said over.' For a similar pair in Modern Italian, compare *raso* and *rasato* 'shaved' in §3.5.10.

Semantic and morphological overlap between adjectives and past participles continues today. Still thriving in Arezzo and Pistoia are short-form 1st-conj. past participles like *trovo* 'found,' reminiscent of short-form past participles in standard Portuguese and in Spanish dialects (see §4.7.8). Rohlfs states that short-form Italian past participles are most commonly encountered in Tuscany and on Corsica but occur elsewhere: from southern Lazio come *tòcco* 'touched,' *tròvo* 'found,' *scòrdo* 'forgotten' (std. *scordato*), *cúleco* 'put to bed' (std. *coricato*), and *desicco* 'dried' (std. *disseccato*). Rohlfs notes—turnabout being fair play—that speakers of some Italian dialects use adjectives as past participles, especially those from PLĒNU 'full' in the sense 'filled' (Rohlfs 1968, 375–79).

---

[58] However, an 1860 decree by Gen. Enrico Cialdini has the phrase *quei compri sicarî* 'those bought-off killers,' with a short-form masc.pl. past participle adjectivized for the nonce (R. Stefanini, p.c.).

3.5.10. Remaining Hesitations and Gaps in Verb Paradigms

Under the modern standard, a few doublets still exist for whole paradigms of certain verbs. Morphological differences mirror semantic or stylistic ones.

Today, more literary 3rd-conj. *radere* 'shave' with its inherited sigmatic p.p. *raso* < RĀSU survives alongside 1st-conj. *rasare*, derived from the old p.p. stem on which was built an unattested frequentative no doubt already equipped with a regular past participle that lay behind today's *rasato*. A second pair of doublets contains a reflex of an old past participle in -ĬTU, one of the few in standard Italian. As noted in §3.5.2.1, the 3rd-conj. infin. *arrogere* 'add, make whole' has the archaic and literary p.p. *arroto* ≠ AD + ROGĀTU, a form also used adjectivally, together with nominalized *arrota* 'addition.' Alongside *arrogere* is 1st-conj. *arrogare* 'arrogate,' with a regular arrhizotonic p.p. *arrogato* (D'Ovidio and Meyer-Lübke, 153).

Like all Romance languages, perhaps more than most, Italian has defective verb paradigms. That the modern standard has yet to select a filler for each slot in each verb is confirmed by the lack of any past-participial form at all for the verbs *competere* 'compete,' *delinquere* 'commit a crime,' *dirimere* 'separate, sunder,' *distare* 'be distant,' *esimere* 'exempt,' *fervere* 'rage,'[59] *incombere* 'impend,' *ostare* 'hinder,' *prudere* 'itch,' *(ri)lucere* 'shine,' *(di)scernere* 'discern,' and *vigere* 'be in force.' Other verbs nowadays— *divergere* 'diverge,' *estollere* 'extol,' and impersonal *urgere* 'urge' among them—also make do without a past participle. A by-form for *esimere* is rare, but regular 1st-conj. *esentare* (p.p. *esentato*) has no doubt been built from the adj. *esente* 'exempt, free.' Meanwhile, *discreto* 'discreet; fairly large,' from the same stem as *discernere* once upon a time, is now used only adjectivally. Perhaps, in the future, Italians will develop the p.p.s *esento* 'exempted' and *dirento* 'sundered' ± infin. *redimere* with p.p. *rendento* 'redeemed.'

Some poetic or literary verbs are highly defective. Besides the past participle already mentioned, *arrogere* 'add' has only imperative forms; the fifteenth-century revival *frendere* 'gnash [teeth]; rage, roil [of water]' has only present and imperfect forms; *molcere* 'flatter' has only 3sg. forms in the present and imperfect indicative and the imperfect subjunctive; *suggere* 'suck' has only 3sg. forms for some noncompound tenses, the usual verb being *succhiare*; and *tangere* 'touch' has only third-person present-tense forms, the usual verb being *toccare*. On the other hand, among finite forms the defective verb *consumere* 'consume, use up' has only preterits for the 1sg., 3sg., and 3pl. slots but, because of a living p.p. *consunto* 'worn-out,' may be used to make compound tenses. Though the verb *recere* 'vomit' < RE + ĪCERE 'throw back' has only the 3sg. present indicative among finite forms, a living p.p. *reciuto* ≠ REJECTU makes possible compound tenses for it as well. All those defectives belong to the 3rd conjugation, but rare *calere* 'be important' and *capere* 'find a place' from the 2nd conjugation also lack past participles, as does *aulire* or *olire* 'be fragrant' from the 4th (Cusatelli, 130–45).

---

[59] It. *fervere* is never used in the literal sense 'boil [of liquids]'; only *bullire* is so used.

This being Italy, at least three verbs have past participles so seldom employed that I call them semi-defective. These three are *convergere* 'converge' with p.p. *converso*, *rifulgere* 'shine' with p.p. *rifulso*, and *soccombere* 'succumb' with p.p. *soccombuto* (Buratti, 160–63).

For defective verbs, one cannot fail to wonder how most of the concepts above are expressed in periphrastic tenses. Granted that many such verbs smell of the lamp—*frendere* 'gnash' being obsolete even among literati—one doubts whether a verb meaning 'itch' would fall into that group, unless *prudere* came back into being as a medical euphemism or as a metaphor for desires more or less honorable. All in all, standard Italian seems to contain more defective verbs than other varieties of Romance because it is the most Latinizing and the most similar to Latin phonetically.

Speakers get around such gaps by using constructions of verbi servili (modals) plus infinitives. Instead of saying *Non ho mai esatto da tei* 'I have never required from you,' they might say *Non ho mai pensato di esigere* 'I never thought of requiring' or *Non mi sono mai sognato di esigere* 'I never dreamed of requiring.' They thus avoid filling a morphological gap by adding nuances of expressivity. Common among the modals used in such constructions are certain 1st-conj. verbs and the high-frequency 2nd-conj. trio *dovere* 'ought,' *potere* 'be able,' and *volere* 'want' (R. Stefanini, p.c.).

If some Italian verbs have no past participle, some have more than one. First, there are pairs of by-forms called verbi sovrabbondanti like *starnutare* and *starnutire* 'sneeze,' each with a regular past participle *starnutato* and *starnutito* respectively. Second, a few verbs retain competing p.p. variants, one stem-stressed and conservative, the other ending-stressed and innovative.[60] And certain ancient forms still linger: note old-style *viso* 'seen' < VĪSU, vaguely cited by Lausberg as being dialectal (251).

Among other verbs with a variant past participle in -*uto*, *cuocere* 'cook' and *nascere* 'be born' have *cotto* < COCTU and *nato* < NĀTU or (supposedly) *cociuto* and *nasciuto*. I say "supposedly" because two consultants denied having ever heard either arrhizotonic past participle from any speaker beyond toddlerhood. In other recent developments, *costruito* 'built' is gaining against old-fashioned *costrutto*, and *risolto* 'resolved' is winning against rare *risoluto*, still adjectival in the sense 'determined, insistent.'[61]

---

[60] For two verbs with competing p.p.s, *visto/veduto* 'seen' and *perso/perduto* 'lost,' the rhizotonic variant tends to prevail in Tuscany more than elsewhere (R. Stefanini, p.c.). By contrast, speakers of nonstd. Tuscan have regular *apparito* 'appeared' for std. sigmatic *apparso* (Rohlfs 1968, 369). For variant arrhizotonics in -*uto* evolved by such speakers, see §3.6.2.

[61] Given Sp. *vuelto* and It. *volto* '[re]turned' ≠ VOLŪTU 'rolled,' I am tempted to see syncopated It. *risolto* ≠ RE + SOLŪTU (cf. Sp. *suelto* 'loose') as a survival, but it may have been formed ± *svelto* 'uprooted,' *scelto* 'chosen.' Cf. also *dissolto* 'dissolved.' Now the REW lists no unlearnèd reflexes of CONSTRUERE 'heap up, build.' One doubts that speakers of Proto-Romance, undoubtedly less skillful at putting new structures together than at pulling old ones apart, had lost their whole lexis for shacks, sheds, and forts. True, It. *costruire* (p.p. *costruito*) looks less learnèd than e.g. Fr. *construire* (p.p. *construit*). Yet the It. form was borrowed from French. A normal [kt] > [t:] assimilation had taken place to yield OIt. *costrutto*.

In standard Italian, the old-fashioned verb *fendere* 'split' may have either *fesso* < FISSU or innovative *fenduto* for its past participle. This verb's replacement by *spaccare, scindere,* or *dividere* may have been hastened by the rise of a slang term *fesso, fessa* 'dumb, foolish' from Sic. *fissa*, based on a misogynistic metonymy. One might have foretold that the rise of that term could have helped *fenduto* to supplant by-form *fesso*, but apparently the whole verb has become contaminated by association. Among standard past participles with an -ĪTU variant today, *seppellire* 'entomb' may have *sepolto* < SEPULTU or arrhizotonic *seppellito*. For 4th-conj. *empire* 'fill, fulfill,' neither regular and more standard *empito* nor irregular and less standard *empiuto* could have sprung from "regular" 2nd-conj. IMPLĒRE with p.p. IMPLĒTU. For the last verb, standard Italian allows an infinitive by-form, 2nd-conj. *empiere*, so that the by-form p.p. *empiuto* would be regular for that class if hardly a classical inheritance.

If one verb embodies the trends in Italian past participles, it has to be semilearnèd *regredire* 'regress, retrogress.' A resuscitated p.p. *regresso* < REGRESSU 'stepped back' is now used almost exclusively as a noun meaning 'regression, abatement,' while regular 4th-conj. *regredito* has taken over the p.p. slot. Regularization has yet to be carried out completely, for users of standard Italian retain a degree of choice for verbs such as *costruire* 'build,' *risolvere* 'resolve, dissolve,' *seppellire* 'bury,' *empire* or *empiere* 'fill, fulfill,' and finally *regredire* 'regress.' But true by-forms are as rare as true synonyms.

3.6. EVIDENCE FROM DIALECTS OF ITALIAN

Even ardent Tuscanizers seldom maintain that a Venetian and a Neapolitan, each speaking dialect, could make much sense of what the other was saying. Several so-called dialects of Italian exhibit such divergence from the standard that they are better regarded as separate languages. In this study, I nonetheless follow convention: apart from Friulian, Ladin, Franco-Provençal, Occitan, and Sardinian, I regard as a "dialect" every nonstandard variant of Romance spoken within the borders of the Republic of Italy. From the Piedmont to Apulia and on to Sicily, these dialects display a wealth of past-participial forms often reminiscent of forms found outside the peninsula. One may observe generally that the standard has kept, evolved, or revived an inventory of rhizotonic ("strong") past participles almost rivaling that of Latin. By contrast, in dialects generally "[i] participi forti vengono molto notevolmente ridotti" [a great many strong forms have been remade] (D'Ovidio and Meyer-Lübke, 154). One could almost say that the only feature shared by all Italian dialects is a set of 1st-conj. endings.

As they do elsewhere, reflexes of old fem. -ĀTA often end deverbal nouns. Examples come from both north and south: Venetian *bagnada* 'bathing,' Milanese *mordüda* 'bite,' Abruzzese *kaskatə* 'great fall,' and Sicilian *trasuta* 'entry' (Telman and Maiden, 120).

This discussion of Italian dialects has been shaped by the availability of data, especially in the series *Profilo dei dialetti italiani* edited by Cortelazzo. By and large, I hold to the spellings used in such published sources, lightly italianizing them only when they prove nearly unreadable otherwise. To increase granularity even further, I focus on past participles from two subdialects: the Val Graveglia in eastern Liguria in §3.6.1.4.1, and San Mango sur Calore in Avellino northeast of Naples in §3.6.2.2.1.

A few points should be made about the dialects under review.

Like the Tuscan-based standard, most dialects north of Rome keep reflexes of -ĀTU, -ĪTU, and -ŪTU as endings on arrhizotonic past participles. Contrary to what one might expect in an area featuring lenition of intervocalic stops, certain morphological archaisms persist. Farther south, the picture is one of archaism and innovation both. Unlike standard Italian but like Sardinian, some southern dialects still have many reflexes of rhizotonic thematic p.p.s in -ĬTU. In other parts of the south, dialects have reduced the number of regular p.p. endings to two, as in Spanish, Portuguese, and Ræto-Romance. While those three keep only reflexes of the -ĀTU and -ĪTU types for regular verbs, dialects in Calabria, Lucania, and Sicily have favored the other arrhizotonic non-1st-conj. past-participial ending: there the -ĪTU type has apparently disappeared after merging with the -ŪTU type. Regularization has gone about as far as it can go. In no language or dialect has the number of regular types dwindled to one.

For a given verb's past participle, by-forms sometimes compete. I have been unable to devise a relative chronology and decide whether an apparently regular form is more recent, or to obtain a frequency count and decide which variant is used more often. Finally, I have replaced certain IPA letters or ones devised by authors with hačeked letters like č.

3.6.1. Survey of Past Participles in Gallo-Italian

Italy appears to have been the main breeding ground for past-participial oddities in ROMANIA. Though far more common in the south, attested reflexes of past participles in atonic -ĬTU survive across the north as well. Wide distribution of that -ĬTU type implies that it once enjoyed greater popularity than it does in the literary language today (Rohlfs 1949, 426–27).

In the north, despite its "regular" CL 2nd-conj. look, Old Veneto *creto* 'believed' goes straight back to CRĒDITU.[62] Meanwhile, syncopated Genoese *futo* 'fled' and Bergamese *pert* 'lost' go back to FUGĬTU and PERDĬTU, yet std. *creduto, fuggito,* and *perduto* or *perso* have all been rebuilt arrhizotonically or sigmatically. By way of comparison across the Adriatic, the Istriano p.p. *zèrto* 'sifted' comes from syncope of a rhizotonic thematic variant also surviving in the std. Italian noun *cérnita* 'sorting, selection,' rather than from the unpopular direct-suffixation type represented by CRĒTU 'sifted.' Likewise,

---

[62] Rhizotonic thematic CRĒDITU 'believed' also has straight reflexes in the Surselvan p.p. *cret* 'idem' and in the Venetian adj. *creto* 'trustworthy' (*REW* no. 2308).

unsyncopated *pióvidu* 'rained' in Romagna and *vívətə* 'drunk' in the Marches go back to rhizotonic thematic variants like *PLUVITU (no CL p.p.) and LL BIBITU for suppletive PŌTU. Compare std. It. *bíbita* 'a drink'; a wholly demotic outcome might have given std. **cerneta*, **béveta*.

On the other hand, certain northern dialects sporadically retain past participles abandoned for longer forms in standard Italian. Thus, Istriano has kept *zi* 'gone' (cf. Fri. *zût* 'idem'), and Venetian has syncopated *sconto* < ABSCONDITU rather than std. *nascosto* 'hidden.' Sigmatic past participles occur in *vínso* 'won' and *spánso* 'expanded' around Burano in the Veneto, for what have to be tautic athematic *vinto* and *spanto* in standard Italian (Zamboni, 35).

Especially around the Veneto, one finds past participles both in *-esto* and less commonly in *-isto*, which resemble those found across the Adriatic in Istriano (see §3.3.3). Old texts from the Veneto contain forms like *movesto* 'moved,' *tolesto* 'taken away,' *poesto* 'been able,' *corresto* 'run,' and *volesto* 'wanted.' In modern Veneto dialects, there may be heard *perdesto* 'lost,' *avesto* 'had,' *vedesto* 'seen,' *veñesto* 'come,' and *piovesto* 'rained.' Other past participles of that type include Ven. *tascesto* 'been quiet,' *credesto* 'believed,' and *podesto* 'been able,' for which cf. std. *taciuto, creduto, potuto* (Zamboni, 22).

Alluding to Rohlfs's view that these *-esto* p.p.s derive from arrhizotonic preterits in -é like *mové* 'moved,' *vedé* 'saw,' and *volé* 'wanted,' Tekavčić goes on to offer his own view of how *-sto* p.p.s came into being: "L'antichità di tali formazioni risulta dal fatto che esse sono dovute all'influsso del passato remoto; ma esse sono probabilmente più antiche e, in ogni modo, probabilmente anteriori alla creazione dei passati remoti arizotonici, perché una forma LEGESTUM si trova addirittura già presso il grammatico Virgilio Marone" (450). [The great age of such forms is attributable to their being influenced by the preterit, but they are probably older still and, in any event, probably came into being before arrhizotonic preterits were created, because a form LEGESTUM 'read' is definitely found in the work of Virgilius Maro]. That is, if anyone can take seriously Virgilius Maro of Toulouse, who portrays grammarians squabbling over the correct vocative of EGŌ 'I.' Nonetheless, such preterits in -é almost give one grounds to suppose that the finite perfectum in -ĒVĪ etc. for old "regular" 2nd-conj. verbs has somehow managed to survive in parts of northern Italy.

According to Carroll (87), Ascoli has also explained forms in *-esto* as a fusion of preterit and the past-participial endings, so that e.g. *vide* 'saw' and *visto* 'seen' would have blended to create *vedesto*. If accurate, Ascoli's explanation would furnish further proof of close morphological links between preterit and past participle. Another influence for such past participles could well have been existing forms in *-sto* related to std. *posto* 'put,' *chiesto* 'asked,' *visto* 'seen,' as Tekavčić himself suggests (451). By analogy with the tonic vowel in 4th-conj. infinitives, past participles in *-isto* also appear around the Veneto. As one might expect, similar forms—e.g., *duvisto* 'had to,' *pudisto* 'been able,' and *savisto* 'known'—appear in

Dignanese Istriano over the water. Three more from Istriano are *paresto* 'seemed,' *valesto* 'been worth,' *vivesto* 'lived.'

Looking backward, Tuttle sums up the story of *-esto* past participles as one of expansion followed by contraction. Highly productive in fifteenth-century Venetian, such forms "radiate[d] with the metropolitan acrolect, by which they [were] thereafter abandoned, to live on...in peripheral backwaters" (268). As usual, nothing dates faster than trendiness.

Hesitation between exponents in *-u* and those in *-esto* has occurred across the Italian north. Over a large part of the Veneto today, some past participles for non-1st-conj. verbs still have by-forms ending in either *-u(o)* or *-esto*: *volesto* competes with *volu* 'wanted,' *avesto* with *avu* 'had,' *veñesto* with *veñúo* 'come,' and *saésto* with *savúo* 'known' (Cortelazzo, 169). In Istriano, as shown in §3.3.3, competition occurs between *voresto* and *(v)usu* 'wanted' and between *podesto* and *pusu* 'been able,' though the second in each pair looks innovative even by the slack norms postulated for Late Latin. To the south, endings in *-sto* have spread as far as Ferrarese *vlest* 'wanted' if scarcely as far as Emiliano *vlu* 'idem' (Hajek, 271).

In Venetian and nearby Paduan, sound changes have failed to reduce morphological transparency. Palatalized [t] and [d] in certain infinitive stems turned into affricates that later reduced to fricatives, as in Portuguese and French. Unconsciously forestallinig greater allomorphy, speakers generalized the fricatives throughout the paradigms of such verbs. In this way, past participles like *vezuto* 'seen' and *verzo* 'open[ed]' (also adjectival)—as against std. (by-form) *veduto*, *aperto*—have acquired [z] < [dz] < [d], itself coming from CL [t], in local reflexes of past participles for offspring of VIDĒRE 'see' and APERĪRE 'open' (Carroll, 87).

In §§3.6.1.1.–3.6.1.5, five dialects and one subdialect from the Gallo-Italian north are examined in detail. I again remind readers that Istriano, south of Trieste (§3.3.3), belongs in this section morphologically.

3.6.1.1. Lombard

Regular past participles in Milanese, a dialect of Lombard, fall into three conjugational classes. According to Nicoli's *Grammatica milanese* (371), each class may be divided in two morphological groups according to gender and number. Masculine singular and common-gender plural past participles end in *-aa* for 1st-conj. verbs, *-uu* for 2nd- and 3rd-conj. ones, and *-ii* for 4th-conj. ones. More conservatively, feminine singular past participles keep alive a memory of CL [t] to end in *-ada*, *-uda*, and *-ida* respectively.

Examples of masc./fem. p.p. pairs are *parlaa* and *parlada* 'spoken,' *veduu* and *veduda* 'seen,' *scrivuu* and *scrivuda* 'written,' *sentii* and *sentida* 'felt.' (In Milanese orthography, vowels are doubled to mark co-occurring length and stress, consonants are doubled to mark shortness of the preceding vowel, and accents are added to differentiate homonyms.)

As Nicoli points out (307), the *-uu* type of past participle occurs much more often in Milanese than in standard Italian. Based on the present arrhizotonic stem, that type may occur where the standard has kept or devised a sigmatic exponent, as seen in forms like Mil. *corruu* 'run' (std. *corso*), *fonduu* 'melted' (std. *fuso*), *mettuu* 'put' (std. *messo*), *morduu* 'bitten' (std. *morso*), *movuu* 'moved' (std. *mosso*), *renduu* 'given back' (std. *reso*), *riduu* 'laughed' (std. *riso*), and *tenduu* 'stretched' (std. [s]*teso*). That type may also occur where the standard has kept or devised a tautic athematic p.p., as seen in forms like Mil. *leggiuu* 'read' (std. *letto*), *nassuu* 'born' (std. *nato*), *rompuu* 'broken' (std. *rotto*), *storgiuu* 'twisted' (std. [s]*torto*), and *vengiuu* 'won' (std. *vinto*). Rarely, that type may occur where the standard has a past participle in [st], as in *risponduu* 'answered' (std. *risposto*) and *veduu* 'seen' (std. by-form *visto*). Yet most face competition from older rhizotonics.

It is no accident, as Marxists used to say, that French past participles in [y] like *couru* 'run,' *fondu* 'melted,' *mordu* 'bitten,' *m û* 'moved,' *perdu* 'lost,' *rendu* 'given back,' *tendu* 'stretched,' *lu* 'read,' *rompu* 'broken,' *tordu* 'twisted,' *vaincu*, 'won,' *répondu* 'answered,' and *v u* 'seen,' have followed the same tendency, while losing any reflex of intervocalic [t]. Because such -ŪTU p.p.s are found all over ROMANIA, most of them probably go back to LL days, when Milan and Lyon became the largest cities in the western Empire. Moreover, both French and Gallo-Italian lie along Schürr's Romance backbone, bordering mostly on areas of Germanic speech, which extends from the North Sea across northern France through Switzerland before entering northeastern Italy and reaching some distance down the east coast (Bertoni, 55–56).

Milanese has yet to choose a single past participle for all verbs (Nicoli, 308–9), but then again neither have several standard tongues. Competition between past-participial forms may involve a sigmatic one and a present-based one, the latter usually ending in -*uu*. Thus, infin. *accénd* 'kindle, light' has either *accés* < ACCĒNSU or *accenduu* for its past participle; *côrr* 'run' has *côrs* < CURSU or *coruu*; *decìd* 'decide' has *decìs* < DĒCĪSU or *deciduu*, just as *divìd* 'divide' has *divìs* < DĪVĪSU or *dividuu*; *mètt* 'put' has *miss* < MISSU or *mettuu*; and *sospénd* 'hang' has *sospés* < SUSPĒNSU or *sospenduu*.

At times, alongside a present-based past participle, Milanese has a sigmatic one untraceable to Latin but present in standard Italian and hence probably a relic of innovation long ago. For instance, infin. *moeuv* 'move' has p.p. *mòss* (cf. std. *mosso*) or *movuu*; infin. *parì* 'appear' has p.p. *pars* (cf. std. *parso*) or *paruu*; infin. *perd* 'lose' has p.p. *pers* (cf. std. by-form *perso*) or *perduu* (cf. std. by-form *perduto*), infin. *varè* 'be worth' has p.p. *vals* (cf. std. *valso*) or *varuu* with intervocalic rhotacism.

Competition may occur between a tautic athematic past participle and a present-based one. Thus, infin. *coeus* 'cook' has p.p. *còtt* < COCTU or *cosuu*; infin. *corég* 'correct' has p.p. *corètt* < CORRĒCTU or *coregiuu*; infin. *fing* 'feign' has p.p. *fint* < FICTU plus [n] or *fingiuu*; infin. *risòlv* 'solve' has p.p. *risolt* or *risolvuu*; infin. *rômp* 'break' has p.p. *rott* < RUPTU or *rompuu*.

Among sigmatic-tautic past participles, *vist* 'seen' competes with *veduu* based on the 2nd-conj. infin. *vedè*, just as *visto* and *veduto* compete in standard Italian. Mil. *rispost* 'answered' (cf. std. *risposto*) competes with *risponduu* based on the 3rd-conj. infin. *rispônd*. Without any sure source, could I suggest that the rhizotonic by-forms are used in more formal registers than the arrhizotonic ones?

Several high-frequency verbs in Milanese have regularized their past participles to accord with their infinitive class. Thus, 4th-conj. *dì* 'say' may have *ditt* < DICTU or regularized *dii*, while 3rd-conj. *scriv* 'write' may have *scritt* < SCRĪPTU or *scrivuu*. If 3rd-conj. *rad* 'shave' has inherited a still current p.p. *ras* < RĀSU, the verb has also acquired a 1st-conj. p.p. *rasaa* from an infinitive based on that past-participial inheritance; compare std. *raso*, *rasato*.

Competition may also take places between past participles for two verb classes. The 4th-conj. infinitive *sentì* 'feel' has either expected *sentii* or innovative *sentuu*, the latter perhaps ± *tegnì* 'hold' and *vegnì* 'come,' which themselves have only *tegnuu* and *vegnuu* for past participles. As in French and standard Italian, reflexes of TENĒRE 'hold' and VENĪRE 'come' tend to have evolved together, both now with -ŪTU past participles. In any event, no reflex of rhizotonic SĒNSU 'felt,' TENTU 'held,' or VENTU 'come' has lasted in Milan.

Two more verbs in Milanese have three competing past participles. Thus, 4th-conj. *dorì* 'grieve, hurt' may have expected *dorii*, ending-changed *doruu*, or sigmatic *dorsuu*; compare *dorsuto* 'idem' in dialectal Florentine. Meanwhile, 2nd-conj. *vorè* 'want' may have for past participles expected *voruu* or the sigmatic duo *vorsuu* or *volsuu*, variations that sound suggestive of Tuscan *voluto* 'wanted' with its nonstandard variants *volsuto* and *vorsuto*. Dialects separated by hundred of miles may move along the same morphological pathways.

Rhizotonic past participles lacking any arrhizotonic competition include Mil. *còlt* and *racòlt* 'gathered,' *fritt* 'fried,' *mort* 'died,' *offert* 'offered,' *ròs* 'gnawn,' and *tolt* 'taken,' the last of these replacing reflexes of PRĒNSU 'grabbed' in Milanese as across most of northern Italy. (But note that French has lost anything like std. It. *togliere* 'take away'; so much for a Romance Center.) As elsewhere, certain old Milanese past participles have been restricted to adjectival use: that has been the fate of *apert* 'open' < APERTU, for in the p.p. sense 'opened,' the regularized 4th-conj. form *dervii* from *dervì* < DĒ + APERĪRE is used.

3.6.1.2. Piedmontese

For masculine singular past participles in the three great arrhizotonic conjugations, Piedmontese has undergone syncope and loss of any reflex of a dental stop, even lengthening of the vowel that once preceded it as in Lombard (§3.6.1.1). Resultant Pied. endings are *-a* < -ĀTU, *-u* < -ŪTU, and *-i* < -ĪTU. More conservatively, Piedmontese resembles Milanese in having regular feminine singular past participles that end in *-ada*, *-uda*, and *-ida* respectively.

In their anatomization of past-participial morphology in Piedmontese, Iliescu and Mourin (420–21) mention few irregular forms, normally the ones

highlighted in any such study. Tautic athematics include *cheuit* 'gathered' <
COLLĒCTU, *dit* 'said, told' < DICTU more or less, and *fait* 'done/made' <
FACTU (infins. *cujì* or *cheuje*, *dì*, *fè*). This last ultra-high-frequency p.p., with
[it̯] < [kt], has exerted morphological attraction on several 1st-conj. past
participles with endings that ought to come from -ĀTU, viz. *andait* 'gone,' *dait*
'given,' *stait* 'stood,' and *estait* 'been'; compare the by-form *andà* 'gone' <
AMBULĀTU?, which shows no such attraction. Given the frequent identity of
stressed vowels in infinitives and past participles across ROMANIA, perhaps
the starting point for those Piedmontese remodelings was the fronting and
raising of the 1st-conj. infin. ending to produce forms like *andé* 'go,' *dè* 'give,'
and *stè* 'stand.' In what might be called illusory conservativism, the Pied.
infin. *esse* 'be' < LL ESSERE has lost -*re* to resume the shape it had in Latin.

Often, rhizotonic past participles compete with arrhizotonics based on an
infinitive stem, but many infinitives hesitate between the 4th and the 3rd
conjugations. Such p.p. by-forms include *mort* and *murì* 'died' (infin. *murì* or
meuire), *ofert* and *ofrì* 'offered' (infin. *ofrì* or *ufrì* or *eufre*), and also *sufert*
and *sufrì* 'suffered' (infin. *sufrì* or *seufre*). In the competitions between *cuvert*
and *curvì* 'covered' (infin. *curvì* or *cheurve*) and between *duvert* and *durvì*
'opened' (infin. *durvì*), consonant clusters in the two supposedly regularized
past participles have undergone metathesis. Other surviving irregularities
face competition as well: Pied. *na* 'born' < NĀTU competes with *nassù* (infin.
nasse), sigmatic-tautic *vist* 'seen' competes with *vejù* and *vëddù* (infin. *vèje*
or *vëdde*), and sigmatic *vorsù* 'wanted' competes with rare and asigmatic
vorù (infin. *vorèj*). All in all, a fairly un-Tuscan dialect.

3.6.1.3. Romagnolo

Pelliciardi's *Grammatica del dialetto romagnolo* says plainly that Romagnolo
(Rml.) retains four infinitive types: 1st-conj. verbs end in -*êr*, 2nd-conj. ones
in -*ér*, 3rd-conj. ones in unstressed -*ar*, 4th-conj. ones in -*ìr*.

In past-participial morphology, the picture looks more complicated. For all
types except reflexes of -ĀTU etc., distinctions of number have been leveled
among masculine forms. Therefore, Rml. masc.sg./pl. *putù* 'been able,' *durmì*
'slept,' and *vèst* 'seen' do duty for both numbers; the corresponding feminine
forms like sg. *putùda* and pl. *putùdi*, sg. *durmìda* and pl. *durmìdi*, sg. *vèsta*
and pl. *vèsti* retain number marking. Only in 1st-conj. past participles are
distinctions made between e.g. masc.sg. *lavê* and masc.pl. *lavé* 'washed.' As in
other conjugations, fem.sg. *lavêda* differs in its final vowel from fem.pl.
lavêdi (Pelliciardi, 127).

In Romagnolo as in Portuguese and nonstandard Tuscan, many 1st-conj.
verbs have both a regular long-form past participle and a shortened variant
consisting of the root alone. For example, the Rml. infin. *švigêr* 'wake up'
(std. *svegliare*) has for its past participle both *švigê* and reduced *švèg*; the
infin. *tuchêr* 'touch' (std. *toccare*) has both *tuchê* and reduced *tòch*; the infin.
distêr 'stir up, rouse' (std. *destare*) has both *distê* and reduced *dèst* (Pelliciardi,
127–28). Because the short forms have a vowel closer to that of the standard, I

suppose that the tonic vowel has risen in the local infinitive and long-form past participle to harmonize with their high final vowels. Short-form past participles thus exhibit conservatism in one respect, innovation in another.

Like speakers of standard Italian, speakers of Romagnolo have competing by-forms for some verbs. They have however merged pairs of verbs still quite distinct in the standard. Besides verbi sovrabbandanti like *scruvar* and *scuvir* 'discover,' both with p.p. *scvért* (cf. std. *scoperto*), and *piašer* and *piéšar* 'please,' both with p.p. *piašù* (cf. std. *piaciuto*), speakers of Romagnolo have what Pelliciardi terms falsi sovrabbondanti, pairs of verbs that have fallen together. Thus, Rml. *šbarêr* and its p.p. *šbarê* may mean either 'kick[ed]' or 'block[ed],' but the two verbs are still distinct in std. It. *scalciare* and *sbarrare*. Partly as a result of metathesis in the local reflex of TREMERE, Rml. *tarmêr* and its p.p. *tarmê* may mean either 'become motheaten' or 'tremble[d], quiver[ed],' a pair still distinct in std. It. *tarmare* and *tremare*.

The term falsi sovrabbondanti may also apply to pairs of verbs whose infinitives differ merely by conjugational ending, and sometimes by stress as well, but whose past participles remain distinct. Examples from Romagnolo are *cùsar* 'cook' and *cusîr* 'sew' with p.p.s *cöt* and *cusî*, or else *parer* 'prepare' and *parér* 'seem' with p.p.s *parê* and *pêrs*, or again *valêr* 'sift, bolt' and *valér* 'be worth' with p.p.s *valê* and *vêls* (Pelliciardi, 135–37). Locals put up with homonymy here as elsewhere.

3.6.1.4. Ligurian

Among dialects of Ligurian reviewed in this section, I consider the dialect of Genoa on the mainland and that of Sisco on Corsica. (For Corsican strictly speaking, a central dialect close to Tuscan, see §3.6.2.1). Data for the first come from Petrucci's *Grammatica sgrammaticata della lingua genovese*; those for the second from Chiodi-Tischer's *Die Mundart von Sisco (Korsika)*. The following subsection, §3.6.1.4.1, deals with the dialect of Val Graveglia in eastern Liguria.

In Genoese, regular 1st-conj. verbs with infinitives in *-â* make their past participles in *-òu*, and regular 4th-conj. verbs with infinitives in *-î* make their past participles in *-îo*. Verbs in these two classes have the same stem throughout. Examples of regular Genoese past participles are 1st-conj. *cantòu* 'sung,' *mangiòu* 'eaten,' *pensòu* 'thought,' 4th-conj. *capîo* 'understood,' *corrîo* 'run,' *sentîo* 'felt, heard' and *doîo* 'hurt, grieved.' So-called regular 2nd-conjugation infinitives in *-éi* and 3rd-conjugation infinitives in *-e* both make their past participles in *-ùo*. Examples of true regularity are 2nd-conj. *taxùo* 'been quiet,' *piäxùo* 'pleased,' and *dovùo* 'had to' for infins. *taxéi, piäxéi, dovéi*, and 3rd-conj. *arrezùo* 'ruled, guided' and *battùo* 'beaten,' for infins. *arréze, batte*.

In the 2nd conjugation, though, an infinitve stem that used to contain an intervocalic consonant may differ from a p.p. stem with sort-of sigmatic marking. Thus, infin. *poéi* 'be able' contrasts with p.p. *posciùo*, infin. *voéi* 'want' with p.p. *vosciùo*, and infin. *paéi* 'appear' with p.p. *parsciùo*. Presumably pronounced [ʃ], this marker could have have been generalized from [s:] in forms resembling std. *posso* 'am able' but its palatal nature suggests rather that it came from inchaotive [sk] before a front vowel.

Everywhere, the 3rd conjugation evinces the greatest number of irregularities. Genoese is no exception. Often, past-participial irregularities appear to have come down from Late Latin or Proto-Romance, if not earlier, and resemble those in standard Italian. Sigmatic past participles include *açceiso* 'lit,' *fuso* 'melted,' *perso* 'lost,' *sparso* 'sprinkled,' for infins. *açcende*, *fonde*, *perde*, *sparze*. Others look semilearnèd, like *alluso* 'alluded,' *discusso* 'discussed,' *diviso* 'divided,' and *persuaso* 'persuaded.' In dealings day to day, I believe, rustics are unlikely to use such verbs; they could well have been borrowed from the standard. (However, infin. *dividde* does not exactly match std. *dividere*.) Sigmatics with long [s:] include *misso* 'put,' *mosso* 'moved,' and *presso* 'squeezed' for infins. *mettere*, *meuve*, and *primme*, which it is hard to imagine rustics' getting along without.

Apparently surviving as a syncopated rhizotonic thematic from Latin times is Gen. *futo* 'fled' < FUGITU. Mentioned in §3.6.1, this rhizotonic has been remade in all standard Romance tongues and syncopated only here.

Tautic athematic past participles in Genoese include *finto* 'feigned,' *frito* 'fried,' *scelto* 'chosen,' and *spanto* 'spread,' for infins. *finze*, *frizze*, *scèglie*, *spande*. Tautic athematics with [t:] include *cheutto* 'cooked' for infin. *cheuxe*. A sigmatic-tautic is *visto* 'seen' for infin. *vedde*, though *assunto* 'assumed' with infin. *assumme* looks as semilearnèd as *protetto* 'protected' with infin. *proteze*. The past participle for *cazze* 'fall,' namely *cheito* 'fallen,' might have arisen ± COLLĒCTU 'gathered,' from peasants' gathering branches or fruit fallen from trees. Irregular 4th-conj. past participles include *morto* 'died' and the pair *coverto* 'covered' and *averto* 'opened' for infins. *moî*, *crovî*, and *arvî*. Here past participles look conservative, infinitives innovative.

Some verbs in Genoese have by-form past participles, the first usually a holdover and the second an innovation along regular lines. By-forms among past participles for 3rd-conj. verbs include *punto* and *punzùo* for infin. *punze* 'sting, prick,' *riso* and *riùo* for infin. *rïe* 'laugh,' and *vinto* and *vinsùo* for infin. *vinçe* 'win,' besides semilearnèd *cesso* and *cedùo* for infin. *cede* 'yield.' Yet infin. *vive* 'live' has two arrhizotonic by forms for its p.p., *visciùo* and *vissùo*, while infin. *tenze* 'dye' has two rhizotonic ones, *tento* and *tinto*. The verb *cianze* 'complain' has three p.p. by-forms: *cento* and *ciento*, and regularized *cianzùo*, all featuring [tʃ] from [pl].

Among remakings of past participles around Genoa, two entail replacement or regularization. Urbanites prefer *preiso* to *piggiòu* 'taken' and also 4th-conj. *soffrîo* to inherited *sofferto* 'suffered.' Conversely, the 3rd-conj. verb *rexiste* 'resist' has an old regular p.p. *rexistùo* and a new irregular one, 4th-conj.-style *rexistîo* (Petrucci, 71–75).

In the village of Sisco, no doubt settled from the north rather than the east, a more conservative variety of Ligurian is spoken, as regards p.p. morphology. Regular masc.sg. past participles end in -*adu* for 1st-conj. verbs, in -*u du* for 2nd- and 3rd-conj. ones, and in -*idu* for 4th-conj. ones. Readers should compare such forms with the pattern encountered in Genoa of 1st-conj. forms in -*ò u*, 2nd-/3rd-conj. forms in -*u o*, and 4th-conj. forms in -*î o*. Examples of regular past participles in Sisco (Lig.: Sis.) are 1st-conj. *kantadu* 'sung,' *mangǎdu* 'eaten,' and *parladu* 'spoken' for infins. *kanta, parla, mangǎ*; 2nd-/3rd-conj. *avudu* 'had,' *kridhudu* 'believed,' *tenudu* 'held,' and *pyegǔdu* 'pleased' for infins. *kredhe, täne, pyäge*; 4th-conj. *finidu* 'ended,' *kabidu* 'understood,' and *durmidu* 'slept' for infins. *fini, kabi, dorme*, but that last infinitive has joined the 3rd conjugation.

Other verbs in Sisco have undergone metaplasm. Infins. *beśte* 'dress, clothe' and *särbe* 'serve' have moved from the 4th conjugation (cf. VESTĪRE, SERVĪRE) to the 3rd and acquired regular past participles for their new class in *biśtudu, serbudu*. Infinitive *mugg̈ǎ* 'bellow, low' has moved from the 4th conjugation (cf. MŪGĪRE) to the 1st and acquired a regular p.p. *mugg̈ǎdu*.

Among irregular past participles in the small corpus are a couple straight from Latin, for the Sis. p.p. *mortu* 'died' still contrasts morphologically with its 3rd-conj. infin. *more*; the Sis. p.p. *kubärtu* 'covered' would probably contrast with its infinitive as well, had the author supplied one. Such forms maintain old allomorphies. In some pairs of infinitives and past participles, allomorphy has increased since Latin times, usually as a result of lenition before front vowels but not before back vowels. Thus, p.p. *bedu* 'drunk' contrasts with infin. *beye*, and p.p. *gózu* or *gududu* 'enjoyed' contrasts with infin. *godhe*. Owing to rhotacism and sigmaticism, p.p. *bursudu* 'wanted' (cf. a nonstd. Tusc. by-form *vorsuto*) contrasts with the more conservative infin. *bulé*. Finally, the slightly irregular Sis. p.p. *pertudu* 'left' and its 3rd-conj. infin. *pärte* provides another instance of metaplasm, considering regular 4th-conj. PARTĪRE 'split, share out' (Chiodi-Tischer, 93–108).

3.6.1.4.1. Val Graveglia

Data for this subsection about a subdialect come from Plomteux's *I dialetti della Liguria orientale odierna: la Val Graveglia*. As usual, I focus on 3rd-conj. verbs, for they display the widest range of past-participial types.

In Val Graveglia (VG), tautic athematic survivals include *fritu* 'fried,' *rutu* 'broken,' and *streytu* 'tightened' (infins. *frize, rumpe* or *rumpi, strenze*). Though infin. *mui* 'die is given (676), the form *murtu* 'dead; corpse' is listed only as an adjective or noun (672). Like their counterparts in standard Italian, the still rhizotonic VG p.p.s *frentu* 'crushed, trodden' ≠ FRĀCTU and *vintu* 'won' ≠ VICTU have imported nasality from the infectum that seems to have raised the tonic vowel; compare the nasal infinitives *franze* and *vinse*.

Sigmatic survivals include *askusu* 'hidden,' *cŏsu* 'shut,' *risu* 'laughed,' and *tunsu* or *tusu* 'shorn' (infins. *askunde, cŏde, riye, tunde*). Other survivals are the triplets *misu* 'put,' *prumisu* 'promised,' *skumisu* 'bet' (infins. *mete, prumete, skumete*). After yod, [s] either voices to [z] or fricativizes to [ts], giving the p.p.s *apeyzu* 'hung,' *apreyzu* 'curdled, clotted,' *ateyzu* 'tended, awaited' (infins. *apende, aprende, atende*), as well as unprefixed p.p. *peyzu* 'hung' for infin. *pende*, a "verbo molto raro" (751) [very rare verb]. In what seems to be the same phonetic environment, s̲ remains at least graphically i n *aseysu* 'lit' and *speysu* 'spent' (infins. *asenze, spende*). Postclassically sigmatic is *persu* 'lost (infin. *perde*), which, unlike its p.p. counterpart in standard Italian, lacks any arrhizotonic by-form.

One VG verb now part of the 4th conjugation still has a sigmatic past participle: *kursu* 'run' for infin. *kuri* ≠ CURRERE. In the p.p. *marsu* 'withered, faded; rotted, spoiled,' s̲ is part of the stem given its 4th-conj. infin. *marsi* ≠ MARCĒRE, so that *marsu* should be ranked as a short-form past participle like those heard elsewhere in Italy (§3.5.9) and in Iberia (§4.7.8). From the same stem comes a masculine noun *marsa* 'clothes-peddler' (659), its extended meaning doubtless attributable to the low quality of apparel hawked door to door along the Val Graveglia.

Two 3rd-conj. arrhizotonics date back to Latin days: *batüu* 'beaten' and *següu* 'followed' (infins. *bate, segwe*). Mast participles remade arrhizotonically in Val Graveglia resemble infectum-based forms found in French, Catalan, Romanian, or standard Italian. A sampler would feature *insernüu* 'sifted,' *kredüu* 'believed,' *kresüu* 'grown,' *nasüu* 'born,' *punzüu* 'stung,' *tesüu* 'woven,' and *vendüu* 'sold' for infins. *inserne, krede, krese, nase, punze, tese, vende*. Both sigmatic and arrhizotonic are the high-frequency rhyming p.p.s *pusüu* 'been able' and *vusüu* 'wanted' (rhyming infins. *puey, vuey*), for two verbs that lacked past participles in Latin.

In Val Graveglia, several 3rd-conj. verbs have acquired 4th-conj.-style past participles with the characteristic *-iyu* ending: *kugĭyu* 'gathered' (infin. *kögĕ*), and the triplets *ingugĭyu* 'wrapped, wound,' *regugĭyu* 'gathered,' *dergugĭyu* 'untangled' (infins. *ingögĕ, regögĕ, dergögĕ*). Of these three, *ingugĭyu* has been remade from p.p. VOLŪTU 'rolled,' probably by a rhyming analogy.

New verbs have evolved in Val Graveglia since Latin times. One is 3rd-conj. *vande* 'winnow' with p.p. *vandüu*, built on the stem of 2nd-decl. VANNU 'winnowing-fan.' (Excrescent [d] after [n] in *vande* suggests that [r] used to be present in all VG infinitives.) Another new verb is 4th-conj. *arenti* 'approach' with p.p. *arentiyu*, built on the present participle of HÆRĒRE 'stick, cling.'

If speakers have developed new verbs, they have merged others: the verbs meaning 'cook' and 'sew'—verbs quite distinct in Latin—are homophonous in Val Graveglia. Not only does p.p. *kötu* mean both 'cooked' < COCTU and 'sewn' ≠ CŌNSŪTU, but infin. *kösĕ* 'cook; sew' is the same as well. Speakers have followed much the same path as those speakers of Spanish who pronounce as [s] the intervocalic consonant in infins. *cocer* 'cook' and *coser* 'sew.' In Val Graveglia, no replacement verb like Sp. *cocinar* 'to kitchen' viz. 'to cook' seems to have been recorded. As always when going by orthography alone, one cannot be aware of phonological distinctions made by speakers but unrecorded on the page.

Among 4th-conj. regularizations is VG *kruviyu* ≠ COOPERTU 'covered' (infin. *krui*). Note also p.p. *veñiu* 'come ≠ VENTU (infin. *veñi*), though the usual ending for that class is written *-iyu*. One form that has remained win the same class is *partiyu* 'left' (infin. *parti*).

Enough VG verbs have p.p. by-forms to prove it unyoked to a literary standard. One type of by-form entails differences in tonic vowels: *cănze* 'lament' has *cĕntu* versus rare *căntu*. The verb *cŏe* 'rain' has for past participles 4th-conj.-style *cŭviyu* versus rare 2nd-/3rd-conj.-style *cŭvüu* (no CL p.p.). The verb *tenze* 'dye' has for past participles old-style *tentu* < TĪNCTU versus regularized but rare *tenzüu*. As seen for Romanian and standard Italian, continued hesitation between sigmatic and tautic athematic p.p. variants often affects past participles for reflexes of TORQUĒRE 'twist.' In Val Graveglia, *intorse* 'twist' takes only the sigmatic p.p. *intorsu*, while unprefixed *torse* 'wring, squeeze' usually takes *tortu* but may also take *torsu*.

One morphological differentiation by age has emerged. Most speakers still say *askusu* 'hidden,' but the by-form *askuzu* used in Statale, is heard elsewhere only among the young (141). *Askuzu* could well prevail in the end if its partisans outlive its adversaries and no new adversaries come along. As for relics, *gasŏw* 'frozen' (cf. std. It. *ghiacciato*) is all that remains of an old 1st-conj. verb, *zea* now being used instead to mean 'freeze' (431).

Between Rome and Val Graveglia, some semantics have shifted. As in std. Italian, the local reflex of RE + ICERE 'throw back' has come to mean 'vomit'; in the VG verb *rey* (p.p. *reyu*), another arrhizotonic has won out for past participle. Moreover, the 1st-conj. verb *brua* (p.p. *bröu*), glossed as "bruciare" [burn, scorch, singe], has a semantic range startling for its narrowness. VG speakers use the verb solely in two circumstances: "quando una capra è morsicata nelle memmelle dalla vipera, in generale non dà più latte dalla parte infrettata; quando il sole estivo rovina la vigna, fa cadere le foglie..." (228) [when a nanny-goat gets bitten in the teats by a viper, she generally gives no more milk from the affected part; when the summer sun blasts a grape-vine and makes the leaves drop off].

Here and there, Plomteux notes that a few VG verbs lack any past participle: *paey* 'seem, appear,' *porze* 'hand over.' Plomteux also notes that the verb *prebugĭ* 'unglue; simmer' is used only in the infinitive and the past participle, the latter being regular 4th-conj. *prebugĭyu* (785).

Regrettably often in his 1,180-page, two-volume dictionary, Plomteux fails to give any past participle for a verb listed. Verbs from the 2nd conjugation denied full coverage are *avey* 'have,' *savey* 'know,' *vaey* 'be worth,' and *vey* 'see.' Verbs from the 3rd conjugation denied full coverage are *di* 'say, tell,' *fute* 'ram; send away,' *kunusĕ* 'know,' and *zunze* 'add, join.' As for 1st-conj. *da* 'give' and *sta* 'stand, stay,' for 4th-conj. *sŭrbi* 'swallow,' *sŭrti* 'go out,' *tusĭ* 'cough,' and *zemi* 'wail, whine,' one may infer but not imply that each has a regular past participle for its class. Plomteux sometimes leaves morphological roles unclear, as when he gives adjectival *avertu* 'open' (153) and *spresu* 'squeezed' (954) without specifying whether they also serve as past participles for infins. *arvi* and *spreme*. Again, while noting that the verb *munze* 'milk' survives in the high valley, being replaced elsewhere by presumably regular 1st-conj. *alayta*, Plomteux gives no past participle for either of them.

Since Plomteux comments that *incĭ* 'fill' has grown rare, being used only in the present indicative, no one would expect him to give a disused (p.p.) form. That by-form *incĭ* has been replaced by *impi*, which does have p.p. *impiyu* 'filled' ≠ IMPLĒTU (431). One would like to learn how speakers in Val Graveglia have dealt with other cases of allomorphy that survived from imperial days or evolved later on.

3.6.1.5. Lunigiana: A Transition Dialect?

Before turning to past-participial outcomes in central-southern Italy, I consider past participles from Lunigiana. That dialect has been termed a dialect of transition between Gallo-Italian and Tuscan, but it looks more northern than central-southern. Examples come from Bellucci's *Lunigiana*.

Lunigiana has roughly the expected Gallo-Italian outcomes for arrhizotonic past participles in e.g. 1st-conj. *parlá* 'spoken,' 2nd-/3rd-conj. *tašü* 'been quiet' and *pardü* 'lost,' and no doubt 4th-conj. *dormí* 'slept.' Retained rhizotonic past participles include *cot* 'cooked,' *let* 'read,' *frit* 'fried,' *fat* 'done/made,' and *mort* 'died,' all of which used to have -TU suffixed to a consonant-final root. A sigmatic reflex is Lun. *cüs̆* 'closed'; sigmatic-tautics are *armast* 'stayed' and *vist* 'seen.' Though *sta* 'been,' *(a)ü* 'had,' and *nda* 'gone,' along with other past participles like *pudü* 'been able,' *vursü* 'turned,' and *saü* 'known,' no longer show a trace of final [t], that stop remains graphically at least in *dat* 'given' < DĂTU, perhaps by analogy with [t] < [kt] in *fat* 'done/made' < FACTU (Bellucci, 59). Regrettably few data have been made available.

3.6.2. Survey of Past Participles in Central-Southern Dialects

South of the line linking La Spezia and Rimini, the past-participial picture becomes quite unlike that found at the Romance Center of France, Catalonia, and northern Italy. A common class in Latin but extinct nearly everywhere in Romance, past participles in reflexes of -ĪTU have survived best in the south of Italy and on Sardinia, if apparently not at all in heel-of-the-boot Apulian (§3.6.2.4). For examples, see Table 3–7 on page 180.

At times, I confess to having been unable to classify each form. Halfway down the east coast, at Agnone in Abruzzia, are found past participles like *vutə* 'wanted' (no CL p.p.), alongside such forms as *íntə* 'filled' ≠ IMPLĒTU, and *nínguətə* 'snowed' (no CL p.p. but cf. infin. NING(U)ERE). These all show innovation, but is there a common thread? Clearly, unsyncopated ONeap. *tòlleto* 'taken away' goes back to a rhizotonic thematic form built on the root of infin. TOLLERE (cf. LL TULLITU). At the same time, ONeap. *chiòppeto* 'rained' (no CL p.p.), along with *cúrzeto* 'run' ≠ CURSU and *mòsseto* 'moved' ≠ MŌTU, represent innovations along -ĪTU lines. Still in the south, South

Lucanian *víppətə*, Campagnan *víbbətə*, and Neapolitan *víppeto* 'drunk' all go back to a postclassical slot-filler BIBITU, unlike the (probably later) arrhizotonic remodeling that turned into std. It. *bevuto*. Another South Lucanian p.p., *sappətə* 'known,' implies that here a rhizotonic thematic variant unlike std. It. *saputo* was developed to fill a past-participial slot left empty in literary Latin. Note also Calabrian *sísitu* 'sensitive' ≠ SĒNSU 'felt,' now purely adjectival.

Table 3–7 illustrates rhizotonic thematic outcomes for the past participles meaning 'drunk,' 'rained,' and 'moved.'

Table 3–7

Rhizotonic Thematic Past Participles
in Southern Dialects of Italian

By-forms are starred

Latin	Neapolitan	Abruzzese	Lucanian
LL BIBITU	víppeto	vévətə	bíppete
[no CL p.p.]	chiuóppeto°	čòbbətə	ćoppete
MŌTU ≠	muóppeto	[muostə]	moppete°

Even speakers in a pocket of Gallo-Italian in Lucania (Luc.GI), who use such un-southern-looking forms as *alluccadu* 'shouted,' *avudu* 'had,' and *ondu* 'oiled' with voicing of [t], have such rhizotonic thematics. Two examples are p.p. *accòvitu* 'welcomed' (infin. *accuogliere*) and the noun *bívita* 'a drink' versus p.p. *bevù* 'drunk' (infin. *bìvere* or *bévere*). Perhaps the Luc.GI by-form *carùttu* 'fallen,' competing with arrhizotonic *carudu* and *cadudu*, syncopated from an old rhizotonic thematic variant like *[káditu], later reinforced by the stem of infin. *caré* or *cadé*. So at any rate I deduce from Mennonna in *I Dialetti gallitalici della Lucania*.

That preterit vocalism could influence p.p. vocalism is as evident in the forms *misso* 'put' and *ditto* 'said' found on Elba and around Arezzo as it is in parallel *misso* and *itto* encountered in Lucca. As happened in Fr. *mis* and *dit* but not in std. It. *messo* or *detto*, speakers drew the tonic vowels of those past participles not from the old p.p.s DICTU and MISSU with tonic [I] but rather from pfs. DĪXĪ, MĪSĪ that had tonic [i:] in Latin (Giannelli, 63, 75, 82).

Within the past system, a tonic vowel of a preterit can influence that of its past participle: Elban has *sutto* < SUCTU 'sucked' rather than std. *succhiato* 'sucked' from Germanic. A consonant from the preterit may appear in the past participle, as witness Laz. *possuto* 'been able' (std. *potuto*). Just as speakers of what became standard Italian brought nasality from the present stem into past participles like *finto* 'feigned,' *(di)pinto* 'painted,' and *vinto* 'won,' speakers in the Marches have used a present stem resembling the one in NING(U)ERE 'snow' to fill a p.p. slot left empty in Latin, but they have marked it with [t]. The resulting form, Marc. *ninto* 'snowed,' shows far greater conservatism than does std. *nevicato* from a paradigm rebuilt on an obl. noun stem NIV- seen in the adj. NIVŌSU 'snowy' (Rohlfs 1949, 422–23). For the corresponding past participles, Romanian has *supt* 'sucked' < SUCTU with labialization of [k] before [t], along with sigmatic *învins* 'won' and *nins* 'snowed.'

In the south of Italy, easy shifts by verbs in *-i-* to the class in *-e-* have been partly responsible for the spread of -ŪTU-style past participles (Rohlfs 1968, 371). Moreover, the -ŪTU type has spread into some past participles still rhizotonic in the latinizing standard. Nonliterary Tuscan has *leggiuto* 'read,' *nasciuto* 'born,' *piangiuto* 'complained,' *vinciuto* 'won,' and *chieduto* 'asked'; Calabrian has *diciuto* 'said,' *mintutu* 'put' with unexplained [n], *scrivutu* 'written,' and *stringiutu* 'clasped' (Tekavčić, 451). To these may be added present-based Neapolitan *arduto* 'burned,' *scennuto* 'cut' (< *scinduto* for std. *scisso*?; cf. std. infin. *scindere*), *corruto* 'run,' *chiagnuto* 'complained,' along with Cal. *aperutu* 'opened,' and *offrutu* 'offered.' In the far southwest, Sicilian has *murutu* 'died,' *nasšutu* 'born,' and *cǐrnutu* 'sifted' (cf. Rom./Cat. *cernut*). As against std. It. *entrato*, South Corsican has *intrutu* 'gone in,' a regular form given the local rhizotonic infin. *éntre* ≠ INTRĀRE (Rohlfs 1949, 422).

Rarely, past participles have come to be doubly marked. In non-std. Tuscan, one encounters rhotic-sigmatic *vorsuto* 'wanted' instead of std. *voluto* (Giannelli, 34). In Lazio, one encounters a similar form namely *volsuto* 'wanted'; this variant is "spesso pronunciato *vorzuto*" [often pronounced [vɔrtsúto]]. At times, though, speakers must feel that old words possess sufficient phonetic body, for Laziale still has disyllabic *ito* 'gone' instead of its std. replacement *andato* (Troncon, 99).

Moves away from arrhizotonicity have taken place, too. One is after all still traveling through Italy. Thus, at least "nei vecchi contadini" [among old peasants], Sienese has sigmatic *creso* 'believed' instead of std. *creduto* together with short-form *spolto* 'stripped' instead of std. *spogliato* (Giannelli, 42–43). These morphological readjustments have happened within Tuscany, but Lazio has *creso*, the Marches *cres*, and Salento *crisu*, all meaning 'believed'; Old Lombard had sigmatic-tautic *cresto* 'idem.' At one time, a sigmatic exponent must have been a powerful competitor for that p.p. slot. Unexpectedly, sigmatic-tautic forms have sprung up here and there across the south, as in Lucanian *mòst* 'moved' and *vòst* 'wanted' (Rohlfs 1968, 372–74).

Within rhizotonic classes, dialects sometimes feature forms divergent from the standard. For instance, Laziale has *scénto* 'gone down' as against std. *sceso* (Troncon, 99).

Though they retain some sigmatic and tautic athematic forms, most dialects in the south have only two types of arrhizotonic past participles, descended from -ĀTU and -ŪTU (but see §3.6.2.4 for an exception). According to Mancarelli's *Salento* (16), for instance, Sal. *turmutu* 'slept,' *sintutu* 'felt, heard,' *furnutu* 'ended,' and *assuto* 'gone out' contrast with std. *dormito, sentito, finito, uscito*. Again, arrhizotonic past participles have grown more widespread around Salento: compare Sal. *cănğŭtu* 'complained' and std. It. *pianto*, Sal. *liğğutu* 'read' and std. *letto*, Sal. *munğŭtu* 'milked' and std. *munto*, Sal. *romputu* 'broken' and std. *rotto*, and Sal. *spinğŭtu* 'pushed, bent' and std. *spinto*.

Competition has arisen between inherited strong and present-based weak forms. As shown in Valente's *Puglia* (34), Apulian has both *fríttə* and *frəsütə* 'fried,' both *sšîsə* and *sənnútə* 'gone down.' Compare the rhizotonics *fritto, sceso* from the banks of the Arno, each unchallenged in the literary standard.

To a speaker of any standard Romance language, the abundance of by-forms thriving in southern dialects makes the past-participial landscape there look more like a jungle than a garden.

3.6.2.1. Corsican

Better termed a central dialect of Italian than a southern one, Corscican (Cors.) strongly resembles Tuscan in past-participial morphology. Data, practically limited to irregulars, come from Albertini's *Précis de grammaire corse*.

Two arrhizotonics are the rhyming pair *tenutu* 'held' and *venutu* 'come,' which on Corsica have the rhyming infinitives *tene* and *vene*.

Rhizotonics are well represented. One old direct-suffixation tautic is Cors. *natu* 'born' (infin. *nasce*). Inheritances in [rt] are *apertu* 'opened' (infin. *apre*) and *cupertu* 'covered' (*copre*). Innovations in [rt], all shared with Tuscan, are *offertu* 'offered' (*offre*), *portu* 'fetched' (*pordie*), and *suffertu* 'suffered' (*soffre*).

Corsican past participles in [nt] are *cintu* 'girded' (infin. *cigne*), *diuntu* 'arrived' < JŪNCTU (*diundie*), *pientu* 'wept (*piendie* or *pienghe*), *tintu* 'dyed' (*tigne* or *tingne*), and *untu* 'oiled' (*ugne* or *ungne*). All come straight from Latin. In contrast, p.p.s *strintu* 'squeezed' (infin. *strigne* or *stringne*) and *vintu* 'won' (*vince*) have nasality imported from the infectum. So does std. It. *vinto* 'won' ≠ VICTU, unlike std. *stretto* 'squeezed' < STRICTU; but cf. the It. adj. *strinto*.

Inherited double-tautics that once contained a [kt] cluster are *custruttu* 'built' (infin. *custruce*), *dettu* 'said, told' (*di*), *fattu* 'done/made' (*fa*), and *prutettu* 'protected' (*prutege*). Two that once contained a [pt] cluster are *rottu* 'broken' (*rompe*) and *scrittu* 'written' (*scrive*). An innovation is *scettu* 'chosen' (*sceglie*), which one would expect to have an [lt] cluster like the std. p.p. *scelto* 'idem' but which has evidently been remade by a rhyming analogy.

Sigmatic *messu* 'put' (infin. *mette*) has been inherited from Latin. Sigmatic *intesu* 'heard, understood' seems to accompany a suppletive infinitive *sente*, rhizotonically reshaped from SENTĪRE 'feel, perceive.' Matching a Tuscan innovation is p.p. *parsu* 'seemed' (infin. *parè*). Also matching mainland innovations are the sigmatic-tautic trio *postu* 'put' (*pone*), *rispostu* 'answered' (*risponde*), and *vistu* 'seen' (*vere* or *vedde*).

For the past participle of *valé* 'be worth,' Albertini gives *valendu*, obviously a present participle. (He gives no filler in the present-participial slot.) Given that oversight, I cannot tell whether Corsican has a sigmatic innovation comparable to std. *valso* 'been worth.'

Somewhat resembling Rom *ştiut* 'known' in being doubly marked is Cors. *sappiutu* 'idem' (infin. *sapé*). Also doubly marked, but in a way found over the water in Tuscany and Lazio, are Cors. *pussutu* 'been able' and *vulsutu* 'wanted' (*pudé, vulé*). All three of these verbs lacked past participles in Latin. Yet another oddity is Cors. *betu* 'drunk' < LL BIBITU ? (infin. *beie*).

Like old and new varieties of Italian (§3.5.9), like standard Portuguese and nonstandard Spanish (§4.7.8), Corsican contains short-form past participles for certain verbs in the 1st conjugation. Albertini gives five of them. First, infin. *trová* or *truvá* has long-form *trovatu* or *truvatu* and short-form *trovu* 'found.' Second, infin. *comprá* or *cumprá* has long-form *compratu* or *cumpratu* and short-form *compru* 'bought.' Third, infin. *troncá* or *truncá* has long-form *troncatu* or *truncatu* and short-form *troncu* 'shattered.' Fourth, infin. *cercá* or *circá* has long-form *cercatu* or *circatu* and short-form *cercu* 'looked for.' Fifth, infin. *guadagná* or *balagná* has long-form *guadagnatu* or *balagnatu* and short-form *guadantu* or *balantu* 'gained, won.' For that last set, the interchange between [gw] and [b] looks positively Sardinian if not Romanian.

In the five sets given above, rhizotonic short forms remain unaffected by the pretonic vowel raising that optionally affects infinitives and long-form past participles. Whether any differentiation, semantic or stylistic, has arisen between short-form and long-form past participles goes unmentioned (Albertini, 83–91).

3.6.2.2. Calabrian

For this section, which deals with Neapolitan, data come from Bichelli's *Grammatica del dialetto napoletano*. In the following subsection, §3.6.2.2.1, I examine the Calabrian dialect of San Mango sul Calore in Avellino.

According to Bichelli, Neapolitan (Neap.) preserves four infinitive endings, as in 1st-conj. *penzà* 'think,' 2nd-conj. *caré* 'fall,' 3rd-conj. *scósere* 'unstitch,' and 4th-conj. *durmi'* 'sleep' but has only two types of regular past participles. All reflexes of 1st-conj. past participles end in -*ato* (*penzato* 'thought,' *dato* 'given'), and all regular reflexes of the other three conjugations end in -*uto* (*caruto* 'fallen,' *scusuto* 'unstitched,' *durmuto* 'slept'). Intervocalic [d] customarily rhotacizes, as in *benerìcere* 'bless' and *malerìcere* 'curse'; compare *dìcere* 'say, tell,' where initial [d] remains. The [rts] cluster in Neap. *kùrzeto* 'run' ≠ CURSU has resulted from a reinforcement of earlier [rs], required by local phonotactics and also evident in e.g. *borza* for std. It. *borsa* 'purse' and *perzona* for std. *persona*.

As it does elsewhere, allomorphy remains highest among 3rd-conj. verbs, here the only ones to preserve final -*re* in infinitives. Irregular past participles may be classified into three groups: (1) those containing [s] or an allophone [ts] after [r], (2) those containing [t] or long [t:] with no theme vowel, (3) those ending in -*eto* < -ÍTU. The third group comes down from forms in -ÍTU, which appear to have enjoyed greater popularity in Late Latin than they had under the classical standard.

Under sigmatic past participles are found Neap. *acciso* 'killed,' *chiuso* 'closed,' *miso* 'sent,' *riso* 'laughed,' and *succieso* 'happened' for infins. *accìrere*, *chiùrere*, *mèttere*, *rìrere*, and *succèrere*. These parallel std. *ucciso* 'killed' and others, except that std. *succedere* 'happen' has by-form past participles, *successo* and *succeduto*. In an instance proving that morphology alone does not determine stylistic register, the Neap. p.p. *spaso* 'spread' is considered vulgar there, but its cognate in standard Italian, *spanso* instead of *spanto*, comes across as learnèd. Neap. past participles with the [ts] allophone include *(j)arzo* 'burned' and *curzo* 'run' (infins. *ardere*, *córrere*).

Under tautic athematic past participles are Neap. *apierto* 'opened,' *muorto* 'died,' *nato* 'born,' *sufferto* 'suffered' for 3rd-conj. *nàscere* and 4th-conj. *arapi'*, *muri'*, *suffri'*. Double-tautics from CL forms in [kt] or [pt] include *cuotto* 'cooked,' *ditto* 'said,' *fritto* 'fried,' and *rutto* 'broken' for infins. *còcere*, *dìcere*, *frìjere*, *rómpere*. Like the standard, Neapolitan also has at least one past participle in [st], namely *visto* 'seen' for infin. *veré*. Past participles in -*eto* include *muóppeto* 'moved,' *scìveto* 'chosen,' and *vìppeto* 'drunk' for infins. *mòvere*, *scégliere*, *vévere*. One may compare these with sigmatic *mosso*, tautic athematic *scelto*, and arrhizotonic *bevuto* in standard Italian.

No one should exclude the possibility that speakers remodeled some past participles long after the Empire's fall. Nevertheless, unlike today's std. *sorriso* 'smiled' and *parso* 'appeared,' doubly marked ModNeap. *sorriésseto* ≠ already sigmatic SUBRĪSU; doubly marked *párzeto* 'appeared' ≠ PĀRITU has acquired sigmatic marking like std. *parso*. For other verbs, pairs of by-form past participles are "usate entrambe indifferentemente": *annascuso* and *annascunnuto* 'hidden,' *perzo* and *perduto* 'lost,' *scurzo* and *scurruto* 'flowed, run,' *stiso* and *stennuto* 'stretched,' *sciso* and *scennuto* 'gone down, come down' (the latter by-form evidently also meaning 'split, cut'), and *strutto* and *strujuto* 'built.' The verb *chiòvere* 'rain' has a past participle in -*eto*, *chiuóppeto*, alongside a regularized one, *chiuvuto* (Bichelli, 178–96). Here again, the conservative variant usually represents a survival from Latin, and the innovative variant has an -*uto* ending added to the bases of infins. *annascónnere*, *pèrdere*, *scénnere*, *scórrere*, *stènnere*, and *strùjere*.

In one respect, Neapolitan bears a vague resemblance to Venetian with its pack of past participles in -*esto*. Speakers around Naples have sometimes favored -*seto* as an ending for preterit-based past participles like *lesseto* 'read,' *sparseto* 'sprinkled,' and even *comparseto* 'bought.' To that last form, compare regular 1st-conj. *comprato* in the standard (D'Ovidio and Meyer-Lübke, 154).

Illuminating again how analogies work, Cal. *staputu* 'been' has probably been modeled on *saputu* 'known' (Rohlfs 1968, 371). Clearly, this analogy was based on sound instead of sense.

3.6.2.2.1. San Mango

Data for this subsection about a subdialect come from Blasi's *Dizionario dialettale di San Mango sur Calore (Avellini)*. Past participles from San Mango (SM), a village leveled by an earthquake in 1980, are close to those from Neapolitan.

In lexis, *crai* < CRĀS 'tomorrow' still thrives in San Mango, though replaced in Neapolitan by something like std. It. *domani*. In phonology, rhotacism of [d] occurs initially in e.g. infins. *rà* 'give' and *rumà* 'tame.' In morphology, Sammanghesi prefer longer variants in e.g. *mozzecà* 'bite' and *rosecà* 'gnaw'; Blasi gives past participles for none of these infinitives. Built from an old present participle is the verb *appezzendi* 'become poor' with p.p. *appezzenduto*; cf. std. It. *pezzente* 'beggar,' the Latin verb being 3rd-conj. PETERE 'go toward; seek, ask, beg.'

Regular p.p. endings will occasion little surprise. In San Mango, past participles in *-ato* go with verbs from the 1st conjugation: *addorcato* 'sweetened,' *scangiato* 'exchanged,' and *sengato* 'signed' for infins. *addorcà*, *scangià*, *sengà*. Blasi gives one 2nd-conj. verb, mentioned below, but no past participle for it. In San Mango, past participles in *-uto* go with verbs from the 3rd conjugation: *arrostuto* 'roasted,' *fottuto* 'fucked; tricked,' and *vestuto* 'clothed' for infins. *arroste*, *fottere*, *vèste*. Forms in *-uto* also go with verbs from the 4th conjugation: *abbivuto* 'brought back to life,' *fuiuto* 'fled,' *iuto* 'gone' for infins. *abbivi*, *fui*, and *i'*. That last verb has a longer by-form past participle *gghiuto* that appears after a modal auxiliary, giving e.g. *so gghiuto* 'I have gone, *è gghiuto* 'he has gone.' After another verb, a similar by-form infinitive is used, giving e.g. *accommenza a gghi'* 'begins to go' (Blasi, 51).

A relic of Latin -ĪTU, an ending in atonic *-ito* occurs in SM *chiuòippito* 'rained' for infin. *chiove* (no CL p.p.). If p.p. coverage were complete, such relics could probably be found elsewhere.

Sammanghesi put certain verbs in different classes than do speakers of standard Italian. If the standard has adj. *cieco* 'blind,' Mango has only p.p.-looking *cecato* in that adjectival sense, also serving as the past participle for the SM infin. *cecà* 'blind' (std. It. *accecare*). Again, SM has *caroluto* 'worm-eaten, moth-eaten,' as against Neap. *caruliato* and std. It. *tarlato* 'idem,' the last a true past participle as well. Finally, SM *arrugginuto* 'rusted' contrasts with std. It. *arrugginito*.

That last SM form reflects the preference of speakers in southern Italy— alien as it sounds to a Spaniard or a Portuguese—for *-uto* over *-ito* as a p.p. ending. For example, Blasi gives a form *abbrustolito* 'roasted' as the past participle for *abbrustolì* (25), which would be regular almost anywhere else in Romance, but adds, "se usa anche la forma *abbrustoluto*" (25) [the form *abbrustoluto* is also used]. I suspect that this *-uto* form really serves as the verb's past participle, the *-ito* form being reserved for adjectival use. After all, a noun or adjective may freely take an ending in *-ito*. Of the two SM nouns that mean 'yeast,' *criscito* derives from an old if nonstandard past participle with the sense 'grown,' while *crescente* derives from the old present participle that meant 'growing' without reference to an moon for Moslems or a butter roll for Viennese.

Speakers in San Mango relish the *-uto* ending, since they apply it to at least two past participles for 1st-conj. verbs that normally end in *-ato*. One such verb has infin. *'nfrostecà* 'frighten; annoy' but p.p. *'nfrostecuto*. Another has infin. *'ngannari* "lure, entice' but p.p. *'ngannaruto*. Both past participles are also adjectival and probably began by being exclusively so.

Sigmatics are scarce here. Two come from what is in effect the same verb with different prefixes. So *appiso* 'hung' and *'mpiso* 'hung' go back to PĒNSU 'idem' (infins. *appènne, 'mpenne*). Minus their prefixes, the third and fourth sigmatic forms, *'nfuso* 'bathed' and *stiso* 'stretched,' go back to FŪSU 'poured' and TĒNSU 'held out' respectively (infins. *nfónne, stènne*).

Like all languages reviewed in Georges, the San Mango dialect has nouns extracted from past participles. The ones I found on Blasi's pages are all feminine. They include *abbiata* 'a start,' *apparata* 'decorating a church with bright banners,' *cignata* 'lash,' *ioccata* 'snow,' and *scordata* 'oversight, neglect.' Compare the 1st-conj. infins. *abbià* 'begin,' *apparà* 'prepare,' *cignà* 'whip,' *ioccà* 'snow,' and *scordà* 'forget.' From the verb *manià* 'handle' comes the p.p.-looking noun *maniata* 'libidinous caress.' The SM verb *frecà* meaning not 'rub' but 'fuck; cheat' has spun off another p.p.-looking noun *frecata* 'coitus.' As a consequence of one *frecata* too many, a young couple may have to run away on a *fuiuta* 'elopement.'

Blasi gives no past participle for the verb *refonne* 'add.' The SM noun *refósa* 'adding, addition' seems to have been built upon its past participle, but I cannot tell whether the expected past participle has stayed current im Volksmund. Also of likely past-participial origin is the noun *remosseta* 'earthquake,' which besides adding to the Sammanghese sigmatic inventory illustrates one more variant of the old -ĬTU ending already seen in SM *chiuòippito* 'rained.' Another likely candidate for a p.p.-derived noun is *vàvito* 'stone hog-trough,' no doubt identical to an old past participle for 1st-conj. reflexive *vaviarsi* 'slobber, drool,' itself presumably with a regular *-ato* p.p. these days. One cannot be sure.

As in the Val Graveglia (§3.6.1.4.1), one regrets that past participles have been given for only a few verbs in San Mango sul Calore. Besides the gaps deplored above, Blasi fails to give past participles for 1st-conj. *quaglià* 'curdle' and *zucà* 'suck,' both presumably regular, but what about a past participle for seemingly 1st-conj. *fa* 'do/make'? Was the local reflex of FACTU 'done/made' kept or lost? Again, Blasi fails to give a past participle for the single 2nd-conj. verb I found, namely *veré* 'see' (which may be 3rd). Blasi fails to give past participles for the 3rd-conj. verbs *arde* 'burn,' *cerne* 'sift,' *còce* or *còcere* 'cook,' *cóse* 'sew,' *énghie* or *egne* 'fill,' *frie* 'fry,' *mónge* 'milk,' *pónge* 'sting,' *régne* 'fill,' *reólle* 'boil,' *rire* 'laugh,' *scénne* 'go down,' *spóne* 'unload,' *ténge* 'dye,' *tremènte* 'look at,' *vatte* 'beat,' and *véve* 'drink.' One would like to know whether Sammanghesi have remodeled or retained past participles like tautic athematic COCTU 'cooked,' PŪNCTU 'stung,' TĪNCTU 'dyed,' like sigmatic ĀRSU 'burned,' RĪSU 'laughed,' VĪSU 'seen,' and others besides.

3.6.2.3. Abruzzese

According to the scanty data given in Giammarco's *Abruzzo* (184), one finds here most of the tendencies already discussed in the survey of southern Italian dialects. Disregarding final schwa, a number of Abru. past participles closely resemble their opposite numbers in the Tuscan-based standard.

Sigmatics here are *risə* 'laughed,' *tesə* 'stretched,' *missə* 'sent,' and *fissə* 'split.' Tautic athematics are *natə* 'born,' *múortə* 'died,' and *túortə* 'twisted.' Double-tautics are *dittə* 'said, told,' *fattə* 'done/made,' *kúottə* 'cooked,' *rottə* 'broken,' and *skrittə* 'written.' As in Lucanian, [t] voices to [d] after [n] in Abru. *mundə* 'milked' ≠ MULCTU and *tində* 'dyed' < TĪNCTU. Voicing of [t] also occurs after [l] in e.g. *ššéldə* 'chosen' ≠ EX + ĒLĒCTU and *kúoldə* 'gathered' ≠ COLLĒCTU (cf. std. *scelto, colto*). These last two evidently derive from old rhizotonic thematics.

Rhizotonic thematic past participles with endings from -ĪTU still flourish, in e.g. *vèvətə* 'drunk,' *cöbbətə* or standard-influenced *pióvətə* 'rained,' *nénghətə* 'snowed,' and *(rə)vévətə* 'lived.' That type may have left traces in p.p. *jində* 'filled' ≠ IMPLĒTU. Conceivably, *apíərtə* 'opened' ≠ APERTU also bears traces of that type, though it looks more like a straight survival; note that [t] fails to voice after [r].

Abruzzese past participles with endings from -ŪTU include *ləǵǵutə* 'read' and, with something like a [g] suffix as in Occitan or Catalan, *vənǵutə* 'come' (see §4.6, especially §4.6.2.3). So popular is the -ŪTU type that it marks past participles of a few 1st-conj. infinitives, as in *bbasˈtutə* 'been enough' and *fətutə* 'bewitched' vefsus std. *bastato, fatato*. Indeed, certain -ŪTU past participles were being used long ago in the deep southeast: *falluta* 'been mistaken,' *feruto* 'struck,' *partuto* 'left,' *rapute* 'kidnapped,' *sbanduti* 'disbanded, straggling,' *sentuto* 'felt,' *salluto* 'gone away,' and *smarruto* 'gotten lost.' Accompanying infinitives from various classes, such archaisms imply that the -ŪTU formant used to be productive.

Today, that productivity may have diminished. According to the even more scanty data in Villa's italianizing *Grammatica e ortografia dei dialetti abruzzesi* (110), 4th-conj. *servi'* 'serve' has two by-form past particfiples: expected southern *servuto* but also *servito*. Given the general scarcity of 4th-conj. p.p. reflexes in the south, *servito* may have been influenced by an identical form in standard Italian. However, nearby Apulian proves exceptional in that regard (see §3.6.2.4).

One gap in coverage remains. Neither of the works consulted mentions any past participle in a reflex of -ĀTU. Has Abruzzese lost a p.p. type found everywhere else? Rather, Giammarco and Villa must have thought that so common a type was unworthy of note.

3.6.2.4. Apulian

Data for this section come from Loporcaro's *Grammatica storica del dialetto di Altamura* (1988), in the province of Bari. I have slightly latinized the continues unrefonted.

Speakers of Altamura Apulian have three types of arrhizotonic past participles. Roughly according to the pattern found across central ROMANIA, 1st-conj. reflexes end in -*eta* (strictly speaking, [ɛtə]), 2nd- and 3rd-conj. reflexes end in -*uta* (strictly, [uu̯tə]), and 4th-conj. reflexes end in -*ita* (strictly, [li̯tə]). Having written final schwa on the words above, Loporcaro 1988 then abandons the practice later; I acquiesce.

Several 4th-conj. verbs, with infinitives ending in -*i*, have acquired 2nd-/3rd-conj.-style past participles: *asut* 'gone out,' *məndut* 'told lies,' *patut* 'suffered, undergone,' and *servut* 'served.' Despite further evidence of metaplasm in Alt. *arəstut* 'roasted' as against std. *arrostito*, Altamura has resisted the trend toward replacing -*it* types with -*ut* types that has swept across the Mezzogiorno. Yet Loporcaro gives no regular past participle from the 4th conjugation, and only one from the 1st. Notable as well, though unmentioned by the author, is the absence of any reflex of the atonic -ĬTU p.p. ending, a type that also thrives across the Mezzogiorno. In past-participial terms, Apulian stands as an outpost in southern Italy of the p.p. vocalism found across the Italian North, Catalonia, and France.

As have speakers of other nonstandard dialects in ROMANIA, speakers from Altamura have leveled past participles along arrhizotonic lines. Such past participles as Alt. *kərut* 'run,' *kjanǧut* 'complained,' *mənǧut* 'milked,' and even the formal p.p. *skrəwut* 'written,' are quite unlike std. It. *corso*, *pianto*, *munto*, and *scritto*. Another kind of innovation comes across in the 1st-conj. p.p. *munəlet* 'cleaned,' built from a reflex of adj. MUNDU 'clean, neat' rather than from something like 'polish.'

Several rhizotonics in Altamura face no competition. Tautic athematics can be classed by their tonic vowel: in [a] is *fat* 'done/made'; in [i] are *aflit* 'distressed,' *dit* 'said, told,' and *frit* 'fried'; in [y] are *strüt* 'worn out' and *anüt* 'carried, brought [toward the speaker].' Sigmatics are *acĭs* 'killed,' *pers* 'lost,' *pərsuweis* 'persuaded,' and *umweis* 'stayed.' Sigmatic-tautics are *pwest* 'put' and *vist* 'seen.'

Under certain conditions, Alt. past participles have tonic vowels that vary by gender. Variance arises if one of each pair, usually the feminine, has a tonic mid vowel; absent that feature, vowels fail to vary. I have found four types of such past participles. Type 1 has a masculine in tonic (*w*)*e* and a feminine in tonic *ö*, giving p.p. pairs like masc. *kwet* and fem. *köt* 'cooked,' masc. *kwelt* and fem. *költ* 'tilled,' masc. *akwelt* and fem. *akölt* 'gathered,' or masc. *selt* and fem. *sölt* 'chosen.' Type 2 has a masculine in *ü* and a feminine in *ò*, giving a pair like masc. *rüt* and fem. *ròt* 'broken.' Type 3 has a masculine in *i* and a feminine in *e*, giving a pair like masc. *apirt* and fem. *apert* 'opened' alongside an arrhizotonic by-form *japrut*. Another such pair, masc. *strind* and fem. *strend* 'tightened, narrowed,' shows the voicing of [t] after [n] also encountered in Lucanian (§3.6.2.5) as well as infectum nasality absent from STRICTU. Perhaps really a Type 2, Altamura Type 4 vowel variation has masc. in *w u*, fem. in *w ò*, giving a masc.-fem. pair like *fwult* and *fwòlt* 'plugged, clogged' alongside an arrhizotonic by-form *fəlčut*. But does such variation remain productive today? None of the verbs above looks like a neologism.

A few reflexes of old present participles survive adjectivally in Altamura. One is *trand* 'too wet [of pasta],' from the verb *tre* 'pull.' That last participle reminds one that, to outsiders, a lexical item in a culture may seem too specific for the bare requirements of communication (Loporcaro 1988, 261–62).

3.6.2.5. Lucanian

Lucanian has regular masculine singular past participles resembling those in Neapolitan: they end in *-at* for reflexes of 1st-conjugation verbs, in *-ut* for reflexes of 2nd-, 3rd-, and 4th-conjugation verbs. Examples are *skupat* 'swept' (1st-conj. infin. *skupá*; cf. SCŌPÆ 'broom') for the first class, and *avut* 'had' (2nd-conj. infin. *avé*), *tenut* 'held' (3rd-conj. infin. *ten*), and *venut* 'come' (4th-conj. infin. *vení*) for the other three. Like Spanish and Portuguese, then, Lucanian has two kinds of arrhizotonic past participle. Like most dialects of southern Italy, Lucanian has generalized reflexes of -ŪTU rather than -ĪTU as its non-1st-conj. ending of choice for past participles.

Most irregulars here resemble those in standard Italian. A number contend with regularized by-forms.

Besides tautic athematics like *mort* 'died' (infin. *murí*), *kot* 'seized' < COLLĒCTU? 'gathered' (infin. *koǵǵ*), and *tort* 'braided, woven' < TORTU 'twisted' (infin. *torc*), Lucanian has double-tautics from the usual two sources in Italian: CL forms in [kt] and in [pt]. Instances of the old [kt] type are *kott* 'cooked' < COCTU (infin. *koc*), *fatt* 'done/made' < FACTU (infin. *fà*), *zitt* 'said' < DICTU (infin. *zic*), and *fritt* 'fried' < FRĪCTU (infin. *friy*). An instance of the old [pt] type is *rutt* 'broken' < RUPTU (infin. *rupp*).

As in standard Italian, many Lucanian verbs with past participles in long [t:] have sigmatic preterits, while other such verbs have preterits in [tʃ]; in Lucanian, such preterits often compete against regularized variants even for high-frequency verbs. Thus, 1sg. *ziss* 'said' < DĪXĪ competes against *zeciv*; and 1sg. *fec* 'did/made' < FĒCĪ competes against *faciv*. In Lucanian, the two p.p. oddities starting with long [s:]—*sset* 'chosen' (infin. *sseǵǵ*) and *ssot* 'undone' (infin. *ssoǵǵ*)—appear to derive from syncopated variants resembling those that gave rise to the std. It. p.p. *volto* 'turned' and adj. *sciolto* 'loose' (cf. Sp.

vuelto, suelto). The two Lucanian p.p. oddities could come from old but postclassical variants in -ÍTU.[63]

Short and long, sigmatic past participles in Lucanian include *accǐs* 'killed' < OCCĪSU (infin. *accǐz*), *ćus* 'closed' < -CLŪSU (infin. *ćuz*), *mis* 'put' < MISSU 'sent' (infin. *mitt*), and by-form *moss* 'moved' (infin. *mov*), to which cf. std. It. *mosso*. As in Neapolitan, Luca. *spas* 'spread' < EXPĀNSU belongs to vulgar registers. Many of these forms parallel sigmatic preterits like 1sg. *mis* 'put' < MĪSĪ 'sent,' now vying with regularized *mettiv*. Sigmatic-tautic past participles are *vist* 'seen' (infin. *viz* or *vezé*), a common type for its verb, and also *vòst* 'wanted' (infin. *vulé*), a much rarer type for its. Both verbs have preterit by-forms, at least one being innovative: 1sg. *vos* ≠ VOLUĪ and regularized *vuliv* 'wanted,' or *vidd* < VĪDĪ and regularized *veziv* 'saw.' What analogy did speakers make to come up with sigmatic *vos*?

Peculiar to Lucanian, Apulian, and southern Abruzzese is a tautic athematic type of past participle with voicing of [t] not between vowels—as one would expect north of La Spezia–Rimini line—but instead after [n] (see §3.6.2.4). Resultant [nd] types occur mostly for verbs whose CL infinitives had an -NG- cluster, and whose LL/PR ancestors had an -NCT- cluster. Examples are Luca. *frand* 'shattered' (infin. *frangǐ*), *ǧind* 'filled' (infin. *gingǐ*), and *tind* 'dyed' (infin. *tingǐ*), to which compare std. It. *franto* 'shattered,' *tinto* 'dyed.' No doubt by chance, this Lucanian type has come to resemble far-western Ptg. *vindo* 'come.' Among Lucanian suppletive verbs are found p.p.s *yut* 'gone' ≠ ÍTU (infin. *yi* < ĪRE) and *stat* 'been' < STATU 'stood, stayed' (infin. *yess* or *yiess* < LL ESSERE 'be'), whose 1sg. preterits are conservative *yiv* 'went' < ĪVĪ and *fuy* 'was' < FUĪ.

As in e.g. Neap. *muóppeto* 'moved,' some Lucanian verbs whose roots end in a labial consonant have a rhizotonic thematic type of past participle incorporating [p:]. Examples include Luca. *bippete* 'drunk' (infin. *biv*), *sappete* 'known' (infin. *sap*), by-form *moppete* 'moved' (infin. *mov*), and *ćoppete* 'rained' (infin. *ćov*). Though the first two had no past participle in Latin, the last two are quite unlike MŌTU, COOPERTU and come from forms based on *u*-stem perfects plus an -ÍTU ending.

In fact, current Lucanian 1sg. preterits whose ending derives from 4th-conj. -ĪVĪ, continue that tradition: *beppiv* 'drank,' *sappiv* 'found out,' *muppiv* 'moved,' and *ćuppiv* 'rained,' the last being purely notional. In Lucanian, this type of preterit ending has spread to the variant *zappiv* 'gave' competing with *ziv* and to the variant *stappiv* 'stood' competing with *stiv* ≠ STETĪ. A similar type of past participle exists in Sardianina, as in Logudorese *appidu* 'had' and *deppidu* 'had to' (see §3.7.3). On that island, however, the post-tonic ending -*idu* has become regular for 2nd- and 3rd-conjugation past participles, and marking in [p:] has spread into far fewer verbs (Iliescu and Mourin, 424–25).

---

[63] The verb meaning 'choose' comes from EX + ĒLIGERE, with the stutter of a doubled prefix; the other verb must be marked o.o.o.

3.6.2.6. Sicilian

If Sicilian shares its vowel system only with the far south of Calabrian and the far south of Apulian, it shares its morphology for past participles with other central-southern dialects that have two arrhizotonic types. According to Consolino's *Vocabulario del dialetto di Vittoria* in the southeast, Sicilian lacks any rhizotonic thematic type like Abruzzese *ninguətə* 'snowed' or Neapolitan *víppeto* 'drunk.' Sicilian therefore contains the purest two-type set of past participles within eastern ROMANIA. An identical reduction of arrhizotonic types is encountered in Ræto-Romance (§4.3), a similar one in Spanish and Portuguese (§4.7).

In Sicilian, regular 1st-conjugation infinitives in *-ari* make their past participles in *-atu*; regular 2nd-/3rd-conjugation infinitives in ´*-iri* and regular 4th-conjugation infinitives in *-íri* all make theirs in *-utu*. Stems remain the same throughout. Examples from the 1st conjugation are *mancătu* 'eaten,' *purtatu* 'carried,' *cămatu* 'named, called,' *církatu* 'looked for,' *muzzikatu* 'bitten' (cf. Rom. *morşecat*, Cat. *mossegat*), and *sukatu* 'sucked,' the last remade from SUCTU much as the doubtful Ist-R form *suptat* has reportedly been. Another 1st-conj. reshaping is Sic. *tiratu* 'pulled, drawn' replacing archaic *tratu* < TRACTU. The whole verb *cǐssare* 'cease' has been built not on the stem of CĒDERE but on that of freq. CESSĀRE, itself based on the same stem as p.p. CESSU (cf. Fr. *cesser*).

Instances of past participles in *-utu* may be divided into three groups: (1) those with infinitives only in ´*-iri*, (2) those with infinitives only in *-íri*, and (3) those with fluctuation between the two types owing to the lack of any standard. In Group 1, which one might term pure 2nd-/3rd-conj. verbs, come the p.p.s *(a)bbattutu* 'beaten' and *futtutu* 'fucked' (infins. [a]*bbáttiri, fúttiri*) from Latin along with innovative *funnutu* 'plowed deep,' *jutu* 'gone,' *nassutu* 'born,' *vincutu* 'won,' *vinnutu* 'sold,' and *vivutu* 'drunk.' In Group 2, which one might term pure 4th-conj. verbs, come the p.p.s *fallutu* 'failed,' *firutu* 'struck,' and *surutu* 'bloomed.' Group 3, by far the largest, might be termed contaminated verbs. They may be divided into three subgroups. If C stands for any consonant or consonant cluster, past participles in the first subgroup have infinitives ending in either [áCiri] or [aCíri], like *karutu* 'fallen,' *partutu* 'left,' *raputu* 'opened, split,' and *trasutu* 'entered.'[64] Past participles in the second subgroup have infinitives ending in either [éCiri] or [iCíri], like *cǐrnutu* 'sifted,' *nissutu* 'gone out,' *pussirutu* 'owned,' *sintutu* 'felt, heard,' *vinutu* 'come,' and *vistutu* 'clothed, dressed.' Past participles in the third subgroup have infinitives ending in either [óCiri] or [uCíri], like *kuggutu* 'gathered,' *kusutu* 'sewn,' and *sacutu* 'mended, patched.' The p.p.

---

[64] Semantic shifts for verbs of motion are exemplified by reflexes of TRĀNSĪRE 'go across.' Sic. *trásiri* means 'go in'; Apul./Cal. *trasire*, Abru. *trasí*, and Neap. *tra sərə* mean 'happen'; Log. *trazire* means 'be astonished'; 1st-conj. Lombard *trazá* means 'waste' (*REW* no. 8855). The Sic. shift could have begun with a narrowing of meaning to 'crossing a threshold.'

liggutu 'read' comes from a verb with three infinitive by-forms (*léggiri,* *liggiri, liggĭri*) and hence escapes ready ranking.

As might seem clear from the above list, many Sicilian verbs waver between the two kinds of non-1st-conj. infinitives, perhaps in part because both take the same kind of past participle. Moreover, several high-frequency verbs have undergone metaplasm into the arrhizotonic non-*are* conjugation: compare Sic. 4th-conj. *avíri* 'have' (p.p. *avutu*), *putíri* 'be able' (p.p. *pututu*), *sapíri* 'know; taste' (p.p. *saputu*), and *vulíri* 'want' (p.p. *vulutu*) with 2nd-conj. std. It. *avere, potere, sapere,* and *volere*. Several verbs belonging to the 4th conjugation in Latin, like Sic. *véniri/viníri* 'come,' now waver between their inherited infinitive class and an innovative 2nd-/3rd-conj. one. One more past participle in this class, *kjuvutu* 'rained,' cannot be assigned an infinitive because the author supplies none (Squartini, 188).

In the reduction of infinitive endings to three and of arrhizotonic p.p. endings to two, one may trace morphological affinities between Sicily and Spain. Just as past participles in -*udo* have grown unfamiliar to speakers of Spanish, a language with only three infinitive types, so past participles in -*itu* have grown unfamiliar to speakers of Sicilian. Actually, the old 4th-conj. -ĪTU type appears scarcely to have survived south of Tuscany; see the end of this section for a fuller discussion.

Turning now to rhizotonic past participles, or former ones now adjectival, I had trouble identifying certain inheritances by morphology alone; p.p. *affisu* 'offended' (infin. *affénniri*) looks as if it ought to mean 'fastened, driven in.' A Romance generalist will recognize others. Sigmatics include adj. *arsu* 'burned' (infin. *ardíri*), *cŭsu* 'closed' < -CLŪSU (infin. *cŭriri*), *misu* 'put' (infin. *míntiri* or *mintíri,* with excrescent [n]), and *persu* 'lost' (infin. *pérdiri*). Tautic athematics come long or short. Longs include *dittu* 'said' (infin. *díri*), *fattu* 'done/made' (infin. *fári*), and *kuottu* 'cooked' (infin. *kócĭri*). Shorts include *juntu* 'arrived; joined' (infin. *júnćiri*) and *kupiertu* 'covered' (infin. *kupríri*). Straight from CRĒDITU but with syncope comes the oddity *krittu* 'believed' (infin. *kríriri* or *kriríri*), to which compare Genoese *futo* 'fled' < FUGITU 'idem' (see §3.6.1).

Certain rhizotonic thematic nouns in Sicilian have the ending -*itu,* which I choose to deem atonic despite the absence of diacritics because reflexes of the same nouns have survived elsewhere. One such noun from Late Latin endures in Sic. *vippita* 'a drink.' That noun competes with arrhizotonic *vivuta* 'idem,' a no doubt more recent remodeling built from the same stem as adj. *vivutu* 'drunk,' itself likely serving as the past participle for the blended infin. *viviri* 'drink; live.' One cannot be certain of this, for Bellestri gives no past participle under *viviri*. A few other rhizotonic nouns beginning with v- are *vagitu* 'whimpering, wailing' *vincita* 'victory, gain,' *vinnita* 'sale,' and *vistitu* 'man's suit.' Compare the infins. *vagiri* 'whimper, wail,' *vinciri* 'win,' *vinniri* 'sell,' and *vistiri* 'clothe,' none of which has a past participle listed (Bellestri, 331–34).

Back to Consolino's study. At times, past participles surviving from Latin compete against regularized by-forms with endings in -*utu*. So, inherited *appisu* 'hung' vies with *appinnutu* (infin. *appénniri*), inherited *frittu* 'fried' with *frijutu* (infin. *fríjiri*), inherited *kunćusu* 'ended' with *kunćurutu* (infin. *kunćúriri*), inherited *śkrittu* 'written' with *śkrivutu* (infin. *śkríviri*), and inherited *tisu* 'stretched, held' with *tinutu* (infin. *téniri* or *tiníri*). Again, *srittu* 'tight[ened]' < STRICTU vies with the p.p. *srinćutu* (infin. *srínćiri*). A difference of register exists in at least one pair of past participles between "standard" *vistu* and archaic, rustic *virutu* 'seen' (infin. *víriri* or *viríri*). By contrast, an arrhizotonic has won out as *rrutu*, now rare, largely yields to *rrumputu* 'broken' as an out-and-out past participle (infin. *rrúmpiri*).

When a verb has such by-forms, the rhizotonic survival has been restricted to serving as an adjective or occasionally as a noun, while the arrhizotonic innovation has come to serve as a past participle. Thus, *frittu* 'fried,' *kunćusu* 'ended,' *śkrittu* 'written' are usually adjectival. As holds true everywhere else, the local reflex of FALSU 'deceived,' here *farsu* 'untrue,' is strictly adjectival, and the p.p. slot is filled by an arrhizotonic, here *fallutu* 'failed.' Somewhat as in Romanian, the local reflex of MORTUU 'died,' *muortu*, has the adjectival sense 'dead' or the nominal one 'corpse,' and a default arrhizotonic, here *murutu* 'died,' fills the p.p. slot (infin. *móriri* or *muríri*). Note also adjectival *abbintu* 'overcome' contrasting with the presumably regular -*utu* p.p. for infin. *abbinciri* 'charm, enthrall.'

In unusual semantic developments, inherited *tintu* < TĪNCTU 'dyed' has come to mean 'bad, lazy,' perhaps passing through the sense 'tainted.' Inherited *motu* < MŌTU 'moved' has acquired the nominal meaning 'apoplexy, stroke' or the adjectival ones 'struck by apoplexy' or 'unable to react,' while infins. *tínćiri* and infin. *móviri* or *muvíri* appear to have (unattested) regular past participles, in all likelihood built from the present stem plus -*utu*. However, *śtuortu* 'twisted' still serves as both adjective and past participle for infin. *śtórciri*. Then again, *śtatu* does double duty both as the only past participle for *éssiri* or *siri* 'be' and as a by-form past participle (along with *śtaputu*) for infin. *śtari* or *śtapíri* 'stand, stay.'

In Sicilian, morphological variation may reflect semantic differentiation. Speakers distinguish between the p.p. *salatu* 'salted' and the adj. *salito* 'idem' (infin. *salari*). The latter item suggests that the -*ito* ending has been limited to adjectival use on Sicily, somewhat as the -*udo* ending has been in Portugal and Spain (§4.7.4.2). Aside from a few dozen rhizotonic inheritances, then, the Vittoria dialect of Sicilian has undergone a thoroughgoing reduction of allomorphy to two p.p. types.

Bellestri provides further evidence that speakers of Sicilian tend to narrow the functional range of the -*itu* and -*utu* endings, the first being nominal or adjectival. From the verb *abbattiri* 'beat' come both the p.p. *abbattutu* 'vanquished, humiliated, reviled' and the noun *abbattitu* 'exhaustion, fatigue.' (I presume that last form to be arrhizotronic.) Specialization of function has remained incomplete, however. If Sicilian past participles never end in -*itu*, Sicilian adjectives sometimes take the -*utu* ending, as witness *ammuḍḍutu* 'softened' and *ammuffutu* 'moldy.' Admittedly, those two forms look exactly like regular past participles—unlisted by the author—for the non-1st-conj. infins. *ammuḍḍiri* 'soften' and *ammuffiri* 'become moldy' (Bellestri, 2, 12). I suppose that, as in a civil case, a preponderance of the evidence would suffice to make one's case here.

3.7. EVIDENCE FROM SARDINIAN

Mosly located (so to speak) northwest of the La Spezia–Rimini line as regards voicing of intervocalic stops and retention of final [s]—though Corsican resembles Tuscan in doing neither—Sardinian remains an intensely conservative tongue. Lexically, Sardinian keeps seemingly unchanged the old neuter nouns *corpus* < CORPUS 'body,' *pecus* 'sheep' < PECUS 'livestock,' and *tempus* < TEMPUS 'time; weather.' Sardinian also keeps the noun *domu* 'house' < DOMU and the adjective *mannu* 'big' < MAGNU. Phonologically, Sardinian tends to keep velar stops before front vowels, as in *kelu* < CÆLU 'sky' along with the verb pair *fákere* 'do/make' and *léghere* 'read' from Nuorese. At least along the coasts, outsiders have ruled the island for fifteen hundred years, but Sardinians resist change more fiercely than any in ROMANIA. This resistance has hardly prevented them from making innovations on their own.

3.7.0. Preliminaries

In dialects across Sardinia, archaic verbs unknown on any mainland include Logurdorese *koyuvare* 'marry' < CONJUGĀRE 'bind together' and Campidanese *yu(β)ilare* 'shout' < JUBILĀRE 'shout for joy' (Contini and Tuttle, 178). Semantics have also shifted in general *apeḍḍare* 'bark' < APELLĀRE 'call' and *turvare* 'drive, herd' < TURBĀRE 'bother' (Jones, 346). Semantics have stayed the same in Log. *dèghere* < DECĒRE 'be seemly,' with no past participle in Latin and none ascertainable in Sardinian.

Regular past participles in Nuorese end in stressed *-átu* for 1st-conj. verbs, unstressed *-itu* for 2nd- and 3rd-conj. verbs, and stressed *-ítu* for 4th-conj. verbs; the corresponding endings for Logudorese are *-ádhu*, *'-idhu*, and *-ídhu*, with the intervocalic consonant written ḏ but pronounced [ð][65] In Campidanese, medial [t] in such endings often vanishes, giving e.g. *cantau* 'sung,' *tímiu* 'been afraid,' *puliu* 'cleaned' (Jones. 332–33). Archaizing orthography normally retains intervocalic ṱ, as in *cantátu*, *tímitu*, *pulítu*. Here I keep to the spellings found in sources.

---

[65] Intervocalic voiceless stops normally voice and fricativize in Loguodorese and Campidanese but remain unchanged in Nuorese. Lexical items from Nuorese are often cited by researchers eager to accentuate the phonological conservatism of Sardinian. One could choose Upper Aragonese, where lenition of intervocalic stops has also failed to occur (§4.7.12), as emblematic of the consesrvatism of Spanish overall.

Syntactically, as Lausberg observes (222), auxiliary verbs still follow the past participle in Sardinian, as they once normally did in Latin; the only other Romance tongue to permit such auxiliary postposition is Romanian, and there it sounds either dialectal or high-flown. Past participles are used passively after conjugated forms of *kérrere* 'want, need' or after preposition *kene* 'without'; no form of *éssere* 'be' is used with a past participle. An example of the former construction would be *kusta kamisa keret lavata* 'this shirt needs washing.' An example of the latter would be *sa petha es' kene mandikata* 'the meat has not been eaten,' or literally 'the meat is without eaten' (Jones, 340).

3.7.1. Athematic Past Participles

As Mourin notes (34, 41, 50), some sigmatic past participles were still in use by speakers of Old Sardinian. Among them were inherited *okkisu* 'killed' < OCCĪSU and *tusu* 'shorn' < TŌNSU, innovated *frissu* 'fried' ≠ FRĪCTU and *binsu* or *bissu* 'won' ≠ VICTU but cf. Rom. *învins* 'won.' Often, however, such sigmatics had been suffixed with a reflex of -ĪTU, perhaps because they seemed insufficiently distinctive as past participles without it. Resultant variants included OSard. *romasidu* 'stayed,' *offensidu* 'offended,' *mossiu* 'bitten,' and *arsidu* 'burned'; compare REMĀNSU, OFFĒNSU, MORSU, and ĀRSU.

According to Table 3–8 on page 196, suffixation in -*idu* was optional for *intesidu* 'held' alongside *intesu* < INTĒNSU 'stretched, strained,' for *lessidu* alongside *lessu* 'read' ≠ LĒCTU (but cf. Rom. *ales* 'chosen') for *missidu* alongside *missu* 'put' < MISSU 'sent,' and apparently also for *passiu* alongside *parsu* 'appeared' ≠ PARITU. Another means of reinforcing an old sigmatic had been to suffix it with [t], a morphological means already available in e.g. syncopated POSTU 'put, set'; the reinforcement gave by-forms like OSard. *infustu* next to *infusu* 'poured' < INFŪSU 'poured in/on.' As in Italian, some sigmatic-tautic forms like *risposto* 'answered' had become the only recognized ones for their slots.

Now *partu* 'appeared' could have syncopated from PĀRITU, and *bittu* 'drunk' from BIBITU, as Rom. *fiert* 'boiled' may have done from something like *FERBITU (no CL p.p.), but let us not multiply entities beyond the bounds of plausibility: as shown by the still disyllabic (Logudorese) Sardinian ending ´-*idu*, that rhizotonic thematic ending has survived on the island and remains identifiable as such, without syncope. OSard. *bistu* 'seen' is of course paralleled in Sp./It. *visto*. As shown by the last column in Table 3–8, rhizotonic thematics in Old Sardinian could be built on bases containing [s], [t], or [f]. For an account of how that last type came into being, see §3.7.5.

Tautic athematics surviving into Old Sardinian included *beneittu* 'blessed,' *istrintu* 'tightened,' *iunctu* 'joined, arrived,' *multu* 'milked,' *natu* 'born,' *puntu* 'stung,' and *suttu* 'sucked' (Mourin, 163). Two other Logudorese verbs given by Blasco Ferrer (1994, 157–61), without etymologies, are missing from Campidanese: p.p. *imbertu* 'hidden' accompanying infin. *imbérghere*, p.p. *isertu* 'gone away' for infin. *isérghere*. Could the first be Germanic? Could the second have acquired an [r] absent from EXITU 'gone out'? Where?

Revealing a thorough lack of standardization, by-forms were common in Old Sardinian. In Table 3–8, the sigmatic column includes sigmatic-tautics. Most of the rhizotonic thematics have stems from the old finite perfectum.

Table 3–8

By-Form Past Participles in Old Sardinian

Inheritances are boldfaced

LATIN	SARDINIAN		
	sigmatic	tautic athematic	rhizotonic thematic
LL BIBITU	bistu	bittu	—
VĪSU	bistu	bittu	—
INTĒNSU	**intesu**	—	intesidu
CRĒTU	kersu	**kertu**	kerfidu
LĒCTU	lessu	**lettu**	lessidu
MISSU	**missu**	—	missidu
PĀRITU	parsu	partu	parfidu, passiu
QUÆSĪTU	kersu	kertu	kerfidu
RĒCTU	arressu	**arrettu**	—
-SESSU	—	settu	settidu

Today, surviving tautic athematic forms include Nuor. *tentu* 'held,' *appertu* 'opened,' *copertu* 'covered,' and *mortu* 'died.' Long tautics that once contained [kt] include *fattu* 'done/made,' *cottu* 'cooked,' *lettu* 'read'; those that once contained [pt] include *ruttu* 'fallen' < RUPTU 'broken.' Those displaying innovation—or perhaps extreme conservatism—include *conottu* 'known' ≠ COGNITU (but cf. unprefixed [G]NŌTU). Matching the sigmatic-tautic type found in Italian, Spanish, and Catalan is Nuor. *postu* 'put,' but Nuor. *bidu* 'seen' looks quite unlike Sp./It. *visto* or Cat. *vist,* and unlike VĪSU besides. Nuorese and Logudorese also have *mantesu* 'kept,' a sigmatic past participle for the 3rd-conj. infin. *mantènnere,* with It. *mantenuto,* Cat. *mantingut,* and Fr. *maintenu* but cf. Rom. *întins₁* 'stretched' and adjectival survivals like Sp. *tieso* 'stiff' (Iliescu and Mourin, 425). Moreover, *mantesu* 'kept' has a rhyming p.p. partner, Log. *intesu* 'felt' for infin. *inténdere.* Another sigmatic apparently surviving is Log. *dezzisu* 'decided' for infin. *dezzídere.*

A sigmatic past participle that appears to have survived as such only on Sardinia is *prasu* 'lunched' < PRĀNSU 'brunched' As against 1st-conj. It. *pranzare* and Vegl. *prandar,* and also 4th-conj. Rom. *a prânzi* (p.p. *prânzit*), only Sard. *prasu* comes straight from Latin. All others look like denominals built on PRANDIU 'brunch,' with regular past participles for their verb classes.

Further rhizotonic survivors on Sardinia include Log. *postu* 'sent,' Nuor. *fatu* 'done/made,' and Cmpi. *lintu* 'licked' < LĪNCTU. Forms that appear to have syncopated an old -ITU ending are Log./Cmpi. *fertu* 'struck' (no CL p.p.) and Nuor. *bittu* 'drunk' (no CL p.p. but cf. LL BIBITU). Surviving from Latin days is *juttu* 'driven' < DUCTU 'led.' Sardinian is like no Romance on earth.

3.7.2. Differences between Dialects

Comparisons and contrasts in this section are drawn from Blasco Ferrer's *La lingua sarda contemporanea* (1986) and *Ello, ellas* (1994). All in all, Logudorese has preserved more rhizotonic past participles than has Campidanese, especially sigmatic ones. Compare pairs like Log. *intesu* 'felt,' *cumpresu* 'understood,' *tusu* 'shorn' with remade Cmpi. *inténdiu,* *cumpréndiu,* and *túndiu.* Compare also a tautic athematic like Log. *letu* 'read' < LĒCTU (also *léghidu*) with Cmpi. *lígiu.* If Logurdorese has by-forms *pássidu* and *partu* seemed, appeared,' Campidanese has only *partu.* Exceptions to this trend include Cmpi. *própiu* 'rained' as against Log. *próghidu* (no CL p.p.).

For past participles meaning 'promised'—PRŌMISSU in Latin—each dialect has a rhizotonic exponent. One, Log. *promissu,* looks sigmatically conservative; the other, Cmpi. *promíttiu,* looks innovative along infectum lines.

Sometimes both dialects have created or retained similar past-participial exponents, as in Log. *pássidu* and Cmpi. *pássiu* 'appeared' ≠ PARITU, Log. *crétidu* and Cmpi. *crétiu* 'believed' (cf. Sic. *crittu*) < CRĒDITU, and occasionally identical ones as in Log./Cmpi. *prenu* 'filled' ≠ PLĒTU (but cf. adj. PLĒNU 'full'). A shared innovative past participle lives on in Log. *bidu* and Cmpi. *biu* 'seen' ≠ VĪSU but is encountering competition from (no doubt) Italian-inspired *bistu.*

Tautic athematics shared by both dialects include Log. *rutu* and Cmpi. *arrutu* 'fallen,' Log./Cmpi. *cotu* 'cooked,' Log. *iscritu* and Cmpi. *scritu* 'written,' and perhaps Log./Cmpi. *allutu* 'lit.' Others are *connotu* 'known' and *postu* 'sent.' Past participles ending in -*rtu* shared by the two dialects are *abertu* 'opened,' *curtu* 'run' ≠ CURSU, *mortu* 'died' or 'killed,' and *fertu* 'struck'; Log. also has *murtu* 'milked.' Shared by both dialects are some past participles in [ntu]: *tentu* 'had, held,' *prantu* 'complained,' *lintu* 'licked,' and *pertuntu* 'pierced' ≠ PERTŪSU. Contrasts emerge between Log. *risu* and Cmpi. *arrísiu* 'laughed' for infins. *ríere* and *arriri*, between Log. *mossu* and Cmpi. *móssiu* 'bitten,' between Log. *móghiu* with infin. *móere* and Cmpi. *móbiu* 'moved' with infin. *móbiri*. Campidanese also has *scípiu* 'known' for infin. *sciri*, a form missing from Logudorese (Blasco Ferrer 1986, 139).

3.7.3. Past Participles in Reflexes of –ĬTU rather than –ŪTU

Sardinian lacks past participles ending in reflexes of -ŪTU. The handful of forms apparently belonging to that class, like *allutu* 'lit' < AD + *LUCTU? (no CL p.p. for LŪCĒRE 'shine'), *iskutu* 'shaken' < EX + *CUTU? (CL QUASSU), and Log. *rutu* 'fallen' < RŬTU 'rushed down, thrown down,' used to belong to other classes. According to Tekavčić (327), this morphological lack means that the -ŪTU type emerged after Sardinia became isolated from the rest of the Latin-speaking world. Though the start of the island's isolation cannot be dated with certainty, Jones (315) adduces views by unnamed scholars that "on purely linguistic grounds...linguistic contact with Rome ceased...possibly as early as the first century BC[E]."

On the island, rhizotonic thematic past participles like *tímitu* 'feared' correspond to stem-stressed infinitives and bear witness to the passage of 2nd-conj. verbs into the 3rd conjugation, as happened in central-southern Italian dialects and sometimes in standard Italian as well (cf. It. *muóvere, lúcere*). Such metaplasm could take place from any of the other three conjugations. Contini and Tuttle (178) cite Log. *bíere* 'see,' *lúghere* 'shine,' *móere* 'go, walk,' *abérrere* 'open,' and *bénnere* 'come,' for which the CL avatars were arrhizotonic 2nd-conj. VIDĒRE, LŪCĒRE, MOVĒRE and 4th-conj. APERĪRE, VENĪRE. Iliescu and Mourin (425) add Nuor. *ténnere* 'hold,' *copérrere* 'cover,' and *férrere* 'strike,' for which the CL avatars were arrhizotonic 2nd-conj. TENĒRE and 4th-conj. COOPERĪRE, FERĪRE. Compare also Nuor. 3rd-conj. *mórrere* 'die' with Ptg. *morrere*. Occasionally, even a 1st-conj. verb has been so affected: Log. *nárrere* 'speak' has changed class since NARRĀRE, but its past participle is unreconstructed *naradu*. Also changing infin. class has been Nuor. *júkere* 'drive,' if it comes from JUGĀRE 'yoke' with "reverse lenition" of the intervocalic stop ([g] > [k]), an outcome perhaps influenced by the [k] in p.p. JŪNCTU 'joined, yoked, harnessed.' If one accepts DŪCERE 'lead' as a better etymon for *júkere*, as I do, no metaplasm need have occurred.

Forms with endings from -ĬTU can fill slots left empty, like Log. *próghidu*, Cmpi. *propiu* 'rained'; CL PLUERE had no past participle. Forms with endings from -ĬTU can take over from tautic athematic forms, like Log. *istérridu* 'stretched, spread.' Forms with endings from -ĬTU can bear originally inchoative marking, like Log. *arbéskidu* and Cmpi. *obrésciu* 'dawned'; CL ALBĒSCERE 'become white' seems to have lacked a past participle. Rarely, forms with endings from -ĬTU have acquired inchoative marking as well, like Log. *connóskidu* ≠ COGNITU 'known'; cf. infin. *connóskere* to appreciate the reduction in allomorphy. Once only, a form with an ending from -ĬTU can take over from regular 4th-conj. marking, like already mentioned Cmpi. *scípiu* 'known.' Nevertheless, Log. *essidu* or *issidu* 'gone out' represent no survival of EXĪTU but rather a 4th-conj. reshaping like the ones found everywhere else in Romance (Blasco Ferrer 1994, 157–62; Pittau, 116).

Despite being rhizotonic, in practice Sardinian past participles like *tímitu* 'feared' play the role of arrhizotonic forms, for their rhizotonicity is a function of their 3rd-conj. rhizotonic infinitives, according to Lausberg (251). Put otherwise, regular verb classes are somewhat predictable in Sardinian, for both arrhizotonic and rhizotonic infinitives normally have past participles stressed like themselves.

As Tekavčić says (452) and as I have repeated in §3.6.2, reflexes of old-style past participles in -ĪTU are also found in southern Italian dialects, though not in Sicilian. Some filled slots left empty in Classical Latin, like Cal. *víppitu* 'drunk' < LL BIBITU and *kjòppitu* 'rained' (no CL p.p. for PLUERE). Some result from remodelings, like Abru. *(rə)vévətə* 'lived,' Neap. *comparseto* 'bought.' Some are retentions, like Rml. *pruìbbətə* 'banned' < PROHIBITU; compare the standard arrhizotonics *bevuto, piovuto, proibito*. In southern Lucanian, one finds forms like *mòppətə* 'moved' and *sàppətə* 'known,' their stems apparently based on the old local preterits *moppi* ≠ MŌVĪ and *sappi* ≠ SAPĪVĪ, which likewise testify to these dialects' retention or creation of proparoxytonic past participles.

Among rhizotonic thematic past participles in Sardinian, many represent retentions of a Latin type that has grown uncommon from Portugal to Romania. A few show consonantal lengthening and devoicing: *áppidu* 'had' < HABITU, *déppidu* 'had to' < DĒBITU, and *créttidu* 'believed' < CRĒDITU. Some fill slots left empty in Latin: *póttidu* 'been able' and *tímitu* 'feared' (no CL p.p.s). Others represent innovations: infectum-based *nàskidu* 'born' ≠ NĀTU and preterit-based *résidu* 'given back' ≠ REDDITU. Still other rhizotonic thematics compete with conservative by-forms: *istetidu* 'been' against *istatu* 'idem' < STĂTU 'stood, stayed.'

3.7.4. Other Past-Participial Oddities

After citing tautic athematic past participles in Sardinian like Cmpi. *líntu* 'licked' < LINCTU and *fértu* 'hit' ≠ suppletive PERCUSSU or ICTU, Wagner stresses the islanders' reluctance to innovate by maintaining that the Log./Cmpi. p.p. *curtu* 'run' "presuppone un lat. *CURTUM anteriore all'innovazione CURSUM." [presupposes a form *CURTUM preceding the sigmatic innovation].[66]

Wagner also cites the sigmatic Log. p.p. *frissu* 'fried' < attested FRIXU, as against FRĪCTU, without claiming that it predates the standard Latin form

---

[66] See Chapter 2, note 78. If it did exist, the supposed p.p. *CURTU 'run' has left no descendants in Latin's daughter languages. In CL, it would have been homonymous with adj. CURTU 'short,' which itself has descendants from Ptg. *curto* to (originally prefixed) Rom. *scurt*. Indeed, the OL p.p. might have been remade precisely to avoid homonymic clash.

(337–38).[67] Nonetheless, the p.p. *frissu* may well have evolved later, with its [s:] borrowed from old preterit forms (cf. std. It. 3sg. *frisse* < FRĪXIT), a morphological tendency toward leveling stems sigmatically that is most manifest in Romanian but also occurs on the Italian mainland. After all, in Old Sardinian, *frittu* still coexisted with *frissu*. Similarly, OSard. *bintu* 'won' coexisted with *binsu*, both ≠ VICTU, while *pertuntu* 'pierced' coexisted with *pertusu*, the latter < PERTŪNSU (Mourin, 163).

A current Sardinian past participle like *curtu* 'run,' without an attested sigmatic by-form, might have been attributable to speakers' unconscious wish to mark a preterit in [s] and a past participle in [t] for that verb (cf. std. It. *giunsi giunto* 'arrived'). Thus, *curtu* could represent a different type of analogical innovation. One might reach the same judgment about p.p. *spartu* ≠ SPARSU 'sprinkled,' except for the lack of an attested OSard. preterit coming from SPARSĪ. More precisely, differing outcomes across ROMANIA for certain past participles could reflect long hesitation between a sigmatic or a tautic athematic exponent and the consequent coexistence of by-forms. See §3.1.5.2 for similar cases in Romanian.

Reflecting a lack of standardization, a few verbs in Old Sardinian had three by-form p.p.s: one tautic thematic, one tautic athematic, and one sigmatic. Such verbs included one meaning 'want' (p.p. *kerfidu*, *kertu*, or *kersu*, all ≠ QUÆSĪTU) and one meaning 'appear' (p.p. *parfidu*, *partu*, or *parsu*, all ≠ PĀRITU). Also with triplet by-forms, the past participles of the verbs meaning 'see' and 'drink' had come to coincide with each other almost completely: compare *bistu*, *bittu*, or *bi(d)u* 'seen' with *bistu*, *bittu*, or *bidu* 'drunk' (Mourin, 114, 163). At least the second *bittu* 'drunk' apparently derived from LL BIBITU; the first *bistu* 'seen' had and has cognates on the mainland.

When tautic athematic and sigmatic forms were perceived as variants in Late Latin, speakers of Sardinian chose the former in *tentu* 'stretched' < TENTU (cf. TĒNSU; the two seem to have passed for by-forms in Late Latin). Sigmatics remain, or used to, in *prasu* 'lunched' < PRĀNSU, as in *arressu* 'ruled' competing with *arrettu* 'idem' (cf. p.p. RĒCTU but pf. RĒXI). All in all, though, sigmatic past participles in Sardinian have inspired only a few analogical forms. Indeed, as suggested by the coexistence of *infusu* with its sigmatic-tautic by-form *infustu*, Lausberg seems to be correct in stating (252) that sigmatics are gradually disappearing as a distinct class.

Because of its low and declining rate of sigmaticism in p.p. morphology, if not its retention and expansion of rhizotonic thematics, Sardinian could be regarded as steadily becoming more like western Romance languages. See §5.5 for a review of three roles played by sigmatic marking across ROMANIA.

---

[67] Fem.sgs. of both by-forms have left reflexes: std. FRĪCTA in Vegl. *frete* 'pancake,' nonstd. FRĪXA in e.g. Pied. *fërsa* 'roast pig drippings' (*REW* nos. 3504, 3522). Much as happened in Romanian with labialization of velar stops in e.g. *copt* < COCTU 'cooked,' Sp. *frito* 'fried' implies a LL form like *FRIPTU, possibly by rhyming analogy with SCRĪPTU 'written.' CL FRĪCTU would regularly have given Sp. *fricho*. Early loss of [k] before [t] in *FRĪTU would have given Sp. *frido*.

3.7.5. Influence of Preterits on Past Participles

In most varieties of Sardinian, only the present and imperfect survive among tenses expressed by one-word exponents. In a sense, though, old preterits still live on today, by having influenced the morphology of past participles.

Verb forms deriving from the CL perfect like *kerfit* 'sought, wanted' < *QUÆRUIT or *bóffidi* 'wanted' < VOLUIT have now been confined to registers like that of dialect poetry; Sardinian has come to use old present-perfect verbs in preterit functions (Jones, 331). Vanished preterits continue to have morphological influence. For the two past participles meaning 'wanted,' both Log. *kérfidu* < [kerfi] < *QUÆRUI and Cmpi. *bóffiu* < [boffi] < VOLUI have been based on old preterits, for the [f] found in both derives from [w] in Latin (Blasco Ferrer 1986, 138). Coming as it does from the same source, such an [f] is somewhat reminiscent of a [g] used in Catalan and Occitan to mark inter alia most past participles for the 2nd and 3rd conjugations (see §4.6.2.3).

Disbelieving in starred etymologies like *QUÆRUI, Togeby (135) suggests that, besides never having past participles in -ŪTU, Sardinian never had arrhizotonic perfects in -UĪ or in -DEDĪ (better, in -DIDĪ). In the light of evidence presented below, it seems likely that -UĪ perfects, at least, did reach the shores of Sardinia.

As Wagner remarks in an overview of past participles used on the island: "Già in antico occorrono forme influenzate dal tema del perfetto...le quali sono ancora molto diffuse" (338) [Even Classical Latin had certain p.p. forms influenced by finite perfectum stems...which forms are still quite widespread]. Thus, both *appi(t)u* 'had' and *deppi(t)u* 'had to' were influenced by the corresponding perfects HABUĪ and DĒBUĪ, for [bw] > [p:], as suggested by the attested OSard. 3sg. pret. *appit* 'had.' Two past participles, *kérfitu* 'wanted' and *dorfitu* 'hurt,' evidently involve an analogical spread of infixed [w] into the perfect systems of QUÆRERE and DOLĒRE, with postconsonantal devoicing of a hypothesized [v] stage. Other past participles reshaped along preterit lines include *pottiu* 'been able' and *steti(d)u* 'stood, been' as against the OSard. 3sg. prets. *pottit* 'was able' < POTUIT and *stettit* 'stood, was' ≠ STETIT, for [tw] > [t:] on the island. By-form *bittu₁* 'seen' ≠ VĪSU appears to have had the same origin as those two past participles but was not inspired by the OSard. 3sg. pret. *vidit* < VĪDIT, as strikingly an old-fashioned form as OSard. *fuit* 'was' < FUIT. Again, the OSard. 3sg. pret. *tennit* 'held' < TENUIT with its still current p.p. *tentu* < TENTU retained great similarities to the Latin, and so did the OSard. 3sg. pret. *bolvit* 'wanted' < VOLUIT. However, VELLE lacked a past participle in Latin, so that one may draw no such conclusion for the still current Sard. p.p. *boffiu*. Paralleling *tennit* in Old Sardinian was the pret. *bennit* 'came' ≠ VĒNIT, with matching p.p. *benniu* (Mourin, 167, 176–77).

For most such past participles, reflexes of [w] have yet to be completely degrammaticalized as perfective markers. Elsewhere in ROMANIA, reflexes of [w] have undergone that fate, unless they completely velarized as the stop [g] from -UĪ perfects extended into past participles like Cat. *hagut* 'had,' inspired by HABUĪ (see §2.14). Perhaps at the same time as pf./pret. marking in [w] or

[v] was being largely degrammaticalized in most areas, p.p. marking in [f] arose and spread on Sardinia. In an outcome possibly imputable to a return of the repressed, Sardinian ended up with its version of the -ŪTU past participles known from Moldova to Catalonia.

As for morphological rapports between the two principal parts within the past system, most appear familiar in the light of Romanian or Italian. Some Old Sardinian verbs might have preterits and past participles both in [s], both in [z], or both in long [s:]. One verb had a preterit in [z] and a past participle in [s:]. Alternations between sigmatic preterits and tautic athematic past participles remained popular: some verbs had preterits in [s] contrasting with past participles in [t]. others had preterits in [z] and past participles in [t:], and yet others had preterits in long [s:] and past participles in long [t:]. Uniquely, one verb had a preterit in [z] and a past participle in [st]. Regrettably, however, "[l]e nombre réduit de parfaits attestés dans les anciens textes ne permet guère de conclusion touchant les rapports auxquels appartenaient les nombreux participes qui semblent isolés" (Mourin, 176) [the few perfects attested in old texts hardly allow us to ascertain past-system patterns involving many participles, which look like isolates].

In fact, not all patterns within the past system were so straightforward as those sketched above. For instance, there was inherited OSard. 3sg. pret. *fekit* or *fesit* < FĒCIT 'did/made' (also *fettit*) as against the still current p.p. *fattu* < FACTU, the two forms differing both vocalically and consonantally. To be sure, Old Sardinian had its share of sigmatic preterits, like 3sg. *parsit* 'appeared,' *lessit* 'read,' *kersit* 'grew' and *krettesit* 'believed,' but all had been innovated from e.g. PĀRUIT, LĒGIT, CRĒVIT, and CRĒDIDIT. Of those preterits, the first three might have either sigmatic or tautic athematic past participles, and the last had a tautic thematic past participle in *crettiu* (Mourin, 176–77). Despite their reputation for conservatism, then, speakers on Sardinia had already innovated more than one might be willing to acknowledge at first sight. They have gone on doing so.[68]

---

[68] Past participles continue to flourish everywhere in Sardinain. However, the Logudorese dialect at least has lost the present participle. Relics of present participles are now felt as adjectives or nouns: *lughente* 'shining,' *diskente* 'apprentice,' and *molente* 'donkey,' the last because by walking around and around it turned the millstone to grind grain (Pittau, 100).

3.8. LOOKING BACK FROM THE ITALIAN
RIVIERA TO THE BLACK SEA

Given the widespread arrhizotonic leveling of past participles to the west, it is tempting to overstate the morphological conservatism of eastern Romance. Each of the two prominent languages of the east has made innovations in its own ways.

Romanian has expanded arrhizotonic and especially sigmatic marking, the latter usually by generalizing preterit stems, and has spun off sigmatic nouns from innovative past participles. Romanian keeps old [pt] clusters intact and labializes old [kt] clusters to [pt] as well. Many forms in Romanian look just like their opposite numbers in Catalan.

Although literary Italian has stayed close to Latin in e.g. evolving double tautics for forms once marked in [kt] or [pt], the Tuscan standard shows signs of sigmatic spread along with the usual three types of arrhizotonic leveling. Nonstandard dialects even in Tuscany show substantial leveling, and Gallo-Italian dialects show more still. Most central-southern dialects of Italian, along with all dialects of Sardinian, preserve reflexes of the old rhizotonic thematic type in -ĪTU, which everywhere else left at most a residuum of syncopated forms no longer identifiable by type. Two rather than three arrhizotonic endings prevail across much of the Mezzogiorno (from -ĀTU and -ŪTU) and on Sardinia (from -ĀTU and -ĪTU). Certain Sardinian past participles in [f] have been influenced by the preterit, now extinct as a tense.

4

Past Participles in Western Romance

> Occasionally, merely for the pleasure of being cruel,
> we put unoffending Frenchmen on the rack with
> questions framed in the incomprehensible jargon of
> their native language, and while they writhed we
> impaled them, we peppered them, we scarified
> them, with their own vile verbs and participles.
>
> Mark Twain, *The Innocents Abroad*

4.0. OVERVIEW

Past participles across western ROMANIA show a greater tendency toward leveling along arrhizotonic lines, and a lesser tendency toward leveling along sigmatic lines, than do past participles in eastern ROMANIA. In this chapter, I look at p.p. corpora from Ræto-Romance, French, Franco-Provençal, Occitan, Catalan, Spanish, and Portuguese, and from selected dialects of these languages. Readers will recall that dialects of Gallo-Italian, generally reckoned western, are dealt with in §3.6.1.

A linguistic archæologist digging into lesser-known varieties of western Romance may observe floor plans resembling those enshrined in literary cathedrals across Tuscany, Castile, or the Ile-de-France. On the ruins of conjugations used by Sallust and Seneca, speakers of Late Latin and Proto-Romance mainly built past participles bearing stress on the theme vowel. Of past participles stressed on the root, they kept a dozen or two as relics set in niches, to which they paid homage every day in speech.

4.0.1. Alpine Romance

In *The Romance Languages* (351), Haiman groups as Ræto-Romance the several varieties of neo-Latin spoken along the crest of the Alps. Haiman notes that, though a phonological description would serve mainly to separate Ræto-Romance from Italian, a description dealing with linguistic innovations would have to recognize a sharp split between the varieties spoken in Switzerland and those spoken in Italy. Because of diverse influences from German or Italian dialects and the lack of political unity of the area, Haiman goes on, "there is nothing we can say about defining properties of Ræto-Romance as a whole" (352).

However that may be, I have found that inventories of past participles differ sharply—notably in speakers' preference for sigmatics—in three Alpine areas. On geographic or phonological grounds, then, Friulian, Ladin, Engadin, and Surselvan could well be assigned to an entity known as Alpine Romance. On morphological grounds, I treat the first two as separate languages and regard Ræto-Romance as consisting in the last two.

4.1. EVIDENCE FROM FRIULIAN

For Friulian spoken in Friuli, data come from Frau's *I Dialetti del Friuli*, but see also the end of this section. In masc.sg., the three major types of past-participial endings in Friulian look like those in Romanian, or for that matter in Occitan or Catalan: 1st-conj. verbs have them in -*at*, 2nd- and 3rd-conj. verbs have them in -*ut*, and 4th-conj. verbs have them in -*it* (Haiman, 358). Examples of the first and last kinds are 1st-conj. *manciât* 'eaten,' *ciapât* 'gotten' and *ciatât* 'gotten' (both from CAPTĀTU 'hunted, caught'?), and 4th-conj. *finît* 'ended.' Probably reflecting LL reshapings are *crepât* 'burst' ≠ CREPĬTU, *ferît* 'hit' (no CL p.p.), *oferît* 'offered' ≠ OBLĀTU, and *soferît* 'suffered' ≠ SUBLĀTU₂. New slot-fillers have most often been -*ût* types: *olût* 'wanted,' *podût* 'been able,' and *savût* 'known' (no CL p.p.s).

For a number of other verbs, speakers of Friulian have reshaped old unpopular types, usually along -*ût* lines.

A direct-suffixation past participle has been remade in *nassût* 'born ≠ NĀTU. Rhizotonic thematics have been remade in *scuindût* 'hidden' ≠ ABSCONDĬTU, *jessût* 'gone out' ≠ EXĬTU, *piardût* 'lost' ≠ PERDĬTU, *tasût* 'been quiet' ≠ TACĬTU, and *zût* 'gone' ≠ ĬTU. For this last, cf. Ist-I 4th-conj.-style *zi* 'gone,' with the same initial consonant but a different theme vowel. In Friulian, certain tautic athematics have likewise been remade: *sponzût* 'stung' ≠ EXPŪNCTU, *rezût* 'ruled' ≠ RĒCTU, *ricevût* 'received' ≠ RECEPTU, *vinzût* 'won' ≠ VĬCTU, and *vivût* 'lived' ≠ VĪCTU.

Sigmatics have been remade in *metût* 'put' ≠ MISSU, *muardût* 'bitten' ≠ MORSU, *ridût* 'laughed' ≠ RĪSU, *respuindût* 'answered' ≠ RESPŌNSU, and the true oddity *viodût* 'seen' ≠ VĪSU. Another sigmatic has succumbed in 4th-conj. *decît* 'decided' ≠ DĒCĪSU. Judging by CL norms, the Friulian p.p. *cerut* 'looked for' ≠ QUÆSĪTU seems to have been remade arrhizotonically in a different way, but cf. the CL infin. QUÆRERE and the Rom. p.p. *cerut* 'asked.'

Among rhizotonics, one type of irregular past participle has a stressed root plus an ending in -ţ. Examples deriving from [kt] include *dit* 'said, told' (infin. *dî*), *fat* 'done/made' (infin. *fâ*), *trat* 'pulled' (infin. *trai*), *cuet* 'cooked' (infin. *cuei*), and *let* 'read' (infin. *lei*). Another tautic athematic survival is *muart* 'died' (infin. *murî*). All are inherited.

As in Italian, Catalan, and French, a handful of ostensibly 4th-conj. verbs make their past participles with stressed -u- instead of -i-: *vignût* 'come' (infin. *vignî*), *tignût* 'held, kept' (infin. *tegni* or *tignî*), *sintût* 'felt' (infin. *sintî*), *scugnût* 'be constrained' (infin. *scugnî*), and *cirût* 'sought' (infin. *cirî*). Suppletive verbs have the p.p.s *lât* 'gone' (infin. *lâ*) and *stât* 'been' (infin. *jessi*). Verbs making past participles in reflexes of -ŪTU include not only expected *vê* 'have' with *vût* 'had' ≠ HABĬTU but also *vai* 'weep' < VĀGĪRE 'whimper' with *vajût* 'wept' ≠ VĀGĪRE, as against It. *vagito* (Iliescu and Mourin, 419–20).[1]

A very few 3rd-conj. verbs make their past participles with an unstressed root plus an -*et* ending: *cjolet* 'taken' (infin. *cjoli*) and *pognet* 'laid eggs' (infin. *pogni*) are examples. Conceivably, that -*et* represents a survival of -ĬTU, replaced for most other verbs, but necessarily entailing a stress shift. "Regular" 2nd-conj. -ĒTU sounds far better phonologically. How likely would it be for that p.p. ending to have survived in a single remote area? At least reflexes of the -ĬTU ending survive in southern Italy and on Sardinia (see §§3.6.2, 3.7.3). Unfortunately, -*et* has to be marked o.o.o. ("of obscure origin"). See §4.2 for similarly inexplicable past participles in Ladin.

As one might expect, old rhizotonic past participles survive in purely adjectival uses. Thus, *viart* < APERTU means 'open' (adj.), but reshaped *viarzût* means 'opened' (p.p.). Again, *stre(n)te*, from an optionally nasalized variant of STRICTU, means 'narrow, tight,' while *strenzût* means 'narrowed, tightened.' Inherited *stuart* < EXTORTU means 'bent, crooked,' but two by-forms compete for the past participle: regularized *stuarzût* and presumably inherited *stuars* (cf. pf. EXTORSĪ) mean 'twisted.'

A review of native-speaker narratives transcribed by Frau (1984, 226–37) reveals some variants and other past participles, including a sigmatic one. From central Friulian (Udine) come *stufat* 'tired' (cf. the std. It. adj. *stufo* 'bored; sick and tired') and *rivat* 'arrived' with aphæresis. From Gorizia come *mesedat* 'dealt' (cf. the std. It. noun *mestiere* 'trade, craft' or [archaic] 'task'), *viart* 'opened' (cf. std. It. *aperto*), and fem.pl. *taádis* 'cut,' to which compare std. It. *tagliate* based on TĀLEA 'a cutting.' From lower southeastern Friulian (Codròipo) comes prefixed *skomensat* 'started off' < EX + CUM + INITIĀTU. From central-eastern Friulian (Ampezzo) come *višat* 'warned, informed' with aphæresis (cf. std. It. *avvisato* 'idem') and also *sucĕdut* 'happened' in which intransitive sense standard Italian has only sigmatic *successo* as a past participle. From Clauzetto come *sucĕdé* 'happened,' fem.pl. *sŭdes* 'gone' ≠ CL EXITĀS, and also *k'apat* 'taken, caught' ≠ CL CAPTU, but cf. freq. CAPTĀTU. From western Friulian (Grado), the form *spakáo* 'cracked, split' (cf. std. It. *spaccato* 'idem') shows complete lenition of intervocalic [t], as does masc.pl. *rivai* 'arrived.' Also from Grado comes the p.p. *meso* 'put' < MISSU 'sent,' the

---

[1] Meyer-Lübke's *REW* (no. 9124) lists no direct descendants of VĀGĪRE 'whimper' anywhere in Romance. In the light of Friulian *vai*, apparently the basic verb meaning 'weep, cry,' one doubts the accuracy of that omission. But did speakers really preserve a reflex of intervocalic [g], especially before a front vowel, an outcome anomalous to say the least?

first sigmatic encountered in all Friuli. Finally, Grado supplies the masc.pl. p.p. *visti* 'seen,' the first sigmatic-tautic encountered here.

So much for Friulian spoken in Friuli. In Pellegrini's *Studi linguistici friulani II* (1970), there appears an article by Vrabie titled "Testi dialettali friulani raccolti in Romania." Most texts gathered by Vrabie come from a consultant born in 1903 in Dobruja by the Black Sea; in 1970, about a hundred families remained. All past participles are written without circumflexes and are marked "Fri.-R" here.

Fri.-R past participles resemble those gathered in Friuli proper. Indeed, *dat* 'given,' *dit* 'said, told,' *fat* 'done/made,' and *muardut* 'bitten' are identical. Any difference between Fri. *nassut* and Fri.-R *nasut* 'born' could be merely graphic.

Of the past participles I have found for Friulian in Romania but not yet for Friulian proper, most belong to the 1st conjugation. Cited more for the sake of thoroughness than for any morphological surprises they might contain, such forms are *acĕtat* 'agreed,' *baiat* 'barked,' *busat* 'kissed,' *cambiat* 'changed,' *clamat* 'called,' *cumincăt* 'begun,' *domandat* 'asked,' *imprestat* 'lent,' *insĕnaglat* 'knelt,' *(in)contrat* 'met, encountered,' *maridat* 'married,' *montat* 'climbed,' *nseñat* 'taught,' *rabiat* 'been angry,' *racontat* 'recounted,' *restat* 'stayed,' *rivat* 'arrived,' *sposăt* 'married,' *spoventat* 'been scared,' and of course *stat* 'been.' A new member of the 1st conjugation is *mugat* 'mooed,' judging by the old 4th-conj. infin. MŪGĪRE 'bellow, low.' Resembling It. *guardato* and Fr. *regardé* 'looked at' is Fri.-R *vardat* 'idem,' from Germanic.

With typical 2nd-/3rd-conj. endings come Fri.-R *batut* 'beaten, knocked,' *divinut* 'become,' *rispondut* 'answered,' *sintut* 'heard,' *tasŭt* 'been silent,' and *vinut* and *rivinut* 'come back.' From the 4th conjugation come *partit* 'left,' *proibit* 'banned,' *surtit* 'gone out.'

Vrabie 1970 shows that past-participial differences between Friulian and Friulian in Romania appear fairly minor. As noted, several forms are the same. Cognates with both Fri.-R *tirat* 'pulled' and Fri. *trat* 'idem,' after all, are found elsewhere in ROMANIA. Fricatives varying in palatalization, and apparently in voicing as well, occur in Fri. *zût* as against Fri.-R *sŭt* 'gone,' but something like the opposite pattern prevails in Fri. *vignût* as against Fri.-R *vinut*. In two cases, Friulian in Romania comes across as more conservative than Friuilian in Friuli, at least the variety briefly examined here. Thus, Fri.-R *vidut* contrasts with Fri. *viodut* 'seen,' which latter has acquired an extra vowel. Fri.-R *vulut* contrasts with Fri. *olût* 'wanted,' which latter has lost its initial consonant.

In the data above, one notes certain divergences between the past participles used by speakers in the homeland and those used by speakers in Romania. It would be rash to ascribe the divergences to a single century of separation. It would appear even more rash to expect Friulian to persist by the Black Sea for century after century. I pass on the past participles above, preserved like a wasp in amber, for the delectation of future connoisseurs.

4.2. EVIDENCE FROM LADIN

Undifferentiated by dialect, data from Pallabazzer's *Lingua e cultura ladina* appear to cover mainly the Val Gardena, discussed in greater detail toward the end of this section. Regular arrhizotonic masc.sg. past participles in this variety of Ladin are marked by tonic vowels: -*a* for 1st-conj. verbs, -*u* for 2nd- and 3rd-conjugation ones, and -*i* for 4th-conjugation ones (Haiman, 358). Graphically at least, the status of final -t appears problematic: 1st-conj. forms (ending in -at) always keep it, 2nd- and 3rd-conj. forms (in -ù) always lose it, and 4th-conj. forms (in -it or -ì) can go either way. Lacking fluency in Ladin, I hold to the spelling given by sources, like dotted s: ṣ.

Instances of regular participles are 1st-conj. *lavat* 'washed' and *manjat* 'eaten,' 2nd- and 3rd-conj. *batù* 'beaten,' *zedù* 'stopped,' and *cïernù* or *zarnù* 'sifted,' 4th-conj. *ferì* 'hit' and *vestì* 'clothed, dressed.' Unlike Friulian, though, Ladin has a 4th-conj. p.p. in *kerì* 'looked for' and a sigmatic plus -ŪTU type in *liesü* 'read.' In Ladin, competition occurs between *cors* 'run' < CURSU and innovative *corù*, but inherited *mors* 'bitten' faces no competition.

Generally, Ladin past participles look close to Friulian ones: most Lad. forms remade since Roman days take endings from -ŪTU. Slot-fillers in that class are *podù* 'been able' and *volù* 'wanted.' Rhizotonic athematics have been remade in *rejù* 'ruled' ≠ RĒCTU, *teñù* 'held' ≠ TENTU, and by-form *tesù* 'woven' ≠ TEXTU. Rhizotonic thematics have been remade in *coñù* 'known,' *credù* 'believed,' and *rendù* 'given back' ≠ COGNĬTU, CRĒDĬTU, REDDĬTU. However, *piert* < PERDĬTU 'lost' competes with regularized *pierdù*. Sigmatics have been remade in *èrdù* 'burned' ≠ ĀRSU, *godù* 'enjoyed' ≠ GĀVĪSU (cf. Fri. 1st-conj. *sgiavât*), *metù* 'put' ≠ MISSU, *spanù* 'spread' ≠ EXPĀNSU, *spenù* 'spent' ≠ EXPĒNSU, *zedù* 'stopped' ≠ CESSU, and *zentù* 'felt' ≠ SĒNSU.

Like its French cousin, Lad. *ri* 'laughed' ≠ RĪSU has lost sigmatic marking, though when this occurred is uncertain. Joining the 4th conjugation has been *tondit* 'shorn' ≠ TŌNSU, but *ṣut* 'gone' ≠ ĬTU seems to have gone the other way. Perhaps deriving from an unattested frequentative in -TĀTU, which would imply a tautic athematic p.p. variant, Lad. *rotat* 'gnawn' ≠ RŌSU has joined the 1st conjugation, and so has Lad. *raṣat* 'shaved' (cf. Fr. *rasé* 'idem').

As should be clear from those last two forms, Ladin still has a few remnants of sigmatic marking. An old sigmatic-tautic has been partly remade as *pasù* 'fed, kept' ≠ PĀSTU. Rhyming partners of that form are *taṣù* 'been silent' ≠ TACĬTU and *piaṣù* 'pleased' ≠ PLACĬTU, along with the old direct-suffixation types *cresù* 'grown' ≠ CRĒTU and *nasù* 'born' ≠ NĀTU. Moreover, as has happened across northern Italy (see §3.5.5.1), new sigmatic-tautics have emerged in Ladin: *ṣaṣést* ≠ JACĬTU 'lain,' *temest* 'feared' (no CL p.p.) are two.

Regular 1st-conj. verbs for which Friulian has p.p. *voltât* and Ladin has p.p. *otat* 'turned around' (cf. It. *voltato*) have come down from a form like *VOLTARE, or possibly *VOLVITARE. Acceptance of the first (originally

frequentative?) etymon would heighten the likelihood that a syncopated
*VOL'TU replaced CL VOLŪTU 'rolled, wound'; acceptance of the second
etymon would heighten the likelihood that -ĪTU p.p.s swelled in popularity
by Late Latin times.

Most irregular past participles in Ladin are tautic athematic. Simple tautic
athematics may derive from forms once containing [kt] like *dit* 'said, told' <
DICTU (infin. *dì*), *fat* 'done/made' < FACTU (infin. *fè*), *trat* 'pulled' < TRACTU
(infin. *trè*), *cuet* 'cooked' < COCTU (infin. *cuejer*), *liet* 'read' < LĒCTU (infin.
liejer), *deriet* 'gotten along, made out' < DIRĒCTU (infin. *deriejer*), and *cundot*
'driven' < CONDUCTU (infin. *condujer*). They may derive from forms once in
[pt] like *scrit* 'written' < SCRĪPTU (infin. *scrì*) and *rot* 'broken' < RUPTU (infin.
rumpì). In at least one instance, a tautic athematic past participle comes from
an old form with a [kst] cluster: by-form *tiet* 'woven' < TEXTU (infin. *tiejer*)
may have resulted from reduction of another [kt] cluster following an
unusual syncope of [s], rather than [k] as in OCat. *test* 'woven.' As shown
below, Ladin speakers have few out-and-out sigmatic past participles.

Their tautic athematic past participles may still end in [nt], [rt], or [lt]. Ones
in [nt] include *depënt* 'painted' with nasal marking (infin. *depënjer*), *destënt*
'faded' (infin. *destënjer*), *spënt* 'hurried' (infin. *spënjer*), *strënt* 'put out (fire)'
(infin. *strënjer*), *spont* 'stung' < EX + PŪNCTU (infin. *spónjer*), and *strapont*
'tacked on, basted on' < EXTRĀ + PŪNCTU 'pricked' (infin. *strapónjer*), along
with the pair *ont* 'oiled' < ŪNCTU (infin. *ónjer*) and *jont* 'joined' < JŪNCTU
(infin. *jonjer*). Ones in [rt] include *mort* 'died' (infin. *murì*) and *tiërt* 'cleaned'
≠ TERSU (infin. *tiërjer*). The p.p. *stravërt* 'wallowed, sprawled' (infin.
stravëujer) could come from EXTRĀ + *VERTU for VERSU 'turned, changed'
(cf. pf. VERTĪ). If so, *tiërt* and *stravërt* provide further evidence of competition
between [s] and [t] as a marker for rhizotonic past participles. By-form *desgort*
'rejected' (infin. *desgòrjer*) may derive from DĒ + EX + CORRĒCTU 'put
straight, set right,' but see below.[2]

As in Italian (§3.5.2.1), one class of Ladin past participles has become
rhizotonic through time. Two of them resemble outcomes in Italian: *ërt*
'raised' ≠ ĒRĒCTU (infin. *ërjer*) and *sport* 'presented' ≠ EX + PORRĒCTU (infin.
spòrjer), for which cf. It. *erto, porto*. As for past participles in [lt], both *assolt*
'shriven' (infin. *assòlver*) and *resolt* 'solved' (infin. *resòlver*) have been
remade from Latin forms in -SOLŪTU. In *frant* 'shattered' ≠ FRĀCTU, nasal
marking has spread from the old infectum; cf. non-nasal Fri. *fret*.

Past participles ending in -u from -ŪTU are *abu* 'had (infin. *avëi*), *sapu*
'known' (infin. *savëi*), *desdrù* 'destroyed' < DĒSTRŪCTU (infin. *desdrer*), *bevù*
or *bu* 'drunk' (infin. *bever*), *du* 'ought to' (infin. *duvëi*), *pedù* 'been able'
(infin. *pudëi*), *pendù* 'hung' (infin. *pënder*), and *respendù* 'answered' (infin.
respuender). Most are paralleled in Italian, Catalan, and French, but not
schendù 'hidden' ≠ ABSCONDĪTU (infin. *scuender*), with the past participle

---

[2] A verb resembling *EXCORRIGERE, with only one prefix, supposedly lies behind It.
scorgere 'perceive, discern' with p.p. *scorto*, and behind OSp. 4th-conj. *escurrir* 'accompany'
with p.p. I know not what (*REW* no. 2986). Yet the semantics look poor for each verb.

perhaps influenced by an arrhizotonic variant of DĒSCĒNSU 'gone down.' Note also *stlut* 'shut' (infin. *stlù*), which given CLAUSU ought to be sigmatic; it appears to have been put together out of a tautic athematic variant of prefixed EXCLŪSU 'shut out.'

Ladin past participles now ending in [əut] include *(de)jëut* 'unwound' (infin. *(de)jëujer* < DĒ + JUGULĀRE? 'yoke'), *mëut* 'milked' (infin. *mëujer* < MULGĒRE) contrasting with *meut* 'moved' (infin. *muever* < MOVĒRE), and *tëut* 'removed' (infin. *tò* < TOLLERE). A few end in [ət]: *dulët* 'hurt' (infin. *dulëi*), *nevët* 'snowed' (infin. *nevëi*), *pluët* 'rained' (infin. *pluëi*), all three of them lacking past participles in CL; they might come from variants in -ĬTU remade postclassically (see §4.1). Notable suppletive past participles are *jit* 'gone' remade from ĬTU (infin. *ji*), and unremade *stat* 'been' < STĂTU 'stood, stayed' (infin. *vester*).

A bit of unique morphology turns up in *toné* 'thundered.' Among forms found in the present research, no other ends in *-é*. Could this be a reflex of the old rhizotonic thematic type TONĬTU, remade elsewhere as a regular 1st-conjugation form?

Sigmatics are almost as scarce in Ladin as in Friulian. Only a few straight reflexes were found: *cors* 'run' < CURSU (infin. *córer*), *mors* 'bitten' < MORSU (infin. *mòrder*). One verb (infin. *ri* 'laugh') has a p.p. *ri* < RĪSU that, as in French, has lost its sigmatic marking. Forms ending in [rs] include by-form *degors* 'rejected' (infin. *desgòrjer*) and *regors* 'flowed' (infin. *regórer*). The second of these comes from RECURSU 'run back'; the first could come from DĒCURSU 'run down' but given the infinitive could well have crossed with something like GURGE 'whirlpool,' ancestor of Fr. *gorge* 'throat' (Iliescu and Mourin, 417–19).[3]

One may get an idea of variance within Ladin from a single past participle. In Urtijei/Ortizei (Gardena), 'welcome' is said *ben uni*, the p.p. coming from **v[e]nítu* with vocalization of the initial consonant. In Val Badia, the same verb's p.p. is *gnü* [ɲy] < **[ve]nútu* with palatalization of the tonic back vowel and the preceding nasal consonant. Those forms may be compared with "standard" Lad. *veñi*, or in italianizing orthography *vegnì* (R. Stefanini, p.c.).

Kramer's *Historische Grammatik des Dolomitenladinischen* contains past participles from five dialects of Ladin: Badiotto (Bad.), Fassano (Fass.), Gardenese (Gard.), Livinallonghese (Liv.), and Marebbano (Marb.), to give them the Italian names used by Kramer. These data show that forms listed side by side in Pallabazzer tend in fact to be differentated by dialect. An analyst proficient in Ladin, as I am not, could probably tell many such variants apart by stylistic level or syntactic function, there being few true by-forms in any tongue. At all events, Table 4–1 on the following page presents p.p. data in the order followed by Kramer. Here readers should concentrate on variations in morphological type rather than, say, phonological features like the retention or fall of final -ṭ.

---

[3] Reflexes of RECURRERE 'run back' are also found from Italian to Spanish (*REW* no. 7138). From the p.p. came 4th-decl. RECURSU 'return, retreat' and a 1st-conj. frequentative.

Table 4–1

Five Dialects of Ladin

(after Kramer)

Latin	Marebbano	Badiotto	Livinal-longhese	Gardenese	Fassano
DĀTU	de		dat		
STATU	šte		štat		
SĒNSU	—		sentu	senti	sentu
VENTU	ñü		veñu	uni	veñu
FACTU	fat				
TRACTU	trat				
DICTU	dit				
SCRĪPTU	škrit			škri	škrit
COCTU	köt		kot	kuet	ket
MULCTU	mut		mout	mëut	mout
REJŪNCTU	aržunt		aržont		
STRICTU	štront	štrant	štrent	štrënt	štrent
[SUBLĀTU]	tut		tout	tëut	tout
ŪNCTU	unt		ont		
VĪCTU	vit		vivu		
VOLŪTU	ot		out		
ĀRSU	vardü		ardu	vardu	ardu
MISSU	metü		metu		
NĀTU	našü		našu		
EXPĒNSU	špenü		—	špendu	špenu
['rained']	ploiu		plovâšt	pluët	pievét
['snowed']	nevü		nevâšt	nevët	nevét
DOLITU	dorü		dolâšt	dulët	dolu
RESPŌNSU	rešponü		rešponu	rešpondu	rešponét
CURSU	korü		korâšt	kors	korét
MŌTU	möt		muot	múet	moét

All five dialects of Ladin have kept high-frequency tautic athematics, apparently along with reflexes of direct-suffixation MŌTU 'moved,' but they have replaced most sigmatic stems with infectum-based arrhizotonic ones. All five have acquired fillers for p.p. slots left empty in Latin. All five have vocalized [l] before another consonant. All five bear traces of p.p. reshapings long ago, such as syncope in VOLŪTU 'turned,' syncope in the infectum-based regularization of SUBLĀTU 'removed,' and the spread of infectum nasality into STRICTU 'tightened.'

Ladin dialects differ past-participially. First comes continued wavering between -ŪTU and -ĪTU types. Thus Gardenese *senti* 'felt' and *uni* 'come' contrast with *veñu* and *sentu* in both Livinallonghese and Fassano. Second comes rhizotonic retention as against arrhizotonic remodeling. Thus *vit* 'lived' in Marebbano and Badiotto represents a rare survival of VĪCTU 'idem,' contrasting with *vivu* in Livinallonghese, Gardenese, and Fassano. Last comes an arrhizotonic remodeling, either with or without an acquired initial consonant that could derive from AB 'from, away.' Thus Marb./Bad. *vardü* and Gar. *vardu* have it, while Liv./Fass. *ardu* lacks it.

In three dialects of Ladin, a handful of verbs display anomalous marking. Livinallonghese resembles Venetian (§3.6.1) in having a number of sigmatic-tautics, here ending in *-âʒ*. Results are Liv. *plovâʒ* 'rained,' *nevâʒ* 'snowed,' *dolâʒ* 'hurt, grieved,' and *korâʒ* 'run'; only Gar. *kors* continues CURSU. Meanwhile, Fassano has several past participles in *-ét*, and Gardenese has several in *-ët*, each a reflex of -ĒCTU that spread. Results are Fass. *pievét* 'rained,' *nevét* 'snowed,' *responét* 'answered,' *korét* 'run,' and *moét* 'moved,' along with Gard. *plu̯ët* 'rained,' *nevët* 'snowed,' and *dulët* 'hurt.' All members of this set contrast with the regular arrhizotonics *ploi̯ü* 'rained,' *nevü* 'snowed,' *dorü* 'hurt,' *reponü* 'answered,' and *korü* 'run' shared by the Badiotto and Marebbano dialects of Ladin (Kramer, 88–9).

4.3. EVIDENCE FROM RÆTO-ROMANCE (ROMANSCH)

Two dialects of Ræto-Romance, Surselvan and Engadin, are recognized. As noted in §4.0.1, the dialects have relatively few distinguishing features as a unique branch of neo-Latin; those few serve mainly to separate Ræto-Romance from Italian (Haiman, 351). Texts originating in the Swiss canton of Graubünden or Grisons include the early-twelfth-century forms *perdudo* 'lost,' *manducado* 'eaten,' and *auirtu* 'opened' (Sampson, 147–49). In the last example, the first u̲ seems to stand for [v].

Little standardization has taken place since. According to Gartner's *Handbuch der rätoromanischen* (224–31), one finds a bewildering variety of verb forms across the Alpine valleys. Among common past participles, for instance, reflexes of PORTĀTU 'carried' may appear as *porta, portat, purta,* or *purtat.* Reflexes of or replacements for VĪSU 'seen' may appear as *vist, vedu, vidu, vis̍o, udu, odu, vedut, vidut,* or *vjodut.* Arrhizotonic replacements for MISSU 'sent' (later 'put') may appear as *metu, matu, motu, betu, metut,* or *mitut.* Arrhizotonic replacements for VENTU 'come' may appear as *venyu, uni, nyu, vinyu,* or *vinyut.* Perhaps one can make sense out of such variety only by limiting oneself to a handful of dialects. (Incidentally, none of the forms listed above appears in the index verborum, unless that form appears elsewhere as well.)

Data for both dialects come mainly from Iliescu and Mourin's *Typologie de la morphologie verbale romane.* Like Romanian, Italian, and French, Engadin and Surselvan maintain four classes of infinitives. Engadin endings are: 1st-conjugation in tonic *-er,* 2nd conjugation in tonic *-air,* 4th conjugation in tonic *-ir.* Surselvan endings are: 1st conjugation in tonic *-a,* 2nd conjugation in tonic *-e,* 4th conjugation in tonic *-i.* Both dialects have 3rd-conj. infinitives in atonic *-er.* By contrast with the three classes of past-participial endings found in Friulian and Ladin, Upper Engadin has reduced regular endings for past participles to two: 1st-conj. forms end in *-o* < -ĀTU, and 2nd-/3rd-/4th-conj. forms end in *-ieu* < -ĪTU, with corresponding fem.sgs. in *-ada* and *-ida* (Iliescu and Mourin, 289, 395). For the more complicated distribution of regular endings in Surselvan, see §4.3.2. Unfortunately, the disappearance of all preterit forms in Surselvan makes it difficult to judge any effect those forms might have had on past participles.[4]

Varieties of Ræto-Romance thus serve as a laboratory for dissecting types of past participle that have survived or arisen across ROMANIA. This dissection begins with an eastern dialect, Engadin, and ends with a western one, Surselvan.

4.3.1. Engadin

Referring to Engadin generally, Velleman in *Grammatica teoretica, pratica ed istorica* notes that of its more than 200 irregular past participles, seventy or so have regular by-forms, arrhizotonic and infectum-based. At times, by-forms have been specialized as different parts of speech, so that e.g. adj. *tort* contrasts with p.p. *tüert* 'twisted.'

Yet morphological trends have not always run toward arrizotonicity: old *craieu* 'believed' has yielded to (apparently) older *cret,* as old *uffrieu* 'offered' has to *offert, infandschieu* 'feigned' to *fint,* and *pardieu* 'lost' to *pers.* Today, the forms *riprendieu* 'taken back' and *proponieu* 'put forward' are usually replaced by *riprais* and *propost.* Within rhizotonic classes, by-forms may also arise: archaic *lijt* is now *let* 'read,' archaic *clit* is now *clet* 'gathered,' and archaic *comprains* is now *comprais* 'understood.' For the simplex, by-forms *prais* and *prandieu* are both obsolete because the whole verb *prender* 'take'

---

[4] Engadin certainly, and Surselvan probably, break Malkiel's Law that a Romance language will have one fewer type of arrhizotonic p.p. ending than it has types of infin. ending. For major languages, Malkiel's Law works. Spanish and Portuguese have three types of infinitive and two types of regular past participle; French, Catalan, Italian, and Romanian have four types of infinitive and three types of regular past participle.

has fallen into disuse. Several by-form past participles go on competing today, like the triplet *revais, revis, revist* 'seen again.'

As suggested by the swarm of replacement forms, the morphological influence of Italian on Engadin has grown stronger through time, if hardly strong enough yet to induce speakers to add a final vowel. Thus, *spüert* yields to *sport* 'offered,' and *güt* to *giunt* 'arrived' (Velleman, 924–25); presumably, g- in *güt* stands for [ʒ] or [dʒ], each a phoneme alien to German. Still, Teutonophiles may admire Engadin p.p.s ending in *-dschieu* for by-form *giundschieu* 'joined, arrived' or *vandschieu* 'won; sold.' Scarcely another spelling in Romance looks half so trans-Alpine.

Within Upper Engadin, surviving simple tautic athematics include by-form *nat* 'born' < NĀTU (infin. *nascher*); the p.p. *conclüt* 'concluded' ≠ CONCLŪSU is no longer sigmatic (infin. *conclüder*). Tautic athematics may also come from forms in [pt] like *ruot* 'broken' < RUPTU (infin. *rumper*), and *scrit* 'written' < SCRĪPTU. As elsewhere, the great majority come from forms in [kt]. No doubt the most common are *cot* 'cooked' < COCTU (infin. *couscher*), *dit* 'said, told' < DICTU (infin. *dir*), *fat* 'done/made' < FACTU (infin. *far*), *trat* 'pulled' < TRACTU (infin. *trer*), and *let* 'read' < LĒCTU (infin. *leger*). Others are *diret* 'guided' < DIRĒCTU (infin. *diriger*), *eret* 'raised' < ERĒCTU (infin. *eriger*), *clet* 'gathered' < COLLĒCTU (infin. *cleger*), *protet* 'protected' < PRŌTECTU (infin. *proteger*), *adüt* 'driven' < ADDUCTU, and *tradüt* 'translated' < TRĀDUCTU (infins. *adü[e]r, tradü[e]l*].

In a class by itself is *miet* 'ground,' remade somehow from MOLĬTU and competing with arrhizotonic *mulieu* (infin. *mouler*).

Irregular past participles ending in [nt] usually come from Latin ones in [ŋkt]: *plaunt* 'complained,' by-form *giunt* 'joined,' *distint* 'distinguished,' *extint* 'put out (fire),' with infins. *plaundscher, giuondscher, distinguer*, and *extinguer*. Outcomes have been slightly different in *assunt* 'assumed' < ASSŪMPTU (infin. *assumer*) and *redemt* 'redeemed' < REDĒMPTU (infin. *redimer*); cf. It. *assunto, redento*. In p.p. *üt* 'oiled' < ŪNCTU, the nasal consonant has vanished, but not in infin. *uondscher*. More often, past participles in this class show creeping nasality from the infectum stem of CL: *depint* 'painted' (infin. *depinger*), *fint* 'pretended' (infin. *finger*), and *spint* 'pushed' (infin. *spinger*), for which cf. It. *dipinto, finto, spinto* ≠ PICTU, FICTU, EX + PĀCTU.

As *üt* 'oiled' above suggests, speakers tend to drop [n] before [t] and after close vowels in monosyllabic past participles. This tendency came out in the OEnga. p.p. *stit* 'put out (fire)' < EXSTĪNCTU, remade as prefixed ModEnga. *destint*. Two further indications of the tendency are [n]-less ModEnga. *tit* 'dyed' < TĪNCTU and *püt* 'stung' < PŪNCTU. Yet [n] often remains in apparently identical phonetic environments: already mentioned *fint* 'feigned,' *depint* 'painted,' and *spint* 'pushed' greatly resemble their opposite numbers in Italian. For one past participle in Engadin, [n] and [nt] alternate in by-forms *convit* and *convint* 'convinced.' For two other past participles, the presence or absence of [n] before [t] marks a semantic distinction: p.p. *vit* 'sold' < VENDITU contrasts with p.p. *vint* 'won' ≠ VĬCTU; cf. It. *vinto*, also with nasality imported from the infectum. In that pair of past participles *vit* and *vint*, the form that had [n] in Latin has lost it; the form that lacked [n] in Latin has gained it. One concludes that phonological drift in Engadin was moving toward effacing [n] after a high vowel and before [t] but that a conservative reaction, or more probably an italianizing one, has begun in favor of keeping [n] in that position. Yet, if so, one would expect to see hypercorrections; none has arisen.

Past participles in -lt- include *accolt* 'greeted' (infin. *accoglier*). Two come from syncope of SOLŪTU: *absolt* 'shriven' (infin. *absolver*) and *scholt* 'undone' (infin. *schoglier*). However, *tot* 'taken away,' from something like LL TOLLĬTU, lost all trace of [l] at some time after syncope. Vocalization of [l] before another consonant is clearly implied by the past participle for infin. *volver*: *vout* 'turned' has no doubt syncopated from VOLŪTU as in Spanish and Italian, but note the prefixed p.p. written *revolt* 'returned' with [l] kept at least graphically.

Along with the inherited [rt] p.p. *mort* 'died' (infin. *murir*), Upper Engadin has the usual foursome of past participles in -*ert*: *cuviert* 'covered' (infin. *cuvrir*), *aviert* 'opened' (infin. *avrir*), *offert* 'offered' (infin. *offrir*), and *sofert* 'suffered' (infin. *sofrir*). As in Catalan, other past participles have been built on that -*ert* model (see §4.6.2.2). If Enga. *spüert* 'presented' (infin. *spordscher*) looks much like unprefixed It. *porto* 'handed over,' and if Enga. *stüert* 'turned' (infin. *stordscher*) looks more like It. *storto* 'twisted,' the same can hardly be said for Enga. *inacchüert* 'noticed' (infin. *inaccordscher*) or *pardert* 'readied' (infin. *parderscher*).

As Mourin notes (160), past participles for suppletive verbs are *gieu* 'had' (infin. *avair*), *ieu* 'gone' (infin. *ir*), and *stat* 'been' (infin. *esser*). Sigmatic-tautics are *provist* 'foreseen' (infin. *proveder*), and *dispost* 'arranged' (infin. *dispuoner*). Looking much like Sicilian *krittu*, another tautic thematic past participle has survived through syncope: Enga. *cret* 'believed' < CRĒDĬTU (infin. *crajer*).

At first glance, several preterits in Upper Engadin may seem to have resulted from metaphony and have come to rhyme with one another: 1sg./3sg. *det* 'gave' < DEDĪ, *stet* 'stood, stayed' < STETĪ, *fet* 'done/made' ≠ FĒCĪ, and *get* 'went' ≠ ĪVĪ. In reality, though, all verbs from the 1st, 2nd, and 3rd conjugations have come to make their 1sg./3sg. preterits in stressed [et], giving e.g. *chantét* 'sang' and *vendét* 'sold'; verbs from the 4th conjugation make their preterits in stressed [it], giving e.g. *partit* 'left.' As in Occitan (§4.6.1.2), the largest preterit class ending in [et] was probably generalized from reflexes of DEDIT 'gave' and STETIT 'stood, stayed,' but here with final [t] extended from 3sg. to 1sg. Final [t] also appears in 1sg./3sg. *füt* 'was' < FUIT, the only preterit having [y] as a tonic vowel. By the evidence of past participles already quoted, trends in preterit formation seem to have had little influence on past-participial formation, except that—as in central-western Iberia—only two morphological classes ended up surviving for both major past-system forms.

As always, morphological irregularities attract the greatest attention. Unlike Friulian, unlike Ladin, Upper Engadin has preserved a great many sigmatic past participles. Among them are not only *miss* 'put' < MISSU 'sent' (infin. *metter*) and *ars* 'burned' < ĀRSU (infin. *arder*) but also OEnga. *vais* and ModEnga. *vis* 'seen' < VĪSU (infin. *vzair*), all of them much like forms surviving in dialects of Italian and Old French. Further sigmatic retentions are the simple p.p.s *fess* 'split' < FISSU (infin. *fendre*), *fus* 'melted' < FŪSU 'poured' (infin. *fuonder*), *müers* 'bitten' < MORSU (infin. *morder*), *respus* 'answered' < RESPŌNSU (infin. *respuonder*), *rus* 'gnawn' < RŌSU (infin. *ruojer*), and *spans* 'strewn, sprinkled' < EXPĀNSU (infin. *spander*). Two other possible members are sigmatic *anness* 'annexed' and *posses* 'owned,' but they could have arrived by an Italian route.

One LL/PR innovation may have been kept in the Germanic-looking p.p. *schmers* 'knocked down' (infin. *schmerdscher*), but this may derive from pleonastic EX + MERSU 'sunk down,' to which compare Rom. *mers* 'gone, walked.'[5] Prefixed past participles in [s] include *defais* 'fought off' < DĒFĒNSU (infin. *defender*), *imprai(n)s* 'learnt' < IN + PRĒNSU (infin. *imprender*), *offais* 'offended' < OFFĒNSU (infin. *offender*), *respus* 'answered' < RESPŌNSU (infin. *respuonder*), *spais* 'spent' < EXPĒNSU 'weighed out' (infin. *spender*), and *stais* 'spread, stretched' < EXTĒNSU (infin. *stender*). Further sigmatic items look more like resuscitations: *discuss* 'talked over' < DISCUSSU, *evas* 'ended, stopped' < ĒVĀSU 'gone out, escaped' (infin. *evader*), and *persvas* 'talked into' < PERSUĀSU (infin. *persvader*).[6] As p.p. *imprai(n)s* indicates, the status of [n] before [s] looks at least as problematic as the status of [n] before [t].

Judging by their semantic fields, certain other forms have the look of survivors: *armes* 'stayed,' *cuors* 'run,' *prais* 'taken,' and *tus* 'shorn.' Others are *scuors* 'sold off' perhaps from EXCURSU 'run out, hurried forth' (infin. *scuorrer*), *succuors* 'helped' < SUCCURSU 'run under; come to aid' (infin. *succuorrer*), and *scuss* 'threshed wheat' < EXCŪSU 'beaten out' (infin. *scuder*). Behind the p.p. *muns* 'milked' (infin. *mundscher* < MUNGERE, demotic by-form for MULGĒRE), there probably lies a sigmatic innovation in Late Latin. Compare Rom. *muls* and OFr. *mos* 'milked' (see footnote 11).

Like Italian, Upper Engadin has sometimes innovated sigmatically in its past participles: *moss* 'moved' (infin. *mouver*) and *pers* 'lost' (infin. *perder*) resemble std. It. *mosso* and by-form *perso*. Yet OEnga. *araes* 'shaved' < RĀSU has been remade (Mourin, 160). Indeed, some interchange between sigmatic and tautic athematic types has taken place: *pretais* 'claimed' ≠ PRÆTENTU 'stretched out, held out' (infin. *pretender*), but compare the unprefixed by-form TĒNSU. Drift has moved in the opposite direction to give p.p. *tert* 'wiped' ≠ TERSU (infin. *terdscher*), but cf. an OFr. by-form *tert* 'idem.'

---

[5] Meyer-Lübke's *REW* has no listing for survivals of ĒMERGERE 'rise, come up' or EX + MERGERE in Romance. I leave it to readers: does the semantic field of this verb suggest revival by experts in statecraft, science, or law?

[6] Also possibly learnèd, the *REW* having no entry for ĒVĀDERE or PERSUĀDĒRE. In each verb, one would expect intervalic [d] to elide by LL times.

An engaging reference to Engadin appears on page 276 in §4.6.1.7, during coverage of the Auvergnat dialect of Occitan.

4.3.2. Surselvan

Reminiscent of Spanish and Portuguese—and Engadin—in apparently retaining reflexes of p.p. morphology from only the 1st and 4th conjugations of Latin, the Surselvan dialect nonetheless makes a distinction between transitive past-participial endings and intransitive or reflexive ones. Transitive verbs have a single past-participial form, unmarked for gender or number, which ends in *-au* for reflexes of -ĀRE verbs like *dar* (p.p. *dau* 'given') and in *-iu* for reflexes of other classes like *ver* (p.p. *viu* 'seen'). Following the same conjugational distribution, regular intransitives and reflexives take *-aus* and *-ius* in masc.sg., *-ai* and *-i* in masc.pl., *-ada* and *-ida* in fem.sg., and *-adas* and *-idas* in fem.pl. (Mendeloff, 51–52).[7]

A number of high-frequency rhizotonic past participles in Surselvan appear to have moved into the stressed -ĪTU class, with disappearance of [t], but some of these result from the fronting and unrounding of the tonic vowel in the -ŪTU past-participial marker (Georges, 20). Examples probably displaying this passage from [u] to [y] to [i] include *giu* 'had' ≠ HABĬTU, *duiu* 'ought to' ≠ DĒBĬTU, and *vendiu* 'sold' ≠ VENDĬTU. Past participles of that type also include *buiu* 'drunk,' *pudiu* 'been able,' *vuliu* 'wanted,' and *saviu* 'known,' for verbs lacking any p.p. slot-filler in CL (Price, 223; Georges, 20, 24).[8] That these seven Surselvan exponents are paralleled by French ones in *-u*, Italian ones in *-uto*, and Romanian ones in *-ut* lends support to the notion that most come down from -ŪTU forms. However, given the remarkable prevalence of regular 4th-conjugation replacements for SĒNSU elsewhere in ROMANIA, the Surs. p.p. *sentiu* 'felt' probably derives from an infectum-based reshaping in -ĪTU traceable to Late Latin or Proto-Romance. Likewise, p.p. *iu* 'gone' derives from a 4th-conj.-style regularization of ĬTU 'idem.' Competing p.p. classes in OFr. *joï* (ModFr. *[en]joui*) contrasting with It. *goduto*, both of them reshaped from GĀVĪSU 'enjoyed,' make it difficult to decide which hypothetical form lay behind Surs. *gudiu* 'enjoyed.' Tracking down the origin of apparently syncopated *priu* 'taken' ≠ PRĒNSU continues to thwart this researcher. Probably, *cartiu* 'believed' used to look something like It. *creduto*, but (unlike Enga. *cret*) it certainly does not continue rhizotonic thematic CRĒDĬTU.

Surselvan contains a fair number of sigmatic past participles, some of them having emerged from the LL/PR restructuring reviewed briefly above.

---

[7] Posner (117) notes that the earliest texts in Surselvan, from the seventeenth century, have residual case marking on past participles as well as on adjectives: nom.sg./obl.pl. *clamaus*, obl.sg. *clamau*, and nom.pl. *clamai* 'called.' The OSurs. system apparently blended OFr./OOc. case marking in zero or *-s* and It. number marking by a change in final vowels.

[8] Between ancient and modern times, the same fronting and unrounding of [u] > [y] > [i] has taken place in Greek.

They include sigmatic *ars* 'burned' < ĀRSU (Surs. infinitive *arder*) and *ruis* 'gnawn' < RŌSU (infin. *ruir* or *ruer*); an innovation is *pruis* 'budded, burgeoned' (infin. *pruir*), the verb evidently coming from 4th-conj. PRŌDĪRE 'advance' that lacked a past participle (Mourin, 160). Other surviving sigmatic past participles in Surselvan include *claus* 'shut' < CLAUSU (infin. *clauder*), *mess* 'put' < MISSU 'sent' (infin. *metter*), *miers* 'bitten' < MORSU, *ris* 'laughed' < RĪSU (infin. *rir*), *spes* 'spent' < EXPĒNSU (infin. *spender*), *spons* 'answered' < (RE)SPŌNSU (infin. *sponder*), and perhaps *possess* 'owned' < POSSESSU (infin. *posseder*). Inflectional -s̲ is kept in intransitive (masc.sg.) *morts* 'died' < MORTUUS.

A form suggestive of Sp. *vuelto* and It. *volto*, namely tautic athematic *inflexion* 'turned' (infin. *volver*), probably comes not from syncope of a tonic vowel in VOLŪTU but from a temporarily popular type in -ĪTU that syncopated later on. What I call semitautic athematic past participles in Surselvan may contain [tʃ] from [kt], as in *cotg* 'cooked' < COCTU (infin. *cuer*), *detg* 'said, told' < DICTU (infin. *dir*), *fatg* < FACTU 'done/made' (infin. *far*), and *tratg* 'pulled' < TRACTU (infin. *trer*). Two others are *fretg* 'fried' < FRĪCTU and *entelgetg* 'understood' < INTELLĒCTU (cf. Rom. *înțelept* 'wise,' an old p.p.). True tautic athematics here have plain [t] from [pt], as in *rut* 'broken' < RUPTU (infin. *romper*) and *scret* 'written' < SCRĪPTU (infin. *scriver*).

Could any morphological feature be called typically Surselvan? By analogy with the many high-frequency p.p.s ending in *-tg* [tʃ], speakers have developed *suffretg* 'suffered' ≠ SUBLĀTU₂ (infin. *suffierer*), *encuretg* 'looked for' ≠ QUÆSĪTU (infin. *encurir*), and *cuvretg* 'covered' ≠ COOPERTU (infin. *cuvierer*). However, the privative partner of this last form, namely *scuviert* 'discovered,' with its infin. *scuvierer*, has so far been unaffected by the spread of the *-etg* ending; *aviert* 'opened' < APERTU likewise remains unaffected (Mourin, 160).

Outstanding lexical anomalies in Surselvan are *dert* 'overturned' < DĒ + ĒRĒCTU and *entschiet* 'begun' < INCEPTU (cf. Rom. *început*, a reshaping). More morphological anomalies stand out in two seemingly reactionary items: *miult* 'ground' may have syncopated from MOLĬTU, while *retschiert* 'received' < RECEPTU with intrusive [r] was conceivably inspired by *aviert* 'opened'; Catalan has similar forms. In Surselvan, the p.p. *sfois* 'searched' might have come from EX + FOSSU 'dug up.' However, the best etymology I can offer for Surs. *fiers* 'thrown,' bearing a morphological if not semantic resemblance to Rom. *fiert* 'boiled,' would be that it might have come from a rhizotonic thematic version of FERĪRE 'hit' (no CL p.p.). As noted in Chapter 2, before the advent of firearms one often had to throw a weapon to strike an enemy.

Table 4–2 shows that, within Ræto-Romance, past participles in Engadin often look more rhizotonically conservative, those in Surselvan more arrhizotonically innovative. Thus, in Engadin, the first and third examples in Table 4–2 have syncopated from Latin; the second and fourth remain sigmatic. In Surselvan, all four have acquired a 2nd-/3rd-conj. default ending for forms apparently based on the infectum stem, and certainly so in the last two instances.

Table 4–2

Engadin and Surselvan

Latin	Engadin	Surselvan
CRĒDITU	cret	cartiu
PR(EH)ĒNSU	prais	priu
VENDITU	vint	vendiu
VĪSU	vis	viu

All in all, the presence of many or few sigmatic past participles typifies eastern and western Romance respectively (see §5.5). Taking a look at all three Alpine languages—Friulian, Ladin, and Ræto-Romance—one notes that all three have been assigned to the western group. In the Alpine east, though, Friulian and Ladin resemble western ROMANIA in having few sigmatic past participles; in the Alpine west, Engadin and Surselvan resemble eastern ROMANIA in having many sigmatic past participles. The geographical chiasmus thus revealed illustrates the limitations of system-building.

4.4. EVIDENCE FROM FRENCH

If the Italian verb has been laid out according to the most latinate plan available today, the garden of French verb morphology shows signs of having been clipped back root and branch. Today, the old and the rustic speak nonstandard northern dialects of French, and "not all that many" speak dialects of Occitan either (Hawkins, 60). No patois has standing in the business of the state.[9]

Regularly evolving masc.sg. past participles display -é [e] from -ĀTU for 1st-conj. verbs, -u [y] from -ŪTU for 2nd- and 3rd-conj. ones, and -i [i] from -ĪTU for 4th-conj. ones. Corresponding infinitives end in -er [e], in -oir [war] or -re [rə] (the latter often dropped), and in -ir [ir].[10]

---

[9] As Wheeler remarks (1988b, 277), "It is hard to be optimistic about the survival of Occitan as a living language *into* the twenty-first century" (italics added). As of this writing, in a year or two analysts will have to stop trusting and start verifying Wheeler's remark.

[10] By the end of the fourteenth century, except in liaison or before a pause, Fr. infinitives ended in [e] for the 1st conjugation, in [wɛ] for the 2nd conjugation, and in [i] for the 4th conjugation. Thus, 1st- and 4th-conj. infinitives were pronounced the same as their masc.sg. past participles. In a retrograde motion, speakers later restored final [i] to 2nd- and 4th-conj. infinitives. In 1st-conj. verbs, homonymy between infin. and p.p. persists (Rickard, 69).

4.4.0. Preliminaries

Distinctively French verbs, represented as usual by their past participles, include Frankish-derived *blessé* 'hurt, wounded,' *choisi* 'chosen,' *frappé* 'hit' (cf. Engl. *rap*), *léché* 'licked,' *sucé* 'sucked,' and *tombé* 'fallen' (cf. Engl. *tumble*). Another verb limited to French is Latin-derived *caché* 'hidden' from a long-form variant of COĀCTĀTU 'compelled' that has now become shorter than the original. One past participle of a verb that resulted from a blend is *brûlé* 'burned' based on USTULĀTU with its initial [br] from a verb like Germ. *brennen*. Another is *craint* 'feared' (no CL p.p.s for infins. TREMERE 'quake with fear,' TIMĒRE 'be afraid') with its initial [k] from Celtic *crem*.

Then again, verbs found everywhere else in ROMANIA are missing from French. The verb represented by p.p. CLĀMĀTU 'called, shouted' has given Rom. *chemat*, It. *chiamato*, Cat. *clamat*, Sp. *llamado*, Ptg. *chamado*; after lasting as far as OFr. *clamé*, the verb has vanished north of the Loire. Likewise vanished as past participles, with their whole verbs, are *ouï* < AUDĪTU 'heard' and *clos* < CLAUSU 'shut.' Though *clamé* means nothing anymore, *ouïe* 'sense of hearing' and *clos* 'enclosure; vineyard' live on as independent nouns. Each lives on as half a noun phrase: *ouï-dire* 'hearsay,' *huis clos* 'no exit' (see §4.4.9).

Like Occitan and Franco-Provençal, French has specialized the local reflex of TRAHERE 'pull' to mean 'milk.' That shift came about in part because the local 3rd-conj. reflex of 2nd-conj. MULGĒRE 'milk' came to sound indistinguishable from the local reflex of 3rd-conj. MOLERE > *moldre* > *moudre* 'grind' with p.p. *moulu* (Ernout and Meillet, 418).[11] Since the Franks took over northern Gaul, in fact, at least seven verbs once of more general application have narrowed or shifted in meaning along farmyard lines (see Table 4–3). Only French has them all.

To the farmyard verbs listed in Table 4–3 one is tempted to add the shift from TŪTĀRĪ 'protect' to *tuer* 'kill'; cf. Cat. *tudar* 'harm.' Even without *tuer*, the verbs below form a semantic constellation far removed from the elegance and refinement later associated with the language. Merely by learning them, one feels as if one were stepping into la France profonde 'down-home France.' All seven verbs—with their p.p.s *couvé* 'hatched,' *labouré* 'plowed,' *mené* 'led,' *mué* 'molted,' *pondu* 'laid eggs,' *sevré* 'weaned,' and *trait* 'milked'—remain current.

Having worn away much of the phonetic body in their verbs as in their other parts of speech, the French have tried to repair the damage by importing less abraded variants. During the past few centuries, lightly gallicized Latin originals have come back into French by a semilearnèd route. Two examples are *muter* 'transfer' with unlenited [t] and *séparer* 'part, disperse' with unlenited [p] (p.p.s *muté*, *séparé*).

---

[11] Despite homonymic clash with the verb meaning 'grind,' another chore in peasant villages, *moldre* 'milk' (p.p. *mos*) became obsolete only in the fifteenth century (Pope, 408). Long before, speakers must have devised a means of disambiguation; I cannot say what it was.

Table 4–3

Farmyard Verbs in French

(after Du Nay, 45)

Latin	French
CUBĀRE 'lie down'	couver 'brood, hatch'
LABŌRĀRE 'work'	labourer 'plow'
MINĀRE 'threaten'	mener 'lead, drive'
MŪTĀRE 'change'	muer 'molt, shed'
PŌNERE 'put, set'	pondre 'lay eggs'
SĒPARĀRE 'sever'	sevrer 'wean'
*TRAGERE 'pull'	traire 'milk'

Three more verbs phonologically repristinated have been OFr. *désloer* remade as *disloquer* because of DISLOCĀRE 'set apart,' OFr. *runer* remade as *ruminer* because of RŪMINĀRE 'chew the cud,' and OFr. *visder* remade as *visiter* because of VĪSITĀRE 'see often.'

4.4.0.1. French Exceptionalism in ROMANIA

What would the Latin of the future France have sounded like to a visitor up from Latium for a year? Researchers have to judge largely by nonstandard orthography. After examining inscriptions from Roman Gaul, Herman (1990, 158) has concluded that consonants stayed relatively stable while vowels were relatively mobile. Addressing verb morphology, Herman notes (160) that "...il n'y a rien dans le système flexionnel du verbe qui n'apparaisse ailleurs et il n'y a pas de faits dans les autres régions qui ne laissent des traces en Gaule" (160) [There is no feature of verb flexion that cannot be found elsewhere, and there is no feature in other areas that cannot also be found in Gaul]. Through time, the mobility of vowels would endure; the stability of consonants would diminish. Endings on verbs would therefore tend increasingly to resemble other verb endings. Several would wear away to nothing.

How could demotic Latin in the far north have changed almost beyond recognition, after the legionnaires of Rome had withdrawn east of the

Adriatic or been killed in battle against barbarians from east of the Rhine? How could 1st-conj. infinitives whose endings came from -ĀRE and their past participles whose endings came from -ĀTU have ended up with the same ending, [e]? How, for a time, could a similar merger to [i] have also affected 4th-conj. infinitives with endings from -ĪRE and their past participles with endings from -ĪTU?

4.4.0.2. Latin Wordstock, Frankish Speechways

French came into being north of the Loire in what had been part of Transalpine Gaul, conquered by the Franks in the fifth century CE and renamed after them. Yet conquered Gaul enslaved her conqueror. Descendants of the new settlers learned to speak Gallo-Romance, still written by a local notion of the CL norm, according to their own habits. In turn enslaved themselves, Gallo-Romans seem to have picked up Frankish habits, notably a strong expiratory or stress accent on words if not yet on whole clauses.

As a result, from the flatlands by the North Sea to the foothills of the Jura, Gallo-Romans and Franks spoke their Latin less and less by the colloquial norms of even a few centuries earlier. They tended to append on-glides or off-glides to stressed vowels, thus creating un-Latin diphthongs or triphthongs that were later reduced; they tended to elide unstressed vowels, thus bringing into contact un-Latin clusters of consonants that were later reduced (Pope, 15). No doubt as early as Proto-French times, before the ninth century, these stress-related changes in pronunciation had already caused the neo-Latin spoken across northern France to differ "very sharply from the speech of any other Romance area" (Rickard, 22).

Perhaps, when scribes translating the Franks' Salic Law wrote PRESI 'I grabbed, took' where CL would have had PRÆHENDĪ, they were trying to write down the most conservative form of that preterit known to them, plus a final vowel no longer pronounced. Certainly by the eighth century—when a scribe spelling in Latin gave still-current equivalents for terms out of the *Vulgate* no longer known to the reasonably literate—entries in the *Reichenau Glosses* include past participles like semantically shifted *subportata* 'lifted; endured' (CL: 'carried up to') defining SUBLĀTA, arrhizotonically remade *sepelita* 'buried' for SEPULTA, semantically shifted *necati* 'drowned' (CL: 'killed') for SUBMERSĪ, and innovative *carcati* 'laden' for ONERĀTĪ (Studer and Waters, 14–19). From tetrasyllabic *CARRICATI, last past participle *carcati* shows part of the syncope of unstressed vowels that shrank it to disyllabic OFr. *chargié* [tʃardʒjé] and to syncopated [ʃarʒé] now.

4.4.0.3. Open or Closed Syllables

Two habits of speech have been at war throughout the history of the language: a Germanic tolerance of consonant clusters against a Latinate love of syllables ending in a vowel. Current odds appear to favor the Germanic side. French has been importing from English a swarm of consonant-final monosyllables, many of them clipped or nonstandard to start with: *spot* 'spotlight,' *cross* 'cross-country race,' *clap* 'clapper board,' *off* 'off-the-record,' *stick* 'illegal cigarette,' and *shit* 'hashish.' From English has come a new French phoneme, final [ŋ], in clippings or adaptations like *living* 'living-room,' *building* 'high-rise,' and *zapping* 'channel-switching.' From English as well come word-final consonant clusters in terms like *self* 'self-service,' *hard* 'computer hardware,' *film* 'movie,' and *fast* 'fast food' (Harris 1988, 243; George, 161, 164; Noreiko, 178). In these ways, speakers of French have been acquiring a new set of final consonants to mute when they will.

After a millennium and a half, the series of interplays between Germanic and Latinate speech habits has resulted in a string of victories for the southern side, most words now being vowel-final in speech. Because words seldom receive independent stress any longer, whole clauses pronounced like a single word will by definition usually end in a vowel.

Often appearing at the end of a clause-word, reflexes of past participles like CANTĀTU 'sung,' BATTŪTU 'beaten,' DORMĪTU 'slept' retain no trace of either the original post-tonic vowels or the dental stops that once preceded them. Two of the three tonic vowels have fronted, to [e] and [y]. Only the CL free [i:] never fronted in French, but then it could not. For past participles in Catalan, Italian, and Romanian, CL tonic free [a:], [i:], [u:] have stayed recognizably the same, minus length. So have [a:] and [i:] in Spanish and Portuguese.

In arrhizotonic masc. past participles, then, originally intervocalic [t] voiced, fricativized, devoiced, and vanished; except in quotations, I omit any reflex of it until Table 4–6 on page 249. On rhizotonics, marking wore away nearly as much. Postconsonantal inherited [t] remained in Old French, as also after reduction of a [kt] or [pt] cluster in e.g. *dit* 'said, told' < DICTU or *escrit* 'written' < SCRĪPTU. OFr. [t] from such sources has since muted in masc. forms. In corresponding fem. forms, the fall of final [ə] has made [t] word-final in speech. As for sigmatic marking, originally intervocalic [s] became final and then muted in masc. forms. In corresponding fem. forms, [s] remained intervocalic and then voiced to [z], becoming word-final in speech with the fall of final [ə]. Along the way, marking for number disappeared.

When one recalls that all masc.acc.sg. and neut.nom./acc.sg. Latin past participles had ended in -TUM or -SUM, and that when speakers stopped using interdentals those endings either disappeared altogether as in OFr. *amé* 'loved' or were reduced to a single consonant as in OFr. *mort* 'died' or *mis* 'put,' one has to agree with Brunot and Bruneau's conclusion that, as early as the High Middle Ages, "il n'y avait plus de caractéristique de participe passé" (467) [French no longer had any marking specific to past participles].

4.4.1. Metaplasm in Proto-French and Later

A great many infinitives and past participles appear to have been remodeled during Proto-French times (see §4.4.2). Like their cousins elsewhere in western ROMANIA, speakers of neo-Latin between the Loire and the Moselle generally preferred arrhizotonic variants and reshaped much of their past-participial inheritance. Since the vernacular long lacked any written standard, certain older forms bequeathed by Rome's legions persisted alongside innovative reshapings.

In the tenth-century *Jonah Fragment*, notes for a sermon written half in Latin and half in early Old French, certain verbs show metaplasm: *entelgir* 'understand' remade from INTELLEGERE (the verb surviving also in Romanian and Engadin), *delir* 'destroy' remade from DĒLĒRE (also in Occitan), and *comburir* 'burn' remade from COMBŪRERE. Leaving the 2nd or 3rd conjugation, all had joined the 4th. The first was never seen again in French (Rickard, 36; Bartsch, 5–6). None has lasted till now. Likewise ill-fated were certain compound verbs like OFr. (*r*)*amentevoir* 'bring back to mind' < RE + AD + MENTE + HABĒRE with p.p. (*r*)*amenteü* 'remembered' or OFr. *clofire* < CLĀVU FĪGERE 'drive in a nail' with p.p. *clofis* 'nailed' (Bartsch, 340, 344).

If most verbs in French have held true to their old conjugations, so that *avoir* 'have' comes straight from 2nd-conj. HABĒRE and *vendre* 'sell' comes straight from 3rd-conj. VENDERE, ModFr. *croire* 'believe' must come from an assumed 2nd-conj. variant of CRĒDERE. In a reverse shift, OFr. *plaire* 'please' and *taire* 'be silent' seem to derive from assumed 3rd-conj. variants of PLACĒRE, TACĒRE but competed against the by-forms *plaisir* and *taisir*. Often, infinitives ending in -ĒRE preceded by a palatal seem to have joined reflexes of the -ĪRE class, so that JACĒRE 'lie, recline' and LICĒRE 'be allowed' became OFr. *gésir* and *loisir*. If some of these had the infinitive by-forms *plaire* and *taire*, perhaps by analogy with *faire* 'do/make,' their p.p.s *geü*, *leü*, *pleü*, and *teü* all ended in [-əy] and certainly failed to continue rhizotonic thematic JACĬTU, LICĬTU, PLACĬTU, TACĬTU. Anomalous past participles show that these verbs had hardly joined the 4th-conjugation forms across the board. Likewise, *luisir* 'shine' with by-form *luire* had the p.p. *luit*, perhaps syncopated from a postclassical variant in -ĬTU (no CL p.p. but cf. infin. LŪCĒRE).

Thoroughly 4th-conjugation arrivals by Proto-French times included once 2nd-conj. *fleurir* 'bloom' and *emplir* 'fill,' once 3rd-conj. *fuir* 'flee,' all with regular past participles in tonic [i]: *fleuri*, *empli*, *fui*. (Recall that FLŌRĒRE 'bloom' had had no past participle, IMPLĒRE 'fill' a "regular" 2nd-conj. one.) Meanwhile, if 2nd-conj. MUCĒRE 'get moldy' (no CL p.p.) became 4th-conj. *moisir* by palatal raising, it also acquired a regular p.p. *moisi*; the verb had lacked that principal part in CL.

From Proto-French times on, the largest verb class has continued to acquire new members. For instance, OFr. 1st-conj. *paver* 'pave' (p.p. *pavé*) shows metaplasm from 4th-conj. PAVĪRE 'beat, pound flat' unless as Darmesteter maintains (4: 139) it was backformed from the noun *pavement* 'paving' < PAVĪMENTU. Today, the 1st conjugation still attracts new members, as witness popular *mouver* 'move' with its regular p.p. *mouvé* replacing irregular but std. *mouvoir*, p.p. *mû*. For other recent reshapings, see Table 4–4 on page 239.

A number of OFr. by-forms had arisen because of fluctuations between or among non-ĀRE conjugations back in Late Latin and Proto-Romance.

Verbs from the 2nd conjugation that developed 3rd-conj. by-forms included MANĒRE 'stay' and MOVĒRE 'move' with *manoir* and *maindre*, *mouvoir* and *mouvre*.[12] Verbs from the 3rd conjugation that developed 2nd-conj. by-forms included RECIPERE 'receive' with *reçoivre* and *recevoir*. Verbs from the 3rd conjugation that developed 4th-conj. by-forms—the most common kind, as *entelgir* and *comburir* in the *Jonah Fragment* would suggest—included TOLLERE 'take away' with *tol(d)re* and *tollir*, COLLIGERE 'gather' with *cueldre* and *coillir*, CURRERE 'run' with *corre* and *corir*, and QUÆRERE 'seek' with *querre* and *querir*. In early Old French, reflexes of 3rd-conj. CADERE 'fall' were found in 4th-conj. *cha(d)ir*, *che(d)ir* and in 2nd-conj. *che(d)eir*, *cha(d)eir*, all of them arrhizotonic. From an active remaking of the 3rd-conj. deponent SEQUĪ 'follow' came OFr. *sivre*, *siure*, and *sivir*, two of them admittedly rhizotonic.[13] Verbs from the 4th conjugation that developed 3rd-conj. by-forms included BULLĪRE 'bubble' (later 'boil') with *bolir* and *boudre*, and also EXĪRE 'go out' with *issir* and *istre* (Kibler, 114–15, 224; Einhorn, 151).

It could happen that speakers used a mere difference of conjugation to mark a distinction of meaning between two verbs. So, in French, 3rd-conj. GEMERE 'sigh, groan' has given rise to both 3rd-conj. *geindre* 'whine, whimper' and 4th-conj. *gémir* 'moan, wail,' with distinct p.p.s *geint* < GEMĬTU and the regular 4th-conj. reshaping *gémi*. Again in French, from the root of 3rd-conj. FALLERE 'fail, trick, lack' derive both 2nd-conj. *falloir* 'be required' and 4th-conj. *faillir* 'almost do something,' with the distinct and regular p.p.s *fallu, failli*. Generally, only one variant has been chosen for each infinitive still in use.

4.4.2. Changes within the Perfectum

This section examines how analogical remodelings of preterits and past participles made them resemble one another more closely before Old French was first written. Realignment could operate either way or could come from outside. Today, though, any such reshaping would be unlikely to occur, the preterit (locally termed "passé simple") having been replaced by the present perfect except in highly formal registers.

4.4.2.1. Reshaping of Preterits

By Proto-French times, a number of ways of making finite perfectum forms had been reduced to relics. Of perfect finite verbs entailing either

---

[12] Though the Fr. forms have given Engl. *remain* and *move*, both are at best obsolescent in current French, with the first being replaced by 1st-conj. *rester* and the second by 1st-conj. *bouger*.

[13] Fourth-conj. *coillir* represents the "regular" outcome for a 3rd-conj. verb that developed a palatalized stem. No such inspiration can be found for the other 4th-conj. variants given.

reduplication or direct suffixation in CL, only reflexes of a few high-frequency ones survived to be attested in Old French preterits. Of the two with reduplication, exemplified by 1sg. DEDĪ 'gave' and STETĪ 'stood, stayed,' the first had been replaced by reflexes of DŌNĀVĪ 'presented, gifted' > *donai*, and the second was reshaped to end in -UĪ (see next paragraph).[14] Almost the sole 1sg. strong preterits to last into Old French were the direct-suffixation fivesome FĒCĪ >*fiz* > *fis* 'did/made,' VĪDĪ > *vit* > *vi* 'saw,' VĒNĪ > *vin* 'came,' its rhyming partner *tin* 'held' ≠ TENUĪ, and FUĪ >*fui* 'was.'

Such anomalies aside, there thrived in northern Transalpine Gaul only four kinds of preterit: arrhizotonic reflexes of -ĪVĪ and -ĀVĪ, rhizotonic reflexes of -UĪ and -SĪ.[15] As multiple analogies might well have been competing in speakers' minds, by-form preterits often emerged, fitted into one of those four classes whenever the CL type came to be felt as anomalous. Some verbs therefore appear more than once in the paragraphs that follow.

As hypothesized by Pope (370), unpopular types of preterits were refashioned in Proto-French times. Among old reduplicated preterits, some would have been remade in -UĪ, like **cadui* 'fell,' **currui* 'ran' and **stetui* 'stood' ≠ CECIDĪ, CUCURRĪ, and STETĪ. Some would have been remade in -SĪ, like **cursi* 'ran,' **morsi* 'bit,' and **tanxi* 'touched' ≠ CUCURRĪ, MOMORDĪ, and TETIGĪ. Some would have been remade in -ĪVĪ, like **falii* 'failed' ≠ FEFELLĪ) or in -ĀVĪ (**stavi* 'stood' later 'stopped' ≠ STĒTĪ). At any rate, reflexes of those CL preterits failed to last.

Among old direct-suffixation preterits, Pope goes on, some would have been remade in -UĪ, giving **bibui* 'drank' ≠ BIBĪ and **legui* 'read' ≠ LĒGĪ. Others would have kept raised tonic vowels but added -UĪ endings, thus giving doubly marked **cepui* 'took' ≠ CĒPĪ, **jecui* 'threw' ≠ JĒCĪ, and **fregui* 'shattered' ≠ FRĒGĪ. Still others would have added sigmatic marking to give **lexi* 'read' ≠ LĒGĪ, **franxi* 'shattered' ≠ FRĒGĪ, and **fusi* 'poured' (later 'melted') ≠ FŪDĪ. Still others would have been remade in arrhizotonic -ĪVĪ to yield **fendii* 'split' ≠ FIDĪ, **fodii* 'dug' ≠ FŌDĪ, **fugii* 'fled' ≠ FŪGĪ, **rumpii* 'broke' ≠ RŪPĪ, and **vertii* 'turned' ≠ VERTĪ.

One should recall that, during Merovingian and into Carolingian times, the literate kept trying to write according to CL norms. Therefore, a putative verb morphology for Proto-French has to be retrojected from attestations found in texts written much later. Remodeling of 2nd- and 3rd-conj. preterits and past participles no doubt continued for centuries. One would probably do better to focus on where the remodeling ended up than to imagine, in the absence of evidence, the pathways that remodeling might have followed.

---

[14] Generalization of the DEDĪ type (-DIDĪ in compounds) to the preterits of some twenty-five verbs resulted in 3sg. and 3pl. forms like *vendié(t)* and *vendierent* 'sold,' *perdié(t)* and *perdierent* 'lost.' Until the early thirteenth century, such preterits remained morphologically distinct from regular 4th-conj. ones like *feri(t), ferirent* 'hit' (Kibler, 216).

[15] Throughout OFr. times, verbs with stems ending in a palatal consonant, or a reflex of one, remained distinct from regular 1st-conj. verbs in the 3pl. preterit, giving e.g. *baillierent* 'they gave' contrasting with unpalatal *chanterent* 'they sang' (Kibler, 208).

Evidently choosing to overlook the hazards inherent in trying to read the minds of speakers long gone, Pope (370) deduces analogies with other verbs that appear to have lain behind certain preterits retrojected to Proto-French. Replacing SAPIĪ or SAPĪVĪ 'knew,' a -UĪ preterit would have developed ± *o i* < HABUĪ 'had,' perhaps ± *poi* 'could' < POTUĪ, to give OFr. *soi*.[16] Some extensions of sigmatic preterits, with nasal consonants from the infectum, would have been replacements for FRĒGĪ 'shattered' and TETIGĪ 'touched' ± *plains* < PLĀNXĪ 'complained' and a replacement for PEPUGĪ 'stung' ± *joins* < JŪNXĪ 'joined'; the latter development might have been inspired by p.p.s PŪNCTU, JŪNCTU, already rhyming in Latin. A replacement for NOCUĪ 'harmed' would have developed ± *duis* 'led' < DŪXĪ.[17] Double replacements might occur when one remade preterit inspired another: **quesi* 'sought' would have come about ± **presi* 'took' > OFr. *pris*, itself ± p.p. PRESSU and replacing pf. PREHENDĪ. Speakers seem to have based such analogies on rhymes or near-rhymes rather than on semantic likenesses. There is no way to tell when they might have done so, or for that matter whether they did.

No uniformity of conjugation was reached. Strong perfects once in the same class might therefore develop in different ways, owing to their phonology. By Old French times, when they had become rhizotonic, 3pl. sigmatic preterits had developed three variants. Where [s] had been intervocalic, it voiced to [z], giving e.g. *closdrent* 'shut' and *misdrent* 'put'; where the fricative had been long [s:] or had been supported by another consonant, it failed to voice, giving e.g. *distrent* 'said, told' and *arstrent* 'burned.' At a remove, one has to deduce voicing not from written s̲, pronounceable as either [s] or [z] medially, but from excrescent d̲ [d] or t̲ [t].[18] Of verbs in that class in early Old French, only the very high-frequency *faire* 'do/make' had a 3pl. preterit with another ending, syncopated *firent*, with a by-form *fistrent* being "rare but possible" (cf. CL FĒCĒRUNT). Nevertheless, short-form *firent* was to provide the model for leveling. By the thirteenth century, analogical *dirent* 'said, told,' *prirent* 'took,' and *quirent* 'sought' had largely supplanted etymological *distrent* and others, as they continue to do i n formal written French (Kibler, 220–22).

Meanwhile, in the Picard dialect used by writers like Froissart, inspiration for leveling in such preterits came from sigmatic 1sg. *fis* < FĒCĪ 'did/made.' On the basis of that form, with or without voicing of [s], there developed 3pl. *fisent*, *misent*, and *dissent* (Gossen, 111–12). For the last two of these, inspiration might also have come from reflexes of the old sigmatic pfs. MĪSĪ 'sent' and DĪXĪ 'said, told.'

---

[16] Attested LL pf./pret. SAPUI 'I tasted, knew' may imply that inspiration for that preterit reshaping came from p.p. *SAPUTU > OFr. *seü*. For the OFr. noun *duis* 'lesson, teaching,' perhaps from a newly sigmaticpast participle unlike DOCTU 'taught,' see §4.4.9.3.

[17] Cf. also two sets of rhyming triplet infinitives: (1) FRANGERE 'shatter,' PLANGERE 'lament,' TANGERE 'touch'; (2) JUNGERE 'join,' PUNGERE 'sting,' UNGERE 'oil.' In OFr., *duire* < DŪCERE 'lead' rhymed with by-form *nuire* remade from NOCĒRE 'harm.'

[18] The graphy z̲ was unavailable to represent [z] because it stood for [ts] in Old French.

4.4.2.2. Reshaping of Past Participles

Three ModFr. past participles in the [y] class belonged to the ancestor of that class in CL: *battu* < BATTŪTU 'beaten,' *cousu* < CŌNSŪTU 'sewn,' and *foutu* < FUTŪTU 'fucked.' Old French also had *esteü* 'stood, stopped' < STATŪTU 'set up,' by-form *seü* 'followed' < SECŪTU, and more besides. Certain other past participles traceable to Old French and still ending in [y] like *eu* 'had,' *crû* 'grown,' and *vu* 'seen' naturally presuppose forms in -ŪTU instead of rhizotonic HABĬTU, CRĒTU, VĪSU, though Old French had a by-form *vis* 'seen' kept from Roman days.

In Proto-French, other past participles tended to move into the -ŪTU class and acquire infectum-based stems. They included reflexes of more than a few rhizotonic past participles like thematic CRĒDĬTU 'believed,' DĒBĬTU 'ought to,' and PERDĬTU 'lost,' but also sigmatic RESPŌNSU 'answered,' CURSU 'run,' and PĒNSU 'hung,' as well as tautic athematic VENTU 'come' and VĪCTU 'lived.' Such reshapings give forms now written *cru, dû, perdu, répondu, couru, pendu, venu,* and *vécu*; Old French still had sigmatic by-forms *pois* 'hung' and *respons* 'answered' (also *respost*). By Old French times, moreover, regular 4th-conj. past participles like *senti* 'felt' and *verti* 'turned' had replaced expected *sens* from SĒNSU and *vers* from VERSU. Meanwhile, regular 2nd-/3rd-conj. past participles like *fendu* 'split' and *vendu* 'sold' had replaced expected *fent* from *FINDITU for CL FISSU and *vent* from VENDĬTU (Pope, 386). Both those rhizotonics would have sounded like those verbs' 1sg./3sg. pres.indic. forms. Some of the new arrhizotonic past participles might have arisen from an unconscious wish among speakers to avoid homonymic clash with unrelated words, a problem in the language from that day to this.

Language being language, the trend toward arrhizotonicity failed to sweep all before it. A few rhizotonic past participles prevailed, though in CL their predecessors had featured a stressed theme vowel. Two -ŪTU forms from Latin, SOLŪTU 'loosened' and VOLŪTU 'rolled,' acquired by-forms in Old French: assumed present-based rhizotonic thematic variants yielded *solt* and *volt*, both paralleled in Sp. *suelto* and *vuelto*, It. *-solto* and *volto*. Meanwhile, attested LL SOLSU, VOLSU yielded OFr. *sols* and *vols* (Ewert, 224).[19] A reflex of SOLŪTU survived in OFr. *solu* 'paid, shriven.' No arrhizotonic reflexes of VOLŪTU survived in French or elsewhere: they had been displaced by a predecessor of OFr. *volu* 'wanted,' the only filler for that slot listed by Bartsch (348), Einhorn (165), and Pope (400) and currently thriving as *voulu* [vuly].

Like *solt* and *volt*, a fair number of Old French past participles seem to have become tautic athematic after syncope of a variant in -ĬTU whose stem came from the infectum. Thus, *tolt* 'taken away' ≠ SUBLĀTU₁, but cf. infin. TOLLERE, suggests that -ĬTU past participles expanded their domain in Late Latin or Proto-Romance; see §4.4.9.2 for several relics. Other such past participles used to be OFr. *tont* 'shorn' ≠ TŌNSU, but cf. infin. TONDĒRE, by

---

[19] Infin. *voldre* < VOLVERE and its whole verb became obsolete by the fourteenth century (Pope, 410). Was there a risk of homonymic clash with the verb now written *vouloir* 'want'?

analogy to which was created OFr. *pont* 'laid, set' (also *pons*) ≠ POS(I)TU, but cf. infin. *pondre* < PŌNERE (Pope, 386). As shown in §3.6.2 and §3.7.3, reflexes of that expansion of -ĬTU as a p.p. ending are still to be found, unsyncopated, on Sardinia and in southern Italy.

Old French had yet to lose verbs whose past participles were *doit* 'taught' < DOCTU, *escos* 'shaken' < EX + QUASSU, and *rové* 'asked' < ROGĀTU. Though Modern French keeps *tenir* 'hold' ≠ TENĒRE, it has somewhat regularized the etymological p.p. *tois* 'stretched' < TĒNSU. If the OFr. noun *treü* 'lord's due' came from a form like p.p. TRIBŪTU 'allotted,' the OFr. p.p. *prangié* 'lunched' had been remade from PRĀNSU; the OFr. neologism *ramenteü* 'recalled' had been assembled from RE + AD + MENTE 'mind' plus an arrhizotonic variant of HABĬTU 'had.' Other past participles had been reshaped partly but not wholly: sigmatic *ahers* 'seized' had incorporated an [r] absent from its ancestor ADHÆSU but present in e.g. infin. ADHÆRĒRE 'stick.'

4.4.2.3. Leveling across the Past System

In northern Transalpine Gaul as elsewhere, speakers tended to favor preterits and past participles that bore clear thematic (or sigmatic) marking. For some verbs, speakers of Late Latin or Proto-French kept the infinitive in the same class but regularized the preterit and past participle to accord with that class. Leveling might occur in any of the four conjugations.

Reflecting regularizations across ROMANIA, Fr. *crever* 'burst' < CREPĀRE 'creak, rattle' acquired a regular 1st-conj. pret. *crevai* and a regular 1st-conj. p.p. *crevé*, rather than reflexes of rhizotonic CREPUĬ and CREPĬTU. Other anomalous forms tended to fall to regular ones. Thus, VETUĬ and VETĬTU 'forbade/forbidden' were remade to agree with infin. VETĀRE, resulting inter alia in the OFr. p.p. *veé*. More leveling of allomorphy in the 1st conjugation appears in *sonné* 'rung' ≠ SONĬTU, *tonné* 'thundered' ≠ TONĬTU, and OFr. *domé* 'tamed' ≠ DOMĬTU. Again, LAVĀRE 'wash' regularly gave OFr. *laver*, but pret. *lavai* 'washed' replaced direct-suffixation LĀVĪ; meanwhile, regular LAVĀTU, already a by-form in CL, won out over LAUTU and LŌTU to yield *lavé*.

In other conjugations, past participles had also been regularized by Old French times. Examples from the 2nd or 3rd conjugation, now ending in reflexes of -ŪTU, were *chavu* 'seized' ≠ CAPTU, *cheü* 'fallen ≠ CĀSU, and *tissu* 'woven' ≠ TEXTU. Examples from the 4th conjugation were *charpi* 'shredded' ≠ CARPTU 'plucked,' *compli* 'fulfilled' ≠ COMPLĒTU, *foï* 'fled' ≠ FUGĬTU, *joï* 'enjoyed' ≠ GĀVĪSU, *ravi* 'seized' ≠ RAPTU, and *seveli* 'buried' ≠ SEPULTU. For verbs still in use, the ModFr. p.p.s are *fui, enjoui, ravi, enseveli*.

Preterits and past participles tended to become more alike in Proto-French. Especially where a verb stem ended in a liquid or nasal consonant, that tendency led to the continuance and even expansion of weak perfects in tonic [u] that eventually fronted to [y] (Pope, 370). Thus, the emergence in LL/PR of many past participles ending in -ŪTU strengthened Proto-French preterits that continued CL forms in -UĪ. Pope's remark about double reinforcement might be extended to apply to verbs with both past-tense forms in [s], and to verbs with both in tonic [i]. Pope's remark could be stretched to cover, barely, Old French 1st-conj. verbs with infinitives in [er], past participles in [e] and 3pl. preterits in [-ɛrə(n)t], though not 3sg. preterits in [a].

Within the perfectum as a whole, "the commonest cause of analogical replacement appears to have been...the desire to secure conformity between the associated forms perfect and past participle" (Pope, 370–71). That desire remained alive until people stopped using preterits. Thus, certain sigmatic past participles like *quis* 'sought, asked' and *sors* 'sprung up' cannot have derived from QUÆSĪTU or SURRĒCTU but must have resulted from extension of preterit stems like those in 1sg. **quesi* and **sorsi*, forms regrettably unattested. Between Late Latin and Old French, at least one tautic athematic past participle remained strong but shifted consonantal markers: instead of TORTU, a sigmatic by-form TORSU (deprecated in the *Appendix Probi*) yielded OFr. *tors*, probably helped by the already sigmatic pf. TORSĪ that inspired the Rom. p.p. *întors* 'turned' as well.

Among tautic thematic past participles undergoing a shift toward sigmaticism were ABSCONDĬTU 'hidden' and PERDĬTU 'lost.' Sigmatic by-forms reminiscent of OIt. *nascoso* and still-current It. *perso* lay behind OFr. *ascons* 'hidden' and *pers* 'lost,' probably influenced by sigmatic perfects replacing ABSCONDIDĪ and PERDIDĪ. Itself inspired by pf. POSUĪ, the OFr. by-form p.p. *pos* 'set, laid' resembles Rom. *pus* 'put' in presupposing a straight sigmatic variant of POS(I)TU, or, more likely, influence from perfect (later preterit) forms like 1sg. POSUĪ > *pos* and 3sg. POSUIT > *post*.

Additional Old French preterits influenced by their past participles included 1sg. *ocis* 'killed' ≠ OCCIDĪ, *pris* 'took' ≠ PREHENDĪ, and *sis* 'sat' ≠ SĒDĪ (Ewert, 214). All borrowed [s] from p.p.s OCCĪSU, PRĒNSU, and -SESSU; in turn, past participles for the last two verbs borrowed anaphony to tonic [i] that started in the 1sg. preterit ending. For the verb meaning 'buy back,' speakers of Proto-French continued a reflex of p.p. REDĒMPTU but established a contrast between [s] in e.g. 1sg. pret. *raens* ≠ REDĒMĪ and [t] in p.p. *raent* like that in e.g. *escris escrit* 'wrote/written' < SCRĪPSĪ SCRĪPTU, or like that in some verbs whose stems contained a nasal consonant like *ceins ceint* 'girded' < CĪNXĪ CĪNCTU or *joins joint* 'joined' < JŪNXĪ JŪNCTU. As a result, 1sg. pret. *raens* and p.p. *raent* developed closer morphological affinities than REDĒMĪ REDEMPTU had had, and the forms *ocis, pris, sis* generally did double duty for 1sg. preterit and past participle.

Given the presence of a nasal infix, Old French past participles like *feint* 'pretended,' *peint* 'painted,' and *estreint* 'clasped,' or for that matter by-form *fraint* 'shattered,' could hardly have descended from FICTU 'shaped,' PICTU 'painted,' STRICTU 'tightened,' or FRĀCTU 'shattered,' though cf. the OFr. etymological by-form *frait*. Likewise, the [n] in 1sg. pret. *atains* and p.p. *attaint* 'reached, attained' could hardly have developed from ATTIGĪ, ATTĀCTU, though cf. infin. ATTINGERE, with its nasal infix. Such past participles and preterits had undergone remodeling based on other parts of the verb, notably the present (Pope, 386–87), or more generally from the whole infectum. No doubt they were inspired as well by regularly evolving past participles in [nt] like *esteint* < EXSTĪNCTU 'put out (fire)' and *teint* < TĪNCTU 'dyed' that had 1sg. preterits in [ns] like *esteins* < EXSTĪNXĪ and *teins* < TĪNXĪ; both verbs remain current today. Indeed, nasal consonants from the infectum could be introduced into the past participle, giving unetymological by-forms in Old French like *ront* 'broken' and *prins* 'taken' ± e.g. infins. *rompre* and *prendre* (Mourin, 159). Speakers also created a by-form p.p. *tins* 'held' ± *prins*; the former could not have come down straight from TENTU.[20] Those nasal reshapings have not survived.

Preterits and past participles came to resemble one another often, not always. In Proto-French, perfects derived from -UĪ types were kept solely by verbs whose stems ended in any stop or almost any fricative. Other types of preterits in the -UĪ class blended with those in the -ĪVĪ class and gave rise to Old French preterits like *cosi* 'sewed' and *voil* 'wanted' ≠ CŌNSUĪ, VOLUĪ. Resistance to the trend emerged, so that a few such preterits were reshaped, probably by analogy with their past participles, to give Old French forms like 1sg. *corui* 'ran' and *valui* 'was worth' (Pope, 378).[21] Later reduction of [wi] to [i] explains why some French verbs contrast preterits in tonic [i] with past participles in tonic [y], despite a great deal of analogical remodeling along the way. Such contrasts still occur in 3rd-conj. verbs like *battre* 'beat' with 1sg./2sg. pret. *battis* but p.p. *battu*.

After early Old French times, Rohlfs's observation (1970, 141) that reflexes of -ŪTU past participles often lost the stem-final consonant by analogy with "kindred [3sg.] perfects where the stem element had been dropped" would also apply to 4th-conj. -ĪTU reflexes inspired by their own preterits. However, it could not apply to reflexes of 1st-conj. perfects in -ĀVIT and past participles in -ĀTU: in the *Jonah Fragment*, forms like *laboret* 'worked,' *penet* 'taken pains,' *pretiet* 'preached,' and *mostret* 'shown' already contrasted in their tonic vowels with the 3sg. pret. *donat* 'gave.'[22] Unlike what was happening elsewhere, 1st-conj. verbs heightened morphological distinctiveness between 3sg. preterits in tonic [a] and past participles in tonic [e].

---

[20] Cf. also the p.p. *espriens* 'oppressed' found in line 25 of *Le lai du chèvrefeuille* (Bartsch, 155). The verb's infin. *espriendre* derives regularly from EXPRIMERE 'squeeze out, force out,' but p.p. *espriens* ≠ EXPRESSU shows the spread of nasal marking into the perfectum.

[21] Two others listed by Kibler (223) are 1sg. *bui* 'drank' ≠ BIBĪ and *reçui* 'received' ≠ RECĒPĪ, but the p.p.s *beü* and *receü*, themselves remade from LL BIBĪTU and CL RECEPTU, suggest that the three-vowel series in *[bəyi̯] and *[rətsəyi̯] were simplified early on.

[22] Price remarks (176) that -ĀVIT could, rarely, contract to -ĀT in CL and that -ĀT would regularly give 1st-conj. 3sg. prets. like *donat* 'gave' and *chantat* 'sang' in early Old French. If so, French would be the only major Romance language in the west to have chosen that variant: 3sg. prets. like It. *cantò*, Sp. *cantó*, and Ptg. *cantou* come from another contracted variant, *CANTAUT. Price suggests that forms like *chanta* might have been remodeled ± *a* 'has' < HABET, because the 1st-conj. preterit endings -*a i* < -ĀVĪ and -*as* < -ĀVISTĪ already were the same as those for pres. *a i* < HABEŌ and *as* < HABĒS and all futures. Still, given Romanian 1st-conj. 3sg. aorists like *cîntă* (final [ə] being stressed), I wonder: might the 3sg. variant -ĀT have been generalized by speakers in both Gallia and Dacia?

4.4.3. Morphological Patterns within
the Old French Past System

Within the past-tense system of Old French, substantial leveling had taken place since Latin days. Most preterits and past participles had the same tonic vowel. Some consonantal variation remained.

For instance, 3sg. preterits in *-st* often contrasted with masc.sg. past participles in *-s*, whether directly after a tonic vowel as in pret. *mist* and p.p. *mis* 'put,' *quist* and *quis* 'sought,' *prist* 'took' and *pris* 'taken,' *rist* and *ris* 'laughed,' and *sist* and *sis* 'sat,' or again after a root consonant as in *terst* and *ters* 'wiped,' *arst* and *ars* 'burned,' *esparst* and *espars* 'sprinkled,' *morst* 'bit' and *mors* 'bitten,' and *torst* and *tors* 'twisted.' Most such consonantal differences were traceable straight back to Latin past participles in -SU and perfects in -SIT. Many of the past participles had by-forms in Old French. In further leveling, both pret. *aerst* and p.p. *aers* 'seized' had acquired the [r] present in e.g. infin. ADHÆRĒRE but absent from ADHÆSIT and ADHÆSU 'stuck, clung.'

Among persistent variation in vowels between preterit and past participle, a few Old French verbs like *vesquiet* and *vescu* 'lived,' *nasquiet* and *nascu* (also *né*) 'born' had preterits and past participles in [sk], though the latter ended in tonic [y]. Several high-frequency verbs had 3sg. preterits in [ot] contrasting with past participles in [əy]: *ot* and *eü* 'had,' *pot* 'was able' and *peü* 'been able,' *sot* 'knew' and *seü* 'known,' though other pret. forms like 2sg. *eüs*, *peüs*, *seüs* had the same tonic vowels as their past participles.[23] Certain verbs with preterit by-forms could have p.p. anomalies in [y]: pret. *lut* or *list* 'read' (both ≠ LĒGIT) had p.p. *lit* < LĒCTU or *leü*, and pret. *vit* < VĪDIT or *vist* 'saw' had p.p. *veü* or *veeit* 'seen' along with etymological *vis*. Most of the innovations above appear to have arisen in LL or PR days.

Almost all other morphological distinctions within the past-tense system involved a contrast between e.g. 3sg. preterits in *-st* and past participles in *-t*. Some of the most common after vowels were pret. *dist* and p.p. *dit* 'said, told,' *escrist* 'wrote' and *escrit* 'written,' *frist* and *frit* 'fried,' *prist* 'took' and by-form *prit* 'taken,' and *traist* and *trait* 'pulled, milked.' Some also entailed vocalic variation, like *fist* 'did/made' versus *fait* 'done/made,' *coist* versus *cuit* 'cooked.' Variation between [st] and [t] often occurred after a stem ending in a nasal consonant, as in *ceinst* and *ceint* 'girded,' *joinst* and *joint* 'joined,' *teinst* and *teint* 'dyed'; it could occur after a liquid-final stem, as in *terst* and by-form *tert* 'wiped' (also *ters*) or *esparst* and by-form *espart* 'sprinkled' (also *espars*). Indeed, some verbs with inherited sigmatic preterits still hesitated between an inherited past participle in [s] and an innovative one in [t].

Old French had only a few verbs with irregular preterits but regular past participles. There were sigmatic *valsist* 'been worth' and *volst* 'wanted' (also

---

[23] Variants in *-o-* rather than *-u-* also existed for preterits like (3sg.) *dut* 'had to,' *crut* 'believed,' and *mut* 'moved' (Kibler, 223). No doubt other variants were current as well, many of them differentiated stylistically or semantically in ways no one these days can tell.

volt, voli, or *volsi),* and the rhyming pair *tint* 'held' and *vint* 'came.' All had past participles in *-u,* the last two being *tenu* and *venu.* A few more verbs had regular preterits but irregular past participles. There were tautic athematic *mort* < MORT(U)U 'died' and *ro(u)t* < RUPTU or *ront* 'broken,' together with two pairs of forms ending in *-ert: ouvert* 'opened' and *couvert* 'covered,' *offert* 'offered' and *souffert* 'suffered' (Mourin, 192–94).

4.4.4. Wavering among Verb Variants

To recapitulate: in Old French, which lived in local variants, fluctuation persisted between or among by-form past participles for various verbs.

Although most 1st-conj. verbs had only a single attested past participle, even some of them had competition between pretonic vowels, as in *geté* or *gité* 'thrown' and *eschevé* or *eschivé* 'avoided, prevented,' or between syncopated and unsyncopated pretonic vowels, as in *comparé* or *compré* 'paid for.' For 2nd-, 3rd-, and 4th-conj. verbs with p.p. by-forms, and often with competing infinitive forms as well, most showed fluctuation between [i] and [y], as in *boli* or *bolu* 'boiled,' *coili* or *coillu* 'gathered,' *cosu* or *cosi* 'sewn,' *empli* or *emplu* 'filled,' *issi* or *issu* 'gone out,' *senti* or *sentu* 'felt,' *toli* or *tolu* 'removed,' and *vesti* or *vestu* 'clothed.' Sigmatics had survived in *vis* 'seen' < VĪSU and *mes* or *mas* 'stayed' < MĀNSU, but the first competed with *veü,* the second with *manu* or *masu.* Past participles for the verb *pondre* 'lay eggs' were *pos(t)* < POSTU, *pons, pot, ponu,* or still-current *pondu* (Einhorn, 149–67; Kibler, 272–73).

Variants for consonant-stem verbs included *cremu* or *cremi* or *crient* or *crent* 'feared': the first two were a 2nd-/3rd-conj.-style form and a 4th-conj.-style form based on one infin. *cremir,* and the final two were based on the present stem of by-form infin. *criembre,* now *craindre.* Verbs anomalous in the preterit could also have dueling past participles like *beneoit* or *benit* 'blessed,' *vencu* or *veincu* 'won,' and *nascu, naissu,* or still current *né* 'born.' Past participles for several verbs fluctuated between sigmatic and tautic athematic variants, and sometimes arrhizotonic ones as well: *occis* and *occit* 'slain,' *assis* and *assit* 'sat,' *espars* and *espart* 'sprinkled,' and *assols, assolt,* and *assolu* 'shriven.' Fluctuating between sigmatic and arrhizotonic were *mols* and *molu* 'ground,' *respons* and *respondu* 'answered' (Mourin, 159; Kibler, 272; Pope, 396, 398).

Judging by Old French by-forms, descendants of TOLLERE 'raise, remove' with anomalous pf. (SUS)TULĪ managed to acquire all three popular types of non-1st-conj. perfect/preterit by Proto-French times. A reflex from a nonstd. type in -SU gave OFr. *tols > tous,* one from a nonstd. type in -UĪ gave OFr. *tolui,* and one from a nonstd. type in -ĪVĪ gave OFr. *toli.* That verb's suppletive p.p. (SUB)LĀTU₁ succumbed to three competing replacements: (1) the -ŪTU type yielded OFr. *tolu,* (2) the -ĒCTU type yielded OFr. *toleit > toloit,* and (3) the unstressed -ĬTU type syncopated to yield OFr. *tolt > tout* (Einhorn,

163).[24] The verb having vanished, no one can tell which form would have won, but if need be I would choose *tolu*.

Arrhizotonic variants continued to oust some rhizotonic past participles during Old French times. One early tautic athematic p.p., *ro(u)t* 'broken' < RUPTU, was eventually replaced by still-current *rompu*, again built on the infectum stem of e.g. infin. *rompre* < RUMPERE (Kibler, 273). The two by-form past participles coexisted for centuries. In fact, the first word in line 2102 of the *Chanson de Roland*—reading *romput est li temples, pur ço que il cornat* in the Oxford manuscript—has been amended to *rut ad le temple…* by Müller and Stengel, perhaps on metrical grounds; the Venice IV manuscript has *roto a li temple pur ço chel sonat* 'he has broken his temple because he sounded it.' However, the Oxford manuscript also has in line 2156 *e sun osberc rumput e desmailet* 'and [they have] broken and torn apart his coat of mail,' with the arrhizotonic by-form unadapted (Bartsch, 28, 30).

When writers of Middle French were establishing the literary norm, they chose a single exponent for each past participle still in use. By that time, several strong past participles like sigmatic *ters* 'wiped' and *ascons* 'hidden,' or like tautic athematic *raent* 'redeemed' and of course *tolt* 'taken away,' had vanished along with the verbs to which they had belonged.

4.4.5. Further Leveling of Variation in Preterit Stems

Beginning in the twelfth and thirteenth centuries and continuing till the early seventeenth century, alternations of verb roots in the preterit were steadily leveled. Already, the three most common types of preterit, represented by OFr. 3sg. *chanta* 'sang,' *dormi* 'slept,' and *paru* 'appeared,' were arrhizotonic throughout their paradigms. However, preterit reflexes of some 2nd- and 3rd-conj. verbs had two different roots: rhizotonic ones for all singular slots and 3pl. contrasted with arrhizotonic ones for 1pl. and 2pl. Gradual leveling took place, the shorter rhizotonics usually prevailing.

Suggestive of a type still extant in plenty of Italian preterits—with rhizotonics in 1sg., 3sg., and 3pl. contrasting with arrhizotonics in 2sg., 1pl., and 2pl.—another type of Old French alternation was leveled by modern times. Usually the former group served as the model, once prevocalic [ə] had vanished in the latter. Preterits for OFr. *veoir* 'see' opposed 1sg. *vi*, 3sg. *vit*, 3pl. *virent* to 2sg. *veïs*, 1pl. *veïmes*, 2pl. *veïstes*; preterits for *venir* 'come' and *tenir* 'held' were comparable, with e.g. 1sg. *vin, tin* as against 2sg. *venis, tenis*. By analogy with such verbs, others simplified their stems: OFr. 2sg. *fesis*, 1pl. *fesimes*, and 2pl. *fesistes* 'did/made' first lost intervocalic [z] to become *feïs, feïmes, feïstes* and then syncopated to *fis, fimes, fistes* ± 1sg. *fis*, 3sg. *fit*, 3pl. *firent*. Preterits for *dire* 'say, tell,' *prendre* 'take,' and *querre* 'seek' underwent a comparable evolution. Still, leveling could go the other way: OFr. 1sg. *ploi*, 3sg. *plot*, and 3pl. *plourent* 'pleased' were remade as *plus, plut, plurent* ± 2sg. *ploüs*, 1pl. *ploümes*, 2pl. *ploüstes*, the pretonic vowel having syncopated. The

---

[24] French reflexes of the -ĒCTU type of past participle are discussed in §4.4.9.3.

same development took place in other verbs that had had rhizotonic preterits in [o] in Old French (Price, 211, 214; Kibler, 219–23). No consistent choice was made between such variants. Analogies proved predictable only in that a single preterit stem survived for all such verbs, whose passés simples became solidly rhizotonic.

Later speakers remade more preterit paradigms on the basis of arrhizotonic forms. From one point of view, speakers might seem to have drawn upon forms like the pres.indic.pl., giving e.g. 3sg. *conduisit* 'drove,' *écrivit* 'wrote,' and *joignit* 'joined' for earlier *conduist* < CONDŪXIT, *escrit* < SCRĪPSIT, and *joinst* < JŪNXIT. More precisely, already extant arrhizotonic preterit forms like OFr. 2sg. *conduisis* were generalized, while others like 2sg. *escresis* and *joinsis* had to be recast along infectum lines. For all three verbs, such recasting was based on stems already used for the pres.indic.pl. (1pl. *conduisons, écrivons, joignons*) and also the whole impf.indic. (3sg. *conduisait, écrivait, joignait*). Not only did preterits acquire the same stem throughout, but that stem now matched one found elsewhere in the verb.

Turning to past participles, even in Old French times *suivi* 'followed' came to replace *seü* < SECŪTU along with variant p.p.s *sevi* or *sivi* (Pope, 386). Strictly speaking, though, the new 4th-conj.-style p.p. *suivi* still clashes morphologically with 3rd-conj. *suivre*, which could also be *sivre, siure* or *sivir* in Old French. Replacement of *seü* might have been attributable in part to homonymic clash with the past participle of *savoir* 'know,' also *seü* in Old French and still *su* today, though nowadays p.p. *plu* may still mean either 'pleased' or 'rained.' In another homonymic clash, the ambiguity in OFr. p.p. *peü*—meaning either 'been able' (no CL p.p.) or 'tended, kept' ≠ PĀSTU (but cf. pf. PĀVĪ)—has been resolved by the near disappearance of all verbal forms of OFr. *paistre* 'tend, keep,' now written *paître*.[25]

Other past-participial homonymies have arisen. OFr. *ester* 'stand' and *estovoir* 'be needed' shared the p.p. *esteü*, but both verbs have disappeared, so that no p.p. *étu* appears to have emerged for either. Again, OFr. *croire* 'believe' and *croistre* 'grow' shared the p.p. *creü*, but both verbs have survived and still (formally) share a past participle pronounced [kry]. Graphically, accentless *cru* 'believed' differs from circumflexed *crû* 'grown.'[26]

Resulting from complete lenition of intervocalic stops and from syncope of atonic vowels, homophony among certain past participles has been resolved by the disappearance of one competitor or both.

---

[25] Even in the modern literary language, *paître* 'tend, keep' has become defective, with no preterit, imperfect subjunctive, or past participle (Augé and Augé, 736). Only the infinitive remains in (occasional) use. Another defective verb is *gésir* 'lie, recline': now used only in 3sg., 3pl., 1pl., and 2pl. of the present indicative, all six slots of the imperfect indicative, and present participle *gisant*, the verb no longer has a past participle, which lived as long as OFr. *geü* 'lain' and would no doubt be written *jû* today (Augé and Augé, 451).

[26] French distinguishes orthographically between *cru* 'believed' and *crû* 'grown.' In part because of homonymic clash, speakers now tend to replace *croître* with *pousser* 'push' or *grandir* 'get bigger.' As with *nonchalant* 'carefree,' another present participle has outlived its verb in adjectivized and nominalized *croissant* 'growing; crescent; butter roll.'

4.4.6. Loss of Final Consonants in Past Participles

In line with the disappearance of most final consonants in speech in Middle French, some surviving sigmatic or tautic athematic past participles lost final [s] or [t] in masculine forms. Often that loss has been reflected in French orthography, so that *conclus* 'concluded' < CONCLŪSU, *ris* 'laughed' < RĪSU, *luit* 'shone' < *LUCITU? (no CL p.p.), and *soffit* 'sufficed' < SUFFECTU came to be and still are written *conclu, ri, lui, suffi.* Pope notes (387) that deletion of final consonants took place either in past participles belonging either to little-used verbs or to verbs with rarely used feminine forms, where [z] and [t] would still have been pronounced before final [ə].

Ewert goes further, stating that all such verbs are intransitives conjugated with *avoir* 'have' and therefore never used in the feminine in perfect constructions, "which would account for their readiness to drop a meaningless consonant and join the -i class" (227). One anomaly dating from that time occurs in past participles for the semilearnèd verb *absoudre* 'shrive,' where graphically sigmatic masc. *absous* [apsú] contrasts with tautic athematic fem. *absoute* [apsút]. An identical anomaly occurs between a related pair, masc. *dissous* and fem. *dissoute* 'dissolved.' Here, as with masc. *absous* and fem. *absoute* 'shriven,' leveling has resulted in the survival of masculine sigmatics and feminine tautic athematics.

Undeniably, though, morphological drift has continued to favor arrhizotonicity for past participles in French (see §4.4.7).

4.4.7. Recent Remodelings of Rhizotonic Past Participles

During the sixteenth and seventeenth centuries, speakers of French leveled even more rhizotonic past participles along arrhizotonic lines. Did they do so because forms seldom spoken failed to catch the ear of the young? At all events, OFr. *mors* 'bitten' < MORSU may now be only *mordu ± mordre*, and OFr. *lit* 'read' < LĒCTU, already competing against an ŪTU-type *leü*, has since been displaced by syncopated *lu* (Price, 223–24). Another old form that had lasted was *ars* 'burned' < ĀRSU, replaced by *ardu ± ardre*, though the whole verb has now become obsolescent if not obsolete (1st-conj. *brûler* being the normal verb for 'burn').[27] Beginning in the thirteenth century, infinitives themselves were remodeled: etymological OFr. *reçoivre* 'receive' < RECIPERE, OFr. *boivre* 'drink' < BIBERE, and OFr. *escrivre* 'write' < SCRĪBERE were remade as *recevoir ± devoir, boire ± croire*, and *escrire ± lire*. For this last pair, the rhyming analogy seems to have been also based on overlapping semantic fields that must both have proved attractive to notaries and clerks.

During the age of standard-building, a few 3rd-conj. infinitives now regarded as anomalous were replaced by arrhizotonic variants. At the same time, a few 4th-conj. infinitives moved over to the 1st conjugation. Thus,

---

[27] Augé and Augé (59) list *arder* or *ardre* 'burn'—a 1st-conj. reshaping coming first—as "Vx." [archaic]. Again, a reflex of the old present participle survives in the Fr. adj. *ardent* 'burning.'

courre < CURRERE 'run,' *querre* < QUÆRERE 'seek,' and *secourre* < SUCCUTERE 'shake' were replaced by *courir, quérir, secouer*. Meanwhile, *tistre* 'weave' < TEXERE and its 4th-conj. by-form *tissir* (p.p. *tissu*) were replaced by 1st-conj. *tisser*. Again, Germanic-derived *espeldre* or *espelir* 'spell' was replaced by *épeler*; Latin-derived *grondir* 'roar, growl' and *afligir* 'distress' were replaced by *gronder, afliger*. Similarly, ModFr. *tousser* 'cough' and *puer* 'stink' used to belong to the 4th conjugation as *toussir, puir* (p.p.s *toussi, puï*) until the sixteenth century; the first comes straight from TUSSĪRE and hence has changed conjugation once, but the second, from 2nd-conj. PUTĒRE (no CL p.p.) has changed twice. Several of these acquired regular past participles for their new class in *tissé, épelé, toussé*, and *pué*. Anomalous *couru* and *quis* persisted: the first still does today, and so does the second if only in compounds.[28] By contrast, some 4th-conj. infinitives based on preterit stems, like *nasquir* 'be born,' *vainquir* 'win,' *suivir* 'follow,' failed to thrive beyond the sixteenth century (Ewert, 180–83). Conservatism led to retention or restoration of the rhizotonic 3rd-conj. variants *naître, vaincre, suivre*.

Under the emerging literary standard, by-form past participles from Old French were deprived of verbal function. Hence regularized *ouvri* 'opened' and *offri* 'offered,' *prendu* 'taken,' *nascu* 'born,' and *mouru* 'died'—most of them still encountered today in compositions from Anglophone learners— were replaced by their historically correct by-forms *ouvert* and *offert, pris, né* and *mort*. Meanwhile, infinitive-based competitors ending in [i] drove out idiosyncratic *cueillé* 'gathered,' along with *resplendu* 'gleamed,' *repentu* 'repented,' and *sentu* 'felt, smelled'; only *cueilli, repenti, senti* are acceptable now (Ewert, 226–27). Remade before the seventeenth century were OFr. *mentu* 'told lies,' *partu* 'left,' and now-obsolete *oü* 'heard,' all acquiring regular 4th-conj. forms; even OFr. *arrestu* 'stopped' was remade as a 1st-conj. form; but, no doubt because of several rhyming monosyllabic past participles, the OFr. by-form *teindu* 'dyed' yielded to *teint* < TĪNCTU (*Grand Larousse*, 4017). Yet *vêtu* 'dressed,' *venu* 'come,' and *tenu* 'held' still clash morphologically with their 4th-conj.-style infinitives *vêtir, venir, tenir*.

Another analogical remodeling in Middle French introduced the p.p. *tordu* 'twisted,' based on infin. *tordre* and replacing *tors* or *tort*, for which compare pf. TORSĪ and p.p. TORTU along with nonstd. TORSU. Today, that verb's old past participles serve only as adjectives or nouns: masc. *tors* 'twisted' (as in *fil tors* 'twisted thread') contrasts with fem. *torse* (as in *colonne torse* 'spiraled shaft') and also with fem. *torte* (as in *jambes tortes* 'bandy legs'). Meanwhile, a reflex of masc. TORTU survives as the noun *tort* 'wrong,' appearing most often in an idiom *avoir tort* 'be mistaken' heard with depressing frequency here below.

Table 4–4 sums up the several kinds of p.p. reshaping that took place during and after Middle French. Some forms lost a final consonant; some became arrhizotonic; some already arrhizotonic joined the 1st conjugation.

---

[28] Replaced by *chercher* elsewhere, *quérir* remains in western dialects of French (Battye and Hintze, 308).

Table 4–4

Reshaping of Past Participles in French

( )   verb now archaic

Latin	Old French	Modern French
Loss of final consonant		
CONCLŪSU	conclus	conclu
RĪSU	ris	ri
—	luit	lui
SUFFECTU	suffit	suffi
Arrhizotonic replacement		
ĀRSU	ars	(ardu)
MORSU	mors	mordu
TORTU	tors, tort	tordu
Metaplasm to 1st conjugation		
—	puï	pué
TEXTU	tissu	tissé
TUSSĪTU	toussi	toussé

4.4.8. Recent Leveling of Stem Variation

During further remodelings in Middle French, most apophonous past participles like *amé* 'loved,' *ploré* 'wept,' and *proiié* 'prayed' were leveled on either the arrhizotonic or the rhizotonic stem to yield *aimé, pleuré, prié*. At about the same time, -ié p.p. endings derived from -ĀTU after a palatal consonant—giving e.g. OFr. *chargié* 'loaded,' *cherchié* 'looked for,' *aidié* 'helped,' and *commencié* 'begun'—were leveled to the standard ending -é, just as infinitive endings in -ier from -ĀRE after a palatal were leveled to the regular -er (Price, 222). In these ways, morphological regularity increased in paradigms for 1st -conj. verbs, which all (I believe) now have the same stem throughout.

Perhaps most often, past participles provided the model for verbal reformulations. The two OFr. preterits meaning 'resolved,' 1sg. *resols* and *resolsis*, were both replaced by *je résolus* based on p.p. *résoulu*; the four OFr. preterits meaning 'wanted,' 1sg. *vols, voil, volsis*, and *volis*, were all replaced by *je voulus*, based on p.p. *voulu* from *VOLUTU, just as 1sg. *vesqui* 'lived' was replaced by *je vescus*, based on the p.p. *vescu* from *VIXUTU (Price, 206–11). As Price goes on to comment (212), Old French had four types of weak preterit and a wide range of strong ones; except for *venir* 'come' and *tenir* 'hold' with e.g. 3sg. *vint* and *tint*, Modern French has only three types. In 3sg., these three end in [a], [i], and [y], a distribution eerily reminiscent of the tonic vowels in arrhizotonic past participles during Late Latin and Proto-Romance.

In all but the earliest Old French, certain verb endings outside the 1st conjugation had become formally identical. Old French forms like *paru* 'appeared' had served as both 3sg. preterit and masc.sg.obl. past participle, final [y] here being the outcome for both -UIT and -ŪTU. Meanwhile, forms like *dormi* 'slept' had served as 1sg. and 3sg. preterit and also masc.sg.obl. past participle because final [i] here was the outcome for -ĪVĪ, -ĪVIT, and -ĪTU alike. This formal identity for many verbs, which grew greater following the loss of case marking for past participles, and greater still in speech once final consonants ceased to be pronounced, might have served as a springboard to further regularization of preterit stems along past-participial lines.

4.4.9. Relic Past Participles in French

Like languages already examined, like ones to come, French preserves former past participles now serving as adjectives or nouns. At times, nouns identical to the corresponding verb's past participle have themselves died out, like OFr. *vée* 'ban, prohibition' from a 1st-conj. reshaping of fem. VETITA 'forbidden' (Godefroy, 8.157). At other times, such relics are the sole remnants of verbs that used to come fully equipped with finite forms. Thus, from a 4th-conj. reshaping of CARPERE 'seize, pluck' came OFr. *charpir* 'shred cloth; work wood,' with a regular p.p. *charpi* ≠ CARPTU; from that verb today, there survive only the masc. noun *charpi* 'cooper's block' and the fem. noun *charpie* 'shreds, lint.' For relic past participles in Romanian, see §3.1.5.3; in Italian, §§3.5.2–3.5.3; in Catalan, §4.6.2.5; and in Spanish, §4.7.7.

4.4.9.1. Reflexes of –ŪTU

Past participles in [y] still used today suggest that variants in reflexes of -ŪTU enjoyed great popularity in the Late Latin or Proto-Romance spoken across northern Gaul. The same formant appears in Old French feminine nouns with endings deriving from -ŪTA. Cases of such fossilized morphology include OFr. *ferue* 'blow, wound,' *value* 'worth' (borrowed into English but supplanted by *valeur* in French), and *creüe* 'growth, increase,' a masculine reflex of which survives in *cru* 'vintage.' Another survivor used to be OFr. *mue* 'change, departure,' remade from the direct-suffixation p.p. MŌTU 'moved' (Godefroy, 5.440). One more such noun that lives on today is *chute* 'a fall' built from infectum stem CAD- plus -ŪTA, with an intervocalic [t] missing from the fem. forms above. One suspects borrowing.

As noted in Table 4–4 on page 239, one verb in French exhibits evidence of successive waves of regularization. In northern Gaul, rhizotonic TEXTU 'woven' was replaced by an arrhizotonic variant like It. *tessuto*. The OFr. reflex of that remade past participle, *tissu*, survives mainly as a noun meaning 'fabric, cloth.' Today the old form *tissu* still retains limited past-participial use, or perhaps more accurately adjectival use, as shown by a phrase *un nid tissu de mousse* 'a nest built out of moss' given by Augé and Augé (1032).[29] Since Old French days, the whole verb *tistre* < TEXERE has been remade along 1st-conj. lines, giving infin. *tisser* with regular p.p. *tissé*.

Among other old past participles used adjectivally or nominally, fem. *issue* 'outcome; outlet' shows a reshaping from rhizotonic thematic EXĬTA 'gone out.' Now one would expect French speakers to have remade that past participle along the lines of 4th-conj. infin. EXĪRE > OFr. *issir*, as speakers did elsewhere in forms like Rom. *ieşit*, It. *uscito*, and OSp. *exido*. In fact, that regularized p.p. *issi* was found as an OFr. by-form. Yet fated to endure was the other OFr. by-form p.p. *issu* 'gone out,' which went along with the reshaped 3rd-conj. infin. *istre* ≠ EXĪRE. Both infinitives are obsolete today, but *issu* survives adjectivally in the sense 'born, sprung from' (Augé and Augé, 549).

4.4.9.2. Rhizotonic Thematics

As Price remarks (224–25), some old neut.pl. past participles from Latin were long ago reinterpreted as fem.sg. nouns in French, usually with an abstract meaning. Some old masc.sg. past participles were reinterpreted as masc.sg. nouns. All were rhizotonic. Thus, CL PERDITA 'things lost,' VENDITA 'things sold,' and DĒBITA 'things owed' have become *la perte* 'loss,' *la vente* 'sale,' *la dette* 'debt,' now divergent from the reshaped p.p.s *perdu* 'lost,' *vendu* 'sold,' and *dû* 'owed, had to.'

To this noun group should be added the fem. noun *fuite* 'leak,' from the CL p.p. FUGITA 'fled,' pronounced [fyịtə] in early Old French. Unless its circumflex is as superfluous as the one on *extrême* 'utmost,' the masculine noun *gîte* 'shelter, lair' probably comes from a variant of the std. p.p. JACITU 'lain.' In Old French, the sigmatic-tautic noun would have contrasted with the arrhizotonic p.p. *geü* 'lain,' but that last form has no reflex in Modern French (see footnote 25 to this chapter, page 236).

---

[29] Augé and Augé (1032) define *tistre* as "ancien synonyme de TISSER" [former synonym of…]. Except for the old past participle *tissu*, no form of 3rd-conj. *tistre* remains in use.

Most relic nouns in French bear witness to the spread of rhizotonic thematic marking as a replacement—temporary, as it turned out—for several kinds of athematic marking on past participles. However much such innovations in -ĬTU may now seem to exemplify an evolutionary dead end, they had the same stem as their infectum and were predictably shaped. They hence represented an advance toward the goal of isomorphy.

Ewert (224) unearths fossils based on variants evidently current in northern Gaul at one time. Thus, feminine nouns like *faute* < *falte* 'mistake,' *fente* 'crack, slot,' and *meute* 'crowd, pack' (in OFr. also meaning 'expedition; uprising') preserve infectum-based variants for FALSA 'tricked,' FISSA 'split,' and MŌTA 'moved.' Both these older sets of past participles diverge from *fallu* 'been required' or *failli* 'almost done,' *fendu* 'split,' and *mû* 'moved,' all of them rebuilt arrhizotonically.

Additional leftover p.p. nouns or adjectives cited by Ewert (229) reflect LL/PR reshapings or creations. Feminines include OFr. *boite* 'a drink' < LL BIBITA 'drunk' and ModFr. *voûte* 'vault' from *VOLVITA for VOLŪTA 'rolled.' The first, *boite*, still survives in the sense 'state of wine good to drink.' Two more reflexes of rhizotonic thematic past participles are *suite* from *SEQUITA for SECŪTA 'followed' and *tonte* 'shearing-time' from *TONDITA for TŌNSA 'shorn.'

One is tempted to add the French noun *récolte* 'harvest,' whose stem comes from a rhizotonic thematic variant of COLLĒCTA 'gathered'; preservation of [l] before another consonant suggests that the word has been borrowed, from It. *ricolta*, so that syncope took place well southeast of the Ile-de-France.

Among its nouns, French also has fossils of unattested fem.sg. (or neut.pl.) past participles ending in -ĬTA, whose stems—unlike those of the CL p.p.s— were identical to the stems of their infinitives, or the infectum generally. One fossil is *ponte* 'egg-laying' ≠ POS(I)TA 'put, set,' but cf. infin. PŌNERE, with the [d] in *PONDITA being an excrescence that at first arose only to the infinitive, between [n] and [r]. Other fossils are ModFr. *assiette* 'plate' ≠ ASSESSA 'set beside' (but cf. infin. ASSIDĒRE), *farce* 'interlude' ≠ FARTA 'stuffed' (but cf. infin. FARCĪRE), and OFr. *tolte* 'removal' ≠ SUBLĀTA (but cf. infin. TOLLERE). To these nouns correspond the ModFr. p.p.s *pondu* 'weighed,' *assis* 'sat,' and *farci* 'stuffed' and the OFr. p.p. *tolu, toli,* or *tolloit* 'taken away.'

Ewert gives a sampler of relics deriving from attested rhizotonic thematic past participles in Latin. For instance, OFr. *cointe* 'mannered, dainty' comes from COGNITA 'known' (cf. Engl. *quaint*). OFr. *empleite* 'purchase' comes from IMPLICITA 'folded up' (ModFr. *emplette*) and memorializes packaging methods from long ago. OFr. masc. *repost* 'hideaway' comes from REPOS(I)TU 'stored.' Note also OFr. *molte* 'grinding of grain' from MOLĬTA 'ground;' the term has since been replaced by suffixed *mouture*, also meaning 'mixture of wheat, rye, and barley meal' (Augé and Augé, 679). Other examples, with possible etyma, are presented in Table 4–5.

Table 4–5

Relics of Unclassical Rhizotonic Thematics in French

CL past participle	LL/PR p.p. in Gaul?	French noun
O b s o l e t e		
—	BIBITA	boite
POS(I)TA	*PONDITA	ponte
SUBLĀTA	TOLLITA	tolte
TŌNSA	*TONDITA	tonte
C u r r e n t		
ASSESSA	*ASSEDITA	assiette
FALSA	*FALLITA	faute
FARTA	*FARCITA	farce
FISSA	*FINDITA	fente
MŌTA	*MOVITA	meute
PĒNSA	*PENDITA	pente
REDDITA	*RENDITA	rente
SECŪTA	*SEQUITA	suite
VOLŪTA	*VOLVITA	voûte

Such relics out of northern France match some of the past participles found to this day across southern Italy and on Sardinia. They indicate that, whether directly surviving or based on the infinitive or perfect stem, past participles in atonic -ĪTU more than held their own for a time in broad reaches of the area where Late Latin and Proro-Romance were spoken. More probably, speakers of nascent French gradually transferred reflexes of that ending to nouns, most of them fairly abstract. Undeniably, French speakers came to prefer marking past participles with a tonic vowel or, once in a while, with [s]. To such artifacts of sigmaticism I now turn.

4.4.9.3. Sigmatics

French used to have more sigmatic past participles than it does now. An obsolete noun *duis* 'lesson, teaching' ≠ DOCTU 'taught' shows postclassical reshaping along finite perfectum lines (cf. pf. DŪXĪ). Meanwhile, the similar-sounding OFr. noun, *duit* 'canal, flow' < DUCTU 'led, brought,' looks classical enough (Godefroy, 2.780–81). As for relic nouns today, Price (224–25) cites two that resemble old rhizotonic past participles in -SU: the masc. nouns *mors* 'bit [for horses]' < 4th-decl. MORSU 'a bite, biting' and *cours* 'running' < 4th-conj. CURSU 'a run, running.' To these nominalized relics correspond the arrhizotonic ModFr. p.p.s *mordu* 'bitten' and *couru* 'run,' now of the -ŪTU type with an infectum stem. (Godefroy, 2.781). Note also the noun *remords* 'remorse,' its ahistorical -d- owing to orthographic rapprochement.

Georges (28) adds sigmatic Fr. *réponse* 'answer,' from neut.pl. or fem.sg. RESPŌNSA and contrasting with the end-stressed ModFr. p.p. *répondu* 'answered.' In an example of what could have been competing past participles at one time, alongside remade *fendu* 'split,' a reflex of FISSA survives in *fesse* 'buttock.'

Survival of other sigmatics from CL, most of them now gone, is indicated by OFr. nouns given in Godefroy like *ces* or *cesse* 'end, cessation' < CESSU and CESSA 'stopped,' *defoise* 'defense' < DĒFĒNSA 'fought off,'[30] *remes* 'suet, grease' < REMĀNSU 'stayed, been left,' and *toise* 'six-foot measurement' < TĒNSU 'stretched'[31] Another was *espoise* 'cost' < EXPĒNSA 'weighed out, paid'; Modern French has semilearnèd *dépense* 'cost.' The still current noun *prise* 'a taking' < PRĒNSA,[32] whose meaning in Old French was 'tax collection, right of requisition,' and the OFr. adj. *possis* 'owned' < POSSESSU show metaphony borrowed from the preterit, whose 1sg. form once ended in -Ī. Contrasting with p.p. *mis* 'put' was the OFr. noun *mes₁* 'messenger,' also from MISSU 'sent' but without metaphony. From the same past participle but with different semantics came OFr. *mes₂* 'dish (of food),' earlier 'something put in front of one.' Now respelled *mets*, again owing to rapprochement, this noun must have come into being after MITTERE had shifted to mean 'put' in Gaul. Compare the evident OFr. homonym *mes₃* 'farmhouse, farm, garden' < MĀNSU 'stayed,' with reflexes in Occitan and Catalan.

Deriving from sigmatic past participles that postdated CL were OFr. fem. *asconse* 'dissimulation' < LL ABSCŌNSA 'hidden,' which also gave the OFr. p.p. *ascons*, together with *vols* 'bent, bulging' ≠ VOLŪTU 'turned' and *acquise* 'acquisition' ≠ doubly marked ADQUĪSĪTA 'gotten, acquired.' A suffixed form of by-form VOLSU > OFr. *vols* 'turned' survives in the noun *voussure* 'arching, vaulting' (Ewert, 224).

---

[30] Cf. Cat. *devesa* '[fenced-in] meadow.'

[31] Once equal to 1.949 meters in length, Fr. *toise* still means 'measuring device for conscripts' (illustration in Augé and Augé, 1033: "conscrit sous la toise").

[32] Cf. Sp. *preso* 'prisoner,' also an adjective 'imprisoned' but no longer a past participle.

Today, nearly all past participles for the corresponding verbs are arrhizotonic, whether 2nd-/3rd-conj.-style *tendu* 'held out' and *défendu* 'forbidden,' or 1st-conj.-style *cédé* 'yielded,' *possédé* 'owned,' *voûté* 'bent,' and apparently denominalized *dépensé* 'spent.' There does survive p.p. *acquis* 'acquired,' looking much as it used to.

Even more old sigmatic past participles still survive, in adjectival or nominal senses. For instance, Fr. *ras* 'short-haired' < RĀSU 'shaved' exists alongside p.p. *rasé* 'shaved.' From the same past participle, and developing more normally, comes the preposition *rez* 'even with, level with,' appearing also in a noun phrase *rez-de-chaussée* 'ground floor.' Meanwhile, the old infin. *rere* < RĀDERE 'shave' has vanished with all its finite forms.

More old past participles whose verbs have fallen into disuse include the adj. *épars* 'scanty' < SPARSU and the fem. noun *source* 'spring' ≠ SURRĒCTA 'arisen, sprung.' Now the OFr. p.p. *sors* 'sprung' shows a sigmatic reshaping probably inspired by pf. SURRĒXĪ, even though the tonic vowel would have had to fall; note also the syncopated perfect infin. SURRĒXE. Even if It. *sorto* and OSp. *surto* 'arisen' resulted from syncope of a rhizotonic thematic variant—a question almost impossible to answer at this late date—they would still show that the reshaping might turn out tautic athematic in at least two areas. Nowadays in French, *sourdre* < SURGERE, its semantic field shrunk to 'turn out, result,' may be used only in the infinitive and sometimes in the pres.indic., 3sg. and 3pl. A nominalized p.p. *source* 'spring' has thus been left as an isolate in the modern tongue (Augé and Augé, 971).

In Italian, whose tolerance for sigmatics surpasses that of French, cognates of almost all the forms above remain in use as both nouns and past participles. In Romanian, whose sigmatic tolerance is higher still, many sigmatic nouns identical to past participles have been innovated. In Spanish and Portuguese, few have survived, and none has been innovated. As one would expect from its p.p. inventory—5% sigmatic in the sample—standard Catalan has more sigmatic nouns than French and far more than Spanish, but far fewer than Italian.

4.4.9.4. Tautic Athematics

Additional past-participial relics cited by Price as deriving from old rhizotonics ending in -CTU, where C stands for any consonant but [s], are the fem. nouns *route* 'road' < RUPTA 'broken,' *élite* < ĒLĒCTA 'chosen,' and *recette* 'recipe' < RECEPTA 'received' (Price, 224–25). To these nominalized relics correspond the arrhizotonic ModFr. p.p.s *rompu* 'broken,' *élu* 'selected,' and *reçu* 'received,' all now of the -ŪTU type. Once used as the past participle for a vanished verb *despire* 'despise' < DĒSPICERE, OFr. *despit* < DĒSPECTU 'looked down on' survives as the ModFr. noun *dépit* 'spite.'

Georges (28) adds *la descente* 'decline' from a tautic athematic variant of sigmatic DĒSCĒNSA 'gone down,' contrasting with the end-stressed ModFr. p.p. *descendu* 'gone down.'

French used to have yet another ending for past participles. From -ĒCTU or from -ĪCTU came OFr. *-eit*, which turned into *-oit* in later Old French. Probably on the model of COLLĒCTU 'gathered,' there developed several unetymological past participles in Old French like *chaeit* 'fallen,' *enfoeit* 'dug,' *fu(i)eit* 'fled,' *remaneit* 'stayed,' and *toleit* 'taken away.' What would be the semantic connection between these verbs?

This ending from -ĒCTU or -ĪCTU was to leave descendants in a single adjective, *benêt* 'foolish' < *beneeit*, itself from postclassical BENEDICTU 'blessed' and now sporting a superfluous circumflex. By analogy with infin. *bénir*, the past participle used in perfect constructions now must be regular 4th-conj. *béni*, but there survives a variant *bénit(e)* [benit] used adjectivally in phrases like *eau bénite* 'holy water.'[33] OFr. *maleoit* 'cursed' < MALEDICTU has not been directly continued; remade mostly ± *dire* 'say,' the verb *maudire* has a masc.sg. p.p. *maudit* with fem.sg. *maudite*.[34] In view of the histories of these two verbs, which were originally compounded from adverbs plus DĪCERE 'say, tell,' and which acquired somewhat different meanings in Christian usage, one might say here that a morphological distinction has arisen from a semantic one.

Still another French noun of the -ĒCTU type is *cueillette* 'harvest,' perhaps from an old neut.pl. p.p. COLLĒCTA 'things gathered.' That noun relic contrasts with the arrhizotonic ModFr. p.p. *cueilli* 'gathered.'

Like *value* (§4.4.9.1) and *quaint* (§4.4.9.2), English preserves past-participial nouns long extinct in French. A third is *deceit* < OFr. *déceite* < DĒCEPTA, no doubt an old neut.pl. meaning 'things cheated or beguiled.' Now French makes do with semilearnèd, polysyllabic *déception* 'trickery.'

4.4.10. Past Participles as Roots for French Verbs

On some past-participial roots, speakers built new 1st-conj. infinitives. They created *toser* 'to shear' from a stem like that of p.p. TŌNSU 'shorn'[35] and *fosser* 'to dig' from a stem like that of p.p. FOSSU 'dug,' for the new verbs' consonantism with medial [z] or [s] does not match that of infins. TONDĒRE and FODERE or that of pfs. TOTONDĪ and FŌDĪ. Rather, both variants imply a sigmatic base, as does the verb *fossoyer* 'ditch; dig graves.' Nouns built on the same stems include OFr. *tose* 'girl' (still extant mutatis mutandis in northern Italian dialects) and still extant *fosse* 'trench, pit' < FOSSA.[36]

---

[33] By-form *beneïr* with p.p. *beneï* already existed in Old French but competed with *benedis(t)re* > *beneïs(t)re* (Einhorn, 150). Note also the Fr. adj. *benêt* 'foolish' < BENEDICTU.

[34] Conjugationally, *maudire* 'curse' differs from *dire* 'say, tell' in the pres.indic.pl., impf.indic., and pres.p., where it has the stem *maudiss-* (Augé and Augé, 630).

[35] Cf. It. *tosare* 'clip, crop,' Cat. *tosa* 'shearing,' and Rom. *tuns* 'idem.'

[36] Cf. It. *fossato* 'ditch, moat,' Fr. *fossé* 'trench,' looking like p.p.s for *fossare, *fosser. Spanish may have only *fosa* 'pit, grave' and Ptg. only *fosso* 'trench, ditch,' but Catalan has a series built on the stem of *fossa: fossana* 'grave(yard),' *fossar* 'graveyard,' p.p.-looking *fossat* 'moat,' and *fosser* 'gravedigger.' Since these languages lack a p.p. reflex of FOSSU 'dug'—Cat. *fos* meaning 'melted'—all the items above are probably denominal.

What of other sigmatic bases? From the p.p. *envols* 'wrapped' came OFr. *envolser* 'wrap,' and from the p.p. *ars* 'burned' came OFr. *arser* 'burn'; compare also OFr. *quester* 'seek, pursue' (now *quêter*) built from a rhizotonic variant of p.p. QUÆSĪTU 'sought' if not from the noun. Today's *semonce* 'a scolding, talking-to' came from an OFr. fem.sg. p.p. *semonse* or *somonse* 'urged,' itself from a sigmatic variant of SUBMONITA 'secretly reminded.' In Old French, that sigmatic variant was also nominalized as *semonse* 'assignment, invitation, advice,' continued in the Engl. law term *summons*. In current French usage, the moribund infin. *semondre* from a 3rd-conj. variant of SUBMONĒRE 'remind secretly' has no past participle, but its old one (or the noun) has inspired a new 1st-conj. infin. *semoncer* (p.p. *semoncé*) 'reprimand, rebuke.'

4.4.11. Tautics, Metaphonics, and Prefixoids Today

French keeps a fair number of tautic athematic past participles, with [t] still pronounced in feminine forms like sg. *cuite* 'cooked' < COCTA, *couverte* 'covered' < COOPERTA and *ouverte* 'opened' < APERTA X COOPERTA, *dite* 'said, told' remade from DICTA, *écrite* 'written' < SCRĪPTA, *jointe* 'joined' < JŪNCTA, *morte* 'died' < MORT(U)A, and *faite* 'done/made' < FACTA. Following a large-scale reduction in the number of sigmatic past participles from Old French—rivaling the liquidation of sigmatics in Spanish and Portuguese—at least two high-frequency ones remain in the language today, with [z] still pronounced in feminine forms: *mise* 'put' and *prise* 'taken.'

Yet these two cannot derive straight from MISSA 'sent' or PRĒNSA 'seized, grabbed,' which would regularly have given **messe* and **proise*, cognate with std. It. *messa, presa*. Rather, the tonic vowel of pret. MĪSĪ was analogically extended to that verb's past participle, while past-participial *pris* emerged from a sigmatic preterit that had undergone metaphony (Mendeloff, 37). In the same vein, *dit* 'said, told' cannot come straight from DICTU with short i̯, which would have given **doit* (homonymous with the word for 'finger'); its vowel too comes from the rhizotonic pret. DĪXĪ (Price, 224). The evolution of metaphonic *mis* 'put,' *pris* 'taken,' and *dit* 'said, told' supplies further evidence of morphological leveling across the past system in French. Recently, speakers have further reduced allomorphy by clipping past-participial forms now perceived as anomalous (see §4.4.12).

Once able to stand by themselves, certain verbs now survive only when prefixed. Naturally, the same holds true for their past participles. Thus, OFr. *duit* 'led, brought' still lives in *conduit* 'driven' (infin. *conduire*) and several others. OFr. *chu* 'fallen' lives in *déchu* 'decayed, declined' (infin. *déchoir*) and OFr. *clos* 'shut' in *éclos* 'hatched; blossomed' (infin. *éclore*). Somewhat comparable is the verb *reclure* 'shut away,' its semantics reversed from those of RECLŪDERE 'unclose, reveal': these days, the French verb is used only in the infinitive or in compound tenses built with p.p. *reclus* < RECLŪSU, itself also serving as an adjective or noun (Augé and Augé, 868). A similar case is prefixed *remplir* 'fill' (p.p. *rempli*), much more widespread than *emplir*

'idem' (p.p. *empli*). In these verbs, prefixes have shrunk to the status of
Malkielian prefixoids; see §2.3.1 for similar verbs in Latin.

4.4.12. Reduction to Zero of Gender and Number Marking

As reflexes of Latin [t], arrhizotonic sg. past participles in early Old French
retained intervocalic [ð] for feminines and word-final [θ] for (oblique)
masculines. In the first seventy-three lines of the eleventh-century *Vie de St.
Alexis*, one sees examples of the former in *honurede* 'honored,' *mustrethe*
'shown,' *comandethe* 'ordered,' and examples of the latter in *perdut* 'lost,'
baptizét 'baptized,' *anuitét* 'nightfallen'; line 96 has 4th-conj. *departit* 'divided,
shared.' By later Old French, both interdental fricatives had vanished from
the phonemic inventory.

Since *St. Alexis* was written, marking of gender and number on
arrhizotonic past participles has withered and decayed in speech. Already in
Old French times, final [ə] in e.g. fem.sg. past participles was elided before a
word starting with a vowel. By the late fifteenth or early sixteenth century,
pluralizing final [s] had largely disappeared except before a pause, and so had
final [ə] except as a support vowel. Compensatory lengthening of the now-
final stressed vowel in fem. past participles meant that speakers still
differentiated them from masc. forms with a short final vowel, as in *allé* [ale]
but *allée* [ale:] 'gone,' *fini* [fini] but *finie* [fini:] 'ended,' *bu* [by] but *bue* [by:]
'drunk.' During the nineteenth century, compensatory lengthening ceased to
operate in standard French (Pope, 117–18, 205–6, 219–21; Rickard, 69).

Earlier distinctions of gender and number are still made on paper today. In
speech, each vowel-final past participle has a single form for masculine and
feminine, singular and plural. Marking on 1st-conj. forms like *chanté(e)(s)*
'sung' may be traced by century across the rough-hewn table following.

According to Table 4–6, arrhizotonic past participles—which from the start
have constituted a large majority of all past participles—kept four separate
forms into the High Middle Ages, and potentially, e.g. before a pause, as late
as Ronsard's day in the sixteenth century. A two-way distinction, of gender
but not of number, would still have been made by Voltaire and Rousseau two
hundred years later, and no doubt by Balzac and Vigny in the early
nineteenth century. Throughout, leveling has moved toward the most
radically clipped form among the four, which now serves for all.[37]
Isomorphism has thus been attained for arrhizotonic past participles.

---

[37] Phonemic distinctions of vowel length persist in regional varieties of French. Speakers in
Normandy, for example, distinguish between masc. *couché* [kuʃe] and fem. *couchée* [kuʃe:]
'lain.' Speakers in the Haute-Marne, part of the old province of Champagne, make a similar
distinction (Hawkins, 62). In standard French, only ninety-nine of the 8,000 verbs listed in
Bescherelle's *Art de conjurguer* have past participles with an audible distinction according to
gender. "Ce faible pourcentage explique la précarité des règles d'accord du participe" (*Grand
Larousse*, 4017) [This low proportion, 1.25%, explains why the rules for past-participial
agreement are so precarious].

Table 4–6

Erosion of Gender and Number Marking

on French Past Participles

| | C E N T U R Y | | | | | | | |
	1st	5th?	7th?	9th?	11th	13th	16th	18th	20th
m.sg	[aːtʊ(m)]	[ato]	[adə]	[aɛðᵊ]	[eθ]	[e]	[e]	[e]	[e]
f.sg	[aːta(m)]	[ata]	[ada]	[aɛða]	[eðə]	[eə]	[eː]	[eː]	[e]
m.pl	[aːtoːs]	[atos]	[adəs]	[aɛðᵊs]	[ets]	[es]	[e(s)]	[e]	[e]
f.pl	[aːtaːs]	[atas]	[adas]	[aɛðas]	[eðəs]	[eəs]	[e(s)]	[eː]	[e]

To trace reduction in gender and number marking for the two other types of regular past participles, one need merely replace 1st-conj. tonic [aː] later [e] with tonic [uː] later [y] for 2nd-/3rd-conj. reflexes like *battu(e)(s)* 'beaten,' or with tonic [iː] later [i] for 4th-conj. reflexes like *servi(e)(s)* 'served.'

Today, the minority of past participles from rhizotonics in -SUM and -TUM still make some distinctions by gender. However, the silencing of most final consonants that started in Old French not only made their singular and plural forms sound alike but also resulted in a partial merger of once distinct morphological classes. Today, just like regular 4th-conjugation past participles, masculine sigmatic and tautic athematic past participles no longer contrast in speech either: vowel-final sg./pl. *mis* [mi] 'put' has come to rhyme with vowel-final sg. *dit* or pl. *dits* [di] 'said, told.' For those verbs' feminine past participles, retention of consonants once internal but now final still allows a contrast in speech between e.g. *mise(s)* [miz] and *dite(s)* [dit], at least in formal registers.

In informal registers, such past participles often display no audible marking for gender and probably have not for some time, at least in relative clauses when several words separate them from their antecedents.[38] Thus, the phrase written *les lettres que j'ai écrites* 'the letters I wrote' may be informally pronounced [lelɛt(rə)k(ə)ʒeekri], with no final [t] sounded; the phrase written *les choses que tu as prises* 'the things you took' may be informally

---

[38] As Kibler remarks (274–75), OFr. past participles used with *avoir* tended to agree with direct objects appearing either before or after them. Nonetheless, past participles used with either *avoir* or *estre* might not agree where one would expect them to, or they might agree where one would expect them not to. Instability in agreement marking dates back a long time.

pronounced [leʃozk(ə)t(y)apri], with no final [z] sounded. When such past participles directly follow a fem. noun, audible agreement still normally takes place: *les choses prises* [priz], *les choses dites* [dit]. Still, past participles like *dit* 'said, told' and *écrit* 'written,' *pris* 'taken' and *mis* 'put,' are coming to be treated as if they were regular 4th-conj. forms like *servi* 'served,' long invariable in speech.

In their most recent leveling of morphological distinctions, speakers of French are tending to make old rhizotonics as invariable for gender as arrhizotonics have already become for both gender and number. In that respect, they have moved further toward isomorphism than have speakers of any other Romance language.

In addition, speakers of popular French have simplified their choice of perfect auxiliaries by using *avoir* 'have' in all such (active) constructions, both for the twenty or so "verbs of motion" that are supposed to take *être* 'be' and for reflexive verbs. One therefore hears sentences like *il a tombé* for std. *il est tombé* 'he fell' and *je m'ai mis à genoux* for std. *je me suis mis à genoux* 'I knelt' (George, 167). In having ceased to differentiate between *avoir* and *être* as perfect active auxiliaries, speakers of demotic French resemble their Spanish and Portuguese cousins, except that even the Académies of central-western Iberia no longer decree any such distinction.

4.4.13. Dialects of French

As already noted in note 37 to this chapter, certain dialects of French have retained a morphological contrast between masculine and feminine in p.p. endings. Here I leave the Ile-de-France to examine conservative and innovative features in Norman to the west, Picard to the north, and Burgundian to the east. Spelling has been slightly altered, so that past participles should be read (as far as possible) as if they were standard French; e.g., y = [j] not [y], i̱ = [ʒ] not [j]. Colons mark vowel length.

4.4.13.1. Norman

Data in the first part of this section come from Lepelley's *Le parler norman du Val de Saire* in the départem en t of La Manche (capital Saint-Lô). Speakers of this dialect express gender contrasts in past participles not only by the length of final vowels but also, for most 1st-conj. verbs, by the height of final vowels. Here the short form is used for masculine singular, the long form for masculine plural and feminine singular and plural. Thus, infinitive *akató* 'buy' has an identical masc.sg. p.p. *akató* ending in short [o] from -ĀTU, and a distinctive one for fem.sg./pl. and masc.pl. *akatá:* ending in [a:] from -ĀTA (cf. Fr. *acheté*). Others of the same type are *froumó* and *froumá:* 'shut,' *jostó* and *jostá:* 'jested, joked.'

Val de Saire has two other types of 1st-conj. verbs, both with palatal raising of the tonic vowel; not only [j] but also [ɥ] (spelled ẅ) has had that effect.

Within the past participle, distinctions of gender are made solely by length in those two types. In what could be called long-distance palatalization, the first type opposes masc.sg. in [e] to fem.sg./pl. and masc.pl. in [e:], giving e.g. *nyé* and *nyé:* 'drowned' from a variant of NOCIT- 'harmed,' or *twë* and *twë:* 'killed' from TŪTĀT- 'safeguarded,' and (homonymous with a vulgar verb in standard French) *chié* and *chié:* 'waxed' from *CERĀT-. Palatalization has created others of that type in [e], like *apyé* 'leaned on, supported' from AD + *PODIĀTU, *rwë* 'thrown stones' from *RŪTĀTU 'rushed, tumbled, crumbled,' *kriyé* 'shouted' from QUIRĪTĀTU 'shrieked, screamed,' and perfectly regular *jwé* 'played' from JOCĀTU 'joked.' No long-form variants of these four past participles are given by Lepelley.

The second type of palatalized 1st-conj. verb has been triggered by the sequence [ai̯] plus originally final [s] or [a], which according to Lepelley has given [ji]. In the past participle, masc.sg. in [ji] contrasts with fem.sg./pl. and masc.pl. in [ji:], giving e.g. *vœdyi* as against *vœdyi:* 'emptied' from variants of VIDUĀT- 'deprived of' (cf. OFr. *vuidié*, ModFr. *vidé*), and metaplasmatic *majyi* as against *majyi:* 'eaten' from MANDUCĀT- 'chewed' replacing CL MANSU with short [a] (cf. Fr. *mangé*).

For other verb classes as well, variation by gender and number involves vowel length alone. Most 2nd-/3rd-conj. verbs have past participles in [y], giving pairs like *pounu* and *pounu:* 'laid eggs,' *vlu* and *vlu:* 'wanted.' The p.p. *répounu* 'answered' evidently falls into this class as well, but no long form of it is given by Lepelley. Apparently, where pretonic [ə] survived for a time before [y], the two blended into [œ], as in *b œ* and *bœ:* 'drunk,' *v œ* and *vœ:* 'seen' (cf. OFr. *beü, veü*).

Resembling the second type of palatalized 1st-conj. verbs are reflexes of regular 4th-conj. past participles, which display contrasts like *bwogli* and *bwogli:* 'boiled,' *fglœi* and *fglœi:* 'bloomed' (cf. std. Fr. *bouilli, fleuri*). The p.p.s *vi* 'lived' and *rvi* 'brought back to life' may also fall into this class, but no long forms are given by Lepelley; those two have joined the 4th conjugation.

A handful of rhizotonics have been gathered. In two of them marked by [kt] in Latin, the pattern of morphological variation differs from that of other past participles. A vowel-final masc. sg./pl. form contrasts with a consonant-final fem. sg./pl. form to give *fé* and *fet* 'done/made,' *di* and *dit* 'said, told.' Two have evidently been modeled on preterits to give *prain:* 'taken' and *tain:* 'held, had' (cf. the OFr. by-form prets. *prins* and *tins*). By analogy with those two, nasal-infixed *main:s* 'put' ≠ MISSU 'sent' has emerged.

Most past participles ending in [ẽ] <u>ain</u> or [œ̃] <u>un</u> remain invariable because most are used only with conjugated forms of *avo* 'have.' They include *dormain* 'slept,' *vnun* 'come' and *dévnun* 'become,' *tnun* 'held, had' and *rténun* 'kept, held back.'

Among the morphological curios in Val de Saire are four past participles with the same ending, an ending found nowhere else in ROMANIA. These are *lẅu ẅəzu* 'read,' *nẅu ẅəzu* 'harmed,' *sẅu ẅəzu* 'followed,' and *tchẅu ẅəzu* 'cooked' (Lepelley, 120–24). If they chose, locals could use any of them as a shibboleth to detect outsiders. Conceivably, that -*ẅu ẅəzu* ending arose from a blend of the -ŪTU type, the -CTU type, and the -SU type, but that conception remains guesswork at best.

To the south and east of Val de Saire, a less innovative Norman dialect is spoken around Perche in Orne (capital Alençon). Since Did'huit, Morain, and Simoni-Aurembou use standard French spelling in *Trésor du parler percheron*, one has trouble knowing whether speakers make distinctions of vowel length.

Among the few past participles gathered, those for three verbs have by-forms. Either masc. *iu*, fem. *iue* or masc. *aïu*, fem. *aïue* may be used for p.p.s meaning 'had'; either *pond* or *ponu* may be used for p.p.s meaning 'laid eggs'; either *répond* or *réponu* may be used in the sense 'answered.' Two forms look as if they came from mediæval times: *sentu* and *sentue* 'felt,' *tint* and *tinte* 'held, had.' Now standard-looking *venu* is apparently the local p.p. meaning 'come,' but prefixed *prévint* 'warned, informed' clashes morphologically with the simplex. Although *vu* is apparently the local p.p. meaning 'seen,' it has developed a sigmatic feminine form *vuse*; although *chu* is definitely the local p.p. meaning 'fallen,' it has inherited a tautic athematic feminine form *chute*. P.p. *coudu* 'sewn' as against std. *cousu* shows the spread of [d] across one paradigm, but p.p. *éclous* 'hatched' from *EXCLAUSU for EXCLŪSU 'shut out' resembles std. Fr. *éclos* 'hatched' in remaining sigmatic. Two tautic athematics have been arrhizotonically remade in *atteindu(e)* 'reached, attained' and *éteindu(e)* 'put out (fire)' as against std. Fr. *atteint* and *éteint*. At least *été* 'been' looks familiar (Did'huit, Morain, and Simoni-Aurembou, 206–9).

According to Liddicoat's *Grammar of the Norman French of the Channel Islands*, infinitives and past participles have fallen together in the 1st and 4th conjugations. Therefore, *donnè* 'given' or 'to give' and *dormi* 'slept' or 'to sleep' do double duty, but infin. *vãndr* 'sell' remains distinct from p.p. *vãdy* 'sold.' I cannot do justice here to Liddicoat's precise transcriptions and so have spelled Nor.CI words much as I trust they would appear in standard French.

Most past participles ending in a tonic vowel show a two-way morphological distinction, the masc.sg. having a short vowel and the fem.sg./pl.–masc.pl. having a lengthened vowel. Instances from the three great Nor.CI arrhizotonic conjugations are 1st-conj. masc.sg. *donnè* with fem.sg./pl.–masc.pl. *donnè:* 'given,' 2nd-/3rd-conj. masc.sg. *vnu* with fem.sg./pl.–masc.pl. *vnu:* 'come' (infin. *vnẽ*), and 4th-conj. masc.sg. *dormi* with fem.sg./pl.–masc.pl. *dòrmi:* 'slept.'

Among reflexes of rhizotonics, Liddicoat gives a few sigmatics and a few tautic athematics.

Tautic athematics meaning 'done/made' and 'said, told' show a three-way distinction in the Norman French of the Channel Islands. Shortest are the masc.sg. forms, with *fè, di*, the fem.sg./pl. has final [t] to give *fèt, dit*, while the masc.pl. has vowel lengthening without -t̲ to give *fè:, di:*.

Sigmatic past participles meaning 'put,' 'taken,' and 'held' likewise show a three-way distinction in the Channel Islands. Shortest are the masc.sg. forms, with *m ẽ, prẽ, tẽ*, the fem.sg./pl. adds final [s] to give *m ẽs, prẽs, tẽs*, while the masc.pl. has vowel lengthening without -s̲ to give *m ẽ:, prẽ:, tẽ:* (Liddicoat,

143–51). No doubt nasality has come into the first of these by way of the two etymologically entitled to such marking. Meanwhile, the corresponding infinitives have stayed sharply distinct from one another: *mètr* 'put,' *prãdr* 'take,' and *tnẽ* 'hold.'

4.4.13.2. Picard

In gathering past participles from Picardy, I have drawn upon three works: Eloy's *Constitution du picard* covers the dialect of Guignemicourt near Amiens (Somme), Lesbegue's *Grammaire picard-brayonne* presumably covers the dialect of Bray-sur-Somme (Somme), and Trabelsi-Louguet's *Lexique de l'avenois* covers the dialect of Avesnes-sur-Helpe (Nord).

In Guignemicourt (Ggn.), the five nonstandard past participles gathered are *prê* 'taken,' *seu* 'known,' *yeu* 'had,' *fwé* 'done/made,' and *défwé* 'undone/unmade.' Each of these however co-occurring with standard French forms, "La morphologie du participle ne permet donc pas de distinguer les deux idiomes" (Eloy, 164) [one cannot tell the two apart by p.p. morphology]. Data from two other locales undermine that assertion.

In the Brayon dialect (Pic.: Br.), a regular 1st-conj. past participles are *canté* 'sung' (infin. *canter*), and a regular 4th-conj. past participle is *fini* or *feni* 'ended' (infin. *finir*). Mixed types—with infinitives in -*ir* but past participles in -*u*—are *bouillu* 'boiled,' *couru* 'run,' *seintu* 'felt,' *vêtu* 'dressed, clothed' (infins. *bouillir, courir, seintir, vêtir*). The second and fourth of these are identical to their counterparts in standard French; the first and third were commonly encountered at earlier stages of the language.

High-frequency past participles include *yu* 'had' (infin. *aweir*). In an outcome reminiscent of the corresponding preterits in Spanish, *été* or *'té* means both 'been' and 'gone' (infins. *èt* 'be,' *aller* 'go').

Across Romance, forms have been regularized along infectum lines. Examples here are *coudu* 'sewn,' *plaindu* 'complained,' and *sui* 'followed' now match their 3rd-conj. infins. *coude, plainde*, and *suire* more closely than std. Fr. p.p.s *cousu, plaint, suivi* match std. infins. *coudre, plaindre, suivre*. Wavering between old and new are by-forms *moulu* or *moudu* 'ground' (infin. *moude*); standard French allows only *moulu*. Displaying infectum nasality is p.p. *prins* 'taken' (infin. *preinde*), versus the n-less std. Fr. p.p. *pris*.

Regrettably, Lesbegue gives no past participles for a number Brayon verbs. None is given for 1st-conj. *einweyer* 'send'; none for 2nd-conj. *mouweir* 'move,' *pouweir* 'be able,' *saweir* 'know,' *trouweir* 'find,' or *weir* 'see'; none for 3rd-conj. *bweire* 'drink,' *creire* 'believe,' or *faire* 'do/make'; none for 4th-conj. *assir* 'sit' (remade on the basis of its p.p.?), *tenir* 'hold,' or *venir* 'come.' Do the missing forms match ones out of Paris?

Hard by the Belgian frontier, the dialect of Avesnois (Pic.: Av.) resembles other versions of Picard because of an interchange of [(t)ʃ] ch- and [k] c- relative to standard French. Compare Av. *déquertché* and std. *déchargé* 'unloaded.' After certain palatal consonants, the tonic vowel in 1st-conj. infinitives often rises to -*i* or -*ie*, but past participles for verbs thus affected continue to end in -*é* not *-*i*. Examples are infins. *bougie* 'move,' by-form *débrouillie* 'get by, make out,' *rinvouyie* 'send back,' *réveilli* 'wake up,' but compare p.p.s *bougé, débrouillé, rinvouyé, réveillé.*

After [n], 3rd-conj. infinitives not only lose any trace of [r] but also, undergoing "reverse lenitiion," devoice [d] to [t]. Resulting infinitives are *intinte* or *intinde* 'understand,' *pyerte* 'lose, *réponte* or *réponde* 'answer,' and *rinte* 'give back.' If these [t]'s are word-final in speech, such devoicing may be traceable to Germanic influence. Corresponding regular 2nd-/3rdconj. past participles retain [d] in *intendu* 'heard,' *perdu* or *pyerdu* 'lost,' *répondu* 'answered,' *rindu* 'given back.'

Most past participles in Avesnois are graphically identical to their counterparts in standard French. They are Av. *appris* 'learned,' *assis* 'sat,' *compris* 'understood,' *connu* 'known,' *couru* 'run,' *cuit* 'cooked,' *dit* 'said, told,' *écrit* 'written,' *fait* 'done/made,' *lu* 'read,' *ouvert* 'opened,' *pu* 'been able,' *pris* 'taken,' *ri* 'laughed,' *souffert* 'suffered,' *su* 'known,' *trait* 'milked,' and *vu* 'seen.' Others come in pairs of one variant by-form and one standard-looking by-form: *freumé* or *fermé* 'shut,' *mourt* or *mort* 'died,' *twé* or *tué* 'killed,' *v'nu* or *venu* 'come,' and *volu* or *voulu* 'wanted.' Several also have by-form infinitives. I deal with them no further.

More twin past participles are *allé* or *dallé* 'gone,' *acaté* or standard-influenced *ach'té* 'bought,' *candjé* or standard-influenced *chingé* 'changed,' *caché* or standard-looking *cherché* 'looked for,' and *comminché* or standard-influenced *commincé* 'begun.'

A number of Avesnois verbs have triplet past participles. That holds true for the most common verb of all, with *ésté* or *sté* or standard-looking *été* 'been' (triplet infin. *être, ête,* or *yête*). It holds true for the second most common, with *yeu, yu,* and standard-looking *eu* 'had' (twin infin. *awè* or *avoir*). Another past participle with triplet by-forms is *carryé* or *quertché* or standard-influenced *chargé* 'loaded' (infins. *canger* or standard-looking *changer*). Yet another is *mindgi*, standard-looking *mangé*, or the true oddity *mié* 'eaten' (infin. *mingi* or standard-looking *manger*). There are frankly too many of these to list. That item *mié* 'eaten' looks almost like a borrowing from Spanish *meado* 'pissed,' but a semantic shift from bottom to top of the tract sounds improbable at best.

A handful of Avesnois verbs have quadruplet past participles. That holds true for locally evolving *couqué* and *couchi*, and standard-influenced *couché* and *coutché* 'lain' (infin. *cou[t]chie* or *coucher*). It holds true for *déquindu* or *désquindu*, standard-influenced *déscindu*, and semi-influenced *désquindu* 'gone down' (quadruplet infins. *déquinde, déquinte, déscinde, désquinte*).

Partial regularization has been achieved in the Av. by-form *déféyé* 'undone' alongside standard-looking *défait* (infin. *défaire*); the simplex has so far remained unaffected. Another regularization seems to be the Av. by-form *vi* 'lived' alongside standard-looking *vécu* (infin. *vive*). A new irregularity has arisen in by form *osu* alongside *osé* 'dared'; though no infinitive is given here, cognates everywhere else belong to the 1st conjugation. While in standard French the p.p. *chu* 'fallen' survives only with prefixoids, Avesnois keeps the unprefixed verb alive by having both p.p. *queillu* 'fallen (no infinitive given) and p.p. *tcheu* 'fallen' (infin. *tchéyi*). Moreover, in the p.p. pair *plu* 'pleased' and *pleu* 'rained' (standard-looking infins. *plaire, pleuvoir*), Avesnois has evolved a distinction yet unknown in standard French. A true oddity is the Av. by-form p.p. *léyé* 'let,' next to standard-looking *laissé* (infin. *laissie* or *léyi*). A singleton oddity is Av. *creu* 'believed' (infin. *coire* or *croire*), where [y] has apparently lowered to [ø] as it has in several forms cited above.

Exemplified as usual by their past participles, verbs unknown under the French Academy's standard include Av. *chuché* 'drunk,' *muché* 'hidden,' *ravisé* 'looked at,' *squinté* 'ruined, wrecked,' and *squété* or *desqueté* 'broken.'

4.4.13.3. Burgundian

Data in this section come from Rouffiange's *Le patois et le français rural de Magny-lès-Aubigny*. Spoken in Côte d'Or (capital Dijon), that dialect of Burgundian has the same kind of morphological contrast between masculine and feminine past participles as that encountered in Val de Saire. Only in the 1st conjugation does the masculine have a lower and a shorter vowel, the feminine a higher and longer one. Examples are the 1st-conj. masculine/feminine pairs *ain:mè* and *ain:mè:* 'loved, liked,' *pòtè* and *pòtè:* 'carried.' Perhaps *rvi:rè* 'returned' and *di:gnè* 'dined, eaten' have a similar contrast, but Rouffiange lists only the low-and-short variant for those two.

In the other arrhizotonic conjugations, the distinction is strictly one of vowel length. Verbs in the 2nd and 3rd conjugations have masc./fem. pairs of past participles like *èvu* and *èvu:* 'had,' *sœ:gu* and *sœ:gu:* 'followed' < SECŪTU, *vnu* and *vnu:* 'come,' *vu* and *vu:* 'seen.' Perhaps *chu* 'fallen,' *fyu* 'been required,' *pœ:vu* 'been able,' *sèvu* 'known,' and *vyu* 'wanted' have a similar contrast, but Rouffiange lists only the short variant. Others receiving the same treatment are *bœvu* 'drunk,' *bouyu* 'boiled,' *koudu* 'sewn,' *kouru* 'run,' *mouyu* 'ground' (perhaps ± *bouyu*), and standard-looking *pondu* 'laid eggs,' which was *ponnu* locally in the sixteenth century. Also remade along standard lines have been *tòdu* 'twisted' ≠ TORTU and *mòdu* 'bitten' ≠ MORSU, which likewise have no long variants cited.

The few 4th-conj. examples given—*drœmi* 'slept,' *fni* 'ended,' *œ:vri* 'opened,' and *tœ:si* 'coughed' (cf. OFr. *toussi*)—are all short forms, so that a length distinction may have ceased to operate in that conjugation. Regularized *œ:vri* does not directly continue APERTU; unlike Norman *bwogli*, Burg. *bouyu* has changed class from BULLĪTU 'bubbled.' Again, *étè* looks familiar, but speakers use it to mean either 'been' or 'had.'

In rhizotonic past participles, the picture looks more complicated. Vowel length sometimes distinguishes masculine from feminine forms; they are most often distinguished by a final consonant retained in the feminine but dropped in the masculine. Past-participial pairs with only the consonantal opposition are *mo* and *mot* 'died; dead,' *di* and *dit* 'said, told'; the p.p. *li* 'read' (only the short form is given) may have arisen ± *di*, though cf. OFr. by-form *lit*. Past-participial pairs with both consonantal and vocalic opposition are sigmatic *pri* and *pri:z* 'taken,' tautic athematic *kœt* and *kœ:t* 'cooked,' and *étwain* and *étwain:t* 'put out (fire).' No feminine form is given for *ékou* 'threshed' < EXCŪSU 'beaten out.' In a class by themselves are *kœ:yè* 'gathered' < COLLĒCTU and *lwè* 'tied, bound' ≠ LIGĀTU, for each of which only a short-vowel form is supplied.

Speakers around Magny-lès-Aubigny preserve as nouns at least two old rhizotonic past participles. First, *bwèt* 'a supply of drink' comes down from LL BIBITA 'drunk' and is reminiscent of OFr. *boite* 'a drink,' itself pronounced [bwɛtə] at one stage. Second, *mè:* 'piece of land, often an orchard by a house' comes down from MĀNSU 'stayed'; compare Cat./Oc. *mas*, OFr. *mes₂* 'farm, farmhouse' (Rouffiange, 184–201).

4.5. EVIDENCE FROM FRANCO-PROVENÇAL

Constituting a "zone of linguistic transition," Franco-Provençal (FP) shares some morphological features with French, some with Occitan, some with Italian.

In lexis, Franco-Provençal still keeps *partir* in the meaning 'share' rather than the French sense 'leave.' A semantic innovations is *braire*—meaning 'bray' in standard French—used in the sense 'cry, weep,' thus perhaps illustrating a proclivity among peasants to anthropomorphize their livestock. A syntactic innovation is *dire* 'say, tell' used transitively like *parler* 'talk, speak' in standard French (Battye and Hintze, 303, 308). Among reflexes of FUTUERE 'fuck,' on the Swiss side of the border *fotre* < FUTUERE has come to mean 'put,' while on the French side *fota* or *fotre* has come to mean 'throw.' Both these semantic shifts are mirrored in colloquial French. Unlike nearly all past participles in standard French, invariable in speech, varieties of Franco-Provençal hypercharacterize gender marking.

Four FP dialects are covered here: Naisey in France, Vaux and Vaud in Switzerland, and Val d'Aosta in Italy.

4.5.1. Naisey

Spoken in part of Doubs (capital Besançon), in the old province of Franche-Comté, the Naisey dialect lies at the far northern end of the Franco-Provençal triangle. With its speakers living less than 100 miles from Magny-lès-Aubigny (see §4.4.13.3), the Naisey dialect appears to qualify as a transition dialect between Burgundian French and Franco-Provençal. Data come from Alex's *Le patois de Naisey*.

In Naisey, morphological distinctions of gender are made not only by vowel length but also by vowel height: masculine past participles have a shorter and lower final vowel than do the corresponding feminines. However, 1st-conj. past participles do not vary, so that forms like *chan:tá:* 'sung' or *èstá:* 'sat' (infins. *chan:tá:, s èstá:*) serve for both genders as well as for the infinitive.

For 2nd-/3rd-conjugation past participles as for 4th-conjugation ones, alternations by vowel length and height may be seen between masculine and feminine forms, both of which differ morphologically from their infinitives. One may observe the patterns in *bètù* and *bètú:* 'beaten,' *épon:dù* and *épon:dú:* 'joined,' *ètandù* and *ètandú:* 'waited,' *fon:dù* and *fon:dú:* 'melted,' *kungù* and *kungú:* 'known,' and *kùzù* and *kùzú:* 'sewn.' As listed in Alex (98–115), the 2nd-conj. p.p.s *pyù* 'been able,' *sèvù* 'known,' and *vèyù* 'been worth' (infins. *pyœ, sèvwè, vèyè*) have no long-vowel variants. Neither do the 3rd-conj. p.p.s *bù* 'drunk,' *chù* 'fallen,' *krèyù* 'believed,' *mudyù* 'bitten,' *tudyù* 'twisted,' or *v ù* 'seen' (infins. *bwèr, cho:r, krèr, mo:dyr, to:dyr, vo:r*). Some at least could have long-vowel forms, for most seem to be useable transitively. For 4th-conj. past participles, similar alternations of length and height between masculine and feminine occur in *finì* versus *finí:* 'ended,' *tnì* versus *tní:* 'held, had,' and *vnì* versus *vní:* 'come.'

As listed, the 4th-conj. p.p. *rsì* 'received' (infin. *rsìr*) also appears invariable but could have specifically feminine forms. So could *dì* 'said, told' (infin. *dir*). Yet hyperconservative *lé:* 'read' < LĒCTU (infin. *lé:r*) seems to have only a long-vowel form. Could compensatory lengthening still be in effect?

Among reflexes of rhizotonic past participles, sigmatics are scarce in Naisey. Only two are listed by Alex, and their morphology is dissimilar. Perhaps influenced by standard French, vowel-final masc. *prì* contrasts with fem. *prìz* 'taken' (infin. *pan:r* < **pra:r* by dissimilation). Again, masc. *èku* contrasts with sigmatic fem. *èkus* 'threshed' (infin. *èkur*).

Like sigmatics, reflexes of tautic athematics oppose a vowel-final masculine form to a consonant-final feminine one. Contrasts exist between masc. *sœ:* and fem. *sœ:t* 'followed' (infin. *sœ:r* from **SEQUERE*), between *kon:dù* and *kon:dùt* 'driven' (infin. *kon:dùr*), between *mœyè:* and *mœyè:t* 'ground' (infin. *mœ:r*), and between *fá:* and *fá:t* 'done/made' (infin. *fè:r*). These forms display no distinctions by length or height.

Around Naisey, speakers have blended reflexes of COQUERE 'cook' with those of COLLIGERE 'gather': the resulting infin. *kyœ:r* and its p.p.s—masc. *kyœ:* and fem. *kyœ:t*—are used in both senses. Moreover, in a blending similar to that seen in Burg. *étè* 'been; had,' Nais. *èvù* from **HABUTU* serves as the past participle for both *é:tr* 'be' and *èvwè* 'have.' In past tenses, forms of the verb *alá:* or *òlá:* 'go' (p.p. *alá:* or *òlá:*) are often replaced by forms of *é:tr* 'be,' as in standard seventeenth-century French *nous fûmes hier à Versailles* 'yesterday we were at Versailles' (Alex, 115).

4.5.2. Vaux

In Franco-Provençal as spoken in what Iliescu and Mourin call Vaux in France—presumably Pont de Vaux in Ain (capital Bourg)—regular masc.sg. past participles end in *-a* for 1st-conj. verbs, in *-u* for 2nd- and 3rd-conj. verbs, and in *-i* for 4th-conj. verbs. Verbs in both the 1st conjugation and the 4th have the same form for infinitives as for masculine past participles. In the 1st conjugation, fem.sg. past participles end in *-a*, like masc. ones; in the 2nd and

3rd conjugations, feminines end in -*ya*; in the 4th conjugation, feminines end in -*wa*. Vaux FP has thus attained gender parity for past participles assigned to the largest class of verbs, while hypercharacterizing gender differences for the other two arrhizotonic classes.

Certain differences in gender marking have arisen because a final consonant lost in masc. forms has been kept in fem. ones that also keep final -*a*. Alternations may take place between zero and [z]: masc. *mai* contrasts with fem. *maiza* 'put,' masc. *prai* with fem. *praiza* 'taken.' More often, alternations take place between zero and [t]: masc. *adẅi* and fem. *adẅita* 'driven,' masc. *ekri* and fem. *ekrita* 'written,' masc. *kwe* and fem. *kweta* 'cooked,' masc. *nẅe* and fem. *nẅeta* 'harmed,' masc. *pye* and fem. *pyeta* 'pleased,' masc. *tre* and fem. *treta* 'milked.'

Feminines are conservative consonantally but not always vocalically. Sometimes a tonic vowel in masc. p.p.s is reduced to an on-glide before [a] in fem. p.p.s. Thus, masc. *paru* contrasts with fem. *parẅa* 'appeared' (infin. *paraitre*), or again masc. *kru* contrasts with fem. *krẅa* 'believed' (infin. *kraire*). Speakers have thus kept gender marking at the expense of isomorphism.

For other past participles, along with consonantal differentiation between genders, a tonic vowel has diphthongized in the feminine but not in the masculine. Thus, masc. *mor* 'died' contrasts with fem. *muarta*, and masc. *etyua* 'hatched, blossomed' with fem. *etyossa*. Likewise, masc. *eku* 'threshed' and *sku* 'beaten trees [to make fruit fall]' contrast with fem. *ekuosa* and *skuosa*.[39] In masc. *fni* as against fem. *fña* 'ended,' the feminine shows nasalization absent in the masculine, but in masc. *koñu*, fem. *kon(ẅ)a* 'known' (infin. *koñaitre*) it works the other way around. In masc. *di* 'said, told' as against fem. *deta* (infin. *dere*), the tonic vowels have come to differ; the vowel in the feminine past participle might have developed straight from DICTA or by analogy with the infinitive, while the vowel in the masculine form has no doubt been inspired by preterits from DĪXĪ 'said, told.'

Meanwhile, fem. *byeva* 'drunk' differs from masc. *byu* both in its tonic vowel and in the consonant following it, but here the infinitive *baire* supplies no inspiration for such a shift. Finally, as in French and Italian, irregularities in stressed vowels occur for some verbs between infinitive and past participle: cf. infin. *teñi* 'hold' and p.p.s *teñu*, *teña* as well as infin. *veñi* 'come' and p.p.s *veñu*, *veña* (Iliescu and Mourin, 407–9).

By contrast with the variety in p.p. types, there is basically one set of preterit endings in Vaux. This set seems to have been generalized from those for third-person 4th-conj. verbs. Almost all singular preterits end in -*í*, and almost all plural preterits in -*iará*; one class contains an originally inchoative infix -*ais*-. Thus, a typical 1st-conj. reflex would be sg. *sáti* and pl. *sátiará* 'sang'; an example of the minority type would be sg. *f(e)naisí* and pl. *f(e)naisíará* 'ended.' Several high-frequency singular preterits are composed of a single-

---

[39] Speakers seem to have drawn a morphological as well as a semantic distinction between two by-forms of EXCUSSU 'knocked out, knocked away.'

consonant root, sometimes plus a semivowel, before the ending: *ví* 'saw,' *rí* 'laughed,' *pwí* 'could,' *dyí* 'said, told,' and *fí* 'did/made.'

A handful of high-frequency verbs in Vaux display greater morphological variation in preterit plurals: nasalized endings contrast with unnasalized ones. Thus, sg. *tê* 'held' and *vê* 'came' are set off not only from 1pl. and 3pl. *teñíarã, veñíarã* but also from unnasalized 2pl. *teñíara̧, veñíara̧*. Likewise, sg. *fu* 'was,' *su* 'knew,' and *u* 'had' are set off not only from 1pl. and 3pl. *fuarã, suarã, uarã* but also from unnasalized 2pl. *fuara̧, suara̧*, and *uara̧* (Iliescu and Mourin, 330–32). How did Vaux speakers come up with such a system?

4.5.3. Vaud

The third variety of Franco-Provençal, also termed Romand, comes from the Swiss canton of Vaud (capital Lausanne). Arrhizotonic masc.sg. past participles have the same -*a*, -*u*, or -*i* endings as those in Vaux, but regular fem.sg. past participles differ slightly: 1st-conj. p.p.s end in -*a̧ie*, those for all other classes in -*yá*. Thus, no consonant usually appears in the endings for regular past participles in the singular. One oddity is the p.p. *risu* 'laughed' from *RĪSŪTU, which—after apocope of its final vowel and the preceding consonant—has almost reassumed the shape of CL RĪSU.

As in Vaux and in formal registers of French, rhizotonic feminine past participles retain consonants that vanish word-finally in masculine forms. Such alternations most often involve the presence or absence of [s], as in fem. *messa* as against masc. *mè* 'put' (infin. *mettre*), fem. *chèssa* as against masc. *chè* 'shut' (infin. *cllioûre*), or fem. *fièssa* as against masc. *fiè* 'hit' (infin. *fière*). This type has become especially frequent for local sigmatic variants of past participles with endings from -ŪTU. Examples are fem. *bussa* as against masc. *bu* 'drunk' (infin. *bâire*), fem. *cognussa* as against masc. *cognu* 'known' (infin. *cougnàitre*), fem. *dussa* as against masc. *du* 'ought to' (infin. *dèvai*), fem. *parussa* as against masc. *paru* 'appeared' (infin. *parâitre*), and the fem. by-form *yussa* as against masc. *yu* 'gone' (infin. *allâ*).

Also occurring in p.p.s with endings from -ŪTU is a second local p.p. peculiarity in Vaud. Short past participles with such variation are fem. *suva* 'known,' *cruva* 'believed,' and *uva* 'had' as against masc. *su, cru, u* (infins. *savâi, crâire, avâi*). Longer ones are fem. *mosuva* 'moved,' *càosuva* 'sewn,' *coosuva* 'cooked,' *reçuva* 'received,' *apeçuva* 'perceived' as against masc. *mosu, càosu, coosu, reçu, apeçu* (two infins. *reçâidre, apèçaidre*); some of these have also acquired unetymological sigmatic marking. Still others are fem. *crûva* as against masc. *crû* 'grown' and fem. *viva* as against masc. *vi* 'lived.'

Even the past participle meaning 'gone' ≠ ĬTU has a fem. by-form *yuva* or *uva*. Since the latter form also serves as a by-form past participle for *être* 'be,' fem. *uva* may mean 'been,' 'had,' or 'gone.' Speakers are free to substitute *età̂*, which means only 'been,' or *allâ*, which means only 'gone,' where ambiguity would otherwise exist. Unsurprisingly, they seem to have evolved no substitute for *uva* 'had.'

At times, a diphthong may simplify word-finally but remain medially, thereby heightening gender differences between past participles. Compare fem. sigmatic *prâissa* 'taken' with masc. *prâ(i)*. More striking differences appear when masculines undergo compensatory lengthening attributable to a vanished final consonant: cf. fem. *tossa* and masc. *too* (infin. *toodre* 'twist'?), fem. *morta* and masc. *m o o* 'died' (infin. *mourî*).

Further alternations may involve [t] or its absence. This feature occurs in e.g. fem. *nourrâte* as against masc. *nourrâ* 'fed' (infin. *nourrî*), and in fem. *punîte* as against masc. *puni* 'punished' (infin. *punî*), fem. *ècrite* as against masc. *ècri* 'written' (infin. *ècrire*), and of course fem. *féte* as against masc. *fé* 'done/made' (infin. *fére*). In [nt] clusters, the masculine retains at least the nasal consonant, giving e.g. fem. *crainta* as against masc. *crain* 'feared' (infin. *craindre*) and fem. *djeinta* as against masc. *djein* 'joined' (infin. *djeindre*). In [rt] clusters, judging by one p.p., the masculine may lose both consonants or neither, as in fem. *âoverta*, masc. *âové/âovert* 'opened' (infin. *âovrî*).

Past participles with irregular theme vowels include two found in French and Old Italian: *vetu* 'clothed' (infin. *vetî*) and by-form *vegnu* 'come' (infin. *venî*). Metaplasm may appear to have occurred in masc. *coulyâ* 'gathered' ≠ COLLĒCTU (infin. *coulyî*) and *salyâ* 'gone out' ≠ SALTU 'jumped' (infin. *salyî*), along with *tsesâ* 'fallen' ≠ CĀSU (infin. *tsesî*) and *corrâ* 'run' ≠ CURSU (infin. *corre*), all now looking like 1st-conj. past participles. However, the corresponding fem. forms *coulyâte*, *salyâte*, *tsesâte*, *corrâte* still contain [t], marking them as isolates in contemporary morphology.

In past participles like *parussa* 'appeared' or *suva* 'known,' an apparently suffixed [s] or [v] belongs to the root. In other past participles with endings from -ŪTU, [s] or [v] has been added after the theme vowel, presumably by analogy with forms in which it was etymological. Many sigmatic past participles, not counting etymological ones like *messa*< MISSA, resemble the rare imperfect subjunctives like *usso* 'had' and *fusso* 'was' as well as a few present subjunctives like by-form *dusso* 'ought to.'

Like Vaux Franco-Provençal across the border, Vaud has far less variation in preterits than in past participles, but for a different reason. Here the only verbs still having preterits are *avâi* 'have' with preterit stem *u-* and *ître* 'be' with preterit stem. *fu-*. The only slots to have preterit forms are 3sg. with a zero ending, 1pl. and 2pl. with a blended *-ra* ending, and 3pl. with a *-rant* ending (Iliescu and Mourin, 333, 410–13).

4.5.4. Val d'Aosta

For this dialect of Franco-Provençal, spoken in far northwestern Italy in Val d'Aosta (VA), data come from Chenal's *Franco-provençal valdotain*.

Like other dialects of Franco-Provençal, Val d'Aosta draws sharp morphological distinctions between masculine and feminine past participles. All masculine forms have become invariant by number, French-style; most if not all feminine forms mark number on final vowels, Italian-style. Often, rhizotonics follow the spoken French pattern whereby final consonants have vanished in the masculine but survive in the feminine.

Regular 1st-conj. past participles have lost number marking for both genders: they end in *-à* for masculines and *-àye* for feminines. Regular 2nd-/3rd-conj. past participles end in *-u* for masculines, *-uya* for fem.sg., and *-uye* for fem.pl. Regular 4th-conj. past participles end in *-i* for masculines, *-ia* for fem.sg., and *-ie* for fem.pl. Collating the 2nd-/3rd-conj. type and the 4th-conj. type, one infers that old fem.pl. 1st-conj. forms have invaded the territory of the old fem.sg. ending *-àya*.

The following arrhizotonic past participles are listed by masc.sg. From the 1st conjugation come *amà* 'loved,' *allà* 'gone,' and *ëtà* 'been' (infins. *amé, allé, ëté*). From the 2nd conjugation come *bu* 'drunk,' *cru* 'believed' and *incru* 'been scared of ghosts,' *du* 'owed, had to,' *miu* 'harvested, reaped,' and *vu* 'seen' (infins. *bèire, crèire* and *s'incèire, dèivre, miere, vère*). Clearly infectum-based are 2nd-conj. *possu* 'been able,' *savu* 'known,' *vallu* 'been worth,' and *volu* 'wanted' (infins. *possèi, savèi, vallèi, volèi*). From the 3rd conjugation come *chouyu* 'climbed,' *cognu* 'known,' *mouyu* 'moved,' *paru* 'appeared,' *reçu* 'received,' and *rendu* 'given back' (infins. *choure₁, cognètre, moure, parëtre, recèivre, rendre*). From the 4th conjugation, loss of post-tonic [t] and [r] having made past participles identical to infinitives, come *dormi* or *drumi* 'slept,' by-form *feni* 'ended,' and *parti* 'left' (infins. *dormi* or *drumi, fein, parti*).

Containing evidence of regularization along arrhizotonic lines is a series of morphologically related past participles for 3rd-conj. verbs: *crègnu* 'feared,' *dzoignu* 'joined,' *ëtrègnu* 'squeezed,' and *plèngnu* 'complained' (infins. *crendre, dzoindre, ëtrendre, plendre*). The second, third, and fourth of these hardly resemble CL JŪNCTU, STRICTU, and PLĀNCTU. With infinitive and past participle slightly divergent, owing to vocalization of [l] before [d], are the p.p.s *moulu* 'ground' and *resolvu* 'solved' (infins. *moudre, resoudre*).

Arrhizotonic anomalies, where past-participial class differs from infinitive class, would include p.p.s *impli* 'filled,' *chorti* or *sorti* 'gone out,' *couru* 'run,' *sentu* 'heard,' *tëgnu* 'held' as against the 2nd-conj. infin. *implere*, the 3rd-conj. infin. *chortre* or *sortre*, and the 4th-conj. infins. *couri, senti,* and *teni*. Probably in the same class is p.p. *venu* 'come,' for which Chenal gives no infinitive but which belongs to the 4th-conjugation everywhere else. In a class by itself, as one would expect from a perfectum-based arrhizotonic, is the Val d'Aosta p.p. *vécu* 'lived' (infin. *vivre*).

Tautic athematics may be split into three groups. In the first, the masculine ends in a vowel, thus looking like a regular 1st- or 4th-conj. form, but the fem.sg. ends in -ta: *écri* and *écrita* 'written,' *fri* and *frita* 'fried,' *llià* and *lliata* 'tied, bound,' *sui* and *suita* 'followed' (infins. *écrire, frire, lliére, suivre*). In the second group, the masculine ends in -t, the fem.sg. in -ta: *adzut* and *adzuta* 'brought,' *couét* and *couéta* 'cooked,' *étsut* and *étsuta* 'hatched, bloomed,' *redzut* and *redzuta* 'shut in,' *trét* and *tréta* 'removed,' and *tsouét* and *tsouéta* 'killed' (infins. *adzure, couére, étsure, redzure, trére, tsouére*). In the third group, the masculine ends in a vowel, the fem.sg. in -te: *condui* and *conduite* 'driven,' *deut* and *deute* 'said, told,' *fét* and *féte* 'done/made,' *foui* and *fouite* 'fled,' and *llioui* and *llouite* 'shone' (infins. *conduire, dère, fére, fouire, lliouire*). As with feminine 1st-conj. forms, the fem.pl. in this third group appears to have ousted an earlier, specifically fem.sg. form in *-a*. In the masculine, *fére* also has an allegro form p.p. *fé* 'done/made.'

Three verbs with infinitives in *-i* have past participles in *-ert* (masc.), *-erta* (fem.sg.), and *-erte* (fem.pl.). With masculine only shown here, these should occasion little surprise: *couvert* or *qeuvert* 'covered,' *ivert* or *uvert* 'opened,' and *ofert* 'offered' for infins. *couvri* or *qeuvri, ivri* or *uvri,* and *ofri.* Alongside these consonant-final forms should be ranked masc. *mor* and fem. *morta* 'died' (infin. *mouere*).

Like their cousins across western ROMANIA, speakers in Val d'Aosta have expanded reflexes of the old p.p. ending -ĒCTU. Reflexes have turned into masc.sg./pl. *-et*, fem.sg./pl. *-èite*, with the old fem.pl. again encroaching on the fem.sg. One past participle has an etymological entitlement to that ending: *coueillet* < COLLĒCTU 'gathered,' with fem.sg. *coueillèite* (infin. *coueilli*). All others have been rebuilt since Latin times: *alondzet* 'lengthened,' *creuvet* 'hidden,' *faillet* 'failed, lacked,' and *saillet* 'protruded' (infins. *alondzi, creuvi, failli, sailli*). No infinitive is given for p.p. *nevet* 'snowed.' This -ĒCTU type has spread all the way to a set of p.p. by-forms for infin. *feni* 'end,' namely masc. *fenet* and fem.sg. *fenèite* next to regular 4th-conj. members. A variant set of endings has fem.sg. *-etta*, as in *chouet* and *chouetta* 'sweated,' *pouet* and *pouetta* 'trimmed grape-vines' (infins. *chouere, pouere*). In generalizing that ending, Val d'Aosta has gone farther than Old French.

The VA verb *choure₂* 'result, turn out' has three p.p. by-forms. First comes expected 2nd-/3rd-conj. *chouyu* with fem.sg. *chouyuya.* Second comes another -ĒCTU-style pair, *chovet* with fem. *chovèite.* Third comes the only VA form to have acquired the [v] suffix seen in other dialects of Franco-Provençal, *chouvu* with fem.sg. *chouvuya* 'resulted, turned out.'

Contrasting with an old sigmatic in Latin, masc. *tset* and fem. *tsèite* 'fallen' have both shifted class from rare CĀSU (infin. *tseere*). These days, Val d'Aosta has one sigmatic, or half-sigmatic, remaining. For infin. *prendre,* only fem. past participles like sg. *prèisa* 'taken' bear the marker, masc. *prèi* having lost it in the same way as masc. *écri* 'written' has lost overtly tautic marking. Chenal lists no reflex of MISSU 'sent,' surviving elsewhere in Franco-Provençal in the sense 'put.'

Several sigmatics have adopted 2nd-/3rd-conj. arrhizotonic marking besides. Two doubly marked past participles are *nëssu* 'born' and *plésu* 'pleased' (infins. *nëtre, plére*). Six more are *caousu* 'sewn,' *cliousu* 'shut,' *crèissu* 'grown,' *dzeesu* 'lain,' *lliësu* 'read,' and *plousu* 'rained' (infins. *caoudre, cllioure, crèitre, dzeere, lliëre, ploure*). Of these, only CŌNSŪTU 'sewn' already belonged to that type in Latin, though [s] there made up part of the stem. An early version of *caousu* 'sewn' could have served as a model for reshaping all others (Chenal, 539–84).

Except for one high-frequency form derived from PREHĒNSU 'taken,' then, speakers in Val d'Aosta evidently came to consider [s] insufficient to stand by itself as a past-participial marker. Instead of discarding [s] in that function, as speakers of standard Spanish and Portuguese did, Valdotains kept [s] by suffixing it, as some speakers of Gallo-Italian did. Recall that, like other corpora unearthed here, this one may prove unrepresentative of its species because it highlights irregularities, especially for 2nd- and 3rd-conj. verbs.

I now move southwest from the Alps, to the rolling hills and lowlands of Occitania and Catalonia.

4.6. EVIDENCE FROM OCCITAN AND CATALAN

Occitan and Catalan, ranked as two separate languages, exhibit great similarities in past-participial formation. Most notably, they share a 2nd-/3rd-conj. suffix *-gut* found nowhere else in ROMANIA. Because of these similarities, especially that areal feature of morphology, I evaluate Occitan and Catalan together.

4.6.0. Preliminaries

Easily reachable from Italia by land or by sea, both the future Occitania and the future Catalonia had been thoroughly Romanized all the way from Greek-founded Nice to Carthaginian-founded Barcelona. All through the afterglow of empire, remembrances of Roman tradition seem to have lingered longer there than anywhere outside Italia. Under a ruler Vandal, Visigoth, or Frank, clerks still sent out decrees, scholars taught texts, and judges handed down verdicts in more-or-less Latin. Illiterates spoke as they pleased. By about 800 CE the empire of Charlemagne comprehended the lands on both sides of the Rhine, the Seine, the Po, the Rhone, and the Gironde, as well as (intermittently) a region south of the Pyrenees that was known as the Spanish March.

Close resemblances in morphology between Occitan and Catalan may date from that time, when speakers from north of the mountains commingled with their cousins to the south. Then again, contacts may never have broken off from the sixth century through the eighth.

By the time Charlemagne turned from the warlord of record into the paladin of legend, resemblances in verb morphology had come into being in lands on each side of the Pyrenees. Resemblances might have intensified when troubadours from the north began to sing in their versions of Romance and when warriors from the south won an empire of their own with outposts from Corsica to Greece. As nation-states consolidated later on, Catalans became officially Spanish, and Occitans French. Morphologically, they still hold true to a past-participial Sprachbund perhaps shaped during the lifetime of Charlemagne or, conceivably, during the lifetimes of emperors reigning before a pope ruled at Rome.

4.6.1. OCCITAN

Unless one counts the troubadours' Schriftsprache, lush with outgrowths
from many dialects, no standard for Occitan has ever been established. It
would be unwise to think of Occitan as having preserved the earliest layout of
morphological flora planted by any speakers after Latin's demise. Yet it is
undeniable that, athwart the crossroads of contiguous ROMANIA, speakers of
Occitan have grown nearly every p.p. variety that still flourishes to the north,
southeast, and southwest. More than a few Occitan forms look exactly like
ones found far to the east.

For those familiar with Spanish, French, Italian, or Romanian, distinctive
lexical items in Occitan seem to include the verbs *davalar* 'go down,' *pojar* 'go
up,' *espelir* 'hatch, open,' and *aturar* 'stop' (p.p.s *davalat, pojat, espelit, aturat*),
but versions of all four are found south of the border in Cat. *davallar, pujar,
espellir,* and *aturar* (Wheeler 1988b, 264, 276). In what follows, data are cited
according to spellings found in published sources.

The best-recorded stage and the one of literary worth, the troubadours'
Schriftsprache, now called Old Occitan (OOc.), is the one dealt with here.
According to Paden's *Introduction to Old Occitan*, regular masc.sg. past
participles ended in *-at* for reflexes of -ĀRE verbs (type *amat* 'loved'), in *-it* for
reflexes of -ĪRE verbs (type *fenit* 'ended'), and in *-ut* for reflexes of both -ĒRE
and -'ERE verbs (type *batut* 'beaten'). Identical endings are found in Catalan.

As in CL, infinitive class did not always signal past-participial class.
Remodeling had taken place in Proto-Occitan: the *-ut* marker could be added
to the roots of some verbs whose infinitives ended in *-ir, -er,* or *-re.* Thus,
vengut 'come' corresponded to the 4th-conj. infin. *venir; vezut* 'seen' went
with 2nd-conj. infin. *vezer,* while *batut* 'beaten' and *perdut* 'lost' went with
3rd-conj. infins. *batre* and *perdre.* Since the Middle Ages, past participles in
some dialects have lost final [t] in masc.sg., giving ModOc. *agu* 'had,' *degu*
'ought to,' *begu* 'drunk,' *pouscu* 'been able,' *vougu* 'wanted,' and *sachu*
'known,' while Catalan past participles have maintained [t] (Price, 223).
Complicating an analyst's task, final *-t* still sometimes serves as an
orthographic reminiscence.

Before the earliest known works were sung out in hut or hall, pressures
toward regularization had been at work. Predictably, 1st-conj. verbs with
rhizotonic past participles were remade in the -ĀTU class: OOc. *crebar* 'rattle' <
CREPĀRE had obtained a regular p.p. *crebat* 'burst' instead of a reflex of
rhizotonic CREPĬTU. Reshapings along 4th-conj. lines included *cabit* 'fit into'
≠ CAPTU 'taken,' by-form *eissit* 'gone out' ≠ EXĬTU, by-form *ferit* 'hit' (no CL
p.p.), by-form *clauzit* 'shut' ≠ CLAUSU, *merit* 'earned, deserved' ≠ MERĬTU, by-
form *seguit* 'followed' ≠ SECŪTU, and *taizit* 'been silent' ≠ TACĬTU.

By analogy with *cubrir* 'cover' and *ubrir* 'open' with p.p.s *cubert* <
COOPERTU (also *cubrit*) and *ubert* < APERTU x COOPERTU, the verbs *sufrir*
'suffer' and *ufrir* 'offer' acquired the p.p.s *sufert* (also *sufrit*) ≠ SUBLĀTU₂ and
ufert ≠ OBLĀTU. The OOc. reflex of TENĒRE 'hold,' variously *tener* or *tenir*,
developed a [g] suffix before a regular 2nd-/3rd-conj. p.p. ending to produce

tengut ≠ TENTU as its past participle, and its rhyming partner *venir* 'come' < VENĪRE followed suit with its p.p. *vengut* ≠ VENTU (Grandgent 1905, 119–20). Reflexes of TENĒRE and VENĪRE influenced each other here as elsewhere.

In Occitania, the prefixed p.p. *sotzgeit* 'underlain' was used for *jazer*, the local reflex of JACERE 'lie'; the CL verb had had no p.p., but cf. LL adj. JACĬTŪRU 'reclining,' perhaps implying a Proto-Occitan rhizotonic p.p. *JACITU. As in Spanish or Italian, the OOc. p.p. *volt* 'turned' probably resulted from syncope in a rhizotonic thematic variant of CL VOLŪTU, just as *solt* 'loosened' had resulted from syncope in a variant of SOLŪTU. Syncope had also occurred in *quist* 'asked, sought' and in *conquis* 'conquered' ≠ (CON)QUĪSĪTU.

Past participles for verbs rarely encountered elsewhere in Romance were OOc. *colt* 'venerated' < CULTU 'tilled, tended; worshipped,' *doch* 'taught' < DOCTU, *legut* 'been allowed' ≠ LICĬTU.

Among others, surviving sigmatics were OOc. *ars* 'burned' < ĀRSU, *aucis* 'slain' < OCCĪSU, prefixed-changed *eces* 'lit' < ACCĒNSU or INCĒNSU, *espars* 'sprinkled' < SPARSU, *fos* 'melted' < FŪSU 'poured,' *mes* 'put' < MISSU 'sent,' *mors* 'bitten' < MORSU, *muls* 'milked' < by-form MULSU, *pars* 'spared' < by-form PARSU, *pres* 'taken' < PRĒNSU, *ras* 'shaved' < RĀSU, and *ters* 'wiped, scoured' < TERSU. Innovative sigmatics were (*d*)*ers* 'built' ≠ ĒRĒCTU, *fins* 'pretended' ≠ FICTU 'shaped,'[40] *nos* 'harmed' < NOCĬTU, *sors* 'arisen, surged' ≠ SURRĒCTU, the last with an OFr. cognate and one in Fr. *source* 'spring' (Mourin, 158). Many had arrhizotonic by-forms identical to ones found in Old French, one example being OOc. *aers* 'stuck' came from ADHÆSU plus infectum [r] as found in infin. ADHÆRĒRE.

Tautic athematic past participles in [t] endured in Old Occitan for certain verbs whose infinitives ended in *-ir*, *-er*, or *-re*. Reflexes of [kt] could appear as either [(i)t] or [tʃ]. Those surviving from CL included *dit* or *dich* 'said, told' < DICTU (infin. *dire*), *duit* or *duich* 'brought' < DUCTU 'led' (infin. *dur*), *fait* 'done/made' < FACTU (infin. *faire*), *nat* 'born' < NĀTU and *mort* 'died' < MORT(U)U (infins. *naiser* ≠ NĀSCĪ, *morir* ≠ MORĪ), and *rout* 'broken' < RUPTU (infin. *romper*).[41]

Necessarily brief, the above sketch presents a rather distorted picture of the state of affairs in Old Occitan verb morphology. A truer picture requires more time. To explain why, I look at a few of the pairs, trios, or quartets of past participles that once vied for speakers' allegiance along the lower Rhône.

4.6.1.1. Wavering in Old Occitan Past Participles

Pairs of rhizotonic and arrhizotonic past participles competed in Old Occitan, with the first usually inherited and the second based on the infinitive stem. Su ch pairs were *defes* < DĒFĒNSU and *defendut* 'fought off,' *elig* < ĒLĒCTU and *elegut* 'chosen,' *remas* < REMĀNSU and *remazut* 'stayed,' and *rot* < RUPTU

---

[40] Thoughturning sigmatic, *fins* acquired the infectum nasal infix like It. *finto* and Fr. *feint*.
[41] Tonic vowels changed in *dit*/ *dich* ± [i :] in infin. and pret., but in *duit* by palatal raising.

and *romput* 'broken.' In the sense 'seen,' Old Occitan had four competing past participles: *vis* < VĪSU and *vist* and *vezut* and *veut*, the last three paralleled in It./Sp. *visto*, Rom. *văzut*, and OFr. *veü*.[42]

Like Sp. *escondido* 'hidden,' OOc. *escos* and *escondut* 'idem' show a change of prefix from CL ABSCONDĬTU; the first shows traces of sigmatic remodeling.[43] Sigmatic *redems* 'redeemed,' no doubt based on pf. REDEMPSĪ instead of p.p. REDĒMPTU 'bought back' (as often happens in Romanian), used to compete with arrhizotonic *rezemut* but also with inherited *rezemt*. Besides inherited *escrit* 'written,' *escrich*—no doubt based on *dich* 'said, told'— competed against inherited arrhizotonic *escriut* with its vocalized bilabial stop.[44] Among sigmatics, competition between *mes* and *mis* 'put,' and between *pres* and *pris* 'taken' may be explained by the presence or absence of metaphony from 1sg. preterits MISĪ and PRĒNSĪ originally ending in [i:]; French has metaphonic *mis* and *pris*, but standard Italian has *messo* and *preso* (Grandgent 1905, 121).

Of Old Occitan verbs from the old 2nd and 3rd conjugations of Latin, about half acquired past participles in *-ut*. For some verbs, that ending might be added to the infectum stem, as in *crezut* 'believed,' *molut* 'ground,' *perdut* 'lost,' *respondut* 'answered,' *romput* 'broken,' *temut* 'feared,' *vendut* 'sold,' or *vezut* 'seen' (Grandgent 1905, 119–20). As in Catalan, though, Old Occitan arrhizotonic participles in *-ut* could also be built on perfectum stems. In fact, the preterit-based type was more widespread than the present-based type. Of *nascut* 'born,' *tescut* 'woven,' and *viscut* 'lived,' only the first had pres. [sk] in CL, and it gave OOc. 3sg. *nais* and infin. *naiser*. Past participles built on sigmatic pret. stems were *remazut* 'stayed,' *quesut* 'sought,' and *temsut* 'feared'; the last had no Latin past participle (Meyer-Lübke 1974, 413).

For the OOc. infin. *saber* 'know,' two unusual past participles had emerged, with a [w] evidently carried over from the tonic vowel [u]: the -ŪTU p.p.s *saubut* and *sauput* 'known' (no CL p.p.) were probably made ± preterit *saupi*, itself from a -UĪ variant of SAPIĪ/SAPĪVĪ. Others of the same type were *deceubut* 'tricked' and *receubut* 'received' ≠ DĒCEPTU, RECEPTU, both also with by-forms in *-put*; cf. OFr. *deceü*, *receü*, with loss of an intervocalic labial. During Old Occitan times, analogical remodeling of past participles continued: *nat* and *saubut* encountered competition from more regular *nascut*, *sabut*, built on old infectum stems (Paden, 62–63).

---

[42] Some analysts decline to credit past participles like OOc. *vis* 'seen' as survivals of VĪSU, attributing them to reduction of a final [st] cluster as in still-std. Cat. *vist*. I wouild rather regard such forms as high-frequency irregularities that have persisted since Latin times; cf. Enga. *vis*, dial. It. *viso*.

[43] Speakers' growing preference for prefixation by EX- also turns up in e.g. Sp. *esconder* 'hide,' as in Sp. *escuchar* and OFr. *escolter* 'listen' < AUSCULTĀRE 'hear attentively, overhear' (cf. It. *ascoltare*).

[44] Vocalization of a bilabial has also occurred in e.g. Cat. *lliurar* 'deliver' < LIBERĀRE 'free' and *deure* 'owe, have to < DĒBĒRE, and, with a shift of accent, also in Sp. *beodo* 'drunken' (adj.) < LL p.p. BIBĬTU 'drunk.'

Past participles like *agut* 'had' (competing with *avut* and *aüt*), *degut* 'ought to,' *begut* 'drunk,' and *conegut* 'known' all contained a [g] suffix—discussed more fully in §4.6.2.3—that derived from [w] in perfects like HABUĪ (Mendeloff, 37). The last three of those could not have come from CL rhizotonic HABĬTU 'had,' DĒBĬTU 'owed,' and COGNĬTU 'known,' which would have given forms like *ait*, *deit*, *conot*, just as insufficiently marked to endure as their cousins north of the Loire would have turned out. Applying to verbs lacking a past participle in CL, -*gut* also appeared in e.g. *begut* 'drunk' and *vougut* 'wanted.' That Catalan/Occitan [g] marker came from the same source as the [f] marker in Old Sardinian (see §3.7.5).

How might a present-tense stem inspire the morphology of past-system forms? Sigmatic OOc. *vensut* 'won' acquired [s] from the present stem as in infin. *venser* and could hardly have come straight from CL VICTU. However, [s] in *temsut* 'feared' (no CL p.p.) never occurred in any present-tense form like infin. *temer* and could not have come from the CL pf. TIMUĪ either. Perhaps speakers reinterpreted the last consonant in stems of past participles like *vensut* as a sigmatic marker, then applied the ending -*sut* to the stem of *temer*. If called upon to resolve the point, a Scottish jury might reach a verdict of n o t p r o v e n rather than guilty or not guilty.

4.6.1.2. Morphological Patterns within the Past System

For reflexes of 3rd-conj. verbs within the past-tense system of Old Occitan, many 3sg. preterits could have forms identical to those of masculine past participles. Examples included sigmatics straight from Latin pf./p.p. roots like *ars* 'burned' and *espars* 'sprinkled.' Remodeling on p.p. roots had taken place for some unpopular types of preterits, like *cors* 'ran/run' ≠ pf. CUCURRĪ (but cf. p.p. CURSU), and *fos* 'dug,' ≠ pf. FŌDĪ (but cf. p.p. FOSSU). In the feminine, these past participles all maintained [s] rather than voicing it to [z].[45]

Verbs that had identical 3sg. preterits and masculine past participles also included the sigmatics *aucis* 'killed,' *claus* 'shut,' *mes* 'put,' *pres* 'took/taken,' *ris* 'laughed,' *ros* 'gnawed/gnawn,' *tes* 'held,' *respos* 'answered.' They all voiced their sigmatic marker to [z] in feminine past participles like *auciza*, *clauza*, and *meza*.

For some of those verbs, the 3sg. preterit had evolved differently from the 1sg. preterit, the latter having undergone metaphony. Either 1sg. *mis*, *pris*, and *quis* 'sought' or 3sg. *mes*, *pres*, and *ques* could and did inspire a past-participial form in Old Occitan.

Other verbs combined pret. [sk] with p.p. [sk], but the past participle ended in -*ut*. Here again there were two types: the simple type had a zero 3sg. ending as in pret. *visc* as against p.p. *viscut* 'lived'; the complicated type had a 3sg.

---

[45] Occitan has thus been approaching isomorphy between preterit and past participle, somewhat as English already has for regular verbs (e.g. *I p l a y e d/ h a v e p l a y e d*). For a review of past-tense verbs from past participles in Indo-Iranian and Slavic, see §1.8.

ending generalized from DEDIT 'gave' as in pret. *tesquet* 'wove' as against p.p. *tescut* 'woven,' or pret. *nasquet* as against p.p. *nascut* 'born.'

A few verb forms in the past system, like *saup* 'knew' and *sauput* (also *saubut*) 'known,' showed that the [w] marker from unclassical preterits had metathesized and then spread into the past participle. This clearly happened after CL times, for the verb SAPERE 'taste, know' lacked a past participle. By analogy with *saber* 'know,' other 3rd-conj. verbs whose stems ended in a bilabial stop remodeled their past-tense systems: *decebre* 'deceive' and *recebre* 'receive' had the 3sg. prets. *deceup* and *receup* and the already mentioned p.p.s *deceubut* and *receubut*.

Alternation between sigmatic preterits and tautic athematic past participles remained popular in mediæval Occitania, as in Italy today. The highest-frequency occurrences were 3sg. pret. *dis* as against p.p. *dit* 'said, told,' *duis* as against *duit* 'brought,' *escris* 'wrote' as against *escrit* 'written,' and *tors* as against *tort* 'twisted.' Those consonantal alternations were inherited, even if the vowel in one form or the other had adjusted to that of its past-tense partner. At times, sigmatic preterits contrasted with sigmatic-tautic past participles: *pos* as against *post* 'set, laid' and *respos* as against *respost* 'answered.' Those past participles were innovated, at least from the CL standard POS(I)TU and RESPŌNSU, but are paralleled in e.g. It. *posto, risposto*.

A widespread kind of alternation involved a sigmatic preterit and multiple past-participial forms, the latter partly because old [kt] clusters might turn into either [it] or [tʃ]. Thus, the high-frequency verb *faire* 'do/make' had 3sg. pret. *fes* < FĒCIT, but either *fait* or *fach* (also spelled *fag*) < FACTU in the past-participial slot. Again, the 3sg. prets. *trais* < TRAXIT 'pulled, milked' and *duis* 'brought' < DŪXIT 'led' corresponded to the p.p.s *trait* or *trach* < TRACTU, and *duit* or *duch* < DUCTU. When a verb root ended in a nasal consonant, three past-participial competitors might arise: for infin. *planher* 'lament, complain,' pret. *plai(n)s* < PLĀNXIT could have the inherited p.p. *plaint* < PLĀNCTU along with bare-[ŋk] *planc* and bare-[ɲ] *planh*. To these may be compared the trio *frach, frait, franh*, all but the last from FRĀCTU 'shattered,' but cf. infin. FRANGERE with nasal marking.

Owing to the spread both of -ŪTU past participles and of a [g] marker for them, devoiced to [k] after [s] or when word-final, the most common type of alternation within the past system of 3rd-conj. verbs entailed final [k] in 3sg. preterits and final stressed [gut] in masc.sg. past participles (see 4.6.2.3).[46] One need cite but a few pairs of preterits and past participles to make the point: 3sg. pret. *ac* as against p.p. *agut* 'had,' *bec* 'drank' as against *begut* 'drunk,' *conoc* 'knew' as against *conogut* 'known,' *correc* 'ran' as against *corregut* 'run,' and *tolc* as against *tolgut* 'removed,' along with the ever-rhyming pair *tenc* as

---

[46] Besides coming from [w] in pf. stems like HABU- 'had,' this velar-stop marker may have been reinforced by the high-frequency 1sg. pres.indic. DĪCŌ 'I say,' which gave *dic* or *di* in OOc. Further reinforcement would have come from 1sg. pres.subj. DĪCAM 'I may say' > OOc. *diga*. Note also the by-form 3sg. pres.subj. *digua*, containing both [g] and [w] (Paden, 393). In some Sard. preterits, the same [w] turned into [f] (§3.7.5).

against *tengut* 'held, had' and *venc* 'came' as against *vengut* 'come' mentioned in 4.6.1.1.

Nevertheless, a few preterits in [k] coexisted with inherited tautic athematic past participles. Both were inherited in pret. *coc* < COXIT as against p.p. *cueit* < COCTU 'cooked'; the first was subject to innovation as in *cuberc* ≠ COOPERUĪ as against *cubert* 'covered' < COOPERTU (Mourin, 188–91; Paden, 62–63). Examples given here have severely understated the variations once found in p.p. morphology between the Alps and the Pyrenees

4.6.1.3. More Wavering among Past Participles

As noted in §4.6.1.1, morphological competition existed mainly for verbs whose rhizotonic past participles were inherited and whose arrhizotonic ones were innovated. Further instances were *aces* < ACCĒNSU and *acendut* 'lit, kindled,' *claus* < CLAUSU and *clauzit* 'closed,' *cors* < CURSU and *corregut* 'run,' *nat* < NĀTU and *nascut* 'born,' *remas* < REMĀNSU and *remazut* 'stayed,' *rot* < RUPTU and *romput* 'broken,' *tes* < TEX(T)U and *tescut* or *teissut* 'woven.' For the last of these, compare even more conservative OCat. *test*. Other sets of by-forms came from innovations postdating CL, as in *pagut* or *pascut* ≠ PĀSTU 'fed, grazed,' *tolt* or *tolgut* ≠ SUBLĀTU₁ 'taken away.'

Still other by-forms involved alternations between final [it] and [ut], as often in Old Italian and Old French. In many such pairs, neither competitor can be traced back to CL: (*e*)*issit* or (*e*)*issut* ≠ EXĪTU 'gone out' (infin. *eissir*), *espandit* or *espandut* 'spread' ≠ EXPĀNSU, *ferit* or *ferut* 'struck' (infin. *ferir*). Sometimes, though, one of the two can be: *seguit* or *segut* < SECŪTU 'followed' (infin. *segre*).

Competition between sigmatic and tautic athematic forms occurred in OOc. *tors* and *tort* 'twisted'; cf. Rom. *întors* 'turned.' As in Italian, several sigmatic past participles had optionally become sigmatic-tautic, so that alternations occurred between final [s] and [st], in e.g. *somos* or *somost* 'urged' ≠ SUBMONĪTU, *vis* or *vist* 'seen,' and *respos* or *respost* 'answered.' A similar pair, *escos* and *escost* 'hidden,' alternated with arrhizotonic *escondut* (Fernández González, 365, 390). Such wavering between sigmatic and sigmatic-tautic variants also occurred for a few past participles in Old Italian, where the sigmatic-tautic side usually ended up winning under the nascent standard (see §3.5.5.1).

Certain other variations in the p.p. morphology of Old Occitan might entail the presence or absence of a surviving fricative. Thus, long-form *cazegut* 'fallen' was closer morphologically to rare CĀSU than was short-form *cagut*, and long-form *benezeit* 'blessed' was closer to BENEDICTU than short-form *beneit*, but neither exactly continued the Latin forms (Mourin, 158).

For *aver* 'have,' besides the three by-form past participles given on page 267, Old Occitan had a fourth with nasal marking: *angut* 'had' (Paden, 367). Unless due to a slip of the quill, *angut* must have arisen by analogy with another verb form. The best prospect semantically is p.p. *tengut* 'held.'

4.6.1.4. Changes between Old and Modern Occitan

Modern Occitan continues several kinds of alternations reviewed for OOc. past participles and their infinitives. Even within one dialect, variance endures: speakers may apparently use either *dit* or *dich* 'said, told,' *escrit* or *escrich* 'written,' *trait* or *trach* 'pulled.'

Other alternations extant today may be ranked in several classes, most surviving from Old Occitan. First, tonic vowels may vary in both past participles and in infinitives: *còit* and *quèit* 'cooked' (infin. *còire, quèire, quèze*). Second, the final consonant may fluctuate between [t] and [tʃ], or between two realizations of an ending. Third, the last vowel may fluctuate between [i(t)] and [u(t)], or between two morphological classes. Examples of such fluctuation include *mozut* and *mozit* 'milked' (infin. *mò(l)ze*); see §3.5.7 for parallels in Old Italian. Fourth and most commonly in Occitan, a fricative or stop may be present in one by-form and absent in the other: *cregut* and *cresegut* 'believed' (infin. *creire*), *crescut* and *creissegut* 'grown' (infin. *crèisser*), *parescut* and *paregut* 'appeared' (infin. *pareisse, parestre*), and *plagut* and *plazegut* 'pleased' (infin. *plaire*). In addition, verbs may have multiple by-forms. The infin. *crenhe* 'fear' may have *crent* (as if from *CREMITU), *crengut*, or *crenhegut* for its past participle; the infin. *planhe* 'complain' may have *planh, planhut*, or *plangut*; the infin. *tòrsse* or *torssir* 'twist' may have *tors, torssit*, or *torssegut*, though OOc. *tort* seems to have died out past-participially. Other old past participles like *irat* 'angry' and *clus* 'shut' survive as adjectives (Fernández González, 412–16).

Now and then, an old rhizotonic survives only adjectivally. In Provençal, adj. *cue* < COCTU contrasts with p.p. *cousegu* 'cooked.' For another such pair, a less neat split has arisen: while the Prov. adjective meaning 'broken' must be *rout* < RUPTU, the corresponding past participle may be either *rout* or *roumpu* (Ronjat, 219).

That the most productive verb class continues to attract new members is suggested by the remaking of some 4th-conj. verbs along 1st-conj. lines. Most are semilearnèd. Instances include ModOc. *corregir* now *corrijar* 'correct,' *diferir* now *diferar* 'delay,' *discutir* now *discutar* 'discuss,' *imprimir* now *imprimar* 'print,' and *enrauquir* now *enraucar* 'become hoarse.' All but the last may have been influenced by morphology used to the north, given Fr. *corriger, différer, discuter, imprimer*. Yet at times Occitan has gone its own way. A couple of 4th-conj. verbs have developed 1st-conj. by-forms whose roots come from related nouns or adjectives: *conquerir* 'conquer' competes with *conquistar*, and *emplir* 'fill' with *emplenar*.

Several 1st-conj. Occitan forms include a [g] suffix coming from [k] in the long-form verb ending -ICĀRE etc. Although the alternation between *mordir* or *mòrdre* 'bite' and long-form *mossegar* may be traceable back to LL, that alternation might have inspired other longer variants in Occitan like *gemir* 'moan, groan' competing with *gemegar*, and *punhir* or *punhe(r)* 'sting, prick' with *punhegar*, and *ròire* 'gnaw' with *rozegar* (Fernández González, 408). All those novelties have 1st-conj. past participles in -*at*, so that allomorphy declines. The last item looks as if it had been built on an old p.p. stem like that of RŌSU 'gnawn,' which lasted at least long enough to give OOc. *ros*. That [g] in certain Occitan 1st-conj. p.p.s like *gemegat* 'moaned,' *mossegat* 'bitten,' *punhegat* 'stung,' *rozegat* 'gnawn' fortuitously resembles the [g] in most past participles from the 2nd and 3rd conjugations. However, the [g] 1st-conj. marker appears throughout those verb paradigms, the [g] 2nd-/3rd-conj. marker only in certain verb forms.

Since the days of the troubadours, when it was far from standardized, Occitan has scarcely served as a literary language. As in the past, dialects today may have several competitors for a past-participial slot. Next I review past participles from five other Occitan dialects: a southwestern one, Gascon; two northern ones, Poitevin and Auvergnat; and two southern ones, Gévaudanais and Languedocian.

4.6.1.5. Gascon

Most divergent from other Occitan dialects in both phonology and morphology, Gascon probably differs from them at least as much as Franco-Provençal does. Despite an Old Castilian-style—or Aromanian-style—shift from [f] to [h] in e.g. *huéger* 'flee' < FUGERE or *auherir* 'offer' from a 4th-conj. variant of OFFERRE, and despite unusual verbs like *vàder* 'walk' < VĀDERE 'go, hasten' and *plàver* 'rain' ≠ PLUERE, the location of Gascon within the French cultural sphere has kept it from being reckoned a separate language (Wheeler 1988b, 246).

Darrigrand's *Initiation au gascon* furnishes the following data. Regular past participles are 1st-conj. *cantat* 'sung' and *anat* 'gone,' 2nd-conj. *avut* 'had' and *podut* 'been able,' and 4th-conj. *sentit* 'felt' and *bastit* 'built.' As usual, the past participles of 3rd-conj. verbs, with infinitives in atonic -*er*, are the least predictable morphologically, but the regular ones end in -*ut* and have the same stem as their infinitives.

Tautic athematic past participles inherited from Latin have undergone simplification of the clusters [kt] or [pt]. After [i], [kt] has reduced [t] as in *dit* 'said, told' (infin. *diser*) and *frit* 'fried' (infin. *frir* or *friser* or *fregir*), while [pt] became [u̯t] as in *escriut* 'written' (infin. *escriver*). After non-high vowels, [kt] became [i̯t] as in *hèit* 'done/made' (infin. *har* or *hèr*), or *cuèit* 'cooked' (infin. *còser*). Survivals in [rt] include *mort* 'died' along with *auhèrt* 'offered,' *cobèrt* 'covered,' and *ubèrt* 'opened' (infins. *morir*, *aubrir*, *cobrir*, *orbir*, plus by-forms); survivals in [nt] include *junt* 'joined' (infin. *júnher*). A single sigmatic, inherited *pres* 'taken,' competes with weak-stem *prengut* (infin. *préner*), but sigmatic-tautic *vist* 'seen' (infin. *véder*) has no competition.

As in Catalan and other varieties of Occitan, once inchoative verbs now tend to have pást participles in [skut]: *crescut* 'grown' (infin. *créisher*), *nascut* 'born' (infin. *naisher*), *conescut* 'known' (infin. *conèisher*), *parescut* 'appeared' (infin. *parèisher*), *pescut* 'tended, kept' (infin. *pèisher*). These usually match 2nd- or 3rd-conj. preterits in [sk] like 1sg. *crescoi* 'grew' from present-based

CRESC- + -UĪ, for CRĒDIDĪ. Non-inchoatives with the same type are *tescut* 'woven' (infin. *tèisser*), and *viscut* 'lived' (infin. *viver*), again usually matching [sk] preterits like *viscoi* 'lived' from a metathesized variant of VIXĪ + -UĪ. Moreover, *t(i)engut* 'held' (infin. *tier*) and rhyming *v(i)engut* 'come' (infin. *vier*), belong to infinitives where intervocalic [n] has vanished, but both past participles show reinforcement of the nasal to [ŋg]; consonantally if not vocalically, these past participles match the prets. *tengoi* 'held' < TENUĪ and *vengoi* 'came' ≠ VĒNĪ, both with inserted [g] (§4.6.1.1). Optionally, both these forms have a diphthong in the pretonic syllable, a trait no doubt borrowed from rhizotonic present-tense verb forms as in the French futures *(je) viendrai* 'I shall come' and *(je) tiendrai* 'I shall hold, have.'

Though evidently arising mainly from [w] in LL perfects/preterits, that Occitan/Catalan [g] suffix might have been reinforced by reflexes of [k] in the stem of DĪCERE 'say, tell,' especially the powerful 1sg. pres.indic. DĪCŌ; compare the Gasc. 1sg. pret. *digoi* 'said, told' from the infectum stem plus -UĪ, where [g] seems unlikely to have arisen from [w]. That type could then have been extended to preterits like *cregoi* ≠ CRĒDIDĪ 'believed' and *prengoi* ≠ PRENDIDĪ 'took.' Today, however, many of those [g]-ful forms compete with present-based variants like pret. *disoi, credoi,* and *prenoi* (infins. *diser, créder, préner*). The first and the last of those verbs' past participles fail to match inherited *dit* < DICTU or *pres* < PRĒNSU, but cf. by-form *prengut*. Likewise, the pret. *vii* 'saw' < VĪDĪ competes with present-based *vedoi*, and *hei* 'did/made' < FĒCĪ competes with present-based *hasoi* (infins. *véder, har*, but cf. 1sg. pres.subj. *haci* or *hasqui*). Neither of these Gascon preterits matches its past participle *vist* 'seen' ≠ VĪSU or *hèit* 'done/made' < FACTU.

In the preterit, generalization of endings derived from DEDĪ 'gave,' itself surviving as *dẹi*, into the 1st conjugation has resulted in regular 1sg. prets. like *cantẹi* 'sang,' not matched vocalically by masc.sg. past participles in -*at* like *cantat* < CANTĀTU 'sung' or for that matter *dat* < DATU 'given.' Regular 4th-conj. preterits in (1sg.) -*íi* like *sentíi* ≠ SĒNSĪ 'felt' are matched vocalically by past participles in -*it* like *sentit* ≠ SĒNSU. In the morphology of 2nd- and 3rd-conj. verbs, a once close relation between the pret. ending -*oi* < -UĪ and the p.p. ending -*ut* < -ŪTU has been disguised by phonological changes (Iliescu and Mourin, 322–24, 401–2). Emerging transparencies of conjugation may turn out to be clouded over later on.

According to Darrigrand (277–93), some by-form past participles correspond to by-form infinitives in Gascon. Thus, *créder* 'believe' with by-form *créser* has for a p.p. *credut* or *cregut*. Again, infin. *vier* or *viéner* 'come' has for a p.p. *vienut, vengut,* or *viengut*, and its rhyming partner *tier* or *tiéner* 'hold, have' has *tienut, tengut,* or *tiengut*. Yet the by-forms *har* and *hèr* 'do/make' have only *hèit* < FACTU for a past participle; the by-forms *orbir* or *aubrir* 'open' have only *ubèrt* < APERTU x COOPERTU; three by-form infins. *frir, fríser,* and *frejir* 'fry' all have only *frit* < FRĪCTU. As a final example, infin. *ir* < ĪRE 'go' and its regularized p.p. *it* are still retained by speakers in the Aspe valley (Basses-Pyrénées). Elsewhere, Gascon speakers use *anar*, no doubt < AMBULĀRE 'go back and forth, walk, travel,' with its regular p.p. *anat*. Once again, the lack of a literary standard has allowed variants to thrive.

4.6.1.6. Poitevin and Saintongeais

Data for this northwestern dialect of Occitan come from Gautier's *Grammaire du poitevin-saintongeais*, covering parts of the old provinces of Poitou and Saintonge. Here I leave out a multitude of by-forms from Bas Poitou, the Pays Mellois, the Marais, and Civraisien. Semantically, certain transitive verbs have implicatures when used intransitively: *batre* 'thresh wheat,' *brulàe* 'distill wine into brandy,' *nourir* 'give suck,' *tallàe* 'trim grape-vines,' and *tuàe* 'slaughter a pig' (119). Morphologically, infinitives end thus by conjugation: in *-àe* (1st), in *-oer* (2nd), in *-re* (3rd), and in *-i* (4th). Regular past participles end thus: in *-ai* (1st), in *-u* or *-ut* (2nd and 3rd), and in *-i* (4th).

Examples from the 1st conjugation are *alai* or *nalai* 'gone' and *dounai* 'given' (infins. *alàe, dounàe*). An example from the 2nd conjugation is *valu* 'been worth' (infin. *valoer*), and one from the 4th conjugation is *fini* 'ended' (infin. also *fini*). Examples from the 3rd conjugation are *mendut* 'led' and *muntut* 'climbed' (infins. *mendre, muntre*). As happens everywhere else in ROMANIA, 3rd-conj. forms show the widest variation in Poitou and Saintonge. Many incorporate a [g] suffix, as in p.p. *creghu* 'believed (infin. *crére*). One of these, *veyu* 'seen' (infin. *vére*), seems to have a [j] suffix, conceivably antihiatic. In p.p. *segut* 'followed,' though, [g] makes up part of the stem, as seen in infin. *segre* or *ségre*. If I knew the meaning of p.p. *vitu* (infin. *se vitre*), I would gloss it; perhaps 'glassed in'?

Of mixed arrhizotonic conjugation are p.p. *assi* 'sat' (3rd-conj. infin. *assire*), p.p. *atenu* 'waited' (4th-conj. infin. *ateni*), p.p. *li* 'read' (3rd-conj. infin. *lire*), and p.p. *paessu* 'fed, kept' (1st-conj. infin. *paessàe*),

A handful of tautic athematics subsist in Poitevin: *crent* 'feared' (no CL p.p.), *cheùt* 'cooked' < COCTU, *dit* 'said, told' < DICTU, *mort* 'died' < MORT(U)U, *pllént* 'complained' < PLĀNCTU (infins. *créndre, cheure, dire, mouri, pllendre*). Sigmatics exist only as part of a p.p. ending *-su* [type **8+6**], as in *pllésu* 'pleased' (infin. *pllere* but pret. *pllesi*) and in a few p.p. by-forms reviewed below. Yet Poitevin has kept or evolved multiple sigmatic preterits: (1sg.) *assisi* 'sat,' *cheusi* 'cooked,' *couneùssi* 'knew,' *dessi* or *dissi* 'said, told,' *lisi* 'read,' *naessi* 'was born,' along with sigmatic by-form preterits like *cheusi* 'fell,' *misi* 'put.' All sigmatic past participles have been reshaped with the arrhizotonic suffix from -ŪTU.

Though never sigmatic, preterit influence comes across in several Poitevin past participles. To start with single exponents, if p.p. *prenghu* 'taken' ≠ PR(EH)ĒNSU 'grabbed' hardly looks little like infin. *pren[d]re*, it really looks like pret. *prenghi*. Likewise, p.p. *soghu* 'known' hardly looks like infin. *saver* but really looks like a pret. by-form *soghi*. Again, the rhyming p.p.s *tenghu* 'held, had' ≠ TENTU and *vénghu* 'come' ≠ VENTU hardly look like their infins. *téndre* or *teni* and *véndre* or *veni* but really look like their prets. *tenghi* (also *teni*) and *vénghi*.

Like other dialects of Occitan, Poitevin has a large number of p.p. by-forms. Many twin past participles contrast the presence and absence of a [g] marker. For instance, in the pair *courghu* and *couri* 'run,' both ≠ CURSU, the second has been regularized along the lines of the 4th-conj. infin. *couri*, while the first has the same stem as pret. *courghi*. However, [g] marking has spread to pret. *anghi* 'went' without affecting p.p. *alai* or *nalai* 'gone.' In p.p. pairs like *deghu* and *du* 'owed,' *faughu* and *falu* or *felu* 'been required,' *pareghu* and *paru* 'appeared,' and *vaughu* and *velu* 'wanted' (infins. *devoer; feler* or *felàe* or *fàloer; paraetre, velér*), the [g]-less forms look suspiciously like those in standard French over the Loire.

One Poitevin p.p. twin contrasts intervocalic consonants: *naeçhu* and *naessu* 'born' (infin. *naetre* but pret. *naessi*); what that graphy ch stands for I cannot say. Another twin contrasts a preterit-looking past participle *recevi* 'received' with a French-looking one *reçu* (infin. *recevre* or *recevoer* but pret. *recevi*). The morphology of pret. *repouni* may have inspired the reshaping of p.p. *repounut* 'answered' if not its clipped-looking by-form *répun*, both ≠ RESPŌNSU (infin. *répoundre* or *repounàe*) unless, exceptionally, [n] alone remained from an old [ns] cluster.

Other p.p. twins are more difficult to characterize. One such pair evidently contrasts inherited *ouvért* with regularized *ouvri* 'opened' (infin. *ouvri* or *uvri*). A second pair contrasts inherited *fét* 'done/made' with innovated *fasu* (infin. *faere* but pret. *fasi*). A third pair has *mét* 'put' ≠ MISSU, no doubt remade ± *fét* 'done/made,' contrasting with arrhizotonic *métu*.

Triplet past participles in Poitevin are *béghu* or *beghu* or *bu* 'drunk' (infin. *boere*); *cheù* or *cheùt* or *cheusu* 'fallen' (infin. *cheure*); and *poghu* or *poughu* or *peghu* 'been able' (infin. *pere* or *pever*). A quadruplet is Poit. *couneughu*, *queneùghu* or *couneùssu*, and *queneùssu* 'known' (infin. *counétre* or *queneùtre* but by-form pret. *couneùssi*).

Saintongeais (Sto.) differs from Poitevin chiefly in retaining final -t at least graphically and in hypercharacterizing gender marking in ways reminiscent of Franco-Provençal (§4.5). On the assumption that Sto. graphies "mean what they say," such pairs may contrast [t] and [zə], as in masc. *but* and fem. *buse* 'drunk' or *vut* and *vuse* 'seen.' They may contrast [t] and [tə], as in masc. *chét* and fem. *chéte* 'fallen.' Most often, they contrast [t] and [ə] after a tonic vowel, resulting in masc. *créyut* and fem. *créyue* 'believed'; masc. *dut* and fem. *due* 'owed'; masc. *finit* and fem. *finie* 'ended'; masc. *segut* and fem. *segue* 'followed'; masc. *tendut* and fem. *tendue* 'held, had'; masc. *vendut* and fem. *vendue* 'sold' (Gautier, 96–119).

4.6.1.7. Auvergnat

Data for this northeastern dialect of Occitan, spoken in the old province of Auvergne, come from Bonnaud's *Grammaire générale de l'auvergnat*. Spellings are somewhat standardized.

Auvergnat has four classes of infinitives, with those of the 1st-conj. ones ending in -â, 2nd-conj. ones in -ê, 3rd-conj. ones in -re or rarely -e, and 4th-conj. ones in -î. Infinitives often have by-forms. True, 3rd-conj. *batre* 'beat' and *tracondre* 'disappear' face no competition. Still, several infinitives waver between 3rd-conj. and 4th-conj. by-forms: *eichandre* or *eichandî* 'heat,' *planhe* or *planhî* 'complain,' *partre* or *partî* 'leave,' *so[r]tre* or *sourtî* 'go out,' *tene* or *tenî* 'have, hold.' Nowadays, 4th-conj. *junhî* 'join,' *teisî* 'weave,' *tenhî* 'dye' almost always replace old 3rd-conj. *junhe, teisse, tenhe*, with past-participial consequences left to the imagination since Bonnaud passes them by. One Auv. infinitive has three by-forms: *aveire* or *agure* or *vî* 'have' (as a modal auxiliary); its apparent past participle *düd* 'had,' for which no infinitive is given, matches none of those three forms. At least two Auv. infinitives, meaning 'be able' and 'want,' have four by-forms, listed below after their by-form past participles. The most common verb of all, meaning 'to be,' has five infin. by-forms, but of these only two, *l-esse* and *d-esse*, are really Auvergnat, for the three others, *eitre, l-eitre*, and *l-estre*, being "du français patoisé" (134) [French adapted to the dialect].

Other 3rd-conj. or 4th-conj. verbs yield to replacement verbs from the 1st conjugation. At times, replacement verbs are built on a stem of the old verb. Instead of *ségre* 'follow,' speakers on the plain of Limagne (Puy-de-Dôme) use *segâ*; instead of *vieure* etc. 'live,' speakers in the département of Cantal use *viscâ*, built on the same stem as in (3sg.) preterit *visque* 'lived.' More often, the irregular verb no longer passes current. So speakers of Auvergnat generally replace *maure* 'grind' with *moulinâ, fuje* or *fuji* 'flee' with *se seuvâ* (cf. std. Fr. *se sauver*), and *leure* 'shine' with *lüzentâ*, built on an old present participle. Since the local reflex of COOPERĪRE 'cover,' *crebî*, now refers only to sowing seeds (179: "recouvrir les semailles"), speakers use *coatâ* or *brejâ* to mean 'cover.' With the verb *durbi* 'open' remaining current only in southern Auvergne, speakers elsewhere say *badâ*; in western Auvergne, speakers replace *so[r]tre* 'go out' with *seutâ*. Rare in the south, very rare in the north, *cl[h]aure* 'shut' has been generally replaced by *sarâ* (cf. Sp. *cerrar* 'idem,' Fr. *serrer* 'squeeze'). Presumably, regular past participles go with all these replacement verbs, but I cannot tell.

Auvergnat has three classes of arrhizotonic past participles. Regular 1st-conj. forms end in -àd: *anàd* or *nàd* 'gone,' *blassàd* 'wounded,' *chatàd* 'bought,' *credàd* 'called,' *eitàd* 'been,' *eubledàd* 'forgotten,' *mandàd* 'summoned,' *parlàd* 'spoken,' *saràd* 'shut.' Regular 2nd-/3rd-conj. forms end in -üd: *batüd* 'beaten,' *couzüd* 'sewn,' *sintüd* 'felt.' Regular 4th-conj. forms end in -id: *batîd* 'built' and perhaps *lejid* 'read' (no infinitive given). A few verbs have mixed conjugations: *so[r]tre* 'go out' (also *sourtî*) with p.p. *sourtîd*, and *venî* 'come' with p.p. *vendüd* or *vengüd*. At least two verbs lack past participles: *care* 'seek,' *doure* 'hurt.' The latter is replaced by *faire mau*, literally 'do/make badly,' and also by *padi* or *pati* 'suffer, undergo'; for unlenited [t] here, cf. Cat. *patir* 'idem,' perhaps owing to medical or ecclesiastical conservatism in both.

Rhizotonics with no competition are tautic athematic *fait* or *foet* 'done/made' (infin. *faî, faire*, or *foére*) and *queut* 'cooked' (infin. *queure*).

Sigmatics are represented by the familiar pair *mez* 'put' and *prez* 'taken' (infins. *metre, prene*). A by-form sigmatic is rare *clauz* or *clheuz* 'shut' (infin. *cl[h]aure*). In this dialect, the Franco-Iberian trend toward arrhizotonicity has generally advanced further in northern Auvergne, where one encounters forms like *metüd* 'put,' *prendüd* 'taken'; but northerners retain rhizotonic *eicrit* 'written' while southerners replace it with arrhizotonic *eicrisüd* or *eicridüd*; the infinitive also varies by region, being *eicrî* in the north but *escrioure* in the south. Then again, innovative *dizut* 'said, told' evidently competes with *dit* everywhere in Auvergne (infin. *di* or *dire*).

In its rhizotonic past participles, Auvergnat differs from other Occitan dialects in having (masc.sg.) forms that end in -d̲ rather than -t̲. In the following passage, Gautier evidently considers that lenition has taken place in only two locales west of the Adriatic (133):

> Le participe passé auv. avec -d- a ses correspondants les plus proches dans le groupe rhéto-roman et non dans le groupe d'oc. En haute Engadine...on note même des formes telles que *salüdo, salüdeda* ['greeted'], *rendieu, rendida* ['given back'] qui s'apparentent étroitement aux types auv. originaux à grande extension (*salüdàd, rendüd*) ou tendanciellement bien représentés (*salüdädà*).

> [The Auvergnat past participle in -d̲- has its closest parallels in Ræto-Romance rather than in Occitan. In Upper Engadin...there are even forms like...closely linked to Auvergnat forms once quite common...or well accounted for in other areas....]

More plausibly, such final -d̲'s reflect voicing that originally took place in both masc. and fem. forms where [t] was still intervocalic. Subsequently, final devoicing of [d] failed to occur in Auvergnat; the presence of [d] in both masc. and fem. forms heightens isomorphy in past participles there. A similar development has swept through old sigmatics, going by the spelling, for masc.sg. forms like *mez* 'put' and *prez* 'taken' now end in [z], and so do fem. *meza* and *preza*. However, reflexes of old [kt] clusters have stayed [t] even between vowels, giving fem. p.p.s like *dita* 'said, told,' *faita* or *foeta* 'done/made' in which isomorphy has been heightened in a different way. I do not know whether *eicrit* 'written' has a feminine in t̲, from [pt], for Bonnaud lists no such feminine form.

Like other dialects of Occitan, Auvergnat has a large amount of p.p. variation. Arrhizotonic past participles with a by-form in [d] and a by-form in [g], the second usually less common, are *bedüd* or *begüd* 'drunk,' *choudüd* or *chougüd* 'had to,' *couredüd* or *couregüd* 'run,' *dedüd* or *degüd* 'owed,' *foudüd* or *fougüd* 'been required,' *pleudüd* or *pleugüd* 'rained' (also anomalous *ploiud*), *poudüd* or *pougüd* 'been able,' *tendüd* or *tengüd* 'held, had,' *vedüd*

or *vegüd* 'seen,' *vieudüd* or *vieugüd* 'lived,' and *voudüd* or *vougüd* 'wanted.'
If the Auv. past participle meaning 'come' may be either *vendüd* or *vengüd*,
the Auv. past participle meaning 'sold' must be *vendüd*. Corresponding
infinitives are *beure* or *biure* 'drunk,' *chalê* 'have to,' *coure* 'run,' *d[i]eure*
'owe,' *falê* 'be required,' *pleure* or *plaire* 'rain,' *poudeî* or *poudê* or *poeire* or
pougure 'be able,' *tene* or *tenhe* or *tenî* 'hold, have,' *veî* or *veire* 'see,' *vieure*
or *viure* or *vioure* 'live,' and *voulê* or *vouleî* or *voudre* or *vougure* 'want.'
None of the past participles cited in this paragraph ended in CL -ŪTU.

Unless Auvergnats buck a trend visible across Occitania, one would think
the [g]-ful forms are bound to win out one day.

However, marking in [d] has spread to certain Auv. past participles
unentitled to it etymologically: *leudüd* 'shone' and *moudüd* 'ground' (infins.
leure and *maure* or *moure*). One more case is *veudüd* or *vadüd* 'been worth'
(infin. *valeî* or *vale*). Even p.p. *següd* 'followed' < SECŪTU, whose [g] already
occurs in infin. *ségre*, has a by-form *sedüd* in intervocalic [d]. Marking in both
[d] and [g] has spread to past participles for another verb that keeps a type 8+6
by-form as well, resulting in the triplet *couneisüd*, *counedüd*, and *counegüd*
'known,' all ≠ COGNITU (infin. *couneisse* or *counïtre* or *counütre* or
counioutre). With a past participle only in *-su-* are *creisüd* 'grown' and
toursüd 'twisted' (infins. *creisse*, *tourse* or *tuorse* or *torse*).

Besides marking in [g] or [d], some arrhizotonics are marked in [z].

Past participles with a by-form in [z] are *crezüd* or *cregüd* 'believed,' *rizüd*
or *ridüd* 'laughed' (infins. *crei* or *creire*, *rî*). Despite sigmatic RĪSU 'laughed,'
Auv. [z] here seems unlikely to have come from voicing of [s], reflecting
rather a fricativization of [d] seen in other Occitan dialects—and sometimes in
Romanian—but occurring only sporadically up in Auvergnat. Among single-
exponent past participles, *mouzüd* 'milked' has only [z] like its infin. *mouze*,
while *moudüd* 'ground' and *sufidüd* 'been enough' have only [d] unlike their
infins. *maure* or *moure* and *sufî*. Past participles with another consonantal
variation are *cranhüd* or *cranjüd* 'feared,' which can also be regular *cranîd*. In
that last instance, the three by-form past participles are linked to three out of
the four by-form infinitives *cranhe*, *cranje*, *cranïtre*, or *cranî*.

As in dialects of Occitan generally, verbs whose stems end in a labial
consonant seldom acquire [g] marking on their past participles. An example is
Auv. *cheubud* 'fit into' ≠ CAPTU (infin. *cheubre*). Another is *rassebüd* or
arsebüd 'received' ≠ RECEPTU (infin. *rassebre*, *arsebre*, *rasseure*, *arseure*,
rasseupre, *rassaupre*, etc.). An exception is the verb with infin. *seubre*, *saubre*,
saupre, or *sagure* 'know,' whose past participle may be more or less expected
seubüd, or [g]-ful *sougüd*, or combinatory *seubegüd* 'known' (Bonnaud, 133–
39, 179–85). Double marking scarcely decreases allomorphy.

Perhaps even greater past-participial variation flourishes in the next
dialect of Occitan to be reviewed. As always in this book, though, apparent
plenty or scarcity may be simply artifacts of documentation.

4.6.1.8. Gévaudanais

Past participles for Gévaudanais, spoken in the département of Lozère, come from Buffière's *Dictionnaire occitan-français: dialecte gévaudanais*. Here final [t] in regular masc.sg. forms has been maintained. Some rhizotonics, mostly monosyllabic, still thrive: *ars* 'burned,' *bist* 'seen,' *mort* 'died,' *prés* 'taken' (403: "rarement *prengut -udo*"), *respost* 'answered,' and *tench* 'dyed,' with *lièch* < LĒCTU 'chosen' surviving in the nominal sense 'bride's trousseau.' Note also *counquist* 'conquered,' a sigmatic-tautic syncopated since CL days.

Gévaudanais has no direct reflex of rhizotonic RUPTU; the verb *roumpre* 'break' has regular *roumput* as its only past participle. Unsurprisingly, the dialect contains several old p.p. forms already adjectival in Latin, like *agut* 'sharp' < ACŪTU, *menut* 'tiny' < MINŪTU, and *faus* 'untrue' < FALSU. Among these, *faus* has yielded to *falhit* in the past-participial sense 'lacked.' There are also several others, still past-participial in Latin—*estrech* 'narrow' < STRICTU, *tort* 'wrong' < TORTU, *finto* 'dissimulation' < FICTA plus infectum nasality— that survive only as adjectives or nouns.

Gévaudanais has replaced rhizotonics with arrhizotonics. Many have aligned themselves more closely with the root of their infinitives, even if new irregularities have emerged along the way. Among 2nd- and 3rd-conj. replacements, the tautic athematic p.p. VĪCTU 'lived' has been supplanted by *biscut* (infin. *bieure*), TEXTU 'woven' by *teissut* (infin. *teisse*), and TENTU 'held' by *tengut* (infin. *tene*). Among 4th-conj. replacements, SALTU 'jumped' has vanished in favor of *sallit* 'gone out' (infin. *salli*) and CAPTU 'taken' in favor of *cabit* 'put away, squeezed' (infin. *cabi*, from a 4th-conj. variant of CAPERE 'take'). Sigmatic SĒNSU 'felt' has been replaced by regular *sentit* (infin. *senti*), as it has everywhere, and sigmatic EXPĀNSU 'spread' has been replaced by regular *espanit* (infin. *espani*). Anomalously as in Italian, French, or Catalan, the new arrhizotonic p.p. *bengut* 'come' still does not match the 4th-conj. infin. *beni*, but it can represent no reflex of rhizotonic VENTU. Rhizotonic thematic past participles like VENDĬTU 'sold' and DĒBĬTU 'owed' have been replaced by *degut* and *bendut* (3rd-conj. infins. *deure* or *dieure, bendre*). The verb *durbi* 'open' < DĒ + APERĪRE has evolved a regular arrhizotonic p.p. *durbit* instead of a direct descendant of rhizotonic (DĒ +) APERTU as in Languedocian *dobert* or *dubert*.

Gévaudanais retains vestiges of past-participial choices made long ago by speakers of LL or PR for verbs lacking a past participle in CL. Among others, *balgut* 'been worth,' *begut* 'drunk,' *chagut* 'been needed' (once 'been hot'), *dolgut* 'hurt, grieved,' *estat* 'been,' *ferit* 'hit,' *flourit* 'bloomed,' *jagut* 'lain,' *lusit* 'shone,' and *nebat* 'snowed' have sprung up locally. Arrhizotonic reflexes of stem-lengthened verbs, resembling some in Catalan, are evident in infinitives like *moussiga* 'bite' competing with still-active *mordre* (p.p. *mors* < MORSU), and in *penja* 'hang,' *manja* 'eat,' and *pintra* 'paint' from a variant with inserted [r] perhaps ± LL/PR *PINCTOR 'painter' for PICTOR) rather than PINGERE. Evidently, infin. *casca* 'hit; fall' (shades of CADŌ and CÆDŌ!) has come from the same etymon as Cat./Sp. *cascar* 'crack'; that long infinitive is based on past-participial QUASSU + -ICĀRE rather than present-infinitival QUATERE 'shake.' All five remade 1st-conj. infinitives have acquired masc.sg. past participles in -*at*: *moussigat, penjat, manjat, pintrat,* and *cascat.*

Additional verbs in Gévaudanais have been built on old past-participial stems, notably sigmatic ones. Besides expected *usa* 'use' from *ŪSĀRE and *ausa* 'dare' from *AUSĀRE, each with a regular 1st-conj. past participle (*ausat, usat*), the infin. *esparsa* 'scatter' and its irregular 4th-conj.-style p.p. *esparcit* have both been drawn from p.p. SPARSU rather than infin. SPARGERE, just as *fissa* 'fasten' and its regular p.p. *fissat* have been drawn from p.p. FĪXU rather than infin. FĪGERE, and *remaisa* 'stay' with its regular p.p. *remaisat* have come from p.p. REMĀNSU rather than infin. REMANĒRE. As in French and Catalan, Gév. *ras* 'close-cropped' < RĀSU 'shaved' survives only adjectivally, but on it has been built a regular 1st-conj. verb *rasa* 'shave' with p.p. *rasat*, perhaps traceable to an old Latin frequentative.

Another peculiarity of Gévaudanais may be found in its treatment of PRUĪRE 'itch' (no CL p.p.). The verb survives elsewhere as Cat. *pruir* (p.p. *pruit*) and It. *prudere*. In Gévaudanais, where intervocalic [d] often fricativizes to [z] as in *ausit* 'heard' < AUDĪTU, the current infin. *prusi* and its p.p. *prusegut* appear to derive from a Proto-Romance form resembling the Italian one, which still lacks a past participle. A similar development has taken place in arrhizotonic *cresegut* 'believed' ≠ CRĒDĬTU, though infin. *creire* < CRĒDERE no longer has either [d] or [z].

If one expects an Occitan dialect to have plenty of by-forms, one will seldom be disappointed. In Gévaudanais, some instances of competition among past participles entail vocalization or nonvocalization of preconsonantal [l], like *bolgut* and *bougut* 'wanted' (infin. *boulé*), or pretonic vowel alternations like the ones in *bencut* or *bincut* 'won' (infin. *benci*), in *plòugut* or *pleugut* 'rained' (infin. *plòure* or *plèure*), and in the triplet *ofrit, oufrit,* or *ufrit* 'offered,' from triple infinitives beginning with each of the vowels above. Competing *coulligiat* and *coulligit* 'gathered' are regular matches for their competing infinitives, 1st-conj. *coulligia* and 4th-conj. *coulligi.* These Gév. past participles have replaced rhizotonic VICTU 'won,' OBLĀTU 'forgotten,' and COLLĒCTU 'gathered,' with the other two lacking past participles in CL. A further pair of p.p. competitors is *cubèrt* or *coubèrt* 'covered,' not yet wholly brought into line with the 4th-conj. infin. *cubri.* Other alternations involve different verb classes, so that the 3rd-conj. infin. *sègre* 'follow' may have either inherited *segut* or evolved *seguit* as its past participle; for once, the new form is less regular than the old.

When Gévaudanais has by-form past participles, an etymological inheritance generally competes with a present-based innovation ending in [gut]. Sigmatic past participles facing competition include *claus* versus *claugut* 'shut' (infin. *claure*) and *ris* versus unusual *resegut* 'laughed' (infin. *rire* or *reire*), no doubt with [z] from [d] again. Unetymological sigmatic *nos* vies with the -ŪTU forms *nousut* and [g]-ful *nousegut* 'harmed' (infin. *nose* or *noire*).[47] Thus, in western ROMANIA, sigmatics may survive if suffixed.

A few Gévaudanais past participles that had [kt] in Latin now have either [tʃ] or [(i)t], as in undifferentiated Old Occitan: *dich* and *dit* 'said, told' (infin. *dire* or *díser*), *fach* and *fait* 'done/made' (infin. *faire* or *fa*), *jount* and *jounch* 'joined' (infin. *jounhe*), *punch* and *pount* 'stung' (infin. *pounhe* or *pónhe*), and *trach* and *trait* 'milked,' with sigmatic *trasegut*, too (infin. *traire*).

Nonetheless, *escriure* 'write' has only *escrich* for a past participle, and remade 1st-conj. *ouncha* 'oil' has only inherited *ounch*. If some standardization has taken place without intervention by forty mortals, *ounch* may never be remade. A verb from the same class, with infin. *coire* or *còser* 'cook,' has etymological *cuèch* versus present-based [g]-ful *cousegut* for its p.p. Similarly, *plonhe* or *plànher* 'complain, lament' has p.p. *plonch* versus present-based [g]-ful *planigut*.

In Gévaudanais, the most common type of past-participial alternation occurs between forms in [ut] and forms in [gut]: *chauput* 'fit' versus *chaupegut* (infin. *chaupre* < CAPERE), *courrut* 'run' versus *corregut* (infin. *courre* or *correr*), *cousut* 'sewn' versus *cousegut* (infin. *couse* or *cóse*), already mentioned *nousut* 'harmed' versus *nousegut* and also sigmatic *nos* (infin. *nose* or *noire*), *taisut* 'been quiet' versus *taisegut* (infin. *se taise*), and *temut* 'feared' versus *temegut* (infin. *teme*). Here again, no traces remain of rhizotonic past participles like CAPTU, CURSU, TACĬTU; the verb TIMĒRE 'fear' lacked a p.p. in CL. A 4th-conj.-looking form, *querrit* 'looked for,' competes with [g]-ful *querregut* (infin. *quèrre*) but does not continue QUÆSĪTU.

Further examples of variation within -ŪTU past participles in Gévaudanais are old-style *nascut* 'born' versus newer *naissut*, and also *paregut* 'appeared' versus *pareissut*; the second in each pair is based on the stem of infins. *naisse* or *pareisse*. One wonders why no form like **parescut* has arisen. In *pougut* 'been able' versus *pouscut* (infin. *pouire* or *poire*), the second by-form seems to have been based on the present subjunctive stem, an odd (unconscious) choice for a past-participial analogy.

Typifying the lack of standardization, a few verbs have not two but three competing past participles. In the by-forms *recebut* 'received' versus *reçauput*, the first has been based on infin. *recebre*, the second on a competing infin. *reçaupre*, but a third infin. by-form *reçaure* has inspired no past participle. Neither has CL RECEPTU. In the triple by-forms *sachut*, *sauput*, and *saupegut* 'known' (no CL p.p.), the first again seems to be based on the present subjunctive stem, the second on an infin. by-form *saupre*, and the third on that form plus a [g] suffix deriving from [w] as in -UĪ, but the competing infinitives *sabé* and *saure* seem to have inspired no past participles. For the once inchoative verb *creisse* 'grow' < CRĒSCERE, the [sk] p.p. *crescut* comes from a variant resembling It. *cresciuto*, the sigmatic Gév. p.p. *creissut* is based

---

[47] That form *nos* could have come from sigmatic-tautic **nost* from syncopated **nos'to* < NOCĬTU. Apart from a handful of dubious cases, though, in this book I refrain from hypothesizing that rhizotonic thematics survived outside Sardinia and southern Italy.

on the infin. stem, and the third by-form *cressegut* is based on the second one, with [g] suffixed. None comes from CRĒTU. For the verb *plaire* 'please,' the stem of p.p. *plasut* comes from the present stem, *plagut* shows the default mode for -ŪTU p.p.s, and *plasegut* results from a blend of the two. None comes from rhizotonic thematic PLACĬTU.

For the verb with infin. *couneisse* or *counouisse* 'know,' four past participles exist in Gévaudanais. All show local reflexes of -ŪTU. None comes from rhizotonic COGNĬTU. The shortest of these, *counegut*, is based on the first part of either infinitive given above, plus the [g] suffix; *couneissut* is based on the first infinitive and *counouissut* on the second infinitive; the longest, doubly marked *couneissegut*, represents a blend of types. For the verb *torce* 'twist' and its variant *tosse*, finally, five past participles are current: *tors* and [r]-less *tos* are from pf. TORSĪ, the sigmatic perfect of CL; infinitive-based *torçut* bears traces of the spread of -ŪTU p.p.s in LL or PR; *tourcegut* and [r]-less *toussegut* represent a lengthening of *torçut* with [g] suffixed just before a reflex of -ŪTU. None of these past participles comes from rhizotonic TORTU, which survive as a noun meaning 'wrong.'

In all likelihood, each variant has its own stylistic connotations: sex, age, wealth, career, locale? Lacking native-speaker competence, I cannot give such details here. Rather, I have reviewed past participles from this little-known dialect so that readers may appreciate how lushly allophony must have flourished across ROMANIA before literary standards were contrived and enjoined.

4.6.1.9. Languedocian

Reckoned the most conservative dialect of Occitan, Languedocian has a semantic innovation in *prusir* 'sprout' < PRŌDĪRE 'come out, turn out,' with regular p.p. *prusit* to fill a slot left empty in Latin (see §4.3.2).[48] Retaining final [t] for masc.sg. past participles, Languedocian has also kept a fair number of rhizotonic inheritances from Latin. Data come from Iliescu and Mourin's *Typologie de la morphologie verbale romane.*

Variants may arise between vocalized and unvocalized [l], as in *molt* or *mout* 'ground,' or again *falgut* or *faugut* 'required' and *calgut* or *caugut* 'mattered' but earlier 'heated.' Such inconsistencies may be merely orthographic; the following ones hardly are. Two sets of variants reflect continued wavering in the infinitive among *mòl(d)dre*, *mòu(d)re*, and *mòler*, among *fal(d)re*, *fau(d)re*, and *fàler*; yet only *caler* is accepted. For the class of past participles ending in *-ert*, variants exist in the pretonic back vowel: speakers may say *cobert* or *cubert* 'covered,' *dobert* or *dubert* 'opened,' *ofert* or *ufert* 'offered,' *sofert* or *sufert* 'suffered'; that variation co-occurs in infins. *cobrir* or *cubrir*, *dobrir* or *dubrir*, *ofrir* or *ufrir*, *sofrir* or *sufrir* and could be termed optional metaphony.

---

[48] A reflex of PRŌDĪRE 'come out, go forth' is also found in Engadin *pruir* 'sprout' (*REW* no. 6768). Remnants of an late-ancient or early-mediæval Sprachbund?

Variants still exist between past participles in [tʃ] and in [(i̯)t], both from [kt]: *dich* or *dit* 'said, told,' *fach* or *fait* 'done/made,' and *trach* or *trait* 'pulled,' among others. The same variation exists for *escrich* and *escrit* 'written,' both from a Latin p.p. in [pt]. Among their respective infinitives, *far* and *faire* do compete, but *dire, escriure,* and *traire* are the only accepted forms. Similarly, a Latin [ŋkt] cluster may yield either [ntʃ] or [nt], sometimes with vowel raising in the tautic athematic form. Compare the by-form p.p.s *planch* or *plant* 'complained,' *cench* or *cint* 'girded,' *crench* or *crent* 'feared' (also *crengut*), *pench* or *pint* 'painted' (also *pengut*), *ponch* or *pont* 'stung' (also *pongut*), and *jonch* or *jont* or *junt* 'joined' (also *jongut*).

Infinitives with endings from -NGERE vary, as do their past participles. Alternations may exist between [ɲ] and [ndʒ]: *crénher* or *crénger,* *plànher* or *plànger, cénher* or *cénger, pénher* or *pénger.* The two foursomes *pónher* or *pónger* or *púnher* or *púnger,* and *jónher* or *jónger* or *júnher* or *júnger,* display that variation as well as one between pretonic back vowels. Another set of variant past participles is found in *jait* 'lain,' perhaps syncopated from rhizotonic thematic JACĬTU, and *jagut,* for which there is the single infin. *jaire.* Yet another is partly rhyming *seit* and *segut* 'sat' ≠ SESSU, going with infin. by-forms *sèire* and *sèser.*

Among the large number of past participles with endings from -ŪTU, one notes the unique *tangut* 'touched' (infin. *tànher* or *tànger* < TANGERE), along with forms seen elsewhere like *vencut* 'won' (infin. *véncer* or *vencre*) and *viscut* 'lived' (infin. *viure*). None continues rhizotonic TĀCTU, VĪCTU, or VICTU. Among former inchoatives, one finds expected *pascut* 'tended, grazed,' *crescut* 'grown,' *tescut* 'woven,' and *merescut* 'deserved,' none of which continues rhizotonic PĀSTU, CRĒTU, TEXTU, or MERĬTU, corresponding to infins. *pàisser, créisser, téisser,* and *meréisser.* For infin. *nàisser* 'be born,' competing past participles are *nat* < NĀTU and *nascut.* Past participles containing a syllabic suffix in *-eg-* include *casegut* 'fallen' (infin. *càser* or *caire*), *corregut* 'run' (infin. *córrer*), and a by-form *queregut* 'looked for' competing with 4th-conj.-style *querit* ≠ QUÆSĪTU (infin. *quèrre* or *querir*).

Inheritances in Languedocian are sigmatic *aucis* 'killed' (infin. *aucir*) and *pres* 'taken' (infin. *prendre* or *prene*). A sigmatic pair of past participles, *fos* 'dug' < FOSSU (infin. *fòire*) and *claus* 'shut' < CLAUSU (infin. *claure*), competes with arrhizotonic *fosegut,* and *claugut.* From a by-form MULSU comes Lang. *mols* 'milked,' resembling Rom. *muls* but here competing with *molgut* (infin. *mòlzer*). Sigmatics that probably joined that class in LL/PR days are *tors* 'twisted' ± pf. TORSĪ (infin. *tòrcer*) and also *nos* 'harmed' ≠ NOCUĪ, NOCĬTU (infin. *nòire*), which past participles compete against long-form *torcegut, nosegut.* Sigmatic-tautic *vist* 'seen' (infin. *véser* or *veire*) probably endures from LL and has been joined by (*r*)*escost* 'hidden' (infin. [*r*]*escondre*); cf. It. *visto, nascosto* (Iliescu and Mourin, 402–5).

Relations have been close between past participles and preterits in Languedocian. As elsewhere in Catalonia and Occitania, suffixed [g] occurs within the past system of many verbs, here giving 1sg. prets. in *-guèri* and p.p.s in *-gut.* That [g] may replace a labial consonant, sometimes vocalized to [u̯], in the pres. stem. Examples include 1sg. pret. *aguèri* and p.p. *agut* 'had,' pret. *beguèri* 'drank' and p.p. *begut* 'drunk,' pret. *deguèri* and p.p. *degut* 'had to,' pret. *moguèri* and p.p. *mogut* 'moved,' where [g] corresponds to an old [b] or [v] in the pres. stem of e.g. infins. *aver, beure, deure,* and *mòure.* Another such verb is 3sg. pret. *ploguèt* and p.p. *plogut* 'rained,' for infin. *ploure.* In one verb, pret./p.p. [g] replaces pres. [d]: pret. *poguèri* 'was able' and p.p. *pogut* 'been able' go with infin. *poder.*

A [g] in both preterit and past participle may also seem to replace a fricative [z] or [s], both deriving from [d], that is found in present-tense forms. Instances of such seeming replacement are pret. *riguèri* and p.p. *rigut* 'laughed,' *clauguèri* and by-form *claugut* 'closed,' *plaguèri* and *plagut* 'pleased,' *creguèri* and *cregut* 'believed.' As suggested above, some infinitives have lost an earlier intervocalic consonant, giving e.g. *rire, claure, plaire* (still also *plàser*), and *creire.*

In examples of enhancement instead of replacement, a past-tense [g] may be added to a present root ending in a liquid or nasal consonant. Most often, it is added to [l], as in pret. *solguèri* and p.p. *solgut* 'undone, loosened,' pret. *valguèri* 'was worth' and p.p. *valgut* 'been worth,' pret. *volguèri* and p.p. *volgut* 'wanted.' Note also 3sg. pret. *calguèt* and p.p. *calgut* 'mattered,' 3sg. pret. *falguèt* and p.p. *falgut* 'been required.' The [g] suffix may also be added to present-tense stems ending in [n] to give [ŋg], as in pret. *venguèri* 'came' and p.p. *vengut* 'come,' pret. *tenguèri* 'held' and p.p. *tengut,* pret. *ponguèri* 'put' and p.p. *pongut*; that form is homophonous with a by-form *pongut* 'stung' that competes against *pont* and *ponch.* Yet the [g] suffix does not appear in the corresponding infins. *sòlvre* or *sòlver, valer, caler, voler, fàler* or *fal(d)re, venir, ténir* or *tenir,* and *póner.*

After [s], Lang. [g] usually devoices to [k], as in pret. *visquèri* 'lived' and p.p. *viscut,* pret. *tesquèri* 'wove' and p.p. *tescut* 'woven,' pret. *mesquèri* 'mixed,' pret. *cresquèri* 'grew' and p.p. *crescut* 'grown,' pret. *nasquèri* 'was born' and by-form p.p. *nascut* 'been born,' and pret. *pasquèri* 'tended, kept' and p.p. *pascut.* Again, the corresponding infinitives—*viure, téisser, méisser, créisser, nàisser,* and *pàisser*—show no trace of either velar stop. In another verb, [k] occurs after [ŋ] in pret. *venquèri* 'won' alongside p.p. *vencut,* but a glance at infin. *véncer* or *vencre* shows that [k] was or still is part of the root.

Despite the expansion of this [g] marker in Languedocian, more than a few innovative preterits in [g] have yet to attract their past participles into the same class. As one might expect, some of these independents rank among the highest-frequency verbs in the dialect. Thus, the by-form pret. *faguèri* 'did/made,' competing against *fèri,* has not attracted the p.p. *fach* or *fait.* Compare also pret. *auciguèri* and p.p. *aucis* 'killed,' pret. *diguèri* and p.p. *dit* or *dich* 'said, told,' pret. *escriguèri* 'wrote' and p.p. *escrit* or *escrich* 'written.' Two more perfective pairs that remain distinctive are pret. *prenguèri* 'took' and p.p. *pres* 'taken,' pret. *traguèri* and p.p. *trach* or *trait* 'pulled.' Again, the by-forms *veguèri* and *vegèri* 'saw' have failed to attract *vist* 'seen.' Of five by-forms for the past participle of *coire* or *cueire* 'cook'—*coch, coit, cuèch, cuéit,* and *cuoch*—none has acquired [g], though pret. *coguèri* has. For verbs with a great many variant past participles, one might note that the prets. *penguèri* 'painted' and *jonguèri* 'joined' match the by-form p.p.s *pengut* and *jongut*, if no others.

Other Languedocian preterits in [g] have extended their sway as far as a p.p. by-form, but no further. Most of the [g]-less past participles are inherited, or at any rate appear far older than the their [g]-ful rivals. They include sigmatics, as in pret. *clauguèri* 'shut' with by-form p.p.s *claugut* versus *claus*. In pret. *foguèri* 'dug' with by-form p.p.s *fosegut* versus *fos*, and in pret. *noguèri* 'harmed' with by-form p.p.s *nosegut* versus *nos*, old sigmatic past participles have been extended with *-egut*, but the stems thus created remain distinct from corresponding pret. stems. The inventory of by-form past participles also includes some tautic athematics, as in pret. *jaguèri* 'lay' with by-form p.p.s *jagut* versus *jait* 'lain,' and pret. *seguèri* 'sat' with by-form p.p.s *segut* versus *seit*. Finally, if both pret. *caiguèri* 'fell' and p.p. *casegut* 'fallen' (infin. *càser* or *caire*) have a [g] suffix, their stems remain as distinct as those of the pret/p.p. pairs *foguèri* and *fosegut* 'dug' or *noguèri* and *nosegut* 'harmed' (Iliescu and Mourin, 325–27, 402–5).

With marked dialectal divergences, with few "fluent active native speakers" under age forty (Wheeler 1988b, 277), all dialects of Occitan may soon become of historical interest alone. With a recognized literary standard and thorough training of young speakers, closely related Catalan has been thriving.

4.6.2. CATALAN

What Wheeler terms "a distinctly Catalan part of common vocabulary" (1988a, 206), though much of it is also current in Occitan, includes several verbs etymologically distinct from reflexes in Romanian, Italian, French, and Spanish: *aixecar* 'raise,' *dur* 'bring,' *tancar* 'shut,' *trencar* 'bend; break.'[49] Two other verbs quite different from forms in other major Romance languages are *amargar* 'hide' from Germanic and *rentar* 'wash' from *RECENTARE (cf. RECENTE 'fresh, young.')[50] Except for *dur* (p.p. *dut*), these verbs have the regular 1st-conj. past participles: *aixecat, tancat, trencat, amargat,* and *rentat*.

In the Barcelona-based standard, *dar* 'give' has become partly defective: in forms 1, 2, 3 and 6 of the present indicative and subjunctive, and in the imperative, it has fallen into disuse and been replaced by *donar* 'give' (Oliva and Buxton, 262). This restriction appears not to have affected the regular past

---

[49] Cat. *trencar* 'shut' is paralleled in Sp./Ptg. *trincar*, variants of the TRUNCĀRE 'slice, cut off' that more regularly gave Oc./Cat./Sp./Ptg. *troncar*, Fr. *trancher* (*REW* no. 8953). Cat. *tancar* seems to come from a clipping of a verb that gave Fr. *étancher* 'stanch,' Oc./Cat./Sp./Ptg. *estancar* 'dam up, block, jam,' and OSp. *atancar* 'stop; delay,' but the verb must be marked o.o.o. 'of obscure origin' (*REW* nos. 8225, 8228a). Save for its [k], one might almost derive *tancar* from a variant of STRANGULĀRE 'choke, throttle.'

[50] Reflexes of *RECENTARE are also found in Fri. *rezentá* and OSp. *recentar* 'refresh,' Fr. *rincer* 'rinse,' and Oc. *rezensar* 'cleanse' (*REW* no. 7110).

participle *dat* 'given,' but see §4.6.2.10 for the state of giving in Alguerese Catalan.

Traces of the old long-form -ICĀTU p.p. ending are still evident in 1st-conj. verbs with p.p.s *rossegat* 'gnawn' ≠ RŌSU and in *mossegat* 'bitten' ≠ MORSU (cf. Rom. *muşcat*) and *cascat* 'cracked' ≠ QUASSU 'shaken.' A present participle CREPANTE 'rattled' survives in another 1st-conj. verb with p.p. *crebantat* 'burst.' Other verb stretchers seem to have left traces, in e.g. p.p.s *carejat* 'done without' ≠ CARĬTU or CASSU 'lacked,' *penjat* 'hung' ≠ PĒNSU (cf. Fr. *penché*), and *punxat* 'stung' ≠ PŪNCTU (cf. Sp. *punzado*). Replacing reflexes of UNG(U)ERE 'oil' has been 1st-conj. *untar* with regular p.p. *untat*, the whole verb clearly based on the old past participle ŪNCTU.

Because of items like p.p. *bullit* 'boiled' < BULLĪTU 'bubbled,' Catalan would rank as a language of central ROMANIA. However, certain 4th-conj.-style p.p.s like *decidit* 'decided,' *descendit* 'gone down,' *fingit* 'pretended,' and *tendit* 'held out' look more like Spanish than like French or Italian. Catalan has no straight past-participial reflex of CĪNCTU 'girded' but uses a 1st-conj. verb with p.p. *cinglat*. Owing to conflation of NECĀRE and NEGĀRE, the Catalan verb *negar* (p.p. *negat*) may mean either 'deny' or 'drown'; in comparable past participles, Spanish contrasts prefixed *anegado* 'drowned' with unprefixed *negado* 'denied,' just as Italian contrasts *annegato* with *negato*. Similarly, Romanian contrasts prefixed *înnecat* 'drowned' and unprefixed *negat* 'denied,' with the two also differing in intervocalic stops. Meanwhile, French makes a contrast between pretonic vowels in *noyé* 'drowned' versus *nié* 'denied.'

4.6.2.1. Kinds of Rhizotonic Past Participles

Unlike their arrhizotonic cousins in -*at*, -*it*, or -*ut*, rhizotonic past participles in Catalan are built on the present stem, often with final consonant deletion plus [t], [z], or rarely [st] to form the masc.sg. (Wheeler, 1988a, 187). Among rhizotonics, feminine forms maintain originally—and sometimes still—supported [t], rather than leniting unsupported [t] to [ð] as happens in arrhizotonic forms. Rhizotonic fem.sg. past participles like *feta* 'done/made,' *dita* 'said, told,' and *duta* 'brought' thus contrast with arrhizotonic ones like *anada* 'gone,' *collida* 'gathered,' and *coneguda* 'known.' Such forms also stand apart from sigmatic pairs like masc. *pres* 'taken' with final [s] and fem. *presa* with intervocalic [z].

One group of sigmatics ends in -*mes* 'put' < MISSU 'sent' in e.g. *admès* 'allowed, accepted,' *omès* 'left out,' and *emès* 'given off.' Another group has *pres* 'taken' < PRĒNSU in compounds like *comprès* 'squeezed' and *imprès* 'printed' (with infin. *imprimir*). Two more are *romàs* 'stayed' < REMĀNSU and *clos* 'shut' < CLAUSU.

Sigmatic *pretès* 'sought, claimed,' *estès* 'spread,' and *entès* 'understood' suggest that TĒNSU (still surviving adjectivally as *tès*; cf. Sp. *tieso* 'stiff') rather than TENTU was the preferred past participle meaning 'held' in Proto-Catalan. P.p. forms in -*ès* are also standard for other infinitives ending in -*endre*, like *encès* 'lit' < INCĒNSU, *despès* 'spent' < DĒ + EXPĒNSU and *ofès* 'offended' < OFFĒNSU. Another sigmatic group in Catalan has p.p.s *empès* 'thrust, shoved' ≠ IMPĀCTU 'dashed against' and *atès* 'overtaken' ≠ ATTĀCTU 'touched, arrived' for infinitives *empènyer, atènyer;* yet another infinitive in the same class, *estrènyer,* has the tautic athematic p.p. *estret* 'narrowed' < STRICTU, also used as an adjective. Morphological predictability remains incomplete for verbs with infinitives in *-endre* or *-ènyer.*

Tautic athematic survivals once containing [kt] are by-form *cuit* 'cooked' < COCTU, *fet* 'done/made' < FACTU, and *tret* 'pulled out' < TRACTU 'pulled.' Of those once containing [pt], *scrit* 'written' < SCRĪPTU remains rhizotonic, but RUPTU has been remade as *romput* 'broken.' Survivals in [rt] include *mort* 'died; killed' and adjectival *tort* 'bent, crooked' < TORTU 'twisted.'

Catalan has developed a few sigmatic-tautic past participles. Two, *respost* 'answered' and *vist* 'seen,' display an [st] suffix only half present in RESPŌNSU and VĪSU. A third, *post,* survives from POS(I)TU and has been restricted to the senses 'laid (eggs)' or 'set (sun, moon, stars).' Made of a cluster, the [st] suffix is maintained unvoiced in fem. *resposta* and *vista,* never **respozda* or **vizda* (Mendeloff, 42). Purely adjectival *adust* 'scorched; austere' (cf. Sp. *adusto* 'grim, forbidding') represents a survival of p.p. USTU 'charred'; purely adverbial *tost* 'soon' (cf. Fr. *tôt*) represents a survival of p.p. TOSTU 'parched.'

Away from Sardinia and southern Italy, survivals of the tautic athematic type become doubtful and rare. Romanian may have one in *fiert* 'boiled' (no CL p.p.); Catalan may have another in *mòlt* 'ground,' if it comes from a syncopation of MOLĬTU.

4.6.2.2. Rhizotonics: Remodeling or Retention

Certain forms still current attest to reshapings between Latin and Catalan. There are 1st-conj. *covat* 'brooded, hatched,' *sonat* 'rang,' *segat* 'reaped, mown,' and *vedat* 'forbidden.' There are 2nd-/3rd-conj. *cabut* 'fit into,' and *cernut* 'sifted.' There are 4th-conj. *adherit* 'stuck,' *carpit* 'plucked,' *collit* 'gathered,' *eixit* 'gone out,' *farcit* 'stuffed,' *rendit* 'given back,' *sentit* 'felt,' and *teixit* 'woven.' Catalan p.p.s for verbs lacking them in Latin are *begut* 'drunk,' *ferit* 'hit,' *lluït* 'shone,' *podrit* 'rotted,' *pruit* 'itched,' and *tremit* or *tremut* 'shuddered.' The adj. *tolit* 'crippled' comes from a reshaping of SUBLĀTU₁ 'taken away.' Catalan past participles that show a change of arrhizotonic conjugation include *cosit* 'sewn' ≠ CŌNSŪTU, *delit* 'destroyed' ≠ DĒLĒTU, and *seguit* 'followed' ≠ SECŪTU. A syncopated reflex of VOLŪTU 'rolled' still exists in the 1st-conj. verb *voltar* with p.p. *voltat* 'gone around' (cf. Sp. *voltado*).

Since Old Catalan times, more rhizotonic past participles have been reshaped, as Badía i Margarit makes clear in *Gramàtica històrica catalana.* After remarking that most rhizotonic past participles inherited by Old Catalan have been retained with full verbal value, Badía i Margarit acknowledges (365) that *defès* 'fought off' < DĒFĒNSU, *tort* 'twisted' < TORTU, *elet* 'chosen' < ĒLĒCTU, *fuyt* 'fled' (still dialectal) < FUGĬTU, and *tint* 'dyed' < TĪNCTU have been replaced as past participles in standard Catalan by regular 1st-conj.

defensat, regular 2nd-conj. *torçut*, and regular 4th-conj. *elegit, fugit, tenyit*. Likewise, OCat. *coleyt* 'gathered' < COLLĒCTU has been replaced by *collit*.

At the same time, OCat. *duyt* 'brought' < DUCTU 'led' has lost its yod to resemble any other 2nd-/3rd-conj. past participle in *-ut*. OCat. *feyt* 'done/made,' *treyt* 'pulled out,' and *estreyt* 'tightened' < FACTU, TRACTU, STRICTU have lost yod to become ModCat. *fet, tret*, and *estret* (infins. *fer, treure, estrènyer*). They stand as morphological isolates, for their one-time rhyming partners *freyt* 'fried' and *leyt* 'read' are now 4th-conj. *fregit* and *llegit* ± infins. *fregir* and *llegir*. An Occitan-looking oddity mentioned by Mourin (157), OCat. *crasagut* 'believed,' has yielded to more regular *cregut* (infin. *creure*). Within arrhizotonics, the OCat. p.p. *elegut* 'chosen' has been regularized to match infin. *elegir*; contrasting morphologically with a semilearnèd adj. *electe* 'elect' (Martin i Castell, 61).

Today, the OCat. p.p. *tort* 'twisted' has been practically limited to adjectival use, masc. *tint* and fem. *tinta* 'dyed' to nominal use. One oddity attested into the fifteenth century, *lest* 'read' (Badía i Margarit, 365), seems to have a blend of the pf./pret. stem and the p.p. stem; another etymon might be the LEGESTUM mentioned by Virgilius Maro of Toulouse. No doubt pronounced with an initial [ʎ], *lest* has been replaced, just as *leyt* has been.

Beside *estat* 'been' < STATU 'stood, stayed,' secondary *sigut* 'been' has been shaped from the present subjunctive and imperative stem *sig-* plus the -ŪTU past-participial marker in a way reminiscent of Olt. *suto* 'been.' Though denounced by purists who favor *estat*, the form *sigut* retains its popularity among the unpretentious (J. Sempere, p.c.). The 3sg. pret. *estigué* 'was' resembles both *estat* and *sigut* but has aligned itself wholly with neither. Eastern dialects of Catalan have a different past participle for this verb: ECat. *set* 'been' rhymes with std. *fet* 'done/made' and has probably been made by analogy with that often-used form.

One peculiarity of Catalan has been the spread of past participles in *-ert* beyond the usual retentions and reshapings. Among retentions are *obert* 'opened' and *cobert* 'covered,' the second having influenced vocalism in the first. Among reshapings found elsewhere are Cat. *ofert* 'offered' ≠ OBLĀTU and *sofert* 'suffered' ≠ SUBLĀTU₂. All four verbs have infinitives in *-ir* and 3sg. prets. in *-í*. Apparently by analogy with such forms in *-fert* or *-bert*, speakers have created unetymological past participles that end either in *-plert* like *omplert* 'filled,' *complert* 'accomplished,' *suplert* 'replaced' or in *-blert* like *establert* 'set up' and *reblert* 'crammed.' Those past participles all have infinitives in *-ir*. From the vantage point of "regular" 2nd-conj. IMPLĒTU, COMPLĒTU, and SUPPLĒTU 'made complete,' the Catalan successor forms show intrusive [r], but that explanation could hardly account for the reshaping of 4th-conj. STABILĪTU or (perhaps) of sigmatic REPULSU 'driven back'; cf. 3rd-conj. infin. REPELLERE. Wavering persists in one verb's past participle: for *complir* 'fulfill, carry out,' either innovative *complert* or regular *complit* is recognized as standard. Recall the Italian by-form infins. *empiere* or *empire* 'fill': each has a regular past participle, in *-uto* and in *-ito*, but no variant in *-erto* has ever emerged for this verb (§3.5.10).

4.6.2.3. Spread of Past Participles in –*gut*

As in French, Italian, and Romanian, a reflex of -ŪTU has become the default p.p. ending for 2nd- and 3rd-conj. verbs, giving e.g. Cat. *sabut* 'known' (no CL p.p.). Inherited *batut* 'beaten' and *fotut* 'fucked' continue to thrive. However, in Catalan and Occitan both, a great many such p.p.s end in -*gut* rather than expected -*ut*. Such forms include *begut* 'drunk,' *plogut* 'rained,' and *pogut* 'been able' (no CL p.p.s) Old Catalan also had *legut* 'been allowed,' remade from LICĬTU; Modern Catalan still has *ragut* 'shaved' and rare *solgut* 'been used to,' remade from RĀSU and SOLĬTU.

Table 4–7 illustrates often-shared Romance innovations in -ŪTU.

Table 4–7

Catalan Past Participles in –*gut*

( ) archaic   [ ] unlike Catalan form

Latin	Catalan	Old French	Italian	Romanian
Replacements for rhizotonic thematics				
COGNITU	conegut	coneü	conosciuto	cunoscut
CRĒDIITU	cregut	creü	creduto	crezut
HABITU	hagut	eü	avuto	avut
JACITU	jagut	(geü)	giaciuto	zăcut
PĀRITU	paregut	paru	(paruto)	părut
PLACITU	plagut	pleü	piaciuto	plăcut
VALITU	valgut	valu	(valuto)	—
Replacements for sigmatics				
CURSU	corregut	couru	[corso]	[curs]
-SESSU	segut	[-sis]	seduto	şezut
Replacements for tautic athematics				
TENTU	tingut	tenu	tenuto	ţinut
VENTU	vingut	venu	venuto	[venit]

(Included in parentheses in Table 4–7 are OIt. *paruto* 'appeared' and *valuto* 'been worth,' since reshaped as the std. sigmatics *parso* and *valso*).

Although all major Romance languages east of Castile have such past participles, only Catalan and Occitan have large numbers in *-gut*. Shared forms in *-gut* are in fact my principal criterion for treating Occitan and Catalan together in this book.

As noted, this [g] past-participial marker derives from LL/PR [w] in the perfect of verbs mostly in the 2nd conjugation. Having evolved through a presumed [gw] stage to [g], it came to mark many past participles in both languages. As noted, it could have been reinforced by surviving [g] from CL [k] in some paradigms of the high-frequency verb *dir* < DĪCERE 'say, tell' such as ModCat. 1sg. pres.subj. *digui*, impf.subj. *digués*, pret. *diguí*, together with the form perhaps most commonly said and heard, 1sg. pres.indic. *dic* < DĪCŌ, with what might have sounded like final devoicing.

To be sure, in Catalan the velar [g] has failed to extend itself after past-participial roots ending in the bilabials [b] or [p], paralleling the infectum root. Thus, *cabut* 'gone into' and *rebut* 'received,' and aforementioned *romput* 'broken' and *sabut* 'known' (infins. *cabre, rebre, rompre, saber*) make do without it, but none of these three could derive from CAPTU and RECEPTU or a fortiori from past participles nonexistent in CL. Rather, they most likely come from the same source as the -ŪTU p.p.s encountered in Romania, Italy, and France. These verbs' preterits, typified by 3sg. *cabé, rebé, rompé*, and *sabé*, also lack the [g] marker. Further p.p.s in that group are *concebut* 'imagined,' *decebut* 'tricked,' and *percebut* 'realized.' Likewise, two verbs whose roots end in [m], namely *témer* 'fear' and *trémer* (also *tremir*) 'shudder,' lack that [g] marker in the p.p.s *temut* and by-form *tremut* (also *tremit*).

An exception to the bilabiality rule might appear to be p.p. *hagut* 'had' ≠ HABĬTU (cf. OOc. *agut*), in which the intervocalic bilabial in CL was [b] rather than [p]; that [b] might have weakened to zero after fricativizing to [β] or [v], unlike Rom. *avut* or It. *avuto*. That [g] also appears in preterits like 3sg. *hagué*. In any event, a few other *-ut* p.p.s in Catalan, like *vençut* 'won' and perhaps *venut* 'sold,' were also based on the stems of infinitives, here *vèncer* and *vendre*, or more generally on infectum stems. Corresponding 3sg. preterits are [g]-ful *vengué* 'sold' but [g]-less *vencé* 'won.' Incidentally, that p.p. *venut* (cf. Lad. *venù* 'sold') displays the expected reduction of [nd] to [n] seen inter alia in Cat. *anat* 'gone' as against Sp. *andado*.

Except for verbs with bilabial-final stems and one other—*perdre* 'lose' with p.p. *perdut*—other *-ut* past participles in Catalan contain a [g] suffix. Some of these seem to have been reinforced by voicing of a [k] already extant in presumed LL or PR forms like *plagut* 'pleased' (CL infin. PLACERE) and *jagut* 'lain' (CL infin. JACĒRE). Among this group, one might mention *conegut* 'known' ≠ COGNĬTU, *corregut* 'run' ≠ CURSU, *degut* 'owed, had to' ≠ DĒBĬTU, *mogut* 'moved' ≠ MŌTU, and of course *volgut* 'wanted' for which CL had no p.p. Those past participles have come to match [g]-ful preterits like 3sg. *plagué*, *jagué, conegué, corregué, mogué*, and *volgué*. For identity of roots within the past system if not outside it, compare also 3sg. pret. *caigué* 'fell' and p.p. *caigut* 'fallen' with infin. *caure,* and 1sg./3sg. imperf.indic. *queia.* The p.p. *segut,* which looks as though it ought to come from SECŪTU and mean 'followed,' actually means 'sat down' ≠ -SESSU, minus [d] but plus a [g] suffix also appearing in its 3sg. pret. *segué.* In most, the analogies at work are identifiable in hindsight.

In two verbs, metaphony originating in 1sg. pret. VĒNĪ 'I came' (cf. Sp. *vine,* Ptg. *vim*) has spread across the whole preterit and into the past participle of *venir,* and into those forms for its rhyming partner *tenir* 'hold, own' as well. Yet that development has not prevented the [g] marker from triumphing throughout those verbs' perfect systems in e.g. 3sgs. *vingué, tingué* and p.p.s *vingut, tingut.* All have evolved in parallel.

After a root ending in [s], that [g] suffix devoices to [k] as in Occitan, yielding *crescut* 'grown,' *nascut* 'born' (also rare *nat*), *viscut* 'lived,' and *merescut* 'deserved' together with preterits like 3sg. *cresqué, nasqué, visqué,* and *meresqué.* The first and second of these past participles (infins. *créixer* and *nèixer*) derive from infectum-based stems plus -ŪTU, both of them with an old inchoative infix, rather than from older CRĒTU₁ and NĀTU; the third (infin. *viure*) apparently comes from the preterit stem VIX- as in It. *vissuto* rather than from VĪCTU; the fourth (infin. *merèixer*) seems to have been modeled on the first and cannot derive directly from 2nd-conj. MERĒRE with rhizotonic p.p. MERĬTU.

Again as in Occitan, extension of the [g] marker into the preterit has not always reached the past participle in Catalan. Compare the 3sg. prets. *romangué* 'stayed,' *clogué* 'shut,' *fongué* 'melted,' and *prengué* 'took' with the still sigmatic p.p.s *romàs, clos, fos,* and *pres.* Compare the 3sg. prets. *cogué* 'cooked,' *tragué* 'pulled out,' *digué* 'said, told,' and *dugué* 'brought' with the still tautic athematic p.p.s *cuit, tret, dit,* and *dut;* p.p. *cogut* 'cooked' has however evolved as a by-form for *cuit.* Compare also the 3sg. pret. *respongué* 'answered' with the still sigmatic-tautic p.p. *respost.* Other persistent irregularities in the past system may be seen in 3sg. prets. like *escriví* 'wrote,' *feu* 'did/made,' and *veu* 'saw' contrasting with the past participles *escrit* 'written,' *fet* 'done/made,' and *vist* 'seen.' In such verbs as these, high frequency still delays reduction of allomorphy.

For a few verbs, continued wavering between past participles is reflected in Fabra's prescriptivistic *Gràmatica catalana* (1969). Fabra advises speakers to avoid certain past participles with [sk] analogically extended like *complascut* 'pleased, obliged,' *aparescut* 'appeared, turned up,' and *comparescut* 'appeared [before a lawcourt]' and favors the by-forms in [g] *complagut, aparegut,* and *comparegut.* On the other hand, Fabra recommends as standard both *sabut* 'known' and *cabut* 'fit into.' He cites but disallows two competing past participles, *sapigut* 'known' and *capigut* 'fit into,' which reflect analogical extension of [g] even for a root ending with a bilabial stop, by analogy with pres. subj. *sàpiga, càpiga,* etc., and some imperatives, just as in the standard p.p.s *segut* 'sat,' *begut* 'drunk,' *caigut* 'fallen' are used alongside their present subjunctives *segui, begui, caigui* etc. In Catalonia as elsewhere across ROMANIA, one analogical pressure may well oppose another.

4.6.2.4. Morphological Patterns within the Past System

In several Catalan verbs, past participles and preterits have come to resemble each other more than they did in Latin. Reduction of allomorphy could affect either the stem for all parts of a verb or the stem used within the past system. In the first group, infin. *cerndre* 'sift' has the p.p. *cernut* (cf. Rom. *cernut*), the latter deriving from the present stem of CERNERE rather than pf. CRĒVĪ or p.p. CRĒTU₂. Still in the first group, *estargir* 'wipe, scour' with p.p. *estargit* has been based throughout on the stem of EXTERGERE 'wipe off'; vowel-changed *fos* 'melted' (cf. FŪSU 'poured') aligned itself more closely with the regularly evolving infin. *fondre* < FUNDERE. In that second group, tonic vowels in *dit* 'said, told' < DICTU, and *dut* 'brought' < DUCTU 'led' have been influenced by preterits; otherwise they would have turned into something like **deit*, **doit*.

Despite what one might expect, allomorphy has tended to increase within the past system of 3rd-conj. verbs in Catalan. Preterits and past participles have grown less alike because of the spread of [g] marking to the preterit but not to the past participle: Old Catalan (3sg.) preterits in *-s* or *-x* [ʃ] have been remade in *-gué*, but Old Catalan past participles in *-s*, *-t*, or *-st* have largely remained the same. Thus, Old Catalan had preterit/past-participial pairs like *pos* and *post* 'set,' *pres* 'took/taken,' *dix* and *dit* 'said, told,' *scris* 'wrote' and *scrit* 'written,' *respos* and *respost* 'answered.' These days, the corresponding preterit/past-participial pairs are *pongué* and *post*, *prengué* and *pres*, *digué* and *dit*, *escrigué* and *escrit*, *respongué* and *respost*. Such arrhizotonic preterits have acquired default marking for their class; such rhizotonic past participles have become morphological isolates.

Another type in Old Catalan had preterits in [k] (written c̲ or ch̲) and past participles in [gut]. Examples of that pairing were (3sg.) *ac* and *agut* 'had,' *bech* 'drank' and *begut* 'drunk,' *caich* 'fell' and *caigut* 'fallen,' *correch* 'ran' and *corregut* 'run,' *jach* 'lay' and *jagut* 'lain,' *volch* and *volgut* 'wanted.' A related Old Catalan type had preterits in [sk] and past participles in [skut]: *cresch* 'grew' and *crescut* 'grown,' *nasch* and *nascut* 'born,' *visc* and *viscut* 'lived.' Both [k] and [sk] preterits have since been remade along the lines of the [g]-ful p.p. stem, which itself has stayed unchanged. Thus, the ModCat. preterits are *hagué, begué, caigué, corregué, jagué, volgué* from the first group and *cresqué, nasqué,* and *visqué* from the second group. A mixed type, with a preterit in [sk] and a past participle in [g], was OCat. *posc* 'could' and *pogut* 'been able,' since remade along past-participial lines as ModCat. *pogué* and *pogut*. By contrast with the verbs sketched in the preceding paragraph, those verbs have come closer to isomorphism within the past system used today.

Because of by-forms, two Old Catalan verbs presented a less focused picture: *tenir* 'hold, have' might have 3sg. pret. *tench* or *tingué*, if always p.p. *tingut*; and *venir* 'come' might have 3sg. pret. *vench* or *vingué* and p.p. *vingut* or *vengut*. In Modern Catalan, *(sos)tenir* has only pret. *(sos)tingué* and p.p. *(sos)tingut*, just as *venir* has only pret. *vingué* and p.p. *vingut*. If the past system here has moved nearer to isomorphism, it now differs from the present system in its first vowel, owing to metaphony inspired by the final high vowel in pf. VĒNĪ.

Partial remodeling has taken place for high-frequency *estar* 'be, stand, stay': OCat. *estech* 'was' and *estat* 'been' < STATU 'stood, stayed' are now *estigué* and unchanged *estat*. In another Old Catalan verb, (3sg.) *trasch* and *tret* 'pulled out,' the contrast between preterit and past participle has been reshaped to ModCat. *tragué* and unchanged *tret*. Influence has been exerted here not by these verbs' past participles in [gut] but by other verbs' preterits in arrhizotonic [ge]. In Old Catalan, preterit/past-participial pairs like *cogué* and *cogut* 'cooked,' *rigué* and *rigut* 'laughed,' *nogué* and *nogut* 'harmed' were in use, and they might have served as models for the rest.

Throughout the past system, two common verbs have resisted realignment. OCat. *feu* 'did/made' and *fet* 'done/made' are the same today as they were (infin. *fer*), and OCat. *viu* 'saw' and *vist* 'seen' are almost so as *veu* and *vist* (infin. *veure*); the ModCat. pret. *veu* might have been remade ±*feu*.

To come full circle, a fair number of verbs with remade preterits ending in (3sg.) -*gué* still have rhizotonic participles, whether sigmatic like *clos* 'shut,' *fos* 'melted,' *romàs* 'stayed,' and *tos* 'shorn' or tautic athematic like *mòlt* 'ground' and by-form *cuit* 'cooked.' As noted above, a few sigmatic-tautic past participles like *post* 'put, set' and *respost* 'answered' also coexist with preterits in -*gué* (Mourin, 180–83).

Dialects of Catalan surveyed here are Rossellonese in the northeast, Valencian in the far south, Tamaritan in the northwest, and Alguerese on Sardinia.[51] All four resemble the standard fairly closely. Before examining them, I wish to mention one form occurring in eastern dialects of Catalan: *set* 'been' as a past participle for *ser* (Griera y Gaja, 40). Regularization can scarcely have advanced further than that.

4.6.2.5. Nouns from Past Participles; Relics

In Catalan as in other Romance tongues, certain adjectives and nouns have the same morphology as past participles. Almost always in Catalan, any remodeling of past participles is reflected in the corresponding nouns. Thus, *beguda* 'beverage,' *ferida* 'wound,' and *sabuda* 'knowledge' serve as fem. past participles for verbs lacking that form in CL. The nouns *exida* 'departure' and *fugida* 'escape,' also serving as fem. past participles, reflect regular 4th-conj. realignments long ago. So does adj. *lluït* 'brilliant,' literally 'shone,' for a p.p. slot left vacant in CL.

Old direct-suffixation forms have been remade in *crescuda* 'growth' ≠ CRĒTA and *moguda* 'departure' ≠ MŌTA 'moved.' Old tautic athematics have been remade in *cabuda* 'space, room' ≠ CAPTA 'taken (in),' *rebuda* 'reception' ≠

---

[51] For a discussion of claims by deep-southern separatists to speak a language distinct from Catalan, see "The Valencian Linguistic Heterodoxy" by Joan Sempere Martínez in *Catalan Review* 9, no. 2 (1995: 97–124).

RECEPTA, and *vinguda* 'coming' ≠ VENTA. Old sigmatics have been remade in *caiguda* 'a fall' ≠ CĀSA, *correguda* 'a run' ≠ CURSA, *mossegada* 'a bite' ≠ MORSA, and *resposta* 'answer' ≠ RESPŌNSA. Another sigmatic-tautic is *posta* 'a putting, placing; setting of heavenly bodies,' still showing ancient syncope.

Two nominalized sigmatic past participles are *fes* 'crack, slit' < p.p. FISSU 'split' and *fosa* 'melting, thaw' < p.p. FŪSA 'poured.' A sigmatic pair is *pres* 'prisoner' and *presa* 'a taking.' Unlike, say, Fr. *fesse* 'buttock' contrasting with p.p. *fendu* 'split' or Sp. *preso* 'prisoner' contrasting with p.p. *prendido* 'caught,' each of those Catalan nouns continues to serve as a past participle.

Catalan does have relics stripped of past-participial force. As in French, the old p.p. *ras* < RĀSU 'shaved' survives as an adjective meaning 'short-haired, close-cropped.' As in Spanish *tieso*, the old Catalan p.p. *tes* < TĒNSU 'stretched' survives as an adjective meaning 'stiff, tight,' next to semilearnèd *tens* 'tense, strained' with an [ns] cluster intact; both adjectives have drifted away from 4th-conj. *tenir* 'have, own' and *tendir* 'tend to' with regular p.p.s *tenit, tendit.*

As the data above suggest, Catalan differs from French (§4.4.9.3) and Spanish (§4.7.7) in having few if any nouns that retain morphology abandoned for the corresponding past participles.

4.6.2.6. A Sampler of Nonstandard Forms

At first glance, past participles in Catalan seem to show a degree of conservatism unknown west of Italy. Closer inspection reveals that dialects have leveled outstanding anomalies that persist under the bookish standard. Data are drawn from Alcover's *Flexió verbal en els dialectes catalans* as revised by Moll (1929), a work not done justice to here. Undifferentiated here by dialect or frequency, such forms are marked "*nonstd.* [Cat.]" in the index verborum. Several reappear later on.

Sigmatics leveled along 2nd-/3rd-conj. lines include *clout* 'shut,' *defengut* 'fought off,' *entengut* 'understood,' *fongut* 'melted,' *metut* 'put,' and *prengut* 'taken, caught.' However, ancient vocalism has been kept in nonstd. *fus* 'melted' < FŪSU 'poured.' A new sigmatic has developed in *cres* 'believed,' which looks like something out of the Marches of Italy (see §3.6.2).

In nonstandard Catalan, tautic athematics leveled along 2nd-/3rd-conj. lines include *molgut* or *molut* 'ground,' along with *obrigut* 'opened' and *tragut* or *tregut* 'taken out.' No new tautic athematics appear in these dialects; two sigmatic-tautics do in *rist* 'laughed' and *fost* 'melted,' which last looks like a Romanian 'been.'

Relative to the standard, the p.p. marker [g] may come or go. It comes in nonstd. Cat. *pergut* 'lost,' *repigut* 'received,' and *temegut* 'feared.' It goes in *beüt* 'drunk,' *caüt* 'fallen,' and *valut* 'been worth.' Such wavering implies that speakers of Catalan have yet to determine how much they will rely on that [g] marker.

Past participles leveled along 4th-conj. lines are *lluguit* or *llucit* 'shone,' *obrit* 'opened,' *omplit* 'filled.' Sporadically, other non-1st-conj. verbs get swept up in the -*it* craze, as witness *coneixit* 'known,' *dolit* 'hurt,' *molit* 'ground,' and *rompit* 'broken.' Unsyncopated variants prevail in *recibut* or *recibit* or *recivit* 'received' and perhaps in *capigut* 'fit into'; yet syncope occurs in *corgut* 'run.' Reflexes of [k] before [t] live on in the yods of nonstd. *feyt* 'done/made' and *treyt* 'taken out' (Alcover, 20–170).

Speakers of these dialects have lightened the load on their memory by tending to make almost all verbs regular in p.p. formation. They countenance a range of by-forms that I suppose are differentiated in ways still unexplored.

4.6.2.7. Rossellonese

According to Fouché's *Morphologie historique du roussillonnais*, regular masc.sg. past participles end in -*at* for 1st-conj. verbs, -*ut* for 2nd- and 3rd-conj. verbs, and -*it* for 4th-conj. verbs, as in the Barcelona-based standard. Besides inherited *batut* 'beaten' and *futut* 'fucked,' standard-looking past participles in -*ut* include *agut* 'had,' *begut* 'drunk,' *caigut* 'fallen,' *tingut* 'held' and *vingut* 'come,' together with *venut* 'sold.'

Rossellonese differs from the standard in having evolved a number of 4th-conj.-looking past participles like *creixit* 'grown,' *neixit* 'born,' *peixit* 'fed, kept,' *coneixit* 'known,' and *planyit* 'lamented' for the 3rd-conj. infins. *créixer*, *néixer*, *péixer*, *conéixer*, *plányer*. Another apparent anomaly has emerged for several verbs whose past participles still end in tonic [it] but whose 3rd-conj. infinitives have come to end in atonic [ə]. Thus, morphological transparency has lessened in pairs like *bullit* and *búller* 'boil[ed],' *eixit* and *éixer* 'gone/go out,' *cusit* and *cúser* 'sew[n],' *fugit* and *fúger* 'fled/flee,' and *currit* and *cúrrer* (also 4th-conj. *currir*) 'run.'[52] In standard Catalan today, and no doubt in Old Rossellonese, the infinitives would be *bollir, eixir, cosir,* and *fugir*.

Even if that anomaly did arise fairly recently, Old Rossellonese generally had more irregularities, typified by the old p.p.s *cresegut* 'believed,' now *cregut*, and the true ORoss. oddity *retut* 'given back' (cf. rhizotonic REDDĬTU). ORoss. *desebut* 'deceived' and *resebut* 'received' have been remade as *debut* and *rebut* to match the syncopated infins. *debre* and *rebre*.

Other tautic athematic survivals in Old Rossellonese included *tint* 'dyed' < TĪNCTU (now *tenyit*), *tolt* 'taken away' ≠ SUBLĀTU₁, and *cinta* 'girded' < CĪNCTA, now nominalized in the sense 'belt.' Sigmatic survivals in Old Rossellonese included *atés* 'waited' and *pretés* 'pretended.' Besides *vist* 'seen,' *post* 'set, laid,' and *respost* 'answered,' Old Rossellonese had sigmatic-tautic *request* 'sought' remade from REQUÆSĪTU. Another old p.p. *tort*, literally 'twisted,' now has the adjectival sense 'limping' in Rossellonese rather than 'twisted, bent' as in the standard (Fouché, 171–74).

---

[52] Reduction to [ə] of this infinitive ending apparently takes places after palatal consonants or [r].

4.6.2.8. Valencian

Spoken in southern Catalonia and deemed by some to constitute a Romance language all its own, Valencian has 90–95 percent mutual intelligibility with standard Catalan (Fleischman 1992, 343). One is tempted to suggest that the figure might actually approach 100 percent. Fullana Mira's ambitiously titled *Gramática elemental de la llengua valenciana* offers little evidence for the un-Catalan nature of Valencian past participles. Neither does a *Gramàtica valenciana* by Salvador or *Gramàtica de la llengua valenciana* by Fontelles et al. As diacritics are used differently in each work, I have left them off Valencian words given here.

Standing against the hegemony of Barcelona, Fullana Mira deprecates the shift of some verbs into the 4th conjugation, recommends the p.p. *refos* 'recast, rewritten' over arrhizotonic *refundit*. Fullana Mira then deprecates the truly Catalan infin. *tancar* 'shut,' a verb of obscure origin, and upholds variants in *-ir* over ones in *-re*: "Esta última forma s'usa ya molt pòc, segons ham dit, mes devía conservarse, ya qu'estes formes son més genuines que *tancar* (en llòc de *clòure*), *fundir* (*fòndre*), *incluir* (*inclòure*), *recluir* (*reclòure*), *infundir* (*infòndre*), *refundir* (*refòndre*)" (162) [This last form is used very little now, as we have said, but it should be preserved, since these forms are more authentic than...]. According to Fontelles, though, Valencian tends to prefer 3rd-conj. variant infinitives where the standard has 4th-conj. forms. For instance, Valencian has *tindre* 'have, hold' and *vindre* 'come' as against std. Cat. *tenir, venir*. For other infinitives, Fontelles gives only rhizotonic *soldre* 'be used to' and *valdre* 'be worth,' while Salvador gives each of these as a by-form; the standard allows only arrhizotonic *soler, valer*. Frankly, certain infinitive variations sound inexplicable: off-glides differ in std. *raure* 'shave' and Val. *raire*, tonic vowels differ in std. *treure* and Val. *traure* 'take out, get out,' and a diphthong contrasts with a monophthong in std. *veure* and Val. *vore* 'see.'

How does such variation affect past participles? For some verbs in the two dialects, past participles are the same, or almost so, but infinitives have by-forms in Valencian. So std. Cat. *atès* and Val. *ates* 'overtaken' seem about the same, but for infinitives Valencian allows *atendre* and *atenyer* while Barcelonan allows only the first. For other verbs, infinitives may be similar but past participles dissimilar. If Valencian has kept or evolved a few more rhizotonic infinitives than standard Catalan, in past participles the southern dialect tends to have leveled rhizotonics at least as far as outfitting them with arrhizotonic by-forms.

Given the sampler of nonstandard forms in §4.6.2.6, one might expect Valencian to tolerate greater p.p. variation than does standard Catalan. It does. Valencian has both *establit* and *establert* 'set up,' *reblit* and *reblert* 'crammed,' *sofrit* and *sofert* 'suffered,' *suplit* and *suplert* 'replaced,' but the standard permits only the second of each pair. Often, an inherited rhizotonic competes with an innovative arrhizotonic. According to Fontelles if not Salvador, Valencian allows *imprimit* or *impres* 'prinited,' the standard allows only *imprès*. Both Fontelles and Salvador give *oferit* and *ofert* 'offered,' but the standard receives only *ofert*. Among sigmatics, the standard has limited *ras* < RĀSU to adjectival use and *ragut* to past-participial use, but in Valencian either *ras* or *ragut* serves as the past participle meaning 'shaved,' according to Salvador.

Still, a drive toward rhizotonicity occurs in sigmatic-tautic Val. *rist* 'laughed.' This is the only slot-filler given by Fontelles and Fullana Mira, though according to Salvador *rist* competes with arrhizotonic *rigut*; the standard accepts only arrhizotonic *rigut*.

Variation in Valencian past participles may involve a by-form in *-nyut* competing with one in *-ngut*. Of the Val. p.p. pairs *pertanyut* and *pertangut* 'belonged' given by Salvador, the standard accepts only the latter. For the past participle of two verbs, *fenyer* 'knead and *planyer* 'grieve,' Fontelles gives *fenygut* and *planygut* in [ŋg], and Fullana Mira gives *planygut*; such variants manage to combine Salvador's by-forms *fenyut*, *planyut* and *plangut*. Inconsistently, the standard accepts only *fenyut* 'kneaded,' only *plangut* 'grieved.' Varied morphological outcomes illustrate how arbitrary any choice of shibboleths must be.

As the above examples make clear, authorities disagree at times about what the Valencian form ought to be. Salvador gives *crescut* 'grown,' identical to the standard slot-filler, but Fullana Mira has *creixcut* with palatalization of [s] to [ʃ]. Similarly, Fullana Mira gives *mereixcut* 'deserved,' as against *merescut* in the standard. Val. *conegut* 'known' seems to have no palatalized by-form though it has infin. *coneixer*, resembling *creixer* 'grow'; evidently, palatalization takes place, if at all, only in the presence of an [sk] cluster. Fontelles and Fullana Mira agree in giving Val. *vixcut* 'lived,' which contrasts with unpalatalized *viscut* in the standard. Though Fullana Mira gives *vullgut* 'wanted' in [ʎ], in contrast to std. *volgut*, neither Salvador nor Fontelles mentions any such form.

A few lexical items combine semantic and morphological differences. Salvador gives infin. *toldre* 'take away' with p.p. *tolt*, but the standard has 4th-conj. *tolir* 'cripple'—i.e. from which function has been taken way—with the regular p.p. *tolit*,' also adjectival. In the sense 'give,' standard Catalan has either defective *dar* (p.p. *dat*) or complete *donar* (p.p. *donat*); Valencian apparently has only the former. Moreover, the 3rd-conj. Valencian verb *oldre* 'smell' (p.p. *olgut*), given by both Fontelles and Salvador, has no counterpart in Barcelonan Catalan; the closest equivalent appears to be 1st-conj. *olorar* (p.p. *olorat*).

Highlighting divergences should not obscure the real similarities between Valencian and standard Catalan. Typical Valencian past participles of Fullana Mira's are masc.sg. *salvat* 'saved,' *perdut* 'lost,' and *servit* 'served.' In the feminine, 1st-conj. *-ada* reduces to tonic *-á*, giving e.g. *salvá* 'saved'; orthographically at least, such extreme lenition never occurs the standard.

Valencian shares most of its rhizotonics with standard Catalan. Shared sigmatics, given in my accentless spelling for Valencian, are *clos* 'shut,' *despes* 'spent,' *empes* 'pushed,' *ences* 'lit,' *fos* 'melted,' *mes* 'put,' *pres* 'taken, caught,' *romas* 'stayed,' *suspes* 'hung,' unprefixed *tes* 'reached,' *tos* 'shorn,' Learnèd-looking sigmatics are *emes* 'given off,' *ofes* 'offended,' *permes* 'allowed,' *sotmes* 'subdued,' Shared sigmatic-tautics are *post* 'set, laid' and *vist* 'seen.'

Shared tautic athematics are *dit* 'said, told,' *dut* 'brought,' *escrit* 'written,' *estret* 'squeezed,' *fet* 'done/made,' *molt* 'ground,' *mort* 'died,' *obert* 'opened,' and *tret* 'taken out, gotten out.' One more is given as *cobert* 'covered' in Salvador and Fontelles but as *cubert* in Fullana Mira. Learnèd-looking tautic athematics held in common are *absolt* 'shriven,' *constret* 'forced,' *dissolt* 'dissolved.'

Most 2nd-/3rd-conj. arrhizotonics, accent-free on my Valencian style sheet, are also shared by north and south. They include inherited *batut* 'beaten,' innovated *cabut* 'fit into' and *cernut* 'sifted,' and [g]-ful *begut* 'drunk,' *caigut* 'fallen,' *calgut* 'mattered,' *corregut* 'run,' *cregut* 'believed,' *dolgut* 'hurt,' *jagut* 'lain,' *segut* 'sat,' *solgut* 'been used to,' *valgut* 'been worth,' and *vençut* 'won.' A shared 4th-conj. innovations since Latin times is *collit* 'reaped' ≠ COLLĒCTU.

At times, the Rossellonese and Valencian dialects of Catalan even share a pair of by-forms: *complit* and *complert* 'fulfilled' are accepted by both. So, probably, are *cuit* and *cogut* 'cooked,' although Fontelles cites only the first. Another by-form pair is *tort* and *torçut* 'twisted,' acceptable north and south. However, in prefixed versions of that verb, Valencian has arrhizotonic *destorçut* 'untwisted' and *retorçut* 'entwined,' while the standard allows only rhizotonic *destort, retort* (Fullana Mira, 159–62; Fontelles, 197–99; Salvador, 112–13, 124–27).

Discrepancies among the three grammars show that norms for Valencian have yet to be established. Perhaps secessionists will create a Valencian Academy to standardize orthography and orthoepy by choosing among by-forms. Still and all, the grammars have enough in common to show that, give or take a diacritic or two, Valencian differs but slightly from standard Catalan in lexis and morphology.

4.6.2.9. Tamaritan

In *El dialecto de Tamarite de Litera (Huesca)*, Carpi y Zaidin and Carpi y Cases list a handful of past participles (72–73). Now the Huescan town of Tamarite de Litera lies some 20 kilometers east of Monzón, probably a Spanish name because of final -n after a stressed vowel, and lies some 20 kilometers west of Castelló de Farfanya, definitely a Catalan name because of the graphy ny. How to decide? Since Tamaritan has an inventory of past participles in -*ut*, with most of those in -*gut*, I have no hesitation in identifying it as a dialect of Catalan.

Most Tamaritan past participles are in fact identical to ones in the Barcelona-based standard. From the 1st conjugation comes Tam. *anat* 'gone.' From the 2nd and 3rd conjugations come by-form *agut* 'had,' *caigut* 'fallen,' *cregut* 'believed,' *crescut* 'grown,' *mogut* 'moved,' *nascut* 'born,' *sabut* 'known,' *solgut* 'been used to,' and *valgut* 'been worth.' From the 4th conjugation, according to the authors, comes *dit* 'said, told,' actually a type 9. Irregulars are *dut* 'taken away' (also *endut*), *vist* 'seen,' and *viscut* 'lived.'

If Tam. *convensut* 'convinced' appears to differ only in spelling from std. *convençut*, other divergences are sharper. Out of nowhere there appears an initial palatal nasal in by-form *ñ'agut* 'had,' and there appears a prefix in *endut* 'taken away'; neither exists in the standard. Perhaps under Spanish influence, a pretonic vowel differs in Tam. *cumplit* 'filled, fulfilled' (cf. std. *complit* but Sp. *cumplido*). Two pretonic vowels differ in Tam. *arropliegat* 'gathered' versus std. *arreplegat*. A tonic vowel remains diphthongized in *feit* 'done/made' (std. *fet* but cf. OCat. *feyt*). Then again, the medial consonant in Tam. *llechit* 'read' (std. *llegit*) cannot be attributed to Spanish, which has no such consonant left in *leído* 'read.'

Semantics differ more than phonetics in Tam. *embescat*, glossed as "ensuciado" ['dirtied'] by the authors, versus std. Cat. *envescat* 'smeared with birdlime; trapped.' Probably attributable to the authors' castilianizing orthography—Spanish having lost [ʃ] as a phoneme centuries ago—is the Tam. 1st-conj. form given as *chollat* 'shorn' but written *xollat* in the standard.

Speakers of the Tamaritan dialect have regularized at least three past participles: *confongut* 'confused,' *escrigut* 'written,' and *malmetut* 'hurt, harmed' contrast with conservative std. *confos*, *escrit*, and *malmes*. Indeed, though it has sigmatic-tautic *vist* 'seen,' Tamaritan seems to lack straight sigmatic past participles. Although dialects of Catalan often have fewer sigmatics than the standard (§4.6.2.6), the loss of all of them here may plausibly be ascribed to the influence of Spanish, which has lost all it had.

As Tam. *sigut* 'been' is the only form given in that sense, purists who favor *estat* 'been' in the standard have lost one battle in this dialect; see §4.6.2.2. Given the three regularized past participles a *confongut* 'confused,' *escrigut* 'written,' and *malmetut* 'hurt, harmed,' purists have no doubt lost other battles as well. Sure enough, de Carpi y Zaidin and de Carpi y Cases mention no Tamaritan by-forms resembling innovative std. *complert* 'fulfilled' or (rare) conservative std. *nat* 'born.'

4.6.2.10. Alguerese

For past participles at Alguer (It. Alghero), the Catalan-speaking enclave on the west coast of Sardinia, data come from Blasco Ferrer's *Grammatica storica del catalano e dei suoi dialetti, con speciale riguardo all'algherese*.

In the masculine singular, most Alguerese past participles are identical to those of standard Catalan: the three great arrhizotonic classes end in *-at*, *-ut*, and *-it*. In corresponding feminines, reflexes of intervocalic [t] have rhotacized to yield the endings *-ara*, *-ura*, and *-ira*. In that respect, allophony has increased relative not only to Latin but to standard Catalan as well.

Two archaisms in Alguerese are *nat* 'born' < NĀTU and *dat* 'given' < DĀTU instead of what are usually *nascut* and *donat* in the standard. Although rhotacism has occurred in Alg. *umprit* 'filled,' it more closely resembles OCat.

omplit than it does the standard reshaping *omplert*. All these forms have been reshaped from "regular" 2nd-conj. IMPLĒTU, but the standard form has been reshaped twice.

Innovative levelings in Alguerese are *ascrivit* 'written,' *molgut* 'ground,' *rasibit* 'received, and *vivit* 'lived' as against rhizotonic *escrit* and *mòlt*, syncopated *rebut*, and preterit-inspired *viscut* in the standard. As for the third of these, compare OCat. *resebut* 'received,' still unsyncopated. Alguerese does share with Barcelonan the sigmatic-tautic innovation *vist* 'seen.'

At Alguer, allophony has increased between principal parts for one common verb: pretonic vowels have come to differ in infin. *ésar* 'be' and p.p. *astat* 'been' (std. *estat*). In the Alguerese by-form *vangut* 'sold' beside by-form *venut* ≠ VENDITU, innovation has been piled upon innovation.

A further innovation is Alg. *calgut* 'fallen,' with an intrusive [l] ascribed by Blasco Ferrer to hypercorrection. However, most past participles meaning 'fallen' that the author adduces to support this view—OVal. *cahegut*, ORoss. *cahut*, and even OFr. *cehoit* from a variant in -ĒCTU—have giveaway silent h̲'s. Instead, I believe that [l] might have arisen as an antihiatic alongside [g] or in its absence, much like the intrusive off-glide [i̯] found in std. *caigut* 'fallen' (Blasco Ferrer 1984, 152–54).

4.7. EVIDENCE FROM SPANISH AND PORTUGUESE

Much like Occitan and Catalan, Spanish and Portuguese are considered two separate languages and display striking similarities in past-participial formation. Both have reduced productive types of p.p. endings to only two. Graphically in the two tongues, regular masc.sg. past participles end in -*ado* from -ĀTU for 1st-conj. verbs (Sp. *lavado* 'washed,' *echado* 'thrown,' *fregado* 'rubbed'), and in -*ido* from -ĪTU for reflexes of the other three conjugations of Latin (Sp. *dormido* 'slept,' *fingido* 'pretended'). Despite great phonetic differences between Spanish and Portuguese, differences that loom even larger in irregular high-frequency past participles like Sp. *hecho* [etʃo] versus Ptg. *feito* [fei̯tu] < FACTU 'done/made,' and despite differences in lexis, here I deal with the two languages as if they shared one inventory of past participles.

There being so few p.p. irregularities across central-western Iberia, readers will forgive my citing several more than once.

4.7.0. Preliminaries

Almost as thoroughly Romanized as the future Occitania and Catalonia, Hispania later underwent rule by semibarbaric Visigoths from the center of Europe and by supercivilized Moors and Arabs from beyond the Straits of Gibraltar. Driven back to redoubts on hills in the north, from Galicia to Aragon, ancestors of Spaniards and Portuguese launched a Drang nach Süden that ended in 1492. East of Galicia, the reconquista was largely in the hands of adventurers from Castile, a warlike band whose prestigious phonology and morphology were imitated by more pacific Romance speakers in Toledo, Mérida, Seville, and Granada, once they had been freed from Moorish rule.

As noted in §3.0.1, far-western Spanish and Portuguese share with far-eastern Romanian certain lexical items that died out in central Romance. In Upper Aragon, speakers keep alive a phonological archaism: unlike almost everyone else in western ROMANIA, they preserve CL voiceless stops (Lloyd, 147).[53] As a result, regular past participles used in the Aragonese Pyrenees retain the Tuscan-looking endings -*ato* and -*ito*.

Unproductive rhizotonic types persist in reflexes of CL -CTU (Sp. *hecho* 'done/made' and *dicho* 'said, told'), of LL -STU (*puesto* 'put' and *visto* 'seen'), of CL -LTU (*abierto* 'opened' and *cubierto* 'covered'), and of CL -PTU (*roto* 'broken' and *escrito* 'written').[54] Other rhizotonics have been brought back to life by the learnèd.

Besides borrowings from Germanic like *guardar* 'watch over,' shared with other western Romance languages, Spanish has a number of Arabic loan-verbs like *achacar* 'accuse' and *halagar* 'flatter' (p.p.s *achacado, halagado*) borrowed during 700 years of Moorish rule; Portuguese may have fewer. On the other hand, Portuguese has borrowed far more terms from Occitan and French than Spanish has (Green, 79, 119; Parkinson, 165–66). Verbs quite unlike those in standard French or Italian—listed by p.p.—include Sp. *buscado* 'looked for,' *chupado* 'sucked,' *lamido* 'licked,' *matado* 'killed,' *quebrado* 'brtoken,' *quemado* 'burned,' and *tomado* 'taken,' together with Ptg. *esquecido* 'forgotten,' *ficado* 'stayed,' *receado* 'feared,' *rezado* 'prayed,' and *zangado* 'angered.'[55]

Such arrhizotonics go back a long way: dating from the second half of the tenth century, the *Glosas silenses* contain a form written *kematu* 'burned,' and also one written *cadutu* 'fallen' (Sampson, 20–21). For a review of what happened to reflexes of the -ŪTU type of past participle in Spanish, see §4.7.4.

True, SOLŪTU and VOLŪTU were replaced by the (thematic?) ancestors of *suelto* 'loose' and *vuelto* 'turned, returned.' Nonetheless, Spanish has

---

[53] North of the border, in Béarn, stops have also failed to voice between vowels.

[54] Here L = liquid. To those may be added certain learnèd forms ending in -*lto* like *absuelto* 'shriven' and *resuelto* '[re]solved'; in -*rto* like *absorto* 'absorbed'; in -*nto* like *exento* 'exempted' and *presunto* 'presumed'; in -*so* like *incluso* 'included,' *impreso* 'printed,' *inverso* 'inverted,' and *propenso* 'tended'; and, most obviously, in -*cto* like *abstracto* 'abstracted,' *aflicto* 'afflicted,' and *electo* 'elect, chosen.' Almost all are restricted to adjectival or nominal use.

[55] Sp./Ptg. *tomar* may come from an echoic word meaning 'plop, clunk' that also gave Sp. *tumbar* 'tumble'; Ptg. *esquecer* may come from EX + *CADĒSCERE 'start to fall apart'; Ptg. *rezar* comes from RECITĀRE 'read aloud, dictate' (*REW* nos. 2944, 7123, 8975). Malkiel has explained *tomar* as deriving from an attested variant ÆSTUMĀRE of ÆSTIMĀRE 'appraise, rate, judge.' Sp./Ptg. *matar* may derive from MACTĀRE 'slay, smite' (Posner, 321), though regular phonological evolution would have given Sp. *machar* and Ptg. *mautar*. Sp. *quemar* comes from CREMĀRE with loss of [r], and Sp. *quebrar* 'break' comes from a regularized variant of CREPĀRE 'creak, rattle' (p.p. CREPITU) with metathesis of [r].

overwhelmingly preferred arrhizotonicity across the past system.[56] A few
remade past participles of the non-1st-conj. kind are *crecido* 'grown' ≠ CRĒTU,
creído 'believed' ≠ CRĒDĬTU, *tejido* 'woven' (Ptg. *tecido*) ≠ TEXTU. Note also
lucido 'shone,' and *podido* 'been able' (no CL p.p.s). That trend toward two
conjugations, both mostly arrhizotonic, may go as far back as Visigothic times:
in Pseudo-Isadore, CŌNSUERE 'sew' is glossed as *cusire*, but unfortunately no
past participle is given (Díaz y Díaz, 156). Was it already a 4th-conj. form?

4.7.1. Morphological Patterns within the Past System

Of the several ways in which preterits and past participles were marked in Old
Spanish, many have passed out of use to the benefit of the two arrhizotonic
types. First were verbs with an alternation between [ʃ] (written x) and [t], as in
(3sg.) pret. *cinxo* and p.p. *cinto* 'girded,' or *tinxo* and *tinto* 'dyed.' Second were
verbs with an alternation between [s] and [t], as in *escrisso* 'wrote' and *escrito*
'written.' Third was one verb with an alternation between [sk] and [tʃ]: by-
form pret. *trasco* and p.p. *trecho* 'brought,' with different tonic vowels. Fourth
were verbs with an alternation between [ʃ] and [tʃ], sometimes with shifts in
tonic vowels, as in *dixo* and *dicho* 'said, told,' *traxo* and *trecho* 'brought,' or
coxo and *cocho* 'cooked.' Fifth were verbs with an alternation between [z] and
[st], as in *puso* and *puesto* 'put' or *quiso* and by-form *quisto* 'wanted; loved.'
Sixth were 1st-conj. verbs with an alternation between pret. [uvo] and p.p.
[ado] endings, as in *anduvo* 'went' as against *andado* 'gone.' Of these six
categories, the first three have vanished, and the others have shrunk through
time. If one limits oneself to considering infinitives, preterits, and past
participles, allomorphy has subsisted only for the highest-frequency verbs like
dar 'give' with pret. *dio* versus p.p. *dado*, *ver* 'see' with pret. *vio* versus p.p.
visto, and of course *ser* 'be' and *ir* 'go' with a shared pret. *fue* 'was; went'
versus separate p.p.s *sido* 'been' and *ido* 'gone.'

More than a few verbs in Old Spanish had a regular past participle but an
irregular preterit. Those in [z] or [ʃ] included (3sg.) *miso* 'put into,' *riso*
'laughed,' *remaso* 'stayed,' and *destruxo* 'destroyed'; those in [sk] included
visco 'lived' and *nasco* 'was born.' Almost all have been remodeled. One verb,
venir 'come,' had a metaphonic pret. *vino* that survives. Those ending in
[uCo] included *cupo* 'fit into,' *hubo* 'had,' *plugo* 'pleased,' *pudo* 'could,' *supo*
'knew,' and *tuvo* 'had, held,' which all survive. Still, many other Old Spanish
preterits of that type have been reshaped along more productive lines.

Old Spanish verbs that had a regular preterit but an irregular past
participle included *prender* 'catch,' with the sigmatic p.p. *preso* < PRĒNSU.

---

[56] In Andalusia, the [s] pluralizer for nouns, adjectives, and past participles often weakens
to [h], so that *los hermanos* 'the brothers' becomes [lɔʰ ermanɔʰ]. All trace of the fricative
may be lost, with number marked Italian-style by contrasts between final vowels, as in sg. *la
madre* [la madre] versus pl. *las madres* [læ madre] 'mother[s]' (Green, 85). Outsiders may
be deaf to such a subtle distinction. Unlike spoken French, Spanish still draws morphological
distinctions between masc. and fem., sg. and pl. forms of all past participles.

'grabbed.' For verbs with regular preterits, irregularities subsist in the p.p.s
abierto 'opened' and *cubierto* 'covered,' *muerto* 'died,' *roto* 'broken,' and
vuelto 'turned, returned.'

If one ignores instances of vowel raising in preterits like (3sg.) *durmió*
'slept' (infin. *dormir*) or *pidió* 'asked' (infin. *pedir*), Spanish today has
irregular morphological relations between preterit and past participle for only
nine verbs; even there, p.p.s *dormido* 'slept' and *pedido* 'asked' are regular.
Portuguese has such irregularities for ten verbs; the mediæval language had
two more. Allomorphy has declined owing to leveling of the preterit, of the
past participle, or of both together (Mourin, 183–87).

4.7.2. Early Reduction of Allomorphy

Regularly, Spanish has two types of past participle and two types of preterit.
All arrhizotonic, they constitute what Georges has called a "bipartite weak
perfectum" (see §4.7.4.1). For -*ar* verbs, which have -*ado* p.p.s, 3sg. preterits
end in -*ó* < -AUT < -ĀVIT, and 3pl. preterits end in -*aron* < -ĀVĒRUNT, with a
stress shift. For non-*ar* verbs, which all regularly have -*ido* p.p.s, 3sg. preterits
end in -*ió* < -IUT < -ĪVIT and 3pl. preterits in -*ieron* < -ĪVĒRUNT, with no
stress shift. Such morphological predictability can be traced back to Latin,
where it was already widespread. How did it expand further in Spanish?

4.7.2.1. Reshaped Preterits

In Proto-Spanish if not earlier, almost all rhizotonic perfects ending in -UĪ etc.
changed to the -ĪVĪ type, as shown by forms like (1sg.) *temí* 'feared' ≠ TIMUĪ,
abrí 'opened' ≠ APERUĪ, *debí* 'ought to' ≠ DĒBUĪ, *yací* 'lay' ≠ JACUĪ, and *valí*
'was worth' ≠ VALUĪ. No doubt the earliest attestation of that morphological
shift in Spain comes from the *Corpus Inscriptionum Latinarum* II, 6302:
POSIUT 'put' from something like 4th-conj.-style OL POSIVIT, an attested
variant of CL POSUIT (Carnoy, 119). The few high-frequency -UĪ perfects later
preterits that survived came to be based on high-frequency 1sg. *ove* 'had' <
*[auβe] < HABUĪ, giving e.g. OSp. *tove* 'had' ≠ TENUĪ, *estove* 'was' ≠ STETĪ,
and *andove* 'went' ≠ AMBULĀVĪ. Semantics could have affected morphology,
if reshaping in the first of these inspired reshaping in the second.

Even before the Romance of Iberia was recognized as distinct from Latin,
glossaries in what one might term imitation CL suggest leveling within the
perfectum. For instance, in a glossary from Silos datable to the 10th or early
eleventh century, PRŌMĪSERIT 'will have promised' is glossed as *prometieret*,
and ĀRSERIT 'will have burned' is glossed as *ardierit*. Here old rhizotonic 3sg.
future perfects have been replaced by regular arrhizotonic forms built on
infectum stems like those in the ModSp. infins. *prometer* and *arder* (R.
Wright, 203). Neither replacement verb was sigmatic.

From the earliest attestations, Spanish had hardly any relics of direct-
suffixation perfects in CL. They were remade into non-*ar*-verb preterits with
infectum bases: (1sg.) *leí* 'read' ≠ LĒGĪ, *rompí* 'torn' ≠ RŪPĪ, and *vencí* 'won' ≠

VĪCĪ. "Regular" 2nd-conj. CRĒVĪ was remade as infin.-based *crecí* 'grew.' Only three high-frequency verbs remain in that class: (1sg.) *vi* 'saw' < VĪDĪ, *hice* 'did/made' < OSp. *fize* < FĒCĪ, and *vine* 'came' < VĒNĪ. Compare OFr. *vi(t)*, *fiz, vin* and It. *vidi, feci* but *venni* from a variant of VĒNĪ that ended in -UĪ.[57]

Early on, speakers in Spain had arrhizotonically reshaped almost all reduplicated perfects as well, giving (1sg.) *corrí* 'ran' ≠ CUCURRĪ, *mordí* 'bit' ≠ MOMORDĪ, and *caí* 'fell' ≠ CECIDĪ. Reflexes of two old reduplicated forms survive: *di* 'gave' < DEDĪ, which looks like a direct inheritance, and *estuve* 'was,' twice remade from OSp. *estide* < STETĪ 'stood, stayed' (Lathrop, 144–48).

Other types of inherited preterits might last for a while: OSp. (1sg.) *mise* 'put into' < MĪSĪ 'sent,' *cinxe* 'girded' < CĪNXĪ, *conuve* 'knew' < COGNŌVĪ, and *escrise* 'wrote' < SCRĪPSĪ; analogical ones included *sove* 'was' and *crove* 'believed.' Most were already competing with regularized arrhizotonic forms like *metí, ceñí, conocí, escribí,* and *creí* that have since prevailed.

To observers familiar with eastern Romance, what may seem surprising has been the unwillingness of Spanish speakers to continue sigmatic preterits, still less evolve new ones. True, Old Spanish still had the inheritance *visque* 'lived' < VĪXĪ, but in the fourteenth century a competitor arose in *viví*, now the only filler for that slot. Increasingly, Spanish speakers preferred to reserve the [s] marker for different morphological uses (see §5.5).

4.7.2.2. Reshaped Past Participles

Dating from LL or PR times, dozens of reshaped past participles in Spanish are paralleled elsewhere in Romance. They include (2nd-/3rd-) 4th-conj. *huido* 'fled' ≠ FUGĬTU, *sorbido* 'swallowed' ≠ SORBĬTU, and *herido* 'hit' (no CL p.p.). They used to include OSp. *exido* 'gone out' ≠ EXĬTU, with a regular 4th-conj. infinitive. They still include 1st-conj. *domado* 'tamed' ≠ DOMĬTU, *quebrado* 'broken' ≠ CREPĬTU 'rattled, creaked,' *segado* 'reaped, mown' ≠ SECTU, *sonado* 'rung' ≠ SONĬTU, and *vedado* 'forbidden' ≠ VETĬTU, each with a regular 1st-conj. infectum in Latin.

Early on, Spanish seems to have gone farther than French, Catalan, or Italian in remaking past participles along default lines. Among remade sigmatics are *adherido* 'stuck' ≠ ADHÆSU, *corrido* 'run' ≠ CURSU, *fundido* 'melted' ≠ FŪSU 'poured,' *medido* 'measured' ≠ MĒNSU, *pendido* 'hung' ≠ PĒNSU, *raído* 'shaved' ≠ RĀSU, *reído* 'laughed' ≠ RĪSU, *respondido* 'answered' ≠ RESPŌNSU, *roído* 'gnawn' ≠ RŌSU, *tendido* 'held out' ≠ TĒNSU, *tundido* 'shorn' ≠ TŌNSU, and *urdido* 'warped cloth' ≠ ŌRSU. Again, one is struck by the unwillingness of speakers to continue sigmatic past participles or to evolve new ones, while their cousins toward the east were doing both (see §§3.1.5, 3.5.3.2). That unwillingness was not quite absolute; for deviations from the anti-sigmatic trend, see the end of §4.7.5.

---

[57] Proto-It. **venui* was almost certainly inspired by pret. TENUĪ 'held, had.' In a series of mutual metaplasms, various forms of the two verbs have come to rhyme in Romance languages.

Among rhizotonic thematics remade along the same lines are Sp, *gemido* 'whined, whimpered' ≠ GEMĬTU, *molido* 'ground' ≠ MOLĬTU, *placido* 'pleased' ≠ PLACĬTU, *rendido* 'given back' ≠ REDDĬTU plus infectum nasal, and of course *habido* 'had' ≠ HABĬTU. Note also *leído* 'read' ≠ LĒCTU.

Across central-western Iberia, "regular" 2nd-conj. -ĒTU p.p.s appear to have been drawn early into the class ending in *-ido*. Thus, Spanish reflexes of COMPLĒTU and IMPLĒTU were and are *cumplido* 'fulfilled,' *henchido* 'filled' (Lathrop, 152). Meanwhile, a reflex of QUIĒTU 'rested' survives in adj. *quedo* 'quiet, still' (cf. Fr. *coi*, It. *cheto*) as well as in a 1st-conj. verb built from it, *quedar* 'stay' with p.p. *quedado*.

Exemplifying early reduction in allophony, a number of Spanish 2nd-/3rd-conj. verbs have infinitives ending in *-cer*, (3sg.) preterits in *-ció*, and past participles in *-cido*. Those verbs contain reflexes of an old [sk] infix, originally inchoative and limited to the infectum but now found across the perfectum as well. Leveling might have happened in Late Latin or Proto-Spanish. Resultant past participles include *carecido* 'lacked' ≠ CARĬTU or CASSU, *conocido* 'known' ≠ COGNĬTU, *fallecido* 'died' ≠ FALSU 'tricked; failed,' *merecido* 'deserved' ≠ MERĬTU, *ofrecido* 'offered' ≠ suppletive OBLĀTU, and *parecido* 'appeared' ≠ PĀRĬTU. Allomorphy has again declined. For the verb STABILĪRE 'make firm,' CL already had a regular 4th-conj. arrhizotonic p.p. STABILĪTU, which could have given **estabelido*, but the spread of inchoative marking shifted that infinitive into the 2nd/3rd conjugation: *establecer* has acquired a regular non-*ar*-verb p.p. *establecido*. Here, by ceding to analogical pressures from other formerly inchoative verbs, Spanish has sacrificed some regularity, for infinitive and past participle no longer share a theme vowel.[58]

4.7.3. Avoidance of Homonymic Clash between Preterit and Past Participle

In the preterit, reduplicative compounds of (3sg.) DEDIT 'gave' like PERDIDIT 'lost,' REDDIDIT 'gave back,' TRĀDIDIT 'handed over, gave up,' and VENDIDIT 'sold' could normally have been expected to produce 3sg. forms in Old Spanish like **perdido*, **vendido*. According to Craddock (186–88), such preterits would have eventually coincided with the p.p.s *perdido, vendido* for the same verbs. Except for the still extant nonstd. pret. *vido* 'saw,' which had and has a distinctive irregular p.p. *visto* 'seen,' all attested Old Spanish (3sg.) preterits in *-ido* belonged to 1st-conj. verbs: *estido* 'was,' *andido* 'went,' *demandido* 'asked,' *catido* 'sampled,' and *entrido* 'went in.' Such *-ido* preterits could never have coincided morphologically with their past participles, all of them regular forms in *-ado*:

Craddock explains the emergence of the 3sg. non-*ar*-preterit ending *-ió* as resulting from recomposition of DEDI(T) and its compounds in -DIDI(T) during Proto-Spanish times: 1sg. **dedi* 'gave' underwent metaphony to yield

---

58 Fr. *établir* and It. *stabilire* have the regular 4th-conj. p.p.s *établi* and *stabilito*.

*dídi, which then syncopated to di. and was generalized to old compounds of DARE, giving 1sg. forms like perdí. The consequent reduction of 3sg. *dedut to *dèw(t) produced dió, perdió, vendió as against p.p.s dado < DATU, and also perdido, vendido (the last two with OSp. by-forms in -udo, by the way).[59]

Owing to its high frequency, that ending in -ió from dió 'gave' came to be generalized to all 3sg. preterits for weak non-ar verbs like temió 'feared,' pidió 'asked,' durmió 'slept.' In that way, speakers kept such preterits morphologically distinct from p.p.s temido 'feared' etc. One might make a circular argument that speakers of Spanish consider such distinctions important, because they have kept them for every verb they use (see §1.8).

4.7.4. Adjectives and Past Participles in Reflexes of –ŪTU

In Latin, speakers used the ending -ŪTUM > -ŪTU to make past participles for u-stem verbs as well as adjectives for u-stem nouns. Both types were fairly rare. Aside from perhaps a score of past participles like SECŪTU 'followed,' SOLŪTU 'loosened,' and VOLŪTU 'rolled,' Latin had a number of adjectives derived from 4th-decl. nouns, like ASTŪTU 'clever' from ASTU 'adroitness, craft' and VERŪTU 'armed with a javelin' from VERU 'dart, javelin.'

A few Latin adjectives ending in -ŪTU applied to body parts of humans or animals, sometimes with augmentative force. Many derived from 4th-decl. u-stem nouns, giving e.g. CORNŪTU 'horned' from CORNU 'horn' and MANŪTU 'big-handed' from MANU 'hand.' In CL, the -ŪTU ending could be added to a fair number of adjectives or nouns from other classes to create e.g. CĀNŪTU 'gray-haired' from 1st/2nd-decl. CĀNA/CĀNU 'whitish-gray' and NĀSŪTU 'big-nosed' from 2nd-decl. NĀSU 'nose.'

During the past fifteen hundred years, reflexes of -ŪTU have specialized in the far east and the far west of ROMANIA. Which of the two functions once performed by -ŪTU has survived in each area?

4.7.4.1. Past Participles in –udo

Thriving from Catalonia to Romania, the suffix deriving from -ŪTU never became firmly established for past participles in central and western Ibero-Romance, according to Lloyd (313). Lausberg agrees, stating (250) that such past participles attested for Old Spanish and Old Portuguese were literary Gallicisms that, at the height of trans-Pyrenean prestige, attained a merely written popularity in epics and lyrics south of the mountains.[60]

In contrast, Alessio (187) considers that Spanish and Portuguese both came to replace earlier -udo p.p.s with -ido ones, but supplies no explanation for

---

[59] Homonymic clash would have become unlikely if perder 'lose' and vender 'sell' had had -udo p.p.s but -ido 3sg. preterits. Through time, I suppose, Spanish speakers came to restrict -ido to past-participial or adjectival use.

[60] Once again, I wonder: how would a Spaniard or Portuguese have heard a past-participial [y] delivered by someone from north of the Pyrenees?

that shift in p.p. tonic-vowel preference. García de Diego (191) agrees with Alessio, stating that -*udo* p.p.s were first adopted in Spain for reflexes of 2nd- and 3rd-conj. verbs from CL, as they usually were from Gallia to Dacia.

One might wonder whether -*udo* p.p.s seen in mediæval works, like the *metudo* 'put into' and *vençudo* 'won' occurring in the *Cid* (ca. 1200) or the *sabudo* 'known,' *temudo* 'feared,' *abatudo* 'beaten,' and *corrompudo* 'corrupted' occurring in the *Libro de Alexandre* (ca. 1200) should truly be classed as imports from farther east or north. Other such forms found in Old Spanish include *perdudo* 'lost,' *conosçudo* 'known,' *esparzudo* 'scattered,' *ardudo* 'burned,' and *defendudo* 'fought off; banned' (Menéndez Pidal, 231). Table 4–8 illustrates the survival or reshaping of a few such past participles between Latin and Spanish.

Table 4–8

Spanish Outcomes for Past Participles in –ŪTU/–*udo*

Latin Past Participle	Old Spanish Past Participle	Modern Sp. Past Participle	Cf. Infinitive
I n h e r i t a n c e			
BATTŪTU	batudo	batido	bater
TRIBŪTU	trevudo	—	—
I n n o v a t i o n			
ĀRSU	ardudo	ardido	arder
COMĒSU	comudo	comido	comer
N e w 4 t h - c o n j . f o r m			
SECŪTU	seguido	*idem*	seguir
S y n c o p e			
SOLŪTU	suelto	—	—
VOLŪTU	vuelto	*idem*	volver

Had these been imports, they would also have been inserted into Old Portuguese texts, which contain past participles like *ascondudo* 'hidden,' *avudo* 'had,' *movudo* 'moved,' and again *corrompudo* 'corrupted' (Martins Sequeira, 176). After all, the phonological evolution of OSp. *trevudo* 'paid taxes' < TRIBŪTU 'allotted' looks far from learnèd, given its marked lenition of two intervocalic stops; cf. ModSp. *tributo* 'tribute, tax' and the derived verb *tributar* 'pay taxes' (p.p. *tributado*), all of them lacking lenition.

At times, judging by attested *apercebudo* 'provided, warned,' *venudo* 'come,' and *encanudo* 'gone gray-haired,' even certain 4th-conj. verbs in Old Spanish like *apercebir, venir, encanir* (ModSp. *encanecer*) might acquire *-udo* p.p.s (García de Diego, 192); see §3.5.7 for wavering between *-uto* and *-ito* in certain Old Italian past participles. As none of these attested OSp./OPtg. *-udo* forms may be traced back to CL rhizotonic thematics like PERDĬTU, HABĬTU, COGNĬTU, or to sigmatics like SPARSU, ĀRSU, DĒFĒNSU, it seems reasonable to agree with Lathrop (152) that the ending from -ŪTU not only survived across Iberia but also "spread analogically to a number of verbs" in Old Spanish, and in Old Portuguese as well.

That is the view held by Williams in *From Latin to Portuguese* (185): *-udo* was the normal past-participial outcome for Old Portuguese reflexes of 2nd- and 3rd-conj. verbs from Latin. As happened elsewhere in e.g. It. *venuto*, Fr. *venu*, and Cat. *vingut*, the OPtg. by-form p.p. *vĩudo* 'come' did not match the 4th-conj. class of its infin. *vẽir > vĩir > vir*, but the ModPtg. p.p. *vindo* [bĩdu] resembles *findo* 'ended' < FINĬTU in coming from a regular or regularized 4th-conj. form attested centuries ago. The OPtg. p.p.s *tẽudo* and *teudo* 'had' were regular given the 2nd-/3rd-conj. infin. *tẽer > ter*. Both p.p. variants have since been replaced by analogical *tido*, using the same non-*ar*-verb default morphology seen in unsyncopated Sp. *tenido* (Williams, 237–38, 241–42).

That most of those mediæval *-udo* p.p.s are paralleled morphologically elsewhere in ROMANIA, except on Sardinia and in part of southern Italy, leads one to suspect that they originated in Late Latin if not indeed under the twelve Cæsars. One's suspicion is heightened by some of Väänänen's attestations in *Introduction au latin vulgaire*, of nonstandard forms in -ŪTU (see §2.14.1). Given that *-udo* p.p.s began to yield to competitors in *-ido* only in fourteenth-century Spanish and fifteenth-century Portuguese, they most likely lasted beyond the High Middle Ages. One might suppose, then, that in Proto-Spanish most descendants of 2nd- and 3rd -conj. verbs (both with infins. in stressed *-er*) adopted either *-ido* or *-udo* as p.p. endings, so that e.g. either *metido* or *metudo* tended to replace attested *mis[s]o* or *mes[s]o* 'put into' < MISSU 'sent.' Later, *-ido* took over for nearly all non-*ar*-verb past participles. Penny agrees with this view, noting that before literary norms were established the two endings *-ido* and *-udo* alternated freely in the participles of 2nd-/3rd-conj. *-er* verbs, but that thereafter *-udo* grew steadily less common (1991, 193).

Looking across the millennia, Montgomery (147) recalls that marking certain perfectum slot-fillers with [u] or [w] spread three times during the history of Latin and Spanish. On pre-CL perfects, such marking first spread from the 1st and 4th conjugations into mostly stative verbs of the 2nd, where infin. -*ē*- contrasted with pf. -*u*-: such marking survived into Old Spanish only in disguised form in e.g. *ove* < HABUĪ 'had' (148). Second, in LL such marking became associated with new -ŪTU p.p.s, for "the -*ū*-, supported by the ending -*uī*, [was] an expressive sign apt for the participle, which with the perfect or preterit is the most distinctively perfective verb form" (150). In central-western Iberia, attested -*udo* past participles appear to have long been interchangeable with -*ido* ones, but they went into a decline during the later Middle Ages. At about the same time, [u] came back to life as a tonic-vowel preterit marker for 2nd-/3rd-conj. verbs, giving ModSp. *supe* 'I knew' (infin. *saber*) and *tuve* 'I had' (*tener*), which replaced forms in tonic [o] and joined earlier preterits in [u] like *pude* 'could' < POTUĪ (infin. *poder*) and *puse* 'put' < POSUĪ (infin. *poner*). Only if speakers had preferred [u] to [o] as a "marker of perfectivity," says Montgomery, could that kind of vowel raising have taken place (152). Thus, tonic [u] still occurs in such 1sg. and 3sg. past-tense forms, and more besides.

More briefly, Anderson and Rochet comment (290) that the loss of -UĪ preterits might have contributed to the demise of -ŪTU as a past-participial ending in Spanish and Portuguese.

Along the same lines, Georges (35) provides a structural explanation for past participles in -*udo*. In Castile, the tripartite p.p. system built of -*ado*, -*ido*, and -*udo* was doomed from the start, because -UĪ perfects—the main support of -ŪTU past participles—failed to take root there as they had elsewhere. (Why this should have been so remains unexplained.) Georges notes that, for regular verbs, the -*er* and -*ir* classes became identical early on in their preterit and past-participial paradigms: in contrast with its neighbors to the east and north, Spanish evolved a "bipartite weak perfectum" and hence had room left for only two types of arrhizotonic past participle along with two types of arrhizotonic preterit.

Put another way, regular Spanish reflexes of 1st-conj. verbs like *cantar* 'sing' < CANTĀRE have a 3sg. pret. ending in -*ó* (*cantó* 'sang' < CANTĀVIT) and a masc.sg. past participle ending in -*ado* (*cantado* 'sung' < CANTĀTU). Regular Spanish reflexes of 2nd-/3rd-conj. verbs like *mover* 'move' < MOVĒRE and *caer* 'fall' < CADERE, along with regular reflexes of 4th-conj. verbs like *oir* 'hear' < AUDĪRE, all have a 3sg. preterit ending in -*ió* or -*yó* (*movió*, *cayó*, *oyó*) and a masc.sg. past participle ending in -*ido* (*movido*, *caído*, *oído*). Even when best represented in mediæval manuscripts, after all, many attested -*udo* p.p.s already had by-forms ending in -*ido*. By the sixteenth century, certainly, -*ido* p.p.s had replaced all earlier -*udo* ones for non-1st-conj. verbs in Spanish and Portuguese (Parkinson, 150).

Recently, the scholarly controversy about -*udo* past participles seems to have been resolved. Harris-Northall (1996) has shown that past participles with endings derived from -ŪTUM survived into the High Middle Ages in Spain. As Harris-Northall points out (36–37), certain -*udo* past participles attested in mediæval Spanish texts are for verbs unrepresented north of the Pyrenees, like *comudo* 'eaten' and *seudo* 'been.' Other -*udo* past participles look more innovative than contemporary Gallo-Romance forms, such as *ardudo* 'burned,' *prometudo* 'promised,' *traudo* 'brought' versus OFr./OOc. *ars* < ĀRSU, Fr. *promis* and Oc. *promes* < PRŌMISSU, Fr./Oc. *trait* < TRACTU, the last of which in Gaul had acquired the sense 'milked.' Moreover, OSp. *atrevudo* 'paid taxes' and *batudo* 'beaten' probably represent continuations of ATTRIBŪTU 'assigned, allotted' and BATTŪTU.

In that light, I wonder: how would speakers of central-western Ibero-Romance have heard a past-participial form from -ŪTU delivered by a reciter of lyrics or epics from north of the Pyrenees? They could have heard, listening to early Old French or Old Occitan (ignoring case distinctions), forms ending in [yt] for masc.sg. and in [yðə] for fem.sg. One therefore questions whether Spaniards or Portuguese would have made any sense of forms like those, given that neither [y] nor [ə] was a phoneme in central-western Ibero-Romance, and that words ending in [t] were phonotactically disallowed there. (Pace Walsh, I ignore the question of when intervocalic [d] lenited to [ð].)

In Spanish now, at any rate, three -ŪTU p.p.s popular in Latin have been remade along old 4th-conj. lines: *batido* 'beaten' ≠ BATTŪTU, *hodido* or *jodido* 'fucked' ≠ FUTŪTU, and *cosido* 'sewn' ≠ CŌNSŪTU.

4.7.4.2. Adjectives in −*udo*

For body parts of humans, the semantic field dealt with here, CL had several suffixes for forming body-part adjectives. Among them, the pair -ŌSU and -EU were limited to adjectival use, but -ĀTU, -ĪTU, and increasingly -ŪTU also served as endings for past participles.

In CL, the adjectival suffix in -ĀTU almost always denoted possession of a given part without regard to size and without any emotional coloration. This seems to have been so for BARBĀTU 'bearded,' DENTĀTU 'toothed,' MENTULĀTU 'having a penis,' and OCULĀTU 'having eyes.' A few body-part CL adjectives ended in -ĪTU like AURĪTU 'long-eared.' They seem to have had augmentative force but grew less popular with time. As noted in §4.7.4, a few CL adjectives ended in -ŪTU: from *u*-stem nouns derived CORNŪTU 'horned' and MANŪTU 'big-handed,' while CĀNŪTU 'gray-haired' and NĀSŪTU 'big-nosed' came from adjectives or nouns in other classes. Such -ŪTU adjectives might or might not be augmentative.

Both the -ĀTU and the -ŪTU type of adjective have remained broadly popular in ROMANIA.

In Spanish today, a handful of old-time past participles like *agudo* 'sharp' i.e. 'sharpened' < ACŪTU (already used for 'pointed, sharp' in CL) and *menudo* 'small' i.e. 'shrunken' < MINŪTU (already used for 'tiny' in CL) have acquired or retained adjectival meaning and may no longer be used in a verbal sense. Spanish instead uses *aguzado* 'sharpened' and *menguado* or *disminuido* 'shrunken,' which one could try to trace back to variants of Latin forms but which in any event belong to the only two classes of regular past participles extant today. There still survives adjectival *sabudo* 'knowledgeable.' Some -*udo* forms have survived by switching their ending, like OSp. *entendudo* 'intelligent' now ModSp. *entendido* 'expert, able.' Others have become archaic, like *tenudo* 'beholden' (Montgomery, 150).

Although *-udo* competed with other adjectival markers in Old Spanish, adjectives with that ending today often refer to body parts of humans or animals, usually with augmentative or pejorative force or both. Examples include Sp. *barbudo* 'bearded,' *ojudo* 'pop-eyed,' *narigudo* 'big-nosed,' *orejudo* 'jug-eared,' *bocudo* 'wide-mouthed,' *dentudo* 'bucktoothed,' rare *lengudo* 'talkative,' and archaic *cabezudo* 'swell-headed.' Another category would contain *-udo* adjs. referring to human character or emotion like *corajudo* 'brave' and *confianzudo* 'overtrusting, gullible,' together with *sañudo* 'angry' and the apparent neologism *suertudo* 'lucky dog' (Montgomery, 154).

Many of these Spanish adjectives parallel French ones like *barbu* 'bearded,' *bossu* 'hunchbacked,' *ventru* 'pot-bellied,' *poilu* 'hairy[-bodied],' *têtu* 'headstrong,' *goulu* 'greedy' i.e. 'snouty,' and also parallel Italian ones like *barbuto* 'bearded,' *occhiuto* 'pop-eyed,' and *gambuto* 'thick-legged' (Malkiel 1992, 19). In Romanian, only two such adjectives end in tonic *-ut: cornut* 'horned' < CORNŪTU and *limbut* 'talkative' < LINGUA 'tongue' + -ŪTU. There, evidently after metathesis and dissimilation, CANŪTU 'gray-haired' has yielded *cărunt*, and MINŪTU 'small' has yielded *mărunt*. Other body-part adjectives in Romanian end in *-os*, from -ŌSU.[61]

4.7.4.3. A Three-Way Split

From the data presented above, one sees that a given Romance language may have body-part adjectives with endings from -ŪTU; it may have past participles with endings from -ŪTU; or it may have both kinds of lexical items.

The resultant pattern shows a ROMANIA split in three: a central area of Catalonia, France, and Italy contrasts with the two extremities, Spain and Portugal against Romania. Throughout the core of Romance, past participles and body-part adjectives with endings from -ŪTU both flourish, if less so in French than they used to. Far-western Spanish and Portuguese have a large number of such adjectives, but neither language has any verb form in *-udo* still used as a past participle. Conversely, far-eastern Romanian has many *-ut* past participles but scarcely an adjective with that ending.

At each geographical extreme, then, the formant deriving from -ŪTU has been specialized in one of its two uses presumed for LL or PR and attested in a handful of past participles and adjectives from CL times.

---

[61] For a survey of one class of adjectives across major Romance languages, see Laurent, "Resultados en las lenguas romances de adjetivos con desinencias derivadas de -ŪTUM" in *Revista de Filología Española* LXXVIII (1998: 27–48).

4.7.5. Influence of Preterits on Past-Participial Morphology

Morphological interchanges between preterit and past participle have been seen across ROMANIA. Southwest of the Pyrenees, the stems of a few arrhizotonic Old Spanish past participles derive not from infinitives like *aver* and *querer* but instead from irregular preterits like 3sg. *ovo* and *quiso*; yet the OSp. p.p.s *ovido* 'had' and *quesido* 'wanted' (with [e] kept) have failed to thrive (Penny 1991, 193).

For a time during the Middle Ages, as Craddock has observed, the *-ido* ending grew so popular that it came to be used for some 1st-conj. verbs. Texts from the thirteenth and fourteenth centuries contain other such past participles as *robido* 'stolen; kidnaped,' *amodorrida* 'become drowsy,' and *desmaido* 'faltered; swooned,' for which only *robado*, *amodorrada*, and *desmayado* are possible today (Menéndez-Pidal, 230). Such 1st-conj. *-ido* past participles in Old Spanish remind one of apparently rhizotonic thematic past participles like PROBITU 'approved' and PROCITU 'asked, demanded' that are attested for a few 1st-conj. verbs in Late Latin and that could actually be 4th-conj. forms (see §2.4.3). Here and there, now and then, speakers will pull back along the road they are supposed to be following toward isomorphy.

Speakers of Spanish have pulled back elsewhere, even in a sigmatic direction. As Lloyd remarks (305), a few Old Spanish verbs related to *querer* 'want; love' adopted sigmatic preterits resembling 3sg. *quiso*: *conquerir* 'conquer' and *requerir* 'demand' developed prets. *conquiso* and *requiso*. By analogy with such innovations, a few other verbs acquired sigmatic preterits like *espiso* 'spent,' *priso* 'took.' These clearly cannot have come from EXPENDIT and PREHENDIT, but seem instead to have been altered ± past participles *espeso* < EXPĒNSU 'weighed out' and *preso* < PREHĒNSU 'grabbed.' Being sigmatic, forms like *espiso* and *priso* were swimming against the morphological currents and have in fact sunk along the way to Modern Spanish.

4.7.6. Past Participles Since Old Spanish Times

Since Old Spanish times, speakers have rebuilt most rhizotonic past participles by shifting them into the *-ido* class, which accounts for over 63 percent of the admittedly rather unrepresentative sample provided in Appendix 2. It will occasion little surprise that the remaining rhizotonics are either ultra-high-frequency forms or else learnèd ones.

4.7.6.1. New Arrhizotonics

By regularizing old sigmatics and old tautic athematics, speakers have further promoted arrhizotonicity in past-participial morphology (see Table 4–4).

Several rhizotonics in Old Spanish, deriving from syncope in LL/PR innovations, have since been remade. Akin to It. *tolto* 'taken away,' still in use as a past participle there, OSp. *tuelto* 'idem' came from a tautic thematic replacement for suppletive SUBLĀTU₁ 'raised, removed' as against infin. TOLLERE, pf. SUSTULĪ.[62] With a narrower semantic field, the verb lives on as *tullir* 'cripple,' with pp. *tullido* also used as an adjective meaning 'crippled' (cf. Cat. *tolit* 'idem'). Demotic-looking *surto* 'arisen' ≠ SURRĒCTU has become archaic, yielding to arrhizotonic *surgido*.

Nearly all old rhizotonics, most with infinitives in *-er*, have been remade on arrhizotonic *-ido* lines (see Table 4–9). Five forms in [tʃ] used to be *cocho* 'cooked' < COCTU; *cojecho* 'caught' < COLLĒCTU 'gathered,' *correcho* 'straightened' < CORRĒCTU, *ducho* 'brought' < DUCTU 'led,' *erecho* 'built, raised' < ĒRĒCTU, and *trecho* 'fetched' < TRACTU 'pulled.' The second had a prefixed variant *escoyecho* 'chosen' < EX + COLLĒCTU (Meyer-Lübke 1974, 424). Yet another used to continue the direct-suffixation tradition: OSp. *nado* 'born' < NĀTU, though synchronically this looks like a 1st-conj. form. All the above have been remade as infectum-based *cocido*, *cogido* and *escogido*, *corregido*, *-ducido*, *erguido* or semilearnèd *erigido*, *nacido*, and *traído*. In dialects where the first of these has become homonymous with *cosido* 'sewn,' infinitives *cocer* and *coser* also being homophonous, the former is often replaced by 1st-conj. *cocinar* (p.p. *cocinado*) based on *cocina* 'kitchen.'

Three past participles in [nt] used to be OSp. *tinto* 'dyed' < TĪNCTU has yielded to *teñido* as a past participle, but the old past participle remains in use as an adjective. Likewise, OSp. *cinto* 'girded' < CĪNCTU has yielded to *ceñido*, but the old past participle survives as a pair of nouns, masculine and feminine (see §4.7.7). Identical at least graphically to It. *vinto*, OSp. *vinto* 'won' has yielded to present-based *vencido*.

Sigmatic-tautics have diminished. Thus, *quisto* 'wanted; loved,' from a syncopated variant of QUÆSĪTU 'sought' (also in OPtg.), is now present-based *querido*. Again, prefixed sigmatic-tautic *conquisto* 'conquered' has been reshaped as *conquerido*.

Sigmatics have vanished. Four past participles in [s] used to be *mis[s]o* or *mes[s]o* 'put into' < MISSU 'sent,' and *preso* 'taken' < PREHĒNSU 'grabbed,' *riso* 'laughed' < RĪSU, and *seso* 'felt' < SĒNSU. They are now present-based *metido*, *prendido*, *reído*, *sentido*. Sigmatic *preso* 'prisoner; imprisoned' has been limited to nominal and adjectival use, *seso* 'brain' and fem. *risa* 'laughter' to nominal use. Today, *meso-* 'middle' and *miso-* 'hatred' are usable only as learnèd prefixes. Meanwhile, *opreso* 'squeezed, oppressed' has yielded to *oprimido*. Two more rebuilt sigmatics are OSp. *enceso* 'lit' < INCĒNSU and *defeso* 'fought off' < DĒFĒNSU. They are now present-based *encendido*, *defendido* (Penny 1991, 194; Andres-Suárez, 50). See Table 4–9 for details.

---

[62] Cf. 4th-conj. Sp. *tullir* and Cat. *tollir* 'cripple, maim,' i.e. 'deprive of function,' each with a regular past participle or isomorphic adjective. In Old Spanish, this verb still meant 'take away.' Its thirteenth-century past participle, with an OSp. by-form *tolludo*, appears in a line by Berceo: *e tú has me tollido a mí un capellano* 'and you have taken a priest from me' (Squartini, 187).

Table 4–9

Reshaping of Old Spanish Rhizotonic Past Participles

Latin Past Participle	Old Sp. Past Participle	Modern Past Participle	Cf. Infinitive
S i g m a t i c (- t a u t i c)			
MISSU	messo	metido	meter
PR(HE)ĒNSU	preso	prendido	prender
SĒNSU	seso	sentido	sentir
QUÆSĪTU	quisto	querido	querer
T a u t i c a t h e m a t i c i n [lt], [rt]			
SUBLĀTU₁	tuelto	tullido	tullir
TORTU	tuerto	torcido	torcer
T a u t i c a t h e m a t i c i n [nt]			
CĪNCTU	cinto	ceñido	ceñir
TĪNCTU	tinto	teñido	teñir
VICTU	vinto	vencido	vencer
T a u t i c a t h e m a t i c i n [tʃ]			
COCTU	cocho	cocido	cocer
DUCTU	ducho	-ducido	-ducir
TRACTU	trecho	traído	traer
S y n c o p e			
SURRĒCTU	surto	surgido	surgir

One oddity remains to be discussed. OSp. *(ar)repiso* 'repented,' with tonic [i], had no doubt been shaped by analogy with a by-form p.p. *quiso* 'sought; wanted'; Portuguese still has the p.p. *repêso* 'repented' from REPĒNSU 'reweighed, repaid' for infin. *arrepender* (Williams, 186); for the semantics, note freq. RESPĒNSĀRE 'make up for.' In Spanish, the morphological anomaly has been regularized along non-*ar*-verb lines to give ModSp. *arrepentido* 'repented' (Lapesa, 210–11).

4.7.6.2. Remaining Rhizotonics

Rhizotonic past participles in Spanish today include some tautic athematic ones containing an [lt] or [rt] cluster, like *abierto* 'opened' < APERTU, *cubierto* 'covered' < COOPERTU, *muerto* 'died' < MORTUU, and *vuelto* '[re]turned' ≠ VOLŪTU (cf. It. *volto*, Enga. *vout*). On the west coast, Portuguese has undiphthongized *aberto, coberto, morto*, and *envolto*.

A few rhizotonics derive from old forms in [pt] like *escrito* 'written' and *roto* 'broken,' both paralleled in Portuguese. A few others derive irregularly from old forms in [kt]. One would expect FRĪCTU to give **fricho* instead of std. *frito* 'fried,' competing with *freído* in some areas. Meanwhile, Sp. *bendito* 'blessed' < BENEDICTU looks more semilearnèd than syncopated Ptg. *bento* (see §4.7.6.4).[63] Spanish has also kept two common past participles containing [tʃ] < [kt], *dicho* 'said, told' < DICTU and *hecho* 'done/made' < FACTU, for which the Portuguese exemplars, in [(i)t], have turned into *dito* and *feito*. As in French and Occitan, the tonic vowel in Sp. *dicho* or Ptg. *dito* cannot derive from the [ī] of Latin DICTU, which developed normally in Leon. *decho* and It. *detto*, but rather is analogical with the finite perfectum forms like DĪXĪ (Lloyd, 314); the same applies to OSp. *ducho* 'led, brought' < DUCTU.

Far-western Romance still has two past participles in [st], Sp. *puesto* and Ptg. *pôsto* 'put' along with shared *visto* 'seen.' As noted, the first comes from syncope of POSITU, the second from a sigmatic-tautic variant of VĪSU, or perhaps from syncope of VĪSĬTU 'inspected.' In the latter event, *visto* would amount to a popularized technicality, as It. *senza* 'without' < ABSENTIĀ 'in the absence of' is said to be.

Even within that shrunken inventory of rhizotonic participles, forces of analogy with the two large classes have been at work over the centuries. In Portuguese if not in Spanish, the rhizotonic survivals *morto* 'died,' *junto* 'joined,' and *sôlto* 'loosened' compete with arrhizotonic *morrido, juntado, soltado*. In Spanish, the old p.p.s *junto* 'joined' and *suelto* 'loosened' have been limited to adjectival use, and so has *tuerto* 'one-eyed'< TORTU 'twisted'; speculation about that last semantic leap is best avoided. In both languages, *rompido* has made inroads on *roto* 'broken' < RUPTU in certain areas, even if consultant Sempere claims never to have heard the present-based variant

---

[63] Also regularized Sp. *benedecido* blessed.' Resembling a short-form and long-form pair, Ptg. *bento* 'idem' competes with regular *benzido* (infin. *benzer*).

from a native speaker of Spanish much beyond toddlerhood. For distinctions between these two by-forms, see the next section.

4.7.6.3. Possible Role of Phonetic Symbolism

Why, in past participles above all, has Spanish verb morphology tended to shift away from rhizotonicity? Malkiel (1993a, 312) notes that the regularized p.p. of Sp. *romper* is fully acceptable under the standard in phrases like *ha rompido con sus amigos* 's/he has broken with his/her friends' but, adjectivally, the inherited form must be used in phrases like *algo está roto* 'something is broken,' where the last word comes across as arguably adjectival. Moreover, unprefixed *roto* contrasts with fully regularized *interrompido* 'interrupted' and with semilearnèd *corrupto* 'corrupted' (also adjectival), which itself has an arrhizotonic by-form *corrompido*.[64]

Still according to Malkiel, the survival of *roto* may be attributable to its phonological and semantic similarity such adjectives or nouns as *bobo* 'fool,' *cojo* 'lame,' *flojo* 'weak, lazy,' *sordo* 'deaf,' *tonto* 'stupid,' *zonzo* 'dull,' all built out of [C(C)oCo] or [CoC(C)o] and all insinuative of physical or characterological shortcomings.[65] As Malkiel remarks, "En tal contexto, *roto* llevaba una enorme ventaja a *rompido*; fue esta suggestividad casi fonosimbólica la que, a mi modo de ver, fortaleció la posición medio lábil de *roto* lo suficiente como para garantizarle la supervivencia en medio de las arremetidas de su rival *rompido*" (1993a, 315) [Thus, *roto* had a great advantage over *rompido*, for its almost phonosymbolic suggestiveness, as I see it, strengthened the rather slippery position of *roto* enough to ensure that it would survive attacks by its rival *rompido*]. For that reason, phonetic symbolism would have helped to preserve an increasingly anomalous form that speakers came to feel as adjectival. Unfortunately, to my knowledge Malkiel never used phonosymbolism to explain how other rhizotonic past participles have survived in Spanish. Perhaps the adjectival roles of *abierto* 'open[ed]' and *cubierto* 'covered' could be adduced to that end (see §6.4).

4.7.6.4. Past Participles for Learnèd Verbs

Of tautic athematic past participles officially extant in Spanish, some like *absuelto* 'shriven' or *resuelto* '[re]solved,' may appear semilearnèd because they retain an [lt] cluster that usually turned into [tʃ] in Castilian, as witness *cuchillo* 'knife' < CULTELLU. Nevertheless, diphthongization of [ɔ] to [we] evidently removed the environment for that shift; retention of a [bs] cluster

---

[64] Inherited *escrito* 'written' has supplied the model for p.p.s *transcrito* 'transcribed,' *suscrito* 'subscribed,' *proscrito* 'banished, outlawed,' and *prescrito* 'prescribed, specified.' For these verbs, standard Spanish accepts no past participles in *-escribido*.

[65] In Malkiel's interpretation, breaking something would presumably suggest awkwardness or incompetence rather than deliberate intent (as in 'we have broken the code' or 'they broke through to the treasure').

does look semilearnèd. Plausibly, analogical pressure from often-said *vuelto* 'turned, returned' and especially *suelto* 'loose[ned],' the latter now only adjectival, helped *absuelto* and *resuelto* to prevail in their current guise, at least among the learnèd.

In Spanish as in other languages across ROMANIA, Latin verbs have been brought back to life by the learnèd. Unlike Italian, which usually assigns revived verbs to the 3rd conjugation, or French, which usually assigns them to the 1st, Spanish tends to reshape revived verbs according to the most common non-*ar*-verb norms, those of the fairly productive 4th conjugation. One knows this not merely by the p.p. ending -*ido*, which of course serves for every regular non-*ar*-verb past participle, but by the ending on the infinitive. Thus, defunct DĪVIDERE 'divide' (p.p. DĪVĪSU) has risen again as It. *dividere*, Fr. *diviser*, Sp. *dividir*. In Spain, the fifteenth-century revivals *presumir* 'surmise, conjecture' (cf. 3rd-conj. PRÆSŪMERE) and *persuadir* 'persuade' (cf. 2nd-conj. PERSUĀDĒRE) acquired the asigmatic prets. *presumí* ≠ PRÆSŪMPSĪ and *persuadí* ≠ PERSUĀSĪ; the sixteenth-century revival *ceder* 'transfer, yield' (cf. 3rd-conj. CĒDERE) joined the 2nd/3rd conjugation and acquired the regular asigmatic pret. *cedí* ≠ CESSĪ (R. Wright, 39–41). Along the way, those verbs obtained regular non-*ar*-verb past participles in Spanish: *presumido* ≠ PRÆSŪMPTU, *persuadido* ≠ PERSUĀSU, and *cedido* ≠ CESSU. Compare Fr. *présumé, persuadé,* and *cédé,* It. *presunto, persuaso, ceduto* but -*cesso* in some compounds. None of these has been resuscitated sigmatically in Spain.

These days, rhizotonics like learnèd-looking *absorto, abstracto, aflicto, electo, incluso,* and *excluso* (which need no glosses) tend to be replaced by regularized forms in -*ido* based on the infectum stem: *absorbido, abstraido, afligido, elegido, incluido,* and *excluido.*[66] Many rhizotonic revivals now serve mainly as other parts of speech: *absorto* 'rapt,' *electo* 'select, choice,' *incluso* 'inclusive of.' In addition, short-form past participles like *despierto* 'woken,' *trunco* 'maimed,' *fijo* 'fixed, set,' *harto* 'glutted,' and *enjuto* 'withered' now tend to yield to regularized forms in the still larger -*ado* class, though again many of the old forms survive adjectivally. Here they have the senses 'awake,' 'fed up,' 'lean, gaunt' (Green, 122).[67] Compare also the Sp. adj. *trunco* 'maimed' < TRUNCU with the p.p. *truncado*.

As shown in §4.7.8, short-form past participles have become standard for some Portuguese verbs, optional for others, and are found in dialects of Spanish. Were it not for a continuing semantic overlap between adjectives and past participles, exemplified morphologically by many short forms in nonstandard Italian (§3.5.9), one could almost believe that a Portuguese tendency toward p.p. abbreviation had wafted across the border into Spain.

---

[66] Otherwise, one has to suppose that the speech habits of seventy-five generations have preserved the consonant clusters [kskl], [bstr], or plain [kt] in these forms.

[67] Inherited Ptg. p.p.s include *preso* 'taken, caught' and *frito* 'fried,' competing with regular *prendido* and *frigido* based on the stems in infins. *prender* and *frigir* (Taylor, 655, noting no stylistic or semantic differentiation). For further discussion of short-form p.p.s, see §4.7.8.

4.7.7. Relic Past Participles in Spanish

Certain nouns in Spanish look exactly like the corresponding regular past participles (or adjectives) in tonic [a] or [i]. They may be masculine as in *juzgado* 'tribunal, lawcourt' and *oído* 'hearing,' or they may be feminine as in *helada* 'frost,' *comida* 'food,' and *leída* 'reading.' Other Spanish nouns look like the corresponding past participles that have resisted leveling: *dicha* 'joy, luck,' *puesta* 'setting [e.g., of the sun],' *vista* 'eyesight,' and *vuelta* 'turn, return.' Still other such nouns live on after the corresponding past participles, and sometimes their whole verbs, have vanished from the language: unlike the OSp. p.p. *exido* 'gone out,' regularized from EXĬTU, Sp. *ejido* 'public land, common' remains current.

During the rest of this section, §4.7.7, I deal mostly with p.p. relics whose morphology, by staying the same, has come to contrast with that of past participles now regularized. Such relics appear in §3.1.5.3 for Romanian, §3.5.2 and §3.5.3 for Italian, §4.4.9 for French, and §4.6.2.5 for Catalan. As in the sections on p.p. relics elsewhere, Romance nouns here that seem to continue Latin past participles may in fact derive from Latin nouns, attested or not.

4.7.7.1. Tautic Athematics

Among athematics, the Spanish noun *asalto* 'attack' continues an unattested compound *ASSALTU 'jumped on, leaped on,' though its infin. ASSALĪRE > OSp. *asalir* has since been remade as 1st-conj. *asaltar* (p.p. *asaltado*), apparently on the basis of the old past participle (see §4.7.7.5). One fem.sg. form, *nada* < NĀTA 'born' has become a negative pronoun with the sense 'nothing' but has ceased to have any verbal function.

Again, the noun *llanto* 'lament' continues the CL p.p. PLĀNCTU, though rhizotonic PLANGERE was remade as archaic *llañer* (p.p. *llañido*) or current semilearnèd-looking *plañir* (p.p. *plañido*) with a [pl] cluster that long ago palatalized to [ʎ] in e.g. *llano* < PLĀNU 'flat' or *lleno* < PLĒNU 'full.' The Spanish noun *parto* 'childbirth' continues PARTU 'given birth,' though rhizotonic PĀRERE has been remade as 4th-conj *parir*, with a regular p.p. *parido*.

A rhyming pair of old past participles still survives. First, *tinto* < TĪNCTU 'dyed' remains in use as an adjective meaning 'colored' and, in fem. *tinta*, as a noun meaning 'ink.' Second, *cinto* 'girded' < CĪNCTU remains in use as masc. *cinto* 'belt' and fem. *cinta* 'ribbon, tape.' Corresponding past participles are regular *ceñido* and *teñido*.

Several words identical to old past participles in [tʃ] < -CT- have become adjectival or nominal. A reflex of ĒRĒCTU 'built, raised,' still past-participial in OSp. *erecho* 'idem,' lives on as adjectival *arrecho* 'horny, aroused.' A reflex of TRACTU 'pulled, drawn,' still past-participial in OSp. *trecho* 'idem,' lives on as the noun *trecho* 'distance, space.' If the Sp. adj. *ducho* 'skillful' may seem to come from p.p. DUCTU 'led,' which gave OSp. *ducho* 'idem,' on semantic grounds it more plausibly comes from p.p. DOCTU 'taught,' already a CL adjective meaning 'well-informed; clever, shrewd.' In Spanish, all three forms in [tʃ] have been replaced as past participles by infectum-based variants in -ido.

A noun isolate in Spanish is *bizcocho* 'biscuit; cookie,' which conserves the old past participle *cocho* 'cooked' along with a variant of *bis-* 'twice' (Lathrop, 153). A near-isolate is *fecha* 'date' < FACTA, whose [f] sets it apart from the fem. p.p. *hecha* 'done/made' though hardly from the noun *fechoría* 'misdeed; atrocity,' which has more to do with the variant in h̲- than with the variant in f̲-. Perhaps originally stylistic, a morphological distinction has thus come to embody a semantic one. Equally [f]-less, whether from the Spanish noun *hecho* 'fact, deed' or the identical masc.sg. past participle, additional nouns have been built: *hechizo* 'enchantment, spell' resembles Arom. *faptu* 'idem' morphologically and semantically, while *hechura* 'handiwork; likeness,' looks like an old neut.pl. future participle meaning 'things to be done/made.'

4.7.7.2. Rhizotonic Thematics

Among rhizotonic thematics, two by-forms, *debdo* and *debda* 'debt' < DĒBĬTU, DĒBĬTA 'thing[s] owed'—now only *deuda*—used to contrast with the regular p.p. *debido* 'had to.' Most probably from p.p. DOMITU 'tamed,' masc. *duende* 'goblin; fairy' lacks overt gender marking. Could speakers in Spain have specialized that noun long ago in the sense 'sorcerer's familiar'?

According to Silva Neto (243), a few nouns in Portuguese come from rhizotonic thematic past participles in Late Latin that underwent syncope; see §3.5.2 for similar developments in Italian. Two instances are innovative Sp./Ptg. *falta* 'a lack, dearth' and Sp. *vuelta*, Ptg. *volta* 'turn, return.'[68] At this late date, however, no one can tell exactly how such forms came into being, but there is more evidence to support rhizotonic thematic etyma. A centuries-long flourishing of that type is implied by feminine nouns in Old Spanish like *bóveda* 'arch, vault; cave' < *VOLVITA, *pérdida* 'loss, harm' < PERDĬTA, *réndida* 'rent, income' < REDDĬTA with infectum [n], and *véndida*, *venta*, or *venda* 'sale' < VENDĬTA. One still current is *tienda* 'stall, shop; tent' < *TENDITA for TENTA 'stretched' (Georges, 126–30). Compare the Fr. cognates *voûte, perte, rente, vente,* and *tente.*

4.7.7.3. Sigmatics

Several sigmatic nouns in Spanish used to be identical to past participles in Latin. The nouns *riso* 'laugh' and *viso* 'aspect, appearance' continue 4th-decl. RĪSU and 2nd-decl. VĪSU, as against the current p.p.s *reído* 'laughed' and *visto* 'seen.' Besides, the noun *seso* 'brain' continues 4th-decl. SĒNSU 'feeling' as

---

[68] In Ptg., *envolto* 'wrapped' competes with regular *envolvido*, both with infin. *envolver* (Taylor, 655, without noting any stylistic or semantic differentiation).

against the current p.p. *sentido* 'felt, heard'; the adj. *raso* 'clear, unobstructed' continues 4th-decl. RĀSU 'shave.' Again, the noun *promesa* 'promise' continues the noun PRŌMISSA, as against the ModSp. p.p. *prometido* 'promised' (Georges, 39).[69] Now historical, the noun *corso* 'privateering' evidently came from the same stem as 4th-decl. CURSU 'run.' Moreover, the ecclesiastical noun *responso* 'prayer for the dead' came from 2nd-decl. RESPŌNSU and keeps an [ns] cluster. Compare the Mod.Sp. p.p.s *corrido* 'run,' *respondido* 'answered.'

Clearly demotic because it had its [we], the Old Spanish sigmatic noun *muesso* 'bite' < MORSU used to contrast with the regular p.p. *mordido* 'bitten.' However, the American Spanish noun *mordida* 'bribe' has been remade arrhizotonically. Dating from mediæval times, Sp. *confuso* 'bewildered' < CŌNFŪSU 'poured together; disorderly' survives as an adjective, and regular *confundido* is used as the past participle for *confundir* 'confuse, confound' (Mourin, 185).

The Spanish noun *poseso* 'possession' has clearly been built on POSSESSU 'owned,' past-participial only in Latin. One sign of its semilearnèd origin, no doubt in legal jargon, is that *poseso* also supposedly serves as an by-form past participle, with regular *poseido*, for the verb *poseir* 'own.' One doubts whether p.p. *poseso* is often heard outside courtrooms or the offices of lawyers and notaries.

Other old past participles survive in the adj. *tieso* 'stiff, firm' < TĒNSU 'stretched,' and also in the nouns *dehesa* 'pasture-ground' < DĒFĒNSA 'fought off' and *remesa* 'remittance' < REMISSA 'sent back' (Menéndez Pidal, 231). Sigmatic OSp. *preso* < PR(EH)ĒNSU 'taken, caught' has been limited to the adjectival sense 'arrested' or the nominal one 'prisoner.' Do speakers feel anything past-participial in such adjectives and nouns today?

Many of the terms above may date back to Latin nouns, often 4th-decl. sigmatics, that had the same stems as past participles for the corresponding verbs. Owing to regularization of verb paradigms, they have all turned into morphological isolates, Spanish having no sigmatic past participles left. No feature reviewed in this study better illustrates the morphological chiasmus that has developed geographically, whereby the marker [s] has been specialized in different uses at the extremes of ROMANIA; see §5.5.

4.7.7.4. Sigmatic-Tautics

Except that Spanish has a few sigmatic-tautic past participles left, its sigmatic-tautic nouns have followed the same path as its sigmatic ones. For instance, the Spanish noun *pasto* 'pasture, grazing' continues the 4th-decl. noun PĀSTU 'idem,' identical to p.p. PĀSTU 'fed, kept' in Latin. Through time,

---

[69] Georges adds OSp. *fues(s)a* 'grave, ditch' < FOSSA 'dug,' *llosa* 'fenced-in [private, forbidden] property' < CLAUSA 'shut,' and *molsa* 'bedding, mattress stuffing' < MULSA 'stroked, soothed' (infin. MULCĒRE). For more nouns built from the stem of FOSSU 'dug,', see note 36 to this chapter.

though, rhizotonic PASCERE was remade as OSp. *paçer*, now *pacer*, with regular p.p. *pacido*.[70]

Similarly, the older Ptg. p.p. *quisto* from *QUÆSTU ± *visto* 'seen' survives only in adjectival compounds like *benquisto* 'well-liked, beloved' or *malquisto* 'hated, disliked'—both also usable as past participles for *bemquerer* and *malquerer*—but all p.p. functions for the simplex are now filled by regularized *querido* 'wanted; loved' based on the same stem as that of infin. *querer* (Martins Sequeira, 195; Williams, 232). In Spanish, the old by-form p.p. *quisto* survives only in the phrases *bien quisto* 'well-liked' and *mal quisto* 'disliked,' while the past participle for *querer* must be *querido* 'wanted; loved.'

4.7.7.5. A Few Verbs from Past Participles

Today, what used to be rhizotonic past participles survive as adverbs in *junto* 'near, beside' or *falto* 'for lack of,' as nouns like *cinto* 'belt,' or as adjectives like *estrecho* 'tight, narrow,' the last of these contrasting with the regularized p.p. *estreñido* 'constipated' (Green, 101). Having so to speak come down in the world, such inheritances may no longer be used to build perfective constructions. Nevertheless, as they did in Late Latin (§2.11), past participles have served as bases for new verbs in Spanish.

For instance, OSp. *falto* 'been lacking,' probably from a rhizotonic (thematic?) variant of p.p. FALSU 'tricked; failed,' has inspired 1st-conj. *faltar* 'lack' (p.p. *faltado*). Again, OSp. *junto* 'joined' < JŪNCTU has inspired *juntar* (p.p. *juntado*). A reflex of its rhyming partner ŪNCTU 'oiled' has inspired *untar* (p.p. *untado*), partly replacing reflexes of UNG(U)ERE in Spanish, though there also exists a 4th-conj. doublet *ungir* 'anoint' with regular p.p. *ungido* (Lloyd, 314).

Finally, semilearnèd *responso* 'prayer for the dead' (§4.7.7.4) has spun off a verb *responsar* 'say prayers for the dead,' with a predictable p.p. *responsado*.

4.7.8. Short-Form Past Participles

In Portuguese as in Italian dialects and in nonstandard Spanish, certain 1st-conj. verbs have developed syncopated past participles with stem stress, thus reversing in part the centuries-long drive toward arrhizotonicity. According to Williams (186), two morphological analogies have been at work in creating short forms. Those in -*o* like *ganho* gained, earned' may be traced back to the coexistence in Latin of pairs like ACCEPTU 'taken, received' and its frequentative ACCEPTĀTU; those in -*e* like *entregue* 'delivered' may be traced back to the coexistence in Portuguese of pairs like *firme* and *firmado*, literally

---

[70] It bears repeating this study only touches on possible derivational pathways through nouns or adjectives from Latin. Such forms—most of them relic nouns in Spanish and French, nouns/p.p.s in Italian, and innovations in Romanian—are discussed briefly as part of the coverage of major languages. Future collators may wish to do likewise for dialects of Romance.

'firm[ed] up, signed.' Such by-forms as these point up the adjectival origins of past participles and their continuing quasi-adjectival status in some uses.

From the Portuguese 1st-conj. infinitives *aceitar, entregar,* and *limpar* are derived the short-forms *aceito* or *aciete* 'accepted' alongside regular *aceitado*, *entregue* 'delivered' alongside *entregado*, and *limpo* 'cleaned' alongside *limpado*.[71] Other 1st-conj. short-form by-forms include *safo* 'pulled off, removed' and the rare pair *assente* or *assento* 'laid, placed' (infins. *safar, assentar*).

In fact, for 1st-conj. *gastar* 'spend; waste,' *pagar* 'pay,' *ganhar* 'win, earn,' only the short-form p.p.s *gasto, pago, ganho* remain in the day-to-day speech of the Portuguese. Long-form *gastado* and *pagado* have grown as archaic as Engl. *standen* 'stood' or *washen* 'washed,' while long-form *ganhado* 'gained, earned' is archaic except in fixed expressions like *vintem poupado, vintem ganhado* 'a penny saved is a penny earned.'

Short forms come from other conjugations. From 2nd-/3rd-conj. *atender, acender, encher* < IMPLĒRE are derived std. *atento* 'answered,' *aceso* 'lit,' and *cheio* 'filled; full' next to *atendido, acendido,* and *enchido*. From 4th-conj. *aspergir, erigir, espargir,* and *imprimir* are derived *asperso* 'sprinkled,' *ereto* 'erected,' *esparso* 'strewn,' and *impresso* 'printed,' among others, next to *aspergido, espargido,* and *imprimido*. Generally, the long form is preferred in compound tenses with *ter* 'have,' the short form in passive constructions. However, both *rompido* and *roto* 'broken,' *enchido* and *cheio* 'filled,' *envolvido* and *envolto* 'wrapped' may be used in passives.[72]

In Portuguese by-form past participles, semantic distinctions may surge out of morphological ones. For the 2nd-/3rd-conj. verb *defender,* long-form *defendido* means 'defended,' short-form *defeso* 'forbidden.' For 4th-conj. *concluir,* long-form *concluido* 'concluded' is used in all senses except the legal one of resolving e.g. a court case, where the past participle has to be *concluso* (Taylor, 655).

In Spanish, the same tendency toward short-form past participles appears in mediæval texts, but only for 1st-conj. verbs. In the *Crónica general de España,* there occurs *traye el pie corto,* where *corto* means *cortado* 'cut, slashed.' It still occurs in vulgarisms like Cast. *está pago* (for *pagado*) 'it is paid' or Arag. *estoy canso* (for *cansado*) 'I am tired' (Menéndez Pidal, 230–31). Two others are OSp. *nublo* 'beclouded' and *quito* 'removed,' both now obligatorily with long forms only under the literary standard (Andres-Suárez, 50).

As will be shown, dialects of Spanish teem with short-form past participles. If the only one found in Cartagena was *pago* 'paid' (García

---

[71] According to Taylor, variant *aceite* is used mainly in Portugal. Other short-form p.p.s competing with regular long-form ones include 1st-conj. *farto* 'stuffed,' *findo* 'ended,' and *isento* 'exempted,' and *safo* 'removed, set free, taken off' (infins. *fartar, findar, isentar, safar*). One suspects that, as in Spanish, a great many of the Ptg. forms listed as alternative p.p.s are actually used only as adjectives or nouns.

[72] As Williams observes (186)—a statement perhaps still accurate in 2000 CE—no one has succeeded in drawing any sharp distinction(s) between the Ptg. past participle and the Ptg. adjective. But see §6.4 for a means of syntactic if not morphological disambiguation.

Martínez, 134), two from present-day Burgos are *canso* 'tired' and *nublo* 'clouded' (González Ollé, 37). Certain clippings constantly recur.

In the Burgos-based standard, many short-form past participles listed in the manuals turn out to be limited to adjectival or nominal use. Besides already mentioned *despierto* 'awake,' *harto* 'fed up,' and *enjuto* 'lean, gaunt,' apparent short forms include *absorto* 'absorbed, rapt,' *abstracto* 'abstract,' poetic *aflicto* 'afflicted,' *electo* 'elect[ed],' *fijo* 'fixed, definite,' *propenso* 'keen on,' *sujeto* 'subject [to]' (also a noun), and *maldito* 'cursed.'[73] Such forms are arguably resultative, or almost adjectival, for they usually occur after a stative verb or after a noun. In true past-participial senses, native speakers have to use 1st-conj. *despertado*, *enjugado* 'rinsed,' *fijado*, *hartado* 'stuffed,' or *sujetado*, 2nd-/3rd-/4th-conj. *absorbido*, *abstraído*, *afligido*, *elegido*, *maldecido*, or *propendido* 'tended.'

At times, wavering between long and short forms may end once a verb gets remade. So archaic *sepelir* 'bury' used to have both regular 4th-conj. *sepelido* and short-form *sepulto* for past participles. Built from a stem like that of the old past participle, 1st-conj. *sepultar* 'bury' has p.p. *sepultado*, while *sepulto* lives on adjectivally. Again, *afijar* 'fasten' used to have a long-form p.p. *afijado*, but the verb has grown archaic, with only short-form *afijo* surviving adjectivally and nominally today (Martínez Amador, 1085–6).

In other past-participial pairs, *predicho* 'foretold' comes across as old-fashioned and sounds hypercorrect next to std. *predecido*, an arrhizotonic remodeling. Either *provisto* or regularized *proveído* will pass as the past participle for *proveer* 'supply, furnish' (A. Cortijo, p.c.).

4.7.9. Ongoing Regularizations; Enduring Hesitations

Among the unpretentious, Sp. *nacido* 'born' has almost replaced tautic athematic *nato*, itself evidently semilearnèd (unless it comes from Upper Aragon) because of unlenited [t]; cf. OSp. *nado*. On the east coast, Cat. *nascut* 'born' has almost replaced *nat* 'idem.' Evincing a confusion in speakers' minds between cause and effect, Ptg. *morto* 'died' competes with regular *matado* as a past participle for *matar* 'kill,' as used to happen in Old Spanish and still happens in Catalan phrases like *l'han mort* 'they have killed it.'

In dialects of Spanish, leveling of p.p. anomalies has proceeded further than in the literary standard. Thus, according to Lamano y Beneite's *El Dialecto vulgar salmantino* (61), speakers use the following present-based *-ido* p.p.s in and around the western city of Salamanca: *cubrido* 'covered,' *escrebido* 'written,' *morido* 'died,' *ponido* 'put,' *resolvido* '[re]solved,' *revolvido* 'returned,' and of course *rompido* 'broken.' In the southeastern city of Cartagena, speakers regularize several forms to give Car. *bendecío* 'blessed,' *escribío* 'written,' *volvío* '(re)turned' and *regolvío* 'mixed, stirred,' together with not-so-surprising *rompío* 'broken.' At times, speakers regularize *freído*

---

[73] Cf. also Sp. *El Maldito* 'the devil.' Note the morphological anomaly between p.p. *dicho* 'said' (never *decido*) but prefixed and regularized *maldecido* 'cursed' and *predecido* 'foretold.'

'fried'; only among children, regular *morido* 'died' may be heard (García Martínez, 134).

Observing that *-ido* p.p.s like *rompido* 'broken,' *freído* 'fried,' and *proveído* 'foreseen' will probably end up replacing rhizotonic *roto, frito,* and *provisto,* Menéndez Pidal in *Manual de gramática histórica española* (282) notes that other dialects of Spanish have achieved greater regularization of past participles than the Castilian-based standard has so far done. From preterit roots derive dialectal *dijido* 'said, told,' *supido* 'known,' and *tuvido* 'had'; from present-tense roots derive *decido* 'said, told,' *volvido* '[re]turned,' and most of the forms given by de Lamano y Beneite besides. To these Meyer-Lübke (1974, 414) adds Arag. *supido* 'known' and *plogido* 'pleased,' both from preterit roots like std. 3sg. *supo* and *plugo* (also regularized *plació*). Even present participles acquire preterit stems now and then: from Cartagena come very rare *dijiendo* 'saying, telling' and equally rare *quisiendo* 'wanting' (García Martínez, 133). All these p.p. innovations have acquired the non-*ar*-verb ending *-ido*. Other levelings appear in §4.7.12 for Aragonese, in §4.7.13 for Leonese.

Had no literary standard been established, speakers' remodeling of anomalous past participles might have advanced further still. The question would be whether speakers unconsciously decided to carry out that leveling on solely perfectum lines, or whether they developed a single form to fill all arrhizotonic slots for such verbs. Greater reduction of allomorphy would result from the second option, generally the one chosen from Proto-Spanish times on as it had been in Late Latin times (see §2.13).

Despite centuries of regularization, which often entailed filling empty slots, several verbs remain past-participially defective in Spanish. They include *atañer* 'concern' (the suppletive p.p. *aludido* 'alluded, referred' being used), *acaecer* and *acontecer* 'happen, occur,' *granizar* 'hail, rain hailstones,' and *usucapir* 'usucapt, squat on land.'[74] Past participles for *concernir* 'concern,' *transgredir* 'transgress,' and *soler* 'be accustomed to' are quite rare.[75] Conversely, a few old verbs have left behind only their past participles, usually adjectivized: *aguerrir* 'make war,' *empedernir* 'harden,' *garantir* (now *garantizar*), and *manir* 'wear away by rubbing' survive only in *aguerrido* 'brave, battle-tested,' *empedernido* 'inveterate,' legalese *garantido* 'guaranteed,' and *manido* 'trite, clichéd' (A. Cortijo, p.c.). One would like to descry archaic morphology in such relics, but all are regular 4th-conj. forms.

By contrast, the Spanish verb meaning 'sift' may be either 2nd-/3rd-conj. *cerner* or innovative 4th-conj. *cernir*, with both variants sharing a past

---

[74] I.e., to win legal ownership of property by occupying it for a time. Only the infinitive exists, resuscitated from ŪSŪCAPERE; agent noun *usucapión* 'squatter' h as been resuscitated from abstract ŪSŪCAPIŌNE 'ownership by long-time presence.' If Spanish law resembles English common law, a squatter would have a 90% chance of obtaining title to the property.

[75] *Soler* is used almost exclusively in the present and imperfect; p.p. *solido* occurs only in the present perfect, and that seldom. How often does an English speaker say, 'I have been used to doing something'?

participle in regular non-*ar*-verb *cernido*. For the verb meaning 'rot,' the infinitive is usually *pudrir* and may also be *podrir*, but the past participle must be *podrido*.

Portuguese seems to have fewer defective verbs than Spanish. *Adequar* 'suit, fit' occurs almost exclusively in the infinitive and past participle, as does *antiquar* 'make outdated.' Some writers avoid using *reaver* 'get back, recover' in the preterit or pluperfect indicative and in the imperfect or future subjunctive. Predictable past participles *adequado*, *antiquado*, and *reavido* are in use for all three verbs (Taylor, 656–62).

4.7.10. Some Differences between Spanish and Portuguese

Far more innovative phonologically after the sixteenth century, Portuguese still keeps more rhizotonic past participles than Spanish. Several Portuguese adjectives and nouns derive from rhizotonic -ĬTU p.p.s in Latin and remain proparoxytonic today. Thus, *bêbedo* 'drunken' (also *bêbado*) and *dívida* 'debt' come straight from postclassical BIBĬTU and from CL DĒBĬTA.[76] Again, the Portuguese noun *lêvedo* 'yeast' comes from LEVĬTU, an attested long-form variant of CL LEVE 'light[-weight],' which certainly has a morphological resemblance to a rhizotonic thematic past participle but may be simply a deadjectival noun.[77]

In Old Portuguese as in Old French, an ending generalized from -ĒCTU in e.g. *eleito* 'chosen' < ĒLĒCTU and *colheito* 'gathered' < COLLĒCTU spread to a few other past participles to yield OPtg. *tolheito* 'removed' and *coseito* 'sewn,' but, probably because of the ascendancy of the bipartite weak *perfectum* and a lack of morphological support from the preterit, that fad proved ephemeral and has left hardly a trace in Portuguese today. Feminine *colheita* still exists as a noun; the Spanish cognate *cosecha* [kosétʃa] 'harvest, yield, result' has had its first fricative reshaped from the one in mediæval *cogecha* [ko(d)ʒétʃa] < COLLĒCTA, meaning 'things gathered' if neuter plural or 'a gathering' if feminine singular (Georges, 47).

As in Ptg. *vindo* compared with Sp. *venido* 'come,' syncope has resulted in disyllabic Ptg. *crido* 'believed,' *lido* 'read,' *rido* 'laughed,' compared with trisyllabic Spanish cognates. The differences appear not excessive.

Unlike regularized Sp. *comido*, a CL by-form past participle, COMESTU 'eaten,' was kept as old-style Ptg. *comesto*, a form unknown to the native-speaker consultant but reminiscent of Venetian -*sto* p.p.s discussed in §3.6.1. By analogy with that verb of ingestion, there developed a p.p. *bebesto* 'drunk,' also archaic today according to Williams in *From Latin to Portuguese* (185–86).[78] Around Oporto, other sigmatic-tautics are found resembling those in

---

[76] Sp. *beodo* 'drunken' has undergone a stress shift to become a paroxytone.

[77] Reflexes of LEVĬTU 'light[-weight]' also survive in the It. proparoxytone *lievito* 'yeast' and Sp. *leudo* 'rising [of bread].' Such reflexes have have spun off 1st-conj. verbs like It. *lievitare* and Ptg. *levedar* 'rise [of bread]' (*REW* no. 5005).

[78] Regular non-*ar*-verb *comido* 'eaten' and *bebido* 'drunk' are the only form accepted today.

northeast Italy: by analogy with the sensory p.p. *visto* 'seen' there have developed not only nonstd. *ouvisto* 'heard' but also others like *avisto* 'had' and *compristo* 'filled,' all replacing standard forms in *-ido* (Meyer-Lübke 1974, 417). In far southwest ROMANIA, sigmatic-tautics have thus come back to life.

As *-udo* p.p.s were lost in Portuguese about 150 years later than in Spanish, more *-udo* adjectives and nouns remain in use there today. An example is Ptg. *conteúdo* 'contents,' like Fr. *contenu*, It. *contenuto* but unlike Sp. *contenido* (Georges, 17). Another is Ptg. *manteuda* 'kept woman, mistress,' contrasting with the remade p.p. *mantido* 'maintained.'

Remade from SUBLĀTU$_1$ 'raised, removed' first as a rhizotonic and then as an arrhizotonic, Sp. *tullido* means 'crippled,' while Ptg. *tolhido* means 'hindered, impeded.'

Finally, a few Portuguese verbs have been based on old present-participial stems to give e.g. *espantar* 'scare, frighten'< EX + PAVENT- + -ĀRE.[79] In std. Portuguese, the present stems *quer-* and *traz-* rather than the preterit stems *quis-* and *troux-* serve to form the p.p.s *querido* 'wanted' and *trazido* 'brought.' Analogous Spanish forms show a similar reduction in allophony.

Turning to dialects of Spanish, one observes that Upper Aragon forms an island of archaism in a sea of innovation affecting arrhizotonic p.p. endings. In Upper Aragon, CL intervocalic [t] remains; elsewhere, again and again, the local reflex of that [t] has worn away to zero. Let one dialect stand for many. In the Aragüés Valley (Aragon? Navarre?), one hears 1st-conj. forms like *amau* 'loved,' *cantau* 'sung,' *echau* 'thrown' and non-1st-conj. forms like *bebiu* 'drunk,' *partiu* 'left,' *rompiu* 'broken,' *temiu* 'feared' (González Guzman, 92). In that particular, complete lenition of intervocalic dental stops, many dialects of Spanish have reached the phonological stage that French had crossed before the High Middle Ages. In failing to mute any final vowels, though, Spanish dialects reveal themselves as less innovative today than French had already become a thousand years ago.

4.7.11. Sot de Ferrer (Castilian)

Located 56 kilometers from Castellón, 46 kilometers from Valencia, and 9 kilometers from Segobe, the village of Sot de Ferrer (SF) lies on the Palancia River. Although the place still has a Catalan name, judging by final -t, its inhabitants speak a dialect of Castilian slightly different from the Burgos-based standard. Data come from Ríos García's *El habla de Sot de Ferrer*. As usual, past participles stand for entire verbs.

Abiding Catalan influences on lexis come across in SF *achupido* 'bent, crouched,' *escalfido* 'heated,' and *amanido* 'readied.' In these senses, standard Spanish has *agachado*, *calentado*, and *preparado*, but Catalan has much closer *ajupit*, *escalfat* (before SF metaplasm), and *amanit*.

---

[79] Cf. It. *spaventare* and OFr. *espoenter* (ModFr. *épouvanter*) 'frighten.' The Fr. form appearsto have evolved an anti-hiatic [v].

Owing to sparse data from Sot de Ferrer, it will be well to include present participles in the discussion. The dialect has retained a distinct 4th-conj. present-participial ending, giving e.g. SF *indo* 'going.' Certain SF present participles have been built on preterit roots: *hiciendo* 'doing/making,' *dijendo* 'saying,' *supiendo* 'knowing,' and *trajendo* 'bringing.' For reasons that escape me, Ríos García also includes SF *caendo* 'falling' and *leendo* 'reading' as belonging to that preterit-based class of present participles. More predictably perhaps, a few past participles have been built on preterit stems: *supido* 'known,' *cáido* 'fallen,' *tráido* 'brought.' Does a stress shift vis-à-vis standard Spanish truly signal preterit origin here, as Ríos García maintains? It is unlikely that any of these forms represents a survival of old Type 5's in -ĪTU.

At any rate, many past participles in Sot de Ferrer resemble those found elsewhere in nonstandard Spanish in eliding intervocalic [d] or [ð]. Here elision yields forms like *tronsao* 'tired' and *sobao* 'rubbed, squeezed.' At times, for reasons unexplained by Ríos García, the final vowel in SF past participles is written -u̱ and perhaps pronounced differently from -o̱, giving forms like *sentau* 'felt,' *cansau* 'been tired,' and *tirau* 'pulled' (Ríos García, 33, 44–46).

4.7.12. Aragonese

According to the nameless compiler(s) of *De la Gramática de lo Cheso*, the work deals with "fabla altoaragonesa" [Upper Aragonese speech]. However, because p.p. endings as cited display lenition, I refer to this dialect as Val d'Echo Aragonese (VE), for what in standard Spanish is known as the Valle de Hecho. A second dialect of Upper Aragonese comes Panticosa (Pant.), described in Nagore Lain's *El Aragonés de Panticosa*. Except for persistence of intervocalic [t] in the endings -*ato* and -*ito*, past participles this dialect resemble ones from Portuguese more than ones from Castilian; see §§4.7.14–4.7.15.

In the work treating Val d'Echo Aragonese, one learns that masculine forms drop intervocalic -ḏ- while feminine forms keep it. Most of the discussion accorded to past participles (45–46) centers on distinctions between short forms, called "fuertes" [strong], and long forms, called "floxos" [weak]. Almost all verbs have weak forms; not all have strong forms.

In the long form, VE 1st-conj. past participles end in -*áu* if masculine and in -*ada* if feminine. Examples are masc. *aimáu* and fem. *aimada* 'loved,' masc. *zarráu* and fem. *zarrada* 'shut.' In the long form, VE 2nd/3rd /4th-conj. past participles end in -*íu* if masculine and in -*ida* if feminine. Examples are masc. *fuíu* and fem. *fuida* 'fled,' masc. *texíu* and fem. *texida* 'woven.' Endings on short-form past participles are identical to those on 1st-/2nd-decl. adjectives: in -*o* for masc.sg., in -*a* for fem.sg.

By-forms have arisen because the survival or emergence of many short rhizotonics has been counterbalanced by regularizations evident in long arrhizotonics. Thus, Val d'Echo has kept short *abierto* 'opened,' *cubierto* 'covered,' *dicho* 'said, told,' *escrito* 'written,' *farto* 'stuffed,' *frito* 'fried,' *muerto* 'died,' *nato* 'born,' and *suelto* 'loosened.' Most precisely resemble irregular past participles in standard Spanish, though Sp. *harto* 'fed up' and *suelto* 'loose' have been restricted to adjectival use. At the same time, Val d'Echo Aragonese has developed arrhizotonic long-form variants unknown in standard Spanish: *abríu* 'opened,' *cubríu* 'covered,' *dicíu* 'said, told,' *escribíu* 'written,' *friíu* 'fried,' *moríu* 'died,' and *nacíu* 'born.' Val d'Echo Aragonese has also developed long-form past participles familiar under the standard: matching VE *fartâu* 'stuffed' and *soltáu* 'loosened' are Sp. *hartado, soltado*. In addition, Val d'Echo Aragonese has developed new short forms, equally unknown in standard Spanish, like *canso* 'tired' and *nublo* 'clouded,' alongside the long forms *cansáu, nubláu*. As happens elsewhere, morphological differentiation serves a semantic function, for speakers tend to use short forms more as adjectives and long forms more as past participles.

Only two common rhizotonics seem to have resisted the trend outlined above: *feito* 'done/made' and *visto* 'seen' (infins. *fer, vier*). Two more resist in part, having one by-form like that in standard Spanish, the other an arrhizotonic regularization. For *dicir* 'say, tell,' the dueling past participles are *dicho* and *dicíu*. For *torcer* 'twist,' they are *tuerto* and *torcíu* (45–46; 108–9).

As only three dozen past participles are supplied by Nagore Lain, it will be well to include them all. With one exception, Panticosa divergences from Castilian have to be lexical rather than phonological to win a place here.

Regular Pant. 1st-conj. past participles are *baxato* 'lowered,' *chugato* 'played,' *comprato* 'bought,' *estato* 'been,' *plenato* 'filled,' *puyato* 'lifted, raised' (std. *subido*), *tornato* 'turned, returned' {std. *vuelto*), and *trobato* 'met, encountered' (std. *encontrado*).

Regular Pant. 2nd-/3rd-/4th-conj. past participles are *benito* 'come,' *caíto* 'fallen,' *conozito* 'known,' *creíto* 'believed,' *dormito* 'slept,' *ito* 'gone,' *leíto* 'read,' *metito* 'put into,' *mobito* 'moved,' *nazito* 'born,' *oito* 'heard,' *parezito* 'suffered' after rhotacism, *podito* 'been able,' *querito* 'wanted; loved,' *sapito* 'known,' *sito* 'been,' *torzito* 'twisted,' and *traíto* 'brought.' Variants *muíto* and *muyíto* 'milked' (infin. *muir*) look and no doubt sound almost alike; in standard Spanish, the verb has been replaced by *ordeñar*.

In Panticosa, *tener* 'have' has two by-form past participles, present-based *tenito* next to preterit-based *tubito*; cf. 3sg. pret. *túbo* 'had.' If, as one would expect in central-western Iberia, the Panticosa past participle meaning 'cooked' is arrhizotonic *cozito*, speakers in the Bielsa subdialect cling to rhizotonic *cueto* < COCTU (174).

Castilian influence may be detected in the variant p.p. *llobito* 'rained,' for which the Panticosa locals normally developed *plobito* with its [pl] cluster intact as in *plenato* 'filled.' Though hardly strong enough to induce speakers to glottalize and mute initial [f], Castilian influence also crops up in the Pant. by-form *fecho* 'done/made,' alongside expected *feto*.

The Panticosa verb *caler* 'be lacking, needed' evinces its own morphological lacuna by having failed to fill its past-participial slot. One wonders how locals fill the gap.

Hardly a rhizotonic survives in Panticosa. An expected twosome is *dito* 'said, told.' and *feto* 'done/made,' but for the latter speakers sometimes use a variant *fecho* that sounds like Old Castilian (181). As in Castilian, not a single sigmatic survives in Panticosa. The one sigmatic-tautic uncovered is *bisto* 'seen.'

Once again, past participles for some verbs have gone unlisted by the author of a dialect study. In all likelihood, the past participles for Pant. *baler* 'be worth,' *caper* 'fit into,' *parzer* 'appear,' *reír* 'laugh,' *salir* 'go out' are regular non-*ar*-verb ones in -*ito*. From a distance, one cannot know.

4.7.13. Leonese

Data for Leonese come from Díaz González's *El Habla de Candama* (probably in Asturias) and from Penny's studies of Valle del Pas and the Nansa valley. Orthography has been lightly castilianized. In all three locales, speakers tend to regularize past participles still rhizotonic in standard Spanish. However, speakers in Candama retain rhizotonics already remade in the standard.

Díaz González remarks notes that Candama Leonese assigns certain verbs into the 2nd/3rd conjugation that belong to the 4th in Castilian, and the other way around. Thus, Candama has *ferver* 'boil' and *esparcer* 'scatter' as against std. Sp. *hervir, esparcir*; Candama has *valir* 'be worth' and *tusir* 'cough' as against std. *valer, toser*. Such metaplasms outside the 1st conjugation hardly affect regular p.p. formation in -*ido*.

As in Val d'Echo Aragonese (§4.7.12), masculine past participles in Candama Leonese show no trace of intervocalic -d̲-, while feminine past participles keep -d̲-. Examples are 1st-conj. masc. *ganau* and fem. *ganada* 'gained, earned,' 2nd/3rd/4th-conj. masc. *metíu* and fem. *metida* 'put, put into' or masc. *partíu* and fem. *partida* 'split.'

Retained rhizotonics facing no competition are *dichu* 'said, told,' *fechu* 'done/made,' *mortu* 'died,' and *vistu* 'seen,' all high-frequency ones.

In Candama, several verbs have by-form past participles. At times, arrhizotonic reshapings prevail over inherited rhizotonics: *rumpíu* over *rotu* 'broken' and *escribíu* over *escritu* 'written.' At other times, rhizotonics still prevail: *encesu* 'lit' (also 'bright red'), *presu* 'caught,' *enxiertu* or *injertu* 'grafted, implanted,' and *ensuchu* 'dried.' For these rhizotonics, standard Spanish has arrhizotonic *encendido* 'lit,' *prendido* 'caught,' *injertado* 'grafted, implanted,' and *secado* 'dried,' though cf. the Sp. adjs. *preso* 'imprisoned' and *enjuto* 'lean, gaunt.'

Though listing various other regular past participles like Can. *cucíu* 'cooked,' *turcíu* 'twisted,' and *díu* 'gone' (see §4.7.15), the author declines to specify any arrhizotonic competitors for the rhizotonics above, except for *encendíu* 'lit' (Díaz González, 60–61).

In the Leonese spoken in Val del Pas (VP), surviving rhizotonics without competition are *abiertu* 'opened,' *echu* 'done/made,' *gweltu* 'turned, returned,' *cubiertu* 'covered,' *pwestu* 'put,' and *bistu* 'seen.' Prefixed 4th-conj. *diu* 'gone' looks as if it had undergone metathesis from standard Spanish.

For a few VP verbs, rhizotonic and arrhizotonic past participles coexist: *mwertu* and *muríu* 'died,' *dichu* and *dicíu* 'said, told,' but a derivative of this last verb always has the arrhizotonic p.p. *maldicíu* 'cursed.' For other verbs, a stress shift differentiates rhizotonic forms, used as adjectives, from arrhizotonic ones used in verbal periphrases like perfects. By inserting new rhizotonics into its morphological inventory, this dialect has as it were brought back the thematic type of ending once seen in e.g. HABĬTU 'had.' With the root-stressed form given first, such VP pairs include adj. *góịdu* and p.p. *guyíu* 'heard,' adj. *cáịdu* and p.p. *cayíu* 'fallen,' and adj. *tráịdu* and p.p. *trayíu* 'brought,' which last also has a syncopated by-form *tríu*. However, arrhizotonic *liyíu* 'read' faces no rhizotonic thematic competition.

Certain short forms used only as adjectives are *cansu* 'tired' and *pretu* 'tight'; cf. std. *cansado, apretado*. Adjectives clipped from nonstandard verbs are *djeldu* 'fermented' (evidently from a reflex of LEVITĀRE 'lighten') and *terrenu* 'melted,' conceivably related to std. *aterrenar* 'demolish, raze.'

Two old rhizotonics now used only as adjectives or nouns are VP *pintu* '(bull) painted white and black' and *remansu* 'stagnant water.' Others are *dezgweltu* 'changed shape,' *dispwistu* 'astute,' *escesu* 'afire (with love),' *ribwiltu* 'mischievous, unruly,' *satisfichu* 'satisfied,' and (much as in standard Spanish) *twirrtu* 'one-eyed.' The form *pindju* 'high, steep' seems to have been based on an old rhizotonic thematic replacement for PĒNSU 'hung.' A morphological distinction mirrors a semantic one in adj. *rutu* 'broken' as against p.p. *rumpíu*.

Like the sigmatics just above, reflexes of -ŪTU are extinct as p.p. endings but live on as adjectival ones in the Val del Pas. A few instances are *arcudu* 'big-chested' (from *arca* 'thorax'), *biludu* 'hairy,' and *chipudu* 'hunchbacked (from *chepa* 'hunch'). Several refer only to livestock. A sheep may be called *lanuda* 'woolly,' a cow *zamarruda* 'corpulent' (from *zamarra* 'fat'), a goat *zerrnexuda* 'hairy-haunched.' (In the last two words, z = [ð].)

Preterit stems have invaded the past participle in *quisíu* 'wanted,' *supíu* 'known,' and *traxíu* or *trizíu* 'brought' (Penny 1970, 112, 137–8).

In Tudanca (Tud.), some forms cited end in -u, some in -o; both are apparently realized as [u̯], but only the second triggers anaphony. These days, moreover, forms in -u are encroaching on forms in -o. Here I follow the author's orthography.

Regular arrhizotonics are *cantáu* 'sung,' *mitíu* 'put into,' *rumpíu* 'broken.' Other non-1st-conj. forms are *caío* 'fallen,' *criío* 'believed,' *riío* 'laughed,' *ruío* 'gnawn,' and *uío* 'heard.' Several arrhizotonics have acquired meanings unlike those in standard Spanish. For instance, Tud. *aburríu* means 'gloomy, hateful,' but std. *aburrido* means 'tiresome, boring.' Again, Tud. *acompanáu* means 'gregarious,' but the equivalent in standard Spanish means 'accompanied'; Tud. *bien abláu* means 'polite,' instead of the more literal sense 'well-spoken' that std. *bien hablado* has. Finally, Tud. *descastáu* means 'forgetful of one's family,' but std. Sp. *descastado* means 'exterminated.'

To follow the author's terminology, Tudanca rhizotonics that may appear with conjugated forms of 'have,' i.e. past participles, are *abierto* 'opened,' *bisto* 'seen,' *dicho* 'said, told,' *hecho* 'done/made,' and *muerto* 'died.' Rhizotonics that may not appear with 'have,' i.e. adjectives, are of several kinds. First come inheritances like *pwestu* 'put,' *gweltu* 'turned, returned,' and *rotu* 'broken,' now contrasting with the arrhizotonic p.p.s *punío, gulbío, rumpío.'* Again, a morphological distinction mirrors a semantic one. Second come short forms found elsewhere in Spain like *cansu* 'tired, *pagu* 'paid,' and *pretu* 'tight.' Third come apparent local innovations like *faltu* 'stupid,' *fayu* 'weak,' and *heda* 'woman who has just given birth,' though cf. Cat. *feda* 'fertilized ewe.' For an etymology of the Tud. adj. *dieldu* 'fermented,' see the subsection on Valle del Pas.

Sometimes in Tudanca, the past participle expresses a notion of potentiality that, in standard Castilian, has to be expressed by suffixes like *-izo* or *-able*. So the Tud. fem. adj. *espantáa* or *sobresaltáa* 'timid, scared (referring to cows)' would be rendered *espantadiza* in standard Spanish. Despite their clear dissimilarity, all three terms are built on p.p. stems (Penny 1978, 104–5).

4.7.14. Galician

Galician began in Romance as the homeland of Portuguese. For that reason, I am going to break my own rule about omitting Portuguese forms and am going to cite all the Galician past participles I found, even if most are identical to Spanish ones.

These days, Galician has become heavily castilianized. Indeed, Pena and Rosales devote much of their *Manual de galego urxente* to listing castilianisms no doubt best avoided but clearly widespread today. Right at the start, they deprecate *abatir* for Gal. *abater* 'knock down,' *abotonar* for Gal. *abotoar* 'button,' and *hundir* for Gal. *afundir* 'sink, plunge.' If unlike Spanish, "uncontaminated" Galician is not quite identical to Portuguese, either. Compare Ptg. *abater* and *abotoar* but 1st-conj. *afundar* instead of Gal. *afundir*.

Give or take an occasional diacritic, regular Galician past participles given by Pena and Rosales (45, 100–1) closely resemble their opposite numbers in Portuguese. Accompanying *-ar* infinitives, and with the same stem, are 1st-conj. *cantado* 'sung,' *chegado* 'arrived,' *dado* 'given,' and *estado* 'been.' Accompanying *-er* infinitives, and with the same stem, are 2nd-/3rd-conj. *cabido* 'fit into,' *caído* 'fallen,' *collido* 'gathered,' *habido* 'had,' *podido* 'been able,' *querido* 'wanted; loved,' *sabido* 'known,' *sido* 'been,' *tido* 'had,' *traído* 'brought,' and *valido* 'been worth.' Accompanying *-ir* infinitives, with the same stem, are 4th-conj. *ido* 'gone,' *oído* 'heard,' and *vido* 'come.'

Irregular past participles from Galician line up with the usual foursome in central-western Iberia: *dito* 'said, told,' *feito* 'done/made,' *posto* 'put,' and *visto* 'seen,' here for infins. *dicir, facer, poñer,* and *ver.*

To these unexceptional examples Carvalho Cabero in *Gallego Común* (201–38) adds 1st-conj. *falado* 'spoken,' 2nd-/3rd-conj. *batido* 'beaten,' and 4th-conj. *partido* 'left,' all of them identical to Portuguese forms. Carvalho Cabero notes that the verb *creer* 'believe' has by-form p.p.s, Spanish-looking *creído* and Portuguese-looking *crido*, and, by saying that *leer* 'read' is conjugated like *creer*, implies that by-form past participles exist for that verb as well.

Like Portuguese, Galician has a number of by-form past participles. Those given by Pena and Rosales (45) may be grouped under several headings.

First come Galician verbs that have both long-form and short-form past participles (see §4.7.8): *calmar* has *calmado* and *calmo* 'calm[ed],' *cansar* has *cansado* and *canso* 'tired,' *gañar* has *gañado* and *gaño* 'gained, earned' and *quedar* has *quedado* and *quedo* 'quiet[ed].' Second come Galician verbs that have a regularized past participle vying with an (apparently) inherited one: *acender* has *acendido* and *aceso* 'lit,' *bendicir* has *bendicido* and *bendito* 'blessed,' *coller* has *collido* and *colleito* 'gathered,' *distinguir* has *distinguido* and *distinto* 'distinguished,' and *tinxir* has *tinxido* and *tinto* 'dyed.' Third come Galician verbs that have past participles neither clipped nor inherited. One of these is *envolver* 'wrap,' with expected *envolvido* and innovative *envolveito*, as if its ancestor had once ended in -ĒCTU.

Already encountered in Old Portuguese, another is *comer* 'eat,' with the expected p.p. *comido* and an innovative sigmatic-tautic one *comesto* 'eaten.' Finally, there is the verb *enxugar*, which has the expected p.p. *enxugado* and a truly innovative one *enxoito* 'dried.' Could *enxoito* come from IN +SICCĀTU 'dried,' an etymon with good semantics but poor phonology? P.p. SUCTU 'sucked' looks like a more plausible etymon, with the whole verb then joining the ever-expanding 1st conjugation and hence representing a rare survival in the Romance far west of SŪGERE 'suck.'

As for explaining the different syntactic or stylistic roles assigned to each of these by-forms, Pena and Rosales content themselves with saying that the regular form is used past-participially, the irregular form adjectivally. I find it gratifying to learn that the homeland of Portuguese remains faithful to one feature of the language that came into existence there.

4.7.15. Barranquenho (Portuguese)

Data for this southern dialect of Portuguese, spoken in the province of Alentejo near the border with Spain, come from Leite de Vasconcelos's *Filologia barranquenha*.

Regular 1st-conj. past participles end in -*adu*, giving *êhtadu* 'been,' *labadu* 'washed' (infins. *êhtá, labá*) along with *combidadu* 'invited,' *enfurcadu* 'hung,' and *mandadu* 'ordered, sent.' Regular 2nd-/3rd-conj. past participles end in -*idu*, giving *bebidu* 'drunk,' *çidu* 'been,' *lidu* 'read,' *pudidu* 'been able,' *tidu* 'had,' and *traídu* 'brought' (infins. *bebê, çe, lê, pudê, tê, trazê*). Slightly anomalous here is the syncopated p.p. written *q'ridu* 'wanted' (unsyncopated infin. *querê*). Regular 4th-conj. past participles also end in -*idu*, giving *çaídu* 'gone out,' *çerbidu* 'served,' *partidu* 'left,' *pididu* 'asked,' and *ridu* 'laughed' (infins. *çaí, çerví, partí, pidí, ri*). An oddity is the prefixed 4th-conj. Barr. p.p. *didu* 'gone' (infin. *di*), resembling a variant found in Spanish dialects.

In Barrancos, two rhizotonics look thoroughly Portuguese: *bindu* 'come' (infin. *bi*) and *fètu* 'done/made' (infin. *faze*). There are no sigmatics. Showing that [s] before another consonant has glottalized, or perhaps velarized, are spellings for the old sigmatic-tautic p.p.s *bihtu* 'seen' (infin. *bê*) and *pôhtu* 'put' (infin. *p ô*). Only one verb has past-participial by-forms: regular 4th-conj. *òbidu* 'heard' (infin. *òbí*) competes with *òbi(h)tu*, shaped by analogy with another sensory p.p. *vihtu* 'seen.'

Regrettably, the author provides no past participles for eighteen Barranquenho verbs, here listed by infinitive: 1st-conj. *andá* 'go,' *dá* 'give,' and *jugá* 'play'; 2nd-/3rd-conj. *abê* 'have' [modal auxiliary], *balê* 'be worth,' *cabê* 'fit into,' *çabê* 'know,' *duê* 'hurt,' *mué* 'grind,' *perdê* 'lose,' and *prazê* 'please'; 4th-conj. *bihtí* 'dress, clothe,' *caí* 'fall,' *midí* 'measure,' *mintí* 'tell lies,' *parí* 'give birth,' and *ripití* 'repeat.' Nor does the author provide a past participle, almost surely a reflex of DICTU, for the high-frequency 3rd-conj. Barr. verb *dizê* 'say, tell' (Vasconcelos, 62). For the last time, I am annoyed to find stony ground for gleaning past participles.

4.8. LOOKING BACK FROM THE ATLANTIC TO THE BLACK SEA

Owing to the steady loss of number and gender marking, spoken French has reached isomorphism for all four forms of most past participles; French no longer has any unambiguously past-participial endings. Elimination of both the sigmatic type and the *-udo* type from Spanish and Portuguese has left only *-ado* and *-ido* as arrhizotonic p.p. markers. Engadin and Surselvan have evolved in much the same way.

I set sail on this voyage of discovery half believing that, somewhere on the circle of lands ringing the Mediterranean, I might make landfall at an eden of isomorphy in past-participial formation. Now, looking back 4,000 past participles later, I am at last ready to acknowledge that no Romance language has achieved a one-to-one match between function and form. While sailing through seas where the Romans used to rule, I did sight on languages with only two types of regular past participle, but there old anomalies have persisted while new ones have sprung up. Most short-form past participles in Portuguese—including ones for verbs from Germanic—suggest local innovations inspired by adjectives, but others suggest resuscitation by scholars.[80] Either way, my earlier expectation of a drive toward predictability has been compromised by the revivifying inventiveness of native speakers living in the Romance far west. As they did in the beginning, past participles continue to overlap with adjectives in function and form. Were I to suggest that, morphologically speaking, short-form past participles have returned to their adjectival origins, would I be making a circular argument?

---

[80] But cf. the OSp. noun *ençienso* 'incense' < INCĒNSU, another noun with the same shape as a past participle (Georges, 132).

5

Synopsis of Data

Then Death, so-called, is but old Matter dress'd
In some new Figure, and a vary'd Vest:
Thus all Things are but alter'd, nothing dies;
And here and there th' unbody'd Spirit flies....

Ovid, *Metamorphoses*
[tr. Dryden]

5.1. SURVIVAL OF LATIN STEMS, WITH HEIGHTENED THEMATIC MARKING

Analyzing the corpora reviewed in Chapters 3 and 4, I discern a drift across ROMANIA toward clearer marking of past participles, a drift swelling through the centuries and swelling toward the west. Aside from learnèd verbs still defective or moribund verbs now defective, every verb in Romance has been endowed with a past participle.

Judging by how the morphology turned out, speakers of Late Latin or Proto-Romance might have already differed in their past-participial preferences depending on where they lived. Most notably in Iberia but in Gallia and Italia as well, they extended the common arrhizotonic endings like -ĀTU and above all -ĪTU to verbs with present stems already matching those two classes. Especially in Italia and Dacia, they extended some sigmatic perfect roots to reshape past participles. Several verbs have thus maintained or obtained sigmatic past participles in Italian or Romanian or both. For quite a few verbs, in fact, Romanian stands alone in possessing sigmatic past participles (§3.1.5). For other verbs, Italian stands equally alone in its past-participial sigmaticism, often accompanied by sigmatic preterits unknown elsewhere (§3.5.3.2).

Particularly in Gallia, most of Rætia, Italia, and Dacia, they widened the scope of an arrhizotonic -ŪTU past-participial marker, rare in Latin, to cover

333

verbs lacking past participles and verbs forming them rhizotonically (§2.14).[1]
Across Catalonia and Occitania, a [w] perfective marker, evolving to [g], came
to become infixed before most -ŪTU p.p. endings, eventually spreading into
the preterit indicative and all subjunctive forms of verbs in that class
(§4.6.2.3).

Yet what is one to make of the throng of -ĪTU past participles across the
south of Italy and Sardinia (§§3.6.2, 3.7.3)? Supplanted elsewhere except as
noun fossils, -ĪTU past participles should be seen as part of the same trend
observed for the nom.sg. of formerly imparisyllabic nouns in LL: the old
paradigm had been nom.sg./acc.sg. RĒX RĒGEM 'king,' but the new one was
parisyllabic [rége(s) rége]. In much the same way, speakers of Late Latin might
have reshaped old athematic past participles by inserting the atonic marker of
a (default?) theme class. If so, that reshaping left few traces among past
participles in an arc drawn from Romanian to Portuguese. Yet more than a
few relics of that type survive as adjectives or nouns.

Certainly one observation made about Romance past participles appears
incontestable. Again and again, for 2nd- and 3rd-conj. verbs in major
Romance languages, one notes a pattern of -ŪTU past participles east of Castile
and -ĪTU past participles in (modern) Castile and Portugal. That pattern occurs
in past participles for reflexes of 2nd-conj. DĒBĒRE 'have to,' DOLĒRE 'hurt,
grieve,' HABĒRE 'have,' PLACĒRE 'please,' *POTERE 'be able,' TENĒRE 'hold,'
and VALĒRE 'be worth.' That pattern occurs in past participles for reflexes of
3rd-conj. BIBERE 'drink,' CRĒDERE 'believe,' CRĒSCERE 'grow,' FUTUERE
'fuck,' and VENDERE 'sell.' Yet it remains unclear how the pattern could have
come into being, tonic [u] scarcely appearing in forms other than the past
participle. One might think that forms in [e:] should have won out; see §5.4.2.

5.2. REMAINING UNPREDICTABILITIES

To review, several isoglosses show outcomes underivable by logic alone.
Reflexes of ŪNCTU 'oiled' continue the Latin tradition in Italian and French,
are sigmatic in Romanian, joined the 1st-conj. -at class in Catalan, and, yes,
may have local reflexes of -ĪTU farther west, but by-forms now adjectival
continue the Latin tradition there as well. Past participles for descendants of
SENTĪRE 'feel' and SALĪRE 'jump' derive from -ĪTU across the board, so that
reflexes of rhizotonic SĒNSU and SALTU no longer exist as past participles.
Again, for descendants of CŌ(N)SŪTU 'sewn,' reflexes of -ĪTU past participles
are shared by Spanish, Catalan, and Italian, reflexes of -ŪTU past participles by
Romanian and French. Finally, for descendants of RĪSU 'laughed,' sigmatic
forms prevail, or used to, from Romania to France, but Catalan has an -ŪTU

---

[1] Could the increase in -ŪTU past participles have represented an innovation, arising at
the heart of the Empire in Italia and Gaul then spreading to peripheral Dacia, where it still
thrives, and to Hispania, where it has died out? For a brief discussion of innovation at the
center contrasting with conservatism at the periphery, though involving lexemes rather than
morphemes, see §3.0.1.

past participle next to the expected -ĪTU past participles of Spanish and Portuguese.

In central and western Iberia, -ŪTU past participles may never have flourished widely. Such forms turn up in mediæval Castilian and Portuguese at the height of French influence but seldom afterwards. More probably, however, they remained in wide use for 2nd-/3rd-conj. past participles from the Fall of Rome into the High Middle Ages, by which time they were already competing with variants in -*ido*. Except for perhaps two dozen verbs, rhizotonic past participles were never popular here either and have grown less so with time; thus, Spanish and Portuguese today have almost exclusively -*ado* and -*ido* as past-participial endings, as witness Sp./Ptg. *batido* 'beaten' ≠ BATTŪTU and Sp. *hodido* or *jodido*, Ptg. *fodido* 'fucked' ≠ FUTŪTU. In Gallia, Italia, and northeastern Iberia, reflexes of -ŪTU became the past-participial ending of choice for verbs in the 2nd and 3rd conjugations. This type was likewise to enjoy great success in Dacia: Romanian has gone so far as to develop *făcut* 'done/made,' by contrast with rhizotonic past-participial reflexes of FACTU farther west like It. *fatto*, Fr. *fait*, Sp. *hecho*, and Ptg. *feito*.

5.3. PRETERITS AND PAST PARTICIPLES WITHIN THE PAST-TENSE SYSTEM

Through the centuries, influences of preterits on past participles and vice versa have continued, for closer resemblances between the two led to heightened morphological transparency for both. Sometimes a stem already extant in perfect finite forms in Latin was applied to past participles: speakers appear to have chosen the 3sg. pf. by-form PLŪVIT 'rained' (no CL p.p.) as the basis for a form in -ŪTU that lay behind forms found today in French, Catalan, and Italian, for an -ĪTU past participle behind forms found in Spanish and Portuguese, and for an -ĀTU past participle behind the form found in Romanian. Attested past participles like It. *vinto* ≠ VĪCTU, OFr. *fraint* ≠ FRĀCTU, and *peint* ≠ CL PICTU, imply that infectum nasal infixes in e.g. VINCERE 'win,' FRANGERE 'shatter,' and PINGERE 'paint' had been inserted into past-participial reflexes, just as they already had been in JUNGERE 'join' with its nasal pf. JŪNXĪ and its nasal p.p. JŪNCTU.

Regular 1st-conj. past participles were created for reflexes of SONĀRE 'ring,' TONĀRE 'thunder,' and VETĀRE 'forbid' (CL rhizotonic p.p.s SONĬTU, TONĬTU, VETĬTU). Regular 4th-conj. past participles were created for reflexes of EXĪRE 'go out' FUGERE 'flee,' and SORBĒRE 'swallow' (CL rhizotonic p.p.s EXĬTU, FUGĬTU, SORBĬTU), as also for reflexes of FERĪRE 'hit' (CL suppletive p.p. ICTU or PERCUSSU). For 2nd-conj. MOVĒRE 'move' (CL direct-suffixation p.p. MŌTU), probably both pres. MOVEŌ and pf. MŌVĪ inspired a past participle in -ŪTU that lay behind the French and Catalan forms or one in -ĪTU behind the Spanish form.

As noted more than once in *Past Participles from Latin to Romance*, tonic vowels in some past participles have been influenced by preterits through metaphony. For reflexes of SEDĒRE 'sit,' for instance, the attested French and Italian past participles *assis* and *assiso* could scarcely have derived straight from either pf. SĒDĪ or p.p. -SESSU. Instead, that past participle must have given rise to a new sigmatic preterit *SESSĪ, which became *SĪSSĪ by metaphony. Subsequently, the high front vowel that had developed in the 1sg. preterit was extended to the past participle, giving something like *SĪSSU in the central area of Proto-Italian and Proto-French.

From Romania to Catalonia—and sometimes in Old Spanish and Old Portuguese—at least a dozen verbs that had had -UĪ perfects but either lacked a past participle or had a rhizotonic one appear to have acquired past participles in -ŪTU in Late Latin or Proto-Romance. Meanwhile, the stems of a few perfects like VĪXĪ 'lived' came to serve for the past participle of those verbs as well, as in It. *vissuto*. Still other verbs were rebuilt on their past-participial stems: FARTU 'stuffed,' ŪNCTU 'oiled,' and QUASSU 'shaken' shaped the entire paradigms of verbs like Sp. *hartar* 'stuff' and *untar* 'oil' or Fr. *casser* 'break.' Again, upon p.p. TRACTU 'pulled' (anomalous infin. TRAHERE) and perhaps pf. TRĀXĪ was remade the LL/PR infin. *TRACERE, which itself must lie behind past participles in -ŪTU or in -ĪTU assumed for parts of Romance.

Occasionally, a past participle doubly marked in Latin lost one of its markers: CONQUĪSĪTU 'brought together, gotten together,' which contained both [s] and [i] markers, developed into sigmatic *CONQUĪSU in Italy and France, present-based *CONQUERITU in Catalonia. Another doubly marked form, QUÆSĪTU 'sought, asked' syncopated into *QUESTU in Italy, France, and Spain but was remade on the present stem as *CERUTU in Romania. Here redundancy succumbed to predictability.

Such interchanges of state within the perfectum resulted in fewer stems per verb for LL/PR speakers to keep in mind. For more than twenty verbs, leveling went further still: new past participles evolving in LL/PR were based on the old infectum. In many parts of ROMANIA, stems like CAD- and CED-, CURR- and FEND-, FUND- and MORD- and PEND- have been applied to the past participle; ending in reflexes of tonic -ŪTU or -ĪTU depending on dialect and somewhat on lexical item, such arrhizotonic variants tended to replace the sigmatic past participles CĀSU 'fallen,' CURSU 'run,' FISSU 'split,' and FŪSU 'poured' later 'melted.' At the same time, infectum stems like CRESC-, CERN-, PASC-, and VINC-, with the same arrhizotonic endings, tended to replace the tautic athematic past participles CRĒTU 'grown' or 'sifted,' PĀSTU 'fed, kept,' and VICTU 'won.' For verbs such as these, speakers lightened the load on their memories even further by shrinking the number of stems from two or three to only one.

These days, any question of influence by preterits on past participles or vice versa has become moot in much of ROMANIA. "The perfect [viz., preterit] is the most vulnerable part of the Romance verbal system," notes Togeby (142–43). Across Romance, preterits have "virtually disappeared": in Northern Italian by 1300, in Ræto-Romance and Catalan by 1400, in Sardinian by 1500, in French by 1700, and in Romanian by 1800. In these areas of compound perfect-preterits, which eliminate a distinction between tenses built up since Latin times, the grammatical role of past participles has expanded. Despite the emergence of new anomalies elsewhere in verb paradigms, chiefly in the present tense, past-participial formation has slowly grown more predictable everywhere, though not always in the same ways.

5.4. ANALYSIS OF MORPHOLOGICAL DATA

As reviewed in detail in Appendix 1, verbs already belonging to the two largest conjugations in Classical Latin and those that joined them in Late Latin or Proto-Romance have almost all acquired completely regular past participles. Both classes, particularly the 4th conjugation, have attracted verbs into their orbits. By and large, with the proportions again increasing as one moves west, reflexes of the 2nd and 3rd conjugations have also acquired regular past participles; from Dacia to Catalonia these belong to the -ŪTU type, and in central-western Iberia to the 4th-conj.-style -ĪTU type, now the default non-1st-conj. p.p. marker there. In addition, certain other mixed types, with hypercharacterized marking, have developed sporadically across ROMANIA. A harvest of mediæval and modern past participles is reaped in the appendixes.

From the data listed in Appendix 2 and classified by type in Appendix 3, I have chosen a sample of 296 Latin verbs that survived into major Romance languages. By-forms being counted twice, my sample has 305 p.p. slots, some unfilled in Latin.

A summary of past-participial reflexes yields the following results: percentages from Table C in Appendix 3 (page 433) are reproduced below for the reader's convenience. Archaic varieties of past participles have been left out, learnèd forms left in. By-forms, where distinct morphologically, have been counted twice, but adjectivized past participles have not been counted.

In Table 5–1, each past participle in the Latin and Romance corpora has been assigned to a type according to its ending. Type 1 has past participles in tonic [a:] like AMĀTU 'loved,' type 2 in tonic [e:] like DĒLĒTU 'destroyed,' type 4 in tonic [i:] like DORMĪTU 'slept,' type 5 in atonic [I] like COGNĬTU 'known,' type 6 in tonic [u:] like BATTŪTU 'beaten,' type 8 in [s] or [s:] like RŌSU 'gnawn' or CESSU 'yielded,' and type 9 in [t] directly suffixed to a stem that ends in another consonant (**C**) except [s], like CĪNCTU 'girded,' APERTU 'opened,' SALTU 'jumped.' Since GESTU 'waged' and syncopated POSTU 'put' combine features of types 8 and 9, they are labeled 8+9. Note that types 1, 2, 4, and 6 are arrhizotonic, types 5, 8, and 9 rhizotonic. (No CL past participle falls under type 3 or type 7.).[2]

---

[2] Type numbers refer to both aspects of Latin verbs. Those with a 3rd-conj. infectum go into type 3, those with a reduplicated finite perfectum into type 7. Neither type applies to CL past participles, so the numbers 3 and 7 do not figure here. There were a few nonstd. "type 7" past participles like GIGNITU 'begotten,' PEPERCITU 'spared,' and Trimalchian FEFELLITU 'tricked.' Maybe such forms became (or remained?) marginally productive in Latin but, like most -ŪTU p.p.s, were spurned by literati loath to allow more than one filler for each slot.

Table 5–1

Types of Past Participles in Latin and Romance

Type/Language number>	Latin [305]	Rom. [146]	Italian [242]	French [187]	Catalan [219]	Spanish [208]
1 (-ĀTU)	9.5	22.6	**23.6**	**39.6**	*31.5*	*29.8*
2 (-ĒTU)	2.0	—	—	—	—	—
4 (-ĪTU)	4.6	17.1	16.1	18.7	**33.5**	**63.5**
5 (-ĬTU)	12.8	—	—	—	—	—
6 (-ŪTU)	4.3	24.7	16.9	*28.2*	21.0	—
8 (-SU)	*24.9*	**28.1**	19.8	1.1	5.0	—
9 (-CTU)	**30.5**	5.4	*21.4*	13.9	6.4	4.8
8+4 (-SĪTU)	0.6	—	—	—	—	—
8+9 (-STU)	1.0	0.7	1.7	—	2.8	1.9
8+6 (-SŪTU)	—	—	0.4	0.5	0.5	—
4+6 (-ĪŪTU)	—	1.4	—	—	—	—
None	9.8	—	—	—	—	—

For each language, the type most commonly encountered in my sample is printed in boldface, and the next most common type is printed in italics. Under each heading, I have concentrated on forms fated to appear increasingly anomalous compared with those in -ĀTU and -ĪTU, which together already accounted for more than half the past participles in Latin. Thus, the percentages below should not be taken as applicable to the entire verb corpus of any tongue. Rather, they are intended to highlight the leveling of anomalies, where leveling has taken place, and concomitantly the presence or absence of each p.p. type in Latin and Romance.

Questions arise about how to interpret a few of the forms above. Possibly, Rom. *fiert* 'boiled' < *FERBITU? (no CL p.p.) could be put into type 5; more plausibly, one could consider it tautic athematic, or type 9. Among other syncopated possibilities outside Sardinia and southern Italy is OOc. *nos* 'harmed' < **nost* < NOCITU. Still, sigmatic innovations have arisen in Occitania and Catalonia as well as Italy and Romania (see §4.6), so that *nos* may be one of those.

Table 5–1 shows again that every Latin verb that endured in daily use acquired a past participle. Nearly 10 percent of the CL verbs in my sample, some like ESSE 'be' and VELLE 'want' in the ultra-high-frequency range, have no filler for the past-participial slot. That p.p.-less figure falls nearly to zero for the verbs in each major Romance language, and falls all the way to zero if one ignores (as I do here) verbs either archaic or learnèd or both.

5.4.1. Rhizotonic Past Participles: Major Languages

In Classical Latin, type 9 past participles like FACTU 'done/made' and DICTU 'said, told,' defined as tautic athematics ending in -CTU, accounted for the largest proportion in my sample at more than 30 percent. Every Romance language keeps reflexes of this type, but their occurrence has declined across the board. At 21 percent of its total, conservative Italian still has more than two-thirds of its CL inheritance in that class, but French has less than half (14 percent of its total), while Romanian, Catalan and Spanish each have barely one-sixth (5 percent or so). In these last three languages, type 9 past participles occur almost exclusively for common verbs.

Past participles assigned to type 8, with endings from -SU, present a mixed picture that might serve to summarize general trends in past-participial formation. From being the second most common type in the CL sample (24.9 percent), forms marked like ĀRSU 'burned' have expanded to account in Romanian for over 28 percent of my sample, owing largely to the spread of sigmatic marking from preterits to past participles. In Italian, sigmatics are well maintained at about 20 percent. Farther west, sigmatics represent 5 percent of my standard Catalan sample (though less in dialects) and a sparse 1 percent of my modern French one, having declined since the Middle Ages. Sigmatics represented less than 2 percent of my Old Spanish sample, but all are now archaic. In different zones, the retention, decrease, or loss of sigmatics mirrors the fate of arrhizotonic past participles generally.

Within the group of surviving rhizotonic past participles, some interchange has occurred between the sigmatic type 8 and the tautic athematic type 9. A number of past participles have come to combine the two markers to create sigmatic-tautics like Sp./It. *visto* 'seen.' Accounting for 1 percent of the CL corpus, type 8+9 has remained somewhat productive. In Catalan, the figure for sigmatic-tautics has risen to 2 percent of my corpus.

Almost 13 percent of CL past participles sampled belong to type 5 with endings in -ĪTU, like DĒBĬTU 'had to.' Except for rare and doubtful cases like Rom. *fiert* 'boiled' (no CL p.p.), major Romance languages have not a single past-participial reflex of this type. Unless it could syncopate to yield an phonotactically acceptable cluster like [st] in POSTU 'put' (type 8+9), that atonic ending must have come to seem insufficiently marked to remain adequately distinctive in speech.

5.4.2. Arrhizotonic Past Participles: Major Languages

As noted in Chapter 4, similarities in past-participial formation have led me to treat Catalan and Occitan as one language, and Spanish and Portuguese as another. Readers should therefore understand that, in the following analysis, the term Catalan refers to both that language and Occitan, while the term Spanish refers to both that language and Portuguese.

Across ROMANIA, arrhizotonic past participles thrive. However, the relatively minor type in -ĒTU has fallen from 2 percent of my CL sample to zero in all the Romance ones, despite its tonic vowel echoing that of 2nd-conj. infinitives like HABĒRE 'have.' My working assumption that speakers have been moving toward greater morphological transparency cannot explain the disappearance of this type.[3]

Ranking third and fourth in the CL sample of verbs with past participles are rhizotonic types in -ĀTU and in -ĪTU. Concentrating as it does on the leveling of anomalies, the survey has downplayed the prevalence of such past participles in Latin and its daughter languages. Nevertheless, from less than 10 percent and less than 5 percent respectively in my CL corpus, these two types have expanded everywhere in the post-Roman world. In the Romanian sample, for instance, reflexes of -ĀTU past participles account for 22 percent and reflexes of -ĪTU past participles for 17.5 percent. Both in Italian (23 percent) and in French (33 percent), -ĀTU past participles have become the largest group among descendants of mostly rhizotonic forms in Latin. Meanwhile, the other major type, in -ĪTU, has become the largest group (33 percent) in the Catalan corpus and accounts for a clear majority of the Spanish one (58 percent), which contains only four types.

Representing only about 4 percent of my CL corpus, though I deliberately sought out past participles in that class, the -ŪTU type has become the second most common in the corpora for Romanian (25 percent) and French (26 percent), with the figures for Catalan (21 percent) and Italian (19 percent) only slightly lower. Of this type in the whole Spanish corpus (3 percent), every instance has now been replaced by variants in -ido. In Spanish today, -udo has been limited to serving as an adjectivizer, usually with augmentative and often with pejorative force, for body parts and moral qualities. In Romanian, by contrast, a reflex of the same formant, -ut, occurs in hardly any adjectives; it has almost been limited to serving as a past-participial marker.

If one reviews data gathered over the centuries, a long-term decline in certain types of past participle becomes more striking still. True, the figures for modern Romanian change only slightly, most notably in a decline of type

---

[3] In CL, only a half-dozen verbs seem to have had a "regular" 2nd-conj. perfectum with a pf. in -ĒVĪ and a p.p. in -ĒTU. Already vanishingly rare in Latin, that type was to leave barely a trace in Romance, and no trace past-participially.

9 past participles from 7 percent to 5 percent, but then again Romanian records go back only a few centuries. Italian achieves an even better balance than before among its three arrhizotonic types in reflexes of -ĀTU (24 percent), -ĪTU (16 percent), and -ŪTU (17 percent), and also between its two usual rhizotonic types coming from ones in -CTU (21 percent) and -SU (20 percent).

Farther west, however, the figures for French show that -ĀTU and -ĪTU have come to account for nearly 58 percent of my modern-day corpus, while sigmatics have fallen from 8 percent to 1 percent. Anomalous Fr. *vécu* (OFr. *vescu*) 'lived,' put into type 8+6 faute de mieux, has ceased to be sigmatic in the modern tongue but remains in that class as its single member. In Catalan, examples of -ĪTU have risen to a third of the total, and the two large arrhizotonic classes together represent nearly two-thirds of the modern corpus; sigmatics show a slight decline from 6 percent to 5 percent.

Through time, a shift toward fewer types of p.p. marking has gone furthest in Spanish among major Romance languages. Discounting learnèd revivals, only some ultra-high-frequency verbs still have rhizotonic past participles. After complete elimination of the endings from -ŪTU and -SU, past participles with endings from -ĪTU now account for 64 percent of my sample, and past participles with endings from -ĀTU another 30 percent. The preponderance of those two arrhizotonic types would loom larger still if I had counted every verb in the language, or even half of them. In Spanish today, the only other two types of past participles extant are the tautic athematic as in *abierto* 'opened' and the sigmatic-tautic as in *puesto* 'put.' Only in forms like the latter could one say that sigmaticism for past participles lives on at all in Spain. That leveling of variety in types of p.p. suffixes appears all the more remarkable when one recalls that Hispania was more thoroughly Romanized than most areas in the Empire outside Italia, and that Spanish has generally kept more of the phonetic shape of Latin words than any Romance tongue save Italian. Nonetheless, the presence in dialects of regularized past participles like *decido* 'said,' *morido* 'died,' and *ponido* 'put' suggests that Spanish may eventually end up with only two types of p.p. marking.

5.4.3. Past Participles in Dialects and Minor Languages

Tables D through K of Appendix 3 cover smaller corpora than those gathered for standard Romanian, Italian, French, Catalan, and Spanish (and Portuguese where morphologically distinct from Spanish). Such corpora should be regarded as illustrative rather than indicative. Once again, the data often provide scanty examples of the two or three most common types of past participle but reveal some of the patterns seen elsewhere.

Going by my written sources, one would think that Istriano in Gallo-Italian has only one past participle in a reflex of -ĀTU (type 1), none in -ĪTU (type 4), and a mere four in -ŪTU (type 6); nevertheless, Istriano has nine sigmatics, twenty forms belonging to type 9, and a full thirty-one belonging to type 8+9, here ending in *-isto* or *-esto*. It is doubtful whether these figures accurately reflect the distribution of endings for the whole inventory of

Istriano past participles. Probably, they serve to show that sigmatic-tautics there still enjoy the popularity they used to in Venice over the water.

In eastern Romance, the corpus for Aromanian looks roughly comparable to that for Romanian. The two most common varieties of past participle belong to type 8 from -SU and type 9 from -CTU (each at 27 percent), with type 6 p.p.s from -ŪTU running a fairly close third (15 percent). In Romanian, sigmatics occupy first place unchallenged. Istro-Romanian differs from Aromanian in favoring type 9 past participles at only a bit above 2 percent; here the -ŪTU type takes first place at nearly 30 percent, with sigmatics second at 21 percent. Despite these divergences, all three varieties of Balkan Romance tend to favor arrhizotonic past participles—no surprise anywhere—and ones bearing sigmatic marking—no surprise in eastern Romance. For further details about Balkan Romance, see Table D on page 434.

More than 500 past participles have been gathered from dialects of Italian. Those from the northern area—Gallo-Italian—favor type 6 past participles with endings from -ŪTU twice as often (34 percent) as the standard does (17 percent), suggesting that speakers long uninfluenced by bookish norms tend to level anomalies on their own, yet hardly to the extent that e.g. Spanish has done. In those dialects, type 9 past participles with endings that were or are in -CTU come in second (22 percent), as they do in the standard, but type 8 sigmatics at 13 percent are only about two-thirds as common as in the standard (20 percent). Although standard Italian has only half a dozen or so sigmatic-tautic past participles like *rimasto* 'stayed,' that type accounts for over 8 percent of the northern-dialect sample, past participles in variants of *-suto* (type 8+6) another 1.5 percent. Perhaps identifiable as "semi-sigmatic," such forms partly compensate for the shrinkage in straight sigmatics compared with the standard. Speakers of eastern Gallo-Italian dialects, then, have promoted arrhizotonicity for many past participles but have generalized an [st] marker like the one in POSTU 'put' for many others. Standard Italian has done this for only a few.

Central-southern dialects of Italian match northern ones in preferring type 6 past participles above all (33 percent of my sample), followed by type 9 ones (24 percent). In contrast not only with those dialects and the Italian standard but also with every other Romance standard, central-southern dialects have retained a great many type 5 past participles with endings from atonic -ĬTU. They fill one-tenth (10 percent) of my sample, a small decline from the 13 percent they filled in Latin. Likewise in contrast with every other standard Romance language, most notably Spanish, central-southern dialects of Italian have hardly a type 4 past participle (endings from -ĪTU). Although in some dialects one might posit a higher survival rate of type 4s than in the ones examined here, many dialects in the south have only two arrhizotonic types, deriving from -ĀTU and -ŪTU, so that the figure of 0.7 percent could actually represent imports from Tuscan. In the center and south of Italy, straight sigmatics are well represented at 12 percent; in nearly 5 percent more of the sample, sigmatic marking occurs in combination with other kinds of marking. Thus, more than one-sixth of past participles here bear marking in

[s], compared with 23 percent for the north of Italy. Central-southern dialects, at least Tuscany and Lazio, also contain short-form past participles, taking up practically 5 percent of the sample. For further details about dialects of Italian, from Venice to Palermo, see Table E on page 435.

With eighty-four past participles gathered, Sardinian agrees with central-southern dialects of Italian in preserving or developing a great many type 5 past participles in reflexes of -ĪTU (34 percent), which rank second only to type 9 ones in reflexes of -CTU (42 percent) in my sample. Sigmatic marking remains popular at 11 percent, with sigmatic-tautics accounting for another 5 percent. Still, type 6 past participles with endings from -ŪTU occupy a less important place here than on the peninsula: type 6s account for a mere 5 percent of the Sardinian corpus, compared with 17 percent in standard Italian and 33–34 percent in each of the two great groups of Italian dialects. Indeed, such past participles seem never to have evolved on the island but have most likely been imported from the mainland.

Broadly speaking, the three varieties of Alpine Romance split into two groups according to past-participial morphology. In the eastern group, both Friulian with 96 past participles and Ladin with 112 past participles prefer type 6 forms with endings from -ŪTU, for they take up more than 40 percent of the respective corpora. While type 9 past participles with endings from -CTU account for some 38 percent of the Ladin sample, though, in Friulian that type falls to 5 percent. Moreover, sigmatic-tautics together with straight sigmatics represent some 6 percent of the Ladin corpus but only 1 percent of the Friulian one (which has no sigmatic-tautics). The conclusion appears inescapable: Ladin has kept a greater preference for rhizotonic past participles than Friulian has.

Farther west, the Upper Engadin and Surselvan dialects of Ræto-Romance, with a total of 122 past participles, agree between themselves in having most past participles in rhizotonic type 9 with endings from -CTU, at 53 percent and 40 percent of their respective corpora or 48 percent overall. Both agree in having a high proportion of sigmatic past participles at about 30 percent of each sample, even greater than the 25 percent recorded for Latin and the 28 percent for Romanian. As for type 6 past participles whose endings derive from -ŪTU, Surselvan shows some of the same favoritism toward them that Friulian and Ladin do, at 26 percent of the total, but in Upper Engadin only 8 percent of past participles collected are of that type, making less than 15 percent for both combined. Still, Alpine Romance generally has resisted the trend toward arrhizotonicity observed closer to the Atlantic coastline. For further details about Sardinian and Alpine Romance, see Table F on page 436.

Dialects of French also have plenty of type 6 past participles (endings from -ŪTU). In Norman, Picard, and Burgundian, these represent 39 percent, 36 percent, and 50 percent of the respective corpora, making 40 percent overall. In Norman and Burgundian, type 1 past participles (endings from -ĀTU) are the second most common type, at about 20 percent, but that type comes in first at 45 percent in Picard. Picard also has more sigmatics than the other two but fewer type 4s and type 9s. In Val-de-Saire Norman, four past participles ending in [ɥyɥəezy] constitute a class on their own. Sigmatics account for 3.5 percent. To the east, the transitional dialect of Naisey agrees with French dialects in favoring type 6 past participles the most, at 49 percent, but agrees with Franco-Provençal in giving second place to type 9s at 23 percent. For further details about dialects of French, see Table G on page 437.

Moving to varieties of Romance spoken across the south of France—Franco-Provençal and Occitan—one observes that the highest preference again goes to type 6 past participles (endings from -ŪTU), which range from 38 percent of the Franco-Provençal corpus to 54 percent of Languedocian, 60 percent of Poitevin, and 72 percent of Auvergnat. Oddly, if one wished to document the spread of arrhizotonic types at the expense of rhizotonic ones, it is type 9 past participles (endings from -CTU) that rank second in Franco-Provençal, Languedocian, and Gascon at about 30 percent in each, something that no doubt has to do with the preference given to anomalous forms in Iliescu and Mourin, and in this study as well. In Gévaudanais, type 4 past participles (endings from -ĪTU) come in second in my sample, at 18 percent, but type 9 past participles occur half as often as in the other three dialects, at less than 14 percent. In all these groups, sigmatic type 8 past participles are well represented: they account for 8 percent of the Franco-Provençal corpus and, together with sigmatic-tautics, 14 percent of the Languedocian, 11 percent of the Gévaudanais, and well over 6 percent of the Gascon, but none at all in Poitevin and a mere 2.5 percent in Auvergnat. For all Occitania, the sigmatic score rises to 7 percent when sigmatic-tautics are included; past participles marked in -sut account for 2.5 percent more. Far beyond what is seen in e.g. closely related Catalan, the tendency of speakers of such dialects of Occitan to hold on to stem-stressed past participles bears witness to a conservatism perhaps born of isolation. For further details about dialects of Franco-Provençal and Occitan, see Tables H and I on pages 438–39.

As shown in Table 5–2 on the following page, arrhizotonicity tends to rise toward the west in dialects, much as it does in literary standards. According to my samples, which of course overrepresent irregular past participles for 2nd-conj. and 3rd-conj. verbs, speakers of most dialects west of Italy prefer -ŪTU types above all, except that speakers of Spanish and Portuguese dialects prefer -ĪTU types for non-1st-conj. verbs generally. Sigmatics decline in importance as one moves west.[4]

Data from dialects of Catalan, Spanish, and Portuguese allow for a brief analysis. In the Catalan dialects surveyed, past participles of type 6 (endings from -ŪTU) are well represented at 44 percent; those of type 8 (sigmatics) are well represented overall at 11 percent, though in fact found only in

---

[4] Omitted from Table 5–2, dialect corpora from Friulian, Ladin, and Ræto-Romance also show a preference for -ŪTU types. So do dialects of Gallo-Italian. Among arrhizotonics in the corpus for Aromanian (including Meglenoromanian), an approximate balance prevails at 18 percent for -ĀTU, 16 percent for -ĪTU, and 15 percent for -ŪTU. See Tables D–F of Appendix 3 (pages 434–36)

Valencian. No forms of either type appear farther west: in Spanish or Portuguese, a few sigmatics abide in dialects, but no past participle there ends in -*udo* any longer.

Table 5–2

Western Dialect Corpora

Type/Dialects number>	DIALECTS OF				
	Franco-Prov. [161]	French [171]	Occitan [323]	Catalan [159]	Spanish & Ptg. [221]
1 (-ĀTU)	9.3	32.8	9.6	5.7	13.6
2 (-ĒTU)	—	—	—	—	—
4 (-ĪTU)	9.3	10.5	9.0	16.4	58.4
5 (-ĬTU)	—	—	—	—	—
6 (-ŪTU)	38.5	39.8	55.7	44.0	—
8 (-SU)	8.1	3.5	5.3	10.7	1.4
9 (-CTU)	31.1	11.1	15.8	17.6	16.3
8+4 (-SĪTU)	—	—	—	—	—
8+9 (-STU)	—	—	1.9	5.7	6.3
8+6 (-SŪTU)	5.0	—	2.5	—	—
4+6 (-ĪŪTU)	—	—	—	—	—
Other	—	2.3	0.3	—	8.1

In nonstandard forms west of Catalonia, speakers tend to regularize the few unlearnèd anomalies remaining, though sometimes along preterit rather than infectum or general lines. In every dialect of Spanish and Portuguese surveyed, type 4 (with endings from -ĪTU) accounts for at least half of all forms, the figure climbing to 87 percent for nonstandard Castilian. Again, forms, the figure climbing to 87 percent for nonstandard Castilian. Again, some of these are due to accidents of attestation, for dialectologists tend to highlight forms divergent from those found in standard languages. For further details about dialects of Catalan, Spanish, and Portuguese, see Tables J and K on pages 440–41.

5.5. SIGMATIC MARKING EAST AND WEST

Back in Latin, marking with [s] played a major role in the morphology of nouns and verbs. With the exception of neuters, fated to vanish anyway as a class, nouns ended in [s] in the acc.pl.[5] Latin verbs had sigmatic endings in 2sg. and 2pl. for every tense but perfect indicative. Sigmatic marking also occurred on a great many past participles, amounting to almost one-fourth of the corpus laid out in Appendix 2. Although originally a variant of the [t] marker after another dental consonant in the stem, [s] or [s:] in past participles like RĀSU 'shaven' < *radsu or MISSU 'sent' < *mitsu probably came to be felt as belonging to a separate class by native speakers of Latin.

Scholars of Romance have long noted a phonological isogloss dividing ROMANIA from the time of the earliest texts: in the west, speakers maintained final [s] in noun plurals and in second-person verb endings, but in the east they either dropped it or vocalized it into [i] or [i̯]. It is now accepted that, early in the Empire, final [s] was pronounced; its vanishing or vocalization represented an innovation that had nothing to do with the fall of -S after O or U in Old Latin (Herman 1987, 97). Judging by inscriptions in Late Latin, an apparent morphosyntactic alternation developed between -US and -U in nom.sg. nouns, notably in central-southern Italy, perhaps in the Balkans, and to a lesser extent in Iberia. Herman asks (107) whether that alternation was completely independent of the future disappearance of final [s] in Balkan Romance and in most dialects of Italian. Put otherwise, did that morphological hesitation at one time have anything in common with phonetic developments far in the future? Finally, Herman wonders whether the "dévalorisation" of final [s] in noun flexion contributed to the loss of final [s] in other morphosyntactic roles.

What appears to have gone unnoticed so far is an isogloss, comparable to the one adumbrated long ago, that also divides ROMANIA into two zones according to the frequency of past participles with sigmatic marking.

In Table 5–3, the role of [s] as a number marker on nouns and a person-number marker on verbs (usually excluding the preterit) is contrasted with the role of [s] as a type 8 marker for the corpus of past participles gathered in Appendix 2 and still in use today.

One finds a high proportion of sigmatic past participles in the east and a low proportion of such past participles in the west. Can one establish an inverse relation between p.p. marking with [s] and noun or finite-verb

---

[5] I take no account here of other morphological roles played by often-final [s] in the nominal and adjectival morphology of Latin (scarlet -IBUS es and so forth).

house divided against itself cannot stand, but it is also true that the Romance house has several mansions.

Table 5–3

Sigmatic Marking across Romance

( ) final [s] habitually muted

Sigmatic?	Rom.	Ist-R	It.	Sard.	Fri.	Lad.	Fr.	Cat.	Sp.
Noun plurals	—	—	—	+	+	+	(+)	+	+
2sg. verbs	—	—	—	+	+	+	(+)	+	+
Past participles	28%	11%	20%	11%	2%	4%	1%	5%	0%

How did this split arise, this division of morphological labor? During the transition from Latin to Romance, sigmatic marking seems to have become largely restricted in both western and eastern ROMANIA, but in a different way in each zone. In the west, where 2sg./pl. verb forms continued to end in [s], as did noun plurals deriving from Latin accusative plurals, there survived few and there survive even fewer past participles marked with [s], which have turned into relics of disused morphology. In the east, where 2sg./pl. verb forms and noun plurals both came to end in vowels or semivowels, there survived and survive a far higher proportion of sigmatic past participles, which have expanded in Romance spoken near the Black Sea. Leaving out its role as a pluralizer for nouns, [s] as a morphological marker has been increasingly restricted either to finite verbs or to past participles, in the two great dominions of Romance.[6]

In this feature, Sardinian would have to be ranked as an odd language out: it has sigmatic marking on nouns and finite verbs, but contains as high a proportion of sigmatic past participles as Istro-Romanian does at 11 percent of my corpus. In Switzerland, both Upper Engadin and Surselvan have sigmatic marking on 2sg./pl. verbs along with many sigmatic past participles—Engadin at 31 percent, Surselvan at 30 percent of the corpora—so that the

---

[6] Omitted from Table 5–3, Aromanian (including Meglenoromanian) agrees with the rest of eastern Romance in marking plenty of p.p.s with [s]. Indeed, by racking up a sigmatic score of just over 32% of my corpus, Aromanian outdistances Istro-Romanian (21%) and even Romanian (28%). As noted in §3.1.5, more and more Rom. past participles have recently been swinging sigmatic; if only the records existed to trace a similar swing across all of Balkan Romance!

proposed specialization of sigmatic marking holds no truer for these varieties of Ræto-Romance than it does for Sardinian.[7] Another caveat: in French since the Middle Ages, the percentage of sigmatic past participles listed in the data has sunk from 8 percent to 1 percent, and except in liaison final -s̲ [z] has ceased to be pronounced at all in noun plurals, in 2sg./pl. verb forms, or in (masc.) past participles like *mis* 'put' and *pris* 'taken.' French has thus practically eliminated all three kinds of sigmatic marking present in Latin.

Admittedly, the data for finite verbs may not be strictly comparable with those for past participles, for in Latin [s] occurred word-finally in certain finite-verb forms but intervocalically in sigmatic past participles, even if it became final after apocope in Romanian, Catalan, Occitan, and French.[8] Besides, class marking with [s] never spread to all past participles in any Romance language, while as an ending for all 2sg./pl. verbs such marking flourished in the west and died out in the east. Nevertheless, within the bounds of my understanding, I regard the following statement as implicative if not definitive: at an early date, speakers in the east generally specialized [s] as a morphological marker in a way quite different from the way chosen by their cousins to the west.

5.6. ALLOMORPHY AND ISOMORPHY: LONG-TERM TRENDS

After centuries of regularization, though along different lines, some verbs in major Romance languages retain rhizotonic, asigmatic past participles still. A list of those surviving across all or even most of ROMANIA barely exceeds half a dozen: reflexes of FACTU 'done/made,' DICTU 'said, told,' MORTUU 'died,' SCRIPTU 'written,' RUPTU 'broken,' POS(I)TU 'put,' and *VISTU 'seen' (see §6.6). Even here, modern French fails to continue the rhizotonic past participles POS(I)TU or *VISTU at all, having kept a reflex of PŌNERE only in the Germanic-inspired sense 'lay eggs' with an arrhizotonic p.p. *pondu*, and using regularized *v u* < *VIDUTU for the past participle of the second (but cf. an OFr. by-form *vis* < VĪSU). French continues *route* < RUPTA only as a noun, though OFr. still had *rot* or *rout* 'broken'; Romanian does not continue *VISTU, using *v ắzut*, and derives *scris* 'written' from a fairly recent sigmatic variant, having also restricted the local reflex of *MORTU to adjectival use and made the past participle regular. Even in Italian, sigmatic-tautic *visto* 'seen' competes with regularized *veduto*. Across all four languages together, not a

---

[7] Recall that, under Malkiel's Law, a Romance language should have one fewer type of arrhizotonic past participle than it has types of infinitive. Ræto-Romance breaks Malkiel's Law, for Surselvan has four infin. types but only two p.p. types, and so does Vallader or Lower Engadin (Haiman, 358). Sardinian and southern Italian dialects only appear to break this law (§§3.6.2–3.7). Still, like Lachmann's Law (§1.3.4), Malkiel's may have to be amended.

[8] I would like to have forged a link between a language's acquiring such a newly final [s] and its subsequently losing much or all p.p. sigmaticism. The link looks strongest for French, weaker for Occitan and Catalan, but lacking in Romanian. So much for that breakthrough.

single rhizotonic athematic has survived as a current past participle with the same kind of ending as its Latin etymon (see Table 5–4).

In Italia and Dacia, sigmatic stems, often extended from Latin perfects, have continued to enjoy a great vogue. Indeed, as noted, in Italia speakers of LL or Proto-Italian changed some past participles in -TU to ones in -SU, choosing *mosso* 'moved' over direct-suffix MŌTU and *perso* (also *perduto*) 'lost' over rhizotonic PERDITU, besides evolving *valso* 'been worth' and *parso* 'appeared' for verbs with no past participles in Latin. The first three of these have the same stems as sigmatic *passati remoti* for forms 1, 3, and 6, even if *parvi* etc. remain asigmatic. Romanian has kept *râs* 'laughed,' *rămas* 'stayed' and gone on to develop forms like *dus* 'taken away,' *pus* 'put,' *tras* 'pulled; thrown,' and *zis* 'said' from sigmatic perfects.

Table 5–4

Survival of Rhizotonic Athematics

( ) archaic as p.p.   [ ] metaplasm   √ literary   * competing with by-form

Latin	Spanish	French	Italian	Romanian
APERTU	abierto	ouvert	aperto	—
CLAUSU, -CLŪSU	—	(clos)	chiuso	închis
COCTU	(cocho)	cuit	cotto	copt
COOPERTU	cubierto	couvert	coperto	[acoperit]
DICTU	dicho	dit	detto	[zis]
DUCTU	(ducho)	-duit	-dotto	[dus]
FACTU	hecho	fait	fatto	(fapt)
MISSU	(messo)	mis	messo	-mis
MORT(U)U	muerto	mort	morto	(mort)
POS(I)TU	puesto	(post)	posto√	[pus]
PR(EH)ĒNSU	(preso)	pris	presso	prins
RUPTU	roto	(rot)	rotto	rupt
SCRĪPTU	escrito	écrit	scritto	(script)
VĪSU	[visto]	(vis)	[visto]*	[văzut]

Nevertheless, speakers in Tuscany, Castile, and the Ile-de-France displayed growing reluctance, no doubt starting in Late Latin or Proto-Romance, to preserve past participles built from consonant-final stems and ending in unstressed -ĬTU or -TU. Speakers seem to have unconsciously required clearer marking of past participles, usually with the theme vowel under stress.

All in all, speakers in Gallia displayed the greatest tendency to adopt the three weak types of past-participial formation in -ĀTU, -ĪTU, and -ŪTU (Elcock, 131). Speakers across much of Hispania, in some of southern Italy, and in an Alpine valley or two, were to go them one fewer and end up with two productive types: one for reflexes of -ĀTU, the other for reflexes of the rest.

One could peer close up at curios among Romance past participles instead of stepping back to take in the big picture. One could linger over rhizotonic islands in an arrhizotonic sea, like *vint* 'come' in Moldavian, *prasu* 'lunched' in Sardinian, *vit* 'lived' in two dialects of Ladin, *test* 'woven in Old Catalan,' or *cueto* 'cooked' in Bielsa Aragonese today, whose survival may be credibly attributed to conservatism.[9] One could linger over local singularities like *frand* 'broken' in Lucanian, *muft* 'moved' in Old Engadin, or *rist* 'laughed' in Rossellonese Catalan, which have emerged through analogy with other past participles or through the phonotactics of a given tongue. Then again, one could linger over innovations like sigmatic and suffixed *couneissegut* 'known' in Gévaudanais Occitan or that foursome out of the Val de Saire in Normandy: *lw̌uw̌əzu* 'read,' *nw̌uw̌əzu* 'harmed,' *sw̌uw̌əzu* 'followed,' and *tchw̌uw̌əzu* 'cooked.' One could linger over scattered regularizations like the two found for reflexes of SCRĪPTU 'written' at opposite ends of ROMANIA: 2nd-/3rd-conj.-style *escrigut* in the Tamaritan dialect of Catalan, and 1st-conj.-style *scriat* in the Banat dialect of Moldavian. One could linger over certain adjectives from Val de Pas Leonese like *cáįdu* 'fallen' or *góįdu* 'heard' that almost seem to continue rhizotonic thematics in -ĪTU. Finally, one could linger over forms like Aromanian *diucl'at* 'hit by the evil eye,' Val d'Aosta *incru* 'been scared of ghosts,' or Catalan *espenyat* 'thrown off a cliff,' each of them morphologically unremarkable but semantically outstanding.

To dawdle in any of those ways would amount to gathering pebbles that gleam along the shore of an ocean long seen from dry land and now known beyond sight of land by its winds, currents, and tides.

During the transition toward analytic verb constructions—above all, analytic perfective constructions—from Sagres on the Atlantic to Sulina on the Black Sea, speakers of what were to become Romance languages narrowed the range of means available to shape past participles. Many types of past-participial formation current in Latin ceased to exist. Several of those remaining came to be restricted lexically or geographically. Through time, especially to the west, speakers have tended to make the morphology of their past participles more predictable through arrhizotonicity or sigmaticism.

---

[9] In its tendency to retain rhizotonic preterits and past participles coming down from Latin, std. Catalan should be ranked between innovative Spanish and—for a change—conservative French (Entwhistle, 59). Catalan floats as something like a sigmatic island in an asigmatic sea.

6

Theoretical Implications

This research had long [since] entered
the charmed stage when the quest
overrides the goal....Pnin averted his
mental gaze from the end of his work,
which was so clearly in sight that one
could make out the rocket of an
asterisk, the flare of a "sic!" This line
of land was to be shunned as the
doom of everything that determined
the rapture of endless approximation.

Nabokov, *Pnin*

6.0. A ROLE FOR THEORY

A theory of verb morphology, dealing with the reshaping or retention of
certain markers through time, should be regarded as useful when it can be
shown to work empirically, by preference across a number of languages. Such
a theory should illuminate the road traveled so far. As indicated in §2.15, a
theory is unlikely to point down new pathways of morphological revamping
before speakers blaze the trails themselves. Even to project current trends
would appear little short of foolhardy.

In this final chapter, I review several theories about verb morphology put
forward during the later twentieth century. I consider whether theories help
to clarify the apparently rather similar tastes of Latin speakers in tolerating
extensive allomorphy in past-participial formation, tastes that might after all
represent little more than an artifact of documentation from CL days. I
consider whether these theories help to explain the shift through time toward
the fairly divergent tastes that developed among Romance speakers in past-
participial morphology. If all participated in a trend toward shaping their past
participles along more predictable lines than the Romans had done, their
morphological preferences for doing so diverged somewhat across space as
across time. In carrying out that comparison between Latin and Romance, and

within Romance, I give opinions inspired by theory about why old-time past participles lived on or died out where and when they did.

6.1. TEN FINDINGS

From the evidence gathered so far, ten findings stand out. (Further findings are welcome.) Later, I review each in the light of the contribution that theories may make toward accounting for the past-participial inventory in each Romance language, present and past.[1]

I.   Western Romance languages have or used to have an inflectional suffix -s on noun plurals and 2sg. verb forms, inter alia, but they have almost no sigmatic past participles; eastern Romance languages have no such inflectional suffix -s but have many sigmatic past participles (§5.5).

II.   This morphological gap between eastern and western Romance has widened, and may still be widening, because Romanian has acquired a great many more sigmatic past participles than Latin had (§§3.1.5), while Italian has kept or evolved almost as many as Latin had (§3.5.3.2).

III.   Fairly common in Classical Latin, and apparently even more so in Late Latin, a rhizotonic thematic p.p. type in -ĪTU has died out everywhere but Sardinia and most of southern Italy (§§3.6.2, 3.7.2), leaving only rare and doubtful exceptions elsewhere.

IV.   Quite common in Latin, a rhizotonic athematic p.p. type ending in -CTU has grown steadily scarcer especially toward the west, where reflexes of the type remain in use for high-frequency verbs alone (§§3.1.5, 3.5.3.1, 3.7.1, 4.4.9.4, 4.6.2.2, 4.7.6).

V.   Owing to wide-ranging sound changes since Old French times, modern spoken French has developed for almost all verbs, and is developing for the rest, a new isomorphism making past participles invariant by gender as well as number (§4.4.12).

VI.   Across Romance, there has been an ebb and flow between adjectival and grammaticalized past-participial function through time (passim, especially §4.7.4).

---

[1] This list has been expanded from one provided by an anonymous reviewer of the manuscript.

VII.   For certain verbs in Italian dialects (§3.5.9), and for certain others in Spanish dialects and in standard Portuguese (§4.7.8), there has developed a peculiar use of what appears to be the 1sg. present indicative, or a 1st-/2nd-declension adjective, instead of the 1st-conjugation past participle.

VIII.   In Occitan and Catalan, most past participles from the 2nd and 3rd conjugations, which end in reflexes of -ŪTU from Romanian through French, have incorporated [g] to end in -*gut* rather than in expected -*ut* (§4.6.2.3).

IX.   During the transition to modern Spanish and Portuguese, all attested past participles in -*udo* merged with -*ido* past participles (§4.7.4.1).

X.   Consequently, the number of major types of past participle in Spanish and Portuguese has been reduced to two, from -ĀTU and -ĪTU. Likewise, only two major types, from -ĀTU and -ĪTU, have lasted in Engadin and Surselvan (§§4.3.1–4.3.2). Only two major arrhizotonic types survive in Calabrian, Abruzzese, Lucanian, and Sicilian as well; those two descend from types in -ĀTU and -ŪTU (§§3.6.2.2–3.6.2.3, §§3.6.2.5–3.6.2.6). Yet Apulian still has three arrhizotonic endings because, exceptionally for southern Italy, it keeps reflexes of the -ĪTU type (§3.6.2.4).

One useful way to begin a search for theoretical explanations of past-participial developments is to go back to the past participles of verbs as they were put together in Classical Latin.

6.2. MARKEDNESS BY ASPECT

In *Morphology*, Bybee observes (50–54) that, cross-linguistically, the 3sg. present indicative active most often has zero marking and thus may be regarded as the stem for deriving all other forms of a verb. Referring to Latin and Romance, Bybee notes (60, 63) that a 3sg. present indicative or 2sg. imperative like *ama* serves as the basis for all forms in a regular 1st-conj. verb in Spanish like *amar*, as its ancestor AMA(T) would for all forms of Latin AMĀRE 'love, like'.[2] Here Bybee might profitably have extended analysis of one-stem verbs to account for regular members of the 4th conjugation like SCĪRE 'know.' Yet, as she acknowledges, the single-stem model cannot explain Latin 3rd-conj. verbs, whose stems differ markedly by aspect.

---

[2] Presumably, under Bybee's analysis of verbs like AMĀRE 'love, like,' one is supposed to ignore the 3sg. pres.indic. marker -T. As that marker disappeared almost everywhere by the time Romance began, such simplifications would seem to pose no obstacle to explaining Romance verb forms.

Bybee's evaluation would suggest that each Latin verb—and by extension, each verb in daughter languages—may be assigned to one of two classes. Verbs in the first class are built on a single stem throughout; two stems are required for verbs in the second class. As shown in Chapters 1 and 2 of this book, the single-stem model would be inapplicable not only to all 3rd-conj. verbs but to almost all 2nd-conj. verbs and some 1st- and 4th-conj. verbs in Classical Latin.

In largely limiting the discussion to finite forms of the infectum and perfectum, though mentioning that each aspect has its own infinitive, Bybee notes that the latter aspect may differ from the former in having sigmatic marking, vowel changes, reduplication, or suppletion. In reference to verbs with two stems, she states that infectum and perfectum can be thought of as deriving from two distinct base forms. So far so good. From a past-participial point of view, the chief shortcoming of her explanation is that it fails to account for certain nonfinite verb forms in Latin, namely past participles whose stems differ from those of finite infectum and finite perfectum both, to as great an extent as the two finite aspects differ from each other.

A few of Bybee's own examples of stem variation by aspect could usefully be extended to cover past participles. Within the perfectum, one could not, synchronically at any rate, account for variations in form between perfects and past participles like vowel and consonant changes as in MĪSĪ and MISSU 'sent,' vowel changes as in ĒGĪ 'did, went' and ĀCTU 'done, gone,' reduplication or its lack as in TETIGĪ and TĀCTU 'touched' or DEDĪ 'gave' and DĀTU 'given,' and (apparent) suppletion in TULĪ and LĀTU 'carried.' I conclude that the traditional practice of listing past participles as the fourth principal part of Latin verbs retains its validity for morphological analysis. Survival within the perfectum of such outstanding irregularities as those just reviewed would suggest that past participles remained mostly adjectival and had yet to be fully integrated into the verb system of Classical Latin.

Nevertheless, as Bybee states, "The forms of each aspect are more closely related to one another than they are to forms in the other aspect" (63). The observation that aspectual differences may be reflected by sharply distinct morphology serves as a theoretical basis for explaining steadily declining allomorphy among verb stems in Romance (if, as usual, the present tense gets left out of consideration). In comparison with Latin, for instance, many more 3rd-conj. verbs in Romanian and some more in Italian contrast sigmatic marking in the past system with the absence of such marking in the present system. In the light of Bybee's further observation that "morpho-phonemic changes...tend to eliminate alternations among closely related forms" (64), I am led to conclude that greater morphological likeness through time between sigmatic preterits and past participles in the Romance east provides evidence that Italians and Romanians have come to link past participles to finite past-tense verb forms more tightly than Latin speakers did and hence now rank past participles as part of the past system.

Though Bybee considers it unlikely that a present stem would substitute for the stem of an imperfect or preterit, she acknowledges that "Any alternation among productively related forms can be leveled" (65). Through time, then, greater morphological likeness among stems for all forms of a verb everywhere in ROMANIA provides evidence that speakers have come to link past participles to all other verb forms and hence now rank past participles as verbal rather than nominal.

6.3. COGNITIVE APPROACHES

In *Morphology and Mind*, Hall approaches affixes from the viewpoint of cognitive linguistics. According to Hall (155), regularly suffixed inflected forms appear to be listed as part of the main stem entry; irregularly inflected forms and all derived ones are listed in sub-entries. If so, speakers of Spanish and Portuguese would have far fewer subentries than their Latin-speaking ancestors did, and speakers of Romanian, Italian, and French would have recognizably fewer.

Repeating a point widely acknowledged in the literature on grammaticalization, Hall says that most affixation has resulted from reduction of free lexical items to bound morphemes. Affixation may also come from what Meillet terms *innovations analogiques*: "These constitute a type of lexical (i.e. lexically internal) reanalysis, whereby one affix replaces another in the same functional domain....[either] where equally productive forms compete...or when one form establishes dominance in its domain and squeezes out the competition" (Hall, 89). From my viewpoint, though one form has never become dominant for past participles in any Romance language, the evolution of preferred types implies that, in Late Latin, equally productive ways of forming that principal part were in competition. Though the predominance of -ĀTU p.p.s for 1st-conj. verbs and -ĪTU p.p.s for 4th-conj. verbs became greater than before, competition remained intense for the types of past participle applied to 2nd- and 3rd-conj. verbs.

Of the three types of internal lexical reanalysis cited (91), restructuring of many past participles in Late Latin or Proto-Romance would fall under Hall's type ii). Thus, the -ĀTU and -ĪTU p.p. suffixes, along with the -ŪTU and -SU ones, were "extended to other forms in the same functional domain" as other p.p. suffixes either vanished completely everywhere or were reduced to relics in most areas where Latin lived on.

6.4. ADJECTIVES OR PAST PARTICIPLES?

When many rhizotonic past participles were remade along arrhizotonic lines, some old forms stayed in use as adjectives: Rom. *mort* 'dead' < MORT(U)U; It. *cheto*, Fr. *coi*, Sp. *quedo* 'quiet, still' < QUIĒTU 'rested'; Fri. *stuart* and Cat. *tort* 'bent,' Sp. *tuerto* and Ptg. *torto* 'one-eyed' < (EX)TORTU 'twisted (out).'

In addition, Portuguese and nonstandard Spanish and Italian have some short-form past participles that resemble adjectives or for that matter (in masc.sg.) 1sg. pres.indic. verbs. As noted in §4.7.8, Williams (186) speculates that Ptg. short forms like *côrto* 'cut,' *baptizo* 'baptized,' and *pago* 'paid' started in Late Latin or early Portuguese: speakers aligned them with extant pairs such as short-form AUSU 'dared' and long-form *AUSATU; even the CL standard tolerated both PŌTU and PŌTĀTU 'drunk' as past participles for BIBERE. In Portuguese, short forms ending in -e like demotic *fixe* 'firm, permanent,' alongside long forms in *-ado*, would have arisen by analogy with pairs like *livre* 'free' and *livrado* 'released.'[3]

What appears to be a 1sg. pres.indic. instead of an overtly marked past participle for certain verbs, in dialects of Italian and Spanish and in standard Portuguese, may therefore be identified as a long-standing morphological conflation of (masc.sg.) 2nd-decl. adjective and (masc.sg.) past participle, here realized as identity of form: verb root plus *-o*. Similarly, Ptg. short-form p.p.s ending in *-e* resemble 3rd-decl. adjectives like *grande* 'big' and *verde* 'green' as well as the 3sg. pres.indic. for non-*ar* verbs.

That Romance adjectives and past participles may overlap semantically as well as morphologically is suggested by divergent outcomes for words with the suffix descending from -ŪTU. Speakers of Spanish and Portuguese have assigned them exclusively to the adjectival class, while speakers of Romanian have assigned them almost exclusively to the past-participial class (§4.7.4.3).

It would be helpful to have a clear-cut means of deciding whether a given form is adjectival, past participial, or both. On that point, Williams notes that in Portuguese, "It is difficult to determine whether many of the surviving strong forms are still really participles because the distinction between the verbal use and the adjectival use of the past participle is extremely elusive in Portuguese and has not yet been defined" (186). That statement was made in the early 1960s.

Such a definition is now at hand. In *Lexeme-Morpheme Based Morphology*, Beard has proposed a syntactic test for separating adjectives from past participles in English. The former have a comparative and a superlative and may also be nominalized. The latter are incompatible with the adjectival prefix *un-* and adjectival intensifiers like *very*; they require *not* and *very much/many*.[4] Adjectives, says Beard, are lexically derived, while participles are inflectional derivations. It seems likely that comparable criteria could be applied in Portuguese and other Romance languages, notably Spanish. Italian, and Romanian.

Beard's criteria work well for distinguishing between adjectives and past participles where both have the same form, as in *scratched, bent*, and *swollen*. For such pairs, the great majority of those found in English, he notes that "The formal evidence points directly to different derivation rules marked by identical sets of suffixes" (109). However, he goes too far in implying (107) that no "passive adjective" differs morphologically from the corresponding past

---

[3] Portuguese also has *aceito/aceita* 'accepted' and *fixo/fixa* 'firm, permanent.' Did Latin have any adjectives conjugable in either the 1st/2nd declension or the 3rd declension? Stigmatized forms from the *Appendix Probi* like masc. TRISTUS 'sad' and fem. PAUPERA 'poor' (instead of ambigeneric TRĪSTIS, PAUPER) suggest some fluctuation between classes.

[4] On pp. 105–7, Beard proceeds to draw a similar syntactic distinction between present participles and "active adjectives," which need hardly concern the reader here.

participle. An empirical test reveals that, in English, pairs of adjectives and past participles with the same stem do not always have the same ending. Thus, *shaven/shaved*, *shrunken/shrunk*, and *drunken/drunk* (cf. Sp. *beodo/bebido*) have become quite distinct morphologically. Even more distinct are a few pairs like *molten/melted* and *stricken/struck* that show a vocalic as well as a consonantal contrast, along with a semantic one.[5]

From such semantic restrictions as well as their morphological distinctiveness, it seems likely that former past participles like *molten* and *stricken* have grown less verbal through time. For pairs like adj. *shaven* and p.p. *shaved*, one could apply a morphological as well as a semantic criterion to differentiate one from the other. One could similarly contrast former p.p.s like Rom. *inţelept* 'wise', Ist-R *kopt* 'cooked,' It. *fisso* 'fastened,' Fr./Cat. *ras* 'short-haired,' and Cat. *fart* and Sp. *harto* 'glutted, fed up' with their usually arrhizotonic replacements. One could use similar tests to decide how each form in a pair of forms has been specialized in a different function, like the Rom. p.p. *spars* and adj. *spart* 'cracked' or the It. p.p. *sparito* 'disappeared' and adj. *sparuto* 'lean, meager.' Whether the test would work for a semantic distinction like that drawn between It. *riflesso* 'bounced back light' and *riflettuto* 'thought over' remains open to interpretation, but it is undoubtedly valid in other uses.

Turning to another Romance language, Hella Olbertz in *Verbal Periphrases in a Functional Grammar of Spanish* reviews constructions involving past participles in several uses. Olbertz ends the section on such constructions (194–200) by observing that speakers of Spanish may replace a past participle with an adverb (including *así* 'so, thus' and *cómo* 'as, how'), with a finite clause, with an adjective, or with nothing at all. Olbertz concludes that, in view of the complexity of past-participial constructions—I would say, in view of their morphological ambiguity—an analyst will often have to apply more than one syntactic test, plugging in different parts of speech, to find out the nature of each construction.

6.5. ALLOMORPHY IN PAST PARTICIPLES

In *Allomorphy in Inflexion*, Carstairs devises an inflectional parsimony hypothesis (31) to explain the usual absence of more than one morphological realization for a given slot: each stem selects only one such realization, unless different realizations are associated with some semantic or stylistic distinction. This hypothesis provides a way to understand certain morphological distinctions that have arisen in certain Romance languages.

Thus, in Italian, speakers make a distinction between pure past-participial usage and adjectival usage for two competing past participles of *vedere* 'see': *è veduto* 'he is (being) seen' contrasts with *è ben visto* 'he is well regarded.' Here the arrhizotonic by-form *veduto* has past-participial force, while the

---

[5] Adj. *molten* refers only to materials like metal or rock that have very high boiling points; adj. *stricken* refers to the (usually sudden) onset of serious illness.

rhizotonic by-form *visto* has adjectival force.[6] In Spanish and Portuguese, speakers make a similar distinction not merely in the form of the past participle or adjective but also in the choice between *ser* and *estar* 'be.' Thus, Sp. *es despertado* 'he is being awoken' contrasts with *està despierto* 'he is awake' (and with *es despierto* 'he is clever [i.e. alert]'); Ptg. *foi corrompido* 'he was corrupted' contrasts with *estava corrupto* 'he was corrupt.' Again, at least in such constructions, the arrhizotonic form has past-participial force while the rhizotonic form has adjectival force (Posner, 180).

Regrettably, however enlightening these observations may turn out to be for synchronic analysis of a given tongue, they appear to shed little light on changes in speakers' morphological preferences through time. Carstairs's hypothesis remains at best only implicitly diachronic.

6.6. DOES IRREGULARITY SURVIVE ONLY IN COMMON VERBS?

In *Morphology*, Bybee suggests, using the verb "tend" with suitable caution, that, in any language, certain high-frequency anomalous verb forms heard and said early and often by speakers will tend to stand a better chance of lasting through the generations: "Only the relatively more frequent items tend to be learned by rote, and as a consequence irregularities will be maintained only in the relatively more frequent lexical items or forms of a paradigm" (6–7).

Supplying concrete instances in "Evidence for varying lexical strength," §5.6 of *Morphology*, she observes that reflexes of OEngl. ablauting verbs that have acquired preterits in *-ed* tend to occur far less often than do verbs that still display ablaut. As Bybee puts it, "The proposal that infrequently used forms fade accounts for the tendency to regularize infrequent irregular forms, for an irregular form that is not sufficiently reinforced will be replaced by a regular formation" (119). Unfortunately for my purposes, Bybee leaves past participles outside her analysis. However, the observation that speakers keep anomalous verb forms alive through high frequency ought to apply to that principal part as well.

Does low frequency alone account for leveling? The evidence submitted looks circumstantial, although to be sure a string of circumstantial exhibits will result in conviction often enough. Perhaps the barely numerate should be wary of lexical quantification. At any rate, Engl. *beat* is described as a "regularized strong verb," despite making its preterit with a zero ending rather than *-ed* (and making its past participle with *-en*). Bybee's own data show that *beat* outscores strong-verb *blow* by 66 to 52 in the present tense. In the past, *beat* is tied with *blew* at 12; unfortunately, p.p.s *beaten* and *blown* do not figure in Bybee's analysis. With the single exception of that verb—which suggests that *beat* might be irregular after all, if in a different way from its

---

[6] In this section, Posner does not mention that the It. p.p. by-form *visto* may also be used in a purely verbal sense, in e.g. *non ho visto niente* 'I have seen nothing.'

OEngl. instar *bēatan bēot(on) bēaten*—the least common principal part of a strong verb in each of the three classes outscores the most common principal part of a regularized verb in that class.

How do like Bybee's findings apply to Romance languages? In four books titled *Frequency Dictionary* for Spanish (1964), Romanian (1965), French (1970), and Italian (1973), Julliand et alii have listed lexical items by frequency of occurrence for each of the four languages (see Table 6–1). Numbers after each entry mark its rank in the 500 most common lexical items by frequency of occurrence in each language.

Table 6–1

Irregular Past Participles in Four Romance Languages

competes with regularized by-form

Romanian		Italian		French		Spanish	
fost	4	stato	8	été	4	dicho	29
vrut	27	fatto	22	eu	23	hecho	32
ştiut	48	detto	29	fait	38	visto	39
spus	52	visto#	40	dit	39	puesto	107
zis	56	venuto	51	su	36	escrito	170
rămâns	87	preso	111	venu	66	muerto	257
pus	89	messo	128	dû	75	abierto	340
adus	121	rimasto	167	pris	95	nato	395
înţeles	130	vissuto	209	tenu	115		
dus	145	giunto	217	mis	126		
ajuns	158	aperto	251	connu	137		
mers	205	morto	256	compris	154		
răspuns	221	reso	269	paru	180		
scos	264	apparso	270	vécu	184		
închis	291	chiesto	271	devenu	191		
prins	315	corso	280	permis	208		
deschis	355	scritto	291	reçu	262		
scris	359	risposto	297	suivi	269		
râs	371	chiuso	304	écrit	284		
trimis	397	nato	309	lu	320		
ales	444	perso#	359	ouvert	333		
atins	461	riso	364	offert	366		
cuprins	491	condotto	381	produit	399		
		letto	421	mort	426		
		sceso	445	découvert	487		
		raccolto	472	souffert	493		

As for methodology: from the 500 most common items for each, I have ignored all parts of speech but infinitives, used in those works to stand for all forms of a verb. Among the infinitives, I have chosen only those with irregular past participles. Some prefixed verbs and some (like It. *esistere* 'exist') that sound too high-flown have been left out of Table 6–1. A Rom. past participle not encountered before is *cuprins* 'contained, included' (infin. *cuprinde* < COMPREHENDERE).

In view of the data in Table 6–1, Bybee's conclusion appears generally valid, if not invariably so: "The correlation of irregularity with high frequency can be documented in almost any language" (119). To this conclusion one need add only its converse: low frequency of use tends to promote but cannot guarantee the leveling of morphological variation.

As noted in Table 5–3, three of the four languages here have straight reflexes of FACTU 'done/made,' DICTU 'said,' PR(EH)ĒNSU 'grabbed,' SCRĪPTU 'written,' and MORTUU 'died.' Besides confirming that few past-participial irregularities in Romance are traceable all the way back to Latin, Table 6–1 reveals that not a single irregularity listed is shared by all four languages today. The chart also highlights the scarcity in Spanish of irregular past participles; even both 'be' verbs have regular ones in *estado* and *sido*.

Throughout the history of past participles in CL and Romance, irregularity has likewise tended to remain in the highest-frequency verbs while being leveled in lower-frequency ones. Yet some recent work has called into question the traditional bases of the analogical processes that I have invoked to account for generally observable leveling of p.p. types in Romance in contrast to Latin. It is time to return to the mother language.

6.7. REGULARITY IN LATIN VERB MORPHOLOGY

In *Morphology by Itself*, Aronoff offers another view of regularity within the Latin verb system. Two types had the same theme vowel throughout. A regular 1st-conj. verb like ARMŌ 'arm' had three stems: ARM-Ā for the infectum, ARM-Ā-U for the finite perfectum, and ARM-Ā-T for the "third form," used inter alia for forming past participles. A regular 4th-conj. verb like AUDIŌ 'hear' also had three stems: AUD-Ī for the infectum, AUD-Ī-U for the finite perfectum, and AUD-Ī-T for the third form.

For almost all 2nd-conj. verbs, though, Aronoff notes that the theme vowel Ē was present only in the infectum stem; in the finite perfectum, such verbs had U as a theme vowel, while in the third form they had either -I-T or vowel-less -T. Thus, theme vowels varied by stem in this class.[7]

---

[7] I leave out "regular" 2nd-conj. verbs, for none survived as such into Romance; their perfects and past participles were all remade. I must take issue with Aronoff's decision to regard such verbs as built not from e.g. FLĒ- but from FL-Ē-. The Ē in such verbs cannot be a theme vowel, says Aronoff, because Latin verb roots otherwise are never less than a syllable in length: "If we agree that the ẽ of these five verbs is indeed part of their lexical form, then they are not really second-declension [viz., -conjugation] verbs at all, let alone regular" (48). Aronoff has overlooked verbs like more or less 1st-conj. STĀRE 'stand; stay' (p.p. STĂTU) and DARE

Verbs grouped under the 3rd conjugation could have E or I as a theme vowel, or they could lack any theme vowel; they could have nasal marking, reduplication, or vowel lengthening in the infectum stem, or they could have none of those features. As if that were not enough to illustrate the unpredictability of such verbs, they formed their finite perfectum stems and third-form stems in various ways. All that 3rd-conj. verbs had in common is the selection of endings in the infectum, together with the absence of a theme vowel in the perfectum.[8] As in most verbs from the 2nd conjugation, then, theme vowels (including zero) varied according to stem for 3rd-conj. verbs.

From these data, Aronoff decides that the characteristic 1st-conj. Ā and 4th-conj. Ī theme vowels, and theme vowels in general, were firmly rooted only in the infectum stem. In trying to explain the great variety of 3rd-conj. stems, Aronoff notes that some perfectum stems were based not on the verb root but on the present stem minus the theme vowel. Verbs like FRANGŌ 'shatter,' PINGŌ 'paint,' and JUNGŌ 'join' all had nasal infixes in infectum forms. However, the first had a fully non-nasal perfectum, the second had a nasal perfect but a non-nasal past participle, and the third had a fully nasal perfectum. How to explain this variation? Aronoff makes the following morphological suggestion: "Build nonpresent stems that retain the nasal on the present stem, while those without the nasal would be built on the lexical representation....Normally, this sound form is specified by a constant function across lexemes for a given realization rule, but we see here that this function may be specified lexically in some instances" (50–51).

According to this analysis, between Latin and Romance speakers steadily tended to use the infectum stem as the basis for perfectum forms. In effect, that stem often became the lexical representation, as indicated by the emergence of Fr. *peint* and It./OSp. *pinto* 'painted' as against Latin non-nasal PĪCTU 'idem.' Within a lexeme-based framework, then, between Latin and Romance speakers tended increasingly to make the stems of lexical representations for past participles and preterits identical to present stems, especially west of Italy. Thus, speakers everywhere blurred the old distinction between infectum and perfectum, with a great many verbs coming to have one stem throughout. In far eastern Romance, by contrast, speakers also tended to make many lexical representations for (masc.sg.) past participles

---

'give' (p.p. DĀTU), along with regular 1st-conj. FLĀRE 'blow' (p.p. FLĀTU) and NĀRE 'swim' (no p.p.; what would have been the regular form, NĀTU, meant 'born'). Aronoff has also overlooked more or less 4th-conj. ĪRE 'go' (p.p. ĬTU) and QUĪRE 'be able' (p.p. QUĬTU), along with regular 4th-conj. SCĪRE 'know' (p.p. SCĬTU). These verbs all have roots of less than one syllable.

[8] In saying that 2nd- and 3rd-conj. verbs "never have a theme vowel except in the present stem" (50), Aronoff presumably means that they show no consistent pattern throughout the conjugation, rather than that theme vowels never appear in 3rd-conj. verbs. Otherwise, Aronoff's own data on p. 49 (Table 2.11), which include perfect stems like CREPU- 'rattled,' APERU- 'opened,' and CUPĪV- 'desired,' along with their p.p. stems CREPIT-, APERT-, and CUPĪT-, would remain inexplicable.

identical to those for sigmatic preterit stems, so that the morphological opposition between infectum and perfectum was to some degree maintained.

Aronoff goes on to propose that, for all conjugations, the default method of building finite perfectum stems would be to suffix U to the present stem; the default method of building third stems would be to suffix T to the same stem. Working "almost without exception" for 1st-conj. verbs and some two-thirds of 4th-conj. verbs, Aronoff's default form for the perfectum also helps to explain the spread of -Uī perfects in Late Latin, when the same rules could still have held true. The default form does little to explain the concurrent spread of -Sī pfs. or of -SU p.p.s., encountered far more often in LL than in CL.

What about the spread of -ŪTU p.p.s in Late Latin or Proto-Romance? At first it might seem that, however valid for the classical tongue, Aronoff's default method for past participles would have been replaced by that time. However, by combining the U and T default forms, one might theoretically be able to account for the spread of forms in -ŪTU, especially for verbs that lacked that principal part or had suppletion under the classical standard. In choosing a past participle for BIBERE 'drink,' for example, LL speakers rejected suppletive PŌTU in favor of rhizotonic thematic BIBITU. That they chose BIBITU, rather than the *BIPTU with no theme vowel predicted under Aronoff's CL schema for 3rd-conj. verbs, suggests that the default p.p. ending became -ĪTU in at least some provincial variants of Late Latin. Surviving past participles on Sardinia and in southern Italy (Luca. *bippete*, Neap. *víppeto* 'drunk') seem to offer proof of such a shift. So do relic nouns like Fr. *pente* 'slope' < *PENDITA, *fente* 'slit' < *FINDITA, and indeed OFr. *boite* 'a drink' < BIBITA. Nonetheless, in line with my combination of Aronoff's assumed default forms, most Romance speakers later rejected reflexes of BIBITU and preferred an arrhizotonic resembling Rom. *băut*, It. *bevuto*, and OSp. *bevudo*.

Both of Aronoff's default methods entail suffixation of the infectum stem. In Late Latin, the spread of suffixation in [w] or [u] promoted sharper marking within the perfectum but meant that many 2nd-conj. and 3rd-conj. verbs— both types increasingly built on the same (infectum) stem—ended up with a contrast between theme vowels in the two aspects. Likewise, the LL spread of suffixation in [s] promoted sharper marking within the perfectum but meant that many 2nd- and 3rd-conj. verbs ended up with a contrast between asigmatic and sigmatic marking in the two aspects, as seen most notably in Romanian today. In both types of verbs, perfects (later preterits) and past participles became more like one another if less like their infinitival, present-tense, or imperfect forms. Meanwhile, more verbs like SONĀRE 'ring,' SENTĪRE 'feel,' FUGERE 'flee,' and CAPERE 'take' moved wholly into line with predominant 1st- and 4th-conj. patterns, for they came to display the same theme vowel throughout and no marking anywhere in [s] or [w]/[u], and still less in reflexes of -(I)TU. Especially in Italian, though, greater allomorphy persisted: many 2nd- and 3rd-conj. verbs still have an unmarked present that contrasts with a sigmatic preterit (in 1sg., 3sg., and 3pl.) that in turn contrasts with a tautic athematic past participle.

Another theoretical contribution made by Aronoff provides a means to depict steadily increasing isomorphism within French past participles. I wish to reconsider Aronoff's schematic representation of the morphology of past participles in Latin (36). Somewhat simplified, it reads:

$$\{ \text{[root or derived verb stem]} + \text{(theme vowel)} + \text{T]} + \text{[1st-/2nd-decl. case]} \begin{array}{l} \text{number} \\ \text{gender} \end{array} \}$$

In this schema, past participles are built of the stem plus an optional theme vowel, plus T (the dental suffix realized usually as [t], sometimes as [s]), plus 1st- or 2nd-decl. marking for number, case, and gender.

To adapt Aronoff's schema to living languages, conservative varieties of Romance like Italian or Spanish still have three classes if not declensions of adjectives and nouns. They have kept almost all of the Latin schema, including the dental suffix:

$$\{ \text{[root or derived verb stem]} + \text{(theme vowel)} + \text{T]} + \text{[1/2 class} \begin{array}{l} \text{number} \\ \text{gender} \end{array} \}$$

For regular past participles in -é, -I, or -u used by speakers of French today, by contrast, that representation would have to be truncated further and would come out looking like this:

$$\{ \text{[root or derived verb stem]} + \text{[theme vowel]} \}$$

Aronoff's schema for Latin thus makes it possible to trace in another way the reduction to zero in gender and number marking outlined in §4.4.12. In Carstairs's terms, French would have arrived at what he terms Deviation IV from the ideal of a one-to-one match between meaning and form: as the language has already reached substantial homonymy within most inflectional paradigms for verbs (all sg. and 3pl. being pronounced the same for 1st-conj. verbs in the pres.indic./pres.subj. and for all verbs in the impf.indic.), so French has achieved homonymy within regular past participles by neutralizing gender and number marking altogether.[9] Does such a fate lie in store for past participles in other Romance languages? If so, how could it come about?

---

[9] Would one be justified in regarding past participles as an "inflectional paradigm"? Parallels between the erosion of once-distinct endings on finite verbs and on past participles appear so striking that, for the nonce, I so regard them.

6.8. GENERALIZATION OF IRREGULAR FORMS

After noting in "Irregularity as a Determinant of Morphological Change" that Italian present-tense verbs of the 1st conjugation are relatively invariable, Maiden deals with several alternations that exist in present-tense verbs of the 2nd and 3rd conjugations as well as some in the 4th conjugation: stems may have different vowels in rhizotones from those in arrhizotones; stem-final consonants may be palatalized or not. Maiden's contention that forms originally perceived as irregular may in fact trigger morphological realignments would be borne out by the spread of palatal consonants to It. past-participial forms ending in -*uto*, giving e.g. *cresciuto* 'grown' and *piaciuto* 'pleased' rather than the **crescuto* and **piacuto* that one would expect before a back vowel. The contention would also be borne out by the spread of diphthongs [jɛ] and [wɔ]—supposed to affect only the stem vowels [ɛ] and [ɔ] when stressed in an open syllable—to past participles like *vietato* 'forbidden' and optionally *suonato* 'rung' (§3.5.1).

In reviewing instances of morphological leveling across fifteen hundred years or more, I have concentrated on preterits, past participles, and infinitives. All three have indeed grown more predictable. Not all verb forms have. Apophonous outcomes for present-tense verb forms in Romance, where rhizotonic and arrhizotonic forms differ far more than they did in Latin, would constitute the primary invalidation of the thesis that verbs have tended to acquire the same stem throughout. (The secondary invalidation would be the emergence of double-stemmed preterits in Italian and Old French.) Consequently, I have stayed away from the first type and surveyed the second only in passing.[10]

Maiden goes on to observe that native speakers of Romance languages have had to deal with a typologically mixed system of inflections. What effect has this feature had on speakers' drive toward morphological transparency in past participles? As always, complexity increases upon closer examination: "The universal predisposition to symmetrical form-meaning matching (instantiated through the mechanism of analogical leveling of alternation) encounters a major obstacle in certain morphological paradigms, where violations of the universal principle are especially prominent" (308–9). According to Maiden, speakers have resorted to a number of strategies intended to assign different and conflicting patterns to different grammatical functions. Of these strategies, the one that concerns me here is that of associating invariance with the 1st conjugation and variance with the other two or three conjugations.

---

[10] In French, the number of present-tense verbs displaying allomorphy caused by apophony has diminished markedly since the Middle Ages, because of leveling either on the rhizotonic stem (as in *nous aimons* ≠ OFr. *amons*) or on the arrhizotonic one (as in *je trouve* ≠ OFr. *truef*). Even now, the number of such verbs stands far higher than in Latin.

Maiden's point deserves to be carried further. For past participles, I propose that variance within and across non-1st-conj. verbs may end up as invariance.

Such a development could have begun in the observed hesitation between -*uto* and -*ito* past participles for some verbs in Old Italian (§3.5.7) and in similar hesitation between -*udo* and -*ido* past participles for some in Old Spanish. In standard Italian, both types have survived in the modern distribution. In other parts of ROMANIA—aside from high-frequency unproductive survivals—non-1st-conj. verbs have often acquired a default arrhizotonic type of past participle. At times, this default type reflects the one that used to end in -ĪTU: -*ido* in Spanish and Portuguese, -*ieu* in Upper Engadin, -*iu* in Surselvan. At times, this default type comes down from the one that used to end in -ŪTU: -*utu* in Neapolitan and Sicilian, -*ut* in Lucanian. It remains unexplained why, for that default type, speakers should have chosen a reflex of -ĪTU across most of Iberia but a reflex of -ŪTU in parts of Switzerland and across southern Italy. An answer remains elusive.

Maiden's observation might however be expanded to account for the spread of sigmatic marking on past participles toward the east of ROMANIA. I would add the proviso that, in Romanian, both 1st-conj. and 4th-conj. verbs would have to be considered invariant. Past participles for certain verbs of the 2nd and 3rd conjugations would hence stand at variance from the 1st/4th-conj. "standard"—and from the 2nd-/3rd-conj. p.p. "standard" in -*ut*—but, by acquiring sigmatic marking in e.g. Rom. *dus* 'taken away,' *scris* 'written,' *zis* 'said,' such verbs might be evolving toward something of a new p.p. standard on their own. Meanwhile, a dwindling number of 2nd- and 3rd-conj. verbs still have past participles in reinforced [t] like *rupt* 'torn' or *frânt* 'broken.' The fairly recent remodeling of *fapt* as *făcut* 'done/made' and of *unt* as *uns* 'oiled' indicates two morphological pathways that other p.p. forms in [pt] or [nt] may follow later on.

Likewise, one could apply to Occitan and Catalan the notion of verb variance contrasting with verb invariance. If 1st-conj. and 4th-conj. verbs are regarded as invariant by stem (for arrhizotonic forms), such verbs would contrast with variant-stem verbs in the 2nd and 3rd conjugations. I thus seem to have found a theoretical rationale for the spread of -*gut* p.p.s for most 2nd- and 3rd-conj. verbs in those two tongues. A similar explanation might apply to 2nd- and 3rd-conj. verbs with default-form -ĪTU past participles in Sardinian and in dialects across southern Italy.

It seems likely, in the light of Maiden's observations, that in both western Romance and far eastern Romance "concrete and statistically predominant alternation patterns [have been] analogically generalized" (310), certainly for present-tense verbs. For past participles, though, the two areas differ. Speakers in western Romance have made leveling through arrhizotonicity more and more the norm; speakers in the far eastern Romance have largely limited such leveling to reflexes of -ĀRE and -ĪRE verbs while tending to make the past-tense system sigmatic for reflexes of -ĒRE and ´-ERE verbs. Only speakers of standard Italian, with their abiding closeness to Latin—much less plain north and south of Tuscany—have retained a distribution of past-participial types that approximates the classical one.

6.9. CONCLUSION

Toward the end of Chapter 2, I wondered whether analogies in reshaping verbs could be knowable, or even made to seem predictable; I decided that they might well be, after the fact. In vernaculars before literary standards were established, competition between two or more past-participial by-forms suggests that speakers back then employed a wealth of morphological analogies, as speakers of various dialects still do. Speakers and littérateurs made their choices unconsciously or consciously, without benefit of logic or reason; however much they may have claimed otherwise, rationality almost always served as a poor guide to a language spoken by people rather than by elaborate machines. A few examples should make the point. If it is hardly surprising that a given verb should join the ever-expanding 1st conjugation, giving Rom. *plouat* 'rained' and Fr. *tissé* 'woven,' why should metaplasm have affected reflexes of PLUERE and TEXERE when and where it did? They joined the 1st conjugation nowhere else.[11]

To date, no one taking a theoretical approach to morphology has found credible answers to the following questions. First, why should a certain past-participial type should have won out where it did or when it did for each Latin verb that lived on? Second, why should the morphological pathways trodden by speakers of each daughter language have diverged as they did? Third, why should the resultant retentions or reshapings have produced the melange of past-participial patterns visible today across ROMANIA?

Nor, except to a slight degree for the third question, do I lay claim to having discovered a new world in *Past Participles from Latin to Romance*. I have charted a sea. I cannot tell how the globe came into being, or how its hollows filled with water, or how its coastlines may shrink or swell, rise or fall, for as long as Romance shall last.

---

[11] For another such reshaping, already mentioned in Table 4-4, compare ModFr. *toussé* 'coughed' ≠ OFr. *toussi* with its opposite numbers in Rom. *tușit*, It. *tossito*, Cat. *tossit*, Sp. *tosido*, and Ptg. *tossido*. At least for major languages, all of extra-Gallic ROMANIA continues regular 4th-conj. TUSSĪTU. To explain why this metaplasm took place in French alone, one need merely acquire flawless hindsight (see §2.15.11).

Appendix 1

Stems for Principal Parts of Verbs in Classical Latin and Late Latin

Numbers and letters shown here apply to verbs on the following pages

	Type	Identifying Morphology
Arrhizotonic throughout:	**1** =	-ĀRE type (ERRĀRE, ERĀVĪ, ERRĀTU)
	2 =	"regular" -ĒRE type (FLĒRE, FLĒVĪ, FLĒTU)
	4 =	-ĪRE type (DORMĪRE, DORMĪVĪ, DORMĪTU)
Rhizotonic infecta:	**3** =	-ĔRE type (DĪCŌ, DĪCERE)
	3I =	type 3, with -i- insert in some forms (CAPIŌ, CAPERE)
Other thematic perfecta:	**5** =	past participle in atonic -ĬTU (HABĬTU)
	6 =	perfect / preterit in atonic -UĪ (HABUĪ) or past participle in tonic -ŪTU (BATTŪTU)
Athematic perfecta:	**7** =	reduplicative perfect later preterit (DEDĪ)
	8 =	sigmatic perfect/preterit (CESSĪ) or p.p. (CESSU)
	9 =	tautic athematic past participle (APERTU, FACTU)

N = preconsonantal nasal consonant from present or perfect stem appearing in LL p.p.

Verb forms unmarked by number have conspicuous irregularities,
as in pf. FĒCĪ as against pres. FACIŌ 'do/make'
( ) = archaic

Examples have at least two reflexes in Romance; some verbs appear more than once

Language key: Romanian; Italian; French; Occitan; Catalan; Spanish; Portuguese

UNPOPULAR TYPES OF PAST PARTICIPLES IN LATE LATIN AND PROTO-ROMANCE

Present Infinitive Active	Perfect	Past Participle	LL/PR Past Participle (+ syllabic augment)	

A. CL verbs lacking a past participle

(i) New p.p. in -ĀTU. *Pan-Romance*

'be'	ESSE *LL* *ESSERE 3	FUĪ	—	*STATU 1 [borrowed]	IFCS
'snow'	NINGUERE 3	NĪNXĪ 8	—	*NIVICATU 1 *NIVATU 1	IF CS
'shake'	TREMERE 3	TREMUĪ 6	—	*TREM(UL)ATU 1	RIFCS

(ii) New p.p. in -ĪTU. *Pan-Romance*

'boil'	FERVĒRE 2/ FERVERE 3	FERBUĪ 6/ FERVĪ	—	*FERVITU 4	SP
'hit'	FERĪRE 4	—	—	*FERITU 4	RICS
'bloom'	FLŌRĒRE 2 *LL* FŁORĪRE 4	FLŌRUĪ 6	—	*FLORITU 4	RIFCS
'shine'	LŪCĒRE 2	LŪXĪ 8	—	*LUCITU 4	FCS
'wither'	MARCĒRE 2	—	—	*MARCITU 4	I (F)(C)
'stink'	PŪTĒRE 2	PŪTUĪ 6	—	*PUTITU 4	RSP
'rot'	PUTRĒRE 2	—	—	*PUTRITU 4	IFCS

(iii) New p.p. in -ŪTU. *Popular beyond Castile, where -ĪTU types prevail*

'drink'	BIBERE 3	BIBĪ 7	—	*BIBUTU 6	RIFC
'be hot'	CALĒRE 2	CALUĪ 6	—	*CALUTU 6	FC
'rain'	PLUERE 3	PLUIT 6 PLUVIT	—	*PLUVUTU 6	IFC

	Infinitive	Perfect	Past Participle	LL/PR Past Participle	
'rain'	PLUERE 3	PLUIT 6 PLUVIT	—	*PLUVUTU 6	IFC
'be able'	POSSE *LL* *POTERE 2	POTUĪ 6	—	*POTUTU 6	RIFC
'taste, know'	SAPERE 3	SAPĪVĪ 4/ SAPUI 6	—	*SAPUTU 6	IFC
'fear'	TIMĒRE 2	TIMUĪ 6	—	*TIMUTU 6	RIC
'want'	VELLE *LL* *VOLERE 2	VOLUĪ 6	—	*VOLUTU 6	RIFC

B. Stems of new 1st-conj. verbs based on CL past participle

(i) (Semi-)deponents made active. *Pan-Romance*

'dare'	AUDĒRE 2	AUSU 8	*idem*	*AUSATU	IFCSP
'forget'	OBLIVĪSCĪ 3	OBLĪTU 9	*idem*	*OBLITATU	RF(I)OCSP
'protect'	TUĒRĪ 2	TŪTU 9	*idem*	*TUTATU	FOC
'use'	UTĪ 3	ŪSU 8	*idem*	*USATU	IFCSP

(ii) Nondeponents: new stem based on old tautic p.p. *Generally western*

'fart'	PĒDERE 3	PEPEDĪ 7	PĒDITU 5	*PEDITATU	FCS
'paint'	PINGERE 3	PĪNXĪ 8	PICTU 9	*PI(N)CTATU	RCS
'rest'	QUIĒSCERE 3	QUIĒVĪ 2	QUIĒTU 9	*QUETATU	ICS
'vow'	VOVĒRE 2	VŌVĪ 7	VŌTU 9	*VOTATU	IF

(iii) Nondeponents: new stem based on old sigmatic p.p. *Generally western*

'crush'	FRENDERE 3	—	FRĒ(N)SU 8	*FRESATU	FO
'harm'	LÆDERE 3	LÆSĪ 8	LÆSU 8	*LESATU	FSP
'bite'	MORDĒRE 2	MOMORDĪ 7	MORSU 8	*MORSICATU 1+	RC
'shake'	QUATERE 3I	QUASSĪ 8	QUASSU 8	*QUASSATU *QUASSICATU	IFCS CS
'pledge'	SPONDĒRE 2	SPOPONDĪ 7	SPŌNSU 8	*SPONSATU	IFCS
'shear'	TONDĒRE 2	TOTONDĪ 7	TŌNSU 8	*TOSATU 1	IS

	Infinitive	Perfect	Past Participle	LL/PR Past Participle

C. Regularized past-participial formation

(i) 1st conjugation: CL p.p.s in -ĬTU, new ones in -ĀTU. *Pan-Romance*

'rattle'	CREPĀRE 1	CREPUĪ 6	CREPITU 5	*CREPATU 1	R I F O S
'recline'	CUBĀRE 1	CUBUĪ 6	CUBITU 5	*CUBATU 1	I F C
'tame'	DOMĀRE 1	DOMUĪ 6	DOMITU 5	*DOMATU 1	I (F)
'rub'	FRICĀRE 1	FRICUĪ 6	FRICTU 9/ FRĪCĀTU 1	FRICATU 1	R I F C S
'lend'	PRÆSTĀRE 1	PRÆSTITĪ 7	PRÆSTITU 5	*PRESTATU 1	I F C S
'cut, saw'	SECĀRE 1	SECUĪ 6	SECTU 9	*SECATU 1	I F C S
'ring'	SONĀRE 1	SONUĪ 6	SONITU 5	*SONATU 1	R I F C S
'thunder'	TONĀRE 1	TONUĪ 6	TONITU 5	*T(R)ONATU 1	R I F C S
'forbid'	VETĀRE 1	VETUĪ 6	VETITU 5	*VETATU 1	I (F) C S

(ii) 4th conjugation: CL p.p.s in -TU or -ĬTU, new infectum-based ones in -ĪTU. *Pan-Romance*

'go out'	EXĪRE 4	EXĪVĪ 4	EXITU 5	*EXITU 4	R I C (S)
'stuff'	FARCĪRE 4	FARSĪ 8	FARTU 9	*FARCITU 4	I F C
'jump'	SALĪRE 4	SALUĪ 6	SALTU 9	*SALITU 4	R I F C
'mend'	SARCĪRE 4	SARSĪ 8	SARTU 9	*SARCITU 4	I O C
'bury'	SEPELĪRE 4	SEPELĪVĪ 4	SEPULTU 9	*(IN)SEPELITU 4	I F O (S)
'come'	VENĪRE 4	VĒNĪ	VENTU 9	*VENITU 4	R S P
				*VENUTU 6	I F O C

(iii) New members of 4th conjugation: CL p.p.s mostly in -TU or -ĬTU, new infectum-based ones in -ĪTU. *Pan-Romance, especially across Iberia*

(a) *From 2nd conjugation*

'enjoy'	GAUDĒRE 2	GĀVĪSU 4+8	*idem*	*GAUDITU 4	F O
'swallow'	SORBĒRE 2	SORBUĪ 6	SORBITU 5	*SORBITU 4	R I (C) S P

	Infinitive	Perfect	Past Participle	LL/PR Past Participle	

(b) From 3rd conjugation

'pluck'	CARPERE 3	CARPSĪ 8	CARPTU 9	*CARPITU 4	I(F)COS
'gather'	COLLIGERE 3	COLLĒGĪ	COLLĒCTU 9	*COLLITU 4	FCS
'shape'	FINGERE 3	FĪNXĪ 8	FICTU 9	*FINGITU 4	CS
'fry'	FRĪGERE 3	FRĪXĪ 8	FRĪCTU 9	*FRIGITU 4	CSP
'choose, read'	LEGERE 3	LĒGĪ	LĒCTU 9	*LEGITU 4	CS
'rule'	REGERE 3	RĒXĪ 8	RĒCTU 9	*REGITU 4	FCS
'spring up'	SURGERE 3	SURRĒXĪ 8	SURRĒCTU 9	*SURGITU 4	FCS
'dye'	TINGERE 3	TĪNXĪ 8	TĪNCTU 9	*TINGITU 4	CSP

(c) From 3rd-conjugation i-stems

'take'	CAPERE 3I	CĒPĪ	CAPTU 9	*CAPITU 4	IS
'flee'	FUGERE 3I LL FUGĪRE 4	FŪGĪ	FUGITU 5	*FUGITU 4	RIFCSP
'grab'	RAPERE 3I	RAPUĪ 6	RAPTU 9	*RAPITU 4	RIF

(d) Deponents remade into the 4th conjugation

'die'	MORĪ	MORTUU	idem	*MORITU 4	RP
'snarl'	RINGĪ	RI(N)CTU	idem	*RINGITU 4	CSP

D. Other rhizotonic thematics replaced by arrhizotonics

(i) 2nd conjugation, one stem throughout: CL pfs. in -UĪ, p.p.s in -ĪTU; most new p.p.s in -ŪTU. *Popular beyond Castile, where -ĪTU types prevail*

'owe'	DĒBĒRE 2	DĒBUĪ 6	DĒBITU 5	*DEBUTU 6	IFC
'hurt'	DOLĒRE 2	DOLUĪ 6	DOLITU 5	*DOLUTU 6	RIFC
'have'	HABĒRE 2	HABUĪ 6	HABITU 5	*HABUTU 6	RIFOC
'lie, rest'	JACĒRE 2	JACUĪ 6	JACITU 5	*JACUTU 6	RIFC

	Infinitive	Perfect	Past Participle	LL/PR Past Participle	
'earn'	MERĒRE 2	MERUĪ 6	MERITU 5	*MERITATU 1	I F
'harm'	NOCĒRE 2	NOCUĪ 6	NOCITU 5	*NOCUTU 6	I (F)C
'appear'	PĀRĒRE 2	PĀRUĪ 6	PĀRITU 5	*PARUTU 6	R (I)F C
'please'	PLACĒRE 2	PLACUĪ 6	PLACITU 5	*PLACUTU 6	R I F C
'be silent'	TACĒRE 2	TACUĪ 6	TACITU 5	*TACUTU 6	R I F
'be worth'	VALĒRE 2	VALUĪ 6	VALITU 5	*VALUTU 6	(I)F C

(ii) 3rd conjugation: CL pfs. of various kinds, p.p.s in -ĬTU; most new p.p.s in -ŪTU. *Popular beyond Castile, where -ĪTU types prevail*

	Infinitive	Perfect	Past Participle	LL/PR Past Participle	
'hide'	ABSCONDERE 3	ABSCONDĪ/ ABSCONDIDĪ 7	ABSCONDITU 5	*(IN)ABSCOSU 8 *ABSCONDITU 4 *ABSCONDUTU 6	R I C S (F)(P)
'know'	COGNOSCERE 3	COGNŌVĪ	COGNITU 5	*COGNOSCUTU 6 *COGNOVUTU 6	R I F C
'believe'	CRĒDERE 3	CRĒDIDĪ 7	CRĒDITU 5	*CREDUTU 6	R I F C
'moan'	GEMERE 3	GEMUĪ 6	GEMITU 5	*GEMUTU 6 *GEMITU 4	R I F C S P
'lose'	PERDERE 3	PERDIDĪ 7	PERDITU 5	*PERDUTU 6	R I F C
'sell'	VENDERE 3	VENDIDĪ 7	VENDITU 5	*VENDUTU 6	R I F C

(iii) Verbs with "regular" 2nd-conj. perfecta: new p.p.s from infectum or finite perfectum stems. *Generally eastern*

	Infinitive	Perfect	Past Participle	LL/PR Past Participle	
'grow'	CRĒSCERE 2	CRĒVĪ 2	CRĒTU 2	*CREVUTU *CRESCUTU	F O R I C
'sift'	CERNERE 3	CRĒVĪ 2	CRĒTU 2	*CERNUTU	R C
'fill'	IMPLĒRE 2	IMPLĒVĪ 2	IMPLĒTU 2	*IMPLITU *IMPLUTU	I F O S P R I

	Infinitive	Perfect	Past Participle	LL/PR Past Participle

E. Rhizotonic athematics replaced by arrhizotonics

(i) 2nd or 3rd conjugation, with tautic athematic p.p.s

(a) New p.p.s in -ŪTU, usually based on infectum stem. *Popular beyond Castile, where* -ĪTU *types prevail*

'take'	CAPERE 3I	CĒPĪ	CAPTU 9	*CAPUTU	(F)C
'receive'	RECIPERE 3I	RECĒPĪ	RECEPTU 9	*RECIPUTU 6	I F C
'break'	RUMPERE 3	RŪPĪ	RUPTU 9	*RUMPUTU 6	F C
'hold'	TENĒRE 2	TENUĪ 6	TENTU 9	*TENUTU 6	R I F C (S)
'weave'	TEXERE 3	TEXUĪ 6	TEXTU 9	*TEXUTU 6 *TEXITU 4	R I C S P
'win'	VINCERE 3	VĪCĪ	VICTU 9	*VINCUTU 6N	F C (S)
'live'	VĪVERE 3	VĪXĪ 8	VĪCTU 9	*VIXUTU 8+6	I F C

(b) New p.p.s in -ĀTU for diminutivized 1st-conj. reflexes. *Unpredictable*

'mingle'	MISCĒRE 2	MISCUĪ 6	MIXTU 9	*MISCULATU 1	R I F C S P
'scorch'	ŪRERE 3	USSĪ 8	USTU 8+9	*USTULATU 1	(F)O

(ii) Direct-suffixation perfecta in CL; new infectum-based p.p.s in -ŪTU. *Popular east of Castile, where* -ĪTU *forms prevail*

'move'	MOVĒRE 2	MŌVĪ	MŌTU 9	*MOVUTU 6	F C (P)
'be born'	(G)NASCĪ LL *NASCERE 3	(G)NĀTU	*idem*	*NASCUTU 6	R I
'feed, keep'	PASCERE 3	PĀVĪ	PĀSTU 9	*PASCUTU 6	R I O

	Infinitive	Perfect	Past Participle	LL/PR Past Participle

F. Sigmatics remade arrhizotonically

(i) With new p.p.s in -ĀTU matching 1st-conj., stems being at times suffixed (+). *Unpredictable, like type E (i) (b)*

(a) New -ĀTU p.p. based on infectum stem

	Infinitive	Perfect	Past Participle	LL/PR Past Participle	
'trust'	FĪDERE 3	FĪSU 8	*idem*	*FIDATU 1	IFCOS
'fasten'	FĪGERE 3	FĪXĪ 8	FĪXU 8	*FIGICATU 1+	FCP
'chew, eat'	MANDERE 3	MANDĪ	MĀNSU 8	*MANDICATU 1+	R (I)F
'lunch'	PRANDERE 3	PRANDĪ	PRĀNSU 8	*PRANDIATU 1	I (F)

(ii) With new p.p.s in -ŪTU based on infectum stem. *Popular east and north of Castile, where -ĪTU forms prevail*

	Infinitive	Perfect	Past Participle	LL/PR Past Participle	
'fall'	CADERE 3	CECIDĪ 7	CĀSU 8	*CADUTU 6	RI (F)C
'run'	CURRERE 3	CUCURRĪ 7	CURSU 8	*CURRUTU 6	FC
'split'	FINDERE 3	FIDĪ	FISSU 8	*FINDUTU 6	IF
'pour'	FUNDERE 3	FŪDĪ	FŪSU 8	*FUNDUTU 6	(I)FC
'hang'	PENDERE 3	PEPENDĪ 7	PĔNSU 8	*PENDUTU 6	IF
'answer'	RESPONDĒRE 2	RESPONDĪ	RESPŌNSU 8	*RESPONDUTU 6	IFC
'sit'	SEDĒRE 2	SĒDĪ	SESSU 8	*SEDUTU 6	RIC

(iii) With new p.p.s in -ĪTU based on infectum stem. *Generally popular*

(a) 2nd conjugation

	Infinitive	Perfect	Past Participle	LL/PR Past Participle	
'stick'	ADHÆRĒRE 2	ADHÆSĪ 8	ADHÆSU 8	*ADHERITU 4	ICS

(b) 3rd conjugation

	Infinitive	Perfect	Past Participle	LL/PR Past Participle	
'go down'	DĒSCENDERE 3	DĒSCENDĪ	DĒSCĒNSU 8	*DESCENDITU 4	CSP
'fail'	FALLERE 3	FEFELLĪ 7	FALSU 8	*FALLITU 4	RIFCP
'slay'	OCCĪDERE 3	OCCĪDĪ	OCCĪSU 8	*OCCITU 4	FC

	Infinitive	Perfect	Past Participle	LL/PR Past Participle	
'spread'	SPARGERE 3	SPARSĪ 8	SPARSU 8	*SPARGITU 4	C S
'turn'	VERTERE 3	VERTĪ	VERSU 8	*VERTITU 4	F S

(c) 4th conjugation (by LL times)

	Infinitive	Perfect	Past Participle	LL/PR Past Participle	
'warp cloth'	ORDĪRĪ	ŌRSU 8	*idem*	ORDITU 4	R I F C S
'undergo'	PATĪ	PASSU 8	*idem*	*PATITU 4	R I
'feel'	SENTĪRE 4	SĒNSĪ 8	SĒNSU 8	*SENTITU 4	R I F C S

POPULAR TYPES OF PAST PARTICIPLES IN LATE LATIN AND PROTO-ROMANCE,

RHIZOTONIC OR SIGMATIC

	Infinitive	Perfect	Past Participle		LL/PR Past Participle

G. Tautic athematics that survived

(i) P.p.s once in -RTU. *Popular west of Dacia*

'open'	APERĪRE 4	APERUĪ 6	APERTU 9	*idem*	I S P
			x *COPERTU 9 FC		
'cover'	COOPERĪRE 4	COOPERUĪ 6	COOPERTU 9	*COPERTU 9	I F C S P
'die'	MORĪ	MORTUUM 9	*idem*	*MORTU 9	(R)I F C S
'twist'	TORQUĒRE 2	TORSĪ 8	TORTU 9	*idem*	(R)I F O C

(ii) P.p.s once in -PTU. *Pan-Romance*

'break'	RUMPERE 3I	RŪPĪ	RUPTU 9	*idem*	R I (F)OS P
'write'	SCRĪBERE 3	SCRĪPSĪ 8	SCRĪPTU 9	*idem*	(R)I FOCS P

(iii) P.p.s once in -NCTU, pfs. usually sigmatic. *Popular at the center*

'gird'	CINGERE 3	CĪNXĪ 8	CĪNCTU 9	*idem*	I F (S)
'put out'	EXSTINGUERE 3	EXSTĪNXĪ 8	EXSTĪNCTU 9	*idem*	I F
'join'	JUNGERE 3	JŪNXĪ 8	JŪNCTU 9	*idem*	I F C (S)
'mourn'	PLANGERE 3	PLĀNXĪ 8	PLĀNCTU 9	*idem*	I F
'sting'	PUNGERE 3	PEPUGĪ 7	PŪNCTU 9	*idem*	I F
'dye'	TINGERE 3	TĪNXĪ 8	TĪNCTU 9	*idem*	I F
'oil'	UNGERE 3	ŪNXĪ 8	ŪNCTU 9	*idem*	(R)I F

Infinitive	Perfect	Past Participle	LL/PR Past Participle	

(iv) P.p.s once in -CTU, not preceded by a nasal in CL; usually with sigmatic pfs. *Popular   at   the   center*

(a) Nasal consonant in infectum and/or finite perfectum stem generalized to p.p. *Popular   at   the   center*

	Infinitive	Perfect	Past Participle	LL/PR Past Participle	
'shape'	FINGERE 3	FĪNXĪ 8	FICTU 9	FINCTU 9N	I F
'shatter'	FRANGERE 3	FRĒGĪ	FRĀCTU 9	*FRANCTU 9N	I F
'paint'	PINGERE 3	PĪNXĪ 8	PICTU 9	*(DE)PINCTU 9N	I F (C)(S)
'tighten'	STRINGERE 3	STRĪNXĪ 8	STRICTU 9	*idem*	I C (F)(S)
				*STRINCTU 9N	R I

(b) No nasal consonant in infectum or finite perfectum stem; reflexes of [kt] kept. *Some   are   pan-Romance*

	Infinitive	Perfect	Past Participle	LL/PR Past Participle	
'cook'	COQUERE 3	COXĪ 8	COCTU 9	*idem*	R I F C (S)
'say, tell'	DĪCERE 3	DĪXĪ 8	DICTU 9	*idem*	I F O C S P
'lead'	DŪCERE 3	DŪXĪ 8	DUCTU 9	*idem*	I (F) C (S)
'do/make'	FACERE 3I	FĒCĪ	FACTU 9	*idem*	(R)I F O C S P
'fry'	FRĪGERE 3	FRĪXĪ 8	FRĪCTU 9	*idem*	R I F S
'pull'	TRAHERE 3	TRAXĪ 8	TRACTU 9	*idem*	I F O (S)

H. Sigmatic past participles that survived

(i) Both pf. and p.p. sigmatic in CL. *Most   popular   in   eastern   ROMANIA, least   popular   in   the   far   southwest*

(a) 2nd conjugation

	Infinitive	Perfect	Past Participle	LL/PR Past Participle	
'burn'	ARDĒRE 2	ĀRSĪ 8	ĀRSU 8	*idem*	R I (F) C
'stay'	REMANĒRE 2	REMĀNSĪ 8	REMĀNSU 8	*idem*	R (I)(F) C
'laugh'	RĪDĒRE 2	RĪSĪ 8	RĪSU 8	*idem*	R I S (F)

	Infinitive	Perfect	Past Participle	LL/PR Past Participle	

(b) 3rd conjugation

	Infinitive	Perfect	Past Participle	LL/PR Past Participle	
'shut'	CLAUDERE 3	CLAUSĪ 8	CLAUSU 8	*idem*	R I (F) C
'fasten'	FĪGERE 3	FĪXĪ 8	FĪXU 8	*idem*	I C (S)
'send, put'	MITTERE 3	MĪSĪ 8	MISSU 8	*idem*	I F
'shave'	RĀDERE 3	RĀSĪ 8	RĀSU 8	*idem*	R I C
'gnaw'	RŌDERE 3	RŌSĪ 8	RŌSU 8	*idem*	R I

(c) Sigmatic p.p. kept, but now incorporating [r] from present stem

	Infinitive	Perfect	Past Participle	LL/PR Past Participle	
'stick '	ADHÆRĒRE 2	ADHÆSĪ 8	ADHÆSU 8	*ADHERSU 8	(F) O

(ii) For verbs with a CL reduplicated perfect. *Popular in the east*

	Infinitive	Perfect	Past Participle	LL/PR Past Participle	
'run'	CURRERE 3	CUCURRĪ 7	CURSU 8	*idem*	R I
'stretch'	TENDERE 3	TETENDĪ 7	TENTU 9/ TĒNSU 8	*idem*	R I (F) C
'shear'	TONDERE 3	TOTONDĪ 7	TŌNSU 8	*idem*	R O

(iii) With dental present and (direct-suffix) perfect. *Popular in the east*

	Infinitive	Perfect	Past Participle	LL/PR Past Participle	
'light'	ACCENDERE 3	ACCENDĪ	ACCĒNSU 8	*idem*	I P
	INCENDERE 3	INCENDĪ	INCĒNSU 8	*idem*	R C (S)
'fight off'	DĒFENDERE 3	DĒFENDĪ	DĒFĒNSU 8	*idem*	I (S) P
'pay out'	EXPENDERE 3	EXPENDĪ	EXPĒNSU 8	*idem* *DE+EXPENSU 8	I (S) F C
'kill'	OCCĪDERE 3	OCCĪDĪ	OCCĪSU 8	*idem*	R I (F) O
'answer'	RESPONDĒRE 2	RESPONDĪ	RESPŌNSU 8	*idem*	R (I) (F)
'sit'	SEDĒRE 2	SĒDĪ	-SESSU 8	*idem*	I F

	Infinitive	Perfect	Past Participle	LL/PR Past Participle	

I. U-stem verbs with CL past participle in -UTUM

(i) Survivals. *Popular beyond Castile, where* -ĪTU *types prevail*

'beat'	BATTUERE 3	BATTUĪ 6	BATTŪTU 6	*idem*	RIFC(S)
'sew'	CŌNSUERE 3	CŌNSUĪ 6	CŌNSŪTU 6	*idem*	RFO
				*CO(N)SITU 4	ICSP
'fuck'	FUTUERE 3	FUTUĪ 6	FUTŪTU 6	*idem*	RIFOC

(ii) Remakings, perhaps on the basis of a remade -ĪTU form

'follow'	SEQUĪ 3	SECŪTUM 6	*idem*	*SEQUITU 4	IFCSP
'loosen'	SOLVERE 3	SOLVĪ (6)	SOLŪTU 6	*-SOL'TU 9	FCSP
'roll'	VOLVERE 3	VOLVĪ (6)	VOLŪTU 6	*VOL'TU 9	I(O)S

(iii) Replaced west of Dacia by its frequentative

'sneeze'	STERNUERE 3	STERNUĪ 6	STERNŪTU 6	*freq.*	
				STERNUTATU 1	IFCSP

J. Sigmatic past participle remade as tautic athematic

'spread'	SPARGERE 3	SPARSĪ 8	SPARSU 8	*SPARTU 9	R(I)

K. Tautic athematic past participle remade as sigmatic

'twist'	TORQUĒRE 2	TORSĪ 8	TORTU 9	*TORSU 8	R(F)O

L. Three sigmatic-tautic past participles

'put, set'	PŌNERE 3	POSUĪ 6	POSITU 5/		
			POSTU 8+9	POSTU 8+9	I(F)CSP
'seek'	QUÆRERE 3	QUÆSĪVĪ 8+4	QUÆSĪTU 8+4	*QUESTU 8+9	I (F)(O)S
'see'	VIDĒRE 2	VĪDĪ	VĪSU 8	*idem*	(I) (F)
				*VISTU 8+9	ICSP

Appendix 2

Romance Past Participles,
by Late Latin Etymon

§ influenced by preterit   • semi-learnèd   # competing with regularized by-form
¶ adjectival or nominal only   ( ) archaic   [ ] more distantly related
» verb based on past participle

Space prohibits listing forms from Alpine Romance
Learnèd forms have often been left out. Starred forms are indicative, not definitive.

CL	LL/PR	Romanian Arom. Vegliote Ist-R Mold. Meg.	Italian +(pres.) Sd=Sard. B=Abru.	French (defunct)	Catalan /Occitan Gascon	Spanish /Portuguese
ABSCONDITU 5 'hidden'	idem	—	—	—	—	—
	ABSCŌNSU	ascuns	ascoso		(ascons) (escons)	
	*INABSCONSU		(nascoso) nascosto			
	*EXCONSTU				O escost, rescost	
	*ABSCONDUTU	L schendù		(ascondu)	[escondit <	(ascondudo) escondido]
ACCĒNSU 8 INCĒNSU 8 'lit'	idem idem	încins	acceso	(encis)	encès (O eces)	P aceso# (enceso)
	*INCENDUTU					(encendudo)
ACŪTU 6 'sharp[ened]'	idem *EXACUTITU	ascuţi t	acuto¶	(agu¶) aigu¶	agut¶	agudo¶
ADAUCTU 9 'increased'	idem cf. ADAUXI	adaos? 'adjoined'	—	—	—	—
	*ADAUGATU	adăugat (adăugit) 'added'	—	—	—	—

381

CL	LL/PR	Romanian	Italian	French	Catalan	Spanish
ADHÆSU 8 'stuck to'	idem *ADHERSU —	— — —	— aderito•	— (ahers) (ahert)	— OO aers] adherit•	— adherido•
AFFLĀTU 1 'sniffed out'	idem	aflat 'found'	—	—	—	hallado P achado
ALLŪSU 8 'jested at'	—	—	aluso•	—	—	—
AMBULĀTU 1 'ambled'	idem	umblat	andato, ambiato	allé amblé	anat amblat	andado (amblado)
ANNEXU 8 'tied to'	idem	—	annesso	—	—	—
APERTU 9 'opened'	idem *DĒ + APERTU *APERITU	— A apirită	aperto	[ouvert]	[obert] [O dobert]	abierto P aberto
ĀRSU 8 'burned'	idem *ARDUTU » ASSATU	ars	arso Sd arsidu	(ars) (art) (ardu)	(ars)	[ardido] (ardudo) asado 'roasted'
ASPERSU 8 'sprinkled'	—	—	asperso•	—	—	P asperso•#
ASSUMPTU 9 'taken on'	—	—	assunto•	— [assumé•	assumit•	asumido•]
ATTĀCTU 9 'reached'	idem *ATTINCTU cf. *ATTINXI	— atins	— attinto	— ateint	— atansat? 'approached'	—
AUDĪTU 4 'heard'	idem	auzit A avdzîtă	udito	(ouï)	oit	oído P ouvido
AUSCULTĀTU 'listened'	*ASCULTATU *EXCULTATU	—	ascoltado	(ascolté) écouté	escoltat	escuchado P escutado
AUSU 8 'dared'	idem » *AUSATU	—	oso¶ osato	(os¶) osé	gosat O ausat	osado P ousado

CL	LL/PR	Romanian	Italian	French	Catalan	Spanish
BĀJULĀTU 1 'given'	idem	—	—	(baillé)	O bailat	—
BATTŪTU 6 'beaten'	idem	bătut	battuto	battu	batut	(batudo) [batido]
BENEDICTU 9 'spoke well'	idem	—	benedetto	(beneeit) benêt¶ 'foolish'	beneít (O beneit, benezeit) Cbenet¶	bendito¶ P bento# (P bĕeito)
[no CL p.p.] {'drunk'}	BIBITU 5 *BIBUTU	 băut A biută Is bi[v]u	B vèvətə S dbittu bevuto	 bu	 begut	 [bebido] (P bibesto)
[no CL p.p.] {'blasphemed'}	*BLASPHE- MATU	blestemat] V blasmat 'bad'	 bestimmiato 'cursed'	 blâmé 'blamed'	 blasmat idem	 lastimado 'injured'
BULLĪTU 4 — 'bubbled'	idem	—	bollito 'boiled'	—	boilli boli (bolu)	bullit
CĀSU 8 'fallen' rare	idem *CADUTU *CADITU *CADECTU	— căzut A cădzută	— caduto	— -chu (cheï)	— caigut (O cagut, cazegut) (cheoit)	— caído
[no CL p.p.] {'been hot'}	*CALSU *CALUTU *INCALITU *INCALIDITU	 (încărit) încălzit 'warmed'	(calso?)	 (chalu) 'cared'	 calgut	[calecido P aquecido] [calentado]
CAPTU 9 'taken'	idem *CAPUTU *CAPITU	 — capito 'understood'	(catto•) capito	 (chavu?) 'fit into'	cabut O cabit idem	 cabido idem
freq. CAPTĀTU 1 'hunted, caught'	idem	cătat 'sought' captat•	cattato 'gotten'	—	captat• 'begged'	(catado) 'hunted'

CL	LL/PR	Romanian	Italian	French	Catalan	Spanish
CARPTU 9 *'plucked'*	*idem*	—	—	—	—	—
	*CARPITU 4	—	carpito 'seized'	(charpi) 'twitched'	carpit 'torn up'	carpido *idem*
CASSU 8/	*idem*	—	—	—	—	—
CARITU 5	*idem*	—	—	—	—	—
'lacked'	*CARISCITU	—	—	—	—	carecido
	*CARIDICATU?				carejat	
CESSU 8 *'yielded'*	*idem*	-ces	(cesso)	(cesn.)		
	*CEDUTU		ceduto•			
	*CEDITU				cedit•	cedido•
	*CEDATU	cedat• <Fr.		cédé•		
CĪNCTU 9 *'belted'*	*idem* cf. CĪNXĪ	încins	cinto	ceint	O ceint, cench [cenyido]	(cinto) [ceñido P cingido]
CLAUSU 8 *'closed'*	*idem*	închis	chiuso	(clos)	clos O claus#	—
	*DEEXCLAUSU	deschis 'opened'				
COCTU 9 *'cooked'*	*idem*	copt	cotto Sd cottu	cuit	cuit/	(cocho) [cocido
	*COCUTU	Is kokut	(cociuto+)		cogut	
	*COCTIATU			(coissié) 'wounded'		P coçado 'itched'
freq. COĀCTĀTU *'compelled'*	*COCTATU	—	—	(coitié) 'oppressed'	cuitat 'hurried'	(cochado) 'oppressed'
	*COACTICATU			caché 'hidden'		(P coitado) 'worried'
COGNITU 5 *'known$_1$'*	*idem*		(conto¶) 'suitable' Sd connottu]	(coint¶) 'pretty'	(O coinde)	—
	*COGNOTU					
	*COGNOSCUTU	cunoscut Is kuñusu	conosciuto+			[conocido P conhecido]
	*COGNOVUTU			connu	conegut	

CL	LL/PR	Romanian	Italian	French	Catalan	Spanish
COLLĒCTU 9 'gathered'	idem	Aculeptu¶ Is koleto		(colloit)	(O colt, culhech)	(cogecho) (P colheito)
	*COLLITU 5 cf.COLLEXĪ *COLLITU 4	cules	colto	cueilli	collit (coillu)	cogido P colhido 'caught'
COMĒSU 8/ COMESTU 8+9 'eaten up'	idem idem *COMITU 4 *COMUTU	— —	—	— —	—	— (P comesto) comido (comudo)
COMPLĒTU 2 'fulfilled'	idem *COMPLUTU *COMPLITU	— cumplit¶	— compiuto	— — (compli) accompli	— complit/ complert	— cumplido P cumprido
CONCEPTU 9 'imagined'	idem *CONCEPITU *CONCEPUTU	—	— concepito•	— conçu	— concebut	— concebido
CŌNSTRŪCTU 9 'built up'	—	construit• <Fr	(costrutto)• costruito•	construit•	idem	construido•
CŌNSŪMPTU 9 'used up'	—	—	consunto•	—	—	—
CŌNSŪTU 6 'sewn up'	idem *CONSITU	cusut	[cucito]	cousu (cousi)	cosit O cosegut	cosido (P coseito)
CONVERSU 8 'turned back'	— —		converso•	converti•	convertit•	convertido•
COOPERTU 9 'covered'	*COPERTU *COPERITU	Is koverto acoperit A acupirit	coperto Sd copertu	couvert	cobert O cubert (covri)	cubierto P coberto
CRĒDITU 5 'believed'	idem *CREDUTU	crezut	Sd crétidu creduto (creso)	cru	cregut (C crasagut)	[creído P crido]
CREMĀTU 1 'burned up'	idem	—	cremato• 'cremated'	(cremé) (cremi) (cremu)	cremat	quemado P queimado

CL	LL/PR	Romanian	Italian	French	Catalan	Spanish
[no CL p.p.] {'feared'}	*CREMITU *CREMUTU	—	—	(cr[i]ent) (cremu) craint	Ocrent, cremut, crengut	—
CREPITU 5 'rattled'	*CREPATU 1	crăpat A cripat 'burst'	crepato	crevé	O crebat [C crebantat]	quebrado 'broken'
CRĒTU₁ 2 'grown'	idem	—	Sd kertu, kersu	—	—	—
	*CREVUTU *CRESCUTU	crescut A criscut	cresciuto+	crû	Ocregut] crescut	[crecido P crescido]
CRĒTU₂ 2 'sifted'	idem? *CERNUTU	Is zèrto] cernut	(cernuto)	—	cernut	[cernido]
CUBITU 5 'reclined'	*CUBATU 1	—	covato 'hatched'	couvé	covat O coat	—
CULTU 9 'tilled'	idem	—	colto¶	—	(O colgut)	—
CURSU 8 'run'	idem	curs	curso [Sd kurtu]			(O cors)
	*CURRUTU *RECURSU	[Is koresto]		couru	corregut	[corrido]
DATU± 1 'given'	idem	dat	dato	—	dat	dado
DĒBITU 5 'owed, had to'	idem *DEBUTU	—	Sd deppidu dovuto	dû	degut	[debido P devido]
DĒCEPTU 9 'tricked'	idem *DECEPUTU	— —	— —	— déçu	— decebut O deceubut	— (decebido)
DĒCĪSU 8 'decided'	idem — —	decis• <It —	deciso	décidé•	decidit•	decidido•

CL	LL/PR	Romanian	Italian	French	Catalan	Spanish
DĒFĒNSU 8 'fought off'	idem	—	difeso (difenso)	(defois¶) défendu	defès (O defendut)	(defeso) P defeso# [defendido]
	*DEFENDUTU					
DĒLĒTU 2 'removed, 'destroyed'	idem *DELITU 4	— —	— —	— —	— O delit 'melted [of snow]'	— —
(DĒ)SCĒNSU 8 'gone down'	idem *DESCENDUTU *DESCENDITU	deştins	sceso	descendu	(O deisses) descendit	descendido P descido
DĒSPECTU 9 'looked down on' ['despite']	idem	—	[dispetto]	(despit) [dépit]	[despit]	[despecho] [P despeito]
DĒSTRUCTU 9 'pulled down'	idem cf. DĒSTRUXĪ	distrus	distrutto	détruit	O destruit, destruch	destruido
DICTU 9 'said, told'	idem cf. DIXĪ	Is dito zis A dzîsă	detto ditto§ dial. (Sd ditu)	dit§	dit§	dicho§ P dito§
DIRĒCTU 9 ['right']	idem cf.DIREXĪ	A dreptu¶ diretto dres	[diritto]	[droit]	[dret] [O drech] [O,C adergat]	[derecho] [P dereito]
DISCUSSU 8 'shattered'	— —	discutat•	discusso•	— discuté•	— discutit•	discutido•
DĪVĪSU 8 'divided'	idem —	Is divizo divizat•	diviso	divisé•	(O devis 'decided'] dividit•	dividido•
DOCTU 9 'taught'	idem	—	dotto¶ 'graceful'	(duit, (doit¶) 'skillful'	(Odoch, dueit¶) idem	(P doito¶) idem

CL	LL/PR	Romanian	Italian	French	Catalan	Spanish
DOLITU 5 'hurt, grieved'	idem *DOLUTU	— durut A durută	— doluto (dolso) (dolsuto) Sd dolfidu	— (dolu)	— dolgut	— [dolido P doido]
DOMITU 5 'tamed'	*DOMATU 1 DOMITATU	—	domato	(domé) dompté	domat	domado
DORMĪTU 4 'slept'	idem	dormit	dormito	dormi	dormit	dormido
DUCTU 9 'led'	idem cf.DŪXĪ	dus] A dusă 'left'	-dotto [Sd juttu 'drove'	(duït) -duit	(Cduyt) (O duich) dut 'brought'	(ducho) [-ducido P -duzido]
ĒLĒCTU 9 'chosen'	idem *EXELITU 5 *ELEGUTU *ELEGITU	[ales]	scelto	élu	C elet¶ 'wizard' elegit	electo• (P eleito) elegido
ĒLĪSU 8 'thrust out'	—	elis• <It	eliso•	élidé•	elidido•	—
ĒRĒCTU 9 'set up'	idem *ERITU 5 *ERSU *DE+ERITU	—	erto	— [érigé]	— [erigit•]	(erecho) P ereto# (O [d]ers) [erigido•]
ĒVĀSU 8 'escaped'	idem *EVADATU *EVADITU	evadat• < Fr	evaso	évadé•	evadit•	evadido•
ĒVULSU 8 'uprooted'	idem *EXVELLITU 5	— —	— svelto	—	—	—
[no CL p.p.] {'been'}	*ESSUTU	—	(suto)	—	—	—
EXĀCTU 9 'required'	idem	—	esatto• (esigito esigiuto)	exact¶• [exigé•]	exacte• [exigit•]	exacto• [exigido•]

CL	LL/PR	Romanian	Italian	French	Catalan	Spanish
EXITU 5 'gone out'	*EXITU 4	ieşit *A* işită	(escito) uscito		eixit [*O* eissit, eissut	(exido)
	*EXUTU			(eissu, issu)	'gone']	
EXPĀNSU 8 'extended'	*idem* *EXPANDITU 5 *EXPANDUTU		espanso• (spanto)	épandu répandu	(*O* espandut) [expandit•	expandido•]
EXPĒNSU 8 'weighed out'	*idem* *DEEXPENSU *DEEXPENSATU —	—	speso 'spent'	dépensé	despès	(espeso) [expendido]
EXPLŌSU 8 'hissed off, clapped off'	*idem* » *EXPLOSATU xEXPLICITATU *EXPLODATU	exploadat•	esploso•	explosé• esploité	[explotat•	explotado•]
EXPOSTU 8+9 'set forth'	— *cf.* EXPOSUĪ	— spus 'said'	—	—	—	—
EXPULSU 8 'driven out'	*idem*		espulso•			
EXSTĪNCTU 9 'put out (fire)'	*idem* *cf.*EXSTĪNXĪ	*A* astimtu stins	estinto• 'dead'	éteint 'put out'	extingit•	extingido•
[no CL p.p.] {'sucked out'}	*EXSUCTU	*V* sot¶ 'dry'	asciutto¶ 'narrow-chested'	—	enjuto¶	*P* enxuto¶ 'thin, lean'
	*EXSUCATU 'dried;wiped'		asciugato	essuyé	aixugat	enjugado *P* enxugado
EXTĒNSU 8 'stretched out'	*idem* *EXTENDUTU	extins•	steso	étendu	estès	[extendido•]
FACTU 9 'done/made'	*idem*	(fapt) *A* faptă *Is* fato	fatto *S d* fattu	fait	(feyt) fet *O* fait,fach *G* hèit	hecho *P* feito
	*FACUTU	făcut				

CL	LL/PR	Romanian	Italian	French	Catalan	Spanish
FALSU 8 'failed'	*idem*	fals¶ V fuals¶	falso¶	faux¶	fals¶	falso¶
	*FALLITU 5 » *FALTATU				faltat 'lacked'	(falto) faltado *idem*
	*FALLUTU		(falluto?)	fallu	O falgut]	
	*FALLITU 4	falit <It.	fallito	failli	fallit	P falido [fallecido]
FARTU 9 'stuffed'	*idem*				fart¶	harto# P farto# Sp hartado
	» *FARTATU					
	*FARCITU	—	farcito	farci	farcit	
[no CL p.p.] {'hit'}	*FERITU	ferit 'banned'	ferito		ferit	herido P ferido
	*FERUTU *FERITU 5		(feruto) [Sd fertu]	(feru)	(O ferut#)	
[no CL p.p.] {'boiled'}	*FERBITU 5? *FERVITU 4	fiert	[p.p. missing]	—	—	hervido P fervido
FISUM 8 'trusted'	*idem*	—	—	—	—	—
	*FIDATU	—	fidato	fié	fiat O fizat	fiado
FICTU 9 'shaped'	*idem*	—	—	—	—	—
	FINCTU	—	finto	feint	O f(e)int, fins]	
	*FINGITU 4				[Cfingit•	fingido•]
FINITU 4 'ended'	*idem*	finit• <Fr.] V fenait	finito	(feni) fini	finit	(P findo) [fenecido]
FIRMĀTU 1 'steadied'	*idem*	—	fermato 'stopped'	fermé 'shut'	fermat 'bound'	firmado• 'signed'
FISSU 8 'split'	*idem* *FENDUTU	—	(fesso)/ fenduto	fendu	fes	[hendido P fendido]

CL	LL/PR	Romanian	Italian	French	Catalan	Spanish
FĪXU 8/ FĪCTU 9 'fastened'	idem idem	înfipt 'stuck'	fisso¶ fitto		fix¶	fijo#
	*FIGICATU		ficcato	fiché 'put in'	ficat idem	P ficado 'stayed'] [Sp hincado P fincado
FLEXU 8 'bent'	idem *FLECTITU 4 *FLECTICATU	—	flesso•	— (fléchié) fléchi	[flectit•]	[flejen. 'hoop']
[no CL p.p.] {'bloomed'}	*FLORITU 4	(în)florit	fiorito	fleuri	florit	florido¶ florecido
[no CL p.p.] {'stunk'}	*FŒTITU 4	—	—	—	—	hedido P fedido
FOSSU 8 'dug'	idem FODICATU *FODICULATU	—	foggiato 'shaped'	(enfoeit) [fouillé 'searched']	fotjat 'rooted' O fozilhat idem	O fos# hozado idem
FRĀCTU 9 'shattered'	idem *FRANCTU	frânt	(franto) infranto	(frait) (fraint)	(O frait, frach, franh)	— P frangido?]
FRĒ(N)SU 8 'crushed'	idem » *FRESATU *FRENDITU	— —	— frendito	— fraisé 'drilled'	— fresat idem	— fresado idem
FRICTU 9/ FRĪCĀTU 1 'rubbed'	idem idem	— frecat	— fregato	— frayé	— fregat	— fregado
FRĪCTU 9 'fried'	idem cf. FRĪXĪ *FRIGITU 4	fript Is frito	fritto S d frittu, S d frìssu	frit	(freyt) fregit	frito/ freído
FRŪCTU 9/ FRUITU 5 'used, enjoyed'	*FRUITU 4	—	fruito•	—	fruit•	—

CL	LL/PR	Romanian	Italian	French	Catalan	Spanish
FUGITU 5 'fled'	*idem* *FUGITU 4* *FUGATU*	fugit *A* fudzit *A* fugat	fuggito	(foï) fui (fuieit)	(fuyt) fugit	huido *P* fugido
FŪNCTU 9 'performed'	—	—	funto• *rare*	—	—	—
[no CL p.p.] {'raged'}	*FURICATU	—	(frucato) 'rummaged around'	(furgié)	fugat *idem*	hurgado *idem*
[no CL p.p.] {'been'}	*cf.* pf.FUISTĪ?	*R* fost *A* fută *Mo* fo(st) *Is* (f)os	—	—	—	—
FŪSU 8 'melted'	*idem* *FUNDUTU	—	fuso *S d* infus(t)u (*It* fonduto)	fondu	fos/ fondut	[fundido]
FUTTŪTU 6 'fucked'	*idem*	futut	fottuto	foutu	fotut	[hodido, jodido *P* fodido]
GĀVĪSU 4+8 'enjoyed'	*idem* *GAUDUTU *GAUDITU *GAUDIATU *GAVATIATU	—	goduto gavazzato	(joï) enjoui	*O* gavis¶ *O* gaudit, jauzit] gojat	*P* gouvido
GEMITU 5 'moaned, groaned'	*idem* *GEMUTU *GEMITU 4 *GEMICATU	gemut	gemuto *rare*	geint 'whined'] gémi	gemit gemegat	gemido
HABITU 5 'had'	*idem* *HABUTU	avut *A* avută *Is* bu	*S d* appidu avuto	eu	hagut (*O* aut)	(*P* avudo) (*Sp* ovido) [habido *P* havido]
[no CL p.p.] {'bristled; dreaded'}	*HORRITU 4	urît *A* aurîtă 'hated'	—	—	—	—
HORTĀTU 1 'exhorted'	*CUMHORTATU	—	—	—	(conortat) 'consoled'	(cohortado)

CL	LL/PR	Romanian	Italian	French	Catalan	Spanish
IMPLĒTU 2 'filled'	idem *IMPLUTU *IMPLITU 4 *ADIMPLITU	— umplut	— empiuto/ empito	— empli rempli (aempli)	— O azemplit [omplert]	— henchido P enchido
INCĒNSU	see under ACCĒNSU					
INCEPTU 9 'begun'	idem *INCEPUTU	— început	— —	— —	— —	— —
INDULTU 9 'overlooked' 'overlooked'	—	—	indulto•	indulgé•	[indultat• 'forgiven'	indultado•] idem
INTELLĒCTU 9 'understood'	idem cf. INTELLEXI	înțelept¶ înțeles înțelegut?	—	—	—	—
INTRĪTU 4 'crumbled'	idem *INTRISU	— —	intriso 'kneaded; soaked'	— —	— —	— —
TRŪSU 8 'pushed, forced'	*INTRUSU	—	intruso•	(intrus•¶)	intrús•¶	intruso•¶
INVENTU 9 'found'	idem *REINVENUTU	— —	— rinvenuto	— —	— —	— —
ĪRĀTU 1 'been angry'	idem *IRASCUTU	— —	irato¶	(iré) (irascu)	irat¶ (O irascut)	(irado¶)
ĪTU 5 'gone'	*ĪTU 4	— Is zi	ito dial. gito lit.	—	G it [Aspe]	ido
JACITU 5 'lain'	idem *JACUTU	— zăcut	— giaciuto+	— (geü)	— jagut [O jait#]	— [yacido P jazido]
JACTU 9 'thrown'	idem freq. JACTĀTU	— —	— gettato	— jeté	— gitat	— echado (P geitado) P deitado
freq. JACULĀTU 'shot at'	*JACULITU	—	—	— jailli 'spurted'	(jali)	—

CL	LL/PR	Romanian	Italian	French	Catalan	Spanish
JŬNCTU 9 'joined'	idem		(gionto) giunto Sd iunctu	joint	junt	(junto)
	cf.ADJŬNXĪ	ajuns 'arrived'				
	*JUNCITU 4					uñido, uncido P jungido 'yoked'
LÆSU 8 'harmed'	idem » *LESATU	lezat• <Fr	leso•	lesé•	les•¶	lisiado P lesado
LAMBITU 5 'licked$_1$'	*LAMBITU 4	—	—	—	—	lamido P lambido
LAVĀTU 1 'washed'	idem *LAVUTU? *EXPERLAVATU	lăut¶ spălat	lavato	lavé	llavat	lavado
LĒCTU 9 'chosen; read'	idem cf.ADLEXI	Is leto, [lezesto] R ales 'chosen'	letto S dlettu, lessu	(lit)	(Cleyt)	
	*LEGUTU *LEXUTU *LEXTU *LEGITU 4		(leggiuto+)	lu	(O lescut) (Clest) llegit	leído P lido
LEVĀTU 1 'raised'	idem	luat 'taken' A loată 'received'	levato 'raised'	levé idem	llevat 'removed'	llevado P levado idem
LĪNCTU 9 'licked$_2$'	idem cf. LĪNXĪ	lins	Sd lintu	—	—	—
LICITU 5 'been allowed'	idem *LICUTU	—	licito¶	(leü)	(O legut) (C llegut)	—
[no CL p.p.] {'shone'}	*LUCITU 4	lucit[?]	— Sd alluttu	(luit) lui	lluit	lucido P luzido
LUCRĀTU 1 'gained'	idem	lucrat 'worked' A lucrată	logorato 'worn out'	—	—	logrado 'gotten'

CL	LL/PR	Romanian	Italian	French	Catalan	Spanish
LŪSU 8 'played'	idem	—	—	—	—	—
	*LUITU 4	—	—	—	—	(P loido)
MANSU 8 'chewed'	idem	—	—	—	—	—
	*MANDICATU	mâncat 'eaten'	(manicato) mangiato <Fr	mangé	menjat <Fr (C manugat)	P manjado <Fr
MĀNSU 8 'stayed'	see under (RE)MĀNSU					
[no CL p.p.] {'been faded, withered'}	*MARCITU 4 *MARC(IT)ATU	mărcat¶ 'yogurt'	marcito	(marci)	marcit	marcido, marchitado
MERITU 5 'earned, deserved'	*MERITU 4 [freq. MERITĀTU	meritat• <Fr/It	meritato•	(meri) merité•	(merit) [merescut]	[merecido]
MERSU 8 'sunk'	idem	mers 'gone, walked'	-merso• 'sunk'	[-mergé•]	[-mergit•]	[-mergido•]
METĪTU 4 'measured'	idem	metit	Sd medidu	—	—	medido
MI(N)CTU 9 'pissed'	— [LLMEJATU	—	(minto•)	—	—	meado P mijado
MINŪTU 6 'lessened'	idem *MINUNTU *MINUATU	mărunt¶	minuto¶ menovato	menu¶	menut¶	menudo¶ menguado
MĪRĀTU 1 'wondered, admired'	idem	mirat 'been surprised'	mirato 'lookedat'	(miré) idem	mirat idem	mirado idem
MISSU 8 'sent, put'	idem		messo (miso§) Sd miss(id)u	mis§	—	(miso§, misso§)
	*MITTUTU					(metudo) [metido] 'put into'
	TRĀMISSU 'sentacross'	trimis'sent' Motrimăs				

CL	LL/PR	Romanian	Italian	French	Catalan	Spanish
MIXTU 9 'mingled'	idem		mistopoet. mesciuto+			
	*MISCUTU *MISCITU 4					mecido 'rocked' P mexido
	*MISCITATU	mişcat 'moved'	(meschitato)			
	*MISCULATU		mischiato	mêlé	mesclat>	mezclado, P mesclado
MOLITU 5 'ground'	idem	—			mòlt	
	MOLUTU *MOLSU			moulu (mols)		
	*MOLITU 4		molito dial.			molido P moido
MONITU 5 'warned'	*MONITU 4	—	—	—	—	muñido 'invited'
MORSU 8 'bitten'	idem		morso Sd mossiu	(mors)	(O mors)	
	*MORDUTU			mordu		[mordido]
	*MORSICATU	muşcat	morsicato		mossegat	P mossegado
MORTUU 'died'	*MORTU	mort ¶ 'dead'] Is morto V muárt]	morto Sd mortu	mort	mort	muerto P morto#
	*MORITU 4	murit 'died'				P morrido
MŌTU 'moved'	idem	—	(moto) Sd móghiu			
	*MOVITU 5 *MOSSU *MOSSUTU		mosso			
	*MOVUTU			mû	mogut	(P movudo) [movido P moído]
MULSU 8/ MULCTU 9 'milked'	idem idem	muls	Sd murtu]	(mos)	O muls	
	*MUNGITU 4				(es)munyit	P mungido
	*EXMULCTU	(Mo zmult) 'yanked out'				
MŪTĀTU 1 'shifted, changed'	idem	mutat V muduot	mutato	mué 'shed'	mudat 'changed'	mudado

CL	LL/PR	Romanian	Italian	French	Catalan	Spanish
[no CL p.p.] {'gone moldy'}	*MUCITU 4 [enmohecido]	—	[muffito]	moisi *rare* cramoisi¶	Oc moz-?	
NARRĀTU 1 'recounted'	*idem*	—	narrato Sd natu 'said'	narré•	narrat•	narrado•
NĀTU 'born'	*idem* *NASCUTU	(nat) născut V nascóit	nato [nasciuto+ notstd.]	né (nascu) (naissu)	nat/ nascut	nato•/ [nada 'nothing'] P nado
NECTU 9 'killed'	*idem* *(AD)NECATU	— înecat 'drowned'	— annegato	— noyé	— negat arch.	— anegado
NEGĀTU 1 'denied'	*idem*	—	negato	nié	negat	negado
NEGLĒCTU 9 'overlooked'	— —	neglijat•	negletto•	négligé•	neglegit•	—
[no CL p.p.] {'snowed'}	cf.NĪNXIT *NINGUITU 5 *NIVATU *NIVICATU	nins	B ninguəta nevicato	neigé	nevat	nevado
NOCITU 5 'harmed'	*NOCITU 4 *NOSTU? *NOCUTU	—	nociuto+	(nuït) nui (neü)	(O nos#) (nogut)	[nucido]
NŪTRĪTU 4 'nourished'	*idem*	nutrit	nutrito	nourri	nodrit	(nodrido) nutrido•
OBLĪTU 'forgotten'	*idem* » *OBLITATU	— uitat [also 'looked at']	— (ubbiato) obliato*lit.* <Fr	— oublié	— oblidat	— olvidado
OBTŪSU 8 'thumped'	*idem*	—	ottuso•*usu.*	—	—	—
OCCĪSU 8 'slain'	*idem* *OCCITU	ucis	ucciso Sd okkisu	(ocis) (occit)	O aucis] occit	—

CL	LL/PR	Romanian	Italian	French	Catalan	Spanish
OBLĀTU *idem* 'offered'	*OFFERITU 5	—	— offerto	— offert	— ofert G auhèrt	—
	*OFFERITU	oferit *neol.*		(ofri)		[ofrecido P oferecido]
[no CL p.p.] *OLUTU {'smelled of'}		—	(oluto?) [olezzato]	(olu)	*O* olgut, nolgut	
	*OLITU			(oli) (olé)		olido [*not in P*]
ŌRSU 8 *idem* 'warped cloth' LL ORDITU 4		— urzit	— ordito	— ourdi	— ordit	— urdido
ORTU 9 *idem* 'risen'	*ORICATU	— urcat 'gone up'	—	—	—	—
ŌSU 8(*OL*) *idem* 'hated'	*ODIATU?	— —	— odiato•	—	— odiat•	— odiado•
PARĀTU 1 *idem* 'set; prepared'		apărat 'defended'	parato 'adorned'	paré idem	parat 'put up with'	parado 'detained'
PĀRITU 5 *idem* 'appeared'	*PARSU	—	parso *Sd* parsu, partu *Sd* pássidu	—	—	—
	*PARSITU 5 *PARUTU	părut [*Is* paresto]	(*It* paruto)	paru	paregut	[parecido]
PARSU 8/ *idem* PARCITU 5 *PARCITU 4 'spared'		—	[parco ¶ 'frugal']	—	(*O* pars) parcit	— [parco ¶ 'frugal'']
PĀSTU *idem* 'fed, kept' *PASCUTU *PAVUTU » *PASTATU		păscut	(pasto¶) pasciuto+	(peü) [repu¶]	*O* pascut, pagut [pasturat]	[pacido] [pastado]
PASSU 8 *idem* 'undergone' *PATITU 4		pățit *A* pățîtă	patito (patuto)	—	(padit) patit•	(padido) [padecido]

CL	LL/PR	Romanian	Italian	French	Catalan	Spanish
PAVĪTU 4 'beaten flat'	*PAVATU 1 <Fr.	pavat•	[pavimentato]	pavé	pavat	pavado
PĒDITU 5 'farted'	idem » *PEDITATU	— —	— [spetezzato]	— pété, peté	— petat	— peado P peidado
PĒNSU 8 'hung'	idem PENDUTU *PENDICATU	depins	-peso penduto	(pois) pendu penché	-pès penjat	-penso• [pendido]
PERCEPTU 9 'grasped'	idem *PERCEPITU *PERCEPUTU	— —	— percepito	— perçu	— percebut	— percibido
PERDITU 5 'lost'	idem *PERSU *PERDUTU	— Is perso pierdut	— perso/ perduto	— (pers) perdu	— perdut	— (perdudo) [perdido]
PERSUĀSU 8 'persuaded'	idem *PERSUADATU *PERSUADITU	—	persuaso•	persuadé•	persuadit•	persuadido•
[no CL p.p.] {'thrown by'}	*PERTRAJECUTU	petrecut 'spent'	—	—	—	—
PERTŪSU 8 'bored through'	idem *PERTUSIATU	pătruns	Sd pertusu, pertuntu] pertugiato	percé	O pertusat	—
PETĪTU 4 'asked'	idem	peți t 'asked to marry'	—	—	—	pedido 'asked'
PICTU 9 'painted'	idem PINCTU 9N *PI(N)CTATU *DEPINCTU cf. PĪNXĪ	— pictat• depins	— (pinto) dipinto	— peint	— O pint pintat	[pinto¶] pintado
PISTU 9 'stamped, crushed'	idem » PIS(I)ATU [freq.PISTĀTU	— pisat —	— pigiato pistato	— pisé —	— pisat O pestat	— pisado pistado

CL	LL/PR	Romanian	Italian	French	Catalan	Spanish
PLACITU 5 'pleased'	idem *PLACUTU	plăcut	piaciuto+	(plait) plu	plagut O prazut?	[placido] P prazido]
PLĀNCTU 9 'bewailed'	idem cf.PLĀNXĪ *PLANCUTU	plâns	pianto Sd prantu	plaint	plangut	([llañido]) [plañido]
PLICITU 5/ PLICĀTU 1 'folded'	idem idem	— plecat 'left; bent'	— piegato 'folded'	— plié idem	— plegat idem ployé	— llegado P chegado 'arrived'
[no CL p.p.] {'rained'}	*PLOVITU 5 *PLOVUTU *PLOVATU	plouat [Is pyovesto]	Sd próghidu, proppiu B čòbbətə It piovuto	plu	plogut	[llovido P chovido]
POLLŪTU 6 'befouled, defiled'	— —	—	—	(pollu)	polluit•	—
POSITU 5/ POSTU 9 'put, set'	idem *PONSU *PONUTU cf. POSUI	pus] A dipusă 'gone down'	postolit.	(post, pos) (pons) (ponu) [pondu 'laid eggs'	post O pongut]	puesto P pôsto
PORRĒCTU 9 'fetched'	idem *PORRITU 5	— —	— porto Sd apportu 'presented'	—	— —	— —
POSSESSU 8 'owned'	idem —	posedat• <Fr	posseduto•	(possis?) possédé•	posseit	poseido P possuido
[no CL p.p.] {'been able'}	*POTUTU *POTITU 5	putut A putută	potuto Sd pottidu	pu	pogut	[podido]

CL	LL/PR	Romanian	Italian	French	Catalan	Spanish
PRÆSTITU 5 'lent'	*PRESTATU	—	prestato	prêté	prestat	prestado
PRĀNSU 8 'lunched'	idem *PRANDITU *PRANDIATU	prânzit	Sd prasu pranzato	— (prangié)	—	—
PRĒNSU 8 'grabbed'	idem	prins 'caught'] A preşă 'understood'	preso (presso) 'taken'	pris§ (prins)	pres	(preso) P prêso [prendido] 'caught'
PRŌCESSU 8 'advanced'	idem	purces 'begun' rustic	—	—	—	—
PRŌTĒCTU 9 'covered'	idem —	—	protetto•	[protégé•	protegit•	protegido•]
PŪNCTU 9 'stung, poked'	idem cf.*PUNXI *PUNGITU 4 » *PUNCTIATU	Is ponto împuns	punto ponzato	point	punt punyit > punxat	pungido punzado P punçado
[no CL p.p.] {'stunk'}	*PUTITU 4 *PUTIATU	puţi t	putito puzzato	(puï) pué	pudit	(pudido)
[no CL p.p.] {'rotted'}	*PUTRITU 4 *PUTRESCITU *PUTRICATU	putrezit	imputridito Sd pudrigadu	pourri	podrit O apoirigat	podrido, pudrido podrecido
QUÆSĪTU 8+4/ QUÆSTU 8+9 'sought'	idem idem *QUERUTU *QUERITU 4 *QUERSITU	cerut Me ţirută Is čerši t 'asked'	inquisiton. chiesto 'asked'	(quest) -quis§	(O quist§) queregut O querit	(quesido) (quiso§) (quisto§) querido 'wanted; loved'
QUASSU 8 'shaken'	idem » *QUASSATU » *QUASSIATU » *QUASSICATU » *EXQUASSATU	—	(casso¶) accasciato 'made tired' squassato 'wrecked'	(cas,quas¶) cassé 'broken'	(O cas¶) cassat¶ 'wounded' cascat¶	cansado¶ 'tired' cascado¶

CL	LL/PR	Romanian	Italian	French	Catalan	Spanish
QUIĒTU 2 'rested'	*QUETU	—	cheto¶ 'still']	coi¶ idem	[quedan. 'curfew']	quedo¶ 'still'
	» *QUETATU		chetato 'stayed'		quedat idem	quedado
	» *QUIETIATU			(coisié)'been quiet'		
RAPTU 9 'made off with'	idem *RAPITU 4 [freq. RAPTATU	— răpit	— rapito	— ravi	— rapit• raptat• O rautat	rato n. 'moment' raptado•
RĀSU 8 'shaved'	idem *RADUTU *RASATU	ras	raso	(rés) ras¶ rasé	(ras¶, ragut) O razat	 [raído¶]
RECEPTU 9 'received'	idem *RECEPUTU	—	— ricevuto	— reçu	— rebut O receubut	— — [recibido]
RĒCTU 9 'ruled'	idem cf. RĒXĪ —	—	retto Sd arrettu, arressu	 régi•	 regit•	 regido•
REDĀCTU 9 'brought back'	idem —	—	redatto•	[rédigé•	redactat•	redactado•]
REDĒMPTU 9 'bought back'	idem *REDIMITU 4	—	redento (ridemito)	(ra[i]ent)	(O rezemt) redimit	redimido (P remido)
REDDITU 5 'given back' xTĒNSU/ PRĒNSU	idem *REDATU 1 *RE(N)SU *RENDUTU *RENDITU 4	— redat — [Is rendesto]	— reso (renduto) [Sd residu]	— rendu	— rendit	— rendido
[no CL p.p.] {'gleamed'}	— —	—	rifulso•	—	refulgit•	—
REGRESSU 8 'gone back, come back'	idem — —	—	regresso•/ regredito• 'regressed'	—	 regressat•	 regresado•

CL	LL/PR	Romanian	Italian	French	Catalan	Spanish
(RE)MĀNSU 8 'stayed'	*idem*	rămas *A* armasă *Is* ramås	(rimaso) rimasto	(remes)	romàs	[remanso 'backwater']
	*REMANUTU *REMANSUTU		[*Sd* romasidu]	(remanu) (remasu)	(O remazut)	[P remanseado 'stayed still']
[no CL verb] {'recalled'}	(RE+)AD+MENTE +*HABUTU	—	—	([r]amenteü)	—	—
RESPŌNSU 8 'answered'	*idem* *RESPOSTU	răspuns	(risoso) risposto	(respons) (respos[t]) (respus)	respost	
	*RESPONDUTU			répondu		[respondido]
RIGĀTU 1 'watered'	*idem*	—	(rigato)	(reé) (rigué•)	regat	regado
RI(N)CTU 9 'snarled'	*idem* *RINGITU 4	— —	—	—	— renyit	— reñido P renhido 'quarreled'
	*RINGULATU		ringhiato, rignato			
RĪSU 8 'laughed'	*idem*	râs	riso	(ris) ri	(O ris)	
	*RIDUTU				rigut	[reído P rido]
ROGĀTU 1 'asked, prayed'	*idem*	rugat	rogato• 'prayed'	(rové)	rogat	rogado
RŌSU 8 'gnawn'	*idem*	ros	roso	—	(O ros, rodut) O rozigat	[roído]
	*RODICATU » *ROSICATU [*RUMIGATU		rosicato	rongé]	Crossegat 'screwed'	P roscado
RUPTU 9 'broken'	*idem*	rupt 'torn' *Is* roto	rotto	(rot, rout, ront)	O rout	roto/ rompido P rôto
	*RUMPTU	rumpt *dial.* *A* aruptă				
	*RUMPUTU » *RUPTIATU			rompu	romput	rozado P roçado

CL	LL/PR	Romanian	Italian	French	Catalan	Spanish
RUTU 'rushed, fallen'	idem » *RUTATU » *RUTIULATU?	— —	— — ruzzolato 'tumbled'	— rué 'rushed'	—	—
SALTU 9 'jumped'	idem *SALITU 4 » *ASSALTATU	— sărit	— salito 'climbed' (saluto)	— sailli 'stood out'	— sallit 'gone out'	— salido P saído idem] [asaltado]
SĀNCTU 9 'hallowed'	idem *SANCITU 4	— A sânt¶	santo¶ Sd santu	saint¶	sant¶	san, santo¶ (sencido¶) cencido¶ 'unharmed'
[no CL p.p.] {'known₂'}	*SAPUTU	— [Is savesto]	saputo	su	sabut	(sabudo) [sabido]
SAR(R)ĪTU 4 'weeded, hoed'	idem *SARCULATU	— —	— sarchiato	— sarclé	— sasclat north Cat.	— sachado
SARTU 9 'mended, patched'	idem *SARCITU 4 » *SARTITU 4	— —	— (ri)sarcito	— serti 'set stones'	— sargit O sarcit	— zurcido
SCISSU 8 'torn, split'	idem » *SCIS(S)ATU	—	scisso§•	—	—	— sisado P sizado 'pilfered'
SCĪTU 4 'known₂'	idem *SCIUTU	— știut	L og.iskitu	—	—	—
SCRĪPTU 9 'written'	idem cf.SCRIPSI *SCRIP'ATU?	(script) Is skrit scris A scriirat	scritto	écrit	escrit	escrito
SECTU 9 'cut, sawn'	*SECATU 1	—	segato	scié	segat 'reaped, mown'	segado
SECŪTU 6 'followed'	idem *SEQUITU 4 » *SECUTATU	—	seguito	(seü) (sivi,sevi) [suivi]	(O segut) [seguit O segudat	seguido

CL	LL/PR	Romanian	Italian	French	Catalan	Spanish
SĒNSU 8 'felt'	idem	—	—	—	—	(seso)
	*SENTITU 4	simți t	sentito	senti	sentit	sentido
	*SENTUTU		(sentuto)	(sentu)		
SEPULTU 9 'buried'	idem	—	sepolto/			(sebellido)]
	*SEPELITU 4		sepellito	(seveli)	O	zambullido
				enseveli	sebollit	'dived'
					[sepultat]	sepultado]
-SESSU 8 'sat'	idem		[assiso]	(sis§)	(O asses,	
				[assis]	assis)	
				[assit]		
	*SEDUTU	șezut	seduto		segut	(seído)
	*SEDITU 5		Sd seitu,		O seit#	sido'been'
			settidu			
SICCĀTU 1 'dried'	idem	secat	seccato	séché	[secada	secado
		V sekuot			'drought']	
SOLITU 5 'been used to'	idem	—	sòlito•			
	*SOLITU 4					solido rare
						P soído rare
	*SOLUTU			(solu)	solgut rare	
	*SOL'TU			(solt)		
	*SOLSU			(sols)		
SOLŪTU 6 'loosened'	idem	—	soluto			
	*SOLVITU 5		-solto	-solt	-solt	(suelto)
			sciolto¶	(-sols)	(O solt)	P sôlto#
	» *SOLTATU		'loose'		[soltat]	[soltado]
SONITU 5 'rung'	*SONATU 1	sunat	s[u]onato	sonné	sonat	sonado
						P soado
SORBITU 5 'swallowed'	*SORBITU 4	sorbit	sorbito		(sorbit)	sorbido
						P sorvido
SPARSU 8 'spread'	idem	spars]	sparso	[espars¶]	idem	
	*SPARTU	spart	(sparto)	(epart)		
	*SPARGUTU					(esparzudo)
	*SPARGITU 4				espargit	esparcido
						P esparzido
SPŌNSU 8 'pledged'	idem	—	—	—	—	—
	» *SPONSATU	—	sposato	épousé	esposat	esposado
			'married'	idem	idem	'shackled'

CL	LL/PR	Romanian	Italian	French	Catalan	Spanish
SPŪTU 6	*idem*	—	—	—	—	— —
'spat'	» *SPUTATU	—	sputato	(espué)	Oespudat [esputat•	esputado•
STABILĪTU 4	*idem*	—	stabilito•	établi•		
'steadied'					[establert]	[establecido P
estabelecido]						
STATU± 1	*idem*	stat	stato	été	estat	estado
'stood, stayed'			*'been'*	*idem*	*idem*	*idem*
		Is sta*'been'*	*E* sto			
			Sd istau, istetidu			
STATŪTU 6	*idem*	(stătut)	—	(esteü)	[estatuit	estatuido]
'set up'		*'stood'*		*'stopped'*	*'decreed'*	*idem*
STERNŪTU 6	*idem*	strănut				
'sneezed'	[*freq.* STERNUTĀTU		starnutato	éternué	estornudat	estornudado
STRICTU 9	*idem*		stretto	étroit¶	(estreyt)	estrecho¶
'tightened'					estret	P estreito¶
	*STRINCTU	strâmt¶	strinto¶	étreint		
		Is strento]	*Sd* istrintu			
	cf. STRĪNXĪ	strâns				
	*STRINCTATU	strâmtat				[estreñido]
	*DESTRINCTU			(destreint)		
	'constipated'					
[no CL p.p.]	*STRISU	—	striso	—	—	—
{*'creaked,*			*'shrieked'*			
grated'}			striduto *rare*			
STRŪCTU 9	—	-struit•	strutto•	-struit•	-struit•	-struido•
'heaped'		<*Fr*			<*Fr*	*idem*
SUBLĀTU₁	*idem*	—	—	—	—	—
'suffered'	*SUFFERITU 5		sofferto	souffert	sofert	
	*SUFFERITU	suferit				sofrido
SUBLĀTU₂	*see under* LL TOLLITU					
SUCCESSU 8	*idem*		successo/			
'gone under'	*SUCCEDUTU		succeduto			
				[succédé	succeit	sucedido]

CL	LL/PR	Romanian	Italian	French	Catalan	Spanish
SUCCUSU 8 'shaken, flung'	idem	scos 'taken out' Is skos	scosso [S d iscutu]	(escos) 'shaken' (secos)	(O escos 'threshed')	
	*SUCUTUTU *SECUTATU *SECUTITU 4 *SECUSSIDIATU?	Is skotut		[secoué]	sacudit < sacsejat	sacudido
SUCTU 9 'sucked'	idem	supt Is supt	S d suttu	—	—	—
	*SUCULATU » *SUCTIATU		succhiato	sucé		[P sugido]
SUBMONITU 5 'secretly warned'	idem *SUMMONSU	— —	— —	— (semons 'urged') semoncer	— (O somos, somons)	— —
SURRĒCTU 9 'sprung up'	idem *SURITU 5 *ADSURTU *SURSU *SURGITU 4	— —	— sorto (surto) assurto	— (sors) surgi <	— sorgit, surgit >	— surto# surgido
TACITU 5 'been silent'	idem *TACUTU	— t ăcut A t ăcută [Is tazesto]	— taciuto+	— tu	—	— [OO taizit]
TĀCTU 9 'touched'	idem *TANGUTU	— —	— [p.p. missing]	— —	— O tangut	— [tañido P tangido]
TĒNSU 8 'stretched'	idem EXTĒNSU *TENDUTU *TENDITU 4	întins A teasă	teso Sd intesu] steso	(tois) [toise¶] tendu	[tès¶] (O tes) tendit	tieso¶ 'stiff' tendido
TENTU 9 'held'	idem *TENDITU 5 *TENUTU	Is retènto A timtu, tes, timsu ţinut	Sd tentu tenuto	tenu (tins)	tingut 'had'	[tenido P tido'had'] (tenudo¶) 'beholden' (P tĕudo)

CL	LL/PR	Romanian	Italian	French	Catalan	Spanish
TERSU 8 'wiped, scoured'	idem		tersol *it.*	(ters) (tert)	(O ters)	
	*TERTU					
	*DETERSU		deterso			
	*EXTERSU	şters				
	*EXTERGITU				estergit 'stenciled']	estarcido *idem*
	*DETERGITU 4				detergit	
TEXTU 9 'woven'	idem	—	—	—	(Ctest)	—
	*TEXUTU	ţesut	tessuto	(tissu) tissé	O tescut	
	*TEXITU 4				C teixit	tejido P tecido
[no CL p.p.] {'feared'}	*TIMITU 5		*Sd* tímidu	—		
	*TIMUTU	temut	temuto		temut [O temsut]	(temudo) [temido]
TĪNCTU 9 'dyed'	idem	întins	tinto	teint	(C int)	tinto¶
	*TINGITU 4				tenyit	teñido P tingido
SUBLĀTU₂ 'raised'	idem	—	—	—	—	—
	*TOLLITU 5	—	tolto	(tolt)	(O tolt,	(Sp tuelto)
	*TOLLUTU		'removed'	(tolu)	tolgut)	
	*TOLLECTU			(toloit)	(Ctolt¶)	(P tolheito)
	*TOLLITU 4			(toli)	[tolit¶ 'lame'	tullido 'crippled'
TONITU 5 'thundered'	*TONATU	tunat	tonato	tonné		
	*TRONATU		(tronato)		tronat	tronado P troado
TŌNSU 8 'shorn'	idem	tuns A tumsu, tumtu	[toso,-a 'kid' dial.] Sd tusu		tos	
	*TONDUTU			tondu		
	*TONDITU	Me tumtă				tundido]
	*TONSATU		tosato	(tosé)	O tozat	(a)tusado 'combed'
TORTU 9 'twisted'	idem	(tort)	torto	(tort)	Ctort#	tuerto¶
	cf.TORSI	tors 'spun thread' întors'turned' A toarsă		(tors)	O tors#	'one-eyed' P torto¶
	*TORTUTU			(tortu) tordu	[torçut	torcido]
	.»*TORTIATU		(torciato)		trossat>	trozado] P trousado

CL	LL/PR	Romanian	Italian	French	Catalan	Spanish
TOSTU 8+ 9 'parched, toasted'	idem *TORRATU	tost¶ 'prompt'		tôt¶ 'soon'	tost¶ idem] torrat	[tuesten. 'toasting'] turrado P torrado
TRACTU 9 'pulled, drawn'	idem cf. TRAXI *TRACUTU » *TRACTIATU	A traptă tras	tratto tracchiato	trait 'milked' tracé	(Ctreyt) O trait tragut 'removed' trassat	(Sp trecho) (P treito) [traído P trazido 'brought'] trazado P traçado
TRĀJECTU 9 'thrown across'	idem *TRAJECUTU *TRAJITU	— trecut 'passed'	—	—	— tragitn. 'retching']	— tragido 'passed'
[no CL p.p.] {'trembled, shuddered'}	*TREMATU *TREMULATU — —	tremurat	tremato tremolato	tremblé	tremolat tremit tremut	(tremado) tremolado 'rippled' [temblado]
TRIBŪTU 6 'allotted'	idem	—	—	(treü ¶) 'lord's due'	(trautn.)	(trevudo) 'paid taxes'
TUSSĪTU 4 'coughed'	idem	tuşi t	tossito	(toussi) toussé	tossit	tosido P tussido
TŪTU 9 'protected'	idem » *TUTATU	—	—	— tué 'killed'	— tudat 'wrecked']	—
[no CL p.p.] {'wetted'}	— (ŪDUM 'wet')	udat [A duot¶ 'wet'	—	—	—	—
ŪNCTU 9 'oiled'	idem » *UNCTATU cf. ŪNXĪ	(unt) Is onto uns [A aumsu, aumtu]	unto (onto) (untato)	oint	[ungit•< untat	ungido• P ongido•] untado
[no CL p.p.] {'urged; collided'}?	*URTU » *URTATU *HURTATU?	—	(urto) urtato <Oc.	(hurté) heurté	O urtat	—

CL	LL/PR	Romanian	Italian	French	Catalan	Spanish
USTU 8+9 'singed'	idem *ADUSTU *USTICATU	— uscat A uscată 'dried']	—	—	— adust¶ 'stern'	— adusto¶ idem
	USTULĀTU	usturat	(ostolato)	(uslé)	O usclat	
ŪSU 8 'used'	idem » *USATU	— uzat• <Fr/It	— usato	— usé	— usat	— usado
VĀGĪTU 4 'whimpered'	— —	—	vagito•	vagi•	[vagitn.] 'baby's cry'	—
VALITU 5 'been strong, been worth'	idem *VALUITU *VALUTU	—	— Sd balfidu (valuto) valso (valsuto)	— valu	— valgut	— — [valido]
VENDITU 5 'sold'	idem *VENDUTU	— vândut A vindut Is vindu	— venduto	— vendu	— venut	— [vendido]
VENTU 9 'come'	idem *VENUTU *VENITU 4	Mo vint venit	venuto [Sd bennidu]	venu	vingut (O vengut)	(venudo) (P vĩudo) venido P vindo
VERSU 8 'turned'	idem *VERTITU 4	— învertit	— -vertito•	— (verti•) -verti•	— -vertit•	— vertido 'spilt'
freq. VERSĀTU1 'turned around'	idem	vărsat	versato	versé	vessat O versat	versado P vessado
VESTĪTU 4 'clothed, dressed'	idem *VESTUTU *VESCUTU	(învéştit) (învăscut)	vestito (vestuto)	(vesti) vêtu	vestit	vestido
VETITU 5 'forbidden'	*VETATU 1	—	vietato	(veé)	vedat	vedado

CL	LL/PR	Romanian	Italian	French	Catalan	Spanish
VICTU 9 'won'	idem *VINCTU cf. VĪCĪ+[n] *VINCUTU	— învins învăncut?	— vinto Sd bintu Sd binsu	— (ve[i]ncu) vaincu	— O vencut C vençut	— — [vencido] (vençudo)
VĪCTU 9 'lived'	idem *VIVITU 5 *VIVUTU *VIVITU 4 *VIXU *VIXUTU *VIVATU	— învins înviat 'given life']	— B vévətə (vivuto) (visso) vissuto	— vécu	— viscut	— — vivido
[no CL p.p.] {'thriven'}	*VIGITU 4	—	[p.p. missing]	—	vigit•	[vigente¶•]
VĪSU 8 'seen'	idem VĪS(I)TU *VIDUTU	 Is visto] văzut A vidzută	visod ia l.] visto/ veduto S d bistu, bittu, bi(d)u]	(vis) vu	(O vis) vist O vezut, vegut, veut	 visto
VOLĀTU 1 'flown'	idem EX+VOLĀTU	 zburat	volato	volé [also 'stolen']	volat	volado P voado
[no CL p.p.] {'wanted'}	*VOLUTU *VOLITU?	vrut/ voit [Is (v)usu, voresto]	voluto Sd boffiu	voulu	volgut	—
VOLŪTU 6 'rolled'	idem *VOLITU 5 *VOLSU *VOLSUTU *VOLVATU	 (învolbat)] învolburat 'overflowed'	-voluto volto	 (volt) (vols) (volsu)	 (O volt)	vuelto [not in P]
freq. VOLŪTĀTU 1 'tumbled about'	*VOLTATU 1	—	voltato	(vouté)	voltat	P voltado [volteado]
VŌTU 'vowed'	idem » *VOTATU	— —	— votato	— voué	— [boda	— boda 'wedding']

Replacement Verbs in Romance Standards, Listed by Past Participle

ABSCONDITU
  'hidden'

Fr. *caché* < *COACTICATU; Cat. *amargat* < Germ. *magan* 'be strong'

AMĀTU
  'loved'

Rom. *iubit*, from Slavic

ĀRSU
  'burned'

Fr. *brûlé* < Germ. *brennen* x LL *USTULATU; Cat. *cremat*, Sp. *quemado*, Ptg. *queimado* < *CREMATU

AUDĪTU
  'heard'

Fr. *entendu*

CLAUSU
  'shut'

Fr. *fermé* < FIRMĀTU; OSp. *cerrado* < SERRĀTU?

DĒSCĒNSU
  'gone down'

Rom. *coborît*

DUCTU
  'led'

Fr. *mené*, It. *menato* < MINĀTU 'threatened'

ĒLĒCTU
  'chosen'

Fr. *choisi* < Germ. *kausjan*

EXPĒNSU
  'weighed out'

Rom. *cheltuit*, from Hungarian

EXITU
  'gone out'

Fr. *sorti*, Cat. *sortit* < SORTĪTU 'split'

*FERUTU
  'hit'

Fr. *frappé* < Germ. *hrappen*

FICTU
  'feigned'

Rom. *prefăcut*

FRĀCTU 'broken'	Fr. *cassé* < *QUASSATU; Sp. *quebrado* < *CREPATU 'rattled, crackled'
FŪSU 'melted'	Rom. *topit*, from Slavic
GĀVĪSU 'enjoyed'	Rom. *bucurat*, fromAlbanian
ĬTU 'gone'	OFr. *allé*, It. *andato*, Cat. *anat* < AMBULĀTU?; Rom. *mers* < MERSU 'sunk'
JECTĀTU 'thrown'	Rom. *aruncat*
LĒCTU 'read'	Rom. *citit*, from Slavic
LĪNCTU 'licked'	Fr. *léché*, It. *leccato*, from Germanic
MOLITU 'ground'	It. *maccinato*, Rom. *măcinat* 'machined'
OBLĪTU 'forgotten'	It. *dimenticato*, Ptg. *esquecido*
OCCĪSU 'killed'	Fr. *tué* < *TUTATU; Sp./Ptg. *matado* (o.o.o.)
PĒNSU 'hung'	Rom. *găsit* (o.o.o.)
PETĪTU 'asked'	It. *domandato*, Fr. *demandé* < DĒMANDĀTU
PRĒNSU 'taken'	Sp., Ptg. *tomado* (o.o.o.)
RĒCTU 'ruled'	Rom. *îndreptat* < *DIRECTATU

REMĀNSU 'stayed'	Fr. *resté* < RESTĀTU 'stopped'; Sp. *quedado* < *QUETATU < *QUETATU, from QUIĒTU 'rested, reposed'; Ptg. *ficado* < FIGICATU 'fastened, made secure'
SĀNCTU 'blessed'	Rom. *binecuvîntat*, from BENE + *cuvînt* 'word' < CONVENTU Elsewhere, from the compound BENE + DICTU 'said'
SECŪTU 'followed'	Rom. *urmat* < Gk. *orama*?
SOLITU 'been used to'	Rom. *obişnuit*, from Slavic
SOLŪTU 'loosened'	Rom. *slăbit*, from Slavic Remade rhizotonically in It. *solto*, Sp. *suelto*
SUCTU 'sucked'	Cat. *chuclat*, Sp. *chupado* (onomat.?); Fr. *sucé*
SURRĒCTU 'arisen'	Rom. *scalat*
*TIMUTU 'feared'	Fr. *craint*; Ptg. *receado*
TRACTU 'pulled'	Fr. *tiré*
VOLŪTU 'rolled'	Fr. *tourné*, Cat. *tornat* Remade rhizotonically in It. *volto*, Sp. *vuelto*
VESTĪTU 'dressed'	Rom. *îmbrecat*
VĪCTU 'lived'	Rom. *trîit*, from Slavic
*VOLUTU 'wanted'	OSp. *quisto* et al. < QUÆSTU 'sought'; ModSp. *querido*

Appendix 3

Past Participles by the Numbers

Again classified by type, each Latin past participle from Appendix 2 is assigned a letter and a number, then compared with its reflexes or reshapings from Romanian to Spanish. Some glosses are given in a kind of verbal shorthand. Learnèd examples appear; doubtful ones do not. Only five major languages are included, owing to sparse data from dialects and minor languages.

Types of Latin past participle

1 = regular -ĀRE type (ERRĀTU 'wandered')

2 = "regular" -ĒRE type (FLĒTU 'wept')

4 = regular -ĪRE type (DORMĪTU 'slept')

5 = tautic thematic type in atonic -ĬTU (HABĬTU 'had')

6 = u̯-stem type in in tonic -ŪTU (BATTŪTU 'beaten')

8 = sigmatic type (CLAUSU 'shut,' CESSU 'yielded')

9 = tautic athematic type in -TU after any consonant but [s]
(APERTU 'opened,' FACTU 'done/made')

0 = direct-suffixation type in -TU after root vowels
(MŌTU 'moved,' NĀTU 'born')

S = suppletive (*pres.* OFFERŌ, unlike *pf.* OBTULĪ, and unlike *p.p.* OBLĀTU 'offered')

( ) archaic   ¶ adj. or noun only

= learnèd   * competes with by-form

Latin P.p.		CL Type	LL/PR Type?	Romanian	Italian	French	Catalan	Spanish
A-1	'hide'	5	8	8	(8), 8+9	(8)	—	4
A-2	'kindle'	8	8	8	8	(8)	8	(8), 4
A-3	'sharpen'	6	6	—	6¶	6¶	6¶	6¶
A-4	'increase'	9	1	1?	—	—	—	—
A-5	'stick to'	8	8/4	—	4	(8)	4	4
A-6	'sniff out'	1	1	1	—	—	—	1
A-7	'jest at'	8	8	—	8	—	—	—
A-8	'amble'	1	1	—	1	1	1	1
A-9	'tie to'	8	8	—	8	—	—	—
A-10	'open'	9	9	—	9	9	9	9
A-11	'burn'	8	8	8	8	(8)	(8)	
A-12	'sprinkle'	8	8	—	8	—	—	—
A-13	'take on'	9	9	—	9	—	—	—
A-14	'reach'	9	9	8	—	9	—	—
A-15	'hear'	4	4	4	4	(4)	4	4
A-16	'listen'	1	1	—	1	1	1	1
A-17	'dare'	8	1	—	1	1	1	1
B-1	'give'	1	1	—	(1)	—	—	—
B-2	'beat'	6	6	6	6	6	6	(6), 4
B-3	'speak well'	9	9	—	9	4	4	—
B-4	'drink'	—	6	6	6	6	6	4

Latin P.p.		CL Type	LL/PR Type?	Romanian	Italian	French	Catalan	Spanish
B-5	'blaspheme'	—	1	—	1	1	1	1
B-6	'bubble'	4	4	—	4	4	4	—
C-1	'fall'	8	6	6	6	(6), (4)	6	4
C-2	'be hot'	—	6/4	(4)	(6)	6	—	—
C-3	'take'	9	9/6/4	—	4	(6)	6	4
C-4	'hunt'	1	1	—	—	1	1	—
C-5	'pluck'	9	4	—	4	(4)	4	4
C-6	'lack'	8/5	4/1	—	—	—	1	4
C-7	'yield'	8	8/6/4/1	—	(8), 6	1	4	4
C-8	'gird'	9	9/8	8	9	9	9	(9), 4
C-9	'shut'	8	8	8	8	(8)	8	—
C-10	'cook'	9	9/6	9	9	9	9*/6*	(9), 4
C-11	'compel'	1	1	—	(1), 1	1	(1)	—
C-12	'know'	5	6/4	6a	6a	6b	6b	4
C-13	'gather'	9	9/8/4	8	9	(9), 4	4	4
C-14	'eat up'	8/8+9	4	—	—	—	—	4
C-15	'fulfill'	2	6/4	4¶	6	-4	4*	4
C-16	'imagine'	9	4/6	—	4	6	6	4
C-17	'use up'	9	9	—	9	—	—	—
C-18	'sew up'	6	6/4	6	4	6, (4)	4	4

Latin P.p.	CL Type	LL/PR Type?	Romanian	Italian	French	Catalan	Spanish
C-19 'turn back'	8	8/4	8=	4=	4=	4=	—
C-20 'cover'	9	9/4	4	9	9	9	9
C-21 'believe'	5	6	6	6	6	6	4
C-22 'burn up'	1	1	—	1=	(1)	1	1
C-23 'fear'	—	5	—	5	—	—	—
C-24 'rattle'	5	1	1	1	1	1a	1
C-25 'grow'	2	6	6a	6a	6b	6a	4
C-26 'sift'	2	6	6	—	—	6	4
C-27 'recline'	5	1	—	1	1	1	—
C-28 'till'	9	9	—	9	—	—	—
C-29 'run'	8	8/6/4	8	8	6	6	4
D-1 'give'	1±	1	1	1	—	—	1
D-2 'owe'	5	6	—	6	6	6	4
D-3 'trick'	9	6	—	6	6	—	—
D-4 'decide'	8	8/1/4	—	8	1	4	4
D-5 'defend'	8	8/6	—	8	6	8	(8), 4
D-6 'destroy'	2	4	—	—	—	4	—
D-7 'go down'	8	8/6/4	—	8	6	4	4
D-8 'scorn'	9	9	—	[9]	[9]	[9]	[9]
D-9 'destroy'	9	9/8	8	9	9	4	4
D-10 'say, tell'	9	9/8	8	9	9	9	9

Latin P.p.		CL Type	LL/PR Type?	Romanian	Italian	French	Catalan	Spanish
D-11	'guide'	9	9/8	8	[9]	[9]	[9]	[9]
D-12	'talk of'	8	8/1	—	8	1	—	—
D-13	'divide'	8	8/4/1	—	8	1	4	4
D-14	'teach'	9	9	—	9¶	(9)	—	—
D-15	'hurt'	5	6	6	6	(6)	6	4
D-16	'tame'	5	1	—	1	(1), 1	1	1
D-17	'sleep'	4	4	4	4	4	4	4
D-18	'lead'	9	9/8/6/4	8	-9	-9	(9), 6	(9), 4
E-1	'choose'	9	9/6/4	—	9	6	4	4
E-2	'thrust out'	8	8	—	8	—	—	—
E-3	'set up'	9	9	—	9		4	(9), 4
E-4	'escape'	8	8/1/4	—	8	1=	4	4
E-5	'uproot'	8	9	—	9	—	—	—
E-6	'be'	—	6	—	(6)	—	—	—
E-7	'require'	9	9	—	9, (6), (4)	1=	4=	4=
E-8	'go out'	5	4	4	4	(4)	4	(4)
E-9	'spread'	8	8/9/6/4	—	8, (9)	6	4=	4=
E-10	'pay out'	8	8/9/1/4	—	8, 9	1	8	4=
E-11	'hiss off'	8	8/1	—	8	1=	1=	1=
E-12	'drive out'	8	8	8	8	—	—	—
E-13	'turn off'	9	9/8/4	8	9=	9	4=	4=

Latin P.p.	CL Type	LL/PR Type?	Romanian	Italian	French	Catalan	Spanish
E-14 'suck out'	—	9	—	9¶	—	—	9¶
E-15 'stretch'	8	8/6/4	8=	8	6	8	4=
F-1 'do/make'	9	9	(9), 6	9	9	9	9
F-2 'fail'	8	8/9/6/4	8¶	8¶, 4	8¶, 6, 4	8¶, 4, 1	8¶, 1, 4
F-3 'stuff'	9	9/1/4	—	4	4	9¶, 4	9/1
F-4 'favor'	9	9	—	—	—	9¶	—
F-5 'hit'	—	4/6	4	4, (6)	(6)	4	4
F-6 'boil'	—	9/4	9	—	—	—	4
F-7 'trust'	8	1	—	1	1	1	1
F-8 'shape'	9	9N/4	—	9	9	4	4
F-9 'end'	4	4	—	4	4	4	—
F-10 'firm'	1	1	—	1	1	1	1
F-11 'split'	8	8/6	—	(8), 6	6	8	4
F-12 'fasten'	8/9	8/9/1	9	8¶, 9	1	8¶, 1	8¶, 1
F-13 'bend'	8	8/4/1	—	8=	(1), 4	4=	—
F-14 'bloom'	—	4	4	4	4	4	4
F-15 'stink'	—	4	—	—	—	4	—
F-16 'dig'	8	1	—	1	1	1	1
F-17 'shatter'	9	9/9N	9	9	9	—	—
F-18 'crush'	8	1/4	—	4	1	1	1
F-19 'rub'	9/1	1	1	1	1	1	1

Latin P.p.		CL Type	LL/PR Type?	Romanian	Italian	French	Catalan	Spanish
F-20	'fry'	9	9/4	9	9	9	4	9/4
F-21	'avail'	9/5	4	—	4	—	4	—
F-22	'flee'	5	4	4	4	4	4	4
F-23	'perform'	9	9	—	9	—	—	—
F-24	'rage'	—	1	—	(1)	(1)	1	1
F-25	'melt'	8	8/6	—	8, (6)	6	6	4
F-26	'fuck'	6	6	6	6	6	6	4
G-1	'enjoy'	4+8	6/4/1	—	6, 1	4	1	—
G-2	'moan'	5	6/4/1	6	6	4	4, 1	4
H-1	'have'	5	6	6	6	6	6	4
H-2	'hate'	—	4	4	—	—	—	—
H-3	'exhort'	1	1	—	—	(1)	(1)	—
I-1	'fill'	2	6/4	6	6, 4	4	[-ert]	4
I-2	'begin'	9	6	6	—	—	—	—
I-3	'overlook'	9	9	—	9	—	—	—
I-4	'understand'	9	9	9¶, 8	—	—	—	—
I-5	'crumble'	4	8	—	8	—	—	—
I-6	'push'	8	8	—	8	—	—	—
I-7	'find'	9	6	—	6	—	—	—
I-8	'be angry'	1	1/6	—	1¶	(1¶),(6¶)	1¶	1¶
I-9	'go'	5	4	—	(4)	—	—	4

Latin P.p.		CL Type	LL/PR Type?	Romanian	Italian	French	Catalan	Spanish
J-1	'lie down'	5	6	6	6	(6)	6	4
J-2	'throw'	9	1F	—	1	1	1	1
J-3	'shoot at'	1	4	—	4	—	—	—
J-4	'join'	9	9/8	8	9	9	9	(9), 4
L-1	'harm'	8	8/1	1=	1=	1=	1=	1
L-2	'lick'$_1$	5	4	—	—	—	—	4
L-3	'wash'	0/1	1/6	6	1	1	1	1
L-4	'read'	9	9/8/6/4	8	9, (6)	6	4	4
L-5	'raise'	1	1	1	1	1	1	1
L-6	'lick'$_2$	9	8	8	—	—	—	—
L-7	'allow'	5	5/6	—	5¶	(6)	—	—
L-8	'shine'	—	4	—	4	4	4	—
L-9	'gain'	1	1	1	1	—	—	—
L-10	'play'	8	4	—	—	—	—	(P 4)
M-1	'chew'	8	1	1	(1)	1	1	—
M-2	'fade'	—	4/1	—	4	(4)	4	1
M-3	'earn'	5	4/1/6	—	1	(4), 1=	6	4
M-4	'sink'	8	8	8	8=	—	—	—
M-5	'measure'	4	4	4	—	—	—	4
M-6	'piss'	9	9	—	(9)	—	—	—
M-7	'lessen'	6	6	6±¶	6¶	6¶	6¶	6¶

Latin P.p.	CL Type	LL/PR Type?	Romanian	Italian	French	Catalan	Spanish
M-8 'wonder'	1	1	1	1	(1)	1	1
M-9 'send'	8	8/6	—	8	8	—	(8/6),4
M-10 'mingle'	9	6/1	1	6, 1	1	1	1
M-11 'grind'	5	9/8/6/4	—	(8), 6	9	4	—
M-12 'warn'	5	4	—	—	—	4	—
M-13 'bite'	8	8/1/6	1	8	(8), 6	1	4
M-14 'die'	9	9/4	9¶, 4	9	9	9	9 [P 4]
M-15 'move'	0	8/6	—	8	6	6	4
M-16 'milk'	8/9	8/9/4	8	9	(8)	4	4
M-17 'shift'	1	1	1	1	1	1	1
M-18 'get moldy'	—	4	—	4	—	—	—
N-1 'recount'	1	1	—	1	1	1	1
N-2 'be born'	0	1/6	1, 6	1, (6)	1, (6)	1, 6	1, 4
N-3 'drown'	9	1	1	1	1	1	1
N-4 'deny'	1	1	—	1	1	1	1
N-5 'overlook'	9	9	—	9	1=	4=	—
N-6 'snow'	—	1/8	8	1a	1a	1b	1b
N-7 'harm'	5	4/6	—	6	4, (6)	(6)	—
N-8 'nourish'	4	4	4	4	4	4	4=
O-1 'forget'	0	1	1	(1)	1	1	1
O-2 'thump'	8	8	—	8	—	—	—

Latin P.p.		CL Type	LL/PR Type?	Romanian	Italian	French	Catalan	Spanish
O-3	'slay'	8	8/4	8	8	(8)	4	—
O-4	'offer'	**S**	9/4	—	9	9, (4)	9	4
O-5	'smell of'	—	6/4	—	(6), (4)	—	4	—
O-6	'warp'	8	4	4	4	4	4	4
O-7	'rise'	9	1	1	—	—	—	—
O-8	'hate'	8	1	—	1	—	1	1
P-1	'prepare'	1	1	1	1	1	1	1
P-2	'appear'	5	8/6	6	8, (6)	6	6	4
P-3	'spare'	8/5	4	—	—	4	—	—
P-3	'feed, tend'	9	6/1	6a	6a	(6b)	—	4
P-4	'undergo'	8	4	4	4	—	4	4
P-5	'pave'	4	1	—	—	1	—	—
P-6	'fart'	5	1	—	1	1	1	1
P-7	'hang'	8	8/6/1	—	6, -8	(8), 6	-8, 1	4
P-8	'perceive'	9	4/6	—	4	6	6	4
P-9	'lose'	5	8/6	6	8, 6	(8), 6	6	(6), 4
P-10	'talk into'	8	8/1/4	—	8	1=	4=	4=
P-11	'throw by'	—	6	6	—	—	—	—
P-12	'bore thru'	8	8	8	—	—	—	—
P-13	'ask'	4	4	4	—	—	—	4
P-14	'paint'	9	9N/1	1	9	9	1	1

Latin P.p.		CL Type	LL/PR Type?	Romanian	Italian	French	Catalan	Spanish
P-15	'stamp'	9	1	1	1	1	1	1
P-16	'please'	5	6	6	6	6	6	4
P-17	'bewail'	9	9/8/6	8	9	9	6	4
P-18	'fold'	5/1	1	1	1	1, 1	1	1
P-19	'rain'	—	6/1	1	6	6	6	4
P-20	'befoul'	6	6/4	—	(6=)	4=	—	—
P-21	'put, set'	5/8+9	8/8+9	8	8+9	6	8+9	8+9
P-22	'fetch'	9	9	—	9	—	—	—
P-23	'own'	8	6/1/4	—	6	1=	4=	4=
P-24	'be able'	—	6	6	6	6	6	4
P-25	'lend'	5	1	—	1	1	1	1
P-26	'lunch'	8	1/4	4	1	(1)	—	—
P-27	'seize'	8	8	8	8	8	8	(8), 4
P-28	'advance'	8 8	(8)	—	—	—	—	
P-29	'protect'	9	9/1/4	—	9	1	4	4
P-30	'sting'	9	9/8/1	8	9	9	1	1
P-31	'stink'	—	4/1	4	4, 1	(4), 1	4	—
P-32	'rot'	—	4	4	4	4	4	4
Q-1	'seek'	8+4	8+9/6	6	8+9	(8+9)	6	4
Q-2	'shake'	8	8/1	—	1	(8¶), 1	8¶/8¶, 1	
Q-3	'rest'	2	2	—	2¶	2¶	—	2¶

Latin P.p.		CL Type	LL/PR Type?	Romanian	Italian	French	Catalan	Spanish
R-1	'carry off'	9	4	4	4	4	4=, 1=	1=
R-2	'shave'	8	8/6/1	8	8	(8), 1	(8, 6), 1	(4), 1
R-3	'receive'	9	6	—	6	6	6	4
R-4	'rule'	9	9/4	—	9	4	4	4
R-5	'bring back'	9	9/1	—	9	1a	1b	1b
R-6	'buy back'	9	9/4/	—	9	(9)	4	4
R-7	'give back'	5	1/8/6/4	1	8	6	4	4
R-8	'gleam'	—	8/4	—	8	—	4	—
R-9	'go back'	8	8/4/1	—	8, 4	—	1	1
R-10	'stay'	8	8	8	(8), 8+9	(8)	8	—
R-11	'recall'	—	?	—	—	(6)	—	—
R-12	'answer'	8	8/6	8	(8), 8+9	(8), 6	8+9	4
R-13	'water'	1	1	—	—	1	1	—
R-14	'snarl'	9	4	—	—	4	4	—
R-15	'laugh'	8	8/6	8	8	(8), 4	6	4
R-16	'request'	1	1	1	1=	(1)	—	—
R-17	'gnaw'	8	8/6/1	8	8	[1]	1	4
R-18	'break'	9	9/6	9	9	(9), 6	6	9, 4
R-19	'rush'	0	1, 1	—	1	1	—	—
S-1	'jump'	9	4	4	4	4	4	4
S-2	'hallow'	9	9/4	—	9¶	9¶	9¶	9¶, 4¶

Latin P.p.		CL Type	LL/PR Type?	Romanian	Italian	French	Catalan	Spanish
S-3	'taste'	—	6	—	6	6	6	(6), 4
S-4	'weed'	4	1	—	1	1	1	1
S-5	'mend'	9	4	—	4a	4b	4a	4
S-6	'tear, split'	8	8	—	8	—	—	—
S-7	'know'	4	4+6	4+6	—	—	—	—
S-8	'write'	9	9/8	8	9	9	9	9
S-9	'cut, saw'	9	1	—	1	1	1	1
S-10	'follow'	6	6/4	—	4	4, (6)	4	4
S-11	'feel'	8	4/6	4	4, (6)	4, (6)	4	4
S-12	'bury'	9	9/4	—	9, 4	4	4	(4)
S-13	'dry'	1	1	1	1	1	—	1
S-14	'be used to'	5	4/6	—	(6)	6	4	—
S-15	'loosen'	6	6/9	—	6, -9	-9	-9	9¶
S-16	'ring'	5	1	1	1	1	1	1
S-17	'swallow'	5	4	4	4	—	(4)	4
S-18	'spread'	8	8/9/4	9	8	8¶	8¶	4
S-19	'pledge'	8	1	—	1	1	1	1
S-20	'spit'	6	1	—	1	(1)	1=	1=
S-21	'steady'	4	4	—	4	4	-ert	4
S-22	'stand'	1±	1	1	1	1	1	1
S-23	'set up'	6	6	(6)	(6)	4=	4=	—

Latin P.p.		CL Type	LL/PR Type?	Romanian	Italian	French	Catalan	Spanish
S-24	'sneeze'	6	6/1	6	1	1	1	1
S-25	'tighten'	9	9(N)/8/1	9¶, 1	9¶	9¶	9	9¶
S-26	'creak'	—	8	—	8	—	—	—
S-27	'arrange'	9	9	—	-9	-9	—	—
S-28	'suffer'	**S**	9/4	4	9	9	9	4
S-29	'go under'	8	8/6	—	8, 6	1	4	4
S-30	'fling'	8	8/1/4	8	8	(8), 1	1	4
S-31	'suck'	9	9/1	9	1a	1b	—	—
S-32	'warn'	5	8	—	(8)	—	—	—
S-33	'spring'	9	9/4	—	9	4	4	4
T-1	'be quiet'	5	6	6	6	6	—	—
T-2	'touch'	9	4	—	—	—	4	—
T-3	'stretch'	8	8/6/4	8	8	(8), 6	8¶, 4	4
T-4	'hold'	9	6	6	6	6	6	6¶, 4
T-5	'wipe'	8	8/9/4	8	8	(9)	4	4
T-6	'weave'	9	6/4	6	6	(6), 1	4	4
T-7	'fear'	—	6	6	6	—	6	(6), 4
T-8	'dye'	9	9/4	—	9	9	4	4
T-9	'remove'	**S**	9/6/4	—	9	(9), (4)	4¶	(9)
T-10	'thunder'	5	1	—	1	1	1	1
T-11	'shear'	8	8/6/4/1	8	1	6	8	4, 1

Latin P.p.	CL Type	LL/PR Type?	Romanian	Italian	French	Catalan	Spanish
T-12 'twist'	9	9/8/6	(9), 8	9	(9), 6	6	4
T-13 'parch'	8+9	8+9/1	8+9	8+9¶	8+9¶, 1	—	—
T-14 'pull'	9	9/8/6	8	9	9	6	(9), 4
T-15 'cross'	9	6/4	6	—	—	4	—
T-16 'quake'	—	1/4/6	1	1	1	1, 4, 6	1
T-17 'allot'	6	6	—	(6¶)	—	(6)	—
T-18 'cough'	4	4	4	4	(4), 1	4	4
T-19 'protect'	9	1	—	1	1	—	—
U-1 'wet'	—	1	1	—	—	—	—
U-2 'oil'	9	9/8/1	(9), 8	9, (1)	9	1	1, 4
U-3 'collide'?	—	9/1	—	(9), 1	1	—	—
U-4 'singe'	8+9	8+9/1	1a	1b	8+9¶	8+9¶	—
U-5 'use'	8	1	—	1	1	1	1
V-1 'whimper'	4	4	—	4	4	—	—
V-2 'be worth'	5	6	—	6	6	6	4
V-3 'sell'	5	6	6	6	6	6	4
V-4 'come'	9	6/4	4	6	6	6	(6), 4
V-5 'turn'	8	4	4	-4	-4	—	4
V-6 'spin'	1	1	1	1	1	—	—
V-7 'clothe'	4	4/6	(4), (6)	4, (6)	6, (4)	4	4
V-8 'forbid'	5	1	—	1	(1)	1	1

Latin P.p.	CL Type	LL/PR Type?	Romanian	Italian	French	Catalan	Spanish
V-9 'win'	9	9N/8/6	8, 6	9	6	6	(6), 4
V-10 'thrive'	—	4	—	—	—	4	—
V-11 'see'	8	8/6/8+9	6	6, 8+9	(8), 6	8+9	8+9
V-12 'live'	9	6/4/1/8+6	1	8+6, (6)	8+6	8+6	4
V-13 'fly'	1	1	—	1	1	1	1
V-14 'want'	—	6/4	6	6	6	6	—
V-15 'roll'	6	9	—	9	(9)	—	9
V-16 'tumble'	1	1	—	1	1	1	—
V-17 'vow'	0	1	—	1	1	—	—

TABLE A

Number of Entries by Past-Participial Type

(C = consonant;
direct-suffixation type 0 counts as type 9)

Type	CL	Romanian	Italian	French	Catalan	Spanish
1 (-ĀTU)	29	34	61	85	70	6
2 (-ĒTU)	6	0	0	0	0	0
4 (-ĪTU)	14	27	39	45	75	136
5 (-ĬTU)	39	0	0	0	0	0
6 (-ŪTU)	13	38	50	67	48	8
8 (-SU)	76	43	53	21	13	4
9 (-CTU)	94	11	56	35	15	17
8+4 (-SĪTU)	2	0	0	0	0	0
8+9 (-STU)	3	1	4	2	5	4
8+6 (-SŪTU)	0	0	1	2	1	0
4+6 (-ĪŪTU)	0	2	0	0	0	0
No past participle	30	0	0	0	0	0
T O T A L	306	155	264	256	227	233

TABLE B

Percentages of Each Type Sampled

In each, the most common type is in boldface, the next most common in italics

Type	CL	Romanian	Italian	French	Catalan	Spanish
1 (-ĀTU)	9.5	21.9	**23.1**	**33.2**	*30.8*	27.5
2 (-ĒTU)	2.0	—	—	—	—	—
4 (-ĪTU)	4.6	17.4	14.8	17.6	**33.0**	**58.4**
5 (-ĬTU)	12.7	—	—	—	—	—
6 (-ŪTU)	4.2	24.5	18.9	*26.2*	21.1	3.4
8 (-SU)	*24.8*	**27.7**	20.1	8.2	5.7	1.7
9 (-CTU)	**30.7**	7.1	*21.2*	13.7	6.6	7.3
8+4 (-SĪTU)	0.7	—	—	—	—	—
8+9 (-STU)	1.0	0.6	1.5	0.8	2.2	1.7
8+6 (-SŪTU)	—	—	0.4	0.4	0.4	—
4+6 (-ĪŪTU)	—	1.3	—	—	—	—
No past participle	9.8	—	—	—	—	—

Samples are unrepresentative of these languages' entire p.p. corpora
Because of rounding, percentages may not sum to 100

TABLE C

One Chart Summarizing the Study

For verbs surviving from Latin, percentage of each p.p. type
either continued or remade, excluding archaic and nonstandard variants

| number > | [305] | [146] | [242] | [187] | [219] | [208] |
Type	CL	Romanian	Italian	French	Catalan	Spanish
1 (-ĀTU)	9.5	22.6	**23.6**	**39.6**	*31.5*	*29.8*
2 (-ĒTU)	2.0	—	—	—	—	—
4 (-ĪTU)	4.6	17.1	16.1	18.7	**33.3**	**63.5**
5 (-ĬTU)	12.8	—	—	—	—	—
6 (-ŪTU)	4.3	*24.7*	16.9	*26.2*	21.0	—
8 (-SU)	24.9	**28.1**	19.8	1.1	5.0	—
9 (-CTU)	**30.5**	5.4	*21.4*	13.9	6.4	4.8
8+4 (-SĪTU)	0.6	—	—	—	—	—
8+9 (-STU)	1.0	0.7	1.7	—	2.3	1.9
8+6 (-SŪTU)	—	—	0.4	0.5	0.5	—
4+6 (-ĪŪTU)	—	1.4	—	—	—	—
No past participle	9.8	—	—	—	—	—

Samples are unrepresentative of these languages' entire p.p. corpora

Because of rounding, percentages may not sum to 100

TABLE D

Dialects and Minor Languages
in Balkan Romance

292 forms

Meglenoromanian forms in -ǫt count as type **4**
Oltrenian (with 11 forms) and Moldavian (with 13) do not figure here

[no.] Type	[103] Arom.	%	[65] Meg.	%	[124] Ist-R	%
1	20	19.4	10	15.4	29	19.4
2	0	—	0	—	0	—
4	12	11.7	14	21.5	21	16.9
5	0	—	0	—	0	—
6	15	14.6	10	15.4	**37**	**29.8**
8	**28**	**27.2**	**26**	**40.0**	26	21.0
9	**28**	**27.2**	5	7.7	3	2.4
8+9	0	—	0	—	1	0.8
8+6	0	—	0	—	0	—
8+5	0	—	0	—	0	—
Allegro	0	—	0	—	4	3.2
Short	0	—	0	—	0	—
Other	0	—	0	—	3	2.4

Samples are unrepresentative of these languages' entire p.p. corpora
Because of rounding, percentages may not sum to 100

TABLE E

Dialects of Italian

536 forms

North Italy—Gallo-Italian—includes Istriano
but not the subdialect of Val Graveglia (Ligurian)

South Italy includes central dialects like Tuscan and Laziale
but not the subidalect of San Mango (Calabrian)

[no.] Type	[264] North Italy	%	[272] South Italy	%
1	19	8.3	19	7.0
2	0	—	0	—
4	24	10.2	2	0.7
5	0	—	27	9.9
6	**80**	**34.1**	**90**	**33.1**
8	35	13.2	33	12.1
9	*64*	*22.0*	*65*	*23.9*
8+9	34	8.3	8	2.9
8+6	3	1.5	3	1.1
8+5	0	—	2	0.7
Short	0	—	13	4.8
Other	3	1.5	0	—

Samples are unrepresentative of the entire p.p. corpora for Italian

Because of rounding, percentages may not sum to 100

TABLE F

Sardinian and Alpine Romance

419 forms

Friulian includes forms found in Romania
Ræto-Romance (RR) covers Engadin and Surselvan

[no.] Type	[84] Sard.	%	[96] Fri.	%	[112] Ladin	%	[122] RR	%
1	2	2.4	34	35.4	10	8.9	4	3.3
2	0	—	0	—	0	—	0	—
4	1	1.2	9	9.4	7	6.2	0	—
5	29	34.5	0	—	0	—	2	1.6
6	4	4.8	42	44.7	45	40.2	18	14.8
8	9	10.7	1	1.0	5	4.5	37	30.3
9	35	41.7	5	5.3	42	37.5	59	48.4
8+9	4	4.8	0	—	2	1.8	2	1.6
Other	0	—	0	—	0	—	0	—

Samples are unrepresentative of these languages' entire p.p. corpora
Because of rounding, percentages may not sum to 100

TABLE G

Dialects of French

171 forms

In Norman, type **1** includes forms ending in both [e] and [o]; type **6** includes p.p.s
ending in both [y] and [œ]. "Other" means forms in [ɥyɥəezy] in Val-de-Saire. In
Picard, including Avesnois and Brayon, forms in [ø] are counted as if they ended in [y].

[no.] Type	[49] Norman	%	[86] Picard	%	[36] Burg.	%
1	10	20.4	39	45.4	7	19.4
2	0	—	0	—	0	—
4	6	12.2	6	7.0	6	16.7
5	0	—	0	—	0	—
6	19	38.9	31	36.0	18	50.0
8	1	2.0	4	4.6	1	2.8
9	9	18.4	6	7.0	4	11.1
Other	4	8.2	0	—	0	—

Samples are unrepresentative of the entire p.p. corpus for French
Because of rounding, percentages may not sum to 100

APPENDIX 3

TABLE H

Dialects of Franco-Provençal

161 forms

-ÉCTU reflexes count as Type 9

[no.]	[35]		[61]		[67]	
Type	Naisey	%	Vaux + Vaud	%	Val d'Aosta	%
1	4	11.4	8	13.1	3	4.5
2	0	—	0	—	0	—
4	4	11.4	3	4.9	8	12.0
5	0	—	0	—	0	—
6	17	48.6	23	37.7	22	33.0
8	2	5.7	10	16.4	1	1.5
9	*8*	*22.8*	*17*	*27.9*	**25**	**37.5**
8+9	0	—	0	—	0	—
8+6	0	—	0	—	8	12.0
Other	0	—	0	—	0	—

Samples are unrepresentative of the entire p.p. corpus for Franco-Provençal

Because of rounding, percentages may not sum to 100

TABLE I

Dialects of Occitan

323 forms

from Poitevin (excluding Saintongeais), Auvergnat,
Gascon, Gévaudanais, and Languedocian

[no.] Type	[60] Poit.	%	[80] Auv.	%	[30] Gasc.	%	[88] Gév.	%	[65] Lang.	%
1	3	5.0	*11*	*9.5*	3	10.0	13	14.8	1	1.5
2	0	—	0	—	0	—	0	—	0	—
4	6	10.0	3	3.8	2	6.7	*16*	*18.2*	2	3.1
5	0	—	0	—	0	—	0	—	0	—
6	**36**	**60.0**	**58**	**72.5**	**14**	**46.7**	**37**	**42.0**	**35**	**53.8**
8	0	—	2	2.5	1	3.3	7	8.0	7	10.8
9	*9*	*15.0*	3	3.8	*9*	*30.0*	12	13.6	*18*	*27.7*
8+9	0	—	0	—	1	3.3	3	3.4	2	3.1
8+6	5	8.3	3	3.8	0	—	0	—	0	—
Other	1	1.7	0	—	0	—	0	—	0	—

Samples are unrepresentative of the entire p.p. corpus for Occitan

Because of rounding, percentages may not sum to 100

TABLE J

Dialects of Catalan

159 forms

from Rossellonese, Valencian, Tamaritan, and Alguerese

All -CTU reflexes count as Type 9

[no.] Type	[26] Ross.	%	[95] Val.	%	[27] Tam.	%	[11] Alg.	%
1	0	—	2	2.1	4	14.8	3	27.3
2	0	—	0	—	0	—	0	—
4	11	42.3	10	10.5	2	7.4	3	27.3
5	0	—	0	—	0	—	0	—
6	11	42.3	39	41.1	16	59.2	4	36.4
8	0	—	17	17.9	0	—	0	—
9	0	—	24	25.3	4	14.8	0	—
8+9	4	15.4	3	3.2	1	3.7	1	9.1
Other	0	—	0	—	0	—	0	—

Samples are unrepresentative of the entire p.p. corpus for Catalan

Because of rounding, percentages may not sum to 100

TABLE K

Dialects of Spanish and Portuguese

221 forms

Aragonese = Bielsa, Panticosa, Val d'Echo
Leonese = Candama, Tudanca, Val del Pas
Nonstandard Castilian = Cartagena, Salmantino, Sot de Ferrer
Portuguese = Barranquenho, Galician, Oporto

[no.]	[62]		[52]		[31]		[76]	
Type	Arag.	%	Leon.	%	Cast.	%	Ptg.	%
1	13	21.0	3	5.8	0	—	14	18.4
2	0	—	0	—	0	—	0	—
4	37	59.7	26	50.0	27	87.1	39	51.3
5	0	—	0	—	0	—	0	—
6	0	—	0	—	0	—	0	—
8	0	—	2	3.8	0	—	1	1.3
9	9	14.5	18	34.6	0	—	9	11.8
8+9	2	3.2	3	5.8	0	—	9	11.8
Short	10	16.1	0	—	4	12.9	4	5.3
Other	0	—	0	—	0	—	0	—

Samples are unrepresentative of the entire p.p. corpora for Spanish and Portuguese
Because of rounding, percentages may not sum to 100

References

Adams, James Noel. 1977. *The Vulgar Latin of the Letters of Claudius Terentianus.* Manchester: Manchester University Press.

Aitchison, Jean. 1981. *Language Change: Progress or Decay?* Bungay, Suffolk: Fontana.

Albertini, Jean. 1972. *Précis de grammaire corse.* 2d ed. Rev. Paris: C.E.R.C.

Alcover, Antoni. 1929. *La flexió verbal en els dialectes catalans, recollida personalment a 149 poblacions.* 2d ed. Rev. Francesc de Borja Moll. Barcelona: Balmes.

Alessio, Giovanni. 1955. *Grammatica storica francese.* Vol. 2, *Morfologia.* Bari: da Vinci.

Alex, Paul. 1965. *Le patois de Naisey (canton de Roulans, arrondissement de Besançon* [Doubs]). Paris: Voisin.

Anderson, James Maxwell, and Bernard Rochet. 1979. *Historical Romance Morphology.* Ann Arbor, Mich.: Published for the University of Calgary by University Microfilms International.

Anderson, Stephen R. 1977. "On Mechanisms by Which Languages Become Ergative." *Mechanisms of Syntactic Change,* ed. Charles N. Li, 317–64. Austin: University of Texas Press.

Andres-Suárez, Irene. 1994. *El verbo español: sistemas medievales y sistema clásico.* Madrid: Gredos.

Aronoff, Mark. 1994. *Morphology by Itself: Stems and Inflexional Classes.* Cambridge, Mass.: MIT Press.

Atanasov, Petar. 1990. *Le mégleno-roumain de nos jours.* Hamburg: Buske.

———. 1984. "Meglenoromâna." *Tratat de dialectologie românească,* ed. Valeriu Rusu, 476–550. Craiova: Scrisul Românesc.

Augé, Claude, and Paul Augé, ed. 1940. *Nouveau petit Larousse illustré.* 310th ed. Paris: Augé, Gillon, Hollier-Larousse, Moreau et Cie.

Augerot, James E., and Florin D. Popescu. 1983. *Modern Romanian*. Reprint of 1971 ed. Columbus, Ohio: Slavica.

Bader, Françoise. 1968. "Vocalisme et redoublement au parfait radical en latin." *Bulletin de la société de linguistique* 63: 160–96.

Badía i Margarit, Antoni M. 1981. *Gramàtica històrica catalana*. Trans. of 1951 Spanish ed. Valencia: Tres i Quatre.

Bartoli, Matteo. 1906. *Das dalmatische: altromanische Sprachreste und ihre Stellung in der apennino-balkanischen Romania von Veglia bis Ragusa* 2. Vienna: A. Holder.

Bartsch, Karl. 1968. *Chrestomathie de l'ancien français (VIIIe–XVe siècles)*. 12th ed. Rev. Leo Wiese. Reprint of 1920 ed. New York: Hafner.

Battisti, Carlo. 1949. *Avviamento allo studio del latino volgare*. Bari: da Vinci.

Battye, Adrian, and Marie-Anne Hintze. 1992. *The French Language Today*. London: Routledge.

Beard, Robert. 1988. *Lexeme-Morpheme Based Morphology*. Lewisburg, Pa.: Bucknell University Occasional Papers in Linguistics.

Bechtel, Edward A. 1902. *Sanctæ Silviæ Peregrinatio: The Text and a Study of the Latinity*. Chicago: University of Chicago Press.

Bellestri, Joseph. 1985. *Basic Sicilian–English Dictionary*. Ann Arbor, Mich.: self-published.

Bellucci, Patrizia Maffei. 1977. *Lunigiana*. No. 9/1 in *Profilo dei dialetti italiani*, ed. Manlio Cortelazzo. Consiglio nazionale delle ricerche, Centro di studio per la dialettologia italiana. Pisa: Pacini.

Benveniste, Emile. 1966. *Problèmes de linguistique générale* 1. Paris: Gallimard.

Bertoni, Giulio. 1916. *Italia dialettale*. Milan: Hoepli.

Bichelli, Pirro. 1974. *Grammatica del dialetto napoletano*. Bari: Pegaso.

Bishop, Morris. 1987. *The Middle Ages*. Reprint of 1968 ed. Boston: Houghton Mifflin.

Blasco Ferrer, Eduardo. 1994. *Ello, ellas: grammatica sarda*. Nuoro: Poliedro.

——. 1986. *La lingua sarda contemporanea: grammatica del logudorese e del campidanese.* Cagliari: Edizioni della Torre.

——. 1984. *Grammatica storica del catalano e dei suoi dialetti, con speciale riguardo all'algherese.* Tübingen: G. Narr.

Blasi, Luigi de. 1991. *Dizionario dialettale di San Mango sur Calore (Avellini).* Potenza: Il Salice.

Bonnaud, Pierre. 1990. *Grammaire générale de l'auvergnat à l'usage des arvernisants.* Chamalières [Puy-de-Dôme]: Cercle Terre d'Auvergne.

Bourciez, Edouard. 1946. *Eléments de linguistique romane.* 4th ed. Rev. Jean Bourciez. Paris: Klincksieck.

Braune, Wilhelm. 1973. *Gotische Grammatik.* 18th ed. Rev. Ernst A. Ebbinghaus. Tübingen: Niemeyer.

Brown, Virginia. 1995. *Leveling of Irregular Past Participles in Military English.* Frankfurt and New York: P. Lang.

Browning, Robert. 1933. *Medieval and Modern Greek.* 2d ed. Cambridge: Cambridge University Press.

Brunot, Ferdinand, and Charles Bruneau. 1937. *Précis de grammaire historique de la langue française.* 2d ed. Paris: Masson.

Buck, Carl Darling. 1933. *Comparative Grammar of Greek and Latin.* Chicago: University of Chicago Press.

Buffière, Félix. 1992. *Dictionnaire occitan–français: dialecte gévaudanais.* Gévaudan [Lozère]: Escolo Gabalo.

Buratti, Rosalia. 1993. *Verbi italiani.* Milan: Garzanti.

Burrow, Thomas. 1965. *The Sanskrit Language.* 2d ed. London: Faber and Faber.

Bybee, Joan L. 1985. *Morphology: A Study of the Relation between Meaning and Form.* Typological Studies in Language 9. Amsterdam: Benjamins.

Bybee, Joan L., Revere Perkins, and William Pagliuca. 1994. *The Evolution of Grammar: Tense, Aspect, and Modality in the Languages of the World.* Chicago: University of Chicago Press.

Capidan, Thodor. 1932. *Aromânii: Dialectul aromân*. Academia Româna, Studii şi cercetărim 20. Bucharest: Imprimeria naţională.

———. 1925. *Meglenoromânii. I. Originea şi graiul lor*. Bucharest: Cultura naţională.

Caragiu, Matilda. 1975. *Compendiu de dialectolgie română*. Bucharest: Editura ştiinţifică şi enciclopedică.

Carballo Cabero, Ricardo. 1976. *Grámatica elemental del gallego común*. 6th ed. Vigo: Galazia.

Carnoy, Albert Joseph. 1903. *Le latin d'Espagne d'après les inscriptions: étude linguistique*. Louvain: J.-B. Istas.

Carpi y Zaidin, Joaquin de, and Joaquin de Carpi y Cases. 1981. *El dialecto de Tamarite de Litera (Huesca)*. Tamarite de Litera: Ayuntamiento.

Carroll, Linda L. 1980. *Language and Dialect in Ruzante and Goldoni (Veneto)*. Ravenna: Longo.

Carstairs, Andrew. 1987. *Allomorphy in Inflexion*. London: Croom Helm.

Castellani, Arrigo, ed. 1980. *I più antichi testi italiani*. Bologna: Pàtron.

Chenal, Aimé. 1986. *Le franco-provençal valdotain: morphologie et syntaxe*. Aoste: Musumeci.

Chiodi-Tischer, Uta. 1981. *Die Mundart von Sisco (Korsika)*. Untersuchungen zur romanischen Philologie 2, ed. W. Theodor Elwert, Heinz Kröll, and Kurt Ringger. Frankfurt: Haag und Herchen.

Cioranescu, Alejandro. 1958–1966. *Diccionario etimológico rumano*. Tenerife: Biblioteca filológica [Universidad de la Laguna].

Comrie, Bernard. 1976. *Aspect*. Cambridge: Cambridge University Press.

Consolino, Giovanni. 1986. *Vocabulario del dialetto di Vittoria*. Pisa: Pacini.

Contini, Michel, and Edward F. Tuttle. 1982. "Sardinian." *Trends in Romance Linguistics and Philology*, ed. Rebecca Posner and John N. Green, 171–88. The Hague: Mouton.

Cooper, Frederic Taber. 1975. *Word Formation in the Roman* sermo plebeius. Reprint of 1895 ed. Hildesheim, N.Y.: Olms.

Cortelazzo, Manlio, ed. 1974–1982. *Profilo dei dialetti italiani.* Pisa: Pacini.

——. 1969. *Avviamento critico allo studio della dialettologia italiana.* Pisa: Pacini.

Coteanu, Ion. 1961. *Elemente de dialectolgie a limbii române.* Bucharest: Editura ştiinţifică.

——. 1957. *Cum dispare o limba (istroromâna).* Bucharest: Societatea de Ştiinţe istorice şi filologice.

Craddock, Jerry R. 1993. "A Small Old Spanish Mystery: Why Wasn't *did(e)* the First Singular Preterite of *dar* 'to give'?" *Homenaje a José Durand,* ed. Luis Cortest, 183–86. Madrid: Verbum.

Cremaschi, Giovanni. 1959. *Guida allo studio del latino medievale.* Padua: Liviana.

Cusatelli, Giorgio, ed. 1968. *Il libro Garzanti della lingua italiana.* Milan: Garzanti.

Dahl, Östen. 1985. *Tense and Aspect Systems.* Oxford: Basil Blackwell.

Dardel, Robert de. 1958. *Le parfait fort en roman commun.* Geneva: Droz.

Darmesteter, Arsène. 1914? [undated]. *Cours de grammaire historique de la langue française.* 4 vols. Paris: Delagrave.

Darrigrand, Robert. 1971. *Initiation au gascon.* Poitiers: Per Noste.

Davis, Stuart, and Donna Jo Napoli. 1994. *A Prosodic Template in Historical Change: The Passage of the Latin Second Conjugation into Romance.* Turin: Rosenberg and Sellier.

De la gramática de los Cheso: fabla altoaragonesa. 1990. Zaragoza: Concello de la Villa de Val d'Echo and Grupo d'Estudios de la Fabla Chesa.

Descombes, Françoise. 1985. *Recueil des inscriptions chrétiennes de la Gaule antér.* ures *à la renaissance carolingienne.* Vol. 15, *Viennoise du nord.* Paris: Conseil national de la recherche scientifique.

Devoto, Giacomo, and Gabriella Giacomelli. 1972. *I dialetti delle regioni d'Italia*. Florence: Sansoni.

Díaz y Díaz, Manuel C. 1950. *Antología del latin vulgar*. Madrid: Gredos.

Díaz González, Olga Josefina. 1986. *El habla de Candama: Aspectos morfosintácticos y vocabulario*. Oviedo: Universidad de Oviedo.

Dicţionarul invers. 1957. Bucharest: Institutul de lingvistică.

Dicţionarul limbii române. 1984. Bucharest: Editura Academiei.

Did'huit, Albert, Alain Morain, and Marie-Rose Simoni-Aurembou. 1979. *Trésor du parler percheron*. Mortagne sur Perche [Orne]: Maison des Comtes du Perche.

Dietrich, Wolf. 1983. *El aspecto verbal perifrástico en las lenguas románicas*. Trans. Marcos Martínez Hernández. Madrid: Gredos.

Dinneen, Francis P. 1967. *An Introduction to General Linguistics*. Washington, D.C.: Georgetown University Press.

D'Ovidio, Francesco, and Wilhelm Meyer-Lübke. 1919. *Grammatica storica della lingua e dei dialetti italiani*. 2d ed. Milan: Hoepli.

Du Nay, André [pseud.]. 1977. *The Early History of the Romanian Language*. Edward Sapir Monograph Series in Language, Culture, and Cognition 3. Lake Bluff, Ill.: Jupiter House.

Einhorn, E. 1974. *Old French: A Concise Handbook*. Cambridge: Cambridge University Press.

Elcock, W. D. 1975. *The Romance Languages*. 2d ed. Rev. John N. Green. London: Faber and Faber.

Eloy, Jean-Michel. 1997. *La constitution du picard: une approche à la notion de langue*. Bibliothèque des cahiers de l'Institut de linguistique de Louvain 90. Louvain: Peeters.

Entwhistle, William J. 1938. *The Spanish Language, Together with Portuguese, Catalan, and Basque*. New York: Macmillan.

Ernout, Alfred. 1935. *Morphologie historique du latin*. 2d ed. Paris: Klincksieck.

Ernout, Alfred, and Antoine Meillet. 1959. *Dictionnaire étymologique de la langue latine: histoire des mots*. 4th ed. Paris: Klincksieck.

Ewert, Alfred. 1943. *The French Language*. 2d ed. London: Faber and Faber.

Fabra, Pompeu. 1969. *Gramàtica catalana*. 5th ed. Barcelona: Teide.

Falcone, Giuseppe. 1976. *Calabria*. No. 18 in *Profilo dei dialetti italiani*, ed. Manlio Cortelazzo. Consiglio nazionale delle ricerche, Centro di studio per la dialettologia italiana. Pisa: Pacini.

Fernández González, José Ramón. 1985. *Gramática histórica provenzal*. Oviedo: Universidad de Oviedo.

Figueiredo, Cândido de. 1937. *Novo dicionário da lingua portuguesa*. 6th ed. Lisbon: Bertrand.

Figueiredo, Cândido de, J. M. Nunes, and A. Gomes Ferreira. 1980. *Compêndio de gramática portuguesa*. Oporto: Porto Editora.

Fisher, John. 1976. *The Lexical Affiliations of Vegliote*. Cranbury, N.J.: Associated University Presses.

Fleischman, Suzanne. 1992. "Romance Languages." *International Encyclopedia of Linguistics*, 3, ed. William Bright, 337–43. New York: Oxford University Press.

———. 1982. *The Future in Thought and Language: Evidence from Romance*. Cambridge: Cambridge University Press.

Flobert, Pierre. 1975. *Les verbes déponents latins des origines à Charlemagne*. Paris: Belles Lettres.

Fontelles, Antoni, Joaquim Lanuza, and Laura Garcia. 1987. *Gramatica de la llengua valenciana*. Valencia: Del ceniu al segura.

Fouché, Pierre. 1980. *Morphologie historique du roussillonnais*. Geneva: Slatkine.

Frau, Giovanni. 1984. *I dialetti del Friuli*. Udine: Società filologica friulana.

Fullana Mira, Lluis. 1915. *Gramática elemental de la llengua valenciana*. Valencia: Domenech.

García de Diego, Vincente. 1951. *Gramática histórica española*. Madrid: Gredos.

García Martínez, Ginés. 1986. *El habla de Cartagena: palabras y cosas*. Reprint of 1960 ed. Murcia: Universidad de Murcia; Excmo Ayuntamiento de Cartagena.

Gartner, Theodor. 1910. *Handbuch der rätoromanischen Sprache und Literatur*. Halle: Niemeyer.

Gautier, Michel. 1993. *Grammaire du poitevin-saintongeais*. Mougon [Vienne?]: Union pour la culture populaire en Poitou-Charentes-Vendée.

George, Ken. 1993. "Alternative French." *French Today: Language in its Social Context*, ed. Carol Sanders, 155–70. Cambridge: Cambridge University Press.

Georges, Emanuel S. 1970. *Studies in Romance Nouns Extracted from Past Participles*. Rev. Jerry R. Craddock and Yakov Malkiel. University of California Publications in Linguistics 63. Berkeley: University of California Press.

Gheție, Ion. 1987. "Origine a dialectelor romăne." *Limba româna* no. 2: 130–46.

———. 1987. "Diferențieri dialectale in romăna primitivă." *Limba româna* no. 1: 79–84.

———. 1986. "Româna primitivă." *Limba româna* no. 6: 516–27.

Giammarco, Ernesto. 1979. *Abruzzo*. No. 13 in *Profilo dei dialetti italiani*, ed. Manlio Cortelazzo. Consiglio nazionale delle ricerche, Centro di studio per la dialettologia italiana. Pisa: Pacini.

Giannelli, Luciano. 1976. *Toscana*. No. 9 in *Profilo dei dialetti italiani*, ed. Manlio Cortelazzo. Consiglio nazionale delle ricerche, Centro di studio per la dialettologia italiana. Pisa: Pacini.

Godefroy, Frédéric. 1982. *Dictionnaire de l'ancienne langue française et de tous ses dialectes du IXe au XVe siècle*. Reprint of 1891–1902 ed. Geneva: Slatkine.

Gołąb, Zbigniew. 1984. *The Arumanian Dialect of Kruševo in SR Macedonia, SFR Yugoslavia*. Skopje: Macedonian Academy of Sciences and Arts.

González Guzman, Pascual. 1953. *El habla viva del valle de Aragüés.* Zaragoza: Monografías del Instituto de estudios pirenaicos.

González Ollé, Fernando. 1964. *El habla de La Bureba: Introducción al castellano actual de Burgos.* Madrid: Revista de filología española, anejo 18.

Goodwin, William Watson. 1958. *Greek Grammar.* Rev. Charles Burton Gulick. New York: Ginn.

Gossen, Charles Théodore. 1951. *Petite grammaire de l'ancien picard.* Paris: Klincksieck.

Grand Larousse de la langue française. 1976. 7 vols. Paris: Librairie Larousse.

Grandgent, Charles H. 1927. *From Latin to Italian: An Historical Outline of the Phonology and Morphology of the Italian Language.* Cambridge, Mass.: Harvard University Press.

——. 1905. *An Outline of the Phonology and Morphology of Old Provençal.* 2d ed. Boston: Heath.

Green, John N. 1988. "Spanish." *The Romance Languages,* ed. Martin Harris and Nigel Vincent, 79–150. London: Croom Helm / New York: Oxford University Press.

Griera y Gaja, Antonio. 1949. *Dialectología catalana.* Barcelona: Escuela de Filología.

Grossi Gondi, Felice. 1920. *Trattato di epigrafia cristiana latina e greca del mondo romano occidentale.* Rome: Università gregoriana.

Haadsma, R. A., and J. Nuchelmans. 1963. *Précis de latin vulgaire.* Groningen: J. B. Wolters.

Haiman, John. 1988. "Rhæto-Romance." *The Romance Languages,* ed. Martin Harris and Nigel Vincent, 351–90. London: Croom Helm / New York: Oxford University Press.

Hajek, John. 1997. "Emilia-Romangna." *The Dialects of Italy,* ed. Martin Maiden and Mair Perry. London: Routledge.

Hall, Christopher J. 1992. *Morphology and Mind: Towards a Unified Approach to Explanation in Linguistics.* London: Routledge.

Hall, Robert A., Jr. 1974. *External History of the Romance Languages*. New York: Elsevier.

Harre, Catherine E. 1991. *T e n e r + Past Participle: A Case Study in Linguistic Description*. London: Routledge.

Harrington, K. P., ed. 1997. *Medieval Latin*. 2d ed. Rev. Joseph Pucci. Chicago: University of Chicago Press.

Harris, Martin. 1988. "The Romance Languages." *The Romance Languages*, ed. Martin Harris and Nigel Vincent, 1–25. London: Croom Helm / New York: Oxford University Press.

———. 1982. "The 'Past Simple' and 'Present Perfect' in Romance." *Studies in the Romance Verb: Studies Offered to Joe Cremona on the Occasion of his 60th Birthday*, 42–70. London: Croom Helm.

———. 1978. *The Evolution of French Syntax: A Comparative Approach*. London: Longman.

Harris, Martin, and Nigel Vincent, ed. 1988. *The Romance Languages*. London: Croom Helm / New York: Oxford University Press.

Harris-Northall, Ray. 1996. "The Old Spanish Participle in -UDO: Its Origin, Use, and Loss." *Hispanic Review* 64: 31–56.

Hawkins, Roger. 1993. "Regional Variation in France." *French Today: Language in its Social Context*, ed. Carol Sanders, 55–84. Cambridge: Cambridge University Press.

Heine, Bernd. 1993. *Auxiliaries: Cognitive Forces and Grammaticalization*. New York: Oxford University Press.

Heine, Bernd, Ulrike Claudi, and Friederike Hünnemeyer. 1991. *Grammaticalization: A Conceptual Framework*. Chicago: University of Chicago Press.

Herman, József. 1990. *Du latin aux langues romanes: Etudes de linguistique historique*. Collected by Sandor Kiss. Tübingen: Niemeyer.

———. 1987. "La disparition de -s et la morphologie dialectale du latin parlé." *Latin vulgaire–latin tardif*, ed. József Herman, 97–107. Tübingen: Niemeyer.

Hock, Hans Henrich. 1986. *Principles of Historical Linguistics*. Berlin: Mouton de Gruyter.

Holl, Alfred. 1988. *Romanische Verbalmorphologie und relationen-theoretische mathematische Linguistik*. Tübingen: Niemeyer.

Iliescu, Maria. 1987. "Ce que nous apprend le vocabulaire de base du latin sur la diversification lexicale des langues romanes." *Latin vulgaire–latin tardif*, ed. József Herman, 109–17. Tübingen: Niemeyer.

Iliescu, Maria, and Louis Mourin. 1991. *Typologie de la morphologie verbale romane*. Vol. 1, *Vue synchronique*. Innsbruck: Institut für Sprachwissenschaft.

Iordan, Iorgu, and John Orr. 1970. *An Introduction to Romance Linguistics*. Rev. Rebecca Posner. Berkeley: University of California Press.

Iseley, Nancy V., ed. 1966. *Chançun de Willame*. Chapel Hill: University of North Carolina Press.

Ive, Antonio. 1975. *I Dialetti ladino-veneti dell'Istria*. Reprint of 1900 ed. Bologna: Forni.

Jakobson, Roman. 1962. "The Concept of the Sound Law and the Teleological Criterion." *Selected Writings 1: Phonological Studies*, 1–2. 's-Gravenage: Mouton.

Joffre, Marie-Dominique. 1995. *Le verbe latin: voix et diathèse*. Louvain: Peeters.

Jones, Michael. 1988. "Sardinian." *The Romance Languages*, ed. Martin Harris and Nigel Vincent, 314–50. London: Croom Helm / New York: Oxford University Press.

Jones, Peter V., and Keith C. Sidwell. 1986. *Reading Latin: Grammar, Vocabulary, and Exercises*. Cambridge: Cambridge University Press.

Joseph, John E. 1989. "Inflection and Periphrastic Structures in Romance." *Studies in Romance Linguistics (Selected Papers from the Seventeenth Linguistic Symposium on Romance Languages)*, ed. Carl Kirschner and Janet De Cesaris, 195–208. Amsterdam: Benjamins.

Julliand, Alphonse, and Vincenzo Traversa. 1973. *Frequency Dictionary of Italian Words*. The Romance Languages and Their Structures, 11. The Hague: Mouton.

Julliand, Alphonse, Dorothy Brodin, and Catherine Davidovitch. 1970. *Frequency Dictionary of French Words*. The Romance Languages and Their Structures, F1. The Hague: Mouton.

Julliand, Alphonse, P. M. H. Edwards, and Ileana Julliand. 1965. *Frequency Dictionary of Romanian Words*. The Romance Languages and Their Structures, R1. The Hague: Mouton.

Julliand, Alphonse, and E. Chang-Rodriguez. 1964. *Frequency Dictionary of Spanish Words*. The Romance Languages and Their Structures, S1. The Hague: Mouton.

Kent, Roland G. 1946. *The Forms of Latin: A Descriptive and Historical Morphology*. Baltimore: Waverly.

Kibler, William W. 1989. *An Introduction to Old French*, 2d ed. New York: Modern Language Association.

Kovačec, August. 1984. "Istroromâna." *Tratat de dialectologie româneascǎ*, ed. Valeriu Rusu, 550–91. Craiova: Scrisul Românesc.

———. 1971. *Descrierea istroromânei actuale*. Bucharest: Editura academiei Republicii Socialiste România.

Kramer, Johannes. 1976. *Historische Grammatik des Dolomitenladinischen: Formenlehre*. Gerbrunn bein Würzburg: A. Lehmann.

Kurzová, Helena. 1993. *From Indo-European to Latin: The Evolution of a Morphosyntactic Type*. Current Issues in Linguistic Theory 104. Amsterdam and Philadelphia: Benjamins.

Lamano y Beneite, José de. 1915. *El dialecto vulgar salmantino*. Salamanca: Tipografía popular.

Lapesa, Rafael. 1981. *Historia de la lengua española*. 9th ed. Madrid: Gredos.

Lathrop, Thomas A. 1986. *The Evolution of Spanish*. Newark, Del.: Juan de la Cuesta.

Laughton, Eric. *The Participle in Cicero*. London: Oxford University Press.

Laurent, Richard. 1998. "Resultados en las lenguas romances de adjetivos con desinencias derivadas de -ŪTUM." Trans. Regina Morin. *Revista de filología española* LXXVIII: 27–48.

Lausberg, Heinrich. 1971. *Linguistica romanza.* Vol. 2, *Morfologia.* Trans. Nicolò Pasero. Critica e filologia 6. Milan: Feltrinelli.

Lăzărescu, Paul. 1984. "Subdialectul moldovean." *Tratat de dialectologie românească,* ed. Valeriu Rusu, 208–40. Craiova: Scrisul Românesc.

Lepelley, René. 1974. *Le parler normand du Val de Saire (Manche): phonétique, morphologie, syntaxe, vocabulaire de la vie rurale.* Cahiers des annales de Normandie 7. Caen: Musée de Normandie.

Lesbegue, Philéas. 1984. *Grammaire picard-brayonne.* Publications du centre d'études picardes 23. Amiens: Université de Picardie.

Leumann, Manu. 1977. *Lateinische Laut- und Formenlehre.* 2d ed. Handbuch der Altertumswissenschaft. Vol. 2:2:1. Munich: C. Beck.

Liddicoat, Anthony. 1994. *A Grammar of the Norman French of the Channell Islands.* Berlin and New York: Mouton de Gruyter.

Lloyd, Paul M. 1987. *From Latin to Spanish.* Vol. 1, *Historical Phonology and Morphology of the Spanish Language.* Memoirs of the American Philosophical Society 173. Philadelphia: American Philosophical Society.

Lockwood, William Burley. 1968. *Historical German Syntax.* Oxford: Clarendon Press.

Löfstedt, Einar. 1959. *Late Latin.* Serie A: Forelesninger 25. Oslo: Institutet for sammenlignende kulturfoskning.

Lombard, Alf, and Constantin Gâdei. 1981. *Dictionnaire morphologique de la langue roumaine.* Arlöv, Sweden: Berlings Skeab.

Loporcaro, Michele. 1998. *Sintassi comparata dell'accordo participiale romanzo.* Turin: Rosenberg and Sellier.

——. 1988. *Grammatica storica del dialetto di Altamura.* Pisa: Giardini.

Magnien, Victor. 1948. *Grammaire comparée du grec et du latin.* Vol. 3. Paris: Bordas.

Maiden, Martin. 1996. "Ipotesi sulle origini del condizionale analitico come 'futuro del passato' in italiano." *Italiano e dialetti nel tempo: Saggi di grammatica,* ed. Giulio C. Lepschy, 149–73. Rome: Bulzoni.

——. 1992. "Irregularity as a Determinant of Morphological Change." *Journal of Linguistics* 28: 285–312.

Maiden, Martin, and Mair Perry, ed. 1997. *The Dialects of Italy*. London: Routledge.

Malkiel, Yakov. 1993a. "Español roto frente al francés rompu." *Verbum romanicum: Festschrift für Maria Iliescu*, ed. Johannes Kramer and A. Plangg, 311–15. Romanistik in Geschichte und Gegenwart 28. Hamburg: Bushe.

——. 1993b. *Etymology*. Cambridge: Cambridge University Press.

——. 1992. "La pérdida del participio en *-udo*." *Nueva revista de filología hispánica* XL.1: 11–28.

——. 1987. "Le dernier épanouissement des verbes en -ĒRE." *Latin vulgaire-latin tardif*, ed. József Herman, 167–79. Tübingen: Niemeyer.

——. 1954. *The Coalescence of* EXPEDĪRE *and* PETERE *in Ibero-Romance*. Studies in the Reconstruction of Hispano-Latin Word Families 3. Berkeley: University of California Press.

Mallinson, Graham. 1988. "Romanian." *The Romance Languages*, ed. Martin Harris and Nigel Vincent, 391–419. London: Croom Helm / New York: Oxford University Press.

Mancarella, Giovan Battista. 1975. *Salento*. No. 16 in *Profilo dei dialetti italiani*, ed. Manlio Cortelazzo. Consiglio nazionale delle ricerche, Centro di studio per la dialettologia italiana. Pisa: Pacini.

Mańczak, Witold. 1990. "Les verbes en -ĒRE et -ĪRE en latin et dans les langues romanes." *Latin vulgaire–latin tardif* II, ed. Gualtiero Calboli, 195–200. Tübingen: Niemeyer.

Mann, Paul. 1885. *Das Participium præteriti in Altprovenzalischen nach den Reimen der Trobadors*. Marburg: Universitäts-Buchdruckerei.

Marin, Vitalii, and G. Rusnac, ed. 1991. *Curs de gramatică istorică a limbii române*. Chişinău, Moldova: Lumina.

Martí i Castell, Joan. 1981. *El català medieval: la llengua de Ramon Llull*. Barcelona: Indesinenter.

Martínez Amador, Emilio M. 1954. *Diccionario gramatical*. Barcelona: Ramón Sopena.

Martino, Paolo. 1991. L' "Area Lausberg": isolamento e arcaicità. Bibliotheca di ricerche linguistiche e filologiche 31. Rome: Università di Roma.

Martins Sequeira, Francisco Júlio. 1959. Gramática histórica da lingua portuguesa. 3d ed. Lisbon: Francisco Franco.

Maurer, Theodoro Henrique, Jr. 1951. A unidade da România occidental. Faculdade de filosofia, ciências e letras, Boletim 126. São Paulo: Universidade de São Paulo.

McCray, Stanley. 1988. Advanced Principles of Historical Linguistics. American University Studies Series 8. Vol. 6. New York: Lang.

Meillet, Antoine. 1965. Linguistique historique et linguistique générale 1. Paris: Champion.

——. 1964. Introduction à l'étude comparative des langues indo-européennes. Reprint of 1937 ed. University, Ala.: University of Alabama Press.

Meillet, Antoine, and Joseph Vendryes. 1927. Traité de grammaire comparée des langues classiques. 2d ed. Paris: Champion.

Mendeloff, Henry. 1969. A Manual of Comparative Romance Linguistics: Phonology and Morphology. Washington, D.C.: Catholic University of America Press.

Menéndez Pidal, Ramón. 1934. Manual de gramática histórica española. 5th ed. Madrid: Suárez.

Mennonna, Anotonio Rosario. 1987. I dialetti gallitalici della Lucania, II. Gallatina: Congedo.

Meyer-Lübke, Wilhelm. 1974. Grammaire des langues romanes. Vol. 2, Morphologie. Trans. Auguste and Georges Doutrepont. Reprint of Paris ed. of 1895. Geneva: Slatkine Reprints.

——. 1935. Romanisches etymologisches Wörterbuch. 2d ed. Heidelberg: C. Winter.

——. 1931. Grammatica storica della lingua italiana e dei dialetti toscani. Trans. Matteo Bartoli and Giacomo Braun. Turin: Chiantore.

Mighetto, David, and Per Rosengren. 1985. Diccionario reverso (Spansk Baklängesordbok). Göteborg, Sweden: Institutionen för Romanska Språk.

Migliorini, Bruno. 1952–1953. *Tra il latino e l'italiano: Primordi della lingua italiana 476–960*. N.p.

Moignet, Gérard. 1976. *Grammaire de l'ancien français*. 2d ed. Paris: Klincksieck.

Moll, Francisco. 1952. *Gramática histórica catalana*. Madrid: Gredos.

Monteil, P. 1970. *Eléments de phonétique et de morphologie du latin*. Paris: Fernand Nathan.

Montgomery, Thomas. 1995. "A Latin Linguistic Icon Readapted in Proto-Romance and in Medieval Spanish." *Hispanic Review* 63: 147–55.

Mourin, Louis. 1968. "Etude No. IV: Les participes passés irréguliers"; and "Etude No. V: Les rapports entre les formes irrégulières du parfait et du participe passé." *Contribution à la description comparée de la morphologie verbale des langues romanes*. Vol. 3. Brussels: Presses universitaires de Bruxelles.

Nagore Lain, Francho. 1986. *El aragonés de Panticosa: Gramática*. Huesca: Excma.

Nandris, Octave. 1963. *Phonétique historique du roumain*. Paris: Klincksieck.

Neagoe, Victorela. 1984. "Subdialectul bănăţean." *Tratat de dialectologie românească*, ed. Valeriu Rusu, 240–84. Craiova: Scrisul Românesc.

Nicoli, Franco. 1983. *Grammatica milanese*. Milan: Bramante.

Noreiko, Stephen. "New Words for New Technologies." *French Today: Language in its Social Context*, ed. Carol Sanders, 171–84. Cambridge: Cambridge University Press.

Oder, Eugen. 1901. *Mulomedicina Chironis*. Leipzig: Teubner.

Olbertz, Hella. 1998. *Verbal Periphrases in a Functional Grammar of Spanish*. Berlin and New York: Mouton de Gruyter.

Oliva, Salvador, and Angela Buxton. 1985. *Diccionari català–anglès*. Barcelona: Enciclopèdia catalana.

Paden, William D. 1998. *An Introduction to Old Occitan*. Introductions to Older Languages 4. New York: Modern Language Association.

Pallabazzer, Vito. 1989. *Lingua e cultura ladina: lessico e onomastica*. Belluno: Istituto bellunese di ricerche sociali e culturali.

Palmer, Leonard Robert. 1954. *The Latin Language*. London: Faber and Faber.

Papahagi, Tache. 1974. *Dicţionarul dialectului aromân general şi etimologic*. Bucharest: Editura Academiei Republicii Populare Române.

Parkinson, Stephen. 1988. "Portuguese." *The Romance Languages*, ed. Martin Harris and Nigel Vincent, 131–69. London: Croom Helm / New York: Oxford University Press.

Pattison, David Graham. 1975. *Early Spanish Suffixes: A Functional Study of the Principal Nominal Suffixes of Spanish up to 1300*. Publications of the Philological Society 27. Oxford: Basil Blackwell.

Pellegrini, G. B., ed. 1970. *Studi linguistici friulani II*. Udine: Società filologica friulana.

Pelliciardi, Ferdinando. 1977. *Grammatica del dialetto romagnola: la lengva dla mi tëra*. Ravenna: Longo.

Pena, X. Ramón, and Manuel Rosales. 1991. *Manual de galego urxente*. 3d ed. Rev. Xerais de Galicia.

Penny, Ralph. 1991. *A History of the Spanish Language*. Cambridge: Cambridge University Press.

——. 1978. *Estudio estructural del habla de Tudanca*. Tübingen: Niemeyer.

——. 1970. *El habla pasiega: ensayo de dialectología montañesa*. London: Tamesis.

Petronius. 1959. *The Satyricon*. Trans. William Arrowsmith. New York: New American Library.

Petrovici, Emil. 1964. "L'unité dialectale de la langue roumaine." *Revue roumaine de linguistique* IX: 375–88.

Petrucci, Vito Elio. 1984. *Grammatica sgrammaticata della lingua genovese*. Genoa: Sagep.

Pisani, Vittore. 1955. *Introduzione allo studio delle lingue germaniche*. 3d ed. Rev. Marco Scovazzi. Turin: Rosenberg and Sellier.

Pittau, Massimo. 1991. *Grammatica della lingua sarda: varietà logurdorese.* Sassari: Delfino.

Planta, Robert von. 1897. *Grammatik der Oskisch-Umbrischen Dialekte,* II. Strasburg: Trübner.

Plomteux, Hugo. 1975. *I dialetti della Liguria orientale odierna: la Val Graveglia.* Storia della lingua italiana e dialettologia. 2 vols. Bologna: Patròn.

Politzer, Robert L. 1949. *A Study of the Language of Eighth-Century Lombardic Documents: A Statistical Analysis of the Codice Paleografico Lombardo.* Ph.D. diss., Columbia University.

Pop, Sever. 1948. *Grammaire roumaine.* Bern: Francke.

Pope, Mildred K. 1952. *From Latin to Modern French, with Especial Consideration of Anglo-Norman.* 2d ed. Manchester: Manchester University Press.

Popescu, Radu. 1980. *Graiul Gorjenilor de lîngă munte.* Craiova: Scrisul Românesc.

Posner, Rebecca. 1996. *The Romance Languages.* Cambridge: Cambridge University Press.

Poultney, James Wilson. 1959. *The Bronze Tablets of Iguvium.* Philological Monographs XVII, ed. John L. Heller. Baltimore: American Philological Association.

Price, Glanville. 1973. *The French Language: Present and Past.* London: Arnold.

Prokosch, Eduard. 1939. *A Comparative Germanic Grammar.* Philadelphia: Linguistic Society of America.

Puşcariu, Sextil. 1926, 1929. *Studii istroromâne.* Vols. 2 and 3. Bucharest: Cultura naţională.

Renzi, Lorenzo. 1982. *Introducción a la filología românica.* Madrid: Gredos.

Rey-Debove, Josette, and Alain Rey. 1993. *Le nouveau petit Robert.* 2d ed. Montreal: Dicorobert.

Rickard, Peter. 1974. *A History of the French Language.* London: Hutchinson.

Ríos García, Isabel. 1989. *El habla de Sot de Ferrer*. Castellón: Diputació de Castelló.

Robins, Robert Henry. 1990. *A Short History of Linguistics*. 3d ed. London: Longman.

Rohlfs, Gerhard. 1949. *Grammatik der italienischen Sprache und ihrer Mundarten*. Bern: Francke.

Rohlfs, Gerhard. 1970. *From Vulgar Latin to Old French*. Trans. Vincent Almazon and Lillian McCarthy. Detroit: Wayne State University Press.

———. 1968. *Grammatica storica della lingua italiana e dei suoi dialetti: Morfologia*. Rev. ed. Trans. Temistocle Franceschi. Turin: Einaudi.

———. 1949. *Grammatik der italienischen Sprache und ihrer Mundarten*. Bern: Francke.

Ronjat, Jules. 1980. *Grammaire [h]istorique des parlers provençaux*. Reprint of 1930–1941 Montpellier ed. Geneva: Slatkine / Marseille: Laffitte.

Rosario, Maria Rita. 1979. *Studi sul dialetto trentino di Stivor (Bosnia)*. Florence: Nuova Italia.

Rosetti, Alexandru. 1978. *Istoria limbii române*. Vol. 1. 2d ed. Bucharest: Editura ştiinţifică şi enciclopedică.

Rouffiange, Robert. 1983. *Le patois et le français rural de Magny-lès-Aubigny (Côte d'Or)*. Dijon: Association bourguignonne de dialectologie et d'onomastique.

Rusu, Valeriu, ed. 1984. *Tratat de dialectologie românească*. Craiova: Scrisul Românesc.

Safarewicz, Jan. 1969. *Historische lateinische Grammatik*. Halle: Niemeyer.

Samarin, William J. 1967. *Field Linguistics: A Guide to Linguistic Field Work*. New York: Holt, Rinehart and Winston.

Sampson, Rodney, ed. 1980. *Early Romance Texts: An Anthology*. Cambridge: Cambridge University Press.

Sanders, Carol, ed. 1993. *French Today: Language in Its Social Context*. Cambridge: Cambridge University Press.

Saramandu, Nicolae. 1984. "Meglenoromânia." *Tratat de dialectologie românească*, ed. Valeriu Rusu, 476 et seq. Craiova: Scrisul Românesc.

Sârbu, Richard, with Vasile Frățilă. 1992. *Texte istroromâne cu un studiu introductiv "Istroromâna—azi" și un glosar.* 2d ed. Timișoara: Tiporafia Universitătii din Timișoara.

Schmitz, John Robert. 1984. "Problems in the Analysis of Portuguese Participles in -*do*." *Papers from the XIIth Linguistic Symposium on Romance Languages*, ed. Philip Baldi, 549–64. Amsterdam: Benjamins.

Schwegler, Armin. 1990. *Analyticity and Syntheticity: A Diachronic Perspective with Special Reference to Romance Languages*. Empirical Approaches to Language Typology 6. Berlin: Mouton de Gruyter.

Sedgwick, Walter Bradbury, ed. 1950. *The Cena Trimalchionis of Petronius, Together with Seneca's* Apocolocyntosis *and a Selection of Pompeian Inscriptions*. Oxford: Clarendon Press.

Sempere Martínez, Joan. 1995. "The Valencian Linguistic Heterodoxy." *Catalan Review* IX, no. 2: 97–124.

Seriani, Luca. 1989. *Grammatica italiana*. Turin: Unione tipografico-editrice torinese.

Sihler, Andrew L. 1995. *New Comparative Grammar of Greek and Latin*. New York: Oxford University Press.

Silva Neto, Serafim da. 1952. *História da língua portuguêsa*. Rio de Janeiro: Livros de Portugal.

Smith, Nathaniel B., and Thomas G. Bergin. 1984. *An Old Provençal Primer*. New York: Garland.

Smyth, Herbert Weir. 1956. *Greek Grammar*. Cambridge, Mass.: Harvard University Press.

Sommer, Ferdinand. 1914. *Handbuch der lateinischen Laut- und Formenlehre*. 2d and 3d ed. Heidelberg: C. Winter.

Spano, Giovanni. 1840. *Ortografia sarda nazionale ossia grammatica della lingua logudorese paragonata all'italiana*. Cagliari: Reale Stamperia.

Squartini, Mario. 1998. *Verbal Periphrases in Romance: Aspect, Actionality, and Grammaticalization*. Empirical Approaches to Language Typology 21. Berlin and New York: Mouton de Gruyter.

Studer, Paul, and E. G. R. Waters. 1924. *Historical French Reader*. Oxford: Clarendon.

Sturtevant, Edgar H. 1933. *A Comparative Grammar of the Hittite Language*. Philadelphia: Waverly.

Tagliavini, Carlo. 1962. *Le origini delle lingue neolatine*. 3d ed. Bologna: Pàtron.

———. 1923. *Grammatica della lingua rumena*. Heidelberg: Giulio Gross.

Taylor, James L. 1958. *A Portuguese–English Dictionary*. Stanford, Calif.: Stanford University Press.

Tekavčić, Pavao. 1972. *Grammatica storica dell'italiano*. Vol. 2, *Morfosintassi*. Bologna: Il Mulino.

Telman, Tullio, and Martin Maiden. 1997. "Word Structure and Word Formation." *The Dialects of Italy*, ed. Martin Maiden and Mair Perry, 116–23. London: Routledge.

Togeby, Knud. 1980. "Romance Historical Morphology." *Trends in Romance Linguistics and Philology*. Vol. 1, *Romance Comparative and Historical Linguistics*. The Hague: Mouton.

Trabelsi-Louguet, Annick. 1994. *Lexique de l'avesnois*. Wattignies-la-Victoire [Nord]: A. Trabelsi-Louguet.

Troncon, Antonella, and Luciano Canepari. 1989. *Lingua italiana nel Lazio*. Rome: Jouvance.

Tuttle, Edward. 1997. "The Veneto." *The Dialects of Italy*, ed. Martin Maiden and Mair Perry, 263–70. London: Routledge.

Unbegaun, B. O. 1967. *Russian Grammar*. Oxford: Clarendon Press.

Väänänen, Veikko. 1987. *Le journal-épître d'Egérie* (Itinerarium Egeriæ): *étude linguistique*. Helsinki: Suomalainenn Tiedeakatemia.

———. 1981. *Introduction au latin vulgaire*. 3d ed. Paris: Klincksieck.

Vaillant, André. 1966. *Grammaire comparée des langues slaves*. Vol. 3, *Le Verbe*, and Vol. 5, *La Syntaxe*. Paris: Klincksieck.

Valente, Vincenzo. 1975. *Puglia*. No. 15 in *Profilo dei dialetti italiani*, ed. Manlio Cortelazzo. Consiglio nazionale delle ricerche, Centro di studio per la dialettologia italiana. Pisa: Pacini.

Vasconcelos, J. Leite de. 1981. *Filología barranquenha*. Reprint of 1955 ed. Lisbon: Imprensa nacional–Casa de moeda.

Velleman, Antonius. 1924. *Grammatica teoretica, pratica ed istorica della lingua ladina d'Engiadin*. Vol. 2, *Il Verbo*. Zürich: Füssli.

Villa, Elegio. 1992. *Grammatica e ortografia dei dialetti abruzzesi*. L'Aquila and Rome: Japadre.

Vincent, Nigel. 1988a. "Latin." *The Romance Languages*, ed. Martin Harris and Nigel Vincent, 26–78. London: Croom Helm / New York: Oxford University Press.

———. 1988b. "Italian." *The Romance Languages*, ed. Martin Harris and Nigel Vincent, 279–313. London: Croom Helm / New York: Oxford University Press.

———. 1978. "Towards an Explanation of Some Analogies in Perfect and Past Participle Stems in Latin and Italian." *Semasia* 5: 47–64.

Vrabie, Emil. 1999. *Aromanian: Grammar, Lexicon, and an English–Arumanian Dictionary*. Romance Monographs. University, Miss.: University of Mississippi Press.

———. 1995. "Aromanian Etymologies." *General Linguistics* 33, no. 4: 212–18.

———. 1970. "Testi dialettali friulani raccolti in Romania." *Studi linguistici friulani II*, ed. G. B. Pellegrini, 103–12. Udine: Società filologica friulana.

Vulpe, Magdalena. 1984. "Subdialectu maramureşean." *Tratat de dialectologie românească*, ed. Valeriu Rusu, 320–54. Craiova: Scrisul Românesc.

Wagner, Max Leopold. 1951. *La lingua sarda: storia spirito e forma*. Bern: Francke.

Watkins, Calvert. 1970. "A Further Remark on Lachmann's Law." *Harvard Studies in Classical Philology* 74: 55–65.

Wetzels, Leo. 1984. "Paradigm Leveling in Latin and Old French: A Critical View of Rule Inversion." *Papers from the XIIth Linguistic Symposium on Romance Languages*, ed. Philip Baldi, 579–99. Amsterdam: Benjamins.

Wheeler, Max W. 1988a. "Catalan." *The Romance Languages*, ed. Martin Harris and Nigel Vincent, 170–208. London: Croom Helm / New York: Oxford University Press.

———. 1988b. "Occitan." *The Romance Languages*, ed. Martin Harris and Nigel Vincent, 246–77. London: Croom Helm / New York: Oxford University Press.

Williams, Edwin B. 1962. *From Latin to Portuguese: Historical Phonology and Morphology of the Portuguese Language*. 2d ed. Philadelphia: University of Pennsylvania Press.

Wright, Joseph. 1910. *Grammar of the Gothic Language*. Oxford: Clarendon Press.

Wright, Roger. 1982. *Late Latin and Early Romance in Spain and Carolingian France*. ARCA Classical and Medieval Texts, Papers and Monographs 8. Liverpool: Francis Cairns.

Zamboni, Alberto. 1974. *Veneto*. No. 5 in *Profilo dei dialetti italiani*, ed. Manlio Cortelazzo. Consiglio nazionale delle ricerche, Centro di studio per la dialettologia italiana. Pisa: Pacini.

Zumpt, Carl Gottlob. 1854. *A Grammar of the Latin Language*. Trans. Leonhard Schmitz. Rev. Charles Anton. 3d ed. New York: Harper and Brothers.

Index Verborum

Entries appear under one of four headings: non-Latin languages, Latin, Late Latin, and Romance. Under the fourth heading, an entry like

dormi 'slept' [Fr.], 4.4.8

consists of **1** a word, **2** its gloss in single quotes, **3** its language or dialect in brackets, **4** the chapter(s) and section(s) in which it appears. Under Latin, Late Latin, and non-Latin languages, each entry consists of parts 1, 2, and 4.

COVERAGE

Unless otherwise stated, entries represent past participles or, in early Indo-European languages, verbal adjectives. Except for Latin verbs lacking past participles, infinitives go unlisted here. So do all finite verb forms and prepositions used as prefixes. Other parts of speech are labeled in italics, as in the Latin entry that begins

MATTEA 'meat delicacy' *noun*

The index verborum omits all words given in tables and appendixes.

Especially for Romanian and Aromanian, certain past participles are followed by a note "also noun" or "also adj." At times, the meaning of the noun or adjective remains close to that of the past participle; after the Rom. p.p. *râs* 'laughed,' the note "also noun" indicates that *râs* also means 'laughter.' At times, meanings have diverged widely, as with Rom. *copt* 'baked' also meaning 'ripe,' or Rom. *trimis* 'sent' also meaning 'envoy'); such an adjective or noun receives an entry of its own.

467

Readers are assumed to be familiar with the sound and spelling systems of major Romance languages. For the forgetful, a list of abbreviations follows these prefatory remarks.

Entries from much of Western Romance are identified by dialect alone rather than language plus dialect. Thus,

a g u t 'had' by-f [Tam.], 4.6.2.9

has [Tam.] rather than *[Cat.: Tam] standing for the Tamaritan dialect of Catalan. The same holds true for two subdialects: Val Graveglia [VG] in Ligurian and San Mango [SM] in Calabrian. Such abridgments should not be taken by linguistic separatists as proof that their dialect now enjoys a separate and equal status among the languages of Romance.

CITATION FORMS

Past participles from Latin appear in the neuter nominative/accusative singular, less -M. Nouns and adjectives from Latin likewise appear in the accusative singular less any -M, and Latin present participles appear in the masculine/feminine accusative singular less -M. Past participles from other Indo-European languages, including Romance, almost always appear in the least marked form: masculine singular without a case ending. Yet verbal adjectives from Greek appear in the masculine nominative singular, and forms found for Proto-Romance appear as they have been reconstructed.

Two past participles appearing on the same line are normally to be read as masc.sg. and fem.sg., in that order. In Franco-Provençal, though, an entry like Val d'Aosta *redzut, –a* 'shut in' means that the masc.sg./pl. and the fem.sg. have the same stem, but that fem.sg. adds a final vowel written a̲. In Norman Val de Saire, the first form given serves for masc.sg., while the second serves for fem.sg./pl. as well as masc.pl.

Portuguese forms figure here only when quite unlike cognates in Spanish. Ptg. *feito* and Sp. *hecho* 'done/made' are both listed. Petty discrepancies like that between Ptg. *devido* and Sp. *debido* 'owed, had to' are almost always ignored to the profit of Spanish.

Two past participles with clearly different origins that have fallen together are distinguished by subscript numerals. For example, from Poitevin Occitan come *cheùt₁* 'cooked' and *cheùt₂* 'fallen.' (As readers know by now, the first continues COCTU; the second could be said to discontinue rare CĀSU.)

Appearing in the index verborum are a very few unattested forms, or more accurately forms I never tracked down, like OFr. **serdu* 'sifted.' Each is marked with an asterisk. Three entries come from Franco-Italian (Fr.-It.), an italianized Old French used to render epics for the Lombard market.

ALPHABETIZING AND DIACRITICS

Customs in Romance languages being irreconcilable, entries are alphabetized according to the norms of English. Double letters, digraphs, diacritics, and apostrophes have no effect on alphabetical ranking, except that entries with diacritics come after otherwise identical forms without them. Unique slot-fillers are listed before any by-forms, past participles before identical words used as other parts of speech. In Latin words, vocalic I and U are kept distinct from consonantal J and V.

To clarify pronunciation, diacritics are added to a few words from Old French. In proparoxytonic nouns from Italian like *créscita* 'growth,' stress is marked by an acute accent, a practice that Italians might consider adopting. To enhance readability, words from Romance dialects often lack the diacritics with which transcribers have adorned them, above and below.

Spelling for dialectal entries has often been lightly italianized, gallicized, hispanized, and so on. In Sardinian words like *kelu* 'sky,' though, [k] before front vowels is written k̲ rather than italianate c̲h̲. Various symbols from the International Phonetic Alphabet, or from national schools of transcription, have been replaced by diacriticked Latin letters. Thus, s̬ stands for [ʃ] as in Fr. *cheval* 'horse,' z̬ stands for [ʒ] as in Fr. *jeune* 'young,' c̬ stands for [tʃ] as in It. *certo* 'sure,' and ğ stands for [dʒ] as in It. *giorno* 'day.' Others have been replaced by digraphs: <u>dh</u> stands for [ð] as in Engl. *this,* and <u>th</u> for [θ] as in Engl. *thin.* Still, ə (schwa) has been kept and comes between *e* and *f.* Two words in this index begin with ə.

GLOSSES

Every entry is glossed, wherever possible with a survival from Germanic rather than a borrowing from Latin or Greek. A handful of forms in Istriano (Gallo-Italian) are glossed merely by '?' Likewise owing to authorial ignorance, further glosses may prove more indicative than definitive.

SPECIAL SIGNS

Entries appearing in footnotes are marked by chapter number, plus sign, and note number: 2+74 is to be read "Chapter 2, note 74." Entries preceded by a hyphen (e.g. Sp. *-ducido* 'led, brought') occur only in compounds like Sp. *conducido* 'driven.' Abbreviations after a colon (e.g. [Vegl.: Z], where Z = Zara) denote dialects or subdialects. Terms after a semicolon (e.g. [OIt.; Dante] or [OFr.; <u>St. Alexis</u>]) denote authors or works, the latter being underlined. A solidus / separates by-form entries in the same gender and number (e.g. [fem.sg.] *kona/konwʿa* 'known' in the Franco-Provençal of Vaux). A comma separates two variants (e.g. It. *puzzo, puzza* 'stink' [noun]). For Istro-Romanian, past participles borrowed from Croatian have been put in curly brackets { }, but the privilege has not been extended to e.g. Arom. *mutrit* 'looked at,' also Slavic-derived, or to words borrowed from tongues like Gaulish, Frankish, or English. Doubtful entries are marked by **?**, seemingly semilearnèd ones by •. True oddities, each a judgment call, are marked by **!**

VARIANTS

Before literary standards began spreading outward from Florence and Burgos and Paris, causing most local speechways to shrivel and succumb, speakers of Romance languages tolerated considerable variation in morphology.

Naturally, this tolerance applied to past participles. Here all prestandard forms are marked *O* for "Old," even if they come from the stage fenced off as "Middle" by later researchers in the field. "Old" forms being by definition out of date, they seldom appear here unless quite unlike modern equivalents, but a few exceptions have been made idiosyncratically.

In French, almost every past participle still extant is listed under its modern spelling. Readers should recall four features of French phonology. First, [s] has regularly vanished before another consonant, in e.g. *écrit* from OFr. *escrit* 'written.' Second, [ə] has vanished before another vowel, in e.g. *pu* from OFr. *peü* 'been able.' Third, a diphthong after a palatal has simplfied, in e.g. *caché* from OFr. *cachié* 'hidden.' Fourth, [l] after a vowel and before a consonant has vocalized to [w], the resulting diphthong subsequently being simplified in speech, in e.g. *faux* < FALSU 'untrue.' Yet OFr. *leü* 'been allowed' ≠ LICITU and *geü* 'lain' ≠ *JECITU both appear in the index verborum because they leave no modern heirs. OFr. *vuidié* 'emptied' appears, because it has simplified twice over to turn into mod. *vidé*. With and without vocalization of [l], OOc. *vout* and *volt* 'turned, rolled' are both listed.

BY-FORMS; SHORT, LONG, ALLEGRO FORMS

Throughout the Romance part of this index, the abbreviation "f" stands for "form" in the usage notes *"by-f," "short f," "long f,"* and *"allegro f."* Perhaps loosely, I use "by-form" to mean either (a) variants within the same form-class, like Val d'Aosta *ivert* and *uvert* 'opened,' or (b) variants belonging to different form-classes, like Galician *bendicido* and *bendito* 'blessed.' Variants eventually received into the belletristic wordstock had often developed by the "Old" period of a language. On that account, the presence of the note *"by-f"* may indicate that a version of the modern standard past participle was already current long ago, but its absence should not be taken to imply that past-participial regularization must have come about afterward. Most words labeled *"by-f"* are dialectal or stylistic variants rather than true fungibles like Engl. *lighted* and *lit*. Readers may fail to find their favorite by-forms here.

Romance Abbreviations

Abru.	Abruzzese [It.]	D	Dignanese [Ist-I]
Alg.	Alguerese [Cat.]	ECat.	Eastern Catalan
Amp.	Ampezzo [Fri.]	Elb.	Elban [It.]
Am.Sp.	American Spanish	Enga.	Engadin [RR]
Apul.	Apulian (Pugliese) [It.]	Fass.	Fassano [Lad.]
Arag.	Aragonese [Sp.]	FP	Franco-Provençal
Args.	Aragüés Valley [Sp.]	Fr.	French
Arom.	Aromanian	Fr.-It.	Franco-Italian
Aspe	Aspe Valley [Gasc.]	Fri.	Friulian
Auv.	Auvergnat [Oc.]	Fri-R	Friulian in Romania
Av.	Avesnois [Pic.]	Gal.	Galician [Ptg.]
Bad.	Badiotto [Lad.]	Gar.	Gardenese [Lad.]
Ban.	Banat [Mold.]	Gasc.	Gascon [Oc.]
Barr.	Barranquenho [Ptg.]	Gen.	Genoese [Lig.]
Berg.	Bergamese [It.]	Gév.	Gévaudanais [Oc.]
Bls.	Bielsa [Arag.]	Ggn.	Guignemicourt [Pic.]
Br.	Brayon [Pic.]	Gor.	Gorizia [Fri.]
Burg.	Burgundian [Fr.]	Gra.	Grado [Fri.]
Cal.	Calabrian [It.]	Ist-I	Istriano [It.]
Can.	Candama [Leon.]	Ist-R	Istro-Romanian
Car.	Cartagena [Sp.]	It.	Italian
Cast.	nonstd. Castilian [Sp.]	K	Kruševo [Arom.]
Cat.	Catalan	Lad.	Ladin
CI	Channel Islands [Nor.]	Lang.	Languedocian [Oc.]
Clau.	Clauzetto [Fri.]	Laz.	Laziale [It.]
Cmpa.	Campagnese [It.]	Leon.	Leonese [Sp.]
Cmpi.	Campidanese [Sard.]	Lig.	Ligurian [It.]
Cod.	Codròipo [Fri.]	Liv.	Livinallonghese [Lad.]
Cors.	Corsican [It.]	Log.	Logudorese [Sard.]

Lomb.	Lombard [It.]		Sal.	Salento [It.]
Luca.	Lucanian [It.]		Salm.	Salmantino [Sp.]
Luca-GI	Gallo-Italian in Lucania		Sard.	Sardinian
Lucc.	Luccan [It.]		SCors.	South Corsican [It.]
Lun.	Lunigiana [It.]		SF	Sot de Ferrer [Sp.]
Mara.	Maramur [Mold.]		Sic.	Sicilian [It.]
Marb.	Marebbano [Lad.]		Sien.	Sienese [It.]
Marc.	Marchese [It.]		Sis.	Sisco [Lig.]
Meg.	Meglenoromanian [Arom.]		SIst-R	South Istro-Romanian
Mil.	Milanese [It.]		SLuca.	South Lucanian [It.]
Mold.	Moldavian [Rom.]		SM	San Mango [Cal.]
N	Naisey [FP]		Sp.	Spanish
Neap.	Neapolitan [Cal.]		Sto.	Saintongeais [Oc.]
Nor.	Norman [Fr.]		Surs.	Surselvan [RR]
Nuor.	Nuorese [Sard.]		Ţ	Ţắrneca [Meg.]
O	Old (stage of language)		Tam.	Tamaritan [Cat.]
Oc.	Occitan		Tud.	Tudanca [Leon.]
Oltn.	Oltenian [Rom.]		Tusc.	nonstd. Tuscan [It.]
Opo.	Oporto [Ptg.]		U	Uma [Meg.]
Pad.	Paduan [It.]		Ud.	Udine [Fri.]
Pch.	Percheron [Nor.]		V A	Val d'Aosta [FP]
Pic.	Picard [Fr.]		Val.	Valencian [Cat.]
Pied.	Piedmontese [It.]		Vd.	Vaud [FP]
Pin.	Mt. Pindus area [Arom.]		V E	Val d'Echo [Arag.]
Pnt.	Panticosa [Arag.]		Vegl.	Vegliote
Poit.	Poitevin [Oc.]		Ven.	Veneto [It.]
Prov.	Provençal [Oc.]		V G	Val Graveglia [Lig.]
Ptg.	Portuguese		V P	Val del Pas [Leon.]
Rml.	Romagnolo [It.]		V S	Val de Saire [Nor.]
Rom.	(Daco-)Romanian		Vx.	Vaux [FP]
Ross.	Rossellonese [Cat.]		Z	Zara [Vegl.]
R R	Ræto-Romance			

Non-Latin Languages

PROTO-INDO-EUROPEAN

*gnHtós 'known,' 1.1
*skḷtós 'owed, ought to,' 1.1
*stətós 'stood,' 1.1

SANSKRIT

bhūtás 'become, been,' 1.1
dāntás 'tamed,' 1.1
dr̥ṣṭás 'seen,' 1.8
hinás 'left, abandoned,' 1.1
jātás 'born,' 1.1
ma-ta- 'thought,' 2.4.1
sthitás 'stood,' 1.1
tīrṇás 'crossed,' 1.1

PALI

maññ-ita- 'thought,' 2.4.1

HITTITE

istamasant- 'heard,' 1.7
pānt- 'gone,' 1.7

OLD PERSIAN

krtam 'done,' 1.7, 1.8

TOCHARIAN

kākätwu 'tricked,' 1.3.1
kākotu 'split,' 1.3.1
pāpeku 'cooked,' 1.3.1
sasruku 'killed,' 1.3.1
tatärku 'given leave,' 1.3.1
wawu 'given,' 1.3.1

TURKISH

kör 'blind' *adj.*, 3+17

GREEK

ἀδάκρυτος 'without tears,' 2.14
αἱρετός 'chosen; conquerable,' 1.1
ἀκουστός 'audible,' 1.1
ἀπρᾱκτός 'doing nothing; not done,' 1.1
γνωστός 'understood,' 0+10
γνωτός 'understood' [Homeric], 0+10
γράμμενο 'written' [modern], 1.7
γραπτός 'written,' 1.1
ζωστός 'girded,' 0+10
κέδρος 'cedar' *noun*, 2.1.1
κόλαφος 'blow, punch' *noun*, 2.2.1
λεκτός 'chooseable; chosen,' 1+17
ματτύη 'dainty dish' *noun*, 3+17
μεμπτός 'blamed; blamable,' 1.1
νοητός 'thinkable,' 1.1
ὁρατός 'visible,' 1.1
πεμπτός 'sendable; to be sent,' 1+17
πιστός 'trusting in' *rare*; 'to be
    trusted,' 0+10, 1.1
ῥυτός 'flowing,' 1.1
στατός 'stood,' 1.1
στύππη 'tow, oakum' *noun*, 2.2.1
τόρνος 'lathe' *noun*, 2.2.1
τλᾱτόν 'durable' [Doric], 1.3.5
χυτόν 'flowed, shed,' 1.3.4

BRETON

gwelet 'seen,' 1.7

OLD SLAVONIC

neslǔ 'carried,' 1.8
vŭzbudilǔ 'awoken,' 1.8

POLISH

powiedzał 'said,' 1.8

RUSSIAN

kal 'mud' *noun*, 3.3.2
pravo 'right' *noun*, 1.7
sdelal 'done' *later* 'did,' 1.8
sh ël 'gone' *later* 'went,' 1.8
svyatoy 'holy' *adj.*, 2+85
syn 'son' *noun*, 1.7
videl 'seen' *later* 'saw,' 1.8
vzyal 'taken' *later* 'took,' 1.8

SERBO-CROATIAN

kao 'mud' *noun*, 3.3.2

GOTHIC

bitans 'bitten,' 1.1
budans 'bid, asked,' 1.1
habáiþs 'had,' 1.1
kunþs 'known,' 1.1
numans 'taken,' 1.1
salbōþs 'anointed,' 1.1
skulds 'owing, lawful,' 1.1
staþs 'a place' *old p.p.,* 1.1
þāhts 'thought,' 1.1
þaúrfts 'useful' *old p.p.,* 1.1

GERMAN

alt 'old' *adj.*, 0.4
kalt 'cold' *adj.*, 0.4
Klappe 'flap, valve' *noun*, 3.3.3
Straße 'street' *noun*, 2+37

ENGLISH

beaten, 6.6
been, 0.0, 1.8, 1+41
bent, 6.4
blown, 6.6
burglar *noun*, 2+71
chidden *arch.*, 0.4
daybreak *noun*, 3.3.1
deceit *noun*, 4.4.9.4
done, 0.0, 1.8
drunk, 0.4, 1+41, 6.4
drunken *adj.*, 0.4, 6.4

flown, 1+41
frozen, 1+41
given, 1.8
gone, 1+41
graven *arch.*, 0.4
hitched, 2.11.2
killer *noun*, 2+71
lover *noun*, 2+71
many *adv.*, 6.4
melted, 0.4, 6.4
molten *adj.*, 0.4, 6.4, 6+5
much *adv.*, 6.4
not *adv.*, 6.4
pedlar *noun*, 2+71
played, 4+45
pled *neol.*, 2+82
quaint *adj.*, 4.4.9.2, 4.4.9.4
rung, 1+41
scratched, 6.4
seen, 1.8, 1+41
sewn, 1.4.4
shaven *adj.*, 0.4, 6.4
shrunk, 6.4
shrunken *adj.*, 6.4
smitten *arch.*, 0.4
snatch *noun*, 2.13.3
sown, 1.4.4
spoken, 1+41
standen *arch.*, 4.7.8
stead *noun*, 1.1
stolen, 1+41
street *noun*, 2+37
stricken *adj.*, 0.4, 6.4, 6+5
struck, 0.4, 6.4
summons *noun*, 2.15.9, 4.4.10
swollen, 6.4
sung, 1.3.3, 1+41
swum, 1+41
trodden *arch.*, 0.4
value *noun*, 4.4.9.1, 4.4.9.3
very *adv.*, 6.4
washen *arch.*, 4.7.8
writer *noun*, 2+71
written, 1+41
wrong *noun*, 2+88

Latin

CRĒTU₁ 'grown,' 2.13, 3.1.3, 3.5.6, 4.2, 4.4.2.2, 4.6.1.9, 4.6.2.3, 4.6.2.5, 4.7.0, 5.3

CRĒTU₂ 'sifted,' 0+11, 1.3.4, 2.13, 2.14.2, 3.5.2.2, 3.6.1, 4.6.2.3, 5.3

CRŪDU 'raw' *adj.*, 3.4

CUBITU 'reclined,' 1.3.6, 3.5.1

CULTELLU 'knife' *noun*, 4.7.6.4

CULTU 'tilled,' 0.3.2, 3.5.2.1, 3.6.1, 4.6.1

CULTU 'tidy, smart' *adj.*, 3.5.2.1

CURSU 'run,' 0.3.1, 2.12, 2.15.8, 3.1.5.1, 3.6.1.1, 3.6.2, 3.6.2.2, 3.7.2, 3.7.4, 3+11, 4.2, 4.4.2.2, 4.5.3, 4.6.1.2, 4.6.1.6, 4.6.1.8, 4.6.2.5, 4.7.2.2, 5.3

CURSU 'running' *noun*, 3.1.5.2, 3.5.3.2, 4.4.9.3, 4.7.7.3

*CURTU 'run' *OLat.*, 2+78, 3+66

CURTU 'short' *adj.*, 3+66

CŪSU 'threshed; forged' *by-f*, 1.4.4

CUSSU 'threshed; forged' *by-f*, 1.4.4

DĀTU 'given,' 2.13.1, 3.1.6, 4.6.2.10, 6.2, 6+8

DĒBITU 'owed, had to,' 2.4.3, 3.5.6, 3.7.3, 4.3.2, 4.4.2.2, 4.4.9.2, 4.6.1.8, 4.6.2.2, 4.7.7.2, 5.4.1

DĒCEPTU 'fooled,' 4.4.9.4, 7.6.1

DĒCĪSU 'decided,' 3.6.1.1, 4.1

DĒCRĒTU 'determined,' 2.14.1

DĒCURSU 'run down,' 4.2

DĒDITU 'surrendered,' 2.9

DĒFĒNSU 'fought off,' 2.15.8, 4.3.1, 4.4.9.3, 4.6.1.1, 4.6.2.2, 4.7.4.1, 4.7.6.1, 4.7.7.3

DĒLĒTU 'removed,' 0.3.1, 1.3.6, 2.4.3, 4.6.2.3, 5.4

DĒMANDĀTU 'entrusted,' 3.0.1

DĒMERSU 'plunged,' 3.3.2

DĒMPTU 'subtracted,' 1.4.4

DENTĀTU 'toothed' *adj.*, 4.7.4.2

DĒPOSITU 'laid down,' 3.3.1

DĒSCĒNSU 'gone down,' 3.1.5.1, 3.5.3.2, 4.2, 4.4.9.4

DĒSPECTU 'looked down' *by-f*, 4.4.9.4

DĒSPICĀTU 'looked down' *by-f*, 1.5

DĒSTRŪCTU 'torn down,' 3.1.5.1, 3.3.2, 4.2

DICTĀTU 'said over,' 3.5.9

DICTU 'said, told,' 0.2, 0.3.2, 1.3.5, 2.4.1, 2.13, 3.1.5.1, 3.3.1, 3.3.2, 3.4, 3.5.3.1, 3.5.9, 3.6.1.1, 3.6.1.2, 3.6.2, 3+37, 3+41, 4.2, 4.3.1, 4.4.11, 4.5.2, 4.6.1, 4.6.1.6, 4.6.2.4, 4.7.6.2, 4.7.15, 5.4.1, 5.6, 6.6

DĪRĒCTU 'guided,' 3.1.5.1, 3.3.1, 3.3.1.1, 3.4, 4.2, 4.3.1

DĪVĪSU 'divided,' 1.4.6, 2.11.2, 3.3.2, 3.6.1.1, 4.7.6.4

DOCTU 'taught' *also adj.*, 0.3.2, 4.4.2.2, 4.4.9.3, 4.6.1, 4.7.7.1, 4+16

DOLITU 'hurt, grieved,' 2.13.3, 4.4.2.3

DOMITU 'tamed,' 1.3.6, 3.5.1, 4.7.2.2, 4.7.7.2

DOMU 'house' *noun*, 3.7

DORMĪTU 'slept,' 2.14, 3.4, 4.4.0.3, 5.4

DUCTU 'led,' 0.2, 1.3.5, 3.1.5.1, 3.3.1, 3.7.1, 3+44, 4.2, 4.4.9.3, 4.6.1, 4.6.1.2, 4.6.2.4, 4.7.6.1, 4.7.6.2, 4.7.7.1, 4+16

ĒLĒCTU 'chosen,' 3.3.1, 3.3.1.1, 3.6.2.3, 4.4.9.4, 4.6.1.1, 4.6.2.2, 4.7.10

ĒMPTU 'bought,' 1.3.5, 1.4.4, 2.3

ĒMŪNCTU 'blown one's nose,' 1.4.3

ĒNECTU 'worn out,' 2.13.1

ĒRĒCTU 'raised, built,' 3.5.2.1, 4.2, 4.3.1, 4.6.1, 4.7.6.1, 4.7.7.1

ĒSU 'eaten' *by-f*, 1.3.5, 1.4.1, 2.3.1

ESTU 'eaten' *by-f*, 2.3.1

RESPŌNSU 'answered,' 2.12, 3.1.5.1,
  3.3.3, 3.4, 3.5.5.1, 4.1, 4.3.1, 4.3.2,
  4.4.2.2, 4.4.9, 4.6.1.2, 4.6.1.6,
  4.7.2.2
RESPŌNSU 'answer' *noun*, 3.1.5.2,
  4.4.9.3, 4.6.2.5, 4.7.7.3
RICTU 'snarled' *by-f*, 2.9
RĪNCTU 'snarled' *by-f*, 2.9
RĪSU 'laughed,' 2.4.2, 2.13, 3.1.5.1,
  3.3.1, 3.3.2.1, 4.1, 4.2, 4.3.2, 4.4.9,
  4.5.3, 4.6.1.7, 4.7.2.2, 5.2
RĪSU 'laughter' *noun*, 3.1.5.2, 4.7.7.3
ROGĀTU 'asked,' 3.3.2, 4.4.2.2
RŌRE 'dew' *noun*, 2.2.1, 3+10
RŌSU 'gnawn,' 3.1.5.1, 3.5.3.2, 3+10,
  4.2, 4.3.1, 4.3.2.4, 4.6.2.2, 4.7.2.2,
  5.4
RUDĪTU 'roared, brayed,' 2.3.3
RUNCĀTU 'thinned out,' 3.3.2
RUPTU 'broken,' 1.3.4, 2+37, 3.1.5,
  3.1.7, 3.3.2, 3.4, 3.5.3.1, 3.6.1.1,
  4.2, 4.3.1, 4.4.4, 4.6.1.4, 4.6.1.8,
  4.7.6.2, 5.6
RUTU 'rushed, fallen,' 2.10, 3.7.3

SARCULU 'light hoe' *noun*, 2.5
SALSU 'salted' *old p.p.*, 0.4
SALTU 'jumped,' 1.3.6, 2.10, 2.13,
  2.13.2, 4.5.3, 4.6.1.8, 5.2, 5.4
SĀNCTU 'blessed,' 1.3.6, 2.15.2
SARĪTU 'hoed' *by-f*, 2.5
SARRĪTU 'hoed' *by-f*, 2.5
SARTU₁ 'mended,' 2.11.2, 2.15.9,
  2+35, 3.5.0
SARTU₂ 'hoed' *by-f, rare*, 2.5
SATU 'sown,' 1.3.5, 2.2.1, 2.3.3
SCISSU 'torn, split,' 1.3.4, 2.11.2
SCĪTU 'known,' 2.8, 3.1.4, 6.8

SCRĪPTU 'written,' 0.2, 0.3.2, 1.4.4,
  1.5, 2.1.4, 3.1.5, 3.3.2, 3.4, 3.5.3.1,
  3.6.1.1, 3+67, 4.2, 4.3.1, 4.4.0.3,
  4.4.2.3, 4.4.11, 5.6, 6.6
SECTU 'cut, sawn,' 0.3.2, 1.3.6, 1.4.4,
  4.7.2.2
SECŪTU 'followed,' 1.4.4, 2.11.1,
  2.14.4, 4.4.2.2, 4.4.9.2, 4.4.13.3,
  4.6.1, 4.6.1.7, 4.6.1.3
SĒMEN 'seed' *noun*, 2.2.1
SĒNSU 'felt,' 2.13.1, 3.4, 3.6.1.1,
  3.6.2, 4.2, 4.3.2, 4.4.2.2, 4.6.1.5,
  4.6.1.9, 4.6.1.8, 5.2
SĒNSU 'feeling' *noun*, 4.7.7.3
SEPULTU 'buried,' 2.1.2, 2.6, 4.4.0.1,
  4.4.2.3
SERVĪTU 'served,' 3.3.1.1
-SESSU 'sat,' 1.3.4, 4.4.2.3, 5.3
SEXTU 'sixth' *adj.*, 1.2
SICCĀTU 'dried,' 4.7.12
SITU 'let; left,' 1.3.5, 2.3.3, 2.5
SOLITU 'used to,' 0.3.2, 2.9, 4.6.2.3
SOLŪTU 'loosened,' 0.3.1, 2.14,
  2.15.8, 3+61, 4.3.1, 4.4.2.2, 4.6.1,
  4.7.0
SONITU 'rung,' 3.1.2, 3.5.1, 4.4.2.3,
  4.7.2.2
SORBITU 'swallowed,' 2.6, 3.1.2,
  3.5.0, 4.7.2.2
SPARSU 'strewn,' 3.1.5.2, 3.3.1,
  3.5.3.2, 4.6.1, 4.6.1.8, 4.7.4.1
SPECTU 'beheld' *rare*, 1.4.6, 2.3.1
SPRĒTU 'spurned,' 1.3.5
SPŌNSA, SPŌNSU 'bride(groom)'
  noun, 2.11.2
SPŌNSU 'pledged, engaged,' 2.11.2
SPŪTU 'spat,' 2.3.1
STABILĪTU 'set up,' 4.4.2.2, 4.6.2.1,
  4.7.2.2
STATU 'stood, stayed,' 1.1, 2.7,
  2.13.1, 3.1.6, 3.3.2, 3.5.6, 3.6.2.5,
  3.7.3, 4.2, 4.6.2.2, 6+8

ŪNCTU 'oiled,' 2.10, 3.1.5.1, 3.1.6,
   3.3.1, 3.3.2, 4.2, 4.3.1, 4.3.2, 4.6.2,
   4.7.7.5, 5.1, 5.3
ŪSU 'used,' 1.4.1, 2.11.1, 2.13
USTULĀTU 'scorched,' 3.3.1
USTU 'charred,' 0.3.2, 1.3.5, 1.4,
   2.11.2, 3.3.1, 4.6.2.1

VACĀTU 'been empty,' 3.3.1
VALITU 'been strong, been worth,'
   0.3.1, 2.13.3, 3.5.3.2, 3.5.5
VANNU 'winnowing-fan' *noun*,
   3.6.1.4.1
VECTU 'conveyed,' 1.4.4, 2.3.1
VENDITU 'sold,' 2.4.3, 3.3.2, 3.5.0,
   4.3.1, 4.3.2, 4.4.2.2, 4.4.9.2, 4.6.1.8,
   4.6.2.10, 4.7.7.2
VENTU 'come,' 1.3.3, 2.4.1, 2.6, 2.13,
   3.3.1.1, 3.6.1.1, 4.4.2.2, 4.6.1,
   4.6.1.6, 4.6.1.8, 4.6.2.5
VENTU 'wind' *noun*, 3+25
VERSU 'turned,' 2.5, 3.1.2, 4.2, 4.4.2.2
VERŪTU 'armed with a javelin' *adj.*,
   4.7.4
VESTĪTU 'dressed,' 3.5.7
VETERĀNU 'old, veteran' *adj.*, 3+25
VETITU 'forbidden,' 1.3.6, 3.5.1,
   4.4.8, 4.7.2.2
VEXĀTU 'ravaged,' 1.2
VICTU₁ 'won,' 2.1.1, 2.14.5, 3.1.6,
   3.3.1, 3.3.1.1, 3.6.1.4.1, 3.6.2.1,
   3.7.1, 4.1, 4.3.1, 4.3.2, 4.6.1.1,
   4.6.1.9, 4.6.1.8, 5.3

VICTU₂ 'tied, bound' *by-f*, 1.4.3
VĪCTU 'lived,' 2.15.7, 3.1.6, 3.5.3.2,
   4.1, 4.2, 4.4.2.2, 4.6.1.9, 4.6.1.8,
   4.6.2.3, 5.3
VIDUĀTU 'deprived' *adj.*, 4.4.13.1
VĪGINTĪ 'twenty' *numeral*, 3+20
VĪNCTU 'tied, bound' *by-f*, 1.3.6,
   1.4.3, 2.5
VIOLĀTU 'violated,' 1.2
VĪSITU 'inspected,' 2.15.8, 3.5.2.1,
   4.7.6.2, 5.6
VĪSU 'seen,' 2.11, 2.15.8, 3.1.3, 3.1.6,
   3.3.2, 3.5.5.1, 3.7.1, 4.1, 4.3.1,
   4.4.2.2, 4.4.4, 4.6.1.1, 4.6.2.1,
   4.7.6.2, 4+42, 5.6
VĪTA 'life' *noun*, 2+89
VITIU 'blemish, flaw' *noun*, 3.1.1
VĪVU 'alive' *adj.*, 3.3.1
VOLĀTU 'flown,' 0.3.1
VOLENTE 'wanting' *pres.p.*, 2.7
VOLSU 'yanked' *by-f*, 1.4.2, 2+59
VOLŪTU 'rolled,' 1.4, 2.14, 2.14.4,
   2.15.8, 3.5.5, 3.6.1.4.1, 3+61, 4.2,
   4.3, 4.3.2, 4.4.2.2, 4.4.9.2, 4.4.9.3,
   4.6.1, 4.7.0, 4.7.6.2
VOLVA 'husk' *noun, by-f*, 2+59
VOMITU 'thrown up,' 1.3.6
VŌTU 'vowed,' 2.10
VULSU 'yanked' *by-f*, 1.4.2, 2.11,
   2+59
VULVA 'husk' *noun, by-f*, 2+59

Supines

DICTU 'tell,' 1.2
PETĪTU 'ask,' 1.2
SESSU 'sit,' 1.3.4
STĀTU 'stand,' 1.2, 2.13.1

Future Participles

CALITŪRU 'going to be hot,' 1.2
DOLITŪRU 'going to hurt,' 1.2, 2.13
DORMĪTŪRU 'going to be asleep,'
   2+2
EXITŪRU 'going to go out,' 2.1.2
FERĪTŪRU 'going to hit,' 2+25
FUTŪRU 'going to be,' 1.2
MISSŪRU 'going to send,' 2.1.2
RUITŪRU 'going to rush, fall,' 2.10
SONĀTŪRU 'going to ring,' 1.2
SUBSCRĪPTŪRU 'going to sign,' 2.1.2
VICTŪRU 'going to win,' 2.1.2
VOLITŪRU 'going to want,' 2.7

Suppletives

BIBERE 'drink,' *see* PŌ(TĀ)TU
FERĪRE 'strike,' *see* ICTU, PERCUSSU
FERRE 'carry,' *see* LĀTU

Proper Names

ALBUTIUS, 2.14.1
CREDUTA, 2.14.1
MUTIUS, 2.14.1
VENUTUS, 2.14.1

Verbs Lacking Past Participles, by Infinitive

ALBĒSCERE 'become white,' 3.7.3
CALĒRE 'be hot,' 2.8
DECĒRE 'be seemly,' 3.7.0
ESSE 'be,' 2.7, 3.3.1
FERVĒRE/FERVERE 'boil,' 2.1.4,
   2.8, 3.0.1, 3.1.5, 3.3.1, 3.7.1,
   4.6.2.1, 5.4.1
FLŌRĒRE 'bloom,' 2.8, 4.4.1
FŒTĒRE 'stink,' 2.8
HORRĒRE 'bristle, be rough,' 3.1.4
LŪCĒRE 'shine,' 3.7.3, 4.4.1, 4.4.6,
   4.7.0
MALLE 'prefer,' 2.7
MŪCĒRE 'be moldy,' 2.8, 4.4.1
NING(U)ERE 'snow,' 2.8, 3.6.2
NOLLE 'not want,' 2.7
PAVĒRE 'shake with fear,' 2.2.1
PLUERE 'rain,' 2.8, 3.1.4, 3.6.1, 3.6.2,
   3.7.2, 3.7.3, 4.6.2.3, 5.3
POSSE 'be able,' 2.7, 4.4.5, 4.6.2.3,
   4.7.0
PRUĪRE 'itch,' 4.6.1.9
PŪTĒRE 'stink,' 2.8, 3.1.2, 4.4.7
SAPERE 'taste, know,' 3.4, 4.6.1.1,
   4.6.1.9, 4.6.2.3
SILĒRE 'be silent,' 2.13.2
TIMĒRE 'fear,' 2.8, 3.7.3, 4.1, 4.4,
   4.6.1.1
TREMERE 'quake with fear,' 4.4
VELLE 'want,' 2.7, 3.4, 3.6.2

Late Latin

Romance

abatudo 'beaten' [OSp.; <u>Alex.</u>],
4.7.4.1

abatut 'beaten, hit, hurt' *by-f* [Ist-R],
3.3.2

abbattutu 'beaten' *by-f* [Sic.],
3.6.2.6

abbiata 'beginning' *noun* [SM],
3.6.2.2.1

abbivuto 'brought back to life' [SM],
3.6.2.2.1

abbrustolito 'roasted' *by-f* [SM],
3.6.2.2.1

abbrustoluto 'roasted' *by-f* [SM],
3.6.2.2.1

aberto 'opened' [Ptg.], 4.7.6.2

abertu 'opened' [Cmpi.], 3.7.2

abertu 'opened' [Log.], 3.7.2

abierto 'opened' [Leon.: Tud.],
4.7.13

abierto 'opened' [Sp.], 4.7.0, 4.7.1,
4.7.6.2, 4.7.6.3, 5.4.2

abierto 'opened' *short f* [Arag.:
VE], 4.7.12

abiertu 'opened' [Leon.: VP], 4.7.13

abláu 'spoken' [Leon.: Tud.], 4.7.13

abríu 'opened' *long f* [Arag.: VE],
4.7.12

absolt 'shriven'• [Enga.], 4.3.1

absolt 'shriven'• [Val.], 4.6.2.8

absorbido 'soaked up'• [Sp.], 4.7.8

absorto 'rapt' *usu. adj.*• [Sp.],
4.7.6.4, 4.7.8, 4+54

absous, absoute 'shriven'• [Fr.],
4.4.2.2, 4.4.6

abstracto 'abstract' *adj.*• [Sp.],
4.7.6.4, 4.7.8, 4+54

abstraído 'abstracted'• [Sp.],
4.7.6.4, 4.7.8

absuelto 'shriven'• [Sp.], 4.7.6.4,
4+54

abu 'had' [Lad.], 4.2

aburrido 'tiresome' *adj.* [Sp.], 4.7.13

aburriu 'gloomy, hateful' *adj.*
[Leon.: Tud.], 4.7.13

acaté 'bought' *by-f* [Pic.: Av.],
4.4.13.2

acățat 'hunted, caught,' [Arom.],
3.3.1

acçeiso 'lit' [Gen.], 3.6.1.4

accenduu 'lit' *by-f* [Mil.], 3.6.1.1

accés 'lit' *by-f* [Mil.], 3.6.1.1

acceso 'lit' [It.], 3.1.6

aččis 'killed' [Luca.], 3.6.2.5

acciso 'killed' [Neap.], 3.6.2.2

accolt 'greeted' [Enga.], 4.3.1

accorto 'realized' [It.], 3.5.5

accovitu 'welcomed' [Luca-GI],
3.6.2

aceite 'accepted' *short f, by-f* [Ptg.],
4.7.8, 4+71

aceito 'accepted' *short f, by-f* [Ptg.],
4.7.8, 6+3

acendido 'lit' *by-f* [Gal.], 4.7.14

acendido 'lit' *by-f* [Ptg.], 4.7.8

acendut 'lit' *by-f* [OOc.], 4.6.1.3

aces 'lit' *by-f* [OOc.], 4.6.1.3

aceso 'lit' *by-f* [Gal.], 4.7.14

aceso 'lit' *by-f* [Ptg.], 4.7.8

achacado 'accused' [Sp.], 4.7.0

achado 'found' [Ptg.], 3.0.1

achupido 'bent, bowed' [Sp.: SF],
4.7.11

ačetat 'agreed' [Fri-R], 4.1

acheté 'bought' [Fr.], 4.4.13.1

ach'té 'bought' *by-f* [Pic.: Av.],
    4.4.13.2

acompanáu 'gregarious' *adj.*
    [Leon.: Tud.], 4.7.13

acoperit 'covered' [Rom.], 3.1.2

acquis 'acquired' [Fr.], 3.5.2.2,
    4.4.9.3

acquise 'acquisition' *noun* [OFr.],
    4.4.9.3

acquisto 'purchase' *noun* [It.],
    3.5.2.2

acupirit 'covered' [Arom.], 3.3.1

acut 'acute' *neol.* [Rom.], 3.1.3

adaos 'adjoined' ? *arch.* [Rom.],
    3.1.7

adaptu 'added' *by-f* [Arom.], 3.3.1

adăugat 'added' [Rom.], 3.1.7,
    3.3.1.1

adăugit 'added' *arch.* [Rom.], 3.1.7

adăvgat 'added' *by-f* [Arom.], 3.3.1

addorcato 'sweetened' [SM],
    3.6.2.2.1

adequado 'suited, fitted' [Ptg.],
    4.7.9

aderito 'stuck' [It.], 3.5.0

adherido 'stuck' [Sp.], 4.7.2

adherit 'stuck' [Cat.], 4.6.2.1

adîvdzit 'added' *by-f* [Arom.],
    3.3.1

admès 'allowed, accepted' [Cat.],
    4.6.2.1

admis 'allowed' *neol.* [Rom.],
    3.1.5.3

admitere 'admission' *noun, neol.*
    [Rom.], 3.1.5.3

adunat 'gathered' [Arom.], 3.3.1

adus 'brought' [Arom.], 3.3.1

adus 'brought' [Rom.], 3.3.1, 3.3.2

adust 'scorched; austere' *adj.* [Cat.],
    4.6.2.1

adusto 'grim' *adj.* [Sp.], 4.6.2.1

adüt 'driven' [Enga.], 4.3.1

adwï, –ta 'driven' [FP: Vx.], 4.5.2

adzut, –a 'brought' [FP: VA], 4.5.4

aers 'stuck' [OOc.], 4.6.1

affisso 'posted' [It.], 3.5.4, 3.5.5

affisu 'offended' [Sic.], 3.6.2.6

afflitto 'distressed'• [It.], 3.5.4

afijado 'fastened' *arch.* [Sp.], 4.7.8

afijo 'fastened' *adj.* [Sp.], 4.7.8

aflat 'found' [Ist-R], 3.3.2

aflat 'found' [Rom.], 3.0.1, 3.1.8

aflicto 'afflicted'• *adj., poet.* [Sp.],
    4.7.6.4, 4.7.8, 4+54

afligido 'distressed' [Sp.], 4.7.6.4,
    4.7.8

aflit 'distressed' [Apul.: Alt.],
    3.6.2.4

agu 'had' [Oc.], 4.6.1.4

agudo 'sharp' *adj.* [Sp.], 4.7.4.2

aguerrido 'battle-tested' *adj.* [Sp.],
    4.7.9x

ağunsu 'reached, arrived' *by-f*
    [Arom.], 3.3.1

ağumtu 'reached, arrived' *by-f*
    [Arom.], 3.3.1

agut 'had' [Lang.], 4.6.1.9

agut 'had' [Ross.], 4.6.2.7

agut 'had' *by-f* [Tam.], 4.6.2.9

agut 'had' *by-f* [OOc.], 4.6.1.1,
    4.6.2.3

agut 'sharp' *adj.* [Gév.], 4.6.1.8

aguzado 'sharpened' [Sp.], 4.7.4.2

aimé 'loved, liked' [Fr.], 4.4.8

ain:mè, ain:mè: 'loved, liked'
    [Burg.], 4.4.13.3

aïu, aïue 'had' *by-f* [Nor.: Pch.],
    4.4.13.1

aixecat 'raised' [Cat.], 4.6.2

ajuns 'arrived' [Rom.], 3.1.5.1,
    3.1.5.2, 3.1.6

ajuns 'social climber' *noun*
    [Rom.], 3.1.5.2

ajupit 'bent, bowed' [Cat.], 4.7.11

akait 'vinegar' *noun* [Vegl.], 3.4

akató, akatá: 'bought' [Nor.: VS],
    4.4.13.1

akessidu 'tired' *adj.* [Log.], 2.15.10

akwelt, akölt 'gathered' [Apul.:
    Alt.], 3.6.2.4

alá: 'gone' *by-f* [FP: N], 4.5.1

alai 'gone' *by-f* [Poit.], 4.6.1.6

aleptu 'chosen' [Arom.], 3.3.1,
    3.3.1.1

aleptu 'chosen' [ORom.], 3.1.5

ales 'chosen' [Ist-R], 3.3.2

ales 'chosen' [Rom.], 3.1.5.1, 3.3.1,
    3.7.1

algo 'something' *pron.* [Sp.], 4.7.6.3

alimsu 'licked' *by-f* [Arom.], 3.3.1

alimtu 'licked' *by-f* [Arom.], 3.3.1

allà, –ye 'gone' [FP: VA], 4.5.4

allâ, allaịe 'gone' [FP: Vd.], 4.5.3

allé 'gone' [Fr.], 4.4.12

allé 'gone' *by-f* [Pic.: Av.], 4.4.13.2

alluccadu 'shouted' [Luca-GI], 3.6.2

alluso 'alluded' [Gen.], 3.6.1.4

alluso 'alluded'• [It.], 3.5.3.2

allutu 'lit' [Sard.], 3.7.3

alondzet, alondzèite
    'lengthened' [FP: VA], 4.5.4

aludido 'alluded'• [Sp.], 4.7.9

amanido 'readied' [Sp.: SF], 4.7.11

amanit 'readied' [Cat.], 4.7.11

amargat 'hidden' [Cat.], 4.6.2

amà, –ye 'loved, liked' [FP: VA],
    4.5.4

amat 'loved, liked' [OOc.], 4.6.1

amau 'loved, liked' [Args.], 4.7.10

amenteü 'remembered' [OFr.], 4.4.1

amé 'loved, liked' [OFr.], 4.4.0.3,
    4.4.8

amigos 'friends' *pl. noun* [Sp.],
    4.7.6.3

amintare 'gain' *noun* [Arom.],
    3.3.1

amintat 'gained; born' [Arom.],
    3.3.1

âmnat 'gone' *by-f* [Ist-R], 3.3.2

amodorrado 'become drowsy'
    [Sp.], 4.7.5

amodorrida 'become drowsy'
    [OSp.], 4.7.5

amprins 'lit' *by-f* [Ist-R], 3.3.2

ămpuţǫt 'spoiled, rotted' [Meg.],
    3.3.1.1

anàd 'gone' *by-f* [Auv.], 4.6.1.7

anat 'gone' [Cat.], 4.6.2.1, 4.6.2.3

anat 'gone' [Gasc.], 4.6.1.5

anat 'gone' [Tam.], 4.6.2.9

ăncaldzǫt 'heated' [Meg.], 3.3.1.1

ăncaţat 'shod' [Ist-R], 3.3.2

ancl'is 'shut in' [Meg.], 3.3.1.1

andà 'gone' *by-f* [Pied.], 3.6.1.2

andado 'gone' [Sp.], 4.6.2.3, 4.7.1

andait 'gone' *by-f* [Pied.], 3.6.1.2

andato 'gone' [It.], 3.5.0, 3.6.2

andires 'guided, led' [Meg.], 3.3.1.1

andrupat ' leaned, supported' *by-f*
    [Arom.], 3.3.1

andrupît ' leaned, supported' *by-f*
    [Arom.], 3.3.1

anegado 'drowned' [Sp.], 4.6.2

angut 'had' *by-f* [OOc.], 4.6.2.3

ănmurţǫt 'chilled' [Meg.], 3.3.1.1

annascunnuto 'hidden' *by-f*
    [Neap.], 3.6.2.2

annascuso 'hidden' *by-f* [Neap.],
    3.6.2.2

annat 'gathered' *allegro f* [Arom.:
    Pin.], 3.3.1

annegato 'drowned' [It.], 4.6.2

anness 'attached' [Enga.], 4.3.1

annesso 'attached' [It.], 3.5.3.2

anţiles 'understood' *also adj.*
[Meg.], 3.3.1.1

anţins 'girded' [Meg.], 3.3.1.1

antiquado 'made outdated' [Ptg.],
4.7.9

ântribat 'asked' [Ist-R], 3.3.2

anuitét 'nightfallen' [OFr.; <u>St.
Alexis</u>], 4.4.12

anüt 'carried, brought' [Apul.: Alt.],
3.6.2.4

anvins 'won' [Meg.], 3.3.1.1

ănvirdzǫt 'turned green' [Meg.],
3.3.1.1

âové/âovert, âoverta 'opened'
[FP: Vd.], 4.5.3

aparegut 'appeared' *arch.* [Cat.],
4.6.2.3

aparescut 'appeared' *nonstd.*
[Cat.], 4.6.2.3

apeçu, apeçuva 'perceived' [FP:
Vd.], 4.5.3

apercebudo 'provided, warned'
[OSp.], 4.7.4.1

apert 'open' *adj.* [Mil.], 3.6.1.1

aperto 'opened' [It.], 3.5.3.1, 3.5.5

apertu 'opened' [Cors.], 3.6.2.1

aperutu 'opened' [Cal.], 3.6.2

apeyzu 'hung' [VG], 3.6.1.4.1

apiárt 'opened' [Vegl.], 3.4

apierto 'opened' [Neap.], 3.6.2.2

apiərtə 'opened' [Abru.], 3.6.2.3

apirit 'opened' [Arom.], 3.3.1

apirt, apert 'opened' [Apul.: Alt.],
3.6.2.4

apparata 'hanging a church with
banners' *noun* [SM], 3.6.2.2.1

apparito 'appeared' [Tusc.], 3+60

apparso 'appeared' [It.], 3.5.5, 3+60

appertu 'opened' [Nuor.], 3.7

appeso 'hung' [It.], 3.5.3.2

appezzenduto 'become poor'
[SM], 3.6.2.2.1

appidu 'had' [Log.], 3.6.2.5

appinnutu 'hung' [Sic.], 3.6.2.6

appiso 'hung' [SM], 3.6.2.2.1

appisu 'hung' *usu. adj.* [Sic.],
3.6.2.6

appitu 'had' [Sard.], 3.7.3, 3.7.5

apreasă 'rising (of planets, stars)'
noun [Arom.], 3.3.1

apres 'lit' *by-f* [Arom.], 3.3.1

apreyzu 'curdled' [VG], 3.6.1.4.1

aprimsu 'lit' *by-f* [Arom.], 3.3.1

aprimtu 'lit' *by-f* [Arom.], 3.3.1

aprins 'lit' *by-f* [Ist-R], 3.3.2

appris 'learned' [Pic.: Av.], 4.4.13.2

apretado 'tight' *adj.* [Leon.: VP],
4.7.13

aprokiịét 'brought near' [Mold.],
3.2.2

apropiat 'brought near' [Rom.],
3.2.2

apyé 'leaned on, supported' [Nor.:
VS], 4.4.13.1

ar 'plow' *noun* [Arom.], 3+17

araciŭ 'plowman' *noun* [Arom.],
3+17

araes 'shaved' [OEnga.], 4.3.1

arămas 'stayed' *by-f* [Arom.], 3.3.1

arat *m.*, arata *f.*, arato *n.* 'plowed'
[Ist-R], 3.3.2

aratu 'plowing' *ger.* [Ist-R], 3.3.2

arbéskidu 'dawned' [Log.], 3.7.3

arca 'thorax' *noun* [Leon.: VP],
4.7.13

arcudu 'big-chested' *adj.* [Leon.:
VP], 4.7.13

ardent 'burning' *adj.* [Fr.], 4+27

ardisto 'burned' [Ist-I], 3.3.3

ardu 'burned' [Lad.: Fass.], 4.2

ardu 'burned' [Lad.: Liv.], 4.2

ardu 'burned' *by-f* [OFr.], 4.4.7

ardudo 'burned' [OSp.], 4.7.4.1

arduto 'burned' *by-f* [Neap.], 3.6.2.2

arentiyu 'neared' [VG], 3.6.1.4.1

arəstut 'roasted' [Apul.: Alt.], 3.6.2.4

arîs 'laughed' [Arom.], 3.3.1

armas 'stayed' *by-f* [Arom.], 3.3.1

armást 'stayed' [Lun.], 3.6.1.5

armes 'stayed' [Enga.], 4.3.1

arrecho 'horny' *adj.* [Sp.], 4.7.7.1

arrepentido 'repented' [Sp.], 4.7.6.1

arrepiso 'repented' *by-f* [OSp.], 4.7.6.1

arreplegat 'gathered' [Cat.], 4.6.2.9

arreso 'surrendered' [It.], 3.5.3.2

arressu 'ruled' *by-f* [Sard.], 3.7.4

arrestu 'stopped' [OFr.], 4.4.7

arrettu 'ruled' *by-f* [Sard.], 3.7.4

arrezùo 'ruled' [Gen.], 3.6.1.4

arrísiu 'laughed' [Cmpi.], 3.7.2

arrogato 'arrogated' [It.], 3.5.10

arropliegat 'gathered' [Tam.], 4.6.2.9

arrostito 'roasted' [It.], 3.6.2.4

arrostuto 'roasted' [SM], 3.6.2.2.1

arrota 'addition' *noun* [It.], 3.5.10

arroto 'added, made whole' *arch.* [It.], 3.5.2.1, 3.5.10

arrugginito 'rusty' *adj.* [It.], 3.6.2.2.1

arrugginuto 'rusty' *adj.* [SM], 3.6.2.2.1

arrutu 'fallen' [Cmpi.], 3.7.2

ars 'burned' [Enga.], 4.3.1

ars 'burned' [Gév.], 4.6.1.8

ars 'burned' [Ist-R], 3.3.2

ars 'burned' [Meg.], 3.3.1.1

ars 'burned' [OCat.], 2.12

ars 'burned' [OOc.], 4.6.1, 4.6.1.2, 4.7.4.1

ars 'burned' [Rom.], 2.12, 3.1.5.1

ars 'burned' [Surs.], 2.12, 4.3.2

ars 'burned' *by-f* [OFr.], 2.12, 4.4.3, 4.4.7, 4.4.10, 4.7.4.1

ârs 'laughed' [Ist-R], 3.3.2

arsebüd 'received' *by-f* [Auv.], 4.6.1.7

arsidu 'burned' [OSard.], 3.7.1

arso 'burned' [It.], 2.1.3, 3.5.3.2

arsu 'burned' [Arom.], 3.3.1

arsu 'burned' [Meg.: Ţ & U], 3.3.1.1

arsu 'burned' *adj.* [Sic.], 3.6.2.6

aruptu 'torn' [Arom.], 3.3.1

arzo 'burned' *by-f* [Neap.], 3.6.2.2

asado 'roasted' [Sp.], 2.11

asalto 'attack' *noun* [Sp.], 4.7.7.1

asaltado 'attacked' [Sp.], 4.7.7.1

asciutto 'narrow-chested' *adj.* [It.], 3.4

ascondudo 'hidden' [OPtg.], 4.7.4.1

ascons 'hidden' *by-f* [OFr.], 4.4.2.3, 4.4.4, 4.4.9.3

asconse 'dissimulation' *noun* [OFr.], 4.4.9.3

ascoso 'hidden' [OIt.], 2.15.9, 3.5.3.2

ascoso 'hidden' *lit.* [It.], 2.15.9

ascrivit 'written' [Alg.], 4.6.2.10

ascultat 'listened' [Rom.], 3.3.2

ascuns 'hidden' [Ist-R], 3.3.2

ascutat 'listened' *by-f* [Ist-R], 3.3.2

ascumtu 'hidden' *by-f* [Arom.], 3.3.1

ascuns 'hidden' [Rom.], 2.15.8, 2.15.9, 3.1.6, 3.3.2, 3.5.5.1

ascunsu 'hidden' *by-f* [Arom.], 3.3.1

aseyso 'lit' [VG], 3.6.1.4.1

así 'so, thus' *adv.* [Sp.], 6.4

askusu 'hidden' *by-f* [VG], 3.6.1.4.1

askuzu 'hidden' *by-f* [VG], 3.6.1.4.1

aspartu 'scattered' [Arom.], 3.3.1

avisto 'had' [Ptg.: Opo.], 4.7.10

avóit 'had' [Vegl.], 3.4

avu 'had' *by-f* [Ven.], 3.6.1

avudo 'had' [OPtg.], 4.7.4.1

avudu 'had' [Lig.: Sis.], 3.6.1.4

avudu 'had' [Luca-GI], 3.6.2

avut 'had' *also adj.* [Arom.], 3.3.1

avut 'had' [Gasc.], 4.6.1.5

avut 'had' [Luca.], 3.6.2.5

avut 'had' [Rom.], 2.14.5, 3.1.3, 3.1.6, 4.6.2.3

avut 'had' [Vegl.: Z], 3.4

avut 'had' *by-f* [Ist-R], 3.3.2

avut 'had' *by-f* [OOc.], 4.6.1.1

avuto 'had' [It.], 2.14.5, 3.5.6, 4.6.2.3

avutu 'had' [Sic.], 3.6.2.6

avvisato 'warned' [It.], 4.1

avzit 'heard' [Ist-R], 3.3.2

baiat 'barked' [Fri-R], 4.1

báit 'drunk' [Vegl.], 3.4

balagnatu 'won, gained' *long f, by-f* [Cors.], 3.6.2.1

balantu 'won, gained' *shofr f, by-f* [Cors.], 3.6.2.1

balfidu 'been worth' [Sard.], 3.7.5

balgut 'been worth' [Gév.], 4.6.1.8

baptizét 'baptized' [OFr.; <u>St. Alexis</u>], 4.4.12

baptizo 'baptized' [Ptg.], 6.4

barbu 'bearded' *adj.* [Fr.], 4.7.4.2

barbudo 'bearded' *adj.* [Sp.], 4.7.4.2

barbuto 'bearded' *adj.* [It.], 4.7.4.2

băşit 'farted' [Rom.], 2.11.2

bastato 'been enough' [It.], 3.6.2.3

bastit 'built' [Gasc.], 4.6.1.5

batîd 'built' [Auv.], 4.6.1.7

batido 'beaten' [Gal.], 4.7.14

batido 'beaten' [Sp.], 4.7.4.1, 5.2

bătrân 'old' *adj.* [Rom.], 3+25

battu 'beaten' [Fr.], 4.4.2.2, 4.4.2.3, 4.4.12

battùo 'beaten' [Gen.], 3.6.1.4

battuto 'beaten' [It.], 3.5.0

batù 'beaten' [Lad.], 4.2

batüd 'beaten' [Auv.], 4.6.1.7

batudo 'beaten' [OSp.], 4.7.4.1

batut 'beaten' [Cat.], 4.6.2.3

batut 'beaten, knocked' [Fri-R], 4.1

batut 'beaten' [OOc.], 4.6.1

batut 'beaten' [Ross.], 4.6.2.7

batut 'beaten, hit, hurt' *by-f* [Ist-R], 3.3.2

batut 'beaten' [Val.], 4.6.2.8

bătut 'beaten' [Meg.], 3.3.1.1

bătut 'beaten' [Rom.], 3.1.3

batüu 'beaten' [VG], 3.6.1.4.1

băut 'drunk' [Rom.], 2.8, 2.14.5, 3.1.3, 3.1.6, 3.3.2, 6.7

baxato 'lowered' [Arag.: Pnt.], 4.7.12

bbaštutə 'been enough' [Abru.], 3.6.2.3

bbattutu 'beaten' *by-f* [Sic.], 3.6.2.6

bêbado 'drunken' *adj., by-f* [Ptg.], 4.7.10

bêbedo 'drunken' *adj., by-f* [Ptg.], 4.7.10

bebesto 'drunk' [OPtg.], 4.7.10

bebido 'drunk' [Sp.], 2.8, 6.4

bebidu 'drunk' [Ptg.: Barr.], 4.7.15

bebiu 'drunk' [Args.], 4.7.10

bedu 'drunk' [Lig.: Sis.], 3.6.1.4

bedüd 'drunk' *by-f* [Auv.], 4.6.1.7

beghu 'drunk' *by-f* [Poit.], 4.6.1.6

béghu 'drunk' *by-f* [Poit.], 4.6.1.6

begu 'drunk' [Oc.], 4.6.1.4

begüd 'drunk' *by-f* [Auv.], 4.6.1.7

beguda 'beverage' *noun* [Cat.], 4.6.2.5

cabu da 'space, room' *noun* [Cat.], 4.6.2.5

cabut 'fit into' *std.* [Cat.], 2.14.5, 4.6.2.3

cabut 'fit into' [Val.], 4.6.2.8

caché 'hidden' [Fr.], 4.4.0

caché 'looked for' *by-f* [Pic.: Av.], 4.4.13.2

cădeare 'fall, falling' *noun* [Arom.], 3.3.1

cadu du 'fallen' *by-f* [Luca-GI], 3.6.2

cadu to 'fallen' [It.], 2.8, 3.5.6

cadu tu 'fallen' [Proto-Sp.], 4.7.0

cădzut 'fallen' [Arom.], 3.3.1

caen do 'falling' *pres.p.* [Sp.: SF], 4.7.11

cagut 'fallen' *by-f* [OOc.], 4.6.1.3

cahegut 'fallen' [OVal.], 4.6.2.10

cahut 'fallen' [ORoss.], 4.6.2.10

cáido 'fallen' [Sp.: SF], 4.7.11

caído 'fallen' [Gal.], 4.7.14

caído 'fallen' [Sp.], 2.8, 4.7.4.1

cái̯du 'fallen' *adj.* [Leon.: VP], 4.7.13

çaídu 'gone out' [Ptg.: Barr.], 4.7.15

caigu da 'fall' *noun* [Cat.], 4.6.2.5

caigut 'fallen' [Cat.], 2.8, 4.6.2.3, 4.6.2.10

caigut 'fallen' [Ross.], 4.6.2.7

caigut 'fallen' [Tam.], 4.6.2.9

caigut 'fallen' [Val.], 4.6.2.8

caío 'fallen' [Leon.: Tud.], 4.7.13

caíto 'fallen' [Arag.: Pnt.], 4.7.12

calen tado 'been hot' [Sp.], 2.8

calgut 'fallen' [Alg.], 4.6.2.10

calgut 'mattered' [Cat.], 2.8

calgut 'mattered' [Val.], 4.6.2.8

calgut 'mattered' *by-f* [Lang.], 4.6.1.9

calm ado 'calmed' *long f* [Gal.], 4.7.14

calm o 'calmed' *short f* [Gal.], 4.7.14

calu to 'been hot' [It.], 2.8

calzato 'shod' [It.], 3.3.2

čamatu 'called, named' [Sic.], 3.6.2.6

cambiat 'changed' [Fri-R], 4.1

can djé 'changed' *by-f* [Pic.: Av.], 4.4.13.2

čangutu 'complained' [Sal.], 3.6.2

cannaruto 'gluttonous' *adj.* [SM], 3.6.2.2.1

cansado 'tired' *long f* [Gal.], 4.7.14

cansado 'tired' *adj.* [Sp.], 4.7.13

cansáu 'tired' *long f* [Arag.: VE], 4.7.14

canso 'tired' *short f* [Arag.], 4.7.8

canso 'tired' *short f* [Arag.: VE], 4.7.12

canso 'tired' *short f* [Cast.], 4.7.8

canso 'tired' *short f* [Gal.], 4.7.14

canso 'tired' *adj.* [Sp.], 2.10

cansu 'tired' *adj.* [Leon.: Tud.], 4.7.13

cansu 'tired' *adj.* [Leon.: VP], 4.7.13

cantado 'sung' [Gal.], 4.7.14

cantado 'sung' [Sp.], 1.6, 1+45, 4.7.4.1

cantat 'sung' [Gasc.], 4.6.1.5

căntat 'sung' [Ist-R], 3.3.2

căntat 'sung' [Meg.], 3.3.1.1

cântat 'sung' [Rom.], 3.1.0, 3.1.6

cantato 'sung' [It.], 1.6

cantau 'sung' [Args.], 4.7.10

cantau 'sung' [Cmpi.], 3.7.0

cantáu 'sung' [Leon.: Tud.], 4.7.13

canté 'sung' [Pic: Br.], 4.4.13.2

cantòu 'sung' [Gen.], 3.6.1.4

čantu 'wept' *by-f, usu.* [VG], 3.6.1.4.1

caosu, –ya 'sewn' [FP: VA], 4.5.4

càosu, –va 'sewn' [FP: Vd.], 4.5.3

čapat 'taken' [Lad.], 2.14.5

capigut 'fit into' *nonstd.* [Cat.],
    4.6.2.3, 4.6.2.6

capîo 'understood' [Gen.], 3.6.1.4

capît 'understood' [Fri.], 2.14.5

capito 'understood' [It.], 2.14.5

carecido 'lacked, needed' [Sp.],
    4.7.2.2

carejat 'done without' [Cat.], 4.6.2

caroluto 'worm-eaten, moth-eaten'
    adj. [SM], 3.6.2.2.1

carpido 'plucked' [Sp.], 4.7.2

carpit 'plucked' [Cat.], 4.6.2.2

carpito 'plucked' [It.], 3.5.0

carryé 'loaded' *by-f* [Pic.: Av.],
    4.4.13.2

cartiu 'believed' [Surs.], 4.3.2

carudu 'fallen' *by-f* [Luca-GI], 3.6.2

caruliato 'worm-eaten, moth-eaten'
    adj. [Neap.], 3.6.2.2.1

cărunt 'gray-haired' *adj.* [Rom.],
    4.7.4.2

carùttu 'fallen' *by-f* [Luca-GI], 3.6.2

carutu 'fallen' [Neap.], 3.6.2.2

cas 'broken' *adj., by-f* [OFr.], 2.10

cas 'broken' *adj.* [OOc.], 2.10

cascat 'bruised' [Cat.], 4.6.2.2

cascat 'hit; fallen' [Gév.], 4.6.1.8

casegut 'fallen' [Lang.], 4.6.1.9

casso 'broken' *adj.* [OIt.], 2.10

căst 'fallen' *allegro f* [Mold.], 3.1.3

catto 'taken' [OIt.; Dante], 2.14.5

caudo 'fallen' [OSp.], 2.8

caugut 'mattered' *by-f* [Lang.],
    4.6.1.9

caüt 'fallen' *nonstd.* [Cat.], 4.6.2.6

căutat 'looked for' [Rom.], 3.3.2

cavtat 'looked for' [Ist-R], 3.3.2

cayíu 'fallen' [Leon.: VP], 4.7.13

cazegut 'fallen' *by-f* [OOc.], 4.6.1.3

cazut 'fallen' [Ist-R], 3.3.2

cazut 'fallen' [Oc.], 2.8

căzut 'fallen' [Meg.], 3.3.1.1

căzut 'fallen' [Rom.], 2.8, 3.1.0,
    3.1.6

cecato 'blinded' *also adj.* [SM],
    3.6.2.2.1

cedat 'yielded' *neol.* [Rom.], 2+90,
    3.1.4

cédé 'yielded' • [Fr.], 2.15.10, 3.1.3,
    4.4.9.3, 4.7.6.4

cedido 'yielded' • [Sp.], 2.15.10,
    4.7.6.4

cedit 'yielded' • [Cat.], 2.15.10

cedùo 'yielded' *by-f* [Gen.], 3.6.1.4

ceduto 'yielded' • [It.], 2.15.9, 3.3.3,
    3.5.3.2, 4.7.6.4

cehoit 'fallen' [OFr.], 4.6.2.10

ceint 'girded' [Fr.], 4.4.2.3, 4.4.3

cench 'girded' *by-f* [Lang.], 4.6.1.9

cencido *adj.* 'unharmed' [Sp.],
    2.15.2

ceñido 'girded' [Sp.], 4.7.6.1

cent 'hundred' *numeral* [Fr.], 1+44

cento 'complained' *by-f* [Gen.],
    3.6.1.4

čentu 'wept' *by-f, rare* [VG],
    3.6.1.4.1

cer 'sky' *noun* [Rom.], 3+18

çerbidu 'served' [Ptg.: Barr.], 4.7.15

cercatu 'looked for' *long f, by-f*
    [Cors.], 3.6.2.1

cercati 'laden' *m.pl.* [Proto-Fr.],
    4.4.0.1

cercu 'looked for' *short f* [Cors.],
    3.6.2.1

cernido 'sifted' [Sp.], 4.7.9

cérnita 'sorting' *noun* [It.], 3.5.2.2,
    3.6.1

cernut 'sifted' [Cat.], 2.14.1, 3.0.1,
    3.3.1, 3.6.2, 3+47, 4.6.2.2, 4.6.2.4

cernut 'sifted' [Rom.], 2.14.1, 3.0.1,
    3.3.1, 3.6.2, 3+47, 4.6.2.4

cernut 'sifted' [Val.], 4.6.2.8

chouyu$_1$, -ya 'climbed' [FP: VA], 4.5.4

chouyu$_2$, -ya 'resulted' *by-f* [FP: VA], 4.5.4

chovet, chovèite 'resulted' *by-f* [FP: VA], 4.5.4

chovido 'rained' [Ptg.], 2.8, 3.1.4

chu 'fallen' [Burg.], 4.4.13.3

chù 'fallen' [FP: N], 4.5.1

-chu 'fallen' [Fr.], 4.4.13.2

chu, chute 'fallen' [Nor.: Pch.], 4.4.13.1

chuché 'drunk' [Pic.: Av.], 4.4.13.2

chugato 'played' [Arag.: Pnt.], 4.7.12

chupado 'sucked' [Sp.], 4.7.0

chute 'fall' *noun* [Fr.], 4.4.9.1

cianzùo 'complained' *by-f* [Gen.], 3.6.1.4

ciapât 'taken' [Fri.], 4.1

ciatât 'gotten' [Fri.], 4.1

cibo 'food, meal' *noun•* [It.], 3+51

çidu 'been' [Ptg.: Barr.], 4.7.15

cieco 'blind' *adj.* [It.], 3.6.2.2.1

ciento 'complained' *by-f* [Gen.], 3.6.1.4

cinat 'dined' [Rom.], 3.3.2

cinglat 'girded' [Cat], 4.6.2

cint 'girded' *by-f* [Lang.], 4.6.1.9

cinta 'ribbon, tape' *noun* [Sp.], 4.7.7.1

cîntare 'singing, song' *noun* [Arom.], 3.3.1

cîntat 'sung' [Arom.], 3.3.1

cinto 'girded' [It.], 3.1.6, 3.5.3.1

cinto 'belt' *noun* [Sp.], 4.7.7.1, 4.7.7.5

cinto 'girded' [OSp.], 4.7.1, 4.7.2.2, 4.7.6.1

cintu 'girded' [Cors.], 3.6.2.1

cirat 'dined' [Ist-R], 3.3.2

circatu 'looked for' *long f, y-f* [Cors.], 3.6.2.1

čirkatu 'looked for' [Sic.], 3.6.2.6

čirnutu 'sifted' [Sic.], 3.6.2, 3.6.2.6

cirût 'looked for' [Fri.], 4.1

città 'city' *noun* [It.], 3.5.0

cjolet 'taken' [Fri.], 4.1

clamat 'called' [Fri-R], 4.1

clamat 'called' [Cat.], 4.4.0

clamé 'called' [OFr.], 4.4.0

clap 'clapper-board' *noun* [Fr.], 4.4.0.3

claugut 'shut' *by-f* [Gév.], 4.6.1.8

claugut 'shut' *by-f* [Lang.], 4.6.1.9

claus 'shut' [Surs.], 4.3.2

claus 'shut' *by-f* [Gév.], 4.6.1.8

claus 'shut' *by-f* [Lang.], 4.6.1.9

claus 'shut' *by-f* [OOc.], 4.6.1.2, 4.6.1.3

clauzit 'shut' *by-f* [OOc.], 4.6.1, 4.6.1.3

clet 'gathered' [Enga.], 4.3.1

clit 'gathered' *arch.* [Enga.], 4.3.1

clliousu, –ya 'shut' [FP: VA], 4.5.4

clofis 'nailed' [OFr.], 4.4.1

clogut 'shut' *nonstd.* [Cat.], 4.6.2.6

clos 'shut' [Cat.], 4.6.2.1, 4.6.2.2

clos 'shut' [OFr.], 4.4.0, 4.4.11

clos 'shut' [Val.], 4.6.2.8

clus 'shut' *adj.* [Oc.], 4.6.1.4

čòbbətə 'rained' *by-f* [Abru.], 3.6.2.3

cobert 'covered' [Cat.], 4.6.2.2

cobert 'covered' *by-f* [Lang.], 4.6.1.9

cobert 'covered' *by-f* [Val.], 4.6.2.8

cobèrt 'covered' [Gasc.], 4.6.1.5

coberto 'covered' [Ptg.], 4.7.6.2

coborît 'gone down' [Rom.], 3.1.1

coch 'cooked' *by-f* [Lang.], 4.6.1.9

cocho 'cooked' [OSp.], 4.7.1, 4.7.6.1, 4.7.7.1

cocido 'cooked' [Sp.], 4.7.6.1

comprès 'squeezed' [Cat.], 4.6.2.1

compris 'understood' [Pic.: Av.],
4.4.13.2

compristo 'filled' [Ptg.: Opo.],
4.7.10

compro 'bought' *short* f[Tusc.],
3.5.9, 3+58

compru 'bought' *short* f[Cors.],
3.6.2.1

comudo 'eaten' [OSp.], 2.3.1, 4.7.4.1

con 'with' *prep.* [Sp.], 4.7.6.3

concebut 'imagined' [Cat.], 4.6.2.2

concepito 'imagined' [It.], 3.5.0

concernido 'concerned' *rare•*
[Sp.], 4.7.9

concesso 'granted' [It.], 2.15.10,
3.5.3.2

concluido 'concluded' *std.* [Ptg.],
4.7.8

conclus 'concluded' [Fr.], 4.4.6

concluso 'concluded' *leg.* [Ptg.],
4.7.8

conclüt 'concluded' [Enga.], 4.3.1

conducere 'leadership' *noun*
[Rom.], 3.1.8

condui, −te 'driven' [FP: VA], 4.5.4

conduit 'driven' [Fr.], 4.4.11

conegut 'known' [Cat.], 4.6.2.1,
4.6.2.3

conegut 'known' [OOc.], 4.6.1.1,
4.6.1.2

conegut 'known' [Val.], 4.6.2.8

coneixit 'known' *nonstd.* [Cat.],
4.6.2.6

coneixit 'known' [Ross.], 4.6.2.7

conescut 'known' [Gasc.], 4.6.1.5

confianzudo 'overtrusting' *adj.*
[Sp.], 4.7.4.2

confongut 'confused' [Tam.],
4.6.2.9

confos 'confused' [Cat.], 4.6.2.9

confundido 'confused' [Sp.],
4.7.7.3

confuso 'confused' *adj.* [Sp.],
4.7.7.3

connóskidu 'known' [Log.], 3.7.3

connotu 'known' [Cmpi.], 3.7.2

connu 'known' [Fr.], 2.14.5

connu 'known' [Pic.: Av.], 4.4.13.2

conocido 'known' [Sp.], 4.7.2.2

conosciuto 'known' [It.], 2.14.5,
3.5.1, 3.5.6

conosçudo 'known' [OSp.], 4.7.4.1

conoscut 'known' *by-f* [Ist-R], 3.3.2

conottu 'known' [Nuor.], 3.7

conozito 'known' [Arag.: Pnt.],
4.7.12

conquerido 'conquered' [Sp.],
4.7.6.1

conqueso 'conquered' [OIt.], 3.5.3.2

conquis 'conquered' [OOc.], 4.6.1

conquiso 'conquered' *poet.* [It.],
3.5.3.2

conquisto 'conquered' [OSp.],
4.7.6.1

conscrit 'draftee' *noun* [Fr.], 4+31

constrângere 'constraint' *noun,*
neol. [Rom.], 3.1.5.3

constrâns 'forced' *neol.* [Rom.],
3.1.5.3

constret 'forced'• [Val.], 4.6.2.8

construit 'built' [Fr.], 3+61

consunto 'worn-out, used up'• [It.],
3.5.10

contenido 'contents' *noun* [Sp.],
4.7.10

contenu 'contents' *noun* [Fr.],
4.7.10

contenuto 'contained' *also noun*
[It.], 4.7.10

conteúdo 'contents' *noun* [Ptg.],
4.7.10

couvert, –a 'covered' by-f [FP: VA], 4.5.4

couvert 'covered' [Fr.], 4.4.3, 4.4.11

couzüd 'sewn' [Auv.], 4.6.1.7

covat 'brooded, hatched' [Cat.], 4.6.2.2

covato 'brooded, hatched' [It.], 2.13.3, 3.5.1

coverto 'covered' [Gen.], 3.6.1.4

cozito 'cooked' [Arag.: Pnt.], 4.7.12

cozut 'sewn' by-f [Ist-R], 3.3.2

crai 'tomorrow' adv. [SM], 3.6.2.2.1

craieu 'believed' arch. [Enga.], 4.3.1

crain, crainta 'feared' [FP: Vd.], 4.5.3

craint 'feared' [Fr.], 4.4.0

cranhüd 'feared' by-f [Auv.], 4.6.1.7

cranîd 'feared' by-f [Auv.], 4.6.1.7

cranjüd 'feared' by-f [Auv.], 4.6.1.7

crǎpat 'burst' [Rom.], 3.1.2

crasagut 'believed' [OCat.], 4.6.2.2

crebantat 'burst' [Cat.], 4.6.2

crebat 'burst' [OOc.], 4.6.1

crecido 'grown' [Sp.], 4.7.0

credàd 'called' [Auv.], 4.6.1.7

credere 'belief' noun [Rom.], 3.1.8

credesto 'believed' [Ven.], 3.6.1

credinţǎ 'belief' noun [Rom.], 3.1.8

credù 'believed' [Lad.], 4.2

credut 'believed' by-f [Gasc.], 4.6.1.5

creduto 'believed' [It.], 2.14.5, 3.5.3.2, 3.6.1, 3.6.2

creghu 'believed' [Poit.], 4.6.1.6

crègnu –ya 'feared' [FP: VA], 4.5.4

cregüd 'believed' by-f [Auv.], 4.6.1.7

cregut 'believed' [Cat.], 2.14.5, 4.6.2.2

cregut 'believed' [Lang.], 4.6.1.9

cregut 'believed' [Ross.], 4.6.2.7

cregut 'believed' [Tam.], 4.6.2.9

cregut 'believed' [Val.], 4.6.2.8

cregut 'believed' by-f [Gasc.], 4.6.1.5

cregut 'believed' by-f [Oc.], 4.6.1.4

creído 'believed' by-f [Gal.], 4.7.14

creído 'believed' [Sp.], 4.7.0

creissegut 'grown' by-f [Oc.], 4.6.1.4

creissu 'grown' [FP: VA], 4.5.4

creissut 'grown' by-f [Gév.], 4.6.1.8

creisüd 'grown' [Auv.], 4.6.1.7

creíto 'believed' [Arag.: Pnt.], 4.7.12

creixcut 'grown' by-f [Val.], 4.6.2.8

creixit 'grown' [Ross.], 4.6.2.7

cremat 'burned' [Cat.], 2.12

cremé 'burned' [OFr.], 4.4.4

cremi 'feared' by-f [OFr.], 4.4.4

cremu 'feared' by-f [OFr.], 4.4.4

crench 'feared' by-f [Lang.], 4.6.1.9

crengut 'feared' by-f [Lang.], 4.6.1.9

crengut 'feared' by-f [Oc.], 4.6.1.4

crenhegut 'feared' by-f [Oc.], 4.6.1.4

crent 'feared' [Poit.], 4.6.1.6

crent 'feared' by-f [Lang.], 4.6.1.9

crent 'feared' by-f [Oc.], 4.6.1.4

crent 'feared' by-f [OFr.], 4.4.4

crepât 'burst' [Fri.], 4.1

crepato 'burst; died' [It.], 2.13.3, 3.5.1

cres 'believed' [Marc.], 3.6.2

cres 'believed' nonstd. [Cat.], 4.6.2.6

crescente 'yeast' noun [SM], 3.6.2.2.1

créscita 'growth' noun [It.], 3.5.2.2

cresciuto 'grown' [It.], 2.14.5, 3.5.1, 3.5.2.2, 3.5.6, 3.5.7, 6.8

cresco 'grown' [OIt.; Boiardo, Frezzi], 3.5.8

crescuda 'growth' noun [Cat.], 4.6.2.5

cu cat 'laid, lain down' [Ist-R], 3.3.2

cu chillo 'knife' *noun* [Sp.], 4.7.6.3

cu ci to 'sewn' [It.], 2.14.5

cu cíu 'cooked' [Leon.: Can.], 4.7.13

cu e 'cooked' *adj.* [Prov.], 4.6.1.4

cu èch 'cooked' *by-f* [Gév.], 4.6.1.8

cu èch 'cooked' *by-f* [Lang.], 4.6.1.9

cu eillé 'gathered' *by-f* [OFr.], 4.4.7

cu eillette 'harvest' *noun* [Fr.], 4.4.7

cu eilli 'gathered' [Fr.], 4.4.4, 4.4.7

cu eit 'cooked' [OOc.], 4.6.1.2

cu éit 'cooked' *by-f* [Lang.], 4.6.1.9

cu èit 'cooked' [Gasc.], 4.6.1.5

cu et 'cooked' [Fri.], 4.1

cu et 'cooked' [Lad.], 4.2

cu eto 'cooked' ! [Arag.: Bls.], 4.7.12, 5.6

cu it 'cooked' [Fr.], 4.4.3, 4.4.11

cu it 'cooked' [Pic.: Av.], 4.4.13.2

cu it 'cooked' *by-f* [Cat.], 2.6.4.1, 4.6.2.3, 4.6.2.4

cu it 'cooked' *by-f?* [Val.], 4.6.2.8

cu lcat 'laid, lain' [Meg.], 3.3.1.1

cu lcat 'laid, lain' [Rom.], 3.3.2

cú leco 'put to bed' *short f* [Laz.], 3.5.9

cu leptu 'gathered' *adj.* [Arom.], 3.3.1

cu leptu 'gathered' [ORom.], 3.1.5

cu les 'gathered' *also noun* [Rom.], 3.1.5.1, 3.1.5.2

cu min čat 'begun' [Fri-R], 4.1

cu mplido 'fulfilled' [Sp.], 4.6.2.9, 4.7.2

cu mplit 'fulfilled' [Tam.], 4.6.2.9

cu mpratu 'bought' *long f, by-f* [Cors.], 3.6.2.1

cu mpresu 'understood' [Log.], 3.7.2

cu mpréndiu 'understood' [Cmpi.], 3.7.2

cu ndot 'driven' [Lad.], 4.2

cu noscut 'known' *by-f* [Ist-R], 3.3.2

cu noscut 'known' [Rom.], 2.14.5, 3.1.3

cu nuscut 'known' [Meg.], 3.3.1.1

cu och 'cooked' *by-f* [Lang.], 4.6.1.9

čuólt 'removed' ? [Vegl.], 3.4

cu ors 'run' [Enga.], 4.3.1

cu otto 'cooked' [Neap.], 3.6.2.2

cu pertu 'covered' [Cors.], 3.6.2.1

cu pirit 'covered' [Meg.], 3.3.1.1

cu prins 'contained' [Rom.], 6+7

cu rrit 'run' [Ross.], 4.6.2.7

cu rs 'run' [Oltn.], 3.2.1

cu rs 'run' [Rom.], 2.15.8, 3.1.5.1, 3.1.6

cu rs 'flow' *noun* [Rom.], 3.1.5.2

cu rsă 'fare' *noun, neol.* [Rom.], 3+11

cu rto 'short' *adj.* [Ptg.], 3+66

cu rtu 'run' [Cmpi.], 3.7.2, 3.7.4

cu rtu 'run' [Log.], 2.15.8, 3.7.2, 3.7.4

cu rvì 'covered' *by-f* [Pied.], 3.6.1.2

cú rzeto 'run' [ONeap.], 3.6.2

cu rzo 'run' *by-f* [Neap.], 3.6.2.2

cü š 'shut' [Lun.], 3.6.1.5

ćus 'shut' [Luca.], 3.6.2.5

cu ši 'sewn' [Rml.], 3.6.1.3

cu sit 'sewn' [Ross.], 4.6.2.7

čusu 'shut' [Sic.], 3.6.2.6

cu sut 'sewn' [Rom.], 3.1.3

cu sut 'sewn' *by-f* [Ist-R], 3.3.2

cu vert 'covered' *by-f* [Pied.], 3.6.1.2

cu viert 'covered' [Enga.], 4.3.1

cu vintat 'said' [Ist-R], 3.3.2

čuviyu 'rained' *by-f, usu.* [VG], 3.6.1.4.1

cu vretg 'covered' [Surs.], 4.3.2

čuvüu 'rained' *by-f, rare* [VG], 3.6.1.4.1

cuzut 'sewn' *by-f* [Ist-R], 3.3.2

dado 'given' [Sp.], 4.7.1, 4.7.3

dădut 'given' *by-f* [Oltn.], 3.2.1

dallé 'gone' *by-f* [Pic.: Av.], 4.4.13.2

dait 'given' [Pied.], 3.6.1.2

dat 'given' [Alg.], 4.6.2.10

dat 'given' [Arom.], 3.3.1

dat 'given' [Gasc.], 4.6.1.5

dat 'given' [Ist-R], 3.3.2

dat 'given' [Meg.], 3.3.1.1

dat 'given' [Rom.], 3.1.2, 3.1.6

dát 'given' [Lun.], 3.6.1.5

dat 'given' [Val.], 4.6.2.8

dat 'taken' *less usu.* [Cat.], 4.6.2.8

dat 'given' *by-f* [Oltn.], 3.2.1

dato 'given' [It.], 3.5.4

dato 'given' [Neap.], 3.6.2.2

dau 'given' [Surs.], 4.3.2

daus 'added' [Meg.], 3.3.1.1

davalat 'gone down' [Oc.], 4.6.1

debdo, debda 'debt' *noun* [OSp.], 4.7.7.2

debido 'owed, had to' [Sp.], 4.7.7.2

débito 'debt' *noun* [It.], 3.5.2.2

débrouillé 'made out, gotten along' [Pic.: Av.], 4.4.13.2

debut 'tricked' [Ross.], 4.6.2.7

decebut 'tricked' [Cat.], 4.6.2.2

déceite 'trickery' *noun* [OFr.], 4.4.9.4

déception 'trickery'• *noun* [Fr.], 4.4.9.4

deceuput 'tricked' *by-f* [OOc.], 4.6.1.1

déçu 'disappointed' [Fr.], 4.6.1.1

déchargé 'unloaded' [Fr.], 4.4.13.2

déchu 'decayed' [Fr.], 4.4.1

decho 'said, told' [Sp.: Leon], 4.7.6.2

decidit 'decided' [Cat.], 4.6.2

decido 'said, told' *dial.* [Sp.], 5.4.2

deciduu 'decided' *by-f* [Mil.], 3.6.1.1

decis 'decided' *by-f* [Mil.], 3.6.1.1

deciso 'decided' [It.], 3.5.3.2

decît 'decided' [Fri.], 4.1

dedüd 'owed, had to' *by-f* [Auv.], 4.6.1.7

defais 'fought off' [Enga.], 2.15.8, 4.3.1

défait 'undone' *by-f* [Pic.: Av.], 4.4.13.2

defendido 'fought off' [Ptg.], 4.7.8

defendido 'fought off' [Sp.], 2.15.8, 4.7.6.1

défendu 'fought off; forbidden' [Fr.], 2.15.8, 4.4.9.3

déféndù 'fought off' [Lad.], 2.15.8

defendudo 'fought off; forbidden' *by-f* [OSp.], 4.7.4.1

defendut 'fought off' *by-f* [OOc.], 2.15.8, 4.6.1.1

defengut 'fought off' *nonstd.* [Cat.], 4.6.2.6

defensat 'fought off' *by-f, usu.* [Cat.], 2.15.8

defes 'fought off' *by-f* [OOc.], 4.6.1.1

defès 'fought off' [OCat.], 4.6.2.2

defès 'fought off' *less usu.* [Cat.], 2.15.8

defesa 'meadow; forest' *by-f* [Ptg.], 2.15.8

defeso 'fought off; forbidden' *by-f* [OSp.], 2.15.8, 4.7.6.1

defeso 'forbidden' [Ptg.], 2.15.8, 4.7.8

déféyé 'undone' *by-f* [Pic.: Av.], 4.4.13.2

defois 'forbidden place' *noun* [OFr.], 2.14.5

defoise 'defense' *noun* [OFr.], 4.4.9.3

défwé 'undone/unmade' [Pic.: Ggn.], 4.4.13.2

deghu 'owed, had to' *by-f* [Poit.], 4.6.1.6

degu 'owed, had to' [Oc.], 4.6.1.4

degüd 'owed, had to' *by-f* [Auv.], 4.6.1.7

degut 'owed, had to' [Cat.], 4.6.2.2

degut 'owed, had to' [Gév.], 4.6.1.8

degut 'owed, had to' [Lang.], 4.6.1.9

degut 'owed, had to' [OOc.], 4.6.1.1

dehesa '(fenced-in) meadow' *noun* [Sp.], 2.15.8, 4.7.7.3

dejëut 'unwound' [Lad.], 4.2

delit 'destroyed' [Cat.], 4.6.2.2

demandé 'asked' [Fr.], 3.0.1

dentudo 'buck-toothed' *adj.* [Sp.], 4.7.4.2

departit 'shared' [OFr.; St. Alexis], 4.4.12

dépense 'spending' *noun* [Fr.], 4.4.9.3

dépensé 'spent' [Fr.], 3+44, 4.4.9.3

depënt 'painted' [Lad.], 4.2

depint 'painted' [Enga.], 4.3.1

dépit 'spite' *noun* [Fr.], 4.4.9.4

deppidu 'owed, had to' [Log.], 3.6.2.5

déppitu 'owed, had to' [Sard.], 3.7.3, 3.7.5

depus 'set (sun)' *arch.* [Rom.], 3.3.1

déquertché 'unloaded' [Pic.: Av.], 4.4.13.2

déquindu 'gone down' *by-f* [Pic.: Av.], 4.4.13.2

deret 'guided, led' [Enga.], 4.3.1

derguǧiyu 'untangled' [VG], 3.6.1.4.1

deriet 'gotten along, made out' [Lad.], 4.2

ders 'raised, built' *by-f* [OOc.], 4.6.1

dert 'overturned' [Surs.], 4.3.2

dervii 'opened' [Mil.], 3.6.1.1

descastáu 'neglectful of family' *adj.* [Sp.], 4.7.13

descastado 'exterminated' [Sp.], 4.7.13

descendit 'gone down' [Cat.], 4.6.1

descendu 'gone down' [Fr.], 4.4.9.4

descente 'decline' *noun* [Fr.], 4.4.9.4

déscindu 'gone down' *by-f* [Pic.: Av.], 4.4.13.2

deschis 'opened' [Rom.], 3.1.1, 3.1.5.1

deschis 'bright' *adj.* [Rom.], 3.1.5.1

desdrù 'destroyed' [Lad.], 4.2

desebut 'tricked' [ORoss.], 4.6.2.7

desendóit 'gone down' *neol.* [Vegl.], 3.4

desgors 'rejected' *by-f* [Lad.], 4.2

desgort 'rejected' *by-f* [Lad.], 4.2

desicco 'dried' *short f* [Laz.], 3.5.9

desmaido 'faltered' [OSp.], 4.7.5

desmailet 'torn apart' [Fr.-It.], 4.4.4

desmayado 'faltered' [Sp.], 4.7.5

despes 'spent' [Val.], 4.6.2.8

despès 'spent' [Cat.], 4.6.2.1

despesa 'spending' *noun* [Cat.], 4.6.2.1

despiertado 'woken' [Sp.], 4.7.8, 6.4

despierto 'awake; clever' *adj.* [Sp.], 4.7.6.4, 4.7.8, 6.4

despit 'looked down on' [OFr.], 4.4.9.4

désquété 'broken' *by-f* [Pic.: Av.], 4.4.13.2

désquindu 'gone down' *by-f* [Pic.: Av.], 4.4.13.2

destënt 'faded' [Lad.], 4.2

dèst 'roused' *by-f* [Rml.], 3.6.1.3

deștins 'gone down' [Rom.], 3.1.5.1

destint 'put out (fire)' *by-f* [Enga.], 4.3.1

destorçut 'untwisted' [Val.], 4.6.2.8

destort 'untwisted' [Cat.], 4.6.2.8

destruto 'destroyed' [Ist-I], 3.3.3

det 'said, told' *by-f* [Vegl.], 3.4, 3+37

detg 'said, told' [Surs.], 4.3.2

dette 'debt' *noun* [Fr.], 4.4.9.2

detto 'said, told' [It.], 3.5.3.1, 4.7.6.2

dettu 'said, told' [Cors.], 3.6.2.1

deuda 'debt' *noun* [Sp.], 4.7.7.2

deut, –e 'said, told' [FP: VA], 4.5.4

devesa 'meadow' *noun* [Cat.], 2.15.8, 4+30

devesa 'meadow; forest' *by-f* [Ptg.], 2.15.8

dévnun 'become' [Nor.: VS], 4.4.13.1

dezgweltu 'changed the shape of' [Leon.: VP], 4.7.13

dezmerto 'wasted' [Ist-I], 3.3.3

dezzisu 'decided' [Log.], 3.7.1

dipus 'set (sun)' [Arom.], 3.3.1

dì 'said, told' [FP: N], 4.5.1

di, deta 'said, told' [FP: Vx.], 4.5.2

di, dit 'said, told' [Burg.], 4.4.13.3

di, dit 'said, told' [Nor.: CI], 4.4.13.1

di, dit 'said, told' [Nor.: VS], 4.4.13.1

dich 'said, told' *by-f* [Gév.], 4.6.1.8

dich 'said, told' *by-f* [Lang.], 4.6.1.9

dich 'said, told' *by-f* [Oc.], 4.6.1.4

dich 'said, told' *by-f* [OOc.], 4.6.1, 4.6.1.2

dicha 'joy, luck' *noun* [Sp.], 4.7.7

dicho 'said, told' *short f* [Arag.: VE], 4.7.12

dicho 'said, told' [Leon.: Tud.], 4.7.13

dicho 'said, told' *std.* [Sp.], 4.7.0, 4.7.1, 4.7.6.2, 4+73

dichu 'said, told' [Leon.: Can.], 4.7.13

dichu 'said, told' *by-f* [Leon.: VP], 4.7.13

dicíu 'said, told' *long f* [Arag.: VE], 4.7.12

dicíu 'said, told' *by-f* [Leon.: VP], 4.7.13

diciuto 'said, told' [Cal.], 3.6.2

didu 'gone' [Ptg.: Barr.], 4.7.15

dieldu 'fermented' *adj.* [Leon.: Tud.], 4.7.13

difeso 'fought off' [It.], 2.15.8, 3.5.3.2

difindût 'fought off' [Fri.], 2.15.8

di:gnè 'dined, eaten' [Burg.], 4.4.13.3

dii 'said, told' *by-f* [Mil.], 3.6.1.1

dijendo 'saying, telling' *pres.p.* [Sp.: SF], 4.7.11

dijiendo 'saying, telling' *pres.p., rare* [Sp.: Car.], 4.7.9

dijido 'said, told' *dial.* [Sp.], 5.4.2

diletto 'beloved' *adj.* [It.], 3.5.4

dimenticato 'forgotten' [It.], 3.5.0

dipeso 'relied, depended' [It.], 3.5.3.2

dipinto 'painted' [It.], 3.5.3.1, 3.6.2, 4.3.1, 6.7

dipunat 'gone down' *by-f* [Arom.], 3.3.1

dipus 'gone down' *by-f, also adj.* [Arom.], 3.3.1

distê 'roused' *by-f* [Rml.], 3.6.1.3

distinguido 'distinguished' *by-f* [Gal.], 4.7.14

direptu 'straight' *adj. by-f* [Arom.], 3.3.1

diretto 'guided' *also adj.* [It.], 3.5.4

disatteso 'ignored' [It.], 3.5.3.2

disceso 'gone down' [It.], 3.5.3.2

discl'is 'opened; educated' [Arom.], 3.3.1

discreto 'discreet' *adj.* [It.], 3.5.10

discuss 'talked over' • [Enga.], 4.3.1

discusso 'talked over' • [It.], 3.5.3.2

discusso 'talked over' • [Gen.], 3.6.1.4

diskente 'apprentice' *noun* [Log.], 3+68

disminudo 'shrunken, reduced' [Sp.], 4.7.4.2

dispost 'arranged' [Enga.], 4.3.1

dispwestu 'clever' *adj.* [Leon.: VP], 4.7.13

disseccato 'dried' [It.], 3.5.9

dissolt 'dissolved' • [Val.], 4.6.2.8

dissolto 'dissolved' [It.], 3+62

dissous, dissoute 'dissolved' • [Fr.], 4.4.6

disteso 'stretched out' [It.], 5.3.2

distint 'distinguished' [Enga.], 4.3.1

distinto 'distinguished' *by-f* [Gal.], 4.7.14

distrus 'destroyed' [Rom.], 3.1.5.1

dit 'said, told' [Apul.: Alt.], 3.6.2.4

dit 'said, told' [Cat.], 4.6.2.3, 4.6.2.4

dit 'said, told' [Enga.], 4.3.1

dit 'said, told' [Fr.], 0.2, 3.6.2, 3+38, 4.4.3, 4.4.11, 4.4.12

dit 'said, told' [Fri.], 4.1

dit 'said, told' [Gasc.], 4.6.1.5

dit 'said, told' [Lad.], 4.2

dit 'said, told' [Pic.: Av.], 4.4.13.2

dit 'said, told' [Pied.], 3.6.1.2

dit 'said, told' [Poit.], 4.6.1.6

dit 'said, told' [Tam.], 4.6.2.9

dit 'said, told' [Val.], 4.6.2.8

dit 'said, told' *by-f* [Gév.], 4.6.1.8

dit 'said, told' *by-f* [Lang.], 4.6.1.9

dit 'said, told' *by-f* [Oc.], 4.6.1.4

dit 'said, told' *by-f* [OOc.], 4.6.1, 4.6.1.2

diterso 'cleaned, wiped' [It.], 3.5.3.2

dito 'said, told' [Arag.: Pnt.], 4.7.12

dito 'said, told' [Gal.], 4.7.14

dito 'said, told' [Ist-I], 3.3.3

dito 'said, told' [Ptg.], 4.7.6.2

dito 'said, told' [Venet.], 3+38

ditt 'said, told' *by-f* [Mil.], 3.6.1.1

dittə 'said, told' [Abru.], 3.6.2.3

ditto 'said, told' [Elb.], 3.6.2

ditto 'said, told' [Neap.], 3.6.2.2

ditto 'said, told' [Ven.], 3.6.1, 3+38

dittu 'said, told' [Sic.], 3.6.2.6

ditu 'said, told' [Vegl.: Z], 3.4

díu 'gone' [Leon.: Can.], 4.7.13

díu 'gone' [Leon.: VP], 4.7.13

diucl'at 'hit by the evil eye' [Arom.], 3.3.1, 5.6

diuntu 'arrived' [Cors.], 3.6.2.1

divelto 'uprooted' [It.], 3.5.2.1

dividuu 'divided' *by-f* [Mil.], 3.6.1.1

divinut 'become' [Fri-R], 4.1

divis 'divided' *by-f* [Mil.], 3.6.1.1

divisé 'divided' [Fr.], 3.1.3

diviso 'divided' [Gen.], 3.6.1.4

divizat 'divided' *neol.* [Rom.], 3.1.4

divizo 'divided' [Ist-I], 3.3.3

dívida 'debt' *noun* [Ptg.], 4.7.10

dizvucat 'given birth' [Arom.], 3.3.1

djein, djeinta 'joined' [FP: Vd.], 4.5.3

djeldu 'fermented' *adj.* [Leon.: VP], 4.7.13

dobert 'opened' *by-f* [Lang.], 4.6.1.9

doch 'taught' [OOc.], 4.6.1

doido 'crazy' *adj.* [Ptg.], 2.13.3

doîo 'hurt' [Gen.], 3.6.1.4

doit 'taught' [OFr.], 4.4.2.2

dolâšt 'hurt' [Lad.: Liv.], 4.2

dolgut 'hurt' [Cat.], 2.13.3

dolgut 'hurt' [Gév.], 4.6.1.8

dolgut 'hurt' [Val.], 4.6.2.8

dolido 'hurt' [Sp.], 2.13.3

dolit 'hurt' *nonstd.* [Cat.], 4.6.2.6

dolso 'hurt' [OIt.], 3.5.8

dolsuto 'hurt' [OIt.], 3.5.8

doluto 'hurt' [It.], 2.13.3, 3.3.2, 3.5.8

domado 'tamed' [Sp.], 4.7.2.2

domandat 'asked' [Fri-R], 4.1

domandato 'asked' [It.], 3.0.1, 3.5.0

domat 'tamed' [Cat.], 2.1.1, 4.6.2.2

domato 'tamed' [It.], 2.1.1, 3.5.1

domé 'tamed' [OFr.], 4.4.2.3

dompté 'tamed' [Fr.], 2.1.1

domu 'house' *noun* [Sard.], 3.7

donat 'given' usu. [Cat.], 4.6.2.8,
    4.6.2.10

dondado 'tamed' [Ptg.], 2.1.1

donné 'given' [Fr.], 4.4.0

donnè, donnè: 'given' [Nor.: CI],
    4.4.13.1

dorfidu 'hurt' [Sard.], 3.7.5

dorii 'hurt' *by-f* [Mil.], 3.6.1.1

dormain 'slept' [Nor.: VS], 4.4.13.1

dormáit 'slept' [Vegl.], 3.4

dormi 'slept' *by-f* [FP: VA], 4.5.4

dormi 'slept' *by-f* [Fr.], 4.4.8

dormí 'slept' [Lun.], 3.6.1.5

dormi, dormi: 'slept' [Nor.: CI],
    4.4.13.1

dormido 'slept' [Sp.], 1+45, 4.7,
    4.7.1

dormire 'sleeping' *ger.* [Rom.],
    3.1.8

dormit 'slept' [Rom.], 3.1.0, 3.1.8,
    3.3.2

dormito 'slept' [Arag.: Pnt.], 4.7.12

dormito 'slept' [It.], 3.6.2

dorsuto 'hurt' [Tusc.], 3.6.1.1

dorsuu 'hurt' *by-f* [Mil.], 3.6.1.1

dorü 'hurt' [Lad.: Marb.], 4.2

doruu 'hurt' *by-f* [Mil.], 3.6.1.1

-dotto 'led, brought' [It.], 3.5.5, 3+43

douăzeci 'twenty' *numeral*
    [Rom.], 3+20

dounai 'given' [Poit.], 4.6.1.6

dovùo 'owed, had to' [Gen.], 3.6.1.4

dovuto 'owed, had to' [It.], 3.5.2.2,
    3.5.6, 4.6.2.3

drat 'straight' *adv.* [Vegl.], 3.4

drept 'law, right' *noun* [Rom.],
    3.1.5.1, 3.1.5.2

dreptu 'straight' *adj. by-f* [Arom.],
    3.3.1

dres 'repaired' *also noun* [Rom.],
    3.1.5.1, 3.1.5.2

drœmi 'slept' [Burg.], 4.4.13.3

drumi 'slept' *by-f* [FP: VA], 4.5.4

du 'owed, had to' *by-f* [Poit.], 4.6.1.6

du 'owed, had to' [Lad.], 4.2

du, dussa 'owed, had to' [FP: Vd.],
    4.5.3

du, −ya 'owed, had to' [FP: VA],
    4.5.4

dû 'owed, had to' [Fr.], 4.4.2.2,
    4.4.9.2

dubert 'opened' *by-f* [Lang.], 4.6.1.9

ducho 'led, brought' [OSp.], 4.7.6.1,
    4.7.7.1

ducho 'skillful' *adj.* [Sp.], 4.7.7.1

-ducido 'led, brought' [Sp.], 4.7.6.1

duende 'goblin; fairy' *noun*.[Sp.],
    4.7.7.2

duich 'led, brought' *by-f* [OOc.],
    4.6.1

duis 'lesson, teaching' *noun* [OFr.],
    4.4.9.3, 4+16

duit 'led, brought' *by-f* [OOc.], 4.6.1

duit 'canal, flow' *noun* [OFr.],
    4.4.9.3

duït 'led, brought' [OFr.], 4.4.11

duiu 'owed, had to' [Surs.], 4.3.2

dulët 'hurt' [Lad.: Gar.], 4.2

durmisto 'slept' [Ist-I], 3.3.3

dulisto 'hurt' [Ist-I], 3.3.3

dunat 'gathered' [Meg.], 3.3.1.1

dúot 'wet' *adj.* [Vegl.], 3.4

durbit 'opened' [Gév.], 4.6.1.8

durmì 'slept' [Rml.], 3.6.1.3

durmisto 'slept' [Ist-I], 3.3.3

durmit 'slept' [Ist-R], 3.1.8, 3.3.2

durmit 'slept' [Meg.], 3.3.1.1

durmitu 'sleeping' *ger.* [Ist-R], 3.1.8, 3.3.2

durmuto 'slept' [Neap.], 3.6.2.2

durn'ire 'sleep, sleeping' *noun* [Arom.], 3.3.1

durn'it 'slept' [Arom.], 3.3.1

durut 'hurt; desired' *also adj.* [Arom.], 3.3.1

durut 'hurt' [Ist-R], 3.3.2

durut 'hurt' [Rom.], 2.13.3, 3.1.3, 3.3.2

durvert 'opened' *by-f* [Pied.], 3.6.1.2

durvì 'opened' *by-f* [Pied.], 3.6.1.2

dus 'carried' [Arom.], 3.3.1

dus 'brought' [Ist-R], 3.3.2

dus 'carried' [Meg.], 3.3.1.1

dus 'taken away' [Rom.], 1.8, 3.1.2, 3.1.5.1, 5.6, 6.8

dus 'going' *noun* [Rom.], 3.1.5.2

dut 'carried, taken' [Cat.], 0.2, 4.6.2, 4.6.2.3, 4.6.2.4

dut 'carried, taken' [Tam.], 4.6.2.9

dut 'carried, taken' [Val.], 4.6.2.8

dut 'said, told' *by-f* [Vegl.], 3.4

dut, due 'owed' [Sto.], 4.6.1.6

duvisto 'owed, had to' [Ist-I: D], 3.3.3, 3.6.1

duyt 'carried, taken' [OCat.], 4.6.2.2

dzăcutu 'been silent' [Meg.: Ţ], 3.3.1.1

dzeesu 'lain' [FP: VA], 4.5.4

dzəs 'said, told' [Arom.: K], 3.3.1

dzîcă 'word, speech' *noun* [Arom.], 3.3.1

dzîs 'said, told' [Arom.], 3.3.1

dzîţeare 'saying' *noun, by-f* [Arom.], 3.3.1

dzîţire 'saying' *noun, by-f* [Arom.], 3.3.1

dzoignu, −ya 'joined' [FP: VA], 4.5.4

ecceduto 'gone too far' [It.], 2.15.10

eces 'lit' *by-f* [OOc.], 4.6.1

echado 'thrown' [Sp.], 4.7

échars 'underweight (of coins)' *adj.* [Fr.], 2.6

echau 'thrown' [Args.], 4.7.10

echu 'done/made' [Leon.: VP], 4.7.13

éclos 'hatched' [Fr.], 4.4.13.1

éclous 'hatched' [Nor.: Pch.], 4.4.13.1

écri, −ta 'written' [FP: VA], 4.5.4

ècri, −te 'written' [FP: Vd.], 4.5.3

écrit 'written' [Fr.], 4.4.0.3, 4.4.2.3, 4.4.3, 4.4.11, 4.4.12

écrit 'written' [Pic.: Av.], 4.4.13.2

êhtadu 'been' [Ptg.: Barr.], 4.7.15

eissit 'gone out' *by-f* [OOc.], 4.6.1, 4.6.1.3

eissu 'gone out' *by-f* [OFr.], 2.14.2

eissut 'gone out' *by-f* [OOc.], 4.6.1.3

eitàd 'been' [Auv.], 4.6.1.7

eixida 'leaving' *noun* [Cat.], 4.6.2.5

eixit 'gone out' [Cat.], 4.6.2.2

eixit 'gone out' [Ross.], 4.6.2.7

ejido 'public land' *noun* [Sp.], 4.7.7

ékou 'threshed' [Burg.], 4.4.13.3

ekri, ekrita 'written' [FP: Vx.], 4.5.2

eku, ekuosa 'threshed' [FP: Vx.], 4.5.2

feito 'done/made' [Ptg.], 4.7, 4.7.6.2, 5.2

felu 'been required' *by-f* [Poit.], 4.6.1.6

fenáit 'ended' [Vegl.], 3.4

fendu 'split' [Fr.], 2.14.2, 4.4.2.2, 4.4.9.2, 4.4.9.3, 4.6.2.5

fenduto 'split' *by-f, arch.* [It.], 3.5.3.2, 3.5.10

fenet, −èite 'ended' *by-f* [FP: VA], 4.5.4

feni 'ended' *by-f* [Pic.: Br.], 4.4.13.2

feni, −a 'ended' *by-f* [FP: VA], 4.5.4

fenit 'ended' [OOc.], 4.6.1

fente 'slit' *noun* [Fr.], 2.4.3, 4.4.9.2, 6.7

fenygut 'kneaded' *by-f* [Val.], 4.6.2.8

fenyut 'kneaded' [Cat.], 2.1.1, 4.6.2.8

fenyut 'kneaded' *by-f* [Val.], 4.6.2.8

ferì 'hit' [Lad.], 4.2

ferida 'wound' *noun* [Cat.], 4.6.2.5

ferido 'hit' [Ptg.], 2.8

ferit 'forbidden' [Rom.], 2.8, 3.1.4

ferit 'hit' [Cat.], 2.8, 4.6.2.2

ferit 'hit' [Gév.], 4.6.1.8

ferit 'hit' *by-f* [OOc.], 4.6.1.3

ferît 'hit' [Fri.], 4.1

ferito 'hit' [It.], 2.8

fermé 'shut' *by-f* [Pic.: Av.], 4.4.13.2

fersa 'roast pig drippings' *noun* [Pied.], 3+67

fertu 'hit' [Cmpi.], 3.7.1, 3.7.2, 3.7.4

fertu 'hit' [Log.], 3.7.1, 3.7.2

feru 'hit' [OFr.], 2.8

ferue 'wound' *noun* [OFr], 4.4.9.1

ferut 'hit' *by-f* [OOc.], 4.6.1.3

feruto 'hit' [OAbru.], 3.6.2.3

feruto 'hit' [OIt.], 2.8, 3.5.7

fervido 'boiled' [Ptg.], 2.8, 3.0.1

fes 'split' [Cat.], 2.15.8

fes 'crack, slit' *noun* [Cat.], 4.6.2.5

fess 'split' [Enga.], 4.3.1

fess 'split' [Surs.], 2.15.8

fesse 'buttock' *noun* [Fr.], 2.4.3, 4.4.9.3, 4.6.2.5

fesso 'split' *by-f, arch.* [It.], 2.15.8, 3.5.3.2, 3.5.10

fesso 'fool' *noun* [It.], 3.5.3.2

fet 'done/made' [Cat.], 4.6.2.1, 4.6.2.2, 4.6.2.3, 4.6.2.4, 4.6.2.9

fet 'done/made' [Val.], 4.6.2.8

fét 'done/made' *by-f* [Poit.], 4.6.1.6

fét, −e 'done/made' *by-f* [FP: VA], 4.5.4

feto 'done/made' *by-f* [Arag.: Pnt.], 4.7.12

fetu 'done/made' [Ptg.: Barr.], 4.7.15

feyt 'done/made' [OCat.], 4.6.2.2, 4.6.2.9

feyt 'done/made' *nonstd.* [Cat.], 4.6.2.6

fətutə 'bewitched' [Abru.], 3.6.2.3

fglœi, fglœi: 'bloomed' [Nor.: VS], 4.4.13.1

fiado 'trusted' [Sp.], 2.9

ficado 'stayed' [Ptg.], 4.7.0

fidat 'trusted' [Cat.], 2.9

fidato 'trusted' [It.], 2.9

fié 'trusted' [Fr.], 2.9

fiè, fièssa 'hit' [FP: Vd.], 4.5.3

fiers 'thrown' [Surs.], 4.3.2

fiert 'boiled' ! [Rom.], 2.8, 3.0.1, 3.1.5, 3.1.6, 3.1.7, 3.3.1, 3.3.2, 3.3.3, 3.7.1, 5.4.1

fijado 'fixed, set' [Sp.], 2.11.2, 4.7.8

fijo 'fixed, set' *adj.* [Sp.], 2.11.2, 4.7.6.4, 4.7.8

film 'movie' *noun* [Fr.], 4.4.0.3

findo 'ended' *short f* [Ptg.], 4+71

fingido 'pretended' [Sp.], 4.7

fingiuu 'pretended' *by-f* [Mil.], 3.6.1.1

fini 'ended' [Fr.], 4.4.12

fini 'ended' *by-f* [Pic.: Br.], 4.4.13.2

fini 'ended' [Poit.], 4.6.1.6

finì, finí: 'ended' [FP: N], 4.5.1

finidu 'ended' [Lig.: Sis.], 3.6.1.4

finit, finie 'ended' [Sto.], 4.6.1.6

finît 'ended' [Fri.], 4.1

finito 'ended' [It.], 3.6.2

fins 'pretended' [OOc.], 4.6.1, 4+40

fint 'pretended' [Enga.], 4.3.1

fint 'pretended' *by-f* [Mil.], 3.6.1.1

finto 'pretense' *noun* [Gév.], 4.6.1.8

finto 'pretended' [Gen.], 3.6.1.4

finto 'pretended' [It.], 2.1.1, 3.5.3.1, 3.6.2, 4.3.1, 4+40

fintu 'fake' *adj.* [Sic.], 3.6.2.6

finuto 'ended' [OIt.], 3.5.7

fiore 'flower' *noun* [It.], 3.5.3.2

fiorito 'bloomed' [It.], 2.8

fire 'nature, character' *noun* [Rom.], 3.1.8

firmado 'fastened' [Ptg.], 4.7.8

firme 'steady' *adj.* [Ptg.], 4.7.8

firutu 'hit' [Sic.], 3.6.2.6

fiso 'fastened' *adj., lit.* [It.], 3.5.5

fissat 'fastened' [Gév.], 4.6.1.8

fissə 'split' [Abru.], 3.6.2.3

fisso 'fastened' *by-f* [OIt.], 3+56

fisso 'fastened' *adj.* [It.], 3.5.5, 6.4

fissu 'split' [Sic.], 3.5.10

fitat 'born' [Arom.], 3.3.1

fitto 'fastened' *by-f* [OIt.; Jacopone da Todi], 3+56

fitto 'fastened; thrust' [It.], 3.5.5

fixe 'fixed, set' *adj.•* [Fr.], 2.4

fixe 'lasting' *adj. by-f* [Ptg.], 6.4

fixo 'lasting' *adj. by-f* [Ptg.], 6+3

flat 'found' [Meg.], 3.3.1.1

flesso 'bent'• [It.], 3.5.3.2

fleuri 'bloomed' [Fr.], 4.4.1, 4.4.13.1

flojo 'weak, lazy' *adj.* [Sp.] 4.7.6.3

florecido 'bloomed' [Sp.], 2.8

florido 'flowery' *adj.* [Sp.], 2.8

florit 'bloomed' [Cat.], 2.8

florit 'bloomed' [Rom.] *see* înflorit

flourit 'bloomed' [Gév.], 4.6.1.8

fni 'ended' [Burg.], 4.4.13.3

fni, fña 'ended' [FP: Vx.], 4.5.2

fo 'been' [Mold.: Mara.], 3.2

fodido 'fucked' [Ptg.], 5.2

foet 'done/made' *by-f* [Auv.], 4.6.1.7

foï 'fled' *by-f* [OFr.], 4.4.2.3

fóit 'been' [Vegl.], 2.7, 3.3.1, 3.4

fóit 'fled' ? [Vegl.], 3.4

fondu 'melted' [Fr.], 2.14.2, 3.5.7, 3.6.1.1

fondù, fondú: 'melted' [FP: N], 4.5.1

fonduto 'melted' [OIt.], 3.5.7

fonduu 'melted' [Mil.], 3.6.1.1

fongut 'melted' *nonstd.* [Cat.], 4.6.2.6

fos 'been' *allegro f* [Ist-R], 3.3.2

fos 'melted' [Cat.], 4.6.2.3, 4.6.2.4, 4+36

fos 'dug' *by-f* [Lang.], 4.6.1.9

fos 'melted' [OOc.], 4.6.1.2

fos 'melted' [Val.], 4.6.2.8

fosa 'melt, thaw' *noun* [Cat.], 4.6.2.5

fosa 'pit, grave' *noun* [Sp.], 4+36

fosegut 'dug' *by-f* [Lang.], 4.6.1.9

fossa 'pit, grave' *noun* [Cat.], 4+36

fossana 'grave(yard)' *noun* [Cat.], 4+36

fossar 'graveyard' *noun* [Cat.], 4+36

fossat 'moat' *noun* [Cat.], 4+36

fossato 'trench' *noun* [It.], 4+36

fritt 'fried' [Mil.], 3.6.1.1

frítta 'fried' by-f [Apul.], 3.6.2

fritto 'fried' [It.], 3.1.5, 3.5.3.1, 3.6.2

fritto 'fried' [Neap.], 3.6.2.2

frittu 'fried' usu. adj. [Sic.], 3.6.2.6

frìttu 'fried' [OSard.], 3.7.4

fritu 'fried' [VG], 3.6.1.4.1

frǫns 'broken' [Meg.], 3.3.1.1

frǫnt, frắntắ 'broken' [Meg.: U], 3.3.1.1

froumo, frouma: 'shut' [Nor.: VS], 4.4.13.1

fs 'been' allegro f [Istr.], 3.3.2

fuáls 'untrue' adj. [Vegl.], 3.4

fuát 'done/made' ? [Vegl.], 3.4

fudzit 'fled' by-f [Arom.], 3.3.1

fudzitǎ 'departure' noun [Arom.], 3.3.1

fuessa 'grave, ditch' noun [OSp.], 4+69

fugat 'fled' by-f [Arom.], 3.3.1

fuggito 'fled' [It.], 3.5.2.2, 3.6.1

fugida 'escape' noun [Cat.], 4.6.2.5

fugit 'fled' [Cat.], 4.6.2.2

fugit 'fled' [Ross.], 4.6.2.7

fugit 'fled' [Rom.], 3.1.2, 3.3.2

fui 'fled' [Fr.], 4.4.1

fuíu 'fled' [Arag.: VE], 4.7.12

fuiuta 'elopement' noun [SM], 3.6.2.2.1

fuiuto 'fled' [SM], 3.6.2.2.1

fuite 'leak' [Fr.], 4.4.9.2

fundido 'melted' [Sp.], 4.7.2

funnutu 'broken ground, plowed deep' [Sic.], 3.6.2.6

funto 'performed' rare• [It.], 3.5.0

furnutu 'ended' [Sal.], 3.6.2

fus 'melted' [Enga.], 4.3.1

fus 'melted' non-std. [Cat.], 4.6.2.6

fuso 'melted' [Gen.], 3.6.1.4

fuso 'melted' [It.], 3.5.7, 3.6.1.1

fut 'been' [Arom.], 3.3.1, 3.4

futa 'fleeing' noun [OIt.], 3.4, 3.5.2.2

futeit 'fled' by-f [OFr.], 4.4.9.4

futo 'fled' ! [Gen.], 3.6.1, 3.6.1.4, 3.6.2.6

futtutu 'fucked' [Sic.], 3.6.2.6

futut 'fucked' [Rom.], 3.1.3

fuyt 'fled' [OCat.], 4.6.2.2

fuzit 'fled' [Meg.], 3.3.1.1

fužit 'fled' [Ist-R], 3.3.2

fwult, fwòlt 'clogged, plugged' [Apul.: Alt.], 3.6.2.4

fwé 'done/made' [Pic.: Ggn.], 4.4.13.2

fyu 'been required' [Burg.], 4.4.13.3

gambuto 'thick-legged' adj. [It.], 4.7.4.2

gañado 'earned, gained' long f [Gal.], 4.7.14

ganau 'earned, gained' [Leon.: Can.], 4.7.13

ganhado 'earned, gained' arch. [Ptg.], 4.7.8

ganho 'earned, gained' short f, std. [Ptg.], 4.7.8

gaño 'earned, gained' short f [Gal.], 4.7.14

garantido 'guaranteed' leg. [Sp.], 4.7.9

garantizado 'guaranteed' std. [Sp.], 4.7.9

gǎrire 'humming' noun [Arom.], 3.3.1

gǎsit 'found' [Rom.], 3.2.2

gǎsow 'frozen' [VG], 3.6.1.4.1

gǎst 'found' allegro f [Mold.], 3.2.2

gastado 'spent' arch. [Ptg.], 4.7.8

gasto 'spent' short f, std. [Ptg.], 4.7.8

geint 'whimpered' [Fr.], 4.4.1

gemegat 'moaned' [Oc.], 4.6.1.4

gemido 'whimpered' [Sp.], 4.7.2.2

gémi 'moaned, wailed' [Fr.], 4.4.1

gemut 'groaned' [Rom.], 3.1.2

gemuto 'groaned' *rare* [It.], 3.5.6

gêné 'bothered' [Fr.], 1+44

geü 'lain' [OFr.], 2.13.3, 4.4.1, 4.4.9.2, 4+25

gghiuto 'gone' *by-f* [SM], 3.6.2.2.1

ghiacciato 'frozen' [It.], 3.6.1.4.1

giaciuto 'lain' [It.], 2.13.3, 2.14.5, 3.5.1

gieu 'had' [Enga.], 4.3.1

ǧind 'filled' [Luca.], 3.6.2.5

ǧini 'good, fine' *adj.* [Arom.], 3.3.1

giocato 'played' [It.], 3.5.0

gionto 'arrived' *by-f* [It.], 3.1.6, 3.5.3.1, 3.5.4

gisant 'reclining' *pres.p.* [Fr.], 4.4.9.2

gité 'thrown' [OFr.], 4.4.4

gîte 'shelter, lair' *noun* [Fr.], 4.4.9.2

gito 'gone' *lit.* [It.], 3.5.0

giu 'had' [Surs.], 4.3.2

giundschieu 'joined' *by-f* [Enga.], 4.3.1

giunt 'joined' *by-f* [Enga.], 4.3.1

giunto 'arrived' *by-f* [It.], 3.5.3.1

giut 'joined' *by-f* [Enga.], 4.3.1

giuto 'gone' [OTusc.], 3.5.7

gnü 'come' [Lad.: Bad.], 4.2

godù 'enjoyed' [Lad.], 2.9, 4.2

goduto 'enjoyed' [It.], 2.9, 4.3.2

goi̯du 'heard' *adj.* [Leon.: VP], 4.7.13

gojat 'enjoyed' [Cat.], 2.9

gorge 'throat' *noun* [Fr.], 4.2

gosat 'dared' [Cat.], 2.11.1

goulu 'greedy' *adj.* [Fr.], 4.7.4.2

gouvido 'enjoyed' [Ptg.], 2.9

gozado 'enjoyed' [Sp.], 2.9

gózu 'enjoyed' *by-f* [Lig.: Sis.], 3.6.1.4

grande 'big' *adj.* [Ptg.], 0.2, 6.4

guadagnatu 'won, gained' *long f, by-f* [Cors.], 3.6.2.1

guadantu 'won, gained' *short f* [Cors.], 3.6.2.1

guardato 'looked at' [It.], 4.1

guastato 'wasted' [It.], 3.5.9

guasto 'laid waste' *short f* [OIt.], 3.5.9

guasto 'out of order' *adv.* [It.], 3.5.9

gudiu 'enjoyed' [Surs.], 4.3.2

gudisto 'enjoyed' [Ist-I], 3.3.3

gududu 'enjoyed' *by-f* [Lig.: Sis.], 3.6.1.4

gulbío '(re)turned' [Leon.: Tud.], 4.7.13

gustat 'eaten' [Ist-R], 3.3.2

güt 'joined' *by-f* [Enga.], 4.3.1

guyíu 'heard' [Leon.: VP], 4.7.13

gwelto '(re)turned' *adj.* [Leon.: Tud.], 4.7.13

gweltu '(re)turned' [Leon.: VP], 4.7.13

habido 'had' [Gal.], 4.7.14

habido 'had' [Sp.], 4.7.2.2

hablado 'spoken' [Sp.], 4.7.13

hagut 'had' [Cat.], 3.7.5, 4.6.2.3, 4.6.2.4

halagado 'flattered' [Sp.], 4.7.0

hallado 'found' [Sp.], 3.0.1

hard 'computer hardware' *noun* [Fr.], 4.4.0.3

hartado 'glutted' [Sp.], 2.11.2, 4.7.8, 4.7.12

harto 'fed up' *adj.* [Sp.], 2.11.2, 4.7.6.4, 4.7.8, 4.7.12, 6.4

hechizo 'spell, enchantment' *noun* [Sp.], 4.7.7.1

malastrudha 'star-crossed' [OIt.; Bonvesin], 3.5.6

maldecido 'cursed' [Sp.], 4.7.8, 4+73

maldicíu 'cursed' [Leon.: VP], 4.7.13

maldito 'accursed' adj., noun [Sp.], 4.7.8, 4+73

maleoit 'cursed' [OFr.], 4.4.9.4

malmes 'hurt, harmed' [Cat.], 4.6.2.9

malmetut 'hurt, harmed' [Tam.], 4.6.2.9

malquisto 'disliked' also adj. [Ptg.], 4.7.7.4

mal quisto 'disliked' adj. [Sp.], 4.7.7.4

mâncare 'food' noun [Rom.], 3.1.8

mâncat 'eaten' [Rom.], 3.1.0

mǎncat 'eaten' [Meg.], 3.3.1.1

manciât 'eaten' [Fri.], 4.1

man čatu 'eaten' [Sic.], 3.6.2.6

mandàd 'summoned' [Auv.], 4.6.1.7

mandadu 'ordered, sent' [Ptg.: Barr.], 4.7.15

mandikata 'eaten' f.sg. [Sard.], 3.7.0

manducado 'eaten' [ORR], 4.3

manğadu 'eaten' [Lig.: Sis.], 3.6.1.4

mangé 'eaten' [Fr.], 4.4.13.1

mangé 'eaten' by-f [Pic.: Av.], 4.4.13.2

mangiato 'eaten' [It.], 3.5.8

mangio 'eaten' short f [Tusc.], 3.5.9

mangiòu 'eaten' [Gen.], 3.6.1.4

maniata 'libidinous caress' noun [SM], 3.6.2.2.1

manicato 'eaten' [OIt.], 3.5.8

manido 'trite' adj. [Sp.], 4.7.9

manjat 'eaten' [Gév.], 4.6.1.8

manjat 'eaten' [Lad.], 4.2

mannu 'big' adj. [Sard.], 3.7

mantenuto 'kept' [It.], 3.7.1

mantesu 'kept' [Log./Nuor.], 3.7

manteuda 'kept woman' noun [Ptg.], 4.7.10

mantido 'kept' [Ptg.], 4.7.10

mantingut 'kept' [Cat.], 3.7.1

marcito 'faded, withered' [It.], 3.5.0

maridat 'married' [Fri-R], 4.1

mǎritat 'married' [Ist-R], 3.3.2

marsa 'clothes-peddler' noun [VG], 3.6.1.4.1

marsu 'spoiled, rotted' [VG], 3.6.1.4.1

mǎrunt 'small' adj. [Rom.], 3.1.3, 4.7.4.2

mas 'farm, farmhouse' noun [Oc./Cat.], 4.4.13.3

mas 'stayed' by-f [OFr.], 4.4.4

masu 'stayed' by-f [OFr.], 4.4.4

matado 'killed' [Sp.], 4.7.0

maţǔkior 'vermiform appendix' noun phrase [Arom.], 3+17

maudit 'cursed' [Fr.], 4.4.9.4

mé: 'lot; orchard' noun [Burg.], 4.4.13.3

mẽ, mẽs 'put' [Nor.: CI], 4.4.13.1

mè, messa 'put' [FP: Vd.], 4.5.3

medido 'measured' [Sp.], 4.7.2

mendut 'led' [Poit.], 4.6.1.6

mené 'led' [Fr.], 4.4.0

menguado 'shrunk' [Sp.], 4.7.4.2

mentu 'lied' [OFr.], 4.4.7

menudo 'small' adj. [Sp.], 4.7.4.2

menut 'tiny' adj. [Gév.], 4.6.1.8

merecido 'deserved' [Sp.], 4.7.2.2

mereixcut 'deserved' [Val.], 4.6.2.8

merescut 'deserved' [Cat.], 4.6.2.3, 4.6.2.8

merescut 'deserved' [Lang.], 4.6.1.9

merit 'deserved' [OOc.], 4.6.1

mers 'gone, walked' [Meg.], 3.3.1.1

mers 'gone, walked' [Rom.], 3.1.5.1,
3.1.7, 3.3.2, 4.3.1

mers 'gait, pace; progress' *noun*
[Rom.], 3.1.5.2

mes$_1$ 'messenger' *n o u n* [OFr.],
4.4.9.3

mes$_2$ 'dish (of food)' *n o u n* [OFr.],
4.4.9.3

mes$_3$ 'farm, farmhouse' *n o u n* [OFr.],
4.4.9.3, 4.4.13.3

mes 'put' [Cat.], 4.6.2.1

mes 'gone' [Ist-R], 3.3.2

mes 'put' [Val.], 4.6.2.8

mes 'stayed' *by-f* [OFr.], 4.4.4

mes 'put' *by-f* [OOc.], 4.6.1, 4.6.1.1,
4.6.1.2

meschiato 'mingled' *by-f, usu.* [It.],
3.5.0

meschitato 'mingled' [OIt.], 3.5.0

mesciuto 'mingled' *by-f, rare* [It.],
3.5.0

mesedat 'dealt' [Fri.: Gor.], 4.1

meso 'put' [Fri.: Gra.], 4.1

meso- 'middle' *prefix* [Sp.], 4.7.6.1

mess 'put' [Surs.], 4.3.2

messo 'put' [Ist-I], 3.3.3

messo 'put' [It.], 2.12, 3.3.2, 3.5.3.2,
3.6.1.1, 4.4.11

messo 'put into' *by-f* [OSp.], 2.12,
4.7.6.1

messu 'put' [Cors.], 3.6.2.1

mestiere 'trade, craft' *n o u n* [It.],
4.1

mét 'put' *!by-f* [Poit.], 4.6.1.6

metido 'put into' [Sp.], 4.7.6.1

metit 'measured' [Rom.], 3.1.0

metito 'put in' [Arag.: Pnt.], 4.7.12

metíu 'put, put into' [Leon.], 4.7.13

metóit 'put' *neol.* [Vegl.], 3.4

métu 'put' *by-f* [Poit.], 4.6.1.6

metù 'put' [Lad.], 4.2

mettuu 'put' *by-f* [Mil.], 3.6.1.1

metüd 'put' *by-f* [Auv.], 4.6.1.7

metudo 'put into' *by-f* [OSp.; Cid],
4.7.4.1

metut 'put' *nonstd.* [Cat.], 4.6.2.6

metût 'put' [Fri.], 4.1

meut 'moved' [Lad.], 4.2

mëut 'milked' *by-f* [Lad.], 2.15.6, 4.2

meute 'crowd, pack' *n o u n* [Fr.],
4.4.9.2

mez 'put' *by-f* [Auv.], 4.6.1.7

məndut 'lied' [Apul.: Alt.], 3.6.2.4

mənǧut 'milked' [Apul.: Alt.],
3.6.2.4

miedo 'fear' *noun* [Sp.], 2.14.4

mié 'eaten' ! *by-f* [Pic.: Av.],
4.4.13.2

miers 'bitten' [Surs.], 4.3.2

miet 'ground' [Enga.], 4.3.1

mindgi 'eaten' *by-f* [Pic.: Av.],
4.4.13.2

minto 'pissed' *arch.●* [It.], 3.5.3.1,
3.5.4

mintutu 'put' [Cal.], 3.6.2

mirat 'been surprised' [Rom.], 3.1.8

mirato 'looked at' *lit.* [It.], 3.5.0

mirosat 'smelled' [Mold.], 3.2.2

mirosit 'smelled' [Rom.], 3.2.2

mis 'put' [Fr.], 0.2, 2.12, 3.6.2,
4.4.0.3, 4.4.3, 4.4.9.3, 4.4.11,
4.4.12, 4.6.1.1, 5.5

mis 'put' [Luca.], 3.6.2.5

mis 'put' *by-f* [OOc.], 4.6.1.1

miso 'put' [OIt.; Dante], 2.12, 3.5.8

miso 'put' [Ven.], 3.6.1

miso- 'hatred' *prefix* [Sp.], 4.7.6.1

miss 'put' [Enga.], 4.3.1

miss 'put' *by-f* [Mil.], 3.6.1.1

missə 'sent' [Abru.], 3.6.2.3

missidu 'put' *by-f* [OSard.], 3.7.1

morso 'bit (for horses)' *noun* [It.],
    3.5.3.2

mort 'dead' *adj.* [Rom.], 2.9, 6.4

mort 'died' [Arom.], 3.3.1

mort 'died; killed' [Cat.], 4.6.2.1,
    4.7.9

mort 'died' [Enga.], 4.3.1

mort 'died' [Fr.], 2.9, 4.4.0.3, 4.4.3,
    4.4.7, 4.4.11

mort 'died' [Gasc.], 4.6.1.5

mort 'died' [Gév.], 4.6.1.8

mort 'died' [Lad.], 4.2

mort 'died' [Luca.], 3.6.2.5

mort 'died' [Lun.], 3.6.1.5

mort 'died' [Mil.], 3.6.1.1

mort 'died' [OOc.], 4.6.1

mort 'died' [Poit.], 4.6.1.6

mort 'died' [Val.], 4.6.2.8

mort 'died' *by-f* [Pic.: Av.], 4.4.13.2

mort 'died' *by-f* [Pied.], 3.6.1.2

morto 'died' [Gen.], 3.6.1.4

morto 'died' [It.], 2.9, 3.5.3.1, 3.5.4

morto 'died' *by-f* [Ist-I], 3.3.3

morto 'died; killed' *by-f* [Ptg.], 2.9,
    4.7.6.2, 4.7.9

morts 'died' [Surs.], 4.3.2

mortu 'died' [Lig.: Sis.], 3.6.1.4

mortu 'died' *also adj., noun* [VG],
    3.6.1.4.1

mortu 'died' [Leon], 4.7.13

mortu 'died' [Nuor.], 3.7

mortu 'died; killed' [Cmpi.], 3.7.2

mortu 'died; killed' [Log.], 3.7.2

moru 'died' *by-f* [OFr.], 4.4.7

moruto 'died' [Tusc.], 3.5.7

mos 'milked' [OFr.], 4.3.1, 4+11

moss 'moved' [Enga.], 2.15.9, 4.3.1

moss 'moved' *by-f* [Luca.], 3.6.2.5

mòss 'moved' *by-f* [Mil.], 3.6.1.1

mossa 'movement' *noun* [It.],
    3.5.3.2

mossegada 'bite' *noun* [Cat.],
    4.6.2.5

mossegat 'bitten' [Cat.], 3.0.1,
    4.6.2.2

mossegat 'bitten' [Oc.], 4.6.1.4

mòsseto 'moved' [ONeap.], 3.6.2

mossiu 'bitten' [OSard.], 3.7.1

móssiu 'bitten' [Cmpi.], 3.7.2

mosso 'moved' [Gen.], 3.6.1.4

mosso 'moved' [It.], 2.15.8, 3.5.3.2,
    3.5.5, 3.6.1.1, 3.6.2.2, 5.6

mossu 'bitten' [Log.], 3.7.2

mòst 'moved' [Luc.], 3.6.2

mosto 'moved' [Tusc.], 3.5.5.1

mostret 'shown' [OFr.; Jonah],
    4.4.2.3

mosu, mosuva 'moved' [FP: Vd.],
    2.15.9, 4.5.3

mot 'milked' *by-f* [Lad.], 2.15.6

moto 'moved, changed' [OIt.], 3.5.3.2

motu 'apoplexy' *noun* [Sic.], 3.6.2.6

moudu 'ground' *by-f* [Pic.: Br.],
    4.4.13.2

moudüd 'ground' [Auv.], 4.6.1.7

moulu 'ground' [Fr.], 4.4.0, 4.4.4,
    4.4.13.2

moulu 'ground' *by-f* [Pic.: Br.],
    4.4.13.2

moulu, –ya 'ground' [FP: VA],
    4.5.4

mourt 'died' *by-f* [Pic.: Av.],
    4.4.13.2

moussigat 'bitten' *by-f* [Gév.],
    4.6.1.8

mout 'ground' [OOc.], 2.4.3

mout 'ground' *by-f* [Lang.], 4.6.1.9

mouture 'grinding of grain' *noun*
    [Fr.], 4.4.9.2

mouvé 'moved' *nonstd.* [Fr.], 4.4.1

mouyu 'ground' [Burg.], 4.4.13.3

mouyu, –ya 'moved' [FP: VA],
    4.5.4

oblidat 'forgotten' [Cat.], 2.11.1

obrésciu 'dawned' [Cmp.], 3.7.3

occhiuto 'popeyed' *adj.* [It.], 4.7.4.2

obrigut 'opened' *nonstd.* [Cat.],
   4.6.2.6

obrit 'opened' *nonstd.* [Cat.], 4.6.2.6

ocis 'killed' *by-f* [OFr.], 4.4.2.3, 4.4.4

ocit 'killed' *by-f* [OFr.], 4.4.4

{odgovorit 'answered' [Ist-R],
   3.3.2}

œ:vri 'opened' [Burg.], 4.4.13.3

oferecido 'offered' [Ptg.], 2.8

oferit 'offered' *neol.* [Rom.], 3.1.4

oferit 'offered' *by-f* [Val.], 4.6.2.8

oferît 'offered' [Fri.], 4.1

ofert 'offered' [Cat.], 2.8, 4.6.2.2,
   4.6.2.8

ofert, −a 'offered' [FP: VA], 4.5.4

ofert 'offered' *by-f* [Lang.], 4.6.1.9

ofert 'offered' *by-f* [Pied.], 3.6.1.2

ofert 'offered' *by-f* [Val.], 4.6.2.8

ofes 'offended' [Val.], 4.6.2.8

ofès 'offended' [Cat.], 4.6.2.1

off 'off-the-record' *adj.* [Fr.], 4.4.0.3

offensidu 'offended' [OSard.], 3.7.1

offert 'offered' [Enga.], 4.3.1

offert 'offered' [Fr.], 2.8, 4.4.7

offert 'offered' [Mil.], 3.6.1.1

offerto 'offered' [It.], 2.8, 3.5.3.1,
   3.5.5

offertu 'offered' [Cors.], 3.6.2.1

offes 'offended' [Enga.], 4.3.1

offri 'offered' *by-f* [OFr.], 4.4.7

offrutu 'offered' [Cal.], 3.6.2

ofrecido 'offered' [Sp.], 2.8, 4.7.2.2

ofrì 'offered' *by-f* [Pied.], 3.6.1.2

ofrit 'offered' *by-f* [Gév.], 4.6.1.8

oído 'heard' [Gal.], 4.7.14

oído 'heard' [Sp.], 0.3.1, 4.7.4.1

oído 'hearing' *noun* [Sp.], 4.7.7

oït 'heard' [Cat.], 0.3.1

oíto 'heard' [Arag.: Pnt.], 4.7.12

ojudo 'popeyed' *adj.* [Sp.], 4.7.4.1

okkisu 'killed' [OSard.], 3.7.1

òlá: 'gone' *by-f* [FP: N], 4.5.1

olgut 'smelled' [Val.], 4.6.2.8

olorat 'smelled' [Cat.], 4.6.2.8

olsât 'dared' [Fri.], 2.11.1

olût 'wanted' [Fri.], 4.1

olvidado 'forgotten' [Sp.], 2.11.1

omès 'left out' [Cat.], 4.6.2.1

omorâtor 'killer' *noun* [Rom.],
   3.1.4

omorît 'killed' [Rom.], 3.1.4

omplert 'filled' [Cat.], 4.6.2.2,
   4.6.2.10

omplit 'filled' [OCat.], 4.6.2.10

omplit 'filled' *non-std.* [Cat.],
   4.6.2.6

ondu 'oiled' [Luca-GI], 3.6.2

onto 'oiled' [Ist-I], 3.3.3

opreso 'oppressed' [OSp.], 4.7.6.1

oprimido 'oppressed' [Sp.], 4.7.6.1

ordeñado 'milked' [Sp.], 2.15.6

ordenhado 'milked' [Ptg.], 2.15.6

ordit 'warped cloth' [Cat.], 2.9

ordito 'warped cloth' [It.], 2.9

orejudo 'jug-eared' *adj.* [Sp.],
   4.7.4.2

os 'been' *allegro f* [Ist-R], 3.3.2

os 'daring' *adj.* [OFr.], 2.11.1

osado 'dared' [Sp.], 2.11.1

osato 'dared' [It.], 2.11.1

osberc 'coat of mail' *noun* [OFr.],
   4.4.4

osé 'dared' *also adj.* [Fr.], 2.11.1

osé 'dared' *by-f* [Pic.: Av.], 4.4.13.2

{oslobodit 'freed' [Ist-R], 3.3.2}

oso 'daring' *adj.* [OIt.], 2.11.1

osu 'dared' *by-f* [Pic.: Av.], 4.4.13.2

otat 'turned around' [Lad.], 4.2

{otopit 'drowned' [Ist-R], 3.3.2}

oü 'heard' [OFr.], 4.4.7

oublié 'forgotten' [Fr.], 2.11.1

oufrit 'offered' by-f [Gév.], 4.6.1.8

ouï 'heard' [OFr.], 0.3.1, 4.4.0

ouï-dire 'hearsay' noun [Fr.], 4.4.0

ouïe 'hearing' noun [Fr.], 4.4.0

ounch 'oiled' [Gév.], 4.6.1.8

ourdi 'warped cloth' [Fr.], 2.9

ousado 'dared' [Ptg.], 2.11.1

ouvert 'opened' [Fr.], 4.4.3, 4.4.7, 4.4.11

ouvert 'opened' [Pic.: Av.], 4.4.13.2

ouvert 'opened' by-f [Poit.], 4.6.1.6

ouvido 'heard' [Ptg.], 0.3.1

ouvisto 'heard' [Ptg.: Opo.], 4.7.10

ovido 'had' [OSp.], 4.7.5

ouvri 'opened' by-f [Poit.], 4.6.1.6

ovri 'opened' by-f [OFr.], 4.4.7

pacido 'fed, kept' [Sp.], 2.11.2, 4.7.7.4

padit 'undergone' [OCat.], 4.6.2.2

paessu 'fed, kept' [Poit.], 4.6.1.6

pagado 'paid' arch. [Ptg.], 4.7.8

pago 'paid' short f [OSp.], 4.7.8

pago 'paid' short f [Sp.: Car.], 4.7.9

pago 'paid' short f [Cast.], 4.7.8

pago 'paid' short f, std. [Ptg.], 4.7.8

pagu 'paid' adj. [Leon: Tud.], 4.7.13

pagut 'fed, kept' by-f [OOc.], 4.6.1.3

parato 'readied' [It.], 3.5.0

parco 'thrifty' adj. [It.], 2.1.1

pardert 'readied' [Enga.], 4.3.1

pardieu 'lost' arch. [Enga.], 4.3.1

pardü 'lost' [Lun.], 3.6.1.5

parê 'readied' [Rml.], 3.6.1.3

parecido 'seemed' [Sp.], 4.7.2.2

pareghu 'appeared' by-f [Poit.], 4.6.1.6

paregut 'seemed' by-f [Gév.], 4.6.1.8

paregut 'seemed' by-f [Oc.], 4.6.1.4

pareissut 'seemed' by-f [Gév.], 4.6.1.8

parescut 'seemed' [Gasc.], 4.6.1.5

parescut 'seemed' by-f [Oc.], 4.6.1.4

paresto 'seemed' [Ist-I], 2.15.4, 3.3.3

parezito 'suffered' [Arag.: Pnt.], 4.7.12

parfidu 'seemed' [OSard.], 3.7.1, 3.7.4

parido 'given birth' [Sp.], 4.7.7.1

parlá 'spoken' [Lun.], 3.6.1.5

parlaa 'spoken' [Mil.], 3.6.1.1

parlàd 'spoken' [Auv.], 4.6.1.7

parladu 'spoken' [Lig.: Sis.], 3.6.1.4

pars 'seemed' by-f [Mil.], 3.6.1.1

pars 'spared' [OOc.], 4.6.1

parsciùo 'seemed' [Gen.], 3.6.1.4

parso 'seemed' [It.], 2.15.9, 3.5.3.2, 3.5.4, 3.5.5, 3.6.2.2, 4.6.2.3, 5.6

parsu 'seemed' [Cors.], 3.6.2.1

parsu 'seemed' [Sard.], 3.7.1, 3.7.4

parti, −a 'left' [FP: VA], 4.5.4

partido 'left' [Gal.], 4.7.14

partidu 'left' [Ptg.: Barr.], 4.7.15

partit 'left' [Fri-R], 4.1

partiu 'left' [Args.], 4.7.10

partíu 'split' [Leon.: Can.], 4.7.13

partiyu 'left' [VG], 3.6.1.4.1

parto 'childbirth' noun [Sp.], 4.7.7.1

partu 'seemed' [Cmpi.], 3.7.2

partu 'left' [OFr.], 4.7.7

partu 'seemed' [OSard.], 3.7.1

partu 'seemed' by-f [Log.], 3.7.2

partutu 'left' [OAbru.], 3.6.2.3

partutu 'left' [Sic.], 3.6.2.6

paru 'appeared' [FP: VA], 4.5.4

paru 'appeared' [Fr.], 4.4.8

paru 'appeared' by-f [Poit.], 4.6.1.6

paru, parussa 'appeared' [FP: Vd.], 4.5.3

pierdù 'lost' *by-f* [Lad.], 4.2

pierdut 'lost' [Rom.], 3.1.3, 3.3.1

pièrt 'lost' ! *by-f* [Lad.], 4.2

pi̯evét 'rained' [Lad.: Liv.], 4.2

piggiòu 'taken' *by-f* [Gen.], 3.6.1.4

pigiato 'trodden' [It.], 2.11.2

pimtu 'pushed' [Arom.], 3.3.1

pindju 'high, steep' *adj.* [Leon.:
    VP], 4.7.13

pint 'spotted' *adj.* [Cat.], 2.11.2

pint 'painted' *by-f* [Lang.], 4.6.1.9

pinta 'spot' *noun* [Cat./Sp.], 2.11.2

pintado 'painted' [Sp.], 2.11.2

pintat 'painted' [Cat.], 2.11.2

pintito 'repented' [OIt.], 3.5.8

pinto 'painted' [It.], *see* dipinto

pinto 'repented' *short f* [OIt.], 3+46

pinto 'spotted' *adj.* [Sp.], 2.11.2, 6.7

pintu 'painted white and black (of
    bulls)' *adj.* [Leon.: VP], 4.7.13

pintrat 'painted' [Gév.], 4.6.1.8

piovesto 'rained' [Ven.], 3.6.1

pióvətə 'rained' *by-f, neol.* [Abru.],
    3.6.2.3

pióvidu 'rained' [Rml.], 3.6.1.3

piovù 'rained' *by-f* [Lad.], 2.8

piovuto 'rained' [It.], 2.8, 3.1.4

pisado 'trodden' [Sp.], 2.11.2

pisat 'trodden' [Cat.], 2.11.2

pisat 'trodden' [Rom.], 2.11.2

pisé 'trodden' [Fr.], 2.11.2

pitrumtu 'pierced' [Arom.], 3.3.1

pizat 'trodden' [Oc.], 2.11.2

pjers 'lost' [Vegl.: Z], 3.4

placido 'pleased' [Sp.], 4.7.2.2

plăcut 'pleased' [Rom.], 2.14.5,
    3.1.3

plagut 'pleased' [Cat.], 2.14.5,
    4.6.2.3

plagut 'pleased' *by-f* [Gév.], 4.6.1.8

plagut 'pleased' *by-f* [Oc.], 4.6.1.4

plaindu 'complained' [Pic.: Br.],
    4.4.13.2

plaint 'complained' [Fr.], 4.4.13.2

plaint 'mourned' *by-f* [OOc.], 4.6.1.2

plămtu 'thrust, planted' [Meg.: Ţ],
    3.3.1.1

planc 'mourned' *by-f* [OOc.], 4.6.1.2

planch 'mourned' *by-f* [Lang.],
    4.6.1.9

plangut 'pitied' [Cat.], 4.6.2.7

plangut 'mourned' *by-f* [Oc.], 4.6.1.4

planh 'mourned' *by-f* [Oc.], 4.6.1.4

planh 'mourned' *by-f* [OOc.], 4.6.1.2,
    4.6.1.4

planhut 'mourned' *by-f* [Oc.],
    4.6.1.4

plañido 'wailed'• [Sp.], 4.7.7.1

planigut 'mourned' *by-f* [Gév.],
    4.6.1.8

plăns 'wept' [Ist-R], 3.3.2

plâns 'wept' *also noun* [Rom.],
    3.1.5.1, 3.1.5.2, 3.1.6

plant 'complained' ? [Vegl.], 3.4

plant 'mourned' *by-f* [Lang.], 4.6.1.9

planygut 'pitied' [Val.], 4.6.2.8

planyit 'pitied' [Ross.], 4.6.2.7

plasegut 'pleased' *by-f* [Gév.],
    4.6.1.8

plašù 'pleased' [Rml.], 3.6.1.3

plasut 'pleased' *by-f* [Gév.], 4.6.1.8

plaunt 'mourned' [Enga.], 4.3.1

plazegut 'pleased' *by-f* [Oc.], 4.6.1.4

plenato 'filled' [Arag.: Pnt.], 4.7.12

plègnu 'complained' [FP: VA], 4.5.4

pl'erdut 'lost' *by-f* [Ist-R], 3.3.2

pl'erzut 'lost' [SIst-R], 3.3.2

plésu 'pleased' [FP: VA], 4.5.4

pleu 'rained' [Pic.: Av.], 4.4.13.2

pleudüd 'rained' *by-f* [Auv.],
    4.6.1.7

pleugüd 'rained' *by-f* [Auv.], 4.6.1.7

pleugut 'rained' *by-f* [Gév.], 4.6.1.8

pleuré 'wept' [Fr.], 4.4.8

plîmtu 'wept' [Arom.], 3.3.1

pllént 'complained' [Poit.], 4.6.1.6

pllésu 'pleased' [Poit.], 4.6.1.6

plobito 'rained' *by-f* [Arag. Pnt.], 4.7.12

plogido 'pleased' [Arag.], 4.7.8

plogut 'rained' [Cat.], 2.8, 3.1.4, 4.6.2.3

plogut 'rained' [Lang.], 4.6.1.9

ploi̯ü 'rained' [Lad.: Marb.], 4.2

ploiüd 'rained'! *by-f* [Auv.], 4.6.1.7

plonch 'mourned' *by-f* [Gév.], 4.6.1.8

plǫns, plănsǎ 'wept, mourned' [Meg.: U], 3.3.1.1

ploré 'wept' [OFr.], 4.4.8

plouat 'rained' [Rom.], 2.8, 3.1.4, 6.9

plòugut 'rained' *by-f* [Gév.], 4.6.1.8

plousu 'rained' [FP: VA], 4.5.4

plovâšt 'rained' [Lad.: Liv.], 4.2

plu 'pleased' [Pic.: Av.], 4.4.13.2

plu₁ 'pleased' [Fr.], 2.8, 4.4.1, 4.4.5

plu₂ 'rained' [Fr.], 2.14.5, 3.1.4, 4.4.5

pluët 'rained' [Lad.: Gar.], 4.2

podesto 'been able' *by-f* [Ist-I], 3.3.3, 3.6.1

podesto 'been able' [Ven.], 3.6.1

podido 'been able' [Gal.], 4.7.14

podido 'been able' [Sp.], 4.7.0

podito 'been able' [Arag.: Pnt.], 4.7.12

podrido 'rotted' [Sp.], 4.7.9

podrit 'rotted' [Cat.], 4.6.2.2

podù 'been able' *by-f* [Lad.], 4.2

podut 'been able' [Gasc.], 4.6.1.5

podût 'been able' [Fri.], 4.1

poesto 'been able' [OVen.], 3.6.1

pœ:vu 'been able' [Burg.], 4.4.13.3

poghu 'been able' *by-f* [Poit.], 4.6.1.6

pognet 'laid eggs' [Fri.], 4.1

pogut 'been able' [Cat.], 2.7, 4.6.2.3, 4.6.2.4, 4.6.2.8

pogut 'been able' [Lang.], 4.6.1.9

pôhtu 'put' [Ptg.: Barr.], 4.7.15

{poidit 'eaten' [Ist-R], 3.3.2}

poilu 'hairy(-bodied)' *adj.* [Fr.], 4.7.4.2

pois 'hung, weighed' [OFr.], 4.4.2.2

pojat 'gone up' [Oc.], 4.6.1

ponch 'stung' *by-f* [Lang.], 4.6.1.9

pond 'laid eggs' *by-f* [Nor.: Pch.], 4.4.13.1

pondu 'laid eggs' [Burg.], 4.4.13.3

pondu 'laid eggs' [Fr.], 4.4.0, 4.4.4, 4.4.9.2, 5.6

pongut₁ 'laid eggs' [Lang.], 4.6.1.9

pongut₂ 'stung' *by-f* [Lang.], 4.6.1.9

ponido 'put' [Sp.: Salm.], 4.7.9

ponido 'put' *dial.* [Sp.], 5.4.2

ponnu 'laid eggs' [OBurg.], 4.4.13.3

pons 'set, laid' *by-f* [OFr.], 4.4.2.2, 4.4.4

pont 'set, laid' *by-f* [OFr.], 4.4.2.2

pont 'stung' *by-f* [Lang.], 4.6.1.9

ponte 'egg-laying' *noun* [Fr.], 4.4.9.2

ponto 'stung' *by-f* [Ist-I], 3.3.3

ponu 'laid eggs' *by-f* [Nor.: Pch.], 4.4.13.1

ponu 'set, laid' *by-f* [OFr.], 4.4.4

ponzesto 'stung' *by-f* [Ist-I], 3.3.3

porto 'carried' *short f* [Tusc.], 3.5.9

porto 'handed over' [It.], 3.5.2.1, 3.5.4, 3.5.5, 4.2

portu 'handed over' [Cors.], 3.6.2.1

portuot 'took' [Vegl.: Z], 3.4

pos 'set, laid' *by-f* [OFr.], 4.4.2.3, 4.4.4

predecido 'foretold' *std.* [Sp.], 4.7.8

predicho 'foretold' *arch.* [Sp.], 4.7.8

prediletto 'preferred'• *also adj.* [It.], 3.5.4

predut 'lost' *by-f* [Ist-R], 3.3.2

prèi, −sa 'taken' [FP: VA], 4.5.4

preidut 'lost' *by-f* [Ist-R], 3.3.2

prendido 'taken, caught' *by-f* [Ptg.], 4+67

prendido 'taken, caught' [Sp.], 4.6.2.5, 4.7.6.1, 4.7.13

prendu 'taken' *by-f* [OFr.], 4.4.7

prendüd 'taken' *by-f* [Auv.], 4.6.1.7

prenghu 'taken' [Poit.], 4.6.1.6

prengut 'taken' *nonstd.* [Cat.], 4.6.2.6

prengut 'taken' *by-f* [Gasc.], 4.6.1.5

prengut 'taken' *by-f, rare* [Gév.], 4.6.1.8

prenu 'filled' [Cmpi.], 3.7.2

prenu 'filled' [Log.], 3.7.2

pres 'taken, caught' [Cat.], 4.6.2.1, 4.6.2.3, 4.6.2.4

pres 'taken' [Lang.], 4.6.1.9

pres 'taken, caught' [Val.], 4.6.2.8

pres 'understood' *by-f* [Arom.], 3.3.1

pres 'taken' *by-f* [Gasc.], 4.6.1.5

pres 'taken' *by-f* [OOc.], 4.6.1.1, 4.6.1.2

prés 'taken' *by-f, usu.* [Gév.], 4.6.1.8

pres 'prisoner' *noun* [Cat.], 4.6.2.5

presa 'a takintg' *noun* [Cat.], 4.6.2.5

presa 'hold, grip' *noun* [It.], 3.5.3.2

prescrito 'specified' [Sp.], 4+64

preso 'taken' [It.], 3.5.3.2, 4.4.11

preso 'taken' [OSp.], 2.12, 4.7.1, 4.7.5, 4.7.6.1

preso 'taken, caught' *by-f* [Ptg.], 4+67

preso 'prisoner' *noun* [Sp.], 4.6.2.5, 4.7.6, 4.7.7.3, 4.7.13, 4+32

preśo 'taken' *by-f, urban* [Gen.], 3.6.1.4

presso 'squeezed' [It.], 3.5.5

presso 'squeezed' [Gen.], 3.6.1.4

préstito 'loan' *noun* [It.], 3.5.2.2

presu 'taken, caught' [Leon.: Can.], 4.7.13

présumé 'presumed' [Fr.], 4.7.6.4

presumido 'presumed' [Sp.], 4.7.6.4

presunto 'presumed' [It.], 4.7.6.4

presunto 'presumptive' *adj.* [Sp.], 4+54

pretais 'claimed' [Enga.], 4.3.1

pretés 'pretended' [ORoss.], 4.6.2.7

pretès 'sought, claimed' [Cat.], 4.6.2.1

pretiet 'preached' [OFr.; Jonah], 4.4.2.3

pretu 'tight' *adj.* [Leon.: Tud.], 4.7.13

pretu 'tight' *adj.* [Leon.: VP], 4.7.13

prévint 'warned' [Nor.: Pch.], 4.4.13.1

prez 'taken' *by-f* [Auv.], 4.6.1.7

pri, pri:z 'taken' [Burg.], 4.4.13.3

prì, prìz 'taken' [FP: N], 4.5.1

priceput 'figured out' [Rom.], 3.1.6

prié 'prayed' [Fr.], 4.4.8

primtu 'understood' *by-f* [Arom.], 3.3.1

prins 'caught, taken' [Ist-R], 3.3.2

prins 'caught, taken' [Meg.], 3.3.1.1

prins 'caught, taken' [Rom.], 3.1.0, 3.1.5.1, 3.1.6

prins 'taken' *by-f* [OFr.], 4.4.2.3

prins 'taken' [Pic.: Br.], 4.4.13.2

prinsoare 'bet' *noun* [Rom.], 3.1.5.2

pris 'taken' [Fr.], 2.12, 4.4.2.3, 4.4.3, 4.4.7, 4.4.11, 4.4.12, 4.4.13.2, 4.6.1.1, 5.5

pris 'taken' *by-f* [OOc.], 4.6.1.1

prise 'taking' *noun* [Fr.], 3.3.1, 4.4.9.3

prit 'taken' *by-f* [OFr.], 4.4.3

priu 'taken' [Surs.], 4.3.2

próghidu 'rained' [Log.], 3.7.3

proibit 'banned' [Fri-R], 4.1

proibito 'banned' [It.], 3.7.3

promes 'promised' [OOc.], 4.7.4.1

promesa 'promise' *noun* [Sp.], 4.7.7.3

prometido 'promised' [Sp.], 4.7.7.3

prometudo 'promised' [OSp.], 4.7.4.1

promissu 'promised' [Log.], 3.7.2

promíttiu 'promised' [Cmpi.], 3.7.2

propendido 'tended' [Sp.], 4.7.8, 4+54

propiu 'rained' [Cmp.], 3.7.3

proponieu 'put forward' *by-f, rare* [Enga.], 4.3.1

propenso 'keen on' *adj.* [Sp.], 4.7.8

propost 'put forward' *by-f, usu.* [Enga.], 4.3.1

prosciutto 'ham' *noun* [It.], 2.11.2

proscrito 'outlawed' [Sp.], 4+64

protet 'protected' [Enga.], 4.3.1

protetto 'protected' [Gen.], 3.6.1.4

proveído 'foreseen' *by-f* [Sp.], 4.7.8

provist 'foreseen' [Enga.], 4.3.1

provisto 'foreseen' *by-f* [Sp.], 4.7.8

próghidu 'rained' [Log.], 3.7.2

promis 'promised' *neol.* [Rom.], 3.1.5.3

promisiune 'promise' *noun, neol.* [Rom.], 3.1.5.3

própiu 'rained' [Cmpi.], 3.7.2

pruibbêtê 'banned' [Rml.], 3.6.1.3

pruis 'budded' [Surs.], 4.3.2

pruit 'itched' [Cat.], 4.6.2.2

prumisu 'promised' [VG], 3.6.1.4.1

prusegut 'itched' ! [Gév.], 4.6.1.8

prusit 'sprouted' ! [Lang.], 4.6.1.9

prutettu 'protected' [Cors.], 3.6.2.1

pu 'been able' [Fr.], 2.7, 4.4.3, 4.4.5

pu 'been able' [Pic.: Av.], 4.4.13.2

pudidu 'been able' [Ptg.: Barr.], 4.7.15

pudisto 'been able' [Ist-I: D], 3.6.1

pudit 'stunk' [Cat.], 2.8

pudiu 'been able' [Surs.], 4.3.2

pudü 'been able' [Lun.], 3.6.1.5

pué 'stunk' [Fr.], 2.8, 4.4.1

puesta 'setting (of sun)' *noun* [Sp.], 4.7.7

puesto 'put' *std.* [Sp.], 3.5.5.1, 4.7.0, 4.7.1, 4.7.6.2, 5.4.2

pugut 'been able' [Val.], 4.6.2.8

puï 'stunk' [OFr.], 2.8, 4.4.1

puliu 'cleaned' [Cmpi], 3.7.0

punch 'stung' *by-f* [Gév.], 4.6.1.8

puníu 'put' [Leon.: Tud.], 4.7.13

punhegat 'stung' [Oc.], 4.6.1.4

puni, punite 'punished' [FP: Vd.], 4.5.3

punto 'stung' [It.], 3.1.6

punto 'stung' *by-f* [Gen.], 3.6.1.4

puntu 'stung' *by-f, rare* [VG], 3.6.1.4.1

puntu 'stung' [OSard.], 3.7.1

punxat 'stung' [Cat.], 4.6.2

punzado 'stung' [Sp.], 4.6.2

punzùo 'stung' *by-f* [Gen.], 3.6.1.4

punzüu 'stung' *by-f, usu.* [VG], 3.6.1.4.1

purces 'begun' *rus.* [Rom.], 3.1.4

purtatu 'carried' [Sic.], 3.6.2.6

pus 'put' [Ist-R], 3.3.2

pus 'put' [Megl.], 3.3.1.1

pus 'put' [Rom.], 2.7, 3.1.5.1, 3.3.1, 4.4.2.3, 5.6

pussirutu 'owned' [Sic.], 3.6.2.6

quisiendo 'wanting' *pres.p., rare*
[Sp.: Car.], 4.7.9
quisíu 'wanted' [Leon.: VP], 4.7.13
quiso 'sought, wanted' *by-f* [OSp.],
4.7.1, 4.7.6.1
quisto 'sought, wanted' *by-f* [OSp.],
3.1.3, 3.5.5.1, 4.7.1, 4.7.6.1, 4.7.7.4
quito 'removed' *short f* [OSp.], 4.7.8

rabiat 'been angry' [Fri-R], 4.1
racòlt 'gathered' [Mil.], 3.6.1.1
racontat 'recounted' [Fri-R], 4.1
radé 'leveled off' [Fr.], 2.11.2
raent 'redeemed' *by-f* [OFr.], 4.4.2.3,
4.4.4
ragut 'shaved' [Cat.], 4.6.2.2, 4.6.2.8
ragut 'shaved' *by-f* [Val.], 4.6.2.8
raído 'shaved' [Sp.], 4.7.2
raient 'redeemed' *by-f* [OFr.],
4.4.2.3, 4.4.4
raimit 'lent' [Ist-R], 3.3.2
rămânat 'stayed' [Mold.], 3.2.2
rămas 'stayed' [Ist-R], 3.3.2
rămas 'stayed' [Meg.], 3.3.1.1
rămas 'stayed' [Mold.: Ban.], 3.2
rămas 'stayed' [Rom.], 3.1.5.1,
3.5.5.1
ramenteü 'remembered' [OFr.],
4.4.1
rămînit 'stayed' *by-f* [Oltn.], 3.2.1
rămîns 'stayed' *by-f* [Oltn.], 3.2.1
răpit 'grabbed' [Rom.], 3.1.2
rapito 'grabbed' [It.], 3.5.0
raputu 'kidnaped' [OAbru.], 3.6.2.3
raputu 'opened, split' [Sic.], 3.6.2.6
ras 'shaved' *by-f* [Val.], 4.6.2.8
ras 'short-haired' *adj.* [Cat.], 4.6.2.5,
4.6.2.8, 6.4
ras 'short-haired' *adj.* [Fr.], 4.4.11,
6.4
ras 'shaven' *adj.* [Gév.], 4.6.1.8

ras 'shaved' [OOc.], 4.6.1
ras 'shaved' *also noun* [Rom.],
3.1.5.1, 3.1.5.2, 5.6
ras 'shaved' *by-f* [Mil.], 3.6.1.1
râs 'laughed' *also noun* [Rom.],
3.1.5.1, 3.1.5.2, 3.3.1.1, 5.6
rasaa 'shaved' *by-f* [Mil.], 3.6.1.1
rasat 'shaved' [Gév.], 4.6.1.8
raśat 'shaved' [Lad.], 4.2
rasato 'shaved' [It.], 3.5.10
rascl'is 'opened' [Ist-R], 3.3.2
rasé 'shaved' [Fr.], 2.11.2, 4.2
rasibit 'received' [Alg.], 4.6.2.10
raso 'shaved' *also adj.* [It.], 3.5.3.2,
3.5.10
raso 'clear, open' *adj.* [Sp.], 4.7.7.3
răspuns 'answered' *also noun*
[Rom.], 3.1.5.1, 3.1.5.2, 3.5.5.1
raspus 'answered' [Ist-I], 3.3.3
rassebüd 'received' *by-f* [Auv.],
4.6.1.7
ravisé 'looked at' [Pic.: Av.],
4.4.13.2
reavido 'gotten back' [Ptg.], 4.7.9
reblert 'crammed' [Cat.], 4.6.2.2,
4.6.2.8
reblert 'crammed' *by-f* [Val.], 4.6.2.8
reblit 'crammed' *by-f* [Val.], 4.6.2.8
rebuda 'reception' *noun* [Cat.],
4.6.2.5
rebut 'received' [Cat.], 4.6.2.3,
4.6.2.10
rebut 'received' [Ross.], 4.6.2.7
recadù 'fallen' [Lad.], 2.8
reçauput 'received' *by-f* [Gév.],
4.6.1.8
receado 'feared' [Ptg.], 4.7.0
recebut 'received' *by-f* [Gév.],
4.6.1.8
receduto 'receded' [It.], 2.15.10
recet 'refuge' *noun* [OFr.], 3+50

rente 'income' *noun* [Fr.], 4.7.7.2

renyit 'quarreled' [Cat.], 2.9

repentido 'repented' [Sp.], 4.7.6.1

repentu 'repented' [OFr.], 4.4.7

repêso 'repented' [Ptg.], 4.7.6.1

repigut 'received' *nonstd.* [Cat.], 4.6.2.6

repiso 'repented' *by-f* [OSp.], 4.7.6.1

répond 'answered' *by-f* [Nor.: Pch.], 4.4.13.1

répondu 'answered' [Fr.], 4.4.2.2, 4.4.4, 4.4.9.3

répondu 'answered' [Pic.: Av.], 4.4.13.2

réponse 'answer' *noun* [Fr.], 4.4.9.3

réponu 'answered' *by-f* [Nor.: Pch.], 4.4.13.1

repost 'hideaway' *noun* [OFr.], 4.4.9.2

répounu 'answered' [Nor.: VS], 4.4.13.1

repounut 'answered' *by-f* [Poit.], 4.6.1.6

répun 'answered' *by-f* [Poit.], 4.6.1.6

request 'sought' [ORoss.], 4.6.2.7

rescost 'hidden' *by-f* [Lang.], 4.6.1.9

resebut 'received' [ORoss.], 4.6.2.7

resebut 'received' [OCat.], 4.6.2.10

resegut 'laughed' *by-f* [Gév.], 4.6.1.8

reso 'given back' [It.], 3.5.2.2, 3.5.3.2, 3.5.7, 3.6.1.1

resolt 'solved' [Lad.], 4.2

résolu 'solved' [Fr.], 4.4.8

resolvido '(re)solved' [Sp.: Salm.], 4.7.9

resolvu, –ya 'solved' [FP: VA], 4.5.4

respendù 'answered' [Lad.], 4.2

resplendu 'gleamed' [OFr.], 4.4.7

respondesto 'answered' [Ist-I], 3.3.3

respondido 'answered' [Sp.], 4.7.2.2, 4.7.7.3

respondut 'answered' *by-f* [OOc.], 4.6.1.1

rešponét 'answered' [Lad.: Fass.], 4.2

respons 'answered' *by-f* [OFr.], 4.4.2.2, 4.4.4

responsado 'said prayers for the dead' [Sp.], 4.7.7.3

responso 'decision, report' *noun* [It.], 3.5.3.2

responso 'prayer for the dead' *noun* [Sp.], 4.7.7.3

rešponü 'answered' [Lad.: Bad.], 4.2

rešponü 'answered' [Lad.: Marb.], 4.2

respos 'answered' *by-f* [OOc.], 4.6.1.2, 4.6.1.3

respost 'answered' [Cat.], 4.6.2.1, 4.6.2.3, 4.6.2.4

respost 'answered' [Gév.], 4.6.1.8

respost 'answered' *by-f* [OFr.], 4.4.2.2

respost 'answered' *by-f* [OOc.], 4.6.1.2, 4.6.1.3

respost 'answered' [Ross.], 4.6.2.7

resposta 'answer' *noun* [Cat.], 4.6.2.5

respuindût 'answered' [Fri.], 4.1

respus 'answered' [Enga.], 4.3.1

respwast 'answered' [Vegl.: Z], 3.4

resso 'given back' [OIt.], 3.5.8

restat 'stayed' [Fri-R], 4.1

restrângere 'limitation' *neol.* , *noun* [Rom.], 3.1.5.3

restrâns 'restrained' *neol.* [Rom.], 3.1.5.3

restricţione 'restraint' *neol.*, *noun* [Rom.], 3.1.5.3

resuelto '(re)solved' [Sp.], 4.7.6.4, 4+54

retorçut 'entwined' [Val.], 4.6.2.8

retort 'entwined' [Cat.], 4.6.2.8

retroceduto 'demoted' *by-f* [It.], 2.15.10

retrocesso 'demoted' *by-f* [It.], 2.15.10

retschiert 'received' [Surs.], 4.3.2

retto 'held up, withstood' [It.], 3.5.4, 3.5.5

retut 'given back' ! [ORoss.], 4.6.2.7

réveillé 'woken' [Pic.: Av.], 4.4.13.2

revolt 'returned' [Enga.], 4.3.1

revolvido 'returned' [Sp.: Salm.], 4.7.9

revais 'seen again' *by-f* [Enga.], 4.3.1

revis 'seen again' *by-f* [Enga.], 4.3.1

revist 'seen again' *by-f* [Enga.], 4.3.1

rexistîo 'resisted' *new* [Gen.], 3.6.1.4

rexistùo 'resisted' *old* [Gen.], 3.6.1.4

reyu 'thrown up' [VG], 3.6.1.4.1

rez 'even with' *prep.* [Fr.], 4.4.9.3

rez-de-chaussée 'ground floor' *noun* [Fr.], 4.4.9.3

rezado 'prayed' [Ptg.], 4.7.0

rezemt 'redeemed' *by-f* [OOc.], 4.6.1.1

rezemut 'redeemed' *by-f* [OOc.], 4.6.1.1

rezût 'ruled' [Fri.], 4.1

rəvévətə 'lived' [Abru.], 3.6.2.3

ri 'laughed' [Fr.], 4.4.6

ri 'laughed' [Lad.], 4.2

ri 'laughed' [Pic: Br.], 4.4.13.2

ribwiltu 'mischievous' *adj.* [Leon.: VP], 4.7.13

ricetta 'recipe' *noun* [It.], 3.5.3.1

ricetto 'received' [OIt.], 3.5.3.1

ricetto 'refuge' *noun, poet.* [It.], 3.5.3.1, 3+50

ricevuto 'received' [It.], 3.5.3.1

ricevût 'received' [Fri.], 4.1

ricolta 'harvest' *noun* [It.], 4.4.9.2

rido 'laughed' [Ptg.], 4.7.10

ridu 'laughed' [Ptg.: Barr.], 4.7.15

ridüd laughed' *by-f* [Auv.], 4.6.1.7

ridût 'laughed' [Fri.], 4.1

riduu 'laughed' [Mil.], 3.6.1.1

riflesso 'reflected (light)'• [It.], 3.5.3.2, 6.4

riflettuto 'reflected, thought over'• [It.], 3.5.3.2, 6.4

rifulso 'flashed'• *rare* [It.], 3.5.4, 3.5.10

rignato 'growled' [It.], 2.9

rigut 'laughed' [Cat.], 4.6.2.4, 4.6.2.8

rigut 'laughed' [Lang.], 4.6.1.9

rigut 'laughed' *by-f* [Val.], 4.6.2.8

riío 'laughed' [Leon.: Tud.], 4.7.13

rimaso 'stayed' [OIt.], 3.5.5.1

rimasto 'stayed' [It.], 3.5.5.1, 5.4.3

rimasuglio 'leftover' *noun* [It.], 3.5.5.1

rindu 'given back' [Pic: Br.], 4.4.13.2

ringhiato 'growled' [It.], 2.9

rinvenuto 'found' [It.], 2.11.2

rinvouyé 'sent back' [Pic.: Av.], 4.4.13.2

riprais 'taken back' *by-f, usu.* [Enga.], 4.3.1

riprendieu 'taken back' *by-f, rare* [Enga.], 4.3.1

ris 'laughed' [OFr.], 4.4.3, 4.4.6

ris 'laughed' [OOc.], 4.6.1.2

ris 'laughed' [Surs.], 4.3.2

ris 'laughed' *by-f* [Gév.], 4.6.1.8

risa 'laughter' *noun* [Sp.] 4.7.7.3

risarcito 'mended' [It.], 2.11.2

risə 'laughed' [Abru.], 3.6.2.3

riso 'laughed' [It.], 3.5.3.2, 3.5.5, 3.6.1.1

scos 'taken out' [Meg.], 3.3.1.1

scos 'taken out' [Rom.], 3.1.5.1

scosso 'shaken' [It.], 3.5.3.2

scotut 'taken out' *by-f* [Ist-R], 3.3.2

scret 'written' [Surs.], 4.3.2

scriat 'written' *by-f* [Arom.], 3.3.1

scriată 'fate, destiny' *noun* [Arom.], 3.3.1

scriat 'written' [Mold.: Ban.], 3.2, 5.6

scriptu 'written' [ORom.], 3.1.5, 3.1.5.1, 3.1.5.2

scris 'written' *by-f* [Arom.], 3.3.1

scris 'written' *also noun* [Rom.], 3.1.5.2, 5.6, 6.8

scrisoare 'handwriting' *noun* [Rom.], 3.1.5.2

scrit 'written' [Enga.], 4.3.1

scrit 'written' [Lad.], 4.2

scritt 'written' *by-f* [Mil.], 3.6.1.1

scritto 'written' [It.], 3.1.5, 3.5.3.1, 3.6.2.4

scrittu 'written' [Cors.], 3.6.2.1

scritu 'written' [Cmpi.], 3.7.2

scrivutu 'written' [Cal.], 3.6.2

scrivuu 'written' *by-f* [Mil.], 3.6.1.1

scugnût 'been constrained' [Fri.], 4.1

scuindut 'hidden' [Fri.], 4.1

şculat 'gotten up, arisen' [Ist-R], 3.3.2

scuns 'hidden' [Ist-R], 3.3.2

scuns 'hidden' [Meg.], 3.3.1.1

scuors 'sold off' [Enga.], 4.3.1

scurruto 'flowed' *by-f* [Neap.], 3.6.2.2

scurt 'short' *adj.* [Rom.], 3+66

scurzo 'flowed' *by-f* [Neap.], 3.6.2.2

scus 'threshed' [Enga.], 4.3.1

scusuto 'unstitched' [Neap.], 3.6.2.2

scutat 'listened' *by-f* [Ist-R], 3.3.2

şcutat 'listened' *by-f* [Ist-R], 3.3.2

scuviert 'discovered' [Surs.], 4.3.2

scvért 'discovered' [Rml.], 3.6.1.3

secado 'dried' [Sp.], 4.7.13

sedüd 'followed' *by-f* [Auv.], 4.6.1.7

şedut 'sat' *by-f* [Oltn.], 3.2.1

seduto 'sat' [It.], 2.14.5, 3.5.3.2, 3.5.6

segado 'reaped, mown' [Sp.], 2.7.2

segat 'reaped, mown' [Cat.], 4.6.2.2

segato 'cut, sawn' [It.], 2.13.3

segnato 'marked, branded' [It.], 3.5.9

seguido 'followed' [Sp.], 2.14.4

seguit 'followed' [Cat.], 4.6.2.2

seguit 'followed' *by-f* [Gév.], 4.6.1.8

seguit 'followed' [OOc.], 4.6.1, 4.6.1.2

seguito 'followed' [It.], 2.14.4

següd 'followed' *by-f* [Auv.], 4.6.1.7

segut 'sat' [Cat.], 4.6.2.3

segut 'followed' [Poit.], 4.6.1.6

segut 'sat' [Val.], 4.6.2.8

segut 'followed' *by-f* [Gév.], 4.6.1.8

segut 'sat' *by-f* [Lang.], 4.6.1.9

segut, segue 'followed' [Sto.], 4.6.1.6

següu followed' [VG], 3.6.1.4.1

seintu 'felt' [Pic.: Br.], 4.4.13.2

seit 'sat' *by-f* [Lang.], 4.6.1.9

sekúot 'dried' [Vegl.], 3.4

self 'self-service' *noun* [Fr.], 4.4.0.3

self, sölt 'lost' [Apul.: Alt.], 3.6.2.4

semoncé 'rebuked' [Fr.], 2.15.9, 4.4.10

semons 'urged, assigned' [OFr.], 2.15.9, 4.4.10

sencido 'unharmed' *adj.* [OSp.], 2.15.2

sengato 'signed' [SM], 3.6.2.2.1

šennutə 'gone down' *by-f* [Apul.], 3.6.2

sentáit 'felt' [Vegl.], 3.4

senti 'smelled, felt' [Fr.], 2.13.3,
   4.4.2.2, 4.4.4, 4.4.7

senti 'felt' [Lad.: Gard.], 4.2

sentido 'felt, heard' [Sp.], 2.13.3,
   4.7.6.1, 4.7.7.3

sentii 'felt' *by-f* [Mil.], 3.6.1.1

sentîo 'felt, heard' [Gen.], 3.6.1.4

sentit 'felt, heard' [Cat.], 2.13.3

sentit 'felt' [Gasc.], 4.6.1.5

sentit 'felt' [Gév.], 4.6.1.8

sentito 'felt, heard' [It.], 2.13.3, 3.6.2

sentiu 'felt' [Surs.], 4.3.2

sento 'marked, branded' *short f*
   [Tusc.], 3.5.9

sentu 'felt' [Lad.: Fass.], 4.2

sentu 'felt' [Lad.: Liv.], 4.2

sentu 'felt' *by-f* [OFr.], 4.4.4

sentu, −e 'felt' [Nor.: Pch.], 4.4.13.1

sentu, −ya 'heard' [FP: VA], 4.5.4

sentuto 'felt' [OAbru.], 3.6.2.3

sentuto 'felt, heard' [OIt.], 3.5.7

sentuto 'felt, heard' [Tusc.], 3.5.7

sentuu 'felt' *by-f* [Mil.], 3.6.1.1

senza 'without' *prep.* [It.], 4.7.6.2

séparé 'parted, dispersed' [Fr.], 4.4.0

sepelido 'buried' *arch.* [Sp.], 4.7.8

sepelita 'buried' *f.sg.* [Proto-Fr.],
   4.4.0.1

sepolto 'buried' *by-f* [It.], 2.6, 3.5.10

seppellito 'buried' *by-f* [It.], 2.6,
   3.5.10

sepultado 'buried' [Sp.], 4.7.8

sepulto 'buried' *adj.* [Sp.], 4.7.8

serbudu 'served' [Lig.: Sis.], 3.6.1.4

*serdu 'sifted' [OFr.], 3+47

serti 'inset' [Fr.], 2.11.2

servi 'served' [Fr.], 4.4.12

servit 'served' [Val.], 4.6.2.8

servito 'served' *by-f* [Abru.], 3.6.2.3

servut 'served' [Apul.: Alt.], 3.6.2.4

servuto 'served' *by-f* [Abru.],
   3.6.2.3

servuto 'needed' [OIt.], 3.5.7

seso 'felt' [OSp.], 4.7.6.1

seso 'brain' *noun* [Sp.], 4.7.7.3

set 'been' [ECat.], 4.6.2.2

seu 'known' [Pic.: Ggn.], 4.4.13.2

seü 'followed' *by-f* [OFr.], 4.4.2.2,
   4.4.5

seubüd 'known' *by-f* [Auv.], 4.6.1.7

seudo 'been' [OSp.], 4.7.4.1

seveli 'buried' [OFr.], 4.4.2.3

sevi 'followed' *by-f* [OFr.], 4.4.5

sevré 'weaned' [Fr.], 4.4.0

sè:vu 'known' [Burg.], 4.4.13.3

sèvù 'known' [FP: N], 4.5.1

şezut 'sat' [Ist-R], 3.3.2

şezut 'sat' *by-f* [Oltn.], 3.2.1

şezut 'sat' [Rom.], 2.14.5, 3.1.6, 3.2

şezut 'posterior' *noun* [Rom.],
   3.1.5.2

šənnútə 'gone down' *by-f* [Apul.],
   3.6.2

sfărşot 'ended' [Meg.], 3.3.1.1

sfint 'holy' *adj.* [Rom.], 2+85

sfirşit 'ended' [Rom.], 3.3.1.1

sfois 'searched' [Surs.], 4.3.2

sgiavât 'enjoyed' [Fri.], 4.2

shit 'hashish' *noun* [Fr.], 4.4.0.3

sido 'been' [Gal.], 4.7.14

sido 'been' [Sp.], 2.7, 4.7.1, 6.6

sigut 'been' *nonstd.* [Cat.], 4.6.2.2

sigut 'been' [Tam.], 4.6.2.9

simţit 'felt' [Rom.], 2.13.3

sintüd 'felt' [Auv.], 4.6.1.7

sintût 'heard' [Fri.], 4.1

sintutu 'felt, heard' [Sal.], 3.6.2

sintutu 'felt, heard' [Sic.], 3.6.2.6

sirbit 'worked' [Meg.], 3.3.1.1

sis 'sat' [OFr.], 4.4.2.3, 4.4.3

sisado 'pilfered' [Sp.], 2.11.2

tido 'had' [Ptg.], 2.6, 4.7.4.1

tidu 'had' [Ptg.: Barr.], 4.7.15

tienda 'shop, stall' *noun* [Sp.], 4.7.7.2

tiengut 'held' *by-f* [Gasc.], 4.6.1.5

tienut 'held' *by-f* [Gasc.], 4.6.1.5

tiërt 'wiped, scoured' [Lad.], 4.2

tieso 'stiff' *adj.* [Sp.], 2.15.8, 3.3.1, 3.7.1, 4.6.2.5, 4.7.7.3

tiet 'woven'! *by-f* Lad.], 4.2

tignût 'held, kept' [Fri.], 4.1

tímitu 'feared' [Sard.], 3.7.5

tímiu 'feared' [Cmpi.], 3.7.0

timsu 'stretched' *by-f* [Arom.], 3.3.1

timtu 'stretched' *by-f* [Arom.], 3.3.1

ţimtu 'girded' *by-f* [Arom.], 3.3.1

tind 'dyed' [Luca.], 3.6.2.5

tində 'dyed' [Abru.], 3.6.2.3

tingut 'held' [Ross.], 4.6.2.7

tingut 'held' [Cat.], 2.6, 4.6.2.3, 4.6.2.4

tins 'held' [OFr.], 4.4.2.3

tint 'dyed' [OCat.], 4.6.2.2

tint 'dyed' [ORoss.], 4.6.2.7

tint, tinte 'held' [Nor.: Pch.], 4.4.13.1

tinta 'ink' *noun* [Sp.], 4.7.7.1

tinto 'dyed' *short* *f* [Gal.], 4.7.14

tinto 'colored' *adj.* [Sp.], 4.7.7.1

tinto 'dyed' [It.], 3.5.3.1, 3.6.2.5

tinto 'dyed' [OSp.], 4.7.1, 4.7.6.1

tinto 'dyed' *by-f* [Gen.], 3.6.1.4

tintu 'dyed' [Cors.], 3.6.2.1

tintu 'bad, lazy' *adj.* [Sic.], 3.6.2.6

ţinut 'held' [Rom.], 2.6, 2.14.5, 3.1.3

tinutu 'held, lasted' [Sic.], 3.6.2.6

tinxido 'dyed' *long* *f* [Gal.], 4.7.14

tirat 'pulled' [Fri-R], 4.1

tiratu 'pulled, drawn' [Sic.], 3.6.2.6

ţirut 'held, had' [Ist-R], 3.3.2

ţirut 'asked; begged' [Meg.], 3.3.1.1

ţirut 'asked; begged' [Meg.: U], 3.3.1.1

tissé 'woven' [Fr.], 4.4.7, 4.4.9.1, 6.9

tissu 'woven' [OFr.], 4.4.7

tissu 'cloth' *noun* [Fr.], 4.4.9.1, 4+29

tisu 'straight' *adj.* [Sic.], 3.6.2.6

tit 'dyed' [Enga.], 4.3.1

tnì, tní: 'held' [FP: N], 4.5.1

tnœ 'held' *by-f* [Nor.: VS], 4.4.13.1

toccato 'touched' [It.], 3.5.0.9

tocco 'touched' *short* *f* [OIt.], 3.5.9

tòcco 'touched' *short* *f* [Laz.], 3.5.9

tòch 'touched' *by-f* [Rml.], 3.6.1.3

tòdu 'twisted' [Burg.], 4.4.13.3

tœ:si 'coughed' [Burg.], 4.4.13.3

tois 'stretched' [OFr.], 4.4.2.2

toise 'six-foot unit of length' [arch.]; measuring device for conscripts' *noun* [Fr.], 4.4.9.3, 4+31

toleit 'taken away' *by-f* [OFr.], 4.4.4, 4.4.9.4

tolesto 'taken away' [OVen.], 3.6.1

tolgut 'taken away' *by-f* [OOc.], 4.6.1.2, 4.6.1.3

tolheit 'taken away' [OPtg.], 4.7.10

tolhido 'hindered' [Ptg.], 4.7.10

tolit 'crippled' *also* *adj.* [Cat.], 4.6.2.2, 4.6.2.8, 4.7.6.1

tòlleto 'taken away' [ONeap.], 3.6.2

tollido 'taken away' *by-f* [OSp.], 4+62

tolludo 'taken away' *by-f* [OSp.], 2.8, 4+62

tols 'taken away' *by-f* [OFr.], 4.4.4

tolt 'taken' [Mil.], 3.6.1.1

tolt 'taken away' [ORoss.], 4.6.2.7

tolt 'taken away' [Val.], 4.6.2.8

tolt 'taken away' *by-f* [OFr.], 4.4.2.2, 4.4.4

tolt 'taken away' *by-f* [OOc.], 4.6.1.3

tolte 'removal' *noun* [OFr.], 4.4.9.2

tolto 'taken away' [It.], 2.4.1, 3.3.2, 3.5.2.1, 3.5.5, 4.7.6.1

tolu 'taken away' *by-f* [OFr.], 4.4.4

tomado 'taken' [Sp.], 4.7.0

tombé 'fallen' [Fr.], 4.4.0, 4.4.12

tonato 'thundered' *by-f* [It.], 2.13.3, 3.5.1

tondit 'shorn' [Lad.], 4.2

tondu 'shorn' [Fr.], 2.14.2

toné 'thundered' [Lad.], 4.2

tont 'shorn' [OFr.], 4.4.2.2

tonte 'shearing-time' *noun* [Fr.], 4.4.9.2

tonto 'foolish' *adj.* [Sp.], 4.7.6.3

too, tossa 'twisted' ? [FP: Vd.], 4.5.3

torcegut 'twisted' *by-f* [Lang.], 4.6.1.9

torcido 'twisted' [Sp.], 2.15.5, 4.7.6, 4.7.7.1

torcíu 'twisted' *long f* [Arag.: VE], 4.7.12

torcut 'spun' *by-f, rare* [Ist-R], 3.3.2

torçut 'twisted' *by-f* [Cat.], 2.15.5, 4.6.2.2

torçut 'twisted' *by-f* [Gév.], 4.6.1.8

torçut 'twisted' *by-f* [Val.], 4.6.2.8

tordu 'twisted' [Fr.], 2.15.5, 3.6.1.1, 4.4.7

tornato '(re)turned' [Arag.: Pnt.], 4.7.12

tors 'spun' *by-f, usu.* [Ist-R], 3.3.2

tors 'spun' [Meg.], 3.3.1.1

tors 'spun' *also noun* [Rom.], 2.15.5, 3.1.5.1, 3.1.5.2

tors 'twisted' *by-f* [Gév.], 4.6.1.8

tors 'twisted' *by-f* [Lang.], 4.6.1.9

tors 'twisted' *by-f* [Oc.], 4.6.1.4

tors 'twisted' *by-f* [OFr.], 2.15.5, 4.4.2.3, 4.4.3, 4.4.7

tors 'twisted' *by-f* [OOc.], 4.6.1.2, 4.6.1.3

torssegut 'twisted' *by-f* [Oc.], 4.6.1.4

torssit 'twisted' *by-f* [Oc.], 4.6.1.4

torsu 'spun' [Arom.], 3.3.1

torsu 'squeezed' *by-f* [VG], 3.6.1.4.1

tort 'twisted' *adj.* [Enga.], 4.3.1

tort 'braided, woven' [Luca.], 3.6.2.5

tort 'twisted' [OCat.], 4.6.2.2

tort 'twisted' [ORoss.], 4.6.2.7

tort 'twisted' *by-f* [OFr.], 2.15.5, 4.4.7

tort 'twisted' *by-f* [OOc.], 4.6.1.3, 4.6.1.4

tort 'twisted' *by-f, also adj.* [Cat.], 2.15.5, 4.6.2.1, 6.4

tort 'twisted' *by-f* [Val.], 4.6.2.8

tort 'wrong' *noun* [Gév.], 4.6.1.8

tort 'tow' *noun* [Rom.], 2.15.5, 3.1.5.2

tort 'limping' *adj.* [Ross.], 4.6.2.7

torto 'one-eyed' *adj.* [Ptg.], 2.15.5, 6.4

torto 'twisted' [It.], 2.15.5, 3.6.1.1

tortu 'squeezed' *by-f* [VG], 3.6.1.4.1

tortu 'twisted' *by-f* [OFr.], 2.15.5

tortu 'spun' [ORom.], 3.1.5.2

torzito 'twisted' [Arag.: Pnt.], 4.7.12

tos 'shorn' [Cat.], 2.15.8, 4.6.2.4

tos 'shorn' [Val.], 4.6.2.8

tos 'twisted' *by-f* [Gév.], 4.6.1.8

tosa 'shearing' *noun* [Cat.], 4+35

tose 'girl' *noun* [OFr.], 4.4.10

tosido 'coughed' [Sp.], 6+12

toso 'child, kid' *dial. noun* [It.], 3.1.6

tossido 'coughed' [Ptg.], 6+12

tossit 'coughed' [Cat.], 6+12

tossito 'coughed' [It.], 3.5.0, 6+12

tost 'soon' *adv.* [Cat.], 2.6, 4.6.2.1

tosto 'soon' *lit. adv.* [It.], 2.6

treü 'lord's due' *noun* [OFr.], 4.4.2.2

trevudo 'paid taxes' [OSp.], 4.7.4.1

treyt 'pulled out' [OCat.], 4.6.2.2

tribù 'tribe' *noun* [It.], 3.5.0

tributado 'paid taxes'• [Sp.], 4.7.4.1

tricut 'passed' [Meg.], 3.3.1.1

trié 'sorted' [Fr.], 2.11.2

trimes 'sent' [Meg.], 3.3.1.1

trimis 'sent' [Rom.], 3.1.5.1

trimis 'envoy' *noun* [Rom.], 3.1.5.2

tritato 'minced, hashed' [It.], 2.11.2

{trlit 'fled' [Ist-R], 3.3.2}

trobato 'met' [Arag.: Pnt.], 4.7.12

trocido 'twisted' [Ptg.], 2.15.5

tronato 'thundered' [OIt.], 2.13.3

troncatu 'shattered' *long f, by-f* [Cors.], 3.6.2.1

troncu 'shattered' *short f* [Cors.], 3.6.2.1

trouvé 'found' [Fr.], 3.0.1

trovato 'found' [It.], 3.0.1

trovatu 'found' *long f, by-f* [Cors.], 3.6.2.1

trovo 'found' *short f* [Tusc.], 3.5.9

tròvo 'found' *short f* [Laz.], 3.5.9

trovu 'found' *short f* [Cors.], 3.6.2.1

truncado 'maimed' [Sp.], 4.7.4.6

truncatu 'shattered' *long f, by-f* [Cors.], 3.6.2.1

trunco 'maimed' *adj.* [Sp.], 4.7.4.6

{trupit 'beaten, hit' [Ist-R], 3.3.2}

truvatu 'found' *long f, by-f* [Cors.], 3.6.2.1

tsesâ, tsesâte 'fallen' [FP: Vd.], 4.5.3

tset, tsèite 'fallen' [FP: VA], 4.5.4

tsouét, −a 'killed' [FP: VA], 4.5.4

tu 'been silent' [Fr.], 2.14.5, 4.4.1

tubito 'had' *by-f* [Arag.: Pnt.], 4.7.12

tuchê 'touched' *by-f* [Rml.], 3.6.1.3

tudyù 'twisted' [FP: N], 4.5.1

tué 'killed' [Fr.], 2.11.1

tué 'killed' *by-f* [Pic.: Av.], 4.4.13.2

tüert 'twisted' [Enga.], 4.3.1

tuelto 'taken away' *by-f* [OSp.], 4.7.6.1

tuerto 'twisted' *short f* [Arag.: VE], 4.7.12

tuerto 'one-eyed' *adj.* [Sp.], 2.15.5, 4.7.6.2, 4.7.7.1, 6.4

tuerto 'twisted' [OSp.], 4.7.6.1

tukisto '?' [Ist-I], 3.3.3

tullido 'crippled' *also adj.* [Sp.], 4.7.6.1

tumsu 'shorn' *by-f* [Arom.], 3.3.1

tumtu 'shorn' [Meg.: Ţ], 3.3.1.1

tumtu 'shorn' *by-f* [Arom.], 3.3.1

tunat 'thundered' [Rom.], 3.1.2

tundido 'shorn' [Sp.], 4.7.2

túndiu 'shorn' [Cmpi.], 3.7.2

tuns 'shorn' [Meg.], 3.3.1.1

tuns 'shorn' *also noun* [Rom.], 3.1.5.2, 3.1.6, 4+35

tunsoare 'shearing' *noun* [Rom.], 3.1.5.2

tunsu 'shorn' *by-f* [VG], 3.6.1.4.1

tuonato 'thundered' *by-f* [It.], 2.13.3, 3.5.1

tuortə 'twisted' [Abru], 3.6.2.3

turcíu 'twisted' [Leon], 4.7.13

turmutu 'slept' [Sal.], 3.6.2

tus 'shorn' [Enga.], 4.3.1

tuşit 'coughed' [Rom.], 6+12

tusu 'shorn' *by-f* [VG], 3.6.1.4.1

tusu 'shorn' [Log.], 3.7.2

tusu 'shorn' [OSard.], 3.7.1

tuvido 'had' *dial.* [Sp.], 5.4.2

twé 'killed' *by-f* [Pic.: Av.], 4.4.13.2

twe, twé: 'killed' [Nor.: VS], 4.4.13.1

twirrtu 'one-eyed' *adj.* [Leon.: VP], 4.7.13

u, uva 'had' [FP: Vd.], 4.5.3
ü 'had' *by-f* [Lun.], 3.6.1.5
ubbiato 'forgotten' [OIt.], 3.5.0
ubert 'opened' [OOc.], 4.6.1
ubèrt 'opened' [Gasc.], 4.6.1.5
ucciso 'killed' [It.], 3.6.2.2
ucis 'killed' [Ist-R], 3.3.2
ucis 'killed' [Rom.], 3.1.5.1
ud 'wet' *adj.* [Ist-R], 3.3.2, 3+40
udat 'wetted' ? [Ist-R], 3.3.2
udito 'heard' [It.], 0.3.1, 3.3.3, 3.5.0
ufert 'offered' [OOc.], 4.6.1
ufert 'offered' *by-f* [Lang.], 4.6.1.9
uffrieu 'offered' *arch.* [Enga.], 4.3.1
ufrit 'offered' *by-f* [Gév.], 4.6.1.8
uío 'heard' [Leon.: Tud.], 4.7.13
uitat 'forgotten; looked at' [Rom.], 2.11.1, 3.1.1
uldisto 'heard' *by-f* [Ist-I], 3.3.3
uldó 'heard' ! *by-f* [Ist-I], 3.3.3
umplut 'filled' [Rom.], 3.1.3
umtu 'oiled' *by-f* [Meg.: U], 3.3.1.1
unweis 'stayed' [Apul.: Alt.], 3.6.2.4
uncido 'yoked' *by-f* [Sp.], 2.10
ungido 'oiled' [Sp.], 4.7.7.5
uni 'come' [Lad.: Urtijei, Ortizei], 4.2
uni 'come' [Lad.: Gar.], 4.2
uñido 'yoked' *by-f* [Sp.], 2.10
uns 'oiled' [Meg.], 3.3.1.1
uns 'oiled' [Rom.], 3.1.5.1, 3.1.6
unsoare 'grease, ointment' *noun* [Rom.], 3.1.5.2
unsu 'oiled' *by-f* [Meg.: U], 3.3.1.1
unt 'butter' *noun* [Rom.], 3.1.5.2
untado 'oiled' [Sp.], 2.10, 4.7.2.2, 4.7.7.5

untat 'oiled' [Cat.], 4.6.2
unto 'oiled' [It.], 3.1.6
untu oiled' [Cors.], 3.6.2.1
untu 'oiled' [ORom.], 3.1.5.2
urano 'sky' *noun* [Arom.], 3+18
urǎ 'hatred' *noun* [Rom.], 3.1.4
urât 'ugly' *adj.* [Rom.], 3.1.4
urcat 'gone up' [Rom.], 2.2.2
urdido 'warped cloth' [Sp.], 2.9
urdinat 'arranged' [Rom.], 2.15.6
urgido 'urged' [Sp.], 2.12
urgit 'urged' [Cat.], 4.6.2
urît 'hated' [Rom.], 3.1.4, 3.3.1.1
urǫt 'hated' [Meg.], 3.3.1.1
urtato 'stumbled, bumped into' [It.], 3.5.9
urto 'shoved; crashed' *short f* [OIt.], 2.12, 2+80, 3.5.9
urto 'bump, clash' *noun* [It.], 2.12
urzit 'warped cloth' [Rom.], 2.9
usado 'used' [Sp.], 2.11.1
usat 'used' [Cat.], 2.11.1
usato 'used; worn-out' [It.], 2.11.1
uscat 'dried' [Rom.], 2.11.2
uscat 'dried' [Arom.], 3.3.1
uscito 'gone out' [It.], 3.6.2, 4.4.9.1
usé 'worn out' [Fr.], 2.11.1
uslé 'singed, scorched' [OFr.], 3.3.1
uso 'accustomed' *adj., lit.* [It.], 2.11.1
usu 'wanted' *by-f* [Ist-I], 3.3.3, 3.6.1
usucapión 'squatter' *noun* [Sp.], 4+74
üt 'oiled' [Enga.], 4.3.1
uţis 'killed' [Meg.], 3.3.1.1
uvert, −a 'opened' *by-f* [FP: VA], 4.5.4
uzat 'worn-out' *neol.* [Rom.], 2.11.1,   3.1.1
uzǫt, uzǎtǎ 'heard' [Meg.: U], 3.3.1.1

veinte 'twenty' *numeral* [Sp.], 3+20

vejù 'seen' *by-f* [Pied.], 3.6.1.2

vêls 'been worth' [Rml.], 3.6.1.3

velu 'wanted' *by-f* [Poit.], 4.6.1.6

venáit 'come' *by-f* [Vegl.], 3.4

vencido 'won' [Sp.], 2.14.5, 4.7.6.1

vencu 'won' *by-f* [OFr.], 4.4.4

vençudo 'won' [OSp.; Cid], 2.14.5, 4.7.4.1

vencut 'won' [Lang.], 4.6.1.9

vencut 'won' *by-f* [OOc.], 2.14.5

vençut 'won' [Cat.], 2.14.5, 4.6.2.3

vençut 'won' [Val.], 4.6.2.8

venda 'sale' *noun* [Ptg.], 3+45

venda 'sale' *noun, by-f,* [OSp.], 4.7.7.2

vendida 'sale' *noun, by-f,* [OSp.], 4.7.7.2

vendido 'sold' [Sp.], 4.7.3

véndita 'sale' *noun* [It.], 3.5.2.2

vendiu 'sold' [Surs.], 4.3.2

vendu 'sold' [Fr.], 4.4.2.2, 4.4.9.2

vendut 'sold' [OOc.], 4.6.1.1

vendut, vendue 'sold' [Sto.], 4.6.1.6

vendüd₁ 'sold' [Auv.], 4.6.1.7

vendüd₂ 'come' *by-f* [Auv.], 4.6.1.7

venduto 'sold' [It.], 3.5.0, 3.5.2.2

vendüu 'sold' [VG], 3.6.1.4.1

veñesto 'come' *by-f* [Ven.], 3.6.1

venghu 'come' [Poit.], 4.6.1.6

vengiuu 'won' [Mil.], 3.6.1.1

vengüd 'come' *by-f* [Auv.], 4.6.1.7

vengut 'come' [Lang.], 4.6.1.9

vengut 'come' [OCat.], 4.6.2.4

vengut 'come' [OOc.], 4.6.1, 4.6.1.2

vengut 'come' *by-f* [Gasc.], 4.6.1.5

veñì 'come' [Lad.], 4.2

venido 'come' [Sp.], 2.1.3, 2.6, 3.0.1, 4.7.10

venit 'come' [Oltn.], 3.2.1

venit 'come' [Rom.], 2.1.3, 2.6, 3.1.0, 3.2.2

venit 'income' *noun* [Rom.], 3.1.5.2

veñiu 'come' [VG], 3.6.1.4.1

venóit 'come' *by-f* [Vegl.], 3.4

vensut 'won' *by-f* [OOc.], 4.6.1.1

venta 'sale' *noun, by-f* [OSp.], 4.7.7.2

vente 'sale' *noun* [Fr.], 3+45, 4.4.9.2, 4.7.7.2

venti 'twenty' *numeral* [It.], 3+20

ventru 'pot-bellied' *adj.* [Fr.], 4.7.4.2

venu 'come' [Fr.], 2.6, 4.4.3, 4.4.7, 4.7.4.1

venu 'come' [Nor.: Pch.], 4.4.13.1

venu 'come' *by-f* [Pic.: Av.], 4.4.13.2

venu, –ya 'come' [FP: VA], 4.5.4

venù 'sold' [Lad.], 4.6.2.3

veñu 'come' [Lad.: Fass.], 4.2

veñu 'come' [Lad.: Liv.], 4.2

veñu, veña 'come' [FP: Vx.], 4.5.2

veñúo 'come' *by-f* [Ven.], 3.6.1

venudo 'come' *rare* [OSp.], 4.7.4.1

venut 'come' [Luca.], 3.6.2.5

venut 'sold' [Cat.], 4.6.2.3, 4.6.2.10

venut 'sold' [Ross.], 4.6.2.7

venuto 'come' [It.], 1+55, 2.6, 3.5.6, 3.5.7, 4.7.4.1

venutu 'come' [Cors.], 3.6.2.1

verde 'green' *adj.* [Ptg.], 6.4

verit 'come' [Ist-R], 3.3.2

-verti 'turned' [Fr.], 4.4.2.2

vertido 'spilled; poured' [Sp.], 2.10

-vertito 'turned' [It.], 2.13.3

verzo 'opened' [Pad.], 3.6.1

vèst 'seen' [Rml.], 3.6.1.3

vesti 'dressed' *by-f* [OFr.], 3.5.7, 4.4.4

vestit 'dressed' [Lad.], 4.2

v u 'seen' [Fr.], 2.14.2, 2.15.8, 3.6.1.1,
    4.4.2.2, 4.4.3, 4.4.4, 4.4.13.1,
    4.6.1.1, 5.6

v u, –y a 'seen' [FP: VA], 4.5.4

v ù 'seen' [FP: N], 4.5.1

v u 'seen' [Pic.: Av.], 4.4.13.2

v u, v u : 'seen' [Burg.], 4.4.13.3

v u, v u s e 'seen' [Nor.: Pch.],
    4.4.13.1

v u e l t a '(re)turn' *n o u n* [Sp.], 4.7.7,
    4.7.7.2

v u e l t o '(re)turned' [Sp.], 2.14.4,
    3.5.2.1, 3+61, 4.7.0, 4.7.1, 4.7.6.2,
    4.7.11

v u i d i é 'emptied' [OFr.], 4.4.13.1

v u l i s t o 'wanted' *by-f* [Ist-I], 3.3.3

v u l i u 'wanted' [Surs.], 2.7, 4.3.2

v u l l g u t 'wanted' [Val.], 4.6.2.8

v u l s u t u 'wanted' [Cors.], 3.6.2.1

v u l u t 'wanted' [Fri-R], 4.1

v u l u t u 'wanted' [Sic.], 3.6.2.6

v u m e a r e 'vomiting' *n o u n, by-f*
    [Arom.], 3.3.1

v u r s ü 'wanted' [Lun.], 3.6.1.5

v u s i ó 'wanted' ! *by-f* [Ist-I], 3.3.3

v u s u 'wanted' *by-f* [Ist-I], 3.3.3,
    3.6.1

v u š ü u 'wanted' [VG], 3.6.1.4.1

v u t 'had' [Meg.], 3.3.1.1

v u t, v u s e 'seen' [Sto.], 4.6.1.6

v û t 'had' [Fri.], 4.1

v u t ə 'wanted' [Abru.], 3.6.2

v y u 'wanted' [Burg.], 4.4.13.3

x o l l a t 'shorn' [Cat.], 4.6.2.9

y a c i d o 'lain' [Sp.], 2.13.3

y e u 'had' [Pic.: Ggn.], 4.4.13.2

y e u 'had' *by-f* [Pic.: Av.], 4.4.13.2

y i n g h i ţ 'twenty' *numeral by-f*
    [Arom.], 3+20

y i u 'alive' *adj.* [Arom.], 3.3.1

y i y i n ţ 'twenty' *numeral by-f*
    [Arom.], 3+20

y o i t 'wet' *adj.* [Vegl.], 3+40

y u 'had' *by-f* [Pic.: Av.], 4.4.13.2

y u 'had' [Pic.: Br.], 4.4.13.2

y u, y u s s a / y u v a 'gone' [FP: Vd.],
    4.5.3

y u t 'gone' [Luca.], 3.6.2.5

z a c l ' i s 'shut' [Ist-R], 3.3.2

z a c u t 'lain' *by-f* [Ist-R], 3.3.2

z ă c u t 'lain' [Rom.], 2.13.3, 2.14.5

{z a i m i t 'lent' [Ist-R], 3.3.2}

z á i t 'gone' [Vegl.], 3.4

z a m a r r u d u 'fat (of cows)' *adj.*
    [Leon.: VP], 4.7.13

z a n g a d o 'angered' [Ptg.], 4.7.0

z a p p i n g 'channel-switching' *n o u n*
    [Fr.], 4.4.0.3

z a r n ù 'sifted' [Lad.], 4.2

z a r r a u 'shut' [Arag.: VE], 4.7.12

z a ţ a t 'lain' *by-f, rare* [Ist-R], 3.3.2

z e d ù 'stopped' [Lad.], 2.15.10

z e n t ù 'felt' [Lad.], 4.2

z e r r n e x u d u 'hairy-haunched (of
    goats)' *adj.* [Leon.: VP], 4.7.13

z è r t o 'sifted' ! [Ist-I], 3.3.3, 3.6.1

z i 'gone' [Ist-I], 3.3.3, 4.1

z i s 'said, told' [Ist-R], 3.3.2

z i s 'said, told' [Rom.], 3.1.5.1, 5.6,
    6.8

ẓ i t t 'said, told' [Luca.], 3.6.2.5

z m u l s 'yanked out' [Rom.], 3.2.2

z m u l t 'yanked out' *arch.* [Mold.],
    3.2.2

z o n z o 'dull' *adj.* [Sp.], 4.7.6.3

z u r c i d o 'mended, darned' [Sp.],
    2.11.2

z û t 'gone' [Fri.], 3.3.3, 4.1